# The Black Americans

## INTERPRETATIVE READINGS

Edited by

SETH M. SCHEINER
and
TILDEN G. EDELSTEIN

*Rutgers University*

HOLT, RINEHART AND WINSTON
New York   Chicago   San Francisco   Atlanta
Dallas   Montreal   Toronto   London   Sydney

COVER PHOTOS        Courtesy of Mrs. Arcola
Ragland, Birmingham, Alabama, depicting her
grandfather, a former slave, and her son.

Library of Congress Catalog Card Number:    79–157094   3-10-76

ISBN: 0–03–081197–X

Printed in the United States of America

1   2   3   4      090      9   8   7   6   5   4   3   2   1

*To*
ELIAS AND HELEN SCHEINER
*and*
SOL AND BERTEL STARGARDTER

# &PREFACE&

O NE of the great paradoxes of world history is how the United States, steeped in Christianity, political democracy, and personal freedom, could initiate and maintain through much of its history a system of caste and repression against a large segment of its population. Ethnocentrism, racism, and slavery have provided the main foundations for the relationship between white Americans and Afro-Americans. Of course the black victims of this relationship have been profoundly affected and have responded in various ways to it. But Afro-American history by no means has been exclusively a response to white attitudes and actions, for the black heritage has substantial roots in the African past and has evolved in America without total dependence on white ways. To comprehend Afro-American history it is necessary, therefore, to examine not only the historic sources of ethnocentrism, racism, and slavery, but also the historic development of forces in black history which have not been dependent upon white attitudes and actions. The soundness of this approach, and its difficulties, are illustrated in this volume.

The selections that follow will focus upon this dual theme of internal development within the Afro-American community and relations between blacks and whites. Rather than cover all aspects of black history, the editors have elected to develop this theme through selected essays from scholarly journals and excerpts from monographs organized into eleven topical or chronological chapters. Each chapter opens with a brief introduction that places the interpretive readings within the broader framework of Afro-American history and highlights significant issues regarding the selections for the reader to consider. The student interested in pursuing particular areas of black history in greater depth will profit from the footnotes and the bibliographical sections noting leading articles and books. To facilitate the use of the bibliographies, each chapter has suggestions for further reading which refer to points raised in the introduction and the readings.

S. M. S.

T. G. E.

New Brunswick, New Jersey
December 1970

# &CONTENTS&

PREFACE          v

CHAPTER ONE    The African Heritage     1
1. *Melville J. Herskovits,* Problem, Method and Theory in
Afroamerican Studies     3
2. *Winthrop D. Jordan,* Initial English Confrontation With Africans     19
3. *Walter Rodney,* African Slavery in the Context of the
Atlantic Slave Trade     38
SUGGESTIONS FOR FURTHER READING     51

CHAPTER TWO    The Colonial Era     53
4. *Leonard Price Stavisky,* Negro Craftsmanship in Early America     55
5. *Paul C. Palmer,* Servant into Slave: The Evolution of the Legal
Status of the Negro Laborer in Colonial Virginia     65
SUGGESTIONS FOR FURTHER READING     78

CHAPTER THREE    Antebellum Slavery     79
6. *Eugene D. Genovese,* Rebelliousness and Docility in the Negro Slave:
A Critique of the Elkins Thesis     82
7. *David Brion Davis,* Slavery     101
8. *Richard B. Morris,* The Measure of Bondage in the Slave States     110
9. *Raymond A. and Alice M. Bauer,* Day to Ray Resistance to Slavery     129
10. *Willie Lee Rose,* The Old Allegiance     152
SUGGESTIONS FOR FURTHER READING     166

CHAPTER FOUR    Free Men in a Slave Nation     168
11. *John Hope Franklin,* The Free Negro in the Economic Life of
Ante-bellum North Carolina     170
12. *Larry Gara,* The Underground Railroad: Legend or Reality?     185

13. *Howard H. Bell*, Expressions of Negro Militancy in the North,
    1840–1860                                                              194
14. *Benjamin Quarles*, The Politics of Freedom                            203
    SUGGESTIONS FOR FURTHER READING                                        217

CHAPTER FIVE    Emancipation and Freedom                                   219
15. *Joel Williamson*, The Meaning of Freedom                              221
16. *August Meier*, Negroes in the First and Second
    Reconstructions of the South                                           241
    SUGGESTIONS FOR FURTHER READING                                        256

CHAPTER SIX    The Withdrawal From Reconstruction                          259
17. *John Hope Franklin*, "Legal" Disfranchisement of the Negro            261
18. *Barton J. Bernstein*,
    Plessy v. Ferguson: Conservative Sociological Jurisprudence            269
19. *George B. Tindall*, South Carolina Negroes in Agriculture, 1877–1900  277
    SUGGESTIONS FOR FURTHER READING                                        289

CHAPTER SEVEN    Black Reaction to Jim Crow                                291
20. *August Meier*, Washington and Du Bois                                 293
21. *Emma Lou Thornbrough*, The National Afro-American
    League, 1887–1908                                                      323
    SUGGESTIONS FOR FURTHER READING                                        337

CHAPTER EIGHT    The Black Ghetto                                          338
22. *Louise P. Kennedy*, The Negro Peasant Turns Cityward                  340
23. *St. Clair and Horace Cayton*, Black Belt—Black Ghetto                 348
24. *Karl E. and Alma F. Taeuber*, The Negro as an Immigrant Group:
    Recent Trends in Racial and Ethnic Segregation in Chicago              365
    SUGGESTIONS FOR FURTHER READING                                        377

CHAPTER NINE    The Militant Twenties                                      379
25. *Wayne Cooper*, Claude McKay and the New Negro of the 1920's           381
26. *Edmund David Cronon*, Black Moses                                     390
    SUGGESTIONS FOR FURTHER READING                                        408

CHAPTER TEN    The Great Depression and The New Deal                       410
27. *Ralph J. Bunche*, A Critique of New Deal Social
    Planning as it Affects Negroes                                         413
28. *Richard M. Dalfiume*, The "Forgotten Years" of the Negro Revolution   420
29. *Thurgood Marshall*, The Supreme Court as Protector of Civil Rights    436
    SUGGESTIONS FOR FURTHER READING                                        448

CHAPTER ELEVEN    Since *Brown v. The Board of Education*                  450
30. *James A. Geschwender*, Social Structure and the Negro Revolution      452
31. *Allen J. Matusow*, From Civil Rights to Black Power                   465
32. *Ronald Steel*, Letter from Oakland: The Panthers                      488
    SUGGESTIONS FOR FURTHER READING                                        501

# CHAPTER ONE 🙊

# The African Heritage

T HERE has been much that has been neglected or distorted in Afro-American history. But the greatest lack has been the failure to acknowledge the cultural and historic contribution of African civilization to the world and to the development of the Afro-American. For centuries, white ethnocentrism and the need to rationalize the oppression of black men led most men with European roots to believe that Africa was a barbaric jungle requiring colonization by whites; its people were considered primitive beings in need of the white man's culture. The shattering of this view has profoundly illuminated American history. And when one realizes that the black American's history begins in Africa, and not in America, a new set of concepts emerges about the nature of Afro-American history.

Melville J. Herskovits has made a momentous contribution to our understanding of Afro-American history by dealing with fundamental questions of African cultural survivals and modifications in the New World. Widening the path laid out by W. E. B. Du Bois and Carter Woodson, the pioneer black historians who emphasized the presence of Africanisms in American black culture, Herskovits employed his skill and reputation as an Africanist and anthropologist to bring scholarly attention to the prevailing ignorance of African culture and showed how that culture influenced both black and white Americans. His concern for an inter-disciplinary approach to Afro-American history and culture is illustrated in selection 1. Noting those Africanisms that either survived, altered, or disappeared as they were transplanted to the Americas, Herskovits focuses attention on the various reasons for cultural survival. Forces seeking to ignore or obliterate that African heritage confront traditions which at times manage to persist.

Herskovits' work has met renewed acceptance in recent years. When ini-tially published, its harshest criticism came from an eminent black sociologist, E. Franklin Frazier, who led an attack on the view that the African past remained viable and operative for black Americans. Frazier argued that assimilation, not African survivals, characterized Afro-American culture; those distinctive black cultural patterns that did exist emanated not from the African heritage but from American economic, political, and social discrimination. Skepticism about African survivals in America has continued, but the new search for a black heritage in particular, and the widening recognition of the pluralistic quality of American cul-ture in general, have increased the appreciation of Herskovits' work.

Another way of viewing the interaction of black and white is demonstrated in the section from Winthrop D. Jordan's White Over Black. Other historians embarked upon the vital search for the historical sources of ethnocentrism, racism, and slavery, have differed significantly in their conclusions. Oscar and Mary F. Handlin had pointed out that slavery was not introduced into the American colonies until the last half of the seventeenth century and only then did racial prejudice arise. Similarly, Kenneth Stampp had denied the existence of earlier patterns of racism by suggesting that they grew out of slavery. Other historians have found evidence of an earlier date for the beginning of American slavery than the Handlins and have disputed the origins of racism. Carl N. Degler had noted that racist attitudes were evident in the colonies prior to slavery and served to cause slavery. Seeking to reconcile these opposing views, Winthrop Jordan, in an early article, suggested that slavery and racial prejudice interacted with each other. But subsequently in White Over Black Jordan discredited his article because when writing it he "was far from comprehending the origins of American slavery." In selection 2 he goes beyond the seventeenth-century American colonies and looks to sixteenth-century Africa for the major roots of ethnocentrism, racism, and slavery. Readers should compare and contrast these earlier attitudes and actions toward Africans with those which would arise in America.

Walter Rodney, in selection 3, treats the cross-cultural impact of slavery. Rodney analyzes the nature of African slavery before and after the white slave traders' arrival. He discusses the role of African chiefs in the slave trade, class distinctions among Africans, and considers the relationship of African slavery to the kind of slavery developed in the New World. Consider how Rodney's article contravenes those whose enthusiasm for the relevance of the African past has led them to idealize it excessively as well as those who have continually sought to denigrate the humanity of African civilization.

# 1

## PROBLEM, METHOD AND THEORY IN AFROAMERICAN STUDIES
*Melville J. Herskovits*

**T**HIS paper will discuss three elements in the scientific study of the New World Negro and his African background that, hitherto in large measure implicit in my writings on the subject, suggest their timeliness for explicit formulation. These comprise a definition and delimitation of the field, which is essential for clarity of purpose in research and for directing future effort; some of the methodological concepts and techniques that have been successfully employed; and some of the hypotheses which have guided investigation and developed out of experience in the field.

It is not always realized how recent is systematic study of the Afroamerican field. Little of the present substantial store of facts concerning New World Negro cultures, or the civilizations from which they derive, or the historical circumstances of their formation were available two decades ago, so that it is apparent why the need to amass data took first place in the attention of students. This continuing emphasis was particularly relevant in view of the vastness of the area in which New World Negroes live and the variety of their cultures, the complexity of the African civilizations from which they derive, the technical difficulties in the way of studying provenience and the intricacy of the acculturative processes to which they have been exposed.

Today, the scientific importance of Afroamerican studies as a field for research is firmly established. A climate of opinion, both lay and scholarly, which encourages further research, has been created, while the body of factual materials and comparative analyses that has been amassed by those working in the field allows hypotheses and procedures to be assessed in terms of collected data and achieved results rather than of probable validity and possible return. It thus appears a logical moment for stock-taking, for the explicit statement of theoretical assumptions, and for a refinement of techniques.

### 2

An outstanding characteristic of the field of Afroamerican studies is its interdisciplinary nature, which must be taken into account whenever problems of definition or method are under discussion. But more than that, Afroamerican studies not only cross disciplines, but are also intercontinental, treating of peoples living in North, South and Central America,

Melville J. Herskovits, "Problem, Method and Theory in Afroamerican Studies," *Phylon*, VII, No. 4 (1946), pp. 337–354. Reprinted by permission of the publisher.

the Caribbean, and Africa. The implications of this interdisciplinary and intercontinental scope, when thought of in terms of the conventional organization of scholarly study, are many. For the field cuts across so many boundaries that it cannot be defined in terms of any commonly accepted categories—a fact that accounts for its late recognition as a definable area of scholarship and for certain practical difficulties that at one time or another have faced those who have worked on its many problems.

That the ramifications of such studies extend into the social sciences, the humanities and the biological sciences, follows from the nature of the data. In this our field is no different from any research that is concerned with obtaining a rounded view of the life of man, or of any group of men. It is nonetheless worthwhile to recall how in Afroamerican studies investigation has had to have recourse to the resources of anthropology, history and psychology to reach an understanding of the social structures, the accepted patterns of behavior, and the past development of the societies studied; how linguistics, musicology and comparative literature have had to be called upon to contribute their techniques for insight into some of the most revealing data in the field; and how such problems as the incidence and effects of race-crossing, of the dynamics of Negro population formation and the like have had to be studied in terms of the techniques and orientations of human biology and demography. Not every student can study every problem, but most students of the Negro have come to realize that their competence in the discipline of their primary affiliation gives them but a starting-point for further effort; and that their field of interest has characteristically broadened as the data have been followed where they led, even when these called for disregard of current delimitation of scholarly concern.

In similar fashion, accepted regional approaches to the ordering of research have had to be transcended. Researches restricted to Latin American problems, or to the United States, or to Africa or to an island of the Caribbean alone, of course, make their contributions to Afroamerican studies. For where data are as sparse as in this field, all contributions are welcome. But those whose perspectives have not been so circumscribed know well how much researches in these areas are enriched by a broader point of view. One of the most telling instances of this is the aid which the study of New World Negro peoples can bring toward a fuller comprehension of the cultures of Africa itself. This is striking because it reverses the customary order of thought, which focuses on African survivals in the New World. That the study of African ways of life is essential to an understanding of survivals of these customs is a truism; but what, it may be asked, can the analysis of survivals contribute to comprehension of their own sources?

Though the matter cannot be documented here, it need merely be recalled that survival is an index of tenacity, which in turn reveals general orientations in parent cultures that may at times not be given proper stress without such background. This is the case as concerns the place of religion in African cultures, whose theoretical importance will be considered in a later page. Furthermore, specific complexes of significance that have been quite overlooked in Africanist studies are to be revealed by investigation on this side of the Atlantic. A recent example of this is had in the instance of the place of drummers, not only in cult-rituals, but in the life of the community as a whole. First noted in a New World Negro culture, it required only brief questioning of Africans to reveal itself as an important facet of social organization in Africa itself, that had hitherto not been explored at all.

Though overlapping many disciplines and a number of geographical regions, the field of Afroamerican studies is distinct from all those on which it impinges, from which it follows that it is therefore often a matter of emphasis and intent just where a given piece of research is to be classified. This is the source of many practical difficulties. Papers on African cultures, deriving from studies stimulated by an interest in the New World descendants of Africa, may appear in Africanist journals where much of their usefulness to those who concentrate on New World Negro societies is lost, while reports on historical aspects of the field, often published in historical journals, are not seen by those studying Afroamerican problems whose primary affiliation is with other disciplines. Conversely Africanists who confine their work to the peoples of that continent, or historians of the Negro whose range of interest is defined by their discipline, fail to benefit from New World studies, or from work on other than historical phases of Negro life that might open new vistas to them.

This may meet with the reasonable suggestion that there is enough justification for the existence of the conventional disciplines in their achieved results to give us pause before we cross their boundaries, tested by time and experience. In the final analysis, however, the ordering of any field must arise from the nature of the materials it deals with; for the most fruitful results can be had only when the facts are studied as they lie, without those preconceptions which, in a case such as that under discussion, lead to distortion if not considered in terms of all interrelated aspects.

This leads us to the nature of the contributions Afroamerican studies can be expected to make, for the point is basic in discussing the importance of the field for scientific research. More than anything else, it comprises data that, because of the available historic controls and the range of related materials, go far toward approximating those laboratory situations which, in the study of man, are more difficult to achieve than any other single methodological factor in the repertory of science. Thus the very fact that to conduct Afroamerican studies calls on the techniques of many disciplines, and is carried on in many different areas, gives it a special significance for the scientific study of man. For here can be prosecuted those comparative researches of mixtures of physical types, of languages and of modes of behavior in terms of known rather than of assumed past contacts. And while in this, Afroamerican research does not differ in kind from studies among other groups of differing backgrounds between whom contact has taken place or is in process, it is to be distinguished from them in degree, as expressed in the very broad variety of situations that, in this field, are to be investigated.

It is not difficult to phrase the manner in which the Afroamerican field differs from the several disciplines on which it draws. To the extent that its problems are to be comprehended within their areas of interest, such problems have an affiliation immediately recognizable. Thus a study of land-tenure in a Caribbean island might find ready reception in a journal devoted to economics, the analysis of a Negro musical style in a musicological publication, the description of the physical characteristics of a North American Negro community in an organ devoted to the problems of physical anthropology. Even where cross-disciplinary considerations have entered, publication can be achieved in journals devoted to the discipline of principal emphasis or, more often, in the subject with which the student is technically affiliated. This is one of the reasons why bibliographic problems are so difficult in Afroamerican research. It is common experience that even after going through the files of journals in several subjects, papers in most unexpected media are come upon, more by chance or hearsay, and despite systematic search.

To draw the line between area fields and Afroamerican research requires somewhat more careful distinctions, for here the problem of efficient historic relationships enters. It is simple to state that study of the Negro in Latin America contributes to the Latin American field; even though, in this sense, we once again encounter overlapping. Yet it is open to question how much a detailed investigation of certain Negro social conventions or music or religious beliefs that have not significantly diffused to other population elements in a given Latin American country is to be regarded as a contribution to the Latin American field, except in a secondary sense.

In the Africanist field, the matter is somewhat different. In earlier years, before the provenience of New World Negroes was known as well as it is at present, it was held that knowledge of African culture in general was essential to effective comparative study of the New World Negro. Today, however, one may ask why, except for general background, this is needed. Field research on the cultures of East Africa, the study of the slave trade in Zanzibar, the analysis of Bushman art, or investigation of Zulu physical types deal with peoples who are outside the range of effective historic impact on New World Negro patterns, since so few individuals from the parts of Africa where they live were brought to the New World that their influence in the formation of New World Negro types and cultures could only have been negligible.

A further point to be made in clarifying the limits of the Afroamerican field has to do with the study of those situations of everyday life in many countries which, as they affect the Negro, present practical problems of great moment that press for immediate solutions. Because the student is also the citizen, with heightened awareness of the needs engendered by these situations, the temptation is great to give over the long-term view in favor of *ad hoc* solutions of such issues. This has been especially true in the United States, where for many years an almost exclusive preoccupation with action programs discouraged the type of broad research which characterizes the Afroamerican field. This is not the place to consider the problem of applied science as against research on a long-term basis, yet it is important that the distinction be made and maintained. For even in the short view, the broader base of comprehension that the results of Afroamerican studies can give those whose task is to frame policies for practical procedures would, of itself, justify the position that such studies must be held distinct from remedial programs in the troubled field of race relations.

Finally, it must be stressed that Afroamerican studies are not to be limited to the study of Negro populations and their cultures alone, but must follow through to assess the contributions Africa has made to the peoples among whom the Negroes live. Thus when race-crossing carries Negroid elements into the genetic composition of the non-Negroid groups, this is quite as significant a subject for research as it is to determine the physical traits of the Negroid group. Parallel cultural phenomena have not been systematically studied at all, except, perhaps, in Brazil. Yet just as race-crossing invariably follows on contact between peoples of different physical types, so cultural borrowing—two-way borrowing—also ensues. The theoretical importance of this fact is clear. Here the problem is stated to emphasize the necessity of including, in the repertory of Afroamerican research, investigation not only into the maintenance of African tradition in the New World, but also into how, and to what extent African custom was diffused to the aboriginal Indian peoples and to those of European derivation who experienced prolonged contact with Africans and their descendants.

3

To the extent that the problems of Afroamerican research fall within the compass of established disciplines, or require interdisciplinary consideration of a type already employed outside the Afroamerican field, the question of method presents no difficulty. A comparative study of Negro music utilizes the techniques of the musicologist, one of language employs the methods of the linguists, research into the present-day Negro family or of living standards of Negro populations use the approaches of the sociologist or of the economist. Overall descriptions of any of these cultures, whether in Africa or the New World, require ethnological field techniques, while analyses of psychological problems arising out of the way of life of Negro people utilize the methods of social psychology. Studies of the slave trade, or of the economics of the plantation, though cross-disciplinary, find research techniques at hand in the modes of investigation employed by economic historians.

Strangely enough, the resources of ethnology and history have only recently been welded into a usable tool. Despite the fact that there are historical schools of ethnology and social historians, there has been but little contact across these disciplines. The "history" of these ethnological schools has been based on the reconstruction of events rather than on documentation; while the social historian, despite the illumination his writings have thrown on the development of the institutions with which he has dealt, has worked primarily as an historian and only rarely and recently has had recourse to the methods of the social sciences. There are, of course, some exceptions to this statement. Studies of certain Indian groups in the United States afford instances of how the use of historic sources has been able to illuminate ethnographic problems, while historians of the American frontier are more and more finding it essential to take into account the relevant ethnographic facts.

Experience is teaching us that the methods of these two disciplines, more than any other two, must be jointly called on if the varying situations that are to be studied comparatively in the Afroamerican field are to be analyzed with comprehension. It must be stressed that this field, consti-tuting as it does a special instance of culture contact, derives its greatest significance from the fact that it so superbly documents the problems of cultural dynamics. Now in studies of culture-contact it is essential to estab-lish the cultural base-lines from which the processes of change began, to know the facts concerning the culture or cultures that have emerged, or are emerging from the contact, and to comprehend how, and under what circumstances, the phenomena as observed in the culture that has resulted from the contact actually developed. The first of these requires ethnographic study, and in some measure the second. But the second also requires his-torical treatment, while the third demands an attack that is essentially historical.

The *ethnohistorical method,* as this combined ethnological and his-torical approach is to be termed, has been basic in systematic Afroamerican research, for until the use of this method was fully established, it was found difficult to achieve perspective, and comparative studies were but elusive. It is through the use of this method, and only by its use, that it has been possible to recover the predominant regional and tribal origins of the New World Negroes and, with this information in hand, to turn to ethnographic research in Africa with a certainty that the materials gathered there would be relevant to the problems of cultural retention and cultural change met with in the New World. Similarly this method has made it possible to test the validity of the rich store of existing documentary information concern-ing slaves and slaving, plantation life and the responses of the Negro to it, and the like, and to realize much of the potential contribution of these materials. Most important, also, has been the continuous comparison of ethnographic facts as found on the two sides of the Atlantic; for ethno-history, as employed in the study of Afroamerican problems, consists essen-tially of the application of a comparative ethnographic technique in unravelling, on the basis of written sources, the historic progression of events that led up to the establishment and functioning of New World Negro cultures as they exist at the present time.

Not only has the ethnohistorical approach been able to fix the African origins of New World Negro cultures, but it has been of great value in accounting for differences that are found between the cultures of Negroes living in different parts of the New World. Thus comparative ethnographic studies have revealed that the cultures of the Dutch Guiana Bush Negroes and of the Maroons of Jamaica manifest their Africanisms predominantly in terms of Gold Coast retentions, while those of Haiti are of Dahomean and Yoruban derivation. The documents tell us that Dutch and English planters preferred Gold Coast slaves, not only because they were more likely to find these for sale by their own nationals, but because of rationalizations that came to be set up concerning the worth of Negroes from tribes of this area compared to other kinds of Negroes. On the other hand, they make it equally clear that Latin slaveowners preferred Dahomean and Yoruban slaves for the same reasons, and thus resolve what would otherwise be a difficult problem.

Another methodological device that has proved of outstanding value in analyzing the problems of Afroamerican research is that of a scale of intensity of Africanisms over the New World. This implies a logically conceived continuum which ranges from retentions that are completely African, or almost so, to those least African and most European—the Indian elements having been so little studied that they cannot be classified. Such a continuum permits an arrangement of the data that gives insight into the process of cultural change by allowing comparisons to be drawn between cultures whose various aspects lie at different points on it. This, in turn, facilitates analysis of the processes that have operated to bring about the cultural changes observed in the course of field research.

It must be emphasized that, as in all scientific study, a classificatory device such as the scale of intensity of Africanisms is but a means to an end rather than an end in itself. In this case, the end that is envisaged is that comprehension of process which alone can lead to valid prediction. To be revealing in terms of this end the classification must be derived through induction, and flow from the data, rather than be imposed upon it after the fashion of a *priori* categories that tend to force materials into groupings that do violence to the scientific reality. Scientific analysis is impossible without classification of data, and herein lies the importance of this series of categories; but it cannot be too strongly emphasized that classification, of itself, can tell us nothing about causes, or relationships, or the processes of change.

A *scale of intensity of Africanisms* was first established somewhat more than a decade ago. At that time, however, the data were meager compared with present resources, so that of necessity the listing was tentative, and had to be in terms of whole cultures or areas or countries. That is, places were assigned to such Negro groups as those of the Guianas or the Virgin Islands, or Haiti, on a scale ranging from most to least African.

A revision of this original statement was made several years later, but still in overall terms, though additional data from various regions were utilized to amplify and rectify the listing. While preferable to the earlier statement, this revision proved to be simpler than the nature of the materials has come to demand. For overall categories of this character do not adequately illuminate the complexities of the data, and often, indeed, hide relationships rather than reveal them, which is their intent.

The scale given in this paper represents an application to Afro-american studies of certain techniques of analyzing cultures that have been increasingly employed as greater acquaintance with human ways of living have been gained. That is, we now know that the broad divisions of culture, even particular institutions, behave differently in different situations. This does not mean that a given body of tradition is to be thought of as other than a unified whole, whose elements are all closely interrelated. But it has come to be recognized that the historic forces that are operative in any given situation—forces which, by their very nature, are unique in each circumstance—will eventuate differently in different instances as far as differing aspects of culture are concerned, or where different institutions within a given cultural category are involved.

The principle of cultural focus, discussed in later pages, is helpful in this connection, since its implications for the dynamics of culture in this situation, as in all others, is that it offers an important leverage to bring about changes in certain aspects of a people's way of life as against others or, under contact, to make for differential resistance to change. Thus pressures from outside the Negro groups to give over economic patterns were far greater in the New World than those militating against the retention of folk-tales or secular musical forms, so that the latter two manifest far more of an African character than the former. On the other hand, inner compulsions derived from the focal concerns of Africans with the supernatural tended to resist varying pressures, in varying countries, employing the different kinds of adjustments that have been described, with the result that Africanisms figure prominently in New World Negro religious behavior everywhere.

A refinement of the earlier scale of intensity of Africanisms, not in terms of total cultures, but of aspects within each culture, such as our data now make possible, is given here. In addition, a further refinement has been achieved by subdividing the areas which earlier appeared as units, where the materials indicate that within a given region districts can be distinguished wherein the pattern and degree of African retentions differ. But since it is apparent that in every part of the New World where Negroes live, excepting only the Guiana Bush, class differences operate so as to make for variation in the number and intensity of Africanisms within each Negro group, our table will record only that degree of retention for each group which is closest to African custom.

Because this point is crucial for a proper reading of the table, and an adequate understanding of its significance, it may be amplified here.

Bahia, for example, is rated as most African in language because only there have certain African tongues been retained, as against retention, at most, of no more than African words or phrases or grammatical structures elsewhere. In their daily usage, as a matter of fact, the Bahian Negroes show perhaps less African elements than elsewhere, since they speak the same Portuguese as is spoken by other Brazilians, with fewer elements of African vocabulary, pronunciation or grammar than is found in the speech of almost any other New World Negro group.

It cannot be too strongly stressed that in every area of the New World, except in the Guiana Bush, variation in African forms of behavior stretches from the point of greatest intensity indicated in our table to almost complete conformity with European ways of life. The problem thus becomes one of accounting for differing degrees of variability in the different populations studied. But since the variation does in almost every case extend to the limit set by the conventions of European custom, it can be seen how significant is the analysis of retentions of African convention if we are to discover how far the distribution extends toward the patterns that made up the cultural endowment of the ancestors of present day Negro populations that are the central concern of Afroamerican research.

Table 1 presents, then, these degrees of intensities of Africanisms, listed by aspect of culture and by region in terms of the most Africanlike manifestation of a given cultural aspect or institution. The assignment of values in each instance has either been on the basis of my own field research in the regions listed, or on the reports of trained and competent observers in areas where I have not had first-hand contact. The weightings given the entries are broadly conceived, as is indicated by the terms used to denote the categories of intensity—"very African," "quite African," and the like. To be more specific would be merely to enlarge the area of possible disagreement between students, and to no purpose, since all classifications of such data must be subjective, at least at this point in our knowledge and with the technical resources for cultural analysis at hand. The sources are indicated in the note appended to the text of this paper.

Greater refinement in the treatment of these data might also be more revealing, but the technique of trait-analysis seems to be too mechanical, and to work too great violence to the unity of the cultural elements involved, to be profitably employed in this case. In like manner, the designations are to be regarded as having been set down for convenience only, and to consider them as anything more than useful symbols would be to introduce a note of spurious accuracy against which too great warning cannot be given.

It is apparent, from scanning the table, that the overall listings in the earlier ratings are in the main borne out by the tabulations of this more refined treatment, the principal clarification being in the direction of indicating variability of retention within a given country. Especially interesting is the indication that extension of the continuum toward the pole of African traditions can be greater in certain traits manifested in centers of population

Table 1 Scale of Intensity of New World Africanisms
(Only the greatest degree of retention is indicated for each group.)

| | Technology | Economic Life | Social Organization | Non-kinship Institutions | Religion | Magic | Art | Folklore | Music | Language |
|---|---|---|---|---|---|---|---|---|---|---|
| Guiana (Cush) | b | b | a | a | a | a | b | a | a | b |
| Guiana (Paramaribo) | c | c | | c | a | a | e | a | a | c |
| Haiti (peasant) | c | | b | c | a | b | d | a | a | c |
| Haiti (urban) | e | d | c | c | b | b | e | a | a | c |
| Brazil (Bahia) | d | d | b | d | a | a | b | a | a | a |
| Brazil (Porto Alegre) | e | e | c | d | a | a | e | ? | a | c |
| Brazil (north-urban) | e | d | c | e | a | b | e | d | a | b |
| Brazil (north-rural) | c | c | b | e | c | b | e | b | b | d |
| Jamaica (Maroons) | c | c | b | b | b | a | e | a | a | c |
| Jamaica (general) | e | d | d | d | c | b | e | a | b | c |
| Trinidad (Toco) | e | d | c | c | c | b | e | b | b | d |
| Trinidad (Port-of-Spain) | e | d | c | b | a | a | e | b | a | c |
| Cuba | ? | ? | ? | c | a | a | ? | ? | b | ? |
| Virgin Islands | e | d | c | d | e | c | ? | b | ? | d |
| Gulla Islands | c | c | c | d | c | b | e | a | b | d |
| United States (rural south) | d | e | c | d | c | c | e | c | b | e |
| United States (north) | e | e | c | d | c | c | e | d | b | e |

a : very African    b : quite African    c : somewhat African    d : a little African    e : trace of African custom, or absent    ? : no report

than in Brazil. Taken as a whole, however, the progression of Guiana, Haiti, Brazil, Jamaica, Trinidad, Cuba, Virgin Islands, the Gulla Islands, and southern and northern United States comprises a series wherein a decreasing intensity of Africanisms is manifest. The series will be filled in after field-work has been carried on in areas as yet unstudied, but there seems little prospect of finding New World Negro cultures more African than those of the interior of Dutch Guiana, nor, in recognizable form, less so than among certain Negro groups in the northern part of the United States.

Turning now to consider the different degree to which differing elements in each of these cultures have responded to contact with non-African ways of life, we see that the carry-over of Africanisms is anything but uniform over the individual cultures, being far greater in some aspects than in others. Certain generalizations can, however, be drawn. Music, folklore, magic and religion, on the whole, have retained more of their African character than economic life, or technology, or art, while language and social structures based on kinship or free association, tend to vary through all the degrees of intensity that are noted.

These differences are probably due to the circumstances of slave-life, and confirm common-sense observations made during the period of slavery. Slave-owners were primarily concerned with the technological and economic aspects of the lives of their slaves, while the conditions of life as a slave also of necessity warped whatever patterns of African social structures the Negroes felt impelled to preserve. On the other hand, what tales were told or the songs that were sung made little difference to the masters, and few external blocks were placed in the way of their retention. In the case of religion, outer controls were of varying kinds and were responded to in varying degree, as is reflected in the intermediate position of this cultural element. Magic, which tends to go under-ground under pressure and can most easily be practised without detection—the force of the specific psychological compulsions here being of special importance—persisted in recognizable form everywhere, particularly since the similarity between African and European magic is so great that the one cultural stream must have operated to reinforce the other. The failure of African art to survive except in Guiana and to a lesser degree in Brazil is understandable when the life of the slave, which permitted little leisure and offered slight stimulus for the production of art in the aboriginal African style or, indeed, in any other style, is recalled.

One further fact which emerges from our table is the differing variability, over the New World as a whole, of the several aspects of the cultures as these have been listed. Only religion and language comprehend in maximum extension toward African patterns all degrees of intensity. Minimum variation in this respect is shown by music, which everywhere has been retained in at least "quite African" form. The degree of variation within each of the groups is likewise interesting, since it is seen how the Bush-Negro culture, the most African, is also most homogeneous as far as the African nature of its several elements is concerned, while the cultures of the

Negroes of the United States, though manifesting a comparable degree of homogeneity, expresses its homogeneous quality at the opposite end of the scale.

The facts thus shown hold both particular and general significance. To students of Afroamerican problems, differentials become manifests which offer leads for further historical and ethnological analysis, since it is to be assumed that the explanation for such differentials is to be discovered in the modes of conducting slaving operations and in the circumstances of slave life, as these reacted upon the aboriginal patterns of individuals derived from the various relevant cultures of Africa. From the broader point of view of understanding culture as a whole, however, such treatment documents the concept of culture as a series of interrelated, but quasi-independent variables that undergo processes of change in accordance with the particular historical situation under which impact of new ideas and new customs has taken place, and the focal concerns of the peoples who, like the Negroes of the New World, made the cultural and psychological adjustments that were called forth by their historical experience.

### 4

The hypotheses that underlie the study of African cultural survivals in the New World derive from a conception of human civilization that holds social behavior to be something learned rather than inborn and instinctive. This means that though there are as many cultures—that is, accepted modes of conduct, configurations of institutions, and systems of values and goals—as there are societies, every culture, or any of its elements, can be mastered by any individual without regard to race, or by any group that has the will and the opportunity to master them.

It follows from our concept of culture as something learned that the borrowing of traditions by one people from another is a simple matter, and research has actually established that cultural borrowing is a universal in human social experience. It is today clear that no two peoples have ever been in contact but that they have taken new ideas and new customs from each other, and this quite independently of whether that contact was friendly or hostile, whether it was between groups of the same size or of unequal size, whether differences of prestige existed between them or they met on a plane of equality.

The conception of culture on which our hypotheses are based thus envisages the operation of the principle of constant change—through borrowing and internal innovation—but at the same time assumes a high degree of stability in every culture, which is assured by the transmission of habits, customs, beliefs and institutions from one generation to the next. That is, the individual member of a society learns how to behave in a given situation, how to operate the techniques which assure his society its living, how to adapt to a given system of drives, rewards and values because he is taught or observes all these things. The resultant cultural conservatism gives

to everyday life a tenaciousness, a toughness—in many writings not sufficiently recognized—which comes to be of special importance in the study
of Africanisms among the Negroes of the New World.

If we assume, then, that culture is in constant change because it is
learned, and not inborn, but is learned by the individuals that constitute
any given society so well that the tendency of human beings to conserve
tradition gives to every culture great stability, the problem next presented
is to resolve this seeming paradox by studying those circumstances in which
changes are instituted, or in which retention of conventions makes for
successful resistance to change. It is essentially the problem of balancing
the drives that induce acceptance of new customs as against the mechanisms
that preserve earlier sanctioned modes of behavior. It is here that the field
of Afroamerican studies can make its greatest contribution.

We may say that the basic hypothesis of culture as something learned
is sharpened when it is perceived that under contact elements of a culture
are the more effectively retained in the degree that they bear resemblance
to newly experienced patterns of behavior or institutions. This, in turn, is
further refined by reference to the process of *syncretism,* the tendency to
identify those elements in the new culture with similar elements in the old
one, enabling the persons experiencing the contact to move from one to the
other, and back again, with psychological ease. The outstanding instance of
syncretism is the identification, in Catholic countries of the New World, of
African deities with the saints of the Church—a phenomenon so well
documented that it need but be mentioned here to make the point.

The discovery that the same principle is operative in West Africa, at
the southern border of Mohammedan influence, where among the Hausa
the pagan *iska* are identified with the *jinn* of the Koran, extends its validity.
But if we turn our analysis to Protestant countries, where syncretism of this
sort is not possible, we find that though the names of African deities have
been but rarely retained, syncretisms take other, more generalized forms.
An example of this is the retention of the African requirement of initiation
into religious groups through its syncretization with the Christian concept
of sanctification achieved through preparation for baptism, or as expressed
in the institution of the "mournin' ground."

At this point another principle must be stated—that of *reinterpretation.* For where it is not possible to set up syncretisms, the force of cultural
conservatism seeks expression in substance, rather than form, in psychological value rather than in name, if the original culture is to survive at all.
Here the hypothesis of the importance of resemblance of the old element
to the new is again involved. Though to a lesser degree than in the instance
of syncretisms, reinterpretation also requires that some characteristic of the
new cultural element be correlated with a corresponding part of the original
one by those to whom it is presented, before the mechanism can operate
effectively.

In this fashion, the pattern of polygynous family structure has come
to be reinterpreted in terms of successive, rather than of simultaneous

plural matings, something which has set in motion an entire train of adjust-ments. Not the least of these has been the rejection, within the Negro group, of the European interpretation of illegitimacy as applied to offspring of unions not sanctioned by law and to legal divorce, since these laws are meaningless in terms of aboriginal conventions. The extent to which new orientations of this kind find distribution among Negroes everywhere in the New World demonstrates the effectiveness of the mechanism, not only to achieve cultural but also psychological adaptation to the new setting. This could also be documented from other aspects of culture—economic life, or religion, or music—if considerations of space permitted. Here, however, the example given suffices to illustrate the principle that has been derived.

Retention of original custom under contact, whether through syn-cretism or reinterpretation is, however, merely one side of the problem, the other being the acceptance of what is newly presented. Here many impon-derables enter, the most important being the degree to which outer accep-tance involves transfer of values and interpretations in the psychological as well as in the institutional sense. This, of course, raises one of the most difficult problems in the entire field of cultural dynamics—whether any element of culture is ever taken over without some degree of reinterpreta-tion, however free the borrowing.

If this particular question be for the moment disregarded, however, it is to be seen that just as syncretism and reinterpretation are means by which retention of the old is achieved, they are by the same token effective in encouraging the adoption of the new. A succession of matings entered into by a man or a woman implies an acceptance of the monogamic prin-ciple, at the same time that it points to the method by which, through reinterpretation, the old polygynous tradition has been retained. Where African gods are syncretized with Catholic saints, the significance of the fact that the Negroes, as professing Catholics, have accepted the new religion must not be lost sight of by focussing attention too closely on the retention of aboriginal deities.

When we press the matter, however, we find that the problem is further complicated by the selective nature of borrowing an another level. On the basis of a comparative analysis of African and New World Negro cultures, it is apparent that even under the compulsions of the dominant culture of the whites, Negroes have retained African religious beliefs and practices far more than they have retained economic patterns. But when we examine the patterns of African cultures, we find that there is no activity of everyday living but that it is validated by supernatural sanctions. And con-sequently, these figure far more in the total life of the people than does any other single facet of the culture such as those matters having to do with making a living, or family structure, or political institutions. This weighting of the concerns of a people constitutes the focus of their culture. *Cultural focus* is thus seen to be that phenomenon which gives a culture its particu-lar emphasis; which permits the outsider to sense its special distinguishing flavor and to characterize its essential orientation in a few phrases.

The role of cultural focus is of such great importance in situations of cultural contact that a further hypothesis may be advanced to the effect that more elements which lie in the area of focus of a receiving culture will be retained than those appertaining to other aspects of the culture, acceptance being greater in those phases of culture further removed from the focal area. Where a culture is under pressure by a dominant group who seek to induce acceptance of its traditions, elements lying in the focal area will be retained longer than those outside it, though in this case retention will of necessity be manifested in syncretisms and reinterpretations.

For example, in the interior of Dutch Guiana almost the only Europeanisms to be found are those which lie in the realm of material culture. In Brazil, where the Negroes accept most of the dominant European economic order, they adjust to the exigencies of the Church by syncretizing their African deities and continuing to worship them as they are worshipped in Africa. In the United States, where pressures have been most severe, almost no African economic patterns have persisted, but adaptation to Protestantism has been marked by the retention of many Africanisms through reinterpretation.

Still another point that must receive attention has to do with the degree to which elements of a culture that may be peripheral to the focal area, but that ride high in the consciousness of the people—that require thought, or call for decision—are retained under contact when compared to those which, so to speak, are carried below the level of consciousness. These may be termed *cultural imponderables*. Prominent among these are linguistic patterns and musical style, and such sanctions as are comprehended in those determinants of behavior that include types of motor habits, systems of values, or codes of etiquette. Research has demonstrated that manifestations of African culture, wherein there is little conscious awareness, have persisted in the New World to a far greater degree than in the case of those cultural elements that lie outside the area of cultural focus. This is not surprising when the factors involved are considered, since the cultural imponderables, being those elements in culture that intrude but slightly upon consciousness, are taken for granted and are thus far more difficult to dislodge from the thought and behavior patterns of individuals subjected to a new culture than those which must be given continuous attention.

Language and musical style may be cited here to illustrate the point. In the case of the former, the analysis of New World Negro dialects in English, French and Spanish, and their African counterparts in English and French, has shown that the underlying structure of the aboriginal tongues persists longest, and is most resistant to change, while vocabulary and pronunciation exhibit the most non-African elements. But it is just the grammatical configurations of any language that lodge deepest in linguistic habit-patterns, and that present the greatest difficulties where a new language is to be learned—far more so than either phonetics or vocabulary, though this last is easier learned than pronunciation. One does not think about the structure of his speech when he uses his own language; he need only "choose his words," as the saying goes.

Such patterns are laid down very early in life, so that, under contact, they are highly persistent. In like manner it is musical style, the "grammar" of music, that most resists change under contact, so that while music proves to be among the most African elements of Negro culture everywhere, yet in such regions as the United States, or in such a country as Peru, where the retention of Africanisms has been least extensive, the elusive elements of style remain in songs where an aspect such as melodic line has given way to a more European type of musical expression.

On the basis of the findings, then, the hypothesis can be advanced that in situations involving change, cultural imponderables are more resistant than are those elements of which persons are more conscious. It is important to stress in this connection, however, the distinction between this assumption and the hypothesis which holds that material culture is more acceptable under contact that non-material culture. All those phenomena which have been mentioned do fall within the latter category, it is true, but this is incidental to the hypothesis that has been advanced, since the principle is one that concerns process and does not concern form.

An exhaustive treatment of the theoretical basis of Afroamerican research would require the statement of still further hypotheses, dealing with such matters as the effect of population mass, of isolation, and of opportunity for acquiring a new culture; or discussion of the operation of such intangibles as pride in an original culture that is under assault, and a resulting determination to retain it against odds. It would require the evaluation, on the basis of available materials, of hypotheses that have been advanced as a result of research in other cultures, or of the more a priori, philosophical speculations such as the principle which correlates a super-naturalistic approach to life with a primitive or rural setting, or that which assumes a special type of mentality for non-European peoples.

Enough hypotheses which have guided Afroamerican research or have developed out of it have been indicated, however, to demonstrate how significant its contribution can be, and indeed, already has been, in furthering the wider ends of the scientific study of man. We have here been concerned with principles that can be applied to culture; we have mentioned one instance where language is to be drawn on; we could, in the same manner, document the point further with reference to the problems of human biology. But whatever the problems to be studied, the advantages presented by the field of Afroamerican studies in the way of breadth of scope and historic control of data make possible the type of approach which, under proper methodological attack, permit assumptions within the field to be tested adequately before advancing them as applicable to other areas, under differing situations of historical development.

Note: The derivations of the listings given in Table 1 are as follows:
   Guiana, Brazil (Bahia and southern Brazil), Trinidad, and Haiti, on field research, and on various published works bearing on the Negro peoples of these countries.

*Brazil* (north-urban and rural), on unpublished reports of field-work by Octavio Eduardo in Maranhao.

*Jamaica,* on first-hand contact with the Maroons and other Jamaican Negroes, though without opportunity for detailed field research; and for the general population, the volume "Black Roadways in Jamaica," by Martha Beckwith.

*Cuba,* on various works by F. Ortiz, particularly his "Los Negros Brujos," and on R. Lachatanere's "Manual de Santeria."

*Virgin Islands,* on the monograph by A. A. Campbell entitled "St. Thomas Negroes—a study of Personality and Culture" (Psychological Monographs, vol. 55, no. 5, 1943), and on unpublished field materials of J. C. Trevor.

*Gulla Islands,* on field-work by W. R. Bascom, some results of which have been reported in a paper entitled "Acculturation among the Gullah Negroes" (*American Anthropologist,* vol. 43, 1941, pp. 43–50).

*United States,* on many works, from which materials of African derivation have been abstracted and summarized in my own work, "The Myth of the Negro Past."

# 2

## INITIAL ENGLISH CONFRONTATION WITH AFRICANS
### Winthrop D. Jordan

E NGLISH voyagers did not touch upon the shores of West Africa until after 1550, nearly a century after Prince Henry the Navigator had mounted the sustained Portuguese thrust southward for a water passage to the Orient. Usually Englishmen came to Africa to trade goods *with* the natives; the principal hazards of these ventures proved to be climate, disease, and the jealous opposition of the "Portingals" who had long since entrenched themselves in forts along the coast. The earliest English descriptions of West Africa were written by adventurous traders, men who had no special interest in converting the natives or, except for the famous Hawkins voyages, in otherwise laying hands on them. Extensive English participation in the slave trade did not develop until well into the seventeenth century. The first permanent English settlement on the African coast was at Kormantin in 1631, and the Royal African Company was not chartered for another forty years.[1] Initially, therefore, English contact with

Winthrop D. Jordan, *White Over Black: American Attitudes Toward the Negro, 1550–1812* (Chapel Hill: University of North Carolina Press, 1968), pp. 3–9, 20–34, 37–40, 43. Reprinted by permission of the publisher.

[1] Kenneth G. Davies, *The Royal African Company* (London, 1957), 38–46; John W. Blake, trans. and ed., *Europeans in West Africa, 1450–1560; Documents to Illustrate the Nature and Scope of Portuguese Enterprise in West Africa, the Abortive Attempt of Castilians to Create an Empire There, and the Early English Voyages to Barbary and Guinea* (*Works Issued by the Hakluyt Society,* 2d Ser., 87 [1942]), II, 254–60.

Africans did not take place primarily in a context which prejudged the Negro as a slave, at least not as a slave of Englishmen. Rather, Englishmen met Negroes merely as another sort of men.

Englishmen found the natives of Africa very different from themselves. Negroes looked different; their religion was un-Christian; their manner of living was anything but English; they seemed to be a particularly libidinous sort of people. All these clusters of perceptions were related to each other, though they may be spread apart for inspection, and they were related also to circumstances of contact in Africa, to previously accumulated traditions concerning that strange and distant continent, and to certain special qualities of English society on the eve of its expansion into the New World.

### THE BLACKNESS WITHOUT

The most arresting characteristic of the newly discovered African was his color. Travelers rarely failed to comment upon it; indeed when describing Negroes they frequently began with complexion and then moved on to dress (or rather lack of it) and manners. At Cape Verde, "These people are all blacke, and are called Negros, without any apparell, saving before their privities,"[2] Robert Baker's narrative poem recounting his two voyages to the West African coast in 1562 and 1563 first introduced the natives with these engaging lines:

> And entering in [a river], we see
>    a number of blacke soules,
> Whose likelinesse seem'd men to be,
>    but all as blacke as coles.
> Their Captaine comes to me
>    as naked as my naile.
> Not having witte or honestie
>    to cover once his taile.[3]

Even more sympathetic observers seemed to find blackness a most salient quality in Negroes: "although the people were blacke and naked, yet they were civill."[4]

---

[2] "The voyage made by M. John Hawkins . . . to the coast of Guinea and the Indies of Nova Hispania . . . 1564," in Richard Hakluyt, The Principal Navigations, Voyages, Traffiques and Discoveries of the English Nation . . . , 12 vols., 1598 ed. (Glasgow, 1903–05), X, 15. See Katherine Beverly Oakes, Social Theory in the Early Literature of Voyage and Exploration in Africa (unpubl. Ph.D. diss., University of California, Berkeley, 1944), 120–23.

[3] "The First Voyage of Robert Baker to Guinie . . . 1562," in Richard Hakluyt, The Principall Navigations, Voiages and Discoveries of the English Nation . . . (London, 1589), 132. The entire poem was omitted in the 1598 edition.

[4] "The Voyage of M. George Fenner . . . Written by Walter Wren" (1566), Hakluyt, Principal Navigations, VI, 270. All ensuing references are to this reprinted 1598 edition unless otherwise indicated.

Englishmen actually described Negroes as *black*—an exaggerated term which in itself suggests that the Negro's complexion had powerful impact upon their perceptions. Even the peoples of northern Africa seemed so dark that Englishmen tended to call them "black" and let further refinements go by the board. Blackness became so generally associated with Africa that every African seemed a black man. In Shakespeare's day, the Moors, including Othello, were commonly portrayed as pitchy black and the terms *Moor* and *Negro* used almost interchangeably.[5] With curious inconsistency, however, Englishmen recognized that Africans south of the Sahara were not at all the same people as the much more familiar Moors.[6] Sometimes they referred to Negroes as "black Moors" to distinguish them from the peoples of North Africa. During the seventeenth century the distinction became more firmly established and indeed writers came to stress the difference in color, partly because they delighted in correcting their predecessors and partly because Negroes were being taken up as slaves and Moors, increasingly, were not. In the more detailed and accurate reports about West Africa of the seventeenth century, moreover, Negroes in different regions were described as varying considerably in complexion. In England, however, the initial impression of Negroes was not appreciably modified: the firmest fact about the Negro was that he was "black."

The powerful impact which the Negro's color made upon Englishmen must have been partly owing to suddenness of contact. Though the Bible as well as the arts and literature of antiquity and the Middle Ages offered some slight introduction to the "Ethiope," England's immediate acquaintance with black-skinned peoples came with relative rapidity. While the virtual monopoly held by Venetian ships in England's foreign trade prior to the sixteenth century meant that people much darker than Englishmen were not entirely unfamiliar, really black men were virtually unknown except as vaguely referred to in the hazy literature about the sub-Sahara which had filtered down from antiquity. Native West Africans probably first appeared in London in 1554; in that year five "Negroes" as the legitimate trader William Towrson reported, were taken to England, "kept till they could speake the language," and then brought back again "to be a helpe to Englishmen" who were engaged in trade with Negroes on the coast. Hakluyt's later discussion of these Negroes, who had said "could wel agree with our meates and drinkes" though "the colde and moyst aire doth

---

[5] Warner Grenelle Rice, Turk, Moor and Persian in English Literature from 1550–1660, with Particular Reference to the Drama (unpubl. Ph.D. diss., Harvard University, 1926), 401–2n; Robert R. Cawley, *The Voyagers and Elizabethan Drama* (Boston, 1938), 31; Samuel C. Chew, *The Crescent and the Rose: Islam and England during the Renaissance* (N. Y., 1937), 521–24; Wylie Sypher, *Guinea's Captive Kings: British Anti-Slavery Literature of the XVIIIth Century* (Chapel Hill, 1942), 26.

[6] An early instance is in "The Second Voyage to Guinea . . ." (1554), in Hakluyt, *Principal Navigations*, VI, 167–68. See the associations made by Leo Africanus, *The History and Description of Africa and of the Notable Things Therein Contained . . .* , trans. John Pory [ca. 1600], ed. Robert Brown, 3 vols. (London, 1896), I, 130.

somewhat offend them," suggests that these "blacke Moores" were a novelty to Englishmen.[7] In this respect the English experience was markedly different from that of the Spanish and Portuguese who for centuries had been in close contact with North Africa and had actually been invaded and subjected by people both darker and more highly civilized than themselves. The impact of the Negro's color was the more powerful upon Englishmen, moreover, because England's principal contact with Africans came in West Africa and the Congo where men were not merely dark but almost literally black: one of the fairest-skinned nations suddenly came face to face with one of the darkest peoples on earth.

Viewed from one standpoint, Englishmen were merely participating in Europe's discovery that the strange men who stood revealed by European expansion overseas came in an astounding variety of colors. A Spanish chronicle translated into English in 1555 was filled with wonder at this diversity: "One of the marveylous thynges that god useth in the composition of man, is coloure: which doubtlesse can not bee consydered withowte great admiration in beholding one to be white and an other blacke, beinge coloures utterlye contrary. Sum lykewyse to be yelowe whiche is betwene blacke and white: and other of other coloures as it were of dyvers liveres."[8] As this passage suggests, the juxtaposition of black and white was the most striking marvel of all. And for Englishmen this juxtaposition was more than a curiosity.

In England perhaps more than in southern Europe, the concept of blackness was loaded with intense meaning. Long before they found that some men were black, Englishmen found in the idea of blackness a way of expressing some of their most ingrained values. No other color except white conveyed so much emotional impact. As described by the *Oxford English Dictionary*, the meaning of *black* before the sixteenth century included, "Deeply stained with dirt; soiled, dirty, foul. . . . Having dark or deadly purposes, malignant; pertaining to or involving death, deadly; baneful, disastrous, sinister. . . . Foul, iniquitous, atrocious, horrible, wicked. . . . Indicating disgrace, censure, liability to punishment, etc." Black was an emotionally partisan color, the handmaid and symbol of baseness and evil, a sign of danger and repulsion.

Embedded in the concept of blackness was its direct opposite— whiteness. No other colors so clearly implied opposition, "beinge coloures utterlye contrary"; no others were so frequently used to denote polarization:

[7] Hakluyt, *Principal Navigations*, VI, 176, 200, 217–18. Just how little Europeans knew about Africa prior to the Portuguese explorations is evident in T. Simar, "La géographie de l'Afrique central dans l'antiquité et au moyen âge," *La Revue Congolaise*, 3 (1912), 1–23, 81–102, 145–69, 225–52, 288–310, 440–41.

[8] Francisco López de Gómara, in Peter Martyr (D'Anghera), *The Decades of the Newe Worlde . . .* , trans. Richard Eden (London, 1555), in Edward Arber, ed., *The First Three English Books on America . . .* (Birmingham, Eng., 1885), 338.

Everye white will have its blacke,
And everye sweete its sowre.[9]

White and black connoted purity and filthiness, virginity and sin, virtue and baseness, beauty and ugliness, beneficence and evil, God and the devil.[10] Whiteness, moreover, carried a special significance for Elizabethan Englishmen: it was, particularly when complemented by red, the color of perfect human beauty, especially *female* beauty. This ideal was already centuries old in Elizabeth's time,[11] and their fair Queen was its very embodiment: her cheeks were "roses in a bed of lillies." (Elizabeth was naturally pale but like many ladies then and since she freshened her "lillies" at the cosmetic table.)[12] An adoring nation knew precisely what a beautiful Queen looked like.

Her cheeke, her chinne, her neck, her nose,
This was a lillye, that was a rose;
Her hande so white as whales bone,
Her finger tipt with Cassidone;
Her bosome, sleeke as Paris plaster,
Held upp twoo bowles of Alabaster.[13]

Shakespeare himself found the lily and the rose a compelling natural coalition.

---

[9] Thomas Percy, *Reliques of Ancient English Poetry . . .* , ed. Robert A. Willmott (London, 1857), 27 (Sir Cauline, pt. 2, stanza 1).

[10] Numerous examples in Middle English, Shakespeare, the Bible, and Milton are given by P. J. Heather, "Colour Symbolism," *Folk Lore,* 59 (1948), 169–70, 175–78, 182–83; 60 (1949), 208–16, 266–76. See also Harold R. Isaacs, "Blackness and Whiteness," *Encounter,* 21 (1963), 8–21; Caroline F. E. Spurgeon, *Shakespeare's Imagery and What It Tells Us* (Boston, 1958), 64, 66–69, 158; Arrah B. Evarts, "Color Symbolism," *Psychoanalytic Review,* 6 (1919), 129–34; Don Cameron Allen, "Symbolic Color in the Literature of the English Renaissance," *Philological Quarterly,* 15 (1936), 81–92; and for a different perspective, Francis B. Gummere, "On the Symbolic Use of the Colors Black and White in Germanic Tradition," *Haverford College Studies,* 1 (1889), 112–62.

[11] Walter Clyde Curry, *The Middle English Ideal of Personal Beauty; As Found in the Metrical Romances, Chronicles, and Legends of the XIII, XIV, and XV Centuries* (Baltimore, 1916), 3, 80–98.

[12] Elkin Calhoun Wilson, *England's Eliza* (Cambridge, Mass., 1939), 337; Charles Carroll Camden, *The Elizabethan Woman* (Houston, N. Y., and London, 1952), chap. 7; Cawley, *Voyagers and Elizabethan Drama,* 85; Elizabeth Jenkins, *Elizabeth the Great* (London, 1958), 62, 100, 159, 296; Gamaliel Bradford, *Elizabethan Women,* ed. Harold O. White (Boston, 1936), 82, 212; Violet A. Wilson, *Queen Elizabeth's Maids of Honour and Ladies of the Privy Chamber* (N. Y., n.d.), 4–5. Hugh Plat, *Delights for Ladies, Written Originally by Sir Hugh Plat, First Printed in 1602, London, England,* ed. Violet and Hal W. Trovillion (Herrin, Ill., 1939), 87–94, 99, 102–3, contains advice on cosmetics.

[13] [George Puttenham?], *Partheniades* (1579), quoted in Wilson, *England's Eliza,* 242.

'Tis beauty truly blent, whose red and white
Nature's own sweet and cunning hand laid on.[14]

By contrast, the Negro was ugly, by reason of his color and also his "horrid Curles" and "disfigured" lips and nose.[15] As Shakespeare wrote apologetically of his black mistress,

My mistress' eyes are nothing like the sun;
Coral is far more red than her lips' red:
If snow be white, why then her breasts are dun;
If hairs be wires, black wires grow on her head.
I have seen roses damask'd, red and white,
But no such roses see I in her cheeks.[16]

Some Elizabethans found blackness an ugly mask, superficial but always demanding attention. . . .


### DEFECTIVE RELIGION

While distinctive appearance set Africans over into a novel category of men, their religious condition set them apart from Englishmen in a more familiar way. Englishmen and Christians everywhere were sufficiently acquainted with the concept of heathenism that they confronted its living representatives without puzzlement. Certainly the rather sudden discovery that the world was teeming with heathen people made for heightened vividness and urgency in a long-standing problem; but it was the fact that this problem was already well formulated long before contact with Africa which proved important in shaping English reaction to the Negro's defective religious condition.

In one sense heathenism was less a "problem" for Christians than an exercise in self-definition: the heathen condition defined by negation the proper Christian life. In another sense, the presence of heathenism in the world constituted an imperative to intensification of religious commitment. From its origin Christianity was a universalist, proselytizing religion, and the sacred and secular histories of Christianity made manifest the necessity of bringing non-Christians into the fold. For Englishmen, then, the

[14] *Twelfth Night*, I, v, 259–60, W. J. Craig, ed., *The Complete Works of Shakespeare* (London, N. Y., Toronto, 1943). For other expressions of this ideal: *A Midsummer-Night's Dream*, I, i, 128–29; III, i, 98–99; III, ii, 137–44.

[15] *Love in Its Ecstacy*, quoted in Cawley, *Voyagers and Elizabethan Drama*, 86n; "A Letter written from Goa . . . by one Thomas Stevens . . . 1579," Hakluyt, *Principal Navigations*, VI, 384. Curry, *Middle English Ideal of Personal Beauty*, 64–66, 113–14, indirectly makes abundantly clear how very far Negro women were from matching prevalent English ideals for beautiful noses, lips, and breasts.

[16] Sonnet CXXX; see also nos. CXXVII, CXXXI, CXXXII. Shakespeare's "Dark Lady" is discussed by George B. Harrison, *Shakespeare under Elizabeth* (N. Y., 1933), 64–67, 310.

heathenism of Negroes was at once a counter-image of their own religion and a summons to eradicate an important distinction between the two peoples.

The interaction of these two facets of the concept of heathenism made for a peculiar difficulty. On the one hand, to act upon the felt necessity of converting Negroes would have been to eradicate the point of distinction which Englishmen found most familiar and most readily comprehensible. Yet if they did not act upon this necessity, continued heathenism among Negroes would remain an unwelcome reminder to Englishmen that they were not meeting their obligations to their own faith—nor to the benighted Negroes. Englishmen resolved this implicit dilemma by doing nothing.

Considering the strength of the Christian tradition, it is almost startling that Englishmen failed to respond to the discovery of heathenism in Africa with at least the rudiments of a campaign for conversion. Although the impulse to spread Christianity seems to have been weaker in Englishmen than, say, in the Catholic Portuguese, it cannot be said that Englishmen were indifferent to the obligation imposed upon them by the overseas discoveries of the sixteenth century. While they were badly out of practice at the business of conversion (again in contrast to the Portuguese) and while they had never before been faced with the practical difficulties involved in Christianizing entire continents, they nonetheless were able to contemplate with equanimity and even eagerness the prospect of converting the heathen. Indeed they went so far as to conclude that converting the natives in America was sufficiently important to demand English settlement there. As it turned out, the well-publicized English program for converting Indians produced very meager results, but the avowed intentions certainly were genuine. It was in marked contrast, therefore, that Englishmen did not avow similar intentions concerning Africans until the late eighteenth century. Fully as much as with skin color, though less consciously, Englishmen distinguished between the heathenisms of Indians and of Negroes.

The suggestive congruence of these twin distinctions between Negroes and Indians is not easy to account for. On the basis of the travelers' reports there was no reason for Englishmen to suppose Indians inherently superior to Negroes as candidates for conversion. While in the sixteenth and seventeenth centuries the Englishmen who had first-hand contact with Africans were not, unlike many of the Portuguese, engaged in missionary efforts, the same may be said of most English contact with Indians. On the other hand, America was not Africa. Englishmen contemplated settling in America, where voyagers had established the King's claim and where supposedly the climate was temperate; in contrast, Englishmen did not envision settlement in Africa, which had quickly gained notoriety as a graveyard for Europeans and where the Portuguese had been first on the scene. Certainly these very different circumstances meant that Englishmen confronted Negroes and Indians in radically different social contexts and that

Englishmen would find it far easier to contemplate converting Indians than Negroes. Yet it remains difficult to see why Negroes were not included, at least as a secondary target, by extension from the program actually directed at the Indians. The fact that English contact with Africans so frequently occurred in a context of slave dealing does not entirely explain the omission of Negroes, since in that same context the Portuguese and Spanish did sometimes attempt to minister to the souls of Negroes (somewhat perfunctorily, to be sure) and since Englishmen in America enslaved Indians when good occasion arose. Given these circumstances, it is hard to escape the conclusion that the distinction which Englishmen made as to conversion was at least in some small measure modeled after the difference they saw in skin color.

Although Englishmen failed to incorporate Negroes into the proselytizing effort which was enjoined by the Christian heritage, that heritage did much to shape the English reaction to Negroes as a people. Paradoxically, Christianity worked to make Englishmen think of Negroes as being both very much like themselves and very different. The emphasis on similarity derived directly from the emphatic Christian doctrine which affirmed that mankind was one. The Old Testament, most notably the book of Genesis, seemed absolutely firm on this point: all men derived from the same act of creation and had at first shared a common experience. So too the New Testament declared all nations to be of one blood. The strength of this universalist strain in Christianity was evident in the assurances offered by a number of English travelers in Africa that they had discovered rudiments of the Word among the most barbarous heathens. In 1623 Richard Jobson exclaimed that "they have a wonderous reference, to the leviticall law, as it is in our holy Bible related; the principalls whereof they are not ignorant in, for they do report concerning *Adam* and *Eve,* whom they call *Adama* and *Evahaha,* talking of *Noahs* flood, and of *Moses,* with many other things our sacred History makes mention of." Another commentator hinted at covert Calvinism in the jungle: "They keep their *Fetissoes* [Fetish] day, one day in seven, and that Tuesday (a Sabbath it seems is natural) more solemnly and stricktly than the *Hollanders* do their Sunday."[17] To call the Sabbath "natural" among heathens was an invitation to the missionary to harvest the seed planted everywhere by God. Such a description also serves to demonstrate how powerfully the Christian tradition operated to make Englishmen and other Europeans consider the new peoples of the freshly opened world as being inherently similar to themselves.

At the same time, Christianity militated against the unity of man. Because Englishmen were Christians, heathenism in Negroes was a fundamental defect which set them distinctly apart. However much Englishmen disapproved of Popery and Mahomedanism, they were accustomed to these

---

[17] Jobson, *Golden Trade,* ed. Kingsley, 78 (probably there was good basis for Jobson's contention since the Negroes he referred to were Muslims); *The Golden Coast,* 80.

perversions. Yet they were not accustomed to dealing face to face with people who appeared, so far as many travelers could tell, to have no religion at all.[18] Steeped in the legacy and trappings of their own religion, Englishmen were ill prepared to see any legitimacy in African religious practices. Judged by Christian cosmology, Negroes stood in a separate category of men.

Perhaps the ambivalence inherent in Christian assessment of heathenism played a part in muting the importance of the Negro's heathenism in the eyes of Englishmen. Probably the increasingly Protestant character of English religious belief also had the same effect, for the Portuguese and Spanish seem to have found the heathenism of Negroes and Indians a more salient and distinct quality than the English did; in the seventeenth and eighteenth centuries this differing reaction among Protestants and Catholics was to become still more obvious upon the slave plantations of the Americas. At any rate, it is clear that during the early period of contact with Africa heathenism was far from being *the* critical attribute which caused Englishmen to view Negroes as a separate kind of people.

Indeed the most important aspect of English reaction to Negro heathenism was that Englishmen evidently did not regard it as separable from the Negro's other attributes. Heathenism was treated not so much as a specifically religious defect but as one manifestation of a general refusal to measure up to proper standards, as a failure to be English or even civilized. There was every reason for Englishmen to fuse the various attributes they found in Africans. During the first century of English contact with Africa, Protestant Christianity was an important element in English patriotism; especially during the struggle against Spain the Elizabethan's special Christianity was interwoven into his conception of his own nationality, and he was therefore inclined to regard the Negroes' lack of true religion as part of theirs. Being a Christian was not merely a matter of subscribing to certain doctrines; it was a quality inherent in oneself and in one's society. It was interconnected with all the other attributes of normal and proper men: as one of the earliest English accounts distinguished Negroes from Englishmen, they were "a people of beastly living, without a God, lawe, religion, or common wealth"[19]—which was to say that Negroes were not Englishmen. Far from isolating African heathenism as a separate characteristic, English travelers sometimes linked it explicitly with barbarity and blackness. They already had in hand a mediating term among these impinging concepts—the *devil*. As one observer declared, Negroes "in colour so in condition are little other than Devils incarnate," and, further, "the Devil . . . has infused prodigious Idolatry into their hearts, enough to rellish his pallat and aggrandize their tortures when he gets power to fry their souls, as the raging Sun has already scorcht their cole-black car-

[18] For example, Hakluyt, *Principal Navigations*, VI, 144.

[19] "Second Voyage to Guinea," *ibid.*, 167.

casses."[20] "Idolatry" was indeed a serious failing, but English travelers in West Africa tended to regard defect of true religion as an aspect of the Negro's "condition." In an important sense, then, heathenism was for Englishmen one inherent characteristic of savage men.

### SAVAGE BEHAVIOR

The condition of savagery—the failure to be civilized—set Negroes apart from Englishmen in an ill-defined but crucial fashion. Africans were *different* from Englishmen in so many ways: in their clothing, huts, farming, warfare, language, government, morals, and (not least important) in their table manners. Englishmen were fully aware that Negroes living at different parts of the coast were not all alike; it was not merely different reactions in the observers which led one to describe a town as "marveilous artificially builded with mudde walles . . . and kept very cleane as well in their streetes as in their houses" and another to relate how "they doe eate" each other "alive" in some places but dead in others "as we wolde befe or mutton."[21] No matter how great the actual and observed differences among Negroes, though, none of these black men seemed to live like Englishmen.

To judge from the comments of voyagers, Englishmen had an unquenchable thirst for the details of savage life. Partly their curiosity was a matter of scientific interest in the "natural productions" of the newly opened world overseas. To the public at large, the details of savage behavior appealed to an interest which was not radically different from the scientist's; an appetite for the "wonderful" seems to have been built into Western culture. It is scarcely surprising that civilized Englishmen should have taken an interest in reports about cosmetic mutilation, polygamy, infanticide, ritual murder and the like—of course *English* men did not really *do* any of these things themselves. Finally, reports about savages began arriving at a time when Englishmen very much needed to be able to translate their apprehensive interest in an uncontrollable world out of medieval, religious terms. The discovery of savages overseas enabled them to make this translation easily, to move from miracles to verifiable monstrosities, from heaven to earth.

As with skin color, English reporting of African customs constituted an exercise in self-inspection by means of comparison. The necessity of continuously measuring African practices with an English yardstick of course tended to emphasize the differences between the two groups, but it

---

[20] Herbert, *Some Years Travels*, 10, 7.

[21] Both seem to be eyewitness reports. "Voyage of Thomas Candish," Hakluyt, *Principal Navigations*, XI, 293; anonymous author on Hawkins' third voyage quoted in James A. Williamson, *Sir John Hawkins: The Time and the Man* (Oxford, 1927), 509. There is an interesting description of (almost certainly) the now well-known symbiotic relationship between Negroes and Pygmies in *The Golden Coast*, 66–67, "I have not found so much faith, nor faithfulness, no not in Israel."

also made for heightened sensitivity to instances of similarity. Thus the Englishman's ethnocentrism tended to distort his perception of African culture in two opposite directions. While it led him to emphasize differences and to condemn deviations from the English norm, it led him also to seek out similarities (where perhaps none existed) and to applaud every instance of conformity to the appropriate standard. Though African clothing and personal etiquette were regarded as absurd, equivalents to European practices were at times detected in other aspects of African culture. Particularly, Englishmen were inclined to see the structures of African societies as analogous to their own, complete with kings, counselors, gentlemen, and the baser sort. Here especially they found Africans like themselves, partly because they knew no other way to describe a society and partly because there was actually good basis for such a view in the social organization of West African communities. . . .[22]

Despite the fascination and self-instruction Englishmen derived from expatiating upon the savage behavior of Africans, they never felt that savagery was as important a quality in Africans as it was in the American Indians. Two sets of circumstances made for this distinction in the minds of Englishmen. As was the case with heathenism, contrasting social contexts played an important role in shaping the English response to savagery in the two peoples. Inevitably, the savagery of the Indians assumed a special significance in the minds of those actively engaged in a program of bringing civilization into the American wilderness. The case with the African was different: the English errand into Africa was not a new or a perfect community but a business trip. No hope was entertained for civilizing the Negro's steaming continent, and Englishmen lacked compelling reason to develop a program for remodeling the African natives. The most compelling necessity was that of pressing forward the business of buying Negroes from other Negroes. It was not until the slave trade came to require justification, in the eighteenth century, that some Englishmen found special reason to lay emphasis on the Negro's savagery.

From the beginning, also, the importance of the Negro's savagery was muted by the Negro's color. Englishmen could go a long way toward expressing their sense of being different from Negroes merely by calling them black. By contrast, the aboriginals in America did not have the appearance of being radically distinct from Europeans except in religion and savage behavior. English voyagers placed much less emphasis upon the Indian's color than upon the Negro's, and they never permitted the Indian's physiognomy to distract their attention from what they regarded as his essential quality, his savagery. Even in the eighteenth century, when the savages of the world were being promoted to "nobility" by Europeans as an aid to self-scrutiny and reform at home, the Negro was not customarily

[22] An early instance is in Clements R. Markham, ed., *The Hawkins' Voyages during the Reigns of Henry VIII, Queen Elizabeth, and James I* (Works Issued by the Hakluyt Soc., 1st Ser., 57 [1878]), 19.

thought of as embodying all the qualities of the noble savage. Certainly he never attained the status of the Indian's primitive nobility. It was not merely that Negroes had by then become pre-eminently the slaves of Europeans in the Americas. The Negro's appearance remained a barrier to acceptance as the noble type. . . .

It would be a mistake, however, to slight the importance of the Negro's savagery, since it fascinated Englishmen from the very first. English observers in West Africa were sometimes so profoundly impressed by the Negro's deviant behavior that they resorted to a powerful metaphor with which to express their own sense of difference from him. They knew perfectly well that Negroes were men, yet they frequently described the Africans as "brutish" or "bestial" or "beastly." The hideous tortures, the cannibalism, the rapacious warfare, the revolting diet (and so forth page after page) seemed somehow to place the Negro among the beasts. The circumstances of the Englishman's confrontation with the Negro served to strengthen this feeling. Slave traders in Africa handled Negroes the same way men in England handled beasts, herding and examining and buying. The Guinea Company instructed Bartholomew Haward in 1651 "to buy and put aboard you so many negers as yo'r ship can cary, and for what shalbe wanting to supply with Cattel, as also to furnish you with victualls and provisions for the said negers and Cattel."[23] Africa, moreover, teemed with strange and wonderful animals, and men that killed like tigers, ate like vultures, and grunted like hogs seemed indeed to merit comparison with beasts. In making this instinctive analogy, Englishmen unwittingly demonstrated how powerfully the African's different culture—for Englishmen, his "savagery"—operated to make Negroes seem to Englishmen a radically different kind of men.

### THE APES OF AFRICA

If Negroes were likened to beasts, there was in Africa a beast which was likened to men. It was a strange and eventually tragic happenstance of nature that the Negro's homeland was the habitat of the animal which in appearance most resembles man. The animal called "orang-outang" by contemporaries (actually the chimpanzee) was native to those parts of western Africa where the early slave trade was heavily concentrated. Though Englishmen were acquainted (for the most part vicariously) with monkeys and baboons, they were unfamiliar with tailless apes who walked about like men.[24] Accordingly, it happened that Englishmen were introduced to

---

[23] Elizabeth Donnan, ed., *Documents Illustrative of the History of the Slave Trade to America,* 4 vols. (Washington, D. C., 1930–35), I, 129.

[24] H. W. Janson, *Apes and Ape Lore in the Middle Ages and the Renaissance* (London, 1952), chap. 11; also Robert M. and Ada W. Yerkes, *The Great Apes: A Study of Anthropoid Life* (New Haven, 1929), 1–26; John C. Greene, *The Death of Adam: Evolution and Its Impact on Western Thought* (Ames, Iowa, 1959), chap. 6. I have oversimplified the confused state of

the anthropoid apes and to Negroes at the same time and in the same place. The startingly human appearance and movements of the "ape"—a generic term though often used as a synonym for the "orang-outang"—aroused some curious speculations.

In large measure these speculations derived from traditions which had been accumulating in Western culture since ancient times. Medieval bestiaries contained rosters of strange creatures who in one way or another seemed disturbingly to resemble men. There were the *simia* and the *cynocephali* and the *satyri* and the others, all variously described and related to one another, all jumbled in a characteristic amalgam of ancient reports and medieval morality. The confusion was not easily nor rapidly dispelled, and many of the traditions established by this literature were very much alive during the seventeenth century. . . .

Given this tradition and the coincidence of contact, it was virtually inevitable that Englishmen should discern similarity between the man-like beasts and the beast-like men of Africa.[25] A few commentators went so far as to suggest that Negroes had sprung from the generation of ape-kind or that apes were themselves the offspring of Negroes and some unknown African beast.[26] These contentions were squarely in line with the ancient tradition that Africa was a land "bringing dailie foorth newe monsters" because as Aristotle himself had suggested many different species came into proximity at the scarce watering places. Jean Bodin, the famous six-teenth-century French political theorist, summarized this wisdom of the ages with the categorical remark that "promiscuous coition of men and animals took place, wherefore the regions of Africa produce for us so many monsters."[27] Despite all these monsters out of Africa, the notion that Negroes stemmed from beasts in a literal sense did not receive wide credence; even the writers who advanced it did not suggest that the Negro himself was now a beast.

---

terminology concerning simians; see M. F. Ashley Montagu, *Edward Tyson, M. D., F. R. S., 1650–1708, and the Rise of Human and Comparative Anatomy in England; A Study in the History of Science* (Phila., 1943), 228, 244–49. By 1600 "baboons," "marmosets," "monkies," "apes" were common in literature; several (probably baboons) were on show in London. Yet a foreign visitor in 1598 did not list any sort of "apes" in the Tower menagerie, though there were lions there. W. Strunk, Jr., "The Elizabethan Showman's Ape," *Modern Language Notes*, 32 (1917), 215–21; Emma Phipson, *The Animal-Lore of Shakespeare's Time* . . . (London, 1883), 5.

[25] Jobson, *Golden Trade*, ed. Kingsley, 186; Thomas Herbert, *A Relation of Some Yeares Travaile, Begunne Anno 1626. Into Afrique and the Greater Asia, Especially the Territories of the Persian Monarchie* . . . (London, 1634), 16–17; Herbert, *Some Years Travels* (1677), 16–17.

[26] Herbert, *Some Years Travels*, 18; Zirkle, "Knowledge of Heredity," Dunn, ed., *Genetics in the 20th Century*, 39–40.

[27] Quotation from Alexander B. Grosart, ed., *The Complete Works of Thomas Nashe*, 6 vols. (London and Aylesbury, 1883–85), I, 160; Aristotle, *Historia Animalium*, trans. D'Arcy W. Thompson, in J. A. Smith and W. D. Ross, eds., *The Works of Aristotle*, IV (Oxford, 1910), 606b; Bodin, *Method for Easy Comprehension of History*, 105.

Far more common and persistent was the notion that there sometimes occurred "a beastly copulation or conjuncture" between apes and Negroes, and especially that apes were inclined wantonly to attack Negro women.[28] The very explicit idea that apes assaulted female human beings was not new; Negroes were merely being asked to demonstrate what Europeans had known for centuries. Englishmen seemed ready to credit the tales about bestial connections, and even as late as the 1730's a well-traveled, intelligent naval surgeon, John Atkins, was not at all certain that the stories were false: "At some Places the *Negroes* have been suspected of Bestiality with them [apes and monkeys], and by the Boldness and Affection they are known under some Circumstances to express to our Females; the Ignorance and Stupidity on the other side, to guide or control Lust; but more from the near resemblances are sometimes met to the Human Species would tempt one to suspect the Fact." Atkins went on to voice the generally received opinion that if offspring were ever produced by such mixtures they would themselves be infertile: "Altho' by the way, this, like other *Hebridous* Productions, could never go no farther; and as such a monstrous Generation would be more casual and subject to Fatality, the Case must be uncommon and rare."[29]

By the time Atkins addressed himself to this evidently fascinating problem, some of the confusion arising from the resemblance of apes to men had been dispelled. In 1699 the web of legend and unverified fact was disentangled by Edward Tyson, whose comparative study of a young "orang-outang" was a masterwork of critical scientific investigation. Throughout his dissection of the chimpanzee, Tyson meticulously compared the animal with human beings in every anatomical detail, and he established beyond question both the close relationship and the non-identity of ape and man.[30] Here was a step forward; the question of the ape's proper place in nature was now grounded upon much firmer knowledge of the facts. Despite their scientific importance, Tyson's conclusions did nothing to weaken the vigorous tradition which linked the Negro with the ape. The supposed affinity between apes and men had as frequently been expressed in sexual as in anatomical terms, and his findings did not effectively rule out the possibility of unnatural sexual unions. Tyson himself remarked that orangs were especially given to venery.[31]

[28] Quotation from Herbert, *Some Years Travels*, 18. Montagu, *Edward Tyson*, 250–52; John Locke, *An Essay Concerning Human Understanding*, 2 vols. in 1 (London, 1721), II, 53 (Bk. III, chap. 6, sec. 23); Phillips, *Journal*, Churchill, comps., *Voyages*, VI, 211; William Smith, *A New Voyage to Guinea* . . . (London, 1744), 52; Zirkle, "Knowledge of Heredity," Dunn, ed., *Genetics in the 20th Century*, 39–40; Janson, *Apes and Ape Lore*, 267–76.

[29] Atkins, *Voyage to Guinea*, 108; also his *Navy Surgeon*, 369.

[30] Edward Tyson, *Orang-Outang, Sive Homo Sylvestris: Or, the Anatomy of a Pygmie Compared with That of a Monkey, an Ape, and a Man. To Which is Added, A Philological Essay Concerning the Pygmies, the Cynocephali, the Satyrs, and Sphinges of the Ancients. Wherein It will Appear That They Are All Either Apes or Monkeys; and Not Men, As Formerly Pretended* (London, 1699); Montagu, *Edward Tyson*, 225–321.

[31] Tyson, *Orang-Outang*, 42.

The sexual association of apes with Negroes had an inner logic which kept it alive without much or even any factual sustenance.[32] Sexual union seemed to prove a certain affinity without going so far as to indicate actual identity—which was what Englishmen really thought was the case. By forging a sexual link between Negroes and apes, furthermore, Englishmen were able to give vent to their feeling that Negroes were a lewd, lascivious, and wanton people.

### LIBIDINOUS MEN

It was no accident that this affinity between Negroes and apes was so frequently regarded as sexual, for undertones of sexuality run throughout many English accounts of West Africa. To liken Africans—any human beings—to beasts was to stress the animal within the man. Indeed the sexual connotations embodied in the terms *bestial* and *beastly* were considerably stronger in Elizabethan English than they are today, and when the Elizabethan traveler pinned these epithets upon the behavior of Negroes he was frequently as much registering a sense of sexual shock as describing swinish manners: "They are beastly in their living," young Andrew Battell wrote, "for they have men in women's apparel, whom they keep among their wives."[33]

Lecherousness among the Negroes was at times merely another attribute which one would expect to find among heathen, savage, beast-like men. A passage in Samuel Purchas's collection makes evident how closely interrelated all these attributes were in the minds of Englishmen: "They have no knowledge of God; those that traffique and are conversant among strange Countrey people are civiller then the common sort of people, they are very greedie eaters, and no lesse drinkers, and very lecherous, and theevish, and much addicted to uncleanenesse: one man hath as many wives as hee is able to keepe and maintaine."[34] Sexuality was what one expected of savages. . . .

Depiction of the Negro as a lustful creature was not radically new, therefore, when Englishmen first met Negroes face to face. Seizing upon and reconfirming these long-standing and apparently common notions about Africa, Elizabethan travelers and literati spoke very explicitly of

[32] Perhaps there was some slight basis in fact for the association, for certain kinds of sexual conduct (though surely not consummation) between apes and human beings are known to be possible and even likely under some circumstances. Earnest Hooton, *Man's Poor Relations* (Garden City, N. Y., 1942), 19, 84–85.

[33] Ernest George Ravenstein, ed., *The Strange Adventures of Andrew Battell of Leigh, in Angola and the Adjoining Regions. Reprinted from "Purchas His Pilgrimes"* (ca. 1607) (*Works Issued by the Hakluyt Soc.*, 2d Ser., 6 [London, 1901]), 18. The term *beastiality* was first used to denote sexual relations with animals early in the 17th century; it was thus used frequently only for about 150 years!

[34] "A Description . . . of Guinea . . ." in Samuel Purchas, *Hakluytus Posthumus or Purchas His Pilgrimes, Contayning a History of the World in Sea Voyages and Lande Travells by Englishmen and Others*, 20 vols. (Glasgow, 1905–07), VI, 251.

Negroes as being especially sexual. Othello's embraces were "the gross clasps of a lascivious Moor." Francis Bacon's *New Atlantis (ca.* 1624) referred to "an holy hermit" who "desired to see the Spirit of Fornication; and there appeared to him a little foul ugly Aethiop." Negro men, reported a seventeenth-century traveler, sported "large Propagators. . . ."[35]

It is certain that the presumption of heightened sexuality in black men was far from being an incidental or casual association in the minds of Englishmen. How very deeply this association operated is obvious in *Othello,* a drama which loses most of its power and several of its central points if it is read with the assumption that because the black man was the hero English audiences were friendly or perhaps indifferent to his blackness.[36] Shakespeare was writing both about and to his countrymen's feelings concerning physical distinctions between kinds of people; the play is shot through with the language of blackness and sex. Iago goes out of his way to soliloquize upon his own motives: "I hate the Moor,/ And it is thought abroad that 'twixt my sheets/ He has done my office." Later, he becomes more direct, "For that I do suspect the lusty Moor hath leaped into my seat." It was upon this so obviously absurd suspicion that Iago based his resolve to "turn her virtue into pitch." Such was his success, of course, that Othello finally rushes off "to furnish me with some means of death for the fair devil." With this contorted denomination of Desdemona, Othello unwittingly revealed how deeply Iago's promptings about Desdemona's "own clime, complexion, and degree" had eaten into his consciousness. Othello was driven into accepting the premise that the physical distinction *matters:* "For she had eyes," he has to reassure himself, "and chose me." Then, as his suspicions give way to certainty, he equates her character with his own complexion:

> Her name, that was as fresh,
> As Dian's visage, is now begrim'd and black
> As mine own face.

This important aspect of Iago's triumph over the noble Moor was a subtly inverted reflection of the propositions which Iago, hidden in darkness, worked upon the fair lady's father. No one knew better than Iago how to play upon hidden strings of emotion. Not content with the straightforward crudity that "your daughter and the Moor are now making the beast with two backs," Iago told the agitated Brabantio that "an old black

---

[35] Rice, Turk, Moor, and Persian, 401; *Othello,* I, i, 127; Spedding, Ellis, and Heath, eds., *Works of Francis Bacon,* III, 152; Ogilby, *Africa,* 451.

[36] See Philip Mason, *Prospero's Magic: Some Thoughts on Class and Race* (London, 1962), chap. 3. The following quotations from *Othello* may be found in I, i, 88–89, 111–12, 117–18, 143; I, ii, 66, 69–71; I, iii, 101, 392–94; II, i, 307–8; II, iii, 369; III, iii, 189, 230, 387–89, 478–79; V, ii, 128–29, 155, 161–62. Shakespeare's play was based on an Italian drama in which Iago told "the Moor" that Desdemona had committed adultery, partly because she was tired of the Moor's color: Kenneth Muir, *Shakespeare's Sources: Comedies and Tragedies* (London, 1957), 124.

ram/ Is tupping your white ewe" and alluded politely to "your daughter cover'd with a Barbary horse." This was not merely the language of (as we say) a "dirty" mind: it was the integrated imagery of blackness and whiteness, of Africa, of the sexuality of beasts and the bestiality of sex. And of course Iago was entirely successful in persuading Brabantio, who had initially welcomed Othello into his house, that the marriage was "against all rules of nature." Brabantio's first reaction betrayed a lurking fear: "This accident is not unlike my dream." Then, as he pondered the prospect, he could only conclude that witchcraft—the unnatural—was responsible; he demanded of Othello what other cause could have brought a girl "so tender, fair, and happy"

> To incur a general mock
> Run from her guardage to the sooty bosom
> Of such a thing as thou.

Altogether a curious way for a senator to address a successful general.

These and similar remarks in the play *Othello* suggest that Shakespeare and presumably his audiences were not totally indifferent to the sexual union of "black" men and "white" women. Shakespeare did not condemn such union; rather, he played upon an inner theme of black and white sexuality, showing how the poisonous mind of a white man perverted and destroyed the noblest of loves by means of bringing to the surface (from the darkness, whence Iago spoke) the lurking shadows of animal sex to assault the whiteness of chastity. Never did "dirty" words more dramatically "blacken" a "fair" name. At the play's climax, standing stunned by the realization that the wife he has murdered was innocent, Othello groans to Emilia, " 'Twas I that killed her"; and Emilia responds with a torrent of condemnation or, rather, of expulsive repudiation: "O! the more angel she,/ And you the blacker devil." Of Desdemona: "She was too fond of her filthy bargain." To Othello: "O gull! O dolt!/ As ignorant as dirt!" Shakespeare's genius lay precisely in juxtaposing these two pairs: inner blackness and inner whiteness. The drama would have seemed odd indeed if his audiences had felt no response to this cross-inversion and to the deeply turbulent double meaning of black *over* white.

It required a very great dramatist to expose some of the more inward biocultural values which led—or drove—Englishmen to accept readily the notion that Negroes were peculiarly sexual men. Probably these values and the ancient reputation of Africa upon which they built were of primary importance in determining the response of Englishmen to Negroes. Whatever the importance of biologic elements in these values—whatever the effects of long northern nights, of living in a cool climate, of possessing light-colored bodies which excreted contrasting lumps of darkness—these values by Shakespeare's time were interlocked with the accretions of English history and, more immediately, with the circumstances of contact with Africans and the social upheaval of Tudor England.[37]

The most obvious of these circumstances was that Englishmen were unaccustomed to West African standards concerning suitable public attire. Many Negroes were (or perhaps merely appeared to trousered Englishmen) utterly "naked."[38] Fully as important were African matrimonial practices, which in fact frequently failed to match the accepted norm for Christian Englishmen. It may be that Englishmen found Negroes free in a primitive way and found this freedom somehow provocative; many chroniclers made a point of discussing the Negro women's long breasts and ease of child-bearing.[39] The life of "savages" had attractions, even if civilized white men were not entirely aware what these attractions were. No doubt these differences between the two colliding cultures helped support the notion that Africans were highly sexed; yet Europeans have not everywhere and always made so much of nudity and polygamy among other peoples, and it seems necessary to inquire briefly concerning certain qualities of thought and feeling in Tudor England which may help account for what seems an unusual hypersensitivity to another people's sexuality.

### THE BLACKNESS WITHIN

The Protestant Reformation in England was a complex development, but certainly it may be said that during the century between Henry VIII and

---

[37] The power of these values may be seen in Thomas Adams, *The White Devil, or the Hypocrite Uncased* . . . (London, 1614), 1–2: "A Devill he was, blacke within and full of rancour, but white without, and skinned over with hypocrisie; therefore to use *Luthers* word, wee will call him the white *Devill.*"

There seem to be no cross-cultural studies of the meaning of color. It clearly would be a mistake to take the English valuations as representing responses to northern (versus Mediterranean) climate or to assume that these valuations were peculiarly Judeo-Christian.

>  On the Day when
>  Some faces will be (lit up
>  With) white, and some faces
>  Will be (in the gloom of) black:
>  To those whose faces
>  Will be black, (will be said):
>  "Did ye reject Faith
>  After accepting it?
>  Taste then the Penalty
>  For rejecting Faith."
>
>  But those whose faces
>  Will be (lit with) white,—
>  They will be in (the light
>  Of) God's mercy: therein
>  To dwell (for ever).

Abdullah Yusuf Ali, trans., *The Holy Qur-an* (Lahore, 1937), Sûrah III, 106–7, where the (Muslim) editor comments, "The 'face' (*wajh*) expresses our Personality, our inmost being. . . . Black is the colour of darkness, sin, rebellion, misery; removal from the grace and light of God."

[38] "The First Voyage Made by Master William Towrson . . ." (1555), Hakluyt, *Principal Navigations*, VI, 184; "A Voyage to Benin . . . Written by James Welsh . . ." (1589), *ibid.*, 457.

[39] An early example is "First Voyage by William Towrson" (1555), *ibid.*, 187.

Oliver Cromwell the content and tone of English Christianity were altered in the direction of Biblicism, personal piety, individual judgment, and more intense self-scrutiny and internalized control. Many pious Englishmen, not all of them "Puritans," came to approach life as if conducting an examination and to approach Scripture as if peering in a mirror. As a result, their inner energies were brought unusually close to the surface, more frequently into the almost rational world of legend, myth, and literature. The taut Puritan and the bawdy Elizabethan were not enemies but partners in this adventure which we usually think of in terms of great literature—of Milton and Shakespeare—and social conflict—of Saints and Cavaliers. The age was driven by the twin spirits of adventure and control, and while "adventurous Elizabethans" embarked upon voyages of discovery overseas, many others embarked upon inward voyages of discovery. Some men, like William Bradford and John Winthrop, were to do both.

Given this charged atmosphere of (self-) discovery, it is scarcely surprising that Englishmen should have used peoples overseas as social mirrors and that they were especially inclined to discover attributes in savages which they found first but could not speak of in themselves. . . .

It was the case with English confrontation with Negroes, then, that a society in a state of rapid flux, undergoing important changes in religious values, and comprised of men who were energetically on the make and acutely and often uncomfortably self-conscious of being so, came upon a people less technologically advanced, markedly different in appearance and culture. From the first, Englishmen tended to set Negroes over against themselves, to stress what they conceived to be radically contrasting qualities of color, religion, and style of life, as well as animality and a peculiarly potent sexuality. What Englishmen did not at first fully realize was that Negroes were potentially subjects for a special kind of obedience and subordination which was to arise as adventurous Englishmen sought to possess for themselves and their children one of the most bountiful dominions of the earth. When they came to plant themselves in the New World, they were to find that they had not entirely left behind the spirit of avarice and insubordination. Nor does it appear, in light of attitudes which developed during their first two centuries in America, that they left behind all the impressions initially gathered of the *Negro* before he became pre-eminently the *slave*.

# 3

## AFRICAN SLAVERY IN THE CONTEXT OF THE ATLANTIC SLAVE TRADE
*Walter Rodney*

**I** T HAS come to be widely accepted that slavery prevailed on the African continent before the arrival of the Europeans, and this indigenous slavery is said to have facilitated the rise and progress of the Atlantic slave-trade. According to P. D. Rinchon, "from the earliest days of the trade, the majority of the Negroes were living in a state of servitude, and the native chiefs did not have far to seek for the human merchandise."[1] Daniel Mannix, in one of the most recent accounts of the Atlantic slave-trade, contends that "many of the Negroes transported to America had been slaves in Africa, born to captivity. Slavery in Africa was an ancient and widespread institution, but it was especially prevalent in the Sudan."[2] In the opinion of J. D. Fage, "the presence of a slave class among the coastal peoples meant that there was already a class of human beings who could be sold to Europeans if there was an incentive to do so. . . . So the coastal merchants began by selling the domestic slaves in their own tribes."[3] The main purpose of this brief study is to test these generalizations with evidence taken from the Upper Guinea Coast—the region between the Gambia and Cape Mount.

Not only did the Upper Guinea Coast have a lengthy association with the Atlantic slave-trade, beginning in the 1460's and extending over four centuries, but it is also a very useful exemplar as far as the present problem is concerned, because the so-called African "slavery" was known to be widespread in this region during the colonial period, and emancipation was eventually brought about by the intervention of the metropolitan powers involved. Sometimes, what resulted was a quasi-feudal exploitation of labour by a ruling *élite,* who received the greater portion of the harvest.[4] More often than not, however, the "domestic slaves," as they have been categorized, were members of their masters' households. They could not be sold, except for serious offences; they had their own plots of land and/or rights to a proportion of the fruits of their labour; they could

Walter Rodney, "African Slavery and Other Forms of Social Oppression on the Upper Guinea Coast in the Context of the Atlantic Slave-Trade," *Journal of African History,* VII, No. 3 (1966), pp. 431–443. Reprinted by permission of the publisher and the author.

[1] D. Rinchon, *La traite et l'esclavage des Congolais par les Européens* (Brussels, 1929), 169.

[2] D. Mannix in collaboration with M. Cowley, *Black Cargoes, a History of the Atlantic Slave Trade* (London, 1963), 43 (44, 45 are also relevant).

[3] J. D. Fage, *Introduction to the History of West Africa* (London, 1959), 78.

[4] See below, p. 43–44.

marry; their children had rights of inheritance, and if born of one free parent often acquired a new status. Such individuals could rise to positions of great trust, including that of chief.[5]

Quite obviously, R. S. Rattray's well-known description of the Ashante "slave,"[6] which is cited in most discussions on this subject,[7] is fully applicable to the Upper Guinea Coast. Rattray was primarily concerned with the "slave child" (Odonko ba), whose privileges were quite different from those of his parents and foreparents. On the Upper Guinea Coast, too, the servants born in the household were distinguished from the individuals who were recruited from captives of war or from those pledged and not redeemed. These latter were vulnerable to sale, being exchanged for goods as well as serving as currency in a number of transactions such as marriage payments. During the latter part of the nineteenth century, after the Atlantic slave-trade had ceased to be conducted from the Upper Guinea Coast, one of the major problems facing the administration of the colony of Sierra Leone was the persistence of the internal slave-trade, mainly supplying victims to the Mande and the Fulas.[8] Thus, an examination of the society of the Upper Guinea Coast at a relatively recent date does reveal the presence of a category of slaves, as well as agricultural serfdom and personal service, which are represented here as "forms of social oppression," though in many cases the oppression was extremely attenuated.

In seeking the roots of the indigenous slavery and serfdom of the Upper Guinea Coast, and in attempting to juxtapose these phenomena with the Atlantic slave-trade, one is struck by the absence of references to local African slavery in the sixteenth or even the seventeenth century, when such evidence could reasonably be construed to mean that the institution preceded the advent of the Atlantic slave-trade. Sometimes, the word "slave" was indeed used, but so loosely as to apply to all the common people. For instance, the Jesuit Alonso de Sandoval reported that, when he was in Cartagena in the early seventeenth century, a priest who came over on a slaveship told him that all the talk about the injustice of slavery was nonsense, because all the Negroes were slaves of absolute kings. Sandoval then went on to pinpoint the king of Casanga on the river Casamance as one such absolute monarch whose subjects were his slaves.[9] In this arbitrary

[5] M. McCulloch, Peoples of Sierra Leone, Ethnographic Survey of Africa, ed. D. Forde (London, 1964), 28, 29, 68.

[6] R. S. Rattray, Ashanti (London, 1923), 40–43, 222, 230.

[7] E.g. Stanley Elkins, Slavery, a Problem in American Institutional and Social Life (New York, 1963), 96; and Basil Davidson, Black Mother (London, 1961), 40. (For a discussion of African "slavery" and "serfdom," see the section on pp. 33–40.)

[8] Christopher Fyfe, A History of Sierra Leone (London, 1962): see index under "slave trade, internal."

[9] Alonso de Sanderval, Natureleza . . . de Todos Etiopes (Seville, 1623).

and figurative sense, the word "slave" is equally applicable not only to the common people of Europe at that time but also to the proletariat of the capitalist world.

There is only one clear instance where labour services on the Upper Guinea Coast were associated with the limitation of the privileges of free men. In Sierra Leone at the beginning of the seventeenth century, when a subject was in danger in one kingdom he could flee to the court of another king and place himself at the mercy of the latter. He became the "slave" of that king, either remaining in his service or liable for sale (to the Europeans).[10] At that time, local customs were already influenced by the presence of slave-buying Europeans, as well as by the arrival of an alien Mande ruling element some decades previously; but the essentials of the practice almost certainly preceded these two external factors. In 1507 the Portuguese chronicler Valentim Fernandes made a statement which could refer to nothing else: "The king has no servants other than his slaves. Sometimes a young stranger arrives and seeks the protection of the king, who looks upon the young man as his own."[11]

When the occasional references to "slaves" on the Upper Guinea Coast in the sixteenth and seventeenth centuries are carefully scrutinized, they therefore point, at the very most, to the presence of a small number of political clients in the households of the kings and chiefs of the area. If they were to have constituted the pad for launching the Atlantic slave-trade, it would never have left the ground.

It is difficult to believe that any observers could possibly have over-looked features such as chattel slaves, agricultural serfs, or even household servants if these had been numerous and markedly disprivileged. Several of the sixteenth- and seventeenth-century Portuguese descriptions of the Upper Guinea Coast are replete with details of the structure of African society on that section of the West African littoral; and the only distinction that they consistently emphasized was the one between rulers and subjects —the *fidalgos* and *plebeus*.[12] For the neighbouring Senegambia, Valentim Fernandes left testimony that the Wolof nobles had several households, each comprising a wife, children and "slaves," the latter working six days for the mistress and one day every week for themselves.[13] Alvares de Almada

---

[10] *Biblioteca de la Real Academia de la Historia* (Madrid)—"Papeles de Jesuitas," tomo 185, no. 1346, report of P. Baltezar Barreira, Sierra Leone, 1606.

[11] Th. Monod, A Texeira da Mota and R. Mauny (eds.), *Description de la côte occidentale d'Afrique (Sénégal au Cap de Monte, Archipels) par Valentim Fernandes (1506–1510)* (Bissau 1951), 82. (To be cited subsequently as "Valentim Fernandes.")

[12] Valentim Fernandes, op. cit. 88; Alvares de Almada, "Tratado Breve dos Rios de Guiné" (1594), in P. Antonio Brasio, *Monumenta missionaria africana, Africa ocidental (1570–1600)*, 2nd series, vol. III (Lisbon, 1964), 323, 324, 333; and Manuel Alvares, "Ethiopia Menor, o descripçao geografica da Provincia de Serra Leoa" (1616), MS. of the *Sociedade de Geografia de Lisboa.*

[13] Valentim Fernandes, op. cit. 10.

in 1594 also referred to Fula "slaves" ruling the Wolofs.[14] Both these writers dealt with the area between the Gambia and Cape Mount at great length, without mentioning any similar phenomena.

On matters of trade, even more than on matters of ethnographic interest, the early Portuguese chroniclers were scrupulous in recording details. In the sixteenth and seventeenth century they knew of the trade routes between the Futa Djalon and the coast, linking the littoral peoples with the Mande and Fula of the interior. Yet, in enumerating the products exchanged, they never once mentioned or hinted that slaves were involved in this commerce.[15] Cloths, pieces of dried indigo and iron bars were noted as being the circulating media in the barter economy of the Upper Guinea Coast, but never slaves in the early period. Non-mention in such circumstances is presumptive of non-existence.

Though one can identify no African slavery, serfdom or the like on the Upper Guinea Coast during the first phase of European contact, that region was one of the first sections of the West African coast from which slaves were exported; and in the sixteenth century the transfer of Africans from the Upper Guinea Coast to the Spanish Indies was already a significant undertaking. No slave-class was necessary to make this possible, because there was in existence a fundamental class contradiction between the ruling nobility and the commoners; and the ruling class joined hands with the Europeans in exploiting the African masses—a not unfamiliar situation on the African continent today.

While the view that African slavery and "domestic slavery" preceded and stimulated the Atlantic slave-trade has been given wide currency, no thought has been spared for any other possible connexion between the two. Was it merely coincidence that it was only after two and a half centuries of slave-trading that the vast majority of the peoples of the Upper Guinea Coast were said to have been living in a state of subjection? Curiously enough, Mungo Park, though he added his authority to the pro-slavery arguments, had posed this question, while absolving himself from answering it. After describing what amounted to both chattel slavery and household service in the Senegambia and the western Sudan, he wrote: "How far it is maintained and supported by the Slave Traffic which, for two hundred years, the nations of Europe have carried on with the natives of the coast, it is neither within my province, nor in my power to explain."[16]

It is a striking fact that the greatest agents of the Atlantic slave-trade on the Upper Guinea Coast, the Mande and the Fulas, were the very tribes who subsequently continued to handle the internal slave-trade, and whose

[14] Alvares de Almada, "Rios de Guiné," 234, 235.

[15] Ibid. 344, 345, 347; and Damiao Peres (ed.), Duas descriçoes seiscentistas da Guiné de Francisco de Lemos Coelho (Lisbon, 1953), 59–61, from the description written in 1669. (To be cited subsequently as "Lemos Coelho.")

[16] Mungo Park, Travels in the Interior Districts of Africa in the Years 1795, 1796 and 1797 (London, 1799), 297, 298.

society came to include significant numbers of disprivileged individuals labouring under coercion. The sequence of events points in the very direction in which Mungo Park had not cared to look too closely. In the first place, the political and religious dominance of the Mande and Fulas over the littoral peoples of the Upper Guinea Coast in the eighteenth century was based on a mixture of motives, among which the desire to sell more slaves to the Europeans featured prominently. Thus the Atlantic slave-trade can immediately be identified as being partly responsible for the vassalage to which the coastal tribes were reduced. In the second place, the raiding of individuals for sale to the Europeans encouraged the marauding tribes to retain numbers of their captives to serve their own needs. When, for example, the Mandinga *Farim Cabo* raided his neighbours to obtain captives for the slave-ships, he retained a small proportion for his own needs.[17]

One of the most direct connexions between the Atlantic slave-trade and the nineteenth-century pattern of social stratification and oppression on the Upper Guinea Coast lay in the fact that numbers of Africans were captured with a view to being sold to the European slavers, but they remained for greater or lesser periods (or sometimes for ever) in the service of their African captors. To begin with, there was usually a time-lag between capture and the moment when a buyer presented himself. Then, there were always individuals whom the Europeans rejected for one reason or another; while the African merchants also decided against carrying through the sale under certain circumstances.

De Almada related that on one occasion on which the Portuguese refused to buy some "pieces" who had been kidnapped by Fulas, the latter killed the victims.[18] Such action might have been taken in isolated instances, but, in general, persons who were offered for sale and who were not purchased by the Europeans were utilized for the economic benefit of their African captors. C. B. Wadstrom, an activist in the movement for the colonization of Sierra Leone, addressed himself to interviewing those engaged in the Atlantic slave-trade in the area on this specific point. First, there was the testimony of the chief of Port Loko, who affirmed that those captives whom the Europeans did not buy were always put to work on the coast. Secondly, "two other intelligent native traders mentioned the great number of slaves now confined on the coast for purchasers: one trader had no fewer than 200 . . . They said that the slaves would certainly not be put to death; for nobody was ever put to death, except in war or for crimes." Further questioning by Wadstrom revealed that, when the average price of slaves fell from 160 "bars" to 120 "bars," the king of the

---

[17] P. Mateo de Anguiano, *Misiones capuchinas en Africa*, ed. P. Buenaventura de Carrocera, II (Madrid, 1950), 136—missionary report of 1686 on the Atlantic slave-trade as pursued on the Upper Guinea Coast. *Cabo* or *Gabu* was a Mandinga province extending between the Gambia and the Corubal. The ruler was called *Farim* or "governor", because he was ostensibly a representative of the emperor of Mali.

[18] Alvares de Almada, "Rios de Guiné," 275.

Fulas, to bring the European slave-traders to terms, forbade his subjects to carry any slaves down to the coast. As a consequence of this manoeuvre, the Fula, Mandinga and Susu territories had become full of slaves who were set to cultivate rice.[19]

For the sake of safety the captives were put to work in small groups.[20] Ever since the seventeenth century (and perhaps earlier) it had been the habit of the Mandinga *Farim Cabo* to disperse his captives among his own subjects, expecting to have them returned when a buyer was available.[21] Those captives thus became for a while literally "household slaves" of the Mandingas. At any given moment, therefore, two of the components of the domestic slave population of the Upper Guinea Coast as viewed by observers at the end of the eighteenth century would have been, first, captives drafted into alien tribes in servile disprivileged positions, as by-products of the Atlantic slaving industry, and, secondly, the real products, who were stock-piled in bond for export.

The majority of the tribes of the Upper Guinea Coast were active participants in the Atlantic slave-trade, and most of them must have retained supplies of slaves for domestic consumption. But the Mandingas, Susus and Fulas stood well to the fore—partly because of their own key role in the slaving operations on the Upper Guinea Coast, and partly because they succeeded in reducing many of the littoral peoples and the inhabitants of the Futa Djalon to a state of vassalage, under the banner of Islam. Military conquest and political ascendancy involved in most cases nothing more than the payment of tribute, but in some instances the Mande or Fula ruling class was directly superimposed on the subjugated peoples. The latter were not dispersed within individual households, but were grouped together in villages, which were economic units producing for the benefit of the master class.

During the latter part of the eighteenth century, some of the Mandinga chiefs on the Upper Guinea Coast had "slave towns" with as many as 1,000 inhabitants.[22] Travelling in Sierra Leone in 1823, Major Laing found that Falaba, the capital of the Sulima Susus, had its own "slave town," Konkodoogorée. Intense agricultural activities were carried on there, and the fields in the area were the best tilled and best laid out that Laing had seen in his travels.[23] The "slave town" was known to the Fulas as the *rounde*.

[19] C. B. Wadstrom, *An Essay on Colonisation* (London, 1795), part 2, pp. 113–117. A "bar" originally signified an iron bar about 9 inches long. It came to be a unit of currency in the trade of the Upper Guinea Coast with a very imprecise and fluctuating value. Wadstrom estimated it at about 3s. (p. 56).

[20] C. B. Wadstrom, op. cit. part 2, p. 117.

[21] P. Cultru, *Premier voyage de Sieur de la Courbe, fait à la Coste d'Afrique en 1685* (Paris, 1913), 252.

[22] John Mathews, *A Voyage to the River Sierra Leone* (London, 1788).

[23] A. G. Laing, *Travels in the Timannee, Kooranko and Soolima Countries* (London, 1825), 221.

The inhabitants *(rimaibe)* worked under the supervision of a *satigi* who was not himself a free man, although he had the full confidence of the Muslim *Alimamy* or chief of the *diwal,* and was in complete control of the *rounde.* At the end of each harvest, the *Satigi* immediately dispatched a bundle of reeds to the *Alimamy,* with the number of stalks indicating the number of loads of grain harvested.[24] This situation has been quite justifiably equated with serfdom, and it was most prevalent in the Futa Djalon after the success of the Muslim *Jihad.*[25]

It was also at the tail-end of the Atlantic slave-trade that evidence was forthcoming about the existence of an internal trade in slaves, and there is every reason to believe that this was an accurate reflexion on the date that it came into being. Captain Canot, who was familiar with the Upper Guinea Coast in the 1820's and 1830's, wrote vividly on both the Atlantic slave-trade and the internal slave-trade, implicitly linking the two. With the Atlantic slave-trade as the main preoccupation of the Susus and Fulas, "a man, therefore, becomes the standard of prices. A slave is a note of hand that may be discounted or pawned; he is a bill of exchange that carries himself to his destination and pays a debt bodily; he is a tax that walks corporately into the chieftain's treasury." As far as the home market was concerned, the victims not only became agricultural labourers, but men were required as personal attendants and women as wives or concubines.[26]

While one major contribution to the rise of "domestic slavery" on the Upper Guinea Coast was made by the coastwards thrust of the interior peoples and their involvement in the slave-trade, an equally great contribution was being made by the European forces acting on the littoral from the seaward side.

In the forts and factories of the Royal African Company, a distinction was made between "sale slaves" and "castle slaves" or "factory slaves." Both were acquired in the same way, but, while the former were destined to face the Middle Passage, the latter were retained around the forts and factories to help in the conduct of trade.[27] The directors took some interest in these "castle slaves." In 1702 they issued instructions that a Negro overseer should be appointed over them. They were to be converted to Christianity, given names, taught to speak English, and be allowed to have one wife (another "castle slave"). Perhaps the most important provision

[24] P. Marty, "Islam in French Guinea" (trans.) in *Sierra Leone Studies* no. xix (old series, 1936), 49–129.

[25] L. Tauxier, *Moeurs et histoire des Peuhls* (Paris, 1937), 9. He renders the word *rimaibe* as "agricultural serfs." The singular is *dimadio.*

[26] Captain Canot, *The Adventures of an African Slaver* (London, 1928), 128, 129. (This account was actually written in 1854 by one Brantz Meyer to whom Canot related his experiences.)

[27] *Public Record Office,* London (to be cited below as *P.R.O.),* T 70/1465: diary of agent Walter Charles, 1728. This mentions "Cayoba, a castle slave who had been made such from a sale slave."

from the company's point of view was that the "castle slaves" should be taught skills to enhance their value and utility. Such workers were not to be sold or transported overseas except for great crimes.[28]

Apparently, no record remains of the number of "castle slaves" in the forts of York and Bence Island and their subsidiary factories, but in 1702 it was felt that there were too many in Sierra Leone, and that some should be transferred to Cape Coast Castle.[29] However, some years later there was talk of shortage. At least, the directors had been made to understand that it was cheaper to use their own slaves than to hire African servants, and they gave their factors authority to purchase slaves for the factories.[30] Walter Charles, the last of the chief factors of the Royal African Company in Sierra Leone, was certainly convinced that, if the Company used their own slaves, it would be cheaper and more convenient; and he urged that some "castle slaves" should be sent to Sierra Leone from the Gambia establishments.[31] The same situation was to be found in the Portuguese trading centre of Cacheu, where the captain-major argued in 1694 that it cost too much to get the help of the Africans.[32]

Apart from the trading companies, private European traders also owned slaves on the coast, so that altogether the numbers of Africans bought by Europeans and remaining in servitude on the Upper Guinea Coast were considerable. The practice probably began with the arrival of Portuguese ships in the fifteenth century, giving rise to the term *grumete* ("sailor's slave"). In practice, the *grumete* (or *grommetto,* as the English came to use the word) was seldom a chattel. More often than not he was a wage-earner, and in many cases African rulers on the Upper Guinea Coast voluntarily sent their children to live with the Europeans and to serve as auxiliaries in the coastal trade.[33] There was a somewhat similar practice in the nineteenth century, involving the sending of children from the hinterland to the colony of Sierra Leone to learn "white man fashion." However, these children were usually only unpaid servants, and, when they grew old enough to realize that they were free, they were sold to the Mande and Fula traders.[34]

Some of the Africans purchased by and remaining in the service of

---

[28] *P.R.O.* T 70/51: instructions to agent Freeman, 4 August 1702.

[29] *P.R.O.* T 70/51: instructions to agent Freeman, 1 December 1702.

[30] *P.R.O.* T 70/60: instructions from the directors, 5 October 1723.

[31] *P.R.O.* T 70/1465: diary of agent Walter Charles.

[32] *Arquivo historico ultramarino,* Lisbon (to be cited below as *A.H.U.),* Guiné, caixa II, no. 230, minute of the Conselho Ultramarino, 30 October 1694.

[33] Alvares de Almada, "Rios de Guiné," 326, and Fr. Francisco de Santiago, "Chronica da Provincia Franciscana de Nossa Senhora da Soledade" (MS.), extracts in A. J. Dias, "Crenças e costumes dos indigenas de Ilha de Bissau no seculo XVIII," *Portugal em Africa,* II, no. 9 (1945), 159–69.

[34] Christopher Fyfe, op. cit. 270.

the resident Europeans were little better off than slaves in the New World. The "castle slaves," like their American counterparts, were branded with their owners' marks.[35] When a "castle slave" committed a crime his punishment was often brutal. In February 1682 the Bence Island factor reported that some of the "castle slaves" had stolen, and he had executed one as an example.[36] Escape and rebellion led to the same fate. If the "castle slave" was not sold, executed or did not die an early natural death, then he could look forward to being freed when he was "old and useless."[37] With the private traders, it was equally obvious that unmitigated chattel slavery prevailed at times. Occasionally, the owners displayed those fits of sadism which afflict those who hold absolute power over human life. When in 1694 Francisco Vaz, member of a prominent Afro-Portuguese trading family, cruelly disposed of twelve of his slaves in his Nunez emporium, the matter reached the ears of the Conselho Ultramarino.[38] In the latter years of the eighteenth century John Ormond, thirty-five years a slave-trader in Baga territory, was notorious for amusing himself at the expense of the lives and limbs of his servants, in much the same way as his contemporaries in Saint Domingue.[39]

The servitude directly introduced on to the Upper Guinea Coast by the Europeans slowly assumed an African character. The slave owners were originally white and foreigners, but the late eighteenth century saw the emergence of powerful mulatto slave-trading chiefs, who were said to own large numbers of "domestic slaves." Wadstrom explains that "if an African slave is impertinent he is sold. The children of such are occasionally sold also. But with the rich traders this is not common."[40] The rich traders he refers to were mulattoes like the Caulkers and the Clevelands, the progeny of English slave dealers and African women. They kept "slaves" not only to serve as crews on the coastal and riverain vessels and to act as porters, but also to provide labour for the production of food and manufactures, which indirectly facilitated the Atlantic slave-trade. In the latter part of the eighteenth century Chief William Cleveland (grandson of the original white Cleveland, who died in 1758) had a large "slave town" on the mainland opposite the Banana Islands. The inhabitants were employed in cultivating extensive rice fields, described as being some of the largest in Africa at the time, and equalled only by the Susu plantations which were also employing forced labour. In another smaller village, whose people

[35] *P.R.O.* T 70/53: instructions to agent Plunkett, 9 February 1721. (He was sent a new branding iron.)

[36] *P.R.O.* T 70/16: letter from agent Edmund Pierce, February 1682.

[37] *P.R.O.* T 70/361: Bence Island accounts, 1682.

[38] *A.H.U.*, Cabo Verde, caixa VI: Bishop of Cape Verde to the Conselho Ultramarino, 27 July 1694.

[39] C. B. Wadstrom, op. cit. part 2, pp. 84, 85, 87.

[40] Ibid. part 2, p. 117.

were said to have been owned by Cleveland, there was a thriving mat and cotton industry.[41]

Whether as agricultural labourers or sailing *grumetes,* whether as temporary members of households or as permanent residents of *roundes,* a large number of Africans on the Upper Guinea Coast at the end of the eighteenth century had been reduced to servile status through the agency of the Atlantic slave-trade. A few quickly emerged as trusted servants and lieutenants, but the majority signalled their oppression by rebelling or escaping when the opportunity presented itself. They had every reason for so doing; because, having been spawned by the Atlantic slave-trade, they in turn constituted the section of the society most liable to be exported. Again it is from Captain Canot's account that the interrelationship between the two phenomena most clearly emerges. When, on one occasion, Canot visited Timbo, the capital of the Futa Djalon, the inhabitants of Findo and Furto, two slave settlements on the outskirts of the city, fled in consternation on hearing that he wanted slaves. They knew that they were earmarked as the first to be exported; and, as it turned out, flight did them no good, because they were hunted by Fulas on horseback, and Canot was provided with his coffle to return to the waterside.[42]

The village of local slaves thus became a warren supplying the Europeans. This was the ultimate degradation to which the Atlantic slave-trade had brought the African society of the Upper Guinea Coast. Without a doubt, as far as this region is concerned, to speak of African slavery as being ancient, and to suggest that this provided the initial stimulus and early recruiting ground for slaves exported to Europe and the Americas is to stand history on its head.[43] When the European powers involved in the area (namely Britain, France and Portugal) intervened to end slavery and serfdom in their respective colonies, they were simply undoing their own handiwork.

While it is the main concern of this paper to demonstrate that the generalization that the Atlantic slave-trade was at its inception stimulated by African slavery and "domestic slavery" cannot be sustained when applied to the Upper Guinea Coast, the validity of the thesis as a whole is open to question. The weaknesses of the generalization can be seen by reverting to the three statements quoted at the outset.

No attempt was made by Rinchon to substantiate his sweeping assertion that the majority of the Africans lived in a state of servitude. Nor does he define "servitude," and it does seem that he is using the word in a

---

[41] British Museum, Add. MS. 12131: papers relating to Sierra Leone, 1792–96, journals by Mr Gray and Mr Watt, 1795.

[42] Captain Canot, op. cit. 168, 169.

[43] J. J. Crooks, in his *A History of the Colony of Sierra Leone* (Dublin, 1903), holds to the view of African slavery being ancient, but he makes no connexion with the Atlantic slave-trade.

very arbitrary and imaginative sense. Propositions stated in this manner cannot be entertained.

J. D. Fage is very careful in defining "domestic slavery" and circumscribing the numbers involved; but he feels that it "nevertheless" gave a fillip to the Atlantic slave-trade. This highlights a certain contradiction. The "domestic slave" was the member of a royal or noble household. What reason is there to suppose that the ruling class would first dispose of the affinal members of their own family? Perhaps the continued employment of the term "slave," however qualified, has some bearing on the conclusion. Rattray himself ended by referring to the "so-called 'slaves' "; and, though perhaps the label "domestic slave" is meant to express this idea, it carries with it the same associations with the Americas which the pro-slavery interests were at pains to evoke, especially since the literature on American slavery has already made familiar the distinction between the domestic or household slave and the field slave on the basis simply of their place of work; while it is well known what constituted the principal "domestic institution" of the Old South.[44]

To recognize that "domestic slavery" is a misnomer is to avoid much confusion, and it does not mean losing sight of the possible existence within fifteenth- and sixteenth-century West African coastal society of authentic chattel slavery and other forms of social oppression such as serfdom and household service with limited rights and onerous obligations. If these can be shown to have prevailed, then the Upper Guinea Coast would be atypical in its social structure and the link with the Atlantic slave-trade would appear extremely credible. But it is quite remarkable that so far no contemporary fifteenth- or sixteenth-century evidence for any West African coastal region has been marshalled behind this imposing generalization.[45]

On the question of identifying African slavery, Mannix gives a much more acceptable picture, legitimately citing Mungo Park to establish a distinction between household servants on the one hand and captives and newly purchased slaves on the other. However, when Park added that these social institutions were ancient and widespread in Africa, he was speculating rather than making a factual observation, so that it is pointless to echo him.[46] It is similarly inconclusive to give a modern ethnographic

[44] See, for example, Eric McKitrick (ed.), Slavery Defended: the Views of the Old South (New Jersey, 1963).

[45] Obviously, the early records of the Portuguese in Benin and the Congo could be of vital importance here. Basil Davidson cited Pacheco Pereira to the effect that there were wars in Benin providing captives for the Europeans, and added that "these wars provided slaves for domestic use, much as in medieval Europe". This is a reasonable presumption, but it is nevertheless an interpolation and not the evidence of Pacheco Pereira (Old Africa Rediscovered, 124, and Esmeraldo de Situ Orbis, ed. Mauny, 134). For the Congo (121, 122) Davidson cites a secondary work: A. Ihle, Das alte Königreich Kongo (1929).

[46] Besides, Mungo Park was heavily influenced by the West Indian slave-owner Bryan Edwards; and it was one of the pro-slavery arguments that, if the majority of Africans were

description (as Fage seems to have done) and leave the impression that this was part of the ancient and traditional order of things in Africa. Here it will be useful to take as an example the contention that people could be enslaved in punishment for a civil or criminal offence, and to test it with evidence from the Upper Guinea Coast.

In describing the societies of the littoral peoples of the Upper Guinea Coast the Portuguese did not omit mention of the regime of law and punishment. It was reported at the beginning of the sixteenth century that the Temnes had no capital punishment, while only murder was punishable by death among the Bulloms. The main punishments were in the form of fines. Adultery, for instance, was easily resolved, the offending male paying the damages.[47] Deprivation of liberty was not listed as a legal penalty at this early date. It makes its appearance in the seventeenth century, when the process of law had become warped under the pressure of the Atlantic slave-trade, and there was hardly an offence which did not carry the penalty of sale into the hands of the Europeans.[48] When therefore a modern ethnographic survey of the region indicates that "punishments formerly included" enslavement for a wide variety of crimes, this itself needs to be placed in historical perspective rather than accepted as historical evidence.[49]

The examples of African slavery documented at an early date which immediately spring to mind come from the western Sudan, with its large centralized expansionist states and its developed system of production and distribution. Not only were slaves exported across the Sahara, but peoples in the region were also being reduced to vassalage and made captives in the large-scale wars that were fought in the open savanna. Their labour was then exploited within an economy which was characterized by some amount of specialization. These would seem to be the prerequisites for a society to incorporate slaves, serfs and the like.

In many respects the Senegambia was an extension of the western Sudan, and so was the Gold Coast area around Mina. The Africans around Mina actually purchased slaves from the Portuguese in the fifteenth and early sixteenth century, those slaves being brought from other sections of the coast and exchanged for gold.[50] In the Senegambia the pattern was even

---

already slaves in Africa, then it would be no improvement in their lot to end the Atlantic slave trade and American slavery. For a discussion of the extent to which Park was influenced by Edwards, see the introduction by John Murray to the publication of Park's second Niger journey, *The Journal of a Mission to Africa in the Year 1805*.

[47] Valentim Fernandes, op. cit. 92, 96.

[48] See, for example, the report of three Spanish Capuchin missionaries on the conduct of the Atlantic slave-trade on the Upper Guinea Coast in the latter part of the seventeenth century in P. Mateo de Anguiano, *Misiones capuchinas en Africa*, II, 132–46 (written in 1686).

[49] M. McCulloch, op. cit. 24, 25.

[50] Raymond Mauny (ed.), *Esmeraldo de Situ Orbis, par Duarte Pacheco Pereira (vers 1506– 1508)* (Bissau, 1956), 134, 126.

more instructive. As indicated earlier, the Portuguese chroniclers did report "household slaves" among the Wolof. They also recorded that the district was exporting slaves in directions other than westwards to the Atlantic. In fact, by a curious cycle of barter, the Portuguese took slaves from the Upper Guinea Coast in the sixteenth century and exchanged them for iron from the Wolofs. The latter apparently handed on most of the slaves to the Moors, while the Portuguese took the iron and bartered it for further captives on the Upper Guinea Coast, making a surplus which was destined for the Spanish Americas.[51] Richard Jobson also bore witness in 1620–21 that slaves were traded inland from the lower and middle Gambia, though "among themselves . . . they make little use thereof."[52]

Two issues would be worth pursuing on the basis of the Mina and Senegambia examples, especially the latter. The first is the extent to which these societies were representative of the West African littoral; and at a glance it would appear that there were far greater areas where the social structure was parallel to the Upper Guinea Coast. The second matter to be noted is the tremendous increase in local slavery in the Senegambia between the voyages of Jobson and Mungo Park—separated by nearly two centuries in which the ruling class has committed itself to a slaving partnership with the Europeans. Quite obviously, Mungo Park's question must have been quite pertinent to the Senegambia,[53] even though slavery and serfdom were encountered in some measure before the arrival of the Portuguese caravels. There must have been some connexion between the status quo at the end of the eighteenth century and the Atlantic slave-trade.

A random selection of examples drawn from farther afield indicates the likelihood of a widespread impact of the Atlantic slave-trade along the lines followed on the Upper Guinea Coast. The Nyamwezi were the great traders in ivory and slaves who supplied the coastal slaving towns in the vicinity of Zanzibar. While they were travelling between the coast and their sources of supply deep in the interior, their lands were worked by slaves acquired for that purpose.[54] In the case of the Nike of eastern Nigeria, the correlation between their participation in the Atlantic slave-trade and their accumulation of slaves was even more definite. Nike acted as the northern agents of the Aro, and were among the principal recruiters of slaves in eastern Nigeria. In the process, they acquired great tracts of land and large numbers of captives remained in their hands, giving rise subsequently to mitigated forms of household service.[55] In this respect, the Ashanti may well repay investigation.

[51] Alvares de Almada, op. cit. 301.

[52] Richard Jobson, The Golden Trade (London, 1933), 108, 109. The "slaves" in the Gambia were owned by the Muslim imams.

[53] See above, p. 434.

[54] R. Oliver and J. D. Fage, A Short History of Africa (London, 1962), 172.

[55] R. K. Udo, "The migrant tenant farmer of eastern Nigeria," in Africa, xxxiv, no. 4 (October, 1964), 333. There is a reference to the regime of household service in southern Nigeria in Black Mother, 39.

The Nyamwezi and the Nike would correspond to the Mande and Fula of the Upper Guinea Coast; while the resident European and mulatto slave-traders of the Upper Guinea Coast also had counterparts elsewhere, notably in Angola. There too, "sale slaves" were employed in agricultural activities for a period of time, while some were kept permanently on the coast. When the Portuguese sought to abolish slavery in Angola in the nineteenth century, what was involved was the ownership of Africans by whites and mulattoes.[56] This can be maintained without contradiction, even if it can be proved that there were tribal slaves within the hierarchical society of the Congo–Angola area in the fifteenth and sixteenth century, and that these constituted the first victims of the Atlantic slave-trade. However, while this latter hypothesis has been shown to be unsatisfactory in many respects, there seems to be at least a *prima facie* case for the counter-assertion that many of the forms of slavery and subjection present in Africa in the nineteenth and twentieth centuries and considered indigenous to that continent were in reality engendered by the Atlantic slave-trade.

[56] James Duffy, *Portugal in Africa* (London, 1962), 61, 62, 69.

## SUGGESTIONS FOR FURTHER READING

THE best surveys of Afro-American history are *John Hope Franklin, *From Slavery to Freedom* (3d ed.; New York, 1967) and *August Meier and Elliott Rudwick, *From Plantation to Ghetto* (New York, 1966). Somewhat briefer but useful is *Benjamin Quarles, *The Negro in the Making of America* (New York, 1964). Two works that look at black history from a sociological perspective are Gunnar Myrdal, *An American Dilemma* (New York, 1944) and E. Franklin Frazier, *The Negro in the United States* (rev. ed.; New York, 1957).

There a number of documentary studies such as *Herbert Aptheker (ed.), *A Documentary History of the Negro People in the United States* (2 vols.; New York, 1951); *Leslie H. Fishel, Jr. and Benjamin Quarles (eds.), *The Negro American: A Documentary History* (Glenview, Ill., 1967); *Albert P. Blaustein and Robert L. Zangrando (eds.), *Civil Rights and the American Negro* (New York, 1968); and *Gilbert Osofsky (ed.), *The Burden of Race* (New York, 1966). *Francis L. Broderick and August Meier (eds.), *Negro Protest Thought in the Twentieth Century* (Indianapolis, Ind., 1965) and *John Hope Franklin, *The Negro in 20th Century America* (New York, 1967) are very useful though more limited in their chronological scope.

There are several bibliographical guides to black history. The most comprehensive, which includes references to other bibliographies, is *Elizabeth Miller (comp.), *The Negro in America* (2d rev. ed.; Cambridge, Mass., 1970).

Informative surveys of African civilization are Maurice Delafosse, *The Negroes of Africa: History and Culture* (Washington, D.C., 1935) and *Basil Davidson, *The Lost Cities of Africa* (Boston, 1959). *Philip Curtin, *African History* (New

York, 1964) is a brief introduction with a selected bibliography. Africa south of the Sahara, the source of most New World black men, is treated in *J. D. Fage, *An Introduction to the History of West Africa* (3d ed.; London, 1962); Samuel Johnson, *The History of the Yorubas* (Evanston, Ill., 1964); and Melville J. Herskovits, *Dahomey* (2 vols.; New York, 1938). Elliot Elisofson, *The Sculpture of Africa* (London, 1958) establishes the quality of African art. Political contributions of African government are analyzed in Joseph Greenberg, "The Negro Kingdoms of the Sudan," *Transactions of the New York Academy of Science*, II (February 1949).

Standard accounts of the horrors of the African slave trade are W. E. B. Du Bois, *Suppression of the African Slave Trade to the United States, 1638–1870*, (Cambridge, Mass., 1896); *Basil Davidson, *Black Mother: The Years of the African Slave Trade* (Boston, 1961); and William S. Howard, *American Slavers and the Federal Law* (Berkeley, Calif., 1963). Philip Curtin, *The Atlantic Slave Trade: A Census* (Madison, Wis., 1969) is a highly important revision of past views about the extent of the trade.

The most trenchant account of African influences in America is *Melville J. Herskovits, *Myth of the Negro Past* (New York, 1941). It may be supplemented by Lorenzo D. Turner, *Africanisms in the Gullah Dialect* (Chicago, 1949) and *James G. Leyburn, *The Haitian People* (New Haven, Conn., 1941). *Frazier's *The Negro in the United States* challenges the relevance of African influences.

The origins of American slavery are argued in Oscar and Mary F. Handlin, "Origins of the Southern Labor System," *William and Mary Quarterly*, XIX (April 1962); Carl N. Degler, "Slavery and the Genesis of American Race Prejudice," *Comparative Studies in Society and History*, II (October 1959); and Winthrop D. Jordan, "Modern Tensions and the Origins of American Slavery," *Journal of Southern History*, XVIII (February 1962). *Winthrop D. Jordan, *White Over Black: American Attitudes Toward the Negro, 1550–1812* (Chapel Hill, N. C., 1968) in which this debate is a pivotal point, also has an extensive bibliographical essay on the subject.

* An asterisk indicates that the book is available in paperback.

# CHAPTER TWO
# The Colonial Era

**W**HILE it is clearly misleading to view the evolution of Afro-American history without giving attention to the African past, the emerging patterns of American race relations and the Afro-American experience must also be seen in the context of American history. The problems and needs of the colonies shaped the contours of race relations to such an extent that by the nineteenth century there existed unmistakable conflicting traditions of slavery and emancipation and varying degrees of racial discrimination and justice.

All the colonies shared a shortage of labor as well as similar attitudes of racial prejudice; but by the end of the seventeenth century it became apparent that the South's plantation agriculture and staple crop system could best utilize slave labor. Free labor and family farming, on the other hand, might have been successful, though less profitable. Although later apologists for slavery would seek to link it to a high-minded aristocratic way of life, the lust for money initially was at the core of the institution's development. The North soon joined the rush for black slaves and maximum economic gain.

Massachusetts legalized slavery as early as 1640 and thirty years later revised its statutes to permit the enslavement of the offspring of slaves. The New England slave trade, however, remained small until the early eighteenth century when the development of the triangular trade route with Africa and the West Indies enabled rum manufactured in New England to be exchanged for slaves. Massachusetts and Rhode Island dominated the colonial slave trade and the ports of Boston and Newport were thriving because of it. Other coastal cities participated to a lesser extent. Fortunes were amassed by the Fanueil, Pepperell, and Brown families, among others, as a wealthy class of slave-trading merchants arose.

The middle colonies contained the greatest number of slaves in the North. On the eve of the American Revolution, New Jersey citizens held about 11,000 slaves; in New York City slaves constituted fifteen percent of the population. Slavery in the middle colonies was as harsh as in the South, while the plight of the New England slaves was eased somewhat by the prevailing belief that slaves were not simply chattels but were entitled to the rights of persons in the possession of their own property and to some protection in civil courts such as trial by jury and the right to testify against whites. Race prejudice and discrimination were widespread in the North, and yet slavery was more markedly an economic system than one of race relations. By the last quarter of the eighteenth century the impact of the humanitarian ideas of the Enlightenment and the decreased economic need for slave labor stimulated a growing sentiment for emancipation in the North. Most New England states freed their slaves soon after the American Revolution. The middle states launched efforts for gradual emancipation, a process which delayed freedom. Not until 1827 in New York and the 1840s in New Jersey did slavery end entirely. Although antislavery societies were numerous in the South until the 1830s, the northern states actually showed the way toward emancipation and some degree of justice for Afro-Americans. The North had contributed substantially, however, to the growth of black slavery and racial discrimination.

The two articles in this chapter analyze the status of the black man in the American colonies. Leonard Price Stavisky, in selection four, challenges the view that plantation slavery only existed in the South and that black slaves were unskilled. Similarly, he dispells the belief that the North utilized slaves solely as domestic servants. For many colonists the question of emancipation was integrally tied to the degree of the slaves' occupational skills. To what extent could slaveholders expect manumitted slaves to be economically self-sufficient?

Paul C. Palmer, in selection five, relates the enslavement of Afro-Americans to the status of white laborers and raises major questions about class conflict in the colonies. Both historians cast doubt upon the alleged fluidity of colonial society in their discussion of Afro-American economic mobility. Palmer's attention to the relationship of law and custom to the Afro-American's status should be recalled when the growth of Jim Crow legislation in the 1890's is examined in Chapter Six.

Stavisky and Palmer illuminate the patterns of race relations inherited by the new nation from the colonies. It should be remembered that the authors of the Declaration of Independence agreed to delete any criticism of slavery from the document and that the supporters of the Constitution voted to protect slavery by allowing each slaveholding state to include three-fifths of its slave population for determining the number of its members in the House of Representatives. The willingness of the Founding Fathers, and the American people who ratified their work, to compromise and achieve a consensus for the legal acceptance of slavery, despite misgivings by some, suggests that readers consider whether it was not only the American Revolution, but also black slavery, which was in the "minds and hearts of the people" of the colonies.

4

## NEGRO CRAFTSMANSHIP IN EARLY AMERICA
*Leonard Price Stavisky*

M ANY Americans continue to harbor ideas of racial hierarchies by believing that the Negro is incapable of performing a series of skilled operations. There are still those who persist in picturing him as the "plantation darky" capable only of work in the cotton fields. Nevertheless, it remains an indisputable fact that Negro labor is gradually changing from agriculture to industry. According to one recent tabulation, the number of Negro tradesmen in the United States totals more than 135,000.[1] This trend is not of recent origin. As early as 1783 a German physician, touring the United States, was astonished to find that "the gentlemen in the country have among their negroes as the Russian nobility among the serfs, the most necessary handicrafts-men, cobblers, tailors, carpenters, smiths, and the like whose work they command at the smallest possible price or for nothing almost. There is hardly any trade or craft," he observed, "which has not been learned and is not carried on by negroes."[2]

The presence of Negro craftsmanship during the first years of political independence from Britain would seem to suggest that this tradition had its origin prior to the advent of the American Revolution. Indeed, there is reason to believe that Negro workers engaged in the crafts while still on the continent of Africa. In the Sudan, almost one thousand years ago, cotton was already being woven. Long before England established colonies in the Western Hemisphere, primitive tanning, weaving, and toolmaking were practiced by the natives of Lake Tchad and Timbuctoo. As one author maintains, "the decorative character manifested in the handicrafts of the black races of Africa is of surpassing character. . . . The native hand derives the maximum of expression from the few elements afforded by the soil."[3]

While African Negroes may have had some experience in the manual arts and crafts, this had little direct influence upon American handiwork. The severance of relations with the African continent resulted in a loss of

Leonard Price Stavisky, "Negro Craftsmanship in Early America," *American Historical Review*, LIV (January, 1941), pp. 315–325. Reprinted by permission of the publisher.

[1] Gordon B. Hancock, "The Changing Status of Negro Labor," *Southern Workman*, LX (August, 1931), 352–53; U.S. Dept. of Commerce, Bureau of the Census, *Sixteenth Census of the United States: 1940* (Washington, 1943), III, 88.

[2] Johann D. Schoepf, *Travels in the Confederation, 1783–1784*, ed. by Alfred J. Morrison (Philadelphia, 1911), II, 221.

[3] George S. Schuyler, "Craftsmen in the Blue Grass," *Crisis*, XLVII (May, 1940), 158; Giles B. Jackson and D. Webster Davis, *The Industrial History of the Negro Race in the United States* (Richmond, 1908), p. 13; W. E. B. Du Bois, *The Negro American Artisan* (Atlanta, 1912), pp. 25–26; P. G. LePage, "Arts and Crafts of the Negro," *International Studio*, LXXVIII (March, 1924), 477–78.

these traditional skills among the later generations of transplanted Negroes. During the early years of American slavery, little thought was given to the possibility of converting imported "savages" into artisans. Slaves were brought to America for agricultural purposes and in most instances were used for no other work. Among the planter class there were those who felt that craftsmanship did nothing more than replace the stock which it consumed and hence was less productive than agriculture.[4] Still others feared that industrialization would bring the slave into contact with free workers and provide access to tools needed for fashioning weapons, thus increasing the danger of insurrection.[5] These factors, together with the hostility of white artisans to slave competition[6] and the widespread belief that black men were inferior in mind and body,[7] served as ample justification for restricting the Negro to predominantly agricultural service.

On the other hand, the steady decline in the price of colonial tobacco, the mainstay of Southern agrarianism, weakened the arguments of its advocates. The handicrafts, even if they created products only commensurate with the value of the materials originally expended, as the

[4] Alexander Hamilton, Works, ed. by John C. Hamilton (New York, 1851), III, 219; Adam Smith, The Wealth of Nations, ed. by Edwin Cannan (New York, 1937), pp. 631–33.

[5] Several of the slaves implicated in the New York "Negro conspiracy" of 1741, which allegedly had as its objective the burning of the city and the murder of its inhabitants, were artisans. Even the preliminary meetings were held at the homes of white tradesmen whom the Negroes probably met while at work. Daniel Horsemanden, The New York Conspiracy, or a History of the Negro Plot (New York, 1810), passim. Aptheker makes reference to this conspiracy as well as to an abortive Virginia plot involving a slave blacksmith who used his skill to fashion three hundred spears for the intended insurrection. Herbert Aptheker, American Negro Slave Revolts (New York, 1943), pp. 114–15, 192–93, 211.

[6] The term "white artisan," as used here, applies primarily to the "journeyman" class rather than to the "master" craftsman, who himself may have employed slave assistants. Such protests by white workers against the competition of slave labor usually were presented in the form of petitions to the colonial authorities. Richard B. Morris, Government and Labor in Early America (New York, 1946), p. 185 n.; Morris, "Labor and Mercantilism," in The Era of the American Revolution (New York, 1939), pp. 79–80; Marcus W. Jernegan, Laboring and Dependent Classes in Colonial America, 1607–1783 (Chicago, 1931), pp. 20–21; John F. Watson, Annals of Philadelphia and Pennsylvania in the Olden Times (Philadelphia, 1844), I, 97–98; Cheesman A. Herrick, White Servitude in Pennsylvania (Philadelphia, 1926), p. 88; Papers of Daniel Horsemanden (MSS.), pp. 175–76 in the library of the New-York Historical Society; Samuel D. McKee, Labor in Colonial New York (New York, 1935), p. 127. For a statement by a colonial office reiterating the grievances of local artisans, see Charles Z. Lincoln, ed., Messages from the Governors (Albany, 1909), I, 260.

[7] Perhaps typical of the eighteenth century Virginia gentry, Colonel George Mason maintained that slavery discouraged the arts and crafts, for it prevented the importation of white laborers "who really enrich and strengthen a country." George Livermore, The Opinions of the Founders of the Republic on Negroes as Slaves, Citizens, and Soldiers (Boston, 1863), p. 56. Similar opinions may be found in Thomas Jefferson, Writings, ed. by H. A. Washington (New York, 1863), VIII, 386; William Byrd to Lord Egmont, July 12, 1736, American Historical Review, I (October, 1895), 89; Lorenzo D. Turner, "Anti-Slavery Sentiment in American Literature," Journal of Negro History, XIV (October, 1929), 386.

planters had maintained, were not completely unproductive. Manufacturing, unlike agriculture, was independent of seasonal weather fluctuations and seemed more conducive to specialization, thereby affording greater opportunity for improvement.[8] Even Thomas Jefferson, the champion of agrarian America, eventually recognized industrialism as one of the major pillars of our prosperity and urged a policy which would plant the manufacturer and husbandman side by side and establish "at the door of every one that exchange of mutual labors and comforts, which we have hitherto sought in distant regions."[9]

Unquestionably the strongest argument for the use of Negro artisans was a scarcity of labor. During most of the colonial period, in spite of constant demand for the products of skilled craftsmanship, the supply of workers who had mastered the trades was generally inadequate. The province of South Carolina in 1731 had only one potter, while Connecticut, the following year, had not enough capmakers to manufacture one half the hats worn by the inhabitants. Writing of New Hampshire, Jeremy Belknap deplored the "want of experienced and industrious workmen."[10] Peter Purry, of Neufchâtel, while advising European emigrants about to depart for the Southern colonies, emphasized the need for tradesmen. Those desirous of going as servants, he remarked, should be carpenters or good laborers. Without referring specifically to the shortage of tailors, Purry notified each to take with him at least three or four good shirts and a suit of clothes.[11] In a similar vein Benjamin Franklin called attention to the "continued demand for artisans of all the necessary and useful kinds to supply those cultivators of the earth with houses and with furniture and utensils of the grosser sorts, which cannot so well be brought from Europe."[12]

This situation gave the few established tradesmen excellent bargaining powers. In many communities the price of labor rose steadily, occasionally becoming almost prohibitive. In New York at the beginning of the

[8] Robert Beverly, The History of Virginia (London, 1722), p. 255; Jernegan, Laboring and Dependent Classes, p. 8; Jernegan, "Slavery and the Beginnings of Industrialism in the American Colonies," American Historical Review, XXV (January, 1920), 222; Hamilton, III, 198–201.

[9] Jefferson's Tammany Society speech, Feb. 29, 1808, in Saul K. Padover, ed., The Complete Jefferson (New York, 1943), pp. 529–30.

[10] J. P. Purry, "A Description of the Province of South Carolina, Drawn up at Charles Town, in September, 1731," in Peter Force, ed., Tracts and Other Papers (Washington, D.C., 1836–46), II, no. XI, 14; Governor and Company of Connecticut to the Board of Trade, October, 1732, in Mary K. Talcott, ed., "The Talcott Papers," Connecticut Historical Society, Collections, IV (Hartford, 1892), 263; Works Project Administration, Federal Writers' Program, New Hampshire: A Guide to the Granite State (Boston, 1938), p. 37.

[11] "Artificers are so scarce at present," Purry observed, "that all sorts of work is very dear; Taylors, Shoemakers, Smiths &c. would be particularly acceptable." Purry, op. cit., pp. 7, 14.

[12] Benjamin Franklin, Works, ed. by Jared Sparks (Boston, 1836–40), II, 471–72.

eighteenth century the "high wages of the labourer" seriously hampered the production of naval stores.[13] To add to the difficulties facing the colonial employer, virgin land was available at reasonable rates. As late as 1779 Dr. Hewit reported that the "artificer and tradesman, after having labored for a few years at their respective employments, and purchased a few negroes, commonly retreat to the country, and settle tracts of uncultivated land."[14] Masters tried to import European workers, but the results were often unsatisfactory. Indentured servants, just as domestic tradesmen, were attracted by the prospects of cheap land. Leaving before their contracts had expired, these men had little difficulty disappearing into the mass of free citizens.[15] As a last resort employers turned to their final source of potential industrial labor—Negro slaves.

The employment of slave mechanics, it was commonly agreed, would restrain the rapid turnover in man power and counteract the excessive wage demands of free workers. In scattered instances American Negroes began working at the trades only a few years after the introduction of slavery. By 1649 one Virginia planter had forty colored helpers whom he instructed in spinning, weaving, and shoemaking. With only about three hundred Negroes in the entire colony, this meant that approximately one out of every seven was receiving instruction in the crafts.[16] Five years later Richard Johnson, a mulatto carpenter, was granted one hundred acres of land in Northampton County, Virginia.[17] In old New Amsterdam Negroes were required to build roads and fortifications, while in 1676 Colonel

---

[13] Robert Livingston to the Lords of Trade, May 13, 1701, in E. B. O'Callaghan, ed., *Documents Relative to the Colonial History of the State of New York* (Albany, 1856–87), IV, 875.

[14] Bartholomew R. Carroll, ed., *Historical Collections of South Carolina* (New York, 1846), I, 377. Also consult Benjamin Franklin, *Observations concerning the Increase of Mankind, Peopling of Countries,* etc. (Boston, 1755), p. 4; Governor William Franklin to the Earl of Hillsborough, June 14, 1768, quoted in *Publications of the Colonial Society of Massachusetts,* VI, *Transactions, 1899, 1900* (Boston, 1904), 360; Albert C. Myers, ed., *Narratives of Early Pennsylvania, West New Jersey, and Delaware, 1630–1707* (New York, 1912), p. 328.

[15] E. B. O'Callaghan, *Documentary History of the State of New York* (Albany, 1849–51), I, 499; Philip A. Bruce, *Economic History of Virginia in the Seventeenth Century* (New York, 1896), II, 413. In addition one could not be certain of the quality of work of imported help. Occasionally inexperienced laborers successfully misrepresented themselves as skilled artisans in order to gain passage to the Western Hemisphere. Even those indentured immigrants who were potentially capable, many colonial employers insisted, viewed America as a land of relaxation, thus performing half-hearted service and refusing to toil for as many hours as they had been accustomed to in Europe. *A Complete Revisal of All the Acts of Assembly of the Province of North Carolina* (New Bern, 1773), p. 79; B. Franklin, *Works,* ed. by John Bigelow (New York, 1905), III, 101; Stella H. Sutherland, *Population Distribution in Colonial America* (New York, 1936), p. 216.

[16] Raymond B. Pinchbeck, *The Virginia Negro Artisan and Tradesman* (Richmond, 1926), p. 15; Evarts B. Greene and Virginia D. Harrington, *American Population before the Federal Census of 1790* (New York, 1932), p. 136.

[17] Pinchbeck, p. 23.

Richard Morris employed sixty to seventy slaves at his New Jersey iron mill and plantation.[18] However, in spite of these early evidences, it was not until the eighteenth century that Negro craftsmanship became a factor of some importance in American economy.

Skilled Negro labor, in one form or another, was present in every province of colonial America,[19] although in no large area did craftsmanship constitute the predominant form of Negro service. The North employed its black inhabitants as household domestics and unskilled laborers, while in the South their capability as field hands overshadowed many attempts to use them extensively for other purposes. Probably the largest proportion of Negro artisans was to be found in the middle provinces, whose flourishing towns served to encourage the development of the trades, and where Negroes could become assistants to established tradesmen. In New York, Philadelphia, and Baltimore, Negroes worked as bakers, brewers, bricklayers, butchers, carpenters, cooks, coopers, distillers, goldsmiths, plasterers, shoemakers, silversmiths, and weavers.[20] Even in the towns of New England, where the number of black inhabitants was always small, Negroes were assimilated into industry. Reflecting the commercial trends of the coastal region, many engaged in various phases of shipbuilding. At a Boston slave auction in October, 1751, five "strong hearty stout Negro men, most of them Tradesmen, such as Caulkers, Sailmakers, etc.," were offered for sale, while in Newport and Providence, Rhode Island, slave workers gave service as anchor makers, mast builders, rope makers, and spinners.[21]

[18] George E. Haynes, *The Negro at Work in New York City* (New York, 1912), p. 66; O'Callaghan, *Docs. Rel. to Col. Hist. of New York,* I, 499, II, 474, III, 307; Marion T. Wright, "New Jersey Laws and the Negro," *Journal of Negro History,* XXVIII (April, 1943), 161.

[19] Slavery was prohibited in the colony of Georgia before 1750, and hence the development of Negro craftsmanship in that region was somewhat retarded.

[20] For examples of Negro craftsmanship in the middle colonies consult: "Eighteenth Century Slaves as Advertised by Their Masters," *Jour. Negro Hist.,* I (April, 1916), 179, 194, 203; *Archives of the State of New Jersey,* 1st series, XX (1898), 8, 263, XXVIII (1916), 48; *Archives of Maryland,* XXVIII (1908), 43; O'Callaghan, *Docs. Rel. New York,* IV, 875, V, 444, 460; *Papers of the Lloyd Family of the Manor of Queens Village, Lloyd's Neck, Long Island, New York, 1654–1826* (New-York Historical Society, *Collections,* LIX, LX, 1927), I, 261, 560; Harry B. Yoshpe, ed., "Record of Slave Manumissions in New York during the Colonial and Early National Periods," *Jour. Negro Hist.,* XXV (January, 1941), 89; Rita S. Gottesman, ed., *The Arts and Crafts in New York, 1726–1776* (New-York Hist. Soc., *Collections,* LXIX, 1938), pp. 48, 140; Alfred C. Prime, ed., *The Arts and Crafts in Philadelphia, Maryland, and South Carolina, 1721–1800* (Philadelphia, 1929–32), I, 48; Prime, *Colonial Craftsmen of Pennsylvania* (Philadelphia, 1925), p. 3; Mrs. A. C. Prime, ed., *Three Centuries of Historic Silver* (Philadelphia, 1938), pp. 52–53; New York *Mercury,* Mar. 1, 1756, Aug. 30, 1756, Dec. 9, 1765; New York *Gazette,* July 6–13; 1730, Aug. 27–Sept. 3, 1733; March 24–31, 1735; New York *Weekly Post-Boy,* Apr. 3, 1749; *Pennsylvania Gazette,* Mar. 21, 1737, Apr. 21, 1761, Aug. 6, 1777; *Pennsylvania Packet,* May 1, 1784.

[21] Boston *Post-Boy,* June 22, 1752, in Elizabeth Donnan, ed., *Documents Illustrative of the History of the Slave Trade to America* (Washington, 1930–35), III, 66; Lorenzo J. Greene, "The New England Negro as Seen in Advertisements for Runaway Slaves," *Jour. Negro Hist.,*

Occupying a unique role in the development of Negro craftsmanship were the Southern colonies. In this region, agriculture dominated the economy, and domestic manufacturing was conceived as ancillary to the traditional agrarian system. On many plantations, slaves, although primarily engaged in planting, found it necessary to have some mechanical knowledge in order to attend to any serious emergency that might arise. From these beginnings emerged a corps of slave artisans whose work was identified with the prevailing agrarian economy and upon whose skills the planters began to depend with increasing frequency. Probably the first trade in which the Southern Negro received instruction was coopering. In preparing the crop for market, large numbers of casks were required, and slaves were therefore taught to cut, bend, and hoop staves into the required shapes. Before the end of the colonial period, one writer insists, every large estate in the rice belt of South Carolina had its own coopering shop. Workers were also needed to construct the small boats on which the shipment was transported to market, while others were given training in the navigation of these vessels, hence the development of Negro ship carpenters and pilots. It is safe to assume that anyone who could not work at the trades himself and did not have slaves who understood these tasks, often found living in the South rather difficult.[22]

With the passage of time the relationship between agriculture and the crafts became even closer. Added numbers of Southern slaves were taught to practice the trades, thus partially relieving dependence upon Europe and the Northern provinces. Often the children of the household servants were encouraged to sew and embroider. Planters also built looms and put their slaves to work at making cloth. George Washington, like countless other slaveowners, had a weaving house on his estate, employing a white supervisor and five Negro girls, who together supplied the clothing for many persons living in the vicinity. Even the medium-sized plantation was equipped with spinning wheel and weaving loom, in this way ensuring the

XXIX (April, 1944), 139; H. Gardner to C. Chaplin, Dec. 23, 1774, *The Commerce of Rhode Island, 1726–1800* (Massachusetts Historical Society, *Collections,* 7th series, IX, X 1914–15), I, 523; Newport *Mercury,* Apr. 27, 1772; Boston *News-Letter,* Jan. 29, 1748, in George F. Dow, ed., *The Arts and Crafts in New England, 1704–1775* (Topsfield, Mass., 1927), p. 197. For other examples of New England Negro tradesmen consult: Boston *Independent Chronicle and the Universal Advertiser,* Jan. 16, 1777; "Advertisements from the Records of Middle-sex County, Virginia, March 5, 1677–78," *William and Mary College Quarterly,* VI (October, 1897), 117; "Eighteenth Century Slaves Advertised," *Jour. Negro Hist.,* I, 165; Boston *News-Letter and Evening Post,* July 11, 1746, in Donnan, III, 66; Providence *Gazette,* July 28, 1770, reprinted in William D. Johnston, *Slavery in Rhode Island, 1755–1776* (Providence, 1894), p. 28; also newspaper extracts in Dow, pp. 62, 187, 188, 189, 195, 197, 202, 304.

[22] W.P.A., Federal Writers' Program, *The Negro in Virginia* (New York, 1940), p. 47; Edward McCrady, *The History of South Carolina under the Royal Government, 1719–1776* (New York, 1899), p. 387; J. Urmstone to the Secretary of the Society for Propagating the Gospel, July 7, 1711, in Ulrich B. Phillips, ed., *Plantation and Frontier Documents* (Cleveland, 1910), II, 272.

profitable use of valuable labor at times when the selling price of tobacco fell below production expenditures.[23]

On the other hand, some of the larger plantations became almost economic units in themselves, having at their disposal sufficient men and equipment to continue operating irrespective of conditions outside. During the most pressing days of the American Revolution, when the British were dangerously near and supplies were virtually unobtainable, many plantations escaped privation because of facilities installed during peacetime. On the plantation of George Mason, for example, were slave "carpenters, coopers, sawyers, blacksmiths, tanners, curriers, shoemakers, spinners, weavers and knitters, and even a distiller." His forest land furnished wood for the carpenters and coopers; his cattle provided skins for the tanners, curriers, and shoemakers; his sheep and his cotton fields supplied the spinners and weavers, while his fruit trees were used by the distillers.[24] John Dixon of Williamsburg, Virginia, owned a host of slave handicraftsmen, including blacksmiths, carpenters, barbers, shoemakers, and plasterers. On another plantation were "several pairs of sawyers, two coopers, two or three indifferent house-carpenters and a ship-carpenter and caulker." The estate of William Byrd of Westover, a mere 43,000 acres, had two hundred and twenty Negroes, "many of them being Tradesmen," who were assessed at 7,000 pounds. According to Philip V. Fithian, Robert Carter operated textile factories, mills, bakeries, salt works, smiths' shops, and iron forges. Carter's slave labor supply, at one time numbering more than five hundred, included one Negro whom the master would not sell for five hundred pounds. Such plantations, having at their disposal extensive working forces, mines, transportation facilities, shops, mills, and tools, seemingly approximated many of the features of modern "vertical" trusts in controlling every aspect of their own production and distribution.[25]

[23] J. Hector St. Jean de Crèvecoeur, *Sketches of Eighteenth Century America,* ed. by Henry L. Bourdin, *et. al.* (New Haven, 1925), p. 143; Jesse W. Parkhurst, "The Role of the Black Mammy in the Plantation Household," *Jour. Negro Hist.,* XXIII (July 1938), 358; Julia C. Spruill, *Women's Life and Work in the Southern Colonies* (Chapel Hill, 1938), p. 75; Frances Little, *Early American Textiles* (New York, 1931), p. 31. As an illustration of the extent of household manufacturing, during the year 1768 George Washington's slave weavers produced more than 1,355 yards of cloth. One of Washington's neighbors, Robert Carter, apparently abandoned the use of white textile workers after once trying Negro labor, although the change may have been influenced by a shortage of white artisans during the American Revolution. Phillips, II, 315, 324–25.

[24] From the MS. Recollections of George Mason, quoted in Thomas J. Wertenbaker, *Patrician and Plebian in Virginia* (Charlottesville, 1912), p. 50.

[25] *South Carolina Gazette,* Jan. 2, 1749, Sep. 19, 1751, reprinted in Thomas J. Wertenbaker, *The Old South* (New York, 1942), pp. 230, 231; William Byrd, *The Secret Diary of William Byrd of Westover, 1709–1712,* ed. by Louis B. Wright and Marion Tinling (Richmond, 1941), p. 186; *Another Secret Diary of William Byrd of Westover, 1739–1741,* ed. by Maude H. Woodfin and Marion Tinling (Richmond, 1942), pp. 324, 325; Philip V. Fithian, *Journal and Letters of Philip Vickers Fithian, 1773–1774: A Plantation Tutor of the Old Dominion,* ed. by Hunter D. Farish (Williamsburg, 1945), pp. xi, 173; Du Bois, *Negro American Artisan,* p. 35;

The individual worker followed a similar pattern. Almost invariably he was responsible for the production of a single item from its first to its last stage. Division of labor during the colonial period was largely nonexistent, and therefore each craftsman was expected to plan, construct, and ornament his own product. Furthermore, every trade carried a very broad implication. Regardless of his occupation the slave artisan usually had to know various other crafts related to his own. Thus the Negro blacksmith often could perform every phase in the production of iron, including the skilled art of fashioning tools, while the carpenter was simultaneously a cabinetmaker, wood turner, builder, coffin and pattern maker, architect, contractor, wheelwright, sawyer, and cooper.[26] To accomplish this required more than an average amount of intelligence and ability. Several slave craftsmen were described as being "very artful," "very sensible," or "ingenious," while a few even mastered two or more foreign languages. In the relatively short period of three months, one Southern planter was able to train thirty Negroes to produce a weekly total of one hundred and twenty yards of cotton and woolen cloth. Two Negro workers in South Carolina were each capable of producing two pairs of shoes per day. Another shoemaker in the same province attended to his master's shop alone for a period of nine years, while in New York an aged shopkeeper pleaded with a court to commute the sentence of a convicted slave blacksmith so that the Negro could continue to support him.[27]

In some instances Negro artisans gained a limited measure of recognition because of their workmanship. Slave craftsmen at Andover, New Jersey, produced superior iron wares which were eventually accepted for high quality on the basis of brand name alone.[28] Even in the "artistic" crafts Negro workers managed to leave their imprint. Serving as pipe carvers, upholsterers, tool and instrument makers, and manufacturers of cabinets, chairs, and other types of furniture, many performed skillfully for their employers. In Boston Thomas Fleet, a printer, kept in his shop three colored helpers who worked at setting type and cutting wooden blocks. One of these printers was responsible for engraving all the pictures found in the

Hugh Jones, *The Present State of Virginia* (London, 1724), pp. 44, 60, 131, 135, in Sabin's *Reprints*, 1865.

[26] Pinchbeck, p. 14; Charles B. Bradley, *Design in the Industrial Arts* (Peoria, Ill., 1946), p. 26; W. E. B. Du Bois, *The Negro Artisan* (Atlanta, 1902), pp. 17, 33; Philip A. Bruce, *The Social Life of Virginia in the Seventeenth Century* (Lynchburg, 1929), p. 120.

[27] "Eighteenth Century Slaves Advertised," *Jour. Negro Hist.*, I, 186, 187, 196, 197; Broadus Mitchell, *The Rise of Cotton Mills in the South* (Baltimore, 1921), p. 13; *South Carolina Gazette*, Jan. 14, 1764, May 24, 1768, reprinted in Jernegan, "Slavery and Industrialism," *Am. Hist. Rev.*, XXV, 234; E. B. O'Callaghan, ed., *Calendar of Historical Manuscripts in the Office of the Secretary of State, Albany, New York* (Albany, 1856–66), Part II, 444.

[28] New York *Gazette and Weekly Mercury*, Mar. 1, 1773; *Pennsylvania Gazette*, June 29, 1774; William Allen, *Extracts from Chief Justice William Allen's Letter Book*, ed. by Lewis B. Walker (Pottsville, 1897), p. 70; Charles S. Boyer, *Early Forges and Furnaces in New Jersey* (Philadelphia, 1931), p. 28.

publications of his master. As a young man Gilbert Stuart, the Republic's first great portrait painter, derived great pleasure from observing the work of Neptune Thurston, a New England slave cooper, who sketched portraits on the heads of the casks in his master's shop. According to J. A. Porter, our only contemporary likeness of Negro poetess Phillis Wheatley, a rough copperplate engraving, was probably the work of a slave.[29]

In other fields of artistic craftsmanship Negro labor was likewise represented. The luxuriously built Southern mansions, notably Jefferson's dwelling at Monticello, as well as the decorative hand-wrought grills and balconies found in the older quarters of New Orleans and Charleston, still attest to the quality of eighteenth century slave labor.[30] One of the original surveyors of our nation's capital at Washington, Benjamin Banneker, the Negro astronomer and mathematician whose contributions evoked praise from Jefferson,[31] once experimented as an amateur handicraftsman. In the province of Maryland in the year 1762 Banneker is reported to have constructed the first clock ever made in America. A factor even more astonishing to his neighbors was that the builder had undertaken the task without ever having seen a clock before. Using a small watch as his model, wood as his raw material, and a pocket knife as his tool, he meticulously assembled a machine which remained in perfect operation for over two decades.[32] Employed at allied occupations in some of the larger towns were Negro goldsmiths, jewelers, and silversmiths. William Ball of Philadelphia, a prominent white silversmith and jeweler, used several Negro assistants. In his Front Street shop, next to the London Coffee House, Ball manufactured "gold and silver in all its branches." In 1778 he was temporarily plagued by a labor shortage, for "three Negro men, viz., Tom, by trade a silversmith,"

[29] New York *Gazette,* Mar. 24–31, 1735; New York *Gazette or Weekly Post-Boy,* Jan. 6 1763; Gottesman, pp. 140, 317; Boston *Gazette,* Jan. 27–Feb. 3, 1728; Boston *News Letter,* Apr. 8–15, 1742; Dow, pp. 195, 272; *South Carolina and American General Gazette,* June 3, 1771; Prime, *Arts and Crafts in Philadelphia,* I, 167; James A. Porter, *Modern Negro Art* (New York, 1943), pp. 15, 16, 18.

[30] Charles S. Johnson, *The Negro in American Civilization* (New York, 1930), p. 11; W.P.A., Writers' Program, *Virginia: A Guide to the Old Dominion* (New York, 1940), p. 77; Albert H. Sonn, *Early American Wrought Iron* (New York, 1928), III, 7–8; J. A. Porter, "Four Problems in the History of Negro Art," *Jour. Negro Hist.,* XXVII (January, 1942), 13–14; Alain Locke, *Negro Art, Past and Present* (Washington, 1936), p. 15; Locke, *The Negro in Art* (Washington, 1940), p. 8; Schuyler, in *Crisis,* XLVII, 158.

[31] Writing to Banneker on August 30, 1791, Jefferson declared: "No body wishes more than I do to see such proofs as you exhibit, that nature has given to our black brethren, talents equal to those of the other colors of men, and that a want of them is owing merely to the degraded condition of their existence both in Africa and America." Thomas Jefferson, *Writings,* ed. by P. L. Ford (New York, 1892–99), V, 377.

[32] Carter G. Woodson, *The Education of the Negro Prior to 1861* (New York, 1915), p. 91; Henry E. Baker, "Benjamin Banneker, the Negro Mathematician and Astronomer," *Jour. Negro Hist.,* III (April, 1918), 105–107, 111; "Benjamin Banneker, the Negro Astronomer," *Atlantic Monthly,* XI (January, 1863), 81, 82–83; Du Bois, *Negro Artisan,* p. 29; Robert Fortenbaugh, "The Learned Negro," *Jour. Negro Hist.,* XIV (April, 1929), 239–42.

left his shop and deserted to the British army.[33] Probably the most famous Maryland craftsman of his day, William Faris of Annapolis, whose many undertakings brought him into the realm of the silversmith, cabinetmaker, jeweler, and clockmaker, also relied on the services of slave helpers. After 1770 Faris became so well established that, unlike other shopkeepers, he found it unnecessary to advertise. Nevertheless, as one biographer maintains: "An appraisal of William Faris' ability as a working silversmith is difficult, as it is impossible to distinguish between the work of his own hand and the silver made in the shop by his workmen."[34]

In some instances such skills as the Negro acquired while in a state of slavery later became a source of employment when he was free. Recognizing this fact, masters, when preparing statements of manumission, often provided that these former servants should be permitted to leave with their tools.[35] On the other hand, the situation confronting the freedman was not always enviable. Thrust into a different environment, deprived of all the protective influence of a master, confronted by the hostility of established white tradesmen, and subjected to almost as many legal restrictions as a slave,[36] the liberated Negro worker encountered great difficulty in trying to

[33] Boston Gazette, Nov. 14, 1752, in Dow, p. 62; New York Mercury, Aug. 30, 1756; New Gazette or Weekly Post-Boy, Feb. 23, 1764, in Gottesman, p. 48; Pennsylvania Gazette, Aug. 6, 1777; Pennsylvania Packet, Oct. 12, 1772, Sept. 1, 1778, May 1, 1784, in Prime, Arts and Crafts in Philadelphia, I, 43–46, 78–79. A less honorable form of the silversmith trade was practiced by those Negroes who stole household plate, stripped off the precious metal, and then sold it to an equally unscrupulous dealer. Governor Hunt of New York to the Lords of Trade, Nov. 14, 1710, in O'Callaghan, Docs. Rel. to New York, IV, 187; South Carolina Gazette, Feb. 22, 1752, Mar. 9, 1752, in Prime, Arts and Crafts in Philadelphia, I, 93, 102.

[34] Of one of his Negro workers, by trade a silversmith, jeweler, and lapidary, Faris once said: "There are few if any better workmen in America." Jacob H. Pleasants and Howard Sill, Maryland Silversmiths: 1715–1830 (Baltimore, 1930), pp. 257–58, 266; Maryland Gazette, Nov. 8, 1759, Dec. 4, 1760, Aug. 25, 1763, Aug. 2, 1764, Jan. 4, 1770, in Prime, Arts and Crafts in Philadelphia, I, 241–42.

[35] Abstracts of Wills on File in the Surrogate's Office of New York, 1665–1784 (New-York Hist. Soc., Collections, XXV-XXXVI, 1892–1903), V, 42; James M. Wright, The Free Negro in Maryland, 1634–1860 (New York, 1921), pp. 154–55 n.

[36] In order to keep the number of manumissions at a minimum, many colonies called for proof that the servant had served meritoriously and required that the master file a complete report and post a bond guaranteeing that the Negro would not become a liability on the community. Furthermore, the freedman was generally prohibited by law from having any dealings with slaves. In some cases the free Negro was compelled to repair the public highways for a specific period each year without receiving remuneration for his labor. Finally, at the discretion of the colonial authorities, adult freedmen who neglected to work or who did not pay their taxes, as well as emancipated minors, could be bound out for service to local employers. Walter Clark, ed., The State Records of North Carolina (Goldsboro, 1895–1906), XXIV, 221; W. W. Hening, ed., The Statutes at Large, being a Collection of all the Laws of Virginia (Philadelphia, 1823), VI, 112; Charles Z. Lincoln, et al., eds., The Colonial Laws of New York from the Year 1664 to the Revolution (Albany, 1894–96), II, 683; Acts and Laws of His Majesty's Province of the Massachusetts Bay in New England (Boston, 1726), p. 176; Acts and Resolves of the Province of Massachusetts Bay (Boston, 1869–1924), I, 519;

assimilate himself into the mass of free citizens. To add to these obstacles, he frequently discovered that much of the instruction which he had received as a slave, especially if he had been trained on a plantation, was elementary in nature and not of the highest standards.[37] It is not surprising that many freedmen either abandoned the crafts or lapsed into a state of servitude.[38] Thus a combination of white prejudice, original inexperience, and a lack of opportunity for improvement served as limiting factors in the early development of skilled Negro craftsmanship in America.

J. H. Trumbull and C. J. Hoadley, eds., *The Public Records of the State of Connecticut, 1776–1780* (Hartford, 1894–95), I, 415–16; Pinchbeck, pp. 20–21; James T. Mitchell and Henry Flanders, eds., *The Statutes at Large of Pennsylvania from 1682–1801* (Harrisburg, 1896–1908), IV, 62–63; B. W. Leigh and W. W. Hening, eds., *The Revised Code of the Laws of Virginia* (Richmond, 1819), I, 434–35; "Court Records Pertaining to Negro Education in Virginia in the Eighteenth Century," *Virginia Magazine of History and Biography*, II (April, 1895), 429.

[37] As the Reverend Hugh Jones of Virginia was quick to observe, the work of slave craftsmen was not always "the aptest or nicest." Plantation artisans had been readily used for minor tasks, but owners did not have complete confidence in the ability of their slaves to handle operations of a more technical nature. It is interesting to note that certain masters, including William Byrd, went to great expense to secure the services of foreign artisans in spite of the availability of Negroes who had been trained in the crafts. Jones, p. 36; DuBois, *Negro Artisans*, p. 13.

[38] Edward R. Turner, *The Negro in Pennsylvania: Slavery-Servitude-Freedom, 1639–1861* (Washington, 1911), pp. 89–91.

# 5

## SERVANT INTO SLAVE: THE EVOLUTION OF THE LEGAL STATUS OF THE NEGRO LABORER IN COLONIAL VIRGINIA
### Paul C. Palmer

THE origin of chattel slavery in the British colonies of North America remains a subject of debate among American historians. Some, such as Oscar and Mary Handlin, assert that the institution began only after several decades during which the lot of the Negro servant scarcely differed from that of the white bondsman. Others seem still to assume that the institution began as early as 1619. Although Carl Degler and Winthrop Jordan have offered some clarification on this

Paul C. Palmer, "Servant into Slave: The Evolution of the Legal Status of the Negro Laborer in Colonial Virginia," *South Atlantic Quarterly*, LXV (Summer, 1966), pp. 355–371. Reprinted by permission of the publisher and the author.

score, further examination is still in order. Other facets remain almost untouched. Did colonial legislatures oppose or promote the growth of slavery and the importation of Negroes? Did they prescribe or simply permit enslavement of Negroes? Was the initial enslavement of Negroes in the British North American colonies legal? Did the institution, once initiated, develop slowly or burst forth full-grown at some definite time? A review of the legal history of the institution in colonial Virginia may be of some value toward achieving at least partial answers.

John Rolfe provided the earliest first-hand account of the introduction of Negroes into the Virginia colony. In a letter to Sir Edwin Sandys he reported that in late August, 1619, a Dutch vessel had arrived at Point-Comfort with "not any thing but 20. and odd Negroes, wch the Governor and Cape Marchant bought for victualle . . . at the best and easyest rate they could."[1] That same year, similar "buying" of English wives was reported in Virginia, and throughout the colonial era "buying" indentured servants was common practice. Misunderstanding has stemmed from the failure of contemporary reporters to consider the distinction between buying one's services and the actual purchase of the person's body. It is apparent that in 1619 neither Negroes nor English bondservants were owned as chattels in Virginia. There is also the fact that several of the first Negroes in Virginia were Christians, which according to English practice automatically "infranchised" them.[2]

The first official record, other than the 1623 census, of a Negro in Virginia shows in November, 1624, one "John Phillip, a Negro Christened in England," acting as witness in the trial of a white man, a duty scarcely to be confused with that of a chattel.[3] Within a year there was a second case involving a Negro; "the negro called by the name of *brase*" was awarded as a servant to Lady Yardley to be paid "monthly for his labor forty pound waight of good marchantable tobacco." Later he was declared by the General Court to "belong to *Sir Francis Wyatt,* Governor . . . As his servant." The matter of wages was not mentioned, but it cannot be concluded that he was a slave.[4]

Not until 1630 is there any evidence of legal distinctions between

---

[1] Susan Myra Kingsbury, ed., *The Records of the Virginia Company of London* (4 vols.; Washington: Government Printing Office, 1933), III, 243.

[2] Helen Tunnicliff Catterall, *Judicial Cases Concerning American Slavery and the Negro* (5 vols.; Washington: Carnegie Institution of Washington, 1926), I, 55. The Christianity of the Negroes is evidenced by their Christian baptismal names. See "Lists of the Livinge and Dead in Virginia, February 16th, 1623," *Colonial Records of Virginia* (Richmond: Public Printing Office, 1874), pp. 37–60.

[3] Henry Read McIlwaine, ed., *Minutes of the Council and General Court of Colonial Virginia 1622–1632, 1670–1676, with Notes and Excerpts from Original Council and General Court Records, into 1683, Now Lost* (Richmond: The Colonial Press, Everett Waddey Co., 1924), p. 33. Hereinafter cited as *Minutes*.

[4] *Minutes*, pp. 72–73.

Negro and white servants in Virginia. In September the General Court ordered "Hugh Davis to be soundly whipped, before an assembly of Negroes and others for abusing himself to the dishonor of God and the shame of Christians, by defiling his body in lying with a negro." It is not completely clear whether Davis was punished for his fornication, because his paramour was a Negro, or perhaps only because she was unbaptized.[5] A clearer distinction was made by an act of the Assembly in January, 1639, providing that "All persons except negroes" should be armed.[6] This was the first of the long train of statutory discriminations that would ultimately make of the Negro a slave.

Servitude for life was first recorded in Virginia in July, 1640, in a case involving runaway servants. All three were sentenced to receive thirty stripes. Two of them, a Scot and a Dutchman, were required to serve an additional four years "after the time of their service is expired . . . ; the third being a negro named John Punch," was ordered to serve "his . . . master or his assigns for the time of his natural life."[7] Service *dura vita* was thereby instituted for at least one Virginia Negro. Only two weeks later another runaway Negro servant was sentenced "to be burnt in the cheek with the letter R, and to work in shakle one year or more as his master shall see cause."[8] It is not improbable that a second Negro was destined to serve in perpetuity.

In 1641 a case furnishing several clues to the legal status of the Virginia Negro in that era was decided by the General Court. John Graweere (or Geaween) brought suit for the possession of his daughter, who was also claimed by his master. Graweere, though a servant, had bought the child from her mother's master, Robert Sheppard. In the decision for Graweere it was stated that he had been "permitted by his said master to keep hogs." It is obvious that Graweere exercised rights unknown in chattel slavery; however, had his status been that of a white servant, no suit would have been necessary to establish his rights to the child he had bought.[9] The fact that Sheppard was able to sell the child suggests that as early as 1641 a Negro servant's children were sometimes considered the property of the mother's master and disposable by him. From this single remarkable case it becomes evident that the position of the Negro was deteriorating in Virginia. In Graweere's case his professed intention to bring up his child "in the fear of God and in the knowledge of religion taught and exercised in the

[5] *Ibid.*, p. 279; William Waller Hening, *The Statutes at Large; Being a Collection of All the Laws of Virginia, from the First Session of the Legislature in the Year 1619* (13 vols.; Richmond: W. W. Hening, 1819–1823), I, 426. Hereinafter cited as *Statutes*.

[6] *Statutes*, I, 226.

[7] *Minutes*, p. 466.

[8] *Ibid.*, p. 467.

[9] *Ibid.*, p. 477; Catterall, *Judicial Cases*, I, 58; "Virginia Council and General Court Records, 1640–1641," *Virginia Magazine of History and Biography*, XI (Jan., 1904), 281.

church of England" clearly influenced the court's decision.[10] Christianity among Negro servants remained an important consideration in determining their legal status until 1667.

Two official actions of March, 1656, succinctly demonstrated the decline of the African's status relative to that of the Indian in Virginia. The Assembly at that time declared that any Indian children in the households of colonists should not be slaves; at the same time the General Court tersely reported a decision involving a mulatto: "Mulatto held to be a slave and appeal taken."[11] It was nevertheless some years before the Indian's status was to be fixed clearly as superior to that of the Negro. In 1658 Indians and Negroes were lumped together in a new act concerning tithables; servants of both races, male and female, were declared subject to the levy, whereas only male white servants were classed as tithable.[12] By 1658, however, Indian servitude was declining, while Negro labor was steadily becoming more important to the tobacco economy of Virginia.[13]

That some Virginia Negroes served for life in the 1640's and 1650's is certain; it is just as certain that many did not. One instance of Negroes bound for a "term of years," as with white servants, occurred in 1647, and others appeared later.[14] It was not until 1661 that perpetual bondage of Negroes in Virginia received statutory recognition, but two acts of the Assembly in 1660 make it appear that they not only recognized that peculiar feature of Negro servitude but seemed inclined to promote its continuation and to encourage increased importation of Negroes. First the Assembly repealed the Irish Servant Act of 1655 as amended in 1658. That act had declared that "all Irish Servants that . . . have bin brought into this collony without indenture . . . shall serve . . . six year" or, if under sixteen, "till they be twenty-four years old." In 1658 it had been amended by the addition of the words "and all aliens to be included in this act."[15] Obviously "all aliens" must include Negroes, although the intent was probably only to cope with an increasingly heterogeneous white immigration. In March, 1660, the Irish Servant Act was replaced with an act which at first glance appears more liberal: "for the future no servant comeing into the country without indentures, of what christian nation soever, shall serve longer than those of our own country."[16] The inclusion of the phrase "of what christian

[10] *Minutes*, p. 477.

[11] *Statutes*, I, 396; *Minutes*, p. 504.

[12] *Statutes*, I, chap. 46. By 1658 being subject to the tithe had become a symbol of one's status as an agricultural laborer.

[13] W. Stitt Robinson, Jr., "The Legal Status of the Indian in Colonial Virginia," *VMH&B*, LVI (July, 1953), 247–259.

[14] "Northampton County Records in the 17th Century," *VMH&B*, IV (April, 1897), 407; *Minutes*, pp. 316, 354, 372.

[15] *Statutes*, I, 411, 471.

[16] *Ibid.*, I, 538–539.

nation soever" makes of this act a sanction for holding in perpetual bondage all Negroes imported in the future from Africa. This interpretation is
supported by the statute which followed. It declared that "the Dutch and
all strangers of what Xpian nation soever" need pay only "two shillings per
hogshead" export duty on tobacco rather than the normal duty charged
foreigners of ten schillings, provided that the tobacco be paid for with
imported Negroes. The Virginia Assembly thus authorized a sizable bounty
for the importation of Negroes, who, in view of the immediately prior repeal
of the Irish Servant Act, might reasonably be expected to serve for life.[17]

The following year perpetual servitude received oblique recognition
in an act of the Virginia Assembly concerning runaway servants. It stated
"That in case any English servant shall run away . . . with any negroes who
are incapable of makeing satisfaction by addition of time . . . [he] shall
serve for the time of the said negroes absence."[18] Although not declaring
that Negroes served for life, the act indicates that such was done and was
legally acceptable. It was in 1662 in amending the above statute that the
Assembly first employed the term, slave, in a law. By that time the most
basic feature of chattel slavery, service for life, was established in practice
and, if only indirectly, in law.[19]

Life servitude naturally involved the question of the status of Negro
offspring. Whether one could be born into slavery was of vital concern both
to the Negroes and their masters. In December, 1662, it was declared by the
Assembly that "Whereas some doubts have arisen whether children got by
any English man upon a negro woman shall be slave or ffree, *Be it enacted*
. . . that all children borne in this country shall be bond or free only according to the condition of the mother." By this legislation life-long servitude
was made self-perpetuating; the children of slaves being property in the
same manner as the natural increase "of livestock or other chattels."[20]

Paganism had been a major excuse for the enslavement of indigenous
races by the Spanish and Portuguese, and slavery so excused was permitted

---

[17] *Ibid.*, I, 540. This law is particularly interesting in view of frequent contentions that Vir-
ginians opposed the importation of large numbers of Negroes.

[18] *Ibid.*, II, 26.

[19] *Ibid.*, II, 116–17; in contrast, another law of the same session forbade Englishmen to sell
Indian servants for any period "longer than English of the like ages should serve." *Ibid.*,
II, 143.

[20] *Ibid.*, II, 170. Oscar and Mary Handlin, in "Origins of the Southern Labor System,"
*William and Mary Quarterly* (3rd series), VII (April, 1950), contend without adequate documentation that Hening altered this passage, presumably substituting "slave" for "bond."
See footnote, p. 216 of the article. Even if such alteration occurred, as is of course possible,
it is difficult to understand how the meaning is changed. Obviously the question of offspring
following their parents into bondage was relevant only in the cases of slaves (and later
the offspring of mulatto bastards of white women). There can be no serious doubt that this
was a slave law. John Codman Hurd, *The Law of Freedom and Bondage in the United
States* (2 vols.; Boston: Little, Brown and Co., 1853), I, 165.

"almost universally."[21] If the paganism of the African was the reason for his enslavement, it followed that Christianization should alter his condition. This logic had obviously influenced the General Court in its decision for Graweere in 1641. John Randolph recorded a case in 1644 in which a baptized mulatto servant, although acquired "as a Slave for Ever," was declared to be not a slave "but to serve as other Christian servants do."[22] In March, 1662, the Assembly ordered an Indian to be freed, although "sold for life," because of his "speaking perfectly the English tongue and desiring baptism."[23] Concerning Negroes, "the opinion prevailed among some that when they ceased to be heathens they were by the very fact, released from slavery."[24] This seems to have been common practice under English law and was the decision of an English court in 1677.[25] It was not to be so for Virginia Negroes. By an act of September, 1667, the General Assembly decreed that in the case of "children that are slaves by birth . . . the conferring of baptisme doth not alter the condition of a person as to his bondage or ffreedome; that divers masters, ffreed from this doubt, may more carefully endeavour the propagation of christianity."[26] This act, despite its pious rationale, markedly reduced the Negro's opportunities for freedom.

It can safely be said that by 1667 the most essential features of chattel slavery had been established in Virginia. The Negro was, however, presumably still accorded many of the legal safeguards enjoyed by bondsmen of other races. One of the most important of those safeguards was removed by "An act about the casuall killing of slaves" passed in October, 1669. The statute was prefaced by the statement that "the only law in force for the punishment of refractory servants resisting their master, mistris or overseer cannot be inflicted upon negroes." That Negroes as a class could not be punished by the normal method of adding to the term of service establishes conclusively that bondage for life had become the accepted rule. Masters of recalcitrant Negroes were to be allowed to use corporal punishment, and if "by the extremity of correction [the slave] should chance to die, . . . his death [would] not be accompted ffelony, but the master . . . be acquit from molestation, since it cannot be presumed that

[21] Hurd, I, 161.

[22] "The Randolph Manuscript," VMH&B, XVII (July, 1909), 232. He was reportedly freed in 1665 after twenty-one years' service, hardly the normal term for "other Christian servants."

[23] Statutes, II, 155.

[24] Charles Campbell, History of the Colony and Ancient Dominion of Virginia (Philadelphia: J. B. Lippincott and Co., 1860), p. 20. See also Philip Neri, "Baptism and Manumission of Negro Slaves in the Early Colonial Period," Records of the American Catholic Society of Philadelphia, LI (Sept.–Dec., 1940), 220–232.

[25] Catterall, I, 55 n.

[26] Statutes, II, 260. The inclusion of the phrase, "slaves by birth," would seem to confirm doubts concerning the Handlins' inferences previously noted. They do not contend that this passage was altered.

prepensed malice . . . should induce any man to destroy his own estate."[27]

Aside from the obvious infringement of his right to life, by the phrase "his owne estate" the Negro servant was clearly designated as a chattel rather than as one whose labor only was the property of his master. That such a concept was current in 1662 is apparent from the fact that a female slave's offspring were slaves by birth. Perhaps it was so as early as 1641 if Graweere's daughter was then considered the disposable property of her mother's master.[28]

It was not until 1670 that slave status was explicitly prescribed for any class of laborers by Virginia law. In that year the Assembly declared "that all servants not being christians imported into this colony by shipping shall be slaves for their lives; but what shall come by land shall serve; if boyes or girles, untill thirty yeares of age, if men or women twelve yeares and no longer."[29] Perhaps the intent was to enslave Africans while providing a milder form of servitude for Indians. But it might well have been, and doubtless was argued, that any Negro brought in from a neighboring colony or a Christian Negro brought in by shipping could demand his freedom at the end of twelve years. Almost exactly twelve years later, in November, 1682, the Assembly repealed the law and substituted one removing all ambiguity. After recounting the hardships worked upon slave merchants as a consequence of the old law, the Assembly declared

*that all servants except Turkes and Moores in amity with his Majestie which . . . shall be . . . imported . . . either by sea or land, whether Negroes, Moors, Mollatoes or Indians, who and whose parentage and native country are not christian at the time of their first purchase . . . by some christian, although . . . before . . . their importation . . they shall be converted to the christian faith . . . are hereby adjudged . . . to be slaves to all intents and purposes, any law, usage or custome to the contrary notwithstanding.*[30]

A more positive statement of the intention of the Assembly that Negroes in Virginia were to be slaves would have been difficult to draft.

If it was the desire of the Assembly that all Negroes in Virginia should serve for life, that hope was thwarted. Instances of free Negroes

---

[27] *Ibid.,* II, 220.

[28] Exactly when the Negro began to be considered property in body as well as service cannot be determined. There was no basis for such ownership in English laws of villeinage. See the discussion of English law in Hurd, Vol. I. Numerous cases involving entailment of slaves, reported in R. T. Barton, *Virginia Colonial Decisions: The Reports by Sir John Randolph and by Edward Barradall of Decisions of the General Court of Virginia, 1728–1741* (2 vols.; Boston: Boston Book Company, 1909), show that the distinction between ownership of service and of body was clear in the eighteenth century.

[29] *Statutes,* II, 283. This also is claimed by the Handlins to be a corruption of the original law. Again it could make little if any difference to substitute the word, "bond," for "slave."

[30] *Ibid.,* II, 490–492.

being reduced to slavery are so rare as to escape notice, but manumissions were rather common. An instance of manumission by will was recorded as early as 1645. Reference to manumitted "or otherwise free" Negroes was made in a law of October, 1670, forbidding Negroes and Indians to own Christian (i.e., white) servants. In the same month one Malack was noted to have been "set free . . . by will." In October, 1672, and again a year later Negroes were set free by the General Court as having fulfilled their indentures. The same was true for "black mary" in April, 1674, and for Phillip Gowen in June of the following year. In June, 1675, March, 1676, and November, 1678, the General Court freed Negroes who had been promised freedom upon the deaths of their masters.[31] By 1691 emancipation had become so common that members of the Assembly were apparently concerned and took action to make it more difficult for masters to free their slaves. In an act of April, 1691, the Assembly declared "that no negro or mulatto be . . . set free by any person . . . whatsoever, unless such person . . . pay for the transportation of such negro . . . out of the countrey within six months" or forfeit ten pounds sterling so that the church wardens might have the Negro transported.[32] Later enactments on the subject were even more stringent. In 1723 the Assembly would decree that not "upon any pretence whatsoever, except for some meritorious services . . . adjudged and allowed by the governor and council," should any slave be freed. If any were set free in contravention of the act, they were to be seized and sold at "public outcry."[33] Such barriers to manumission were among the features that made of American Negro slavery one of the harshest slave systems in all history.[34]

Regardless of the statutory imposition of servitude for life, Negroes in Virginia still possessed certain rights in law. No law had so far denied the right to a measure of self-protection, reasonable freedom of movement, property-holding and the like. As of 1680 Negroes could still sue in court, serve as witnesses, and enjoy other privileges later considered the exclusive province of free whites. Certainly those legal rights had been somewhat restricted in practice earlier. In 1680 further rights were removed by "An act for preventing negroes insurrections." That act provided that no Negro could carry weapons of any nature, offensive or defensive, or go from place to place without written permission, and that if any "negro or other slave" should "presume to lift up his hand in opposition against any christian," he would be punished with thirty lashes. In addition the law

---

[31] "Northampton County Records," *VMH&B,* V (July, 1897), 40; *Statutes,* II, 280; *Minutes* pp. 240, 316, 354, 372–373, 411, 413, 437, 520. Gowen's petition for his freedom is a very interesting document. It can be found (with the names of the principals slightly corrupted) in William P. Palmer, ed., *Calendar of Virginia State Papers* (10 vols.; Richmond: Public Printing Office, 1875), I, 9–10.

[32] *Statutes,* III, 86–88.

[33] *Ibid.,* IV, 132.

[34] Discussed in Frank Tannenbaum, *Slave and Citizen: The Negro in the Americas* (New York: A. A. Knopf, 1947).

stated that "any negroe or other slave . . . lurking in obscure places, comitting injuries to the inhabitants" could be killed by anyone "that shalby any lawfull authority be imployed to apprehend them."[35] In April, 1691, the law was modified to require a sheriff or justice's warrant for arrest of the offending Negro before it was "lawfull . . . to kill and distroy" him. The amended version also allowed compensation from public funds for the value of the dead slave.[36] The protection of the law enjoyed by other servants was being withdrawn from the Negro by the close of the seventeenth century.

Another portion of the act of April, 1691, presented an interesting departure from an established principle of law. Alleging a desire "for the prevention of that abominable mixture and spurious issue," the Assembly breached the principle that a child followed "the condition of the mother." Any bastard born of a white woman by a Negro or mulatto would, by the terms of the act, be bound to service by the church wardens for thirty years. In practice this could be expected to amount to the reduction of such unfortunates to the status of slaves.[37]

In April, 1692, two significant changes in the legal status of the slave in Virginia were embodied in a single act of the Assembly. "An act for the more speedy prosecution of slaves committing Capitall Crimes" inaugurated the use of separate courts for the trial of slaves. The governor, when notified by a county sheriff of the detention of a slave for a capital crime, was charged to "issue out a commission of *oyer* and *terminer*" to any suitable person of the county. The person so commissioned was "to cause the offender to be arraigned and indicted, and to take . . . evidence," judging the case "without the solemnitie of jury." These courts would achieve permanent status, ending only with the end of slavery.[38]

The other modification wrought by this act concerned the property-holding rights of slaves. The anomaly of property owning property was partially resolved by the order "that all horses, cattle and hoggs marked of any negro or other slaves marke . . . be converted by the owner of such slave to the use and marke of the said owner . . . [or] be forefeited to the use of the poore of the parish." Slaves were legally permitted to keep dogs until 1752, when that privilege was removed by the terms of "An act for preserving the breed of Sheep."[39]

---

[35] *Statutes*, II, 481–482.

[36] *Ibid.*, III, 86.

[37] *Ibid.*, III, 86–89. That the act did result in abuses and the virtual enslavement of the original bastard and her offspring is evidenced by two cases recorded in Thomas Jefferson, *Reports of Cases Determined in the General Court of Va. from 1730 to 1740; and from 1768 to 1772* (Charlottesville: F. Carr and Co., 1829), pp. 87, 90; and by an item in the *Virginia Gazette* (Pinckney), May 2, 1766.

[38] *Statutes*, III, 102–103, 269–270; Oliver P. Chitwood, *Justice in Colonial Virginia* (Baltimore: Johns Hopkins University Press, 1905), p. 18.

[39] *Statutes*, III, 102–103; VI, 295.

Chattel slavery had been firmly established in the laws of Virginia by the end of the seventeenth century; the capstone to the edifice would be set in 1705. Several statutes of that year applied in whole or in part to the status of persons of African descent. One of these, entitled "An act declaring who shall not bear office in this country," ventured for the first time to define legally the term "mulatto," frequently employed in slave legislation. It decreed "That the child of an Indian and the child, grand child, or great grand child, of a negro shall be . . . a mulatto." By such wording it remained legally possible for a person of less than one-eighth Negro ancestry to be deemed white until the definition was amended in 1849.[40]

The Virginia Assembly of 1705 fostered further removal of the slave's legal personality, if not his very humanity. First was an act providing punishment for the commission of "adultery or fornication." By the omission of slaves from the terms of the act, the Assembly eliminated the legal responsibility of the Negro bondsman for actions defined as immoral and culpable for the white populace.[41] Another law of the same session forbade and provided punishment for the marriage of servants without the consent of their masters. Though the disability worked upon all bondsmen was great, the effect upon the Negro slave, who served for life, was infinitely greater.[42]

Two laws of October, 1705, dealt with the relationship of the Negro to the courts of Virginia. One was simply a re-enactment in modified form of the law establishing courts of oyer and terminer. A second act decreed "That popish recusants convict, negroes, mulattoes and Indian servants, and others, not being christians, shall be deemed . . . persons incapable to be witnesses in any cases whatsoever."[43] Because the term "Christian" was frequently used to mean white protestant, it is probable that the intention was to exclude all Negroes as witnesses. All ambiguity was finally removed by a law of May, 1732, which barred the testimony of Negroes, bond or free, Christian or pagan, except in the trial of slaves for capital offenses.[44] Another aspect of the slave's legal personality was thereby removed.

The law that perhaps most graphically demonstrated the comparative lack of legal personality on the part of the slave was enacted in October,

---

[40] *Ibid.,* III, 252; James Curtis Ballagh, *A History of Slavery in Virginia* (Baltimore: Johns Hopkins University Press, 1902), p. 61.

[41] *Statutes,* III, 361. An act of 1692 was perhaps of a similar nature. It provided that any damages "committed by any negro or other slave living at a quarter where there is no christian overseer . . . shall be recompensed by the owner of such slave." *Ibid.,* III, 103.

[42] *Ibid.,* III, 441–446. This law also helped make possible the virtual enslavement of mulatto females born of white mothers. Being often unable to marry before the age of thirty-one, their children were frequently born out of wedlock and, following "the condition of the mother," became themselves bondsmen. See cases cited in n. 37.

[43] *Statutes,* III, 269–270, 298.

[44] *Ibid.,* IV, 326–327.

1705. That was the law whereby slaves were "adjudged to be real estate." Although the definition was to apply only in certain cases of inheritance and made no change in the practical condition of the slave, it aptly reveals the decline in the eyes of the law of the slave as a human being.[45]

1705 saw the passage in Virginia of the first law which might properly be called a slave code, part of a general codification begun in 1698. The lengthy "act concerning Servants and Slaves" actually contained little that was new. It was in effect a consolidation of numerous existing laws. Some of its provisions included slight, but significant, departures from the acts which it superseded. The section determining "Who shall be slaves" contained a new clause stating that imported servants who could not "make due proof of their being free in England, or any other Christian country: were to be accounted . . . slaves." To counter English practice a subsequent section provided that "a slave's being in England, shall not . . . discharge him of his slavery."[46]

Other alterations excepted slaves from certain legal safeguards provided for indentured servants. Slaves were not covered by the section which granted other servants the right to "have their complaints received by a justice of the peace."[47] The servant, as well as the slave, was denied the right to buy and sell "without the leave, license, or consent of the master."[48] Such a provision was the natural corollary to the slave's own status as property, but, as it affected servants equally, it was probably enacted only to minimize theft by bondsmen of all classes.

A more important and severe discrimination against the Negro slave was effected by the section of the 1705 code which dealt with "outlying slaves." Previously only persons designated by "lawfull authority . . . to apprehend" fugitives were authorized, and then only in case of resistance, to kill them. By the code of 1705 it was made legal "for any person or persons whatsoever, to kill and destroy such slaves . . . without accusation or impeachment of any crime for the same." For the first time the law prescribed the castration of such "outlying slaves." This punishment was to be legally used—and apparently abused—until 1769, when it was explicitly limited to cases of attempted rape of white females.[49]

Remaining sections of the code of 1705 had little effect upon the condition of the Negro. Several former provisions were made less vague and, in the case of the slave's freedom of movement, slightly more restrictive. Aside from those already noted, perhaps the most significant feature of the code was the simple fact of its compilation. No longer was it possible to overlook or deny the fact that Virginia possessed a fully developed

[45] Ibid., III, 333–335.

[46] Ibid., III, 447–448.

[47] Ibid., III, 448.

[48] Ibid., III, 451.

[49] Ibid., II, 481–482; III, 460–461; Chitwood, p. 98.

legal system of chattel slavery. This may have been partially responsible for the subsequent decline in immigration of English laborers into Virginia. The masters, secure in the possession of Negroes as slaves, furnished a decreased demand for whites as servants, and slavery offered unattractive competition for free laborers.[50]

In the seventy years from 1705 to the outbreak of the Revolution there were relatively few substantial changes in the legal status of the Negroes of the colony. By the terms of a statute of 1723 Negroes were subjected to castration or death for "consulting, plotting or conspiring" in unlawful assemblies of more than five. The same punishment was also prescribed for "going abroad in the night, or running away."[51] Mutilation continued to be practiced in such cases until 1769, when the Assembly, describing it as a penalty "revolting to the principles of humanity," restricted its use.[52]

The act of 1723 also extended by one year the servitude of mulattoes born of white mothers and further declared that any child born during the bondage of its mother should serve for an identical period. The plight of such persons was not alleviated until October, 1765, when the Assembly, deciding that the law worked "an unreasonable severity towards such children," reduced their time of service to twenty-one years for males and eighteen for females.[53]

A major gain was realized by the slaves of Virginia in 1732 regarding their rights before the courts. In January, 1731, a case had arisen in a court of oyer and terminer involving theft by a female slave, Mary Aggie. To the dismay of the court, Governor William Gooch caused a lawyer to enter a plea for benefit of clergy. Feeling unqualified to judge of its applicability to Negroes, the court "Adjourned [the question] into the General Court." The result was a statute passed in May, 1732, explicitly granting benefit of clergy to "any negro, mulatto, or Indian whatsoever." Offenses for which this privilege was extended to Negroes were fewer than for whites, but its passage represented a noteworthy gain.[54]

---

[50] "The Leadership of Virginia in the War of the Revolution; Part I, The Period of the Stamp Act," *William and Mary Quarterly*, 1st series, XVIII (Jan., 1910), 150–151; Abbott E. Smith, *Colonists in Bondage: White Servitude and Convict Labor in America, 1607–1776* (Chapel Hill: University of North Carolina Press, 1947), pp. 29–30, 330.

[51] *Statutes*, IV, 126, 132.

[52] *Ibid.*, VIII, 358; Chitwood, p. 98. Other barbarous punishments were occasionally used in the eighteenth century. In 1746 a Negro woman was buried alive by order of the Orange County Court; in 1737 in the same county a male slave was hanged, his head cut off and displayed on a pole for several weeks. A. G. Grinnan, "The Burning of Eve in Virginia," *VMH&B*, III (Jan., 1896), 307–310.

[53] *Statutes*, IV, 133; VII, 134.

[54] Gooch to Bishop of London, May 28, 1731, printed in G. McLaren Brydon, ed., "The Virginia Clergy: Governor Gooch's Letters to the Bishop of London, 1727–1749, *VMH&B*, XXXII (Dec., 1924), 323–325; *Statutes*, IV, 326.

An act abolishing the classification of Negro slaves as real estate was passed in 1748 but was disallowed in 1751. At the same time a slightly modified slave code was passed and disallowed, only to be re-enacted in 1753.[55] Of no effect on the slave's status, but indubitably affecting his actions, were the militia acts of 1738 and 1754. The former permitted the formation of local slave patrols; the latter required them.[56] If the functions of the patrollers were carried out as prescribed, there can be no doubt that the slave's freedom of movement thereafter suffered as great restrictions in fact as it did already in law.

From examining the evolution of the legal status of the Negro slave in colonial Virginia several conclusions may be derived. It is certain that the system of slavery did not simply arrive in the colony with the first Negroes. To argue that enslavement, when it came, proceeded either from innate racial antipathy or from necessity, economic or climatic, as a single causal element is clearly a futile exercise; the sources simply do not yield that information.[57] Whatever the factors which brought about the institution of chattel slavery in Virginia, its development could scarcely be described as spontaneous. It was a gradual process, no doubt accompanied by many examinations of conscience. Sometimes the legislative verbiage itself reflects those introspections. Few of the earlier laws are couched in terms leading one to believe that the members of the Assembly were actively prescribing the enslavement of the Negro; they seem more often to be describing and giving legal sanction to practices already in existence. If such usages did exist prior to the laws supporting them, it is indisputable that the earliest slavery in Virginia was contrary to English practice and probably illegal. Certainly the laws of England and the early charters of the colony did not establish the institution.

It is equally apparent that the Assembly and governors of the colony made no serious efforts to prevent or to destroy the institution. Few were their attempts to alter even its harshest features for the protection and benefit of the Negro. Occasionally the Assembly appears consciously to have promoted the growth and development of Negro slavery. It is possible that the failure of the early laws to fix unequivocally the slave status of the Negro was due to the apprehension that overt slave legislation would incur the veto of the home government. Judging from similar developments

[55] Statutes, V, 432–443; VI, 356–369; Virginia Gazette (Rind), April 10, 1752.

[56] Statutes, V, 19; VI, 421.

[57] Handlin and Handlin, p. 199. One of the most recent additions to this still lively debate is an article by Winthrop D. Jordan. Although his general conclusions appear to be sound, in the attempt to balance a variety of viewpoints he gives too much credence to some of the arguments for early racial antipathy. This is particularly true when he asserts that the identification of some persons simply as "a negro" rather than by name is evidence that persons so identified had some peculiar status. There are several instances of court decisions from the period wherein Negroes are identified by name and whites merely as Dutchmen, Scots, etc. "Modern Tensions and the Origins of American Slavery," Journal of Southern History, XXVIII, No. 1 (Feb., 1962), 18–30.

in other English colonies during the same period, however, it is almost certain that they had no cause to fear such action.

It is probable that by 1641 some Negroes in Virginia suffered a condition closely akin to slavery. It is clear that many served for life by 1661, and that most of the essentials of slavery were definitely established by 1670. Between that time and 1705 there developed in Virginia a system of chattel slavery as severe as would ever exist in the modern history of the continent. Some ameliorations were effected in the eighteenth century, but for the most part the institution continued unchanged for 160 years.

## SUGGESTIONS FOR
## FURTHER READING

AN indispensable early study of Afro-Americans during the colonial era is *Lorenzo J. Greene, The Negro in Colonial New England, 1620–1776 (New York, 1942); it should be supplemented by Robert C. Twombley and Robert H. Moore, "Black Puritan, the Negro in Seventeenth-Century Massachusetts," William and Mary Quarterly, XXIV (April 1967) and by chapters in Jordan's White Over Black. For the southern context read Frank J. Klingberg, An Appraisal of the Negro in Colonial South Carolina (Washington, D.C., 1941) and *Thad W. Tate, Jr., The Negro in Eighteenth Century Williamsburg (Williamsburg, Va., 1965). Two new state studies of slavery are Edgar J. McManus, A History of Negro Slavery in New York (Syracuse, N.Y., 1966) and Robert McColley, Slavery and Jeffersonian Virginia (Urbana, Ill., 1964). The status of black and white laborers is explored in Richard B. Morris, Government and Labor in Early America (New York, 1946).

*Arthur Zilversmit, The First Emancipation: The Abolition of Negro Slavery in the North (Chicago, 1967) carefully analyzes differences between each state. Afro-Americans fighting for American independence is the focus of *Benjamin Quarles, The Negro in the American Revolution (Chapel Hill, N.C., 1961). A controversial and stimulating book is *Staughton Lynd, Class Conflict, Slavery and the United States Constitution (Indianapolis, Ind., 1967).

* An asterisk indicates that the book is available in paperback.

# CHAPTER THREE

# Antebellum Slavery

**D**ESPITE the existence of slavery, the new nation promised to provide freedom and equality for its citizens. The blot of slavery, some had expected, would fade gradually once the foreign slave trade was legally prohibited in 1808. Colonial traditions of race relations failed to succumb, however, to the spread of freedom and equality in the nineteenth century; the nation intensified its oppression of Afro-Americans. Black slavery emerged as one of the nation's most tenacious institutions. White Americans and the citizens of other countries, nevertheless, continued to identify freedom and equality with the United States. The image of this country as a refuge from oppression brought millions of Europeans here and provided hope for millions of others. Although black Americans often despaired, many of them shared the hope that America would provide them too with relief from oppression. But freedom and equality largely remained the possession of white American men—slavery the exclusive burden of Afro-Americans.

The difficulties in unraveling the complexities of American slavery are illustrated by the articles reprinted in this chapter. Although in any historical field the past is elusive, historians of slavery have been confronted with special source, methodological, and interpretive problems. Slaveowners left ample plantation records, and even with their strong biases (and sometimes because of them) they disclosed much about slavery. White travelers through the South also provided abundant and at times conflicting observations. Few of the four million slaves, however, left comparable primary written accounts of their own experiences. Historians have analyzed slave songs to learn about black responses to the institution. These songs sometimes reveal both overt and hidden aspirations, but it remains uncertain whether they describe reality anymore accurately than the slave laws formulated by slaveholders.

Letters written by slaves were very rare. The most useful and plentiful sources were the narratives written by fugitive slaves who had escaped from the South and related their past experiences while living in the North or in Canada. The best known of these accounts was Frederick Douglass' *Narrative,* but precisely because of his unique genius, historians of slavery cannot assume that he represented the typical slave. And given the facts that a small number of slaves were fugitives and largely from the border states rather than the deep South, most fugitive-slave accounts were not truly representative of the mass of slaves. Also many fugitive-slave narratives were published—and sometimes ghost written—by abolitionists whose antislavery commitment generally made them more interested in condemnations of slavery than in impartial accounts. Fugitive-slave sources, it still may be argued, are no less useful or more biased than the accounts written by slaveowners and white travelers. Despite the need for critical caution in reading them, they are an indispensable source and the clearest voice of the slave. The reader should evaluate the way these various sources are used by the historians reprinted in the following selections.

Difficulties in generalizing about slavery continued to plague historians. Not only were there obvious differences among individual slaves, but among house servants, field hands, and slave drivers as well as between rural and urban slaves. Moreover, slaves might be treated differently by different masters, from place to place, or from one year to the next.

Compounding the historians' difficulties have been their assumptions about the morality of slavery, the need for Civil War, and the nature of the black man. These past assumptions provide a background for the more recent views reprinted in this chapter. Until as recently as twenty-five years ago, Ulrich B. Phillips generally was regarded as the most authoritative historian of slavery. A southerner writing at a time when discrimination against Afro-Americans was greater than anytime since before the Civil War, he presented antebellum slavery as a benignly patriarchal institution sheltering innately submissive slaves. The alleged inherent inferiority of Afro-Americans and their dependent status were assumptions underlying both Phillips' work and the views of most white Americans. Except for a vanguard of civil rights spokesmen, many Americans—and historians—did not reject their own racism until the publicizing of the horrors of Nazi racism. Added to historians' interest in re-examining slavery in the light of equalitarian racial findings of modern anthropology, was the new desire to write social history about the little-known common man rather than to continue to write political history about prominent ones.

The Marxist historian, Herbert Aptheker, provided one of the earliest attacks on Phillips' view of slave submissiveness by enumerating some 250 slave revolts in the South. Kenneth Stampp, avoiding Phillips' racist conservatism and Aptheker's militant Marxism, represented the liberal view of the 1950s and dramatically altered the picture of slavery drawn by Phillips. According to Stampp, the evidence revealed a harsh system sustained by southern racism and the immoral greed of slaveholders. Fugitive-slave narratives and research in a wider variety of plantation records distinguished Stampp's sources from Phillips'. Gone were the happy slaves portrayed by Phillips; in their place were "nothing more, nothing less" than "white men with black skins" who desired freedom.

Stanley Elkins, part of whose work is analyzed here by Eugene Genovese, sought to go beyond the writings of Phillips and Stampp by accepting Phillips' conclusion about the slaves' submissiveness and docility while rejecting his racist explanation of this behavior. Stampp, according to Elkins, was correct in choosing the social sciences but was too limited in applying them to the study of slavery. The findings of social psychology, especially personality theory, suggested to Elkins that docility and childlike behavior could be induced in adults by harsh treatment. Just as Nazi guards brought about these responses in inmates of concentration camps, slave masters caused the same behavior in slaves. Elkins, relying on Frank Tannenbaum's work on South America, further noted that North American slavery when compared to South American, was considerably different because of the general absence of institutional restraints. Protestant sectarianism and laissez-faire capitalism in North America enabled slaveowners to treat their slaves more harshly than in South America where the Roman Catholic Church and Roman law prevailed. Methodologically, Elkins argued that analogy and comparative history reveal far more than a plantation full of manuscript sources.

Eugene Genovese supported Elkins in his skepticism about Stampp's work and his appreciation of Phillips. Phillips, according to Genovese, was right about the South's aristocratic paternalism, but Genovese reminded his readers that paternalism everywhere in the nineteenth century was more often harsh than gentle and permissive. And the issue of slave docility, along with other crucial questions, could best be studied through a more careful use of comparative slavery history than Elkins supplied. However, both Elkins and Genovese considered Herbert Aptheker's catalogue of widespread southern slave revolts a gross exaggeration and rejected it. Analyzing Elkins' views about slave docility and his comparisons of North American slavery with South American, Genovese, in selection 6, challenges the usefulness of psychological analysis.

The monumental task of studying slavery in other countries and in different eras has been the focus of David Brion Davis' work. Consequently, it has become increasingly apparent that American slavery was not a unique system. Worth considering is whether it nevertheless deserves to be called a "peculiar institution"? In selection 7 Davis surveys some of the results of studying comparative history. And Richard B. Morris, in selection 8, treats the varieties of laboring groups in the urban and rural South, raising questions about comparative oppression and compulsion of all laborers, white or black, free or unfree. Readers should note the insights into American slavery gained from such comparisons.

The question of slave docility can be better understood as an empirical problem after considering Raymond A. and Alice M. Bauer's article, selection 9, about varieties of slave resistance. In selection 10 Willie Lee Rose, using a different approach, analyzes the impact of the slave experience by describing its aftereffects once emancipation occurred. To what degree were the slaves broken by the system?

Readers should note the various ways each historian of slavery included in this anthology has sought to overcome the source, methodological, and interpretive problems confronting him. It remains important to decide whether Eugene Genovese is correct in suggesting that "orthodox procedures of historical research" are still needed to solve the problems raised by the new methodological and interpretive direction taken by historians of slavery.

# 6

## REBELLIOUSNESS AND DOCILITY IN THE NEGRO SLAVE: A CRITIQUE OF THE ELKINS THESIS
### Eugene D. Genovese

**D**ESPITE the hostile reception given by historians to Stanley M. Elkins' *Slavery: A Problem in American Institutional and Intellectual Life*,[1] it has established itself as one of the most influential historical essays of our generation. Although Elkins ranges widely, we may restrict ourselves to his most important contribution, the theory of slave personality, and bypass other questions, such as his dubious theory of uncontrolled capitalism in the South. His psychological model would fit comfortably into other social theories and may, up to a point, be analytically isolated.

Elkins asserts that the Sambo stereotype arose only in the United States. He attempts to explain this allegedly unique personality type by constructing a social analysis that contrasts a totalitarian plantation South with a feudal Latin America in which church, state, and plantation balanced one another. To relate this ostensible difference in social structure to the formation of slave personality he invokes an analogy to Nazi concentration camps to demonstrate the possibility of mass infantilization and proceeds to apply three theories of personality: (1) the Freudian, which relates the growth of a personality to the existence of a father figure and which accounts for the identification of a tyrannized child with a tyrannical father; (2) Sullivan's theory of "significant others," which relates the growth of a personality to its interaction with individuals who hold or seem to hold power over its fortunes; and (3) role theory, which relates the growth of a personality to the number and kinds of roles it can play.[2] Elkins assumes that Sambo existed only in the United States and that our task is to explain his unique appearance in the Old South. I propose to show, on the contrary, that Sambo existed wherever slavery existed, that he nonetheless could turn

Eugene D. Genovese, "Rebelliousness and Docility in the Negro Slave: A Critique of the Elkins Thesis," *Civil War History*, XIII (December, 1967), pp. 293–314. Reprinted by permission of the publisher.

[1] Stanley M. Elkins, *Slavery: A Problem in American Institutional and Intellectual Life* (Chicago, 1959). For a brief critique of the book as a whole see Genovese, "Problems in Nineteenth-Century American History," *Science & Society*, XXV (1961). This present paper shall, so far as possible, be limited to questions of method and assumption. A much shorter version was read to the Association for the Study of Negro Life and History, Baltimore, Maryland, Oct., 1966, where it was incisively criticized by Professor Willie Lee Rose of the University of Virginia. Mrs. Rose was also kind enough to read and criticize the first draft of this longer version. I do not know whether or not my revisions will satisfy her, but I am certain that the paper is much better as a result of her efforts.

[2] Elkins, *Slavery*, pp. 115–133 and the literature cited therein.

into a rebel, and that our main task is to discover the conditions under which the personality pattern could become inverted and a seemingly docile slave could suddenly turn fierce.

Elkins asserts that the United States alone produced the Sambo stereotype—"the perpetual child incapable of maturity." He does not, as so many of his critics insist, equate childishness with docility, although he carelessly gives such an impression. Rather, he equates it with dependence and, with a subtlety that seems to elude his detractors, skillfully accounts for most forms of day-to-day resistance. His thesis, as will be shown later, is objectionable not because it fails to account for hostile behavior, but because it proves too much and encompasses more forms of behavior than can usefully be managed under a single rubric.

Elkins' assumption that the existence of a stereotype proves the reality behind it will not stand critical examination either as psychological theory or as historical fact. As psychological theory, it is at least open to question. John Harding and his collaborators have argued that stereotypes, under certain conditions, may in fact be without foundation;[3] this side of the problem may be left to specialists and need not alter the main lines of the argument. Historically, Sambo was emerging in the United States at the same time he was emerging in the French colonies. Negroes, if we would believe the French planters, were childlike, docile, helpless creatures up until the very moment they rose and slaughtered the whites. Accordingly, I have a sporting proposition for Elkins. Let us substitute French Saint-Domingue for the United States and apply his logic. We find a Sambo stereotype and a weak tradition of rebellion. True, there was a century of maroon activity, but only the efforts of Mackandal constituted a genuine revolt. Those efforts were, in the words of C. L. R. James, "the only hint of an organized attempt at revolt during the hundred years preceding the French Revolution."[4] Boukman's revolt ought properly to be regarded as the first phase of the great revolution of 1791 rather than a separate action. In short, when the island suddenly exploded in the greatest slave revolution in history, nothing lay behind it but Sambo and a few hints. Now, let us rewrite history by having the French Jacobins take power and abolish slavery in 1790, instead of 1794. With the aid of that accident the slaves would have been freed as the result of the vicissitudes of Jacobin-Girondist factionalism and not by their own efforts. We would then today be reading a Haitian Elkins whose task would be to explain the extraordinary docility of the country's blacks. As the rewriting of history goes, this excursion requires little effort and ought to make us aware of how suddenly a seemingly docile, or at least adjusted, people can rise in violence. It would be much safer to assume that dangerous and strong currents run beneath that docility and adjustment.

[3] John Harding, et al., "Prejudice and Ethnic Relations," *Handbook of Social Psychology*, Gardner Lindzey (ed.) (Cambridge, 1954), II, 1021–1062, esp. 1024.

[4] C. L. R. James, *The Black Jacobins: Toussaint L'Ouverture and the San Domingo Revolution* (Vintage ed., New York, 1963), p. 21.

Reaching further back into history, we find an identification of Negroes, including Africans, with a Sambo-like figure. As early as the fourteenth century—and there is no reason to believe that it began that late—so learned and sophisticated a scholar as Ibn Khaldun could write:

*Negroes are in general characterized by levity, excitability, and great emotionalism. They are found eager to dance whenever they hear a melody. They are everywhere described as stupid. . . . The Negro nations are, as a rule, submissive to slavery, because (Negroes) have little (that is essentially) human and have attributes that are quite similar to those of dumb animals.*[5]

In 1764, in Portugal, a pamphlet on the slavery question in the form of a dialogue has a Brazilian slaveowning mine operator say: "I have always observed that in Brazil the Negroes are treated worse than animals. . . . Yet, withal the blacks endure this." The conclusion drawn was that this submissiveness proved inferiority.[6]

Sambo appears throughout Brazilian history, especially during the nineteenth century. In the 1830's the ideologues of Brazilian slavery, significantly under strong French influence, assured planters that the black was a "man-child" with a maximum mental development equivalent to that of a white adolescent. This and similar views were widespread among planters, particularly in the highly commercialized southern coffee region.[7] Brazilian sociologists and historians accepted this stereotype well into the twentieth century. Euclides da Cunha, in his masterpiece, *Rebellion in the Backlands,* described the Negro as "a powerful organism, given to an extreme humility, without the Indian's rebelliousness."[8] Oliveira Lima, in his pioneering comparative history of Brazil and Spanish and Anglo-Saxon America, described the Negro as an especially subservient element.[9] Joao Pandía Calógeras, in his long standard *History of Brazil,* wrote:

[5] Ibn Khaldun, *The Muqaddimah* (tr. Franz Rosenthal; New York, 1958), I, 174, 301; the parentheses were inserted by the translator for technical reasons. David Brion Davis maintains that as Muslims extended their hegemony over Africa, they came to regard black Africans as fit only for slavery: *The Problem of Slavery in Western Culture* (Ithaca, 1966), p. 50. Cf. Basil Davidson, *Black Mother* (Boston, 1961), pp. xvii, 7, 45, 92–93 for Sambo's appearance in Africa.

[6] C. R. Boxer (ed.), "Negro Slavery in Brazil" [trans. of *Nova e Curiosa Relacao (1764)*], *Race*, V (1964), 43.

[7] Stanley J. Stein, *Vassouras: A Brazilian Coffee County, 1850–1900* (Cambridge, Mass., 1957), p. 133.

[8] Euclides da Cunha, *Rebellion in the Backlands (Os Sertoes)* (trans. Samuel Putnam; Chicago, 1944), p. 71; for a critical review of some of this literature see Arthur Ramos, *The Negro in Brazil* (Washington, 1939), pp. 22–24.

[9] Manoel de Oliveira Lima, *The Evolution of Brazil Compared with That of Spanish and Anglo-Saxon America* (Stanford, 1914), p. 122.

*The Negro element in general revealed a perpetual good humor, a childish and expansive joy, a delight in the slightest incidentals of life. . . . Filled with the joy of youth, a ray of sunshine illumined his childlike soul. Sensitive, worthy of confidence, devoted to those who treated him well, capable of being led in any direction by affection and kind words, the Negro helped to temper the primitive harshness of the Portuguese colonists.*[10]

One of the leading interpretations in Brazil today regards the blacks as having been subjected to a regime designed to produce alienation and the destruction of the personality by means of the exercise of the arbitrary power of the master. The account given in Kenneth M. Stampp's *The Peculiar Institution* of the efforts to produce a perfect slave has a close parallel in Octavio Ianni's *As Metamorfoses do Escravo*, which analyzes southern Brazil during the nineteenth century.[11]

Nor did Sambo absent himself from Spanish America. The traditional advocacy of Indian freedom often went together with a defense of Negro slavery based on an alleged inferiority that suggests a Sambo stereotype.[12] In 1816, Simón Bolívar wrote to General Jean Marión of Haiti:

*I have proclaimed the absolute emancipation of the slaves. The tyranny of the Spaniards has reduced them to such a state of stupidity and instilled in their souls such a great sense of terror that they have lost even the desire to be free!! Many of them would have followed the Spaniards or have embarked on British vessels [whose owners] have sold them in neighboring colonies.*[13]

[10] Joao Pandía Calógeras, *A History of Brazil* (Chapel Hill, 1939), p. 29. Even today, when Negroes face discrimination in Brazil, whites insist that it is a result of their own incapacities and sense of inferiority. See Fernando Henrique Cardoso and Octavio Ianni, *Côr e mobilidade em Florianópolis* (Sao Paulo, 1964), p. 231.

[11] Kenneth M. Stampp, *The Peculiar Institution* (New York, 1956), p. 148: "Here, then, was the way to produce the perfect slave: accustom him to rigid discipline, demand from him unconditional submission, impress upon him his innate inferiority, develop in him a paralyzing fear of white men, train him to adopt the master's code of good behavior, and instill in him a sense of complete dependence. This at least was the goal."
Octavio Ianni, *As Metamorfoses do Escravo* (Sao Paulo, 1962), pp. 134–135: "Essential to the full functioning of the regime [was] a rigorous, drastic system of control over the social behavior of the enslaved laborer; . . . mechanisms of socialization appropriate to the dominant social strata . . .; the impossibility of vertical social mobility; . . . rules of conduct ordered according to a standard of rigid obedience of the Negroes in front of white men, whether masters or not."
See also Fernando Henrique Cardoso, *Capitalismo e Escravidao no Brasil Meridional* (Sao Paulo, 1962), pp. 312–313. Davis follows Ianni and others and speaks of Brazilian slaves as having been reduced "to a state of psychic shock, of flat apathy and depression, which was common enough in Brazil to acquire the special name of *banzo.*" *Problem of Slavery*, p. 238; cf. Ramos, *Negro in Brazil*, pp. 22, 135–136.

[12] Davis, *Problem of Slavery*, p. 171.

[13] *Selected Writings of Bolivar* (New York, 1951), I, 131.

Elkins cites evidence that the Spanish regarded the Indians as docile and the Negroes as difficult to control, but evidence also exists that shows the reverse. The view of the Indian or Negro as docile or rebellious varied greatly with time, place, and circumstance.[14] Sidney Mintz, with one eye on Cuba and Puerto Rico and the other eye on Brazil, has suggested that, regardless of institutional safeguards, the more commercialized the slave system the more it tended to produce dehumanization. This thesis needs considerable refinement but is at least as suggestive as Elkins' attempt to construct a purely institutional interpretation.[15]

On close inspection the Sambo personality turns out to be neither more nor less than the slavish personality; wherever slavery has existed, Sambo has also.[16] "Throughout history," David Brion Davis has written, "it has been said that slaves, though occasionally as loyal and faithful as good dogs, were for the most part lazy, irresponsible, cunning, rebellious, untrustworthy, and sexually promiscuous."[17] Only the element of rebelliousness does not seem to fit Sambo, but on reflection, even that does. Sambo, being a child, could be easily controlled but if not handled properly, would revert to barbarous ways. Davis demonstrates that by the fifth century B.C. many Greeks had come to regard the submission of barbarians to despotic and absolute rulers as proof of inferiority.[18] By the end of the eighteenth century, America and Europe widely accepted the image of the dehumanized black slave, and even Reynal believed that crime and indolence would inevitably follow emancipation.[19]

Sambo has a much longer pedigree and a much wider range than Elkins appreciates. Audrey I. Richards, in 1939, noted the widespread existence of "fatal resignation" among primitive peoples in Africa and suggested that their psychological and physical sluggishness might be attributable in a large part to poor diet and severe malnutrition.[20] Josué de Castro, former head of the United Nations Food and Agriculture Organization, has made the same point about Brazilian slaves and about people in

---

[14] For an interpretation of the Spanish slave law as holding Negroes to be an especially revolutionary people see Augustín Alcalá y Henke, *Esclavitud de los negros en la América espanola* (Madrid, 1919), p. 51. For a view of Brazilian Indians that sounds much like Sambo see the comments of the famous Dutch sea captain, Dierck de Ruiter, as reported in C. R. Boxer, *Salvador de Sá and the Struggle for Brazil and Angola* (London, 1952), p. 20.

[15] Sidney Mintz, review of Elkins' *Slavery, American Anthropologist*, LXIII (1961), 585.

[16] "Slavery is determined 'pas par l'obeissance, ni par rudesse des labeurs, mais par le statu d'instrument et la réduction de l'homme a l'etat de chose.' " François Perroux, *La Coexistence pacifique*, as quoted by Herbert Marcuse, *One-Dimensional Man: Studies in the Ideology of Advanced Industrial Society* (Boston, 1964), pp. 32–33.

[17] Davis, *Problem of Slavery*, pp. 59–60.

[18] *Ibid.*, pp. 66–67.

[19] *Ibid.*, p. 420.

[20] Audrey I. Richards, *Land, Labour and Diet in Northern Rhodesia: An Economic Study of the Bemba Tribe* (London, 1939), p. 400.

underdeveloped countries in general.[21] As Jean-Paul Sarte has suggested, "Beaten, under-nourished, ill, terrified—but only up to a certain point—he has, whether he's black, yellow, or white, always the same traits of character: he's a sly-boots, a lazybones, and a thief, who lives on nothing and who understands only violence."[22] By constructing a single-factor analysis and erroneously isolating the personality structure of the southern slave, Elkins has obscured many other possible lines of inquiry. We do not as yet have a comparative analysis of slave diets in the United States, Brazil, and the West Indies, although it might tell us a great deal about personality patterns.

It is generally believed that Elkins merely repeated Tannenbaum when he declared Sambo to be a native of the Old South; in fact, the assertion is, for better or worse, entirely his own. I would not dwell on this point were it not that I cannot imagine Tannenbaum's taking so one-sided a view. I intend no disrespect to Elkins by this observation, for, as a matter of fact, his single-mindedness, even when misguided, has helped him to expose problems others have missed entirely. Elkins' greatest weakness, nonetheless, is his inability to accept the principle of contradiction, to realize that all historical phenomena must be regarded as constituting a process of becoming, and that, therefore, the other-sidedness of the most totalitarian conditions may in fact represent the unfolding of their negation. If Sambo were merely Sambo, then Elkins must explain how an overseer could publicly defend his class, without challenge, for having "to punish and keep in order the negroes, at the risk of his life."[23]

Elkins recognizes a wide range of institutional factors as having contributed to the contrast between the Latin and Anglo-Saxon slave systems, but he places special emphasis on the system of law in relation to the structure and policies of Church and Crown.[24] Although in this way Elkins follows Tannenbaum, he necessarily must go well beyond him, and therein lies his greatest difficulty. Tannenbaum's well-known thesis need not be reviewed here, but we might profitably recall his suggestive comment on *Las Siete Partidas:*

*Las Siete Partidas was formed within the Christian doctrine, and the slave had a body of law, protective of him as a human being, which was already there when the Negro arrived and had been elaborated long before he came upon the scene.*[25]

[21] Josué de Castro, *The Geography of Hunger* (Boston, 1952), *passim.*

[22] Jean-Paul Sartre, preface to Frantz Fanon, *The Wretched of the Earth* (New York, 1965), p. 14.

[23] Quoted from the *Southern Cultivator,* VII (Sept., 1849), 140, by William K. Scarborough, "The Southern Plantation Overseer: A Re-evaluation," *Agricultural History,* XXXVIII (1964), 16.

[24] See his explicit summary statement, "Culture Contacts and Negro Slavery," *Proceedings of the American Philosophical Society,* CVII (1963), 107–110, esp. p. 107.

[25] Frank Tannenbaum, *Slave & Citizen: The Negro in the Americas* (New York, 1946), p. 48.

The essential point of Tannenbaum's contrast between this legal tradition and that of the Anglo-Saxon lies in its bearing on the problem of emancipation. Whereas the Hispanic tradition favored and encouraged it, the Anglo-Saxon blocked it.[26] So long as a general contrast can be demonstrated, Tannenbaum's thesis obtains, for he is primarily concerned with the social setting into which the Negro plunged upon emancipation. His thesis, therefore, can absorb criticism such as that of Arnold A. Sio, who argues that the Romans assimilated the rights of their slaves to property despite a legal code which respected the moral personality of the slave. Sio finds evidence of a similar tendency in Latin as well as Anglo-Saxon America.[27] Tannenbaum's thesis would fall only if the tendency were equally strong everywhere, but obviously it was not.[28] Elkins, however, cannot absorb such qualifications, for he necessarily must demonstrate the uniqueness of the southern pattern as well as the absoluteness of the contrast with Latin America. If the contrast could be reduced to a matter of degree, then we should be left with more American than Latin American Sambos, but Elkins' notion of a special American personality pattern and problem would fall.

Elkins, like Tannenbaum, ignores the French slave colonies, but nowhere was the gap between law and practice so startling. The *Code Noir* of 1685 set a high standard of humanity and attempted to guarantee the slaves certain minimal rights and protection. It was treated with contempt in the French West Indies, especially when the islands began to ride the sugar boom. It is enough to quote a governor of Martinique, one of the men charged with the enforcement of these laws: "I have reached the stage of believing firmly that one must treat the Negroes as one treats beasts."[29] On the eve of the Haitian Revolution probably not one of the protective articles of the *Code Noir* was being enforced.[30]

[26] *Ibid.,* pp. 65, 69, and *passim.*

[27] Arnold A. Sio, "Interpretations of Slavery: The Slave Status in the Americas," *Comparative Studies in Society and History,* VII (1965), 303, 308. For a fresh consideration of the problem of slave law in the islands see Elsa V. Goveia, "The West Indian Slave Laws in the Eighteenth Century," *Revista de Ciencias Sociales* (1960), 75–105.

[28] Marvin Harris has counterposed an economic viewpoint to Tannenbaum's. Despite considerable exaggeration and one-sidedness, he does demonstrate the partial applicability of an institutional approach. For a critical analysis of Harris' polemic and the literature it touches see Genovese, "Materialism and Idealism in the History of Negro Slavery in the Americas," *Journal of Social History,* forthcoming.
The experience of the Dutch demonstrates how much religious and national attitudes gave way before the necessities of colonial life. The Dutch experience in Surinam, New Netherland, Brazil, etc. varied enormously. See, e.g., C. R. Boxer, *The Dutch in Brazil* (Oxford, 1957), esp. p. 75; Edgar J. McManus, *A History of Negro Slavery in New York* (New York, 1966), Ch. I.

[29] Quoted by James, *Black Jacobins,* p. 17.

[30] *Ibid.,* p. 56; Davis, *Problem of Slavery,* p. 254 and the literature cited therein.

Elkins offers Brazil as a counterpoint to the Old South and invokes the Iberian legal tradition, together with the power of Church and Crown. Yet, even Gilberto Freyre, on whom Elkins relies so heavily, writes of the widespread murders of slaves by enraged masters.[31] As late as the nineteenth century, slaves were being whipped to death in the presence of all hands. The law might say what it would, but the *fazendeiros* controlled the police apparatus and supported the doctors who falsified the death certificates.[32] The measures designed to prevent wanton killing of slaves do not seem to have been better in Latin America than in Anglo-Saxon America.[33] If Brazilian slaves went to the police to complain about unjust or illegally excessive punishment, the police would, in Freyre's words, give them a double dose.[34] If the law mattered much, we need to know the reason for the repeated reenactment of legislation to protect slaves. The famous Rio Branco Law of 1871, for example, granted slaves rights they were supposed to have enjoyed for centuries, and these too remained largely unrespected.

The Portuguese Crown could legislate in any manner it wished, and so later could the Emperor of Brazil; local power resided with the *fazendeiros,* as the emissaries of the Crown learned soon enough. We may imagine conditions in the first three centuries of colonization from Freyre's succinct comment on conditions in the middle of the nineteenth century: "The power of the great planters was indeed feudalistic, their patriarchalism being hardly restricted by civil laws."[35] Not until that time did a strong central government arise to challenge effectively the great planters.[36] That the contrast with the Old South might have been the reverse of what Elkins thinks is suggested by the diary of an ex-Confederate who fled to Brazil after the war. George S. Barnsley, formerly a Georgia planter and Confederate army surgeon, complained as late as 1904 of the lack of government and the prevalence of virtually feudal conditions.[37]

[31] Gilberto Freyre, *The Masters and the Slaves: A Study in the Development of Brazilian Civilization* (2nd English Language ed., rev.; New York, 1956), p. xxxix.

[32] Stein, *Vassouras,* p. 136.

[33] See, e.g., the discussion of the law of 1797 in Antigua in Elsa V. Goveia, *Slave Society in the British Leeward Islands at the End of the Eighteenth Century* (New Haven, 1966), p. 191.

[34] Gilberto Freyre, *The Mansions and the Shanties: The Making of Modern Brazil* (New York, 1963), p. 226.

[35] Gilberto Freyre, "Social Life in Brazil in the Middle of the Nineteenth Century" *Hispanic American Historical Review,* V (1922), 597–628; see also, Freyre, *Masters,* pp. xxxiii, 24, 42; *New World in the Tropics: The Culture of Modern Brazil* (New York; Vintage ed., 1963), p. 69.

[36] Alan A. Manchester describes 1848 as the turning point. See *British Pre-Eminence in Brazil* (Chapel Hill, 1933), pp. 261–262.

[37] George S. Barnsley MS Notebook in the Southern Historical Collection, University of North Carolina, Chapel Hill.

*Las Siete Partidas* constituted a theoretical work and standard of values, the importance of which ought not to be minimized, but it had little to do with the actual practice on which Elkins' thesis depends.[38] The kind of protection that transcended the theoretical and might have conditioned decisively the personality development of the slave population as a whole probably did not appear until the *Real Cédula* of 1789. As Davis suggests, "There are many indications, moreover, that Spanish planters paid little attention to the law.[39]

Elkins assumes that the strongly centralized Spanish state could and did prevail over the planters. No doubt it did in matters of prime importance to its survival and income. In most matters, notwithstanding its best efforts at institutional control, the planters continued to have their way on their own estates. The Spanish court promulgated humane legislation to protect the natives of the Canary Islands, but attempts at enforcement so far from home proved futile. The problem swelled enormously when transferred to the West Indies, not to mention to the mainland.[40] The fate of the protective features of the Laws of Burgos (1512) and of similar legislation is well known.[41] The British and other foreigners who did business in Spanish America ridiculed the mass of laws and the clumsy administrative apparatus designed to enforce them. As the agent of the South Sea Company at Jamaica noted in 1736, he who wants to deal illegally with the Spanish officials needs only the cash necessary to bribe them.[42] The lot of the slaves could, under such conditions, hardly reflect other than the disposition of the masters. A case study of Jaime Jaramillo Uribe of the judicial system of New Grenada shows that even the reform laws of the eighteenth century could not reach down into the plantations to protect the slaves.[43]

Much of Elkins' treatment of Spanish law deals with Cuba and flows from the work of Herbert Klein.[44] Without attempting a close examination of the intricacies of the Cuban case, we ought to note that it presents a

[38] For a penetrating discussion of these two sides of *Las Siete Partidas* see Davis, *Problem of Slavery*, pp. 102–105.

[39] *Ibid.*, p. 240.

[40] Arthur Percival Newton, *The European Nations in the West Indies, 1493–1688* (London, 1933), p. 3.

[41] For a useful recent summary discussion of the literature see Harris, *Patterns of Race*, pp. 18–20.

[42] Cf., Arthur S. Aiton, "The Asiento Treaty as Reflected in the Papers of Lord Shelburne," *Hispanic American Historical Review,* VIII, (1928), 167–177, esp. p. 167.

[43] Jaime Jaramillo Uribe, "Esclavos y Senores en la sociedad colombiana del siglo XVIII," *Anuario colombiano de historia social y de cultura,* I (1963), 1–22.

[44] Herbert Klein, "Anglicanism, Catholicism and the Negro," *Comparative Studies in Society and History,* VIII (1966), 295–327; *Slavery in the Americas: A Comparative Study of Cuba and Virginia* (Chicago, 1967).

striking picture of a bitter struggle between planters and state officials. The planters, there too, usually won the day. The liberal Governor Concha finally admitted that the resistance of the slave-owners to government intervention was justified by the necessity for controlling the blacks and avoiding any ambiguity in authority. In 1845 the government did seriously challenge the masters' power, but the uproar proved so great that the militant officials had to be removed.[45]

The fate of the law during the sugar boom requires more attention than Elkins and Klein have given it. In its earlier phases Cuban slavery was exceptionally mild and fit much of Elkins' schema. When the Haitian Revolution removed the Caribbean's leading sugar producer from the world market, Cuba entered into a period of wild expansion and prosperity. The status of the slave declined accordingly. The old institutional arrangements did not disappear, but their bearing on the life of the great mass of slaves became minimal or nonexistent.[46]

The legal and political structure of Spanish America in general and of Cuba in particular helped ease the way to freedom by providing a setting in which the slave might be abused brutally but retained a significant degree of manhood in the eyes of society. For Tannenbaum's purpose, this distinction establishes the argument: the slave was abused as a slave but only incidentally as a Negro. The master might rule with absolute authority, but only because he could get away with it, not because it was, by the standards of his own class, church, and society, just and proper. Tannenbaum and Freyre do make too much of this argument. The persistence and depth of racial discrimination and prejudice in twentieth-century Brazil and Cuba ought to remind us that the enslavement of one race by another must generate racist doctrines among all social classes as well as the intelligentsia. Qualitative and quantitative distinctions nonetheless obtain, and Tannenbaum's argument requires correction and greater specificity, not rejection. For Elkins, Tannenbaum's distinction, however qualified, is not enough. If, as seems likely, the great majority of the slaves labored under such absolutism, theoretical or not, their personalities would have been shaped in response to conditions equivalent to those he describes for the United States.

In the United States, as in the British West Indies and everywhere else, custom and conventional moral standards had greater force than the law, as Ulrich B. Phillips long ago argued. Just as the vast range of rights granted the slaves in Latin America usually proved unenforceable in a society in which power was largely concentrated in local planter oli-

---

[45] See H. H. S. Aimes, *A History of Slavery in Cuba, 1511 to 1868* (New York, 1907), pp. 150–151, 175–177.

[46] On this point see Sidney Mintz, foreword to Ramiro Guerra y Sánchez, *Sugar and Society in the Caribbean* (New Haven, 1964), and his review of Elkins' book in the *American Anthropologist*, LXIII (1961), 579–587. Klein, Tannenbaum and Elkins make much of the practice of *coartación*. For a critical assessment see Davis, *Problem of Slavery*, pp. 266–267.

garchies, so in Anglo-Saxon America the quasi-absolute power of the master was tempered by the prevailing ethos. Tannenbaum, and especially Elkins, go much too far in denying that English and American law recognized the moral personality of the slave. As Davis has demonstrated, the double nature of the slave as thing and man had to be, and in one way or another was, recognized in law and custom by every slave society since ancient times. As a result, every southern planter knew intuitively the limits of his power, as imposed by the prevailing standards of decency. If he exceeded those limits, he might not suffer punishment at law and might even be strong enough to prevent his being ostracized by disapproving neighbors. For these reasons historians have dismissed community pressure as a factor. In doing so, they err badly, for the point is not at all what happened to a violator of convention but the extent to which the overwhelming majority of slaveholders internalized conventional values. In this respect the legal structures of Brazil and the United States were important in conditioning those conventional values. Once again, the difference between the two cases suffices for Tannenbaum's thesis but not for Elkins'—which depends entirely on the experience of absolute power by the slave.

Elkins follows Tannenbaum in ascribing a special role to the Catholic Church in the development of Ibero-American slave societies. The Church defended the moral personality of the slave from a position of independent institutional strength, whereas in the Anglo-Saxon world the separation of church and state, the bourgeois notion of property rights, and the divisions within the religious community largely excluded the churches from the field of master-slave relations. The religious as well as the legal structure helped generate a particular climate of moral opinion into which the Negro could fit as a free man. The difference in structure and result satisfies Tannenbaum's argument; it does not satisfy Elkins' argument, which turns on the specific role played by the priesthood in the life of the slave.

Since Brazil, as the largest Catholic slaveholding country, ought properly to serve as a test case, we might profitably begin with a consideration of developments in Angola, which supplied a large part of its slaves. The clergy, including Jesuits and Dominicans, participated in every horror associated with the slave trade; there is little evidence of its having played a mediating role.[47] By the middle of the seventeenth century Catholic proselytism in the Congo and Angola had spent its force. Contemporary Catholic sources admitted that much of the failure was due to the greed of the clergy in pursuing slave-trade profits and to the generally venal character of priests, secular officials and laymen.[48] The governor of Angola, the troops, the bishop, and the entire staff of civil and ecclesiastical officials drew their salaries from the direct and indirect proceeds of the slave trade.

[47] Boxer, *Salvador de Sá*, p. 279.

[48] C. R. Boxer, *Race Relations in the Portuguese Colonial Empire, 1415–1825* (Oxford, 1963), pp. 7–8, 11–12, 21.

The Holy House of Mercy [*Misericordia*] at Luanda, as well as the Municipal Council [*Camara*] lived off the trade. Since the *Junta das missoẽs*, the chief missionary agency, was supported by these proceeds we need not be surprised that it accomplished little.[49]

In Brazil itself the decisive questions concern the number, character, and relative independence of the priests.[50] We have little data on numbers, but in the mid-twentieth century, Brazil, with a population of fifty million, of whom 95 per cent were nominal Catholics, had, according to Vianna Moog, only six thousand priests.[51] We may, nonetheless, assume for a moment that a high ratio of priests to slaves existed. There is good reason to believe that a significant percentage of the priests who ventured to the colonies had questionable characters and that many of good character succumbed to the indolence, violence, and corruption that marked their isolated, quasi-frontier environment. It is no insult to the Church to affirm this state of affairs, for the Church has had to struggle for centuries to raise the quality of its priests and to maintain high standards of perform-ance. Like other institutions of this world it has consisted of men with all the weaknesses of men, and in the difficult circumstances of colonial life the adherence of its men to the high standards of the Church Militant proved erratic and uncertain.

Even if we grant the Brazilian clergy a higher quality than it probably deserved, we confront the question of its relationship to the master class. The local chaplain depended on and deferred to the planter he served more than he depended on his bishop. The Brazilian Church never achieved the strength and cohesion of the Church in Spanish America. The typical sugar planter, in Freyre's words, "though a devout Catholic, was a sort of Philip II in regard to the Church: he considered himself more powerful than the bishops or abbots." Under these conditions the interposition of priest between master and slave was probably little more significant than the interposition of the mistress on a plantation in Mississippi. The analogy assumes particular force when we consider that, increasingly, the Brazilian priesthood was recruited from the local aristocracy.[52] In coffee-growing southern Brazil, in which slavery centered during the nineteenth century,

---

[49] C. R. Boxer, *Portuguese Society in the Tropics: The Municipal Councils of Goa, Macao, Bahia, and Luanda, 1510–1800* (1965), pp. 131–132, Davidson, *Black Mother*, p. 158.

[50] Elkins certainly errs in ascribing a protective role to the Jesuits, whose efforts on behalf of the Indians were not repeated with the Negroes. Jesuit treatment of those Negroes within their reach does not constitute one of the more glorious chapters in the history of the order. The literature is extensive; for a good, brief discussion see Joao Dornas Filho, *A Escravidao no Brasil* (Rio de Janeiro, 1939), p. 105.

[51] Vianna Moog, *Bandeirantes and Pioneers* (New York, 1964), p. 209. Cf., Percy Alvin Martin, "Slavery and Abolition in Brazil," *Hispanic American Historical Review*, XIII (1933), 168: "On most plantations the spiritual life of the slaves received scant attention. Priests were found only on the larger estates."

[52] Freyre, *New World in the Tropics*, pp. 70–71, 87–88; *Mansions*, p. 244.

few priests resided on plantations at all and visits were possibly less common than in the United States. The large number of Africans imported during 1830–1850 received little attention from the Church.[53]

The situation in Spanish America worked out more favorably for Elkins' argument because the Church there came much closer to that independence and crusading spirit which has been attributed to it. Even so, the ruthless exploitation of Indians and Negroes by large sections of the clergy is well documented. The position of the Church as a whole, taken over centuries, demonstrates its growing subservience to state and secular power in respects that were decisive for Elkins' purposes. The bulls of Popes and the decrees of kings proved inadequate to temper the rule of the great planters of the New World, although they did play a role in shaping their moral consciousness.[54] In Cuba the clergy acted more boldly and, according to Klein, had a numerical strength adequate to its tasks. However, the effective interposition of even the Cuban clergy during the sugar boom of the nineteenth century has yet to be demonstrated, and if it were to be, Cuba would stand as an exception to the rule.

That more Brazilian and Cuban slaves attended religious services than did southern is by no means certain, the law to the contrary notwithstanding. That the Catholic clergy of Latin America interposed itself more often and more effectively than the Protestant clergy of the South cannot be denied. On balance, Tannenbaum's case is proven by the ability of the Catholic Church to help shape the ethos of slave society and the relative inability of the Protestant to do the same. But Elkins' case falls, for the difference in the potentialities for and especially the realities of personal interposition remained a matter of degree.

Despite the efforts of law and Church in Latin America it is quite possible that as high or higher a percentage of southern slaves lived in stable family units than did Latin American. The force of custom and sentiment generally prevailed over the force of law or institutional interference. In Brazil, as in the Caribbean, male slaves greatly outnumbered female; in the United States the sexes were numerically equal. This factor alone, which derived primarily from economic and technological conditions, encouraged greater family stability in the United States and therefore casts great doubt on Elkins' thesis. To the extent that participation in a stable family life encouraged the development of a mature personality, the slaves of the South probably fared no worse than others. Elkins argues that the Latin American families could not be broken up because of Church and state restrictions. In fact, they often were broken up in open defiance of both. The greatest guarantee against sale existed not where the law forbade it, but where economic conditions reduced the necessity.

The attendant argument that Latin American slaves could function in the roles of fathers and mothers, whereas southern slaves could not, is

[53] Stein, *Vassouras*, pp. 196–199.

[54] Cf., Rene Maunier, *The Sociology of Colonies* (London, n.d.), I, 293–294.

altogether arbitrary. The feeling of security within the family depended on custom and circumstance, not law, and a great number of southern slaves worked for masters whose economic position and paternalistic attitudes provided a reasonable guarantee against separate sales. In any case, all slaves in all societies faced similar problems. When a slaveowner beat or raped a slave woman in Brazil or Cuba, her husband was quite as helpless as any black man in Mississippi. The duties, responsibilities, and privileges of fatherhood were, in practice, little different from one place to another.

The point of Elkins' controversial concentration camp analogy is not altogether clear. Sometimes he seems to wish to demonstrate only the possibility of mass infantilization, but if this were all he intended, he could have done so briefly and without risking the hostile reaction he brought down on himself. At other times he seems to intend the analogy as a direct device. Although he denies saying that slavery was a concentration camp or even "like" a concentration camp, he does refer to concentration camps as perverted patriarchies and extreme forms of slavery; he finds in them the same total power he believes to have existed on the southern plantations. In the first, restricted, sense the analogy, used suggestively, has its point, for it suggests the ultimate limits of the slave experience. In the second, and broader, sense it offers little and is generally misleading. Unfortunately, Elkins sometimes exaggerates and confuses his device, which only demonstrates the limiting case, with the historical reality of slavery. His elaborate discussion of detachment offers clues but is dangerously misleading. The process did not differ for slaves bound for different parts of the New World; only the post-shock experience of the slave regimes differed, so that we are led right back to those regimes. No doubt Elkins makes a good point when he cites concentration camp and slave trade evidence to show that many participants were spiritually broken by the process, but he overlooks the contribution of newly imported Africans to slave disorders. Everywhere in the Americas a correlation existed between concentrations of African-born slaves and the outbreak of revolts. The evidence indicates that creole slaves were generally more adjusted to enslavement than those who had undergone the shock and detachment processes from Africa to America.[55]

The fundamental differences between the concentration camp and plantation experience may be gleaned from a brief consideration of some of the points made in Bruno Bettelheim's study, on which Elkins relies heavily.[56] Prisoners received inadequate clothing and food in order to test

[55] Elkins seems troubled by this—see p. 102—but he does not pursue it. Onwuka Dike points out that Guineans brought to the trading depots of the Niger Delta had already been prepared psychologically for slavery by the religious indoctrination accompanying the cult of the Aro oracle. See "The Question of Sambo: A Report of the Ninth Newberry Library Conference on American Studies," *Newberry Library Bulletin*, V (1958), 27 and Dike's *Trade and Politics in the Niger Delta, 1830–1885* (Oxford, 1956), Ch. II.

[56] Bruno Bettelheim, "Individual and Mass Behavior in Extreme Situations," *Journal of Abnormal and Social Psychology*, XXXVIII (1943), 417–452. On the general problem of the

their reaction to extremities of inclement weather and their ability to work while acutely hungry. Slaves received clothing and food designed to provide at least minimum comfort. Slaves suffered from dietary deficiencies and hidden hungers, but rarely from outright malnutrition. In direct contrast to prisoners, slaves normally did not work outdoors in the rain or extreme cold; usually, they were deliberately ordered to stay indoors. Pneumonia and other diseases killed too many slaves every winter for planters not to take every precaution to guard their health. Therein lay the crucial differences: prisoners might be kept alive for experimental purposes, but slaves received treatment designed to grant them long life. Prisoners often did useless work as part of a deliberate program to destroy their personality; slaves did, and knew they did, the productive work necessary for their own sustenance. Prisoners were forbidden to talk to each other much of the day and had virtually no privacy and no social life. Slaves maintained a many-sided social life, which received considerable encouragement from their masters. The Gestapo deliberately set out to deny the individuality of prisoners or to distinguish among them. Planters and overseers made every effort to take full account of slave individuality and even to encourage it up to a point. Prisoners were deliberately subjected to torture and arbitrary punishment; those who followed orders endured the same indignities and blows as those who did not. Slaves, despite considerable arbitrariness in the system, generally had the option of currying favor and avoiding punishment. As Hannah Arendt has so perceptively observed: "Under conditions of total terror not even fear can any longer serve as an advisor of how to behave, because terror chooses its victims without reference to individual actions or thoughts, exclusively in accordance with the objective necessity of the natural or historical process."[57] Concentration camp prisoners changed work groups and barracks regularly and could not develop attachments. Slaves had families and friends, often for a lifetime. The Gestapo had no interest in indoctrinating prisoners. They demanded obedience, not loyalty. Masters wanted and took great pains to secure the loyalty and ideological adherence of their slaves. In general, the slave plantation was a social system, full of joys and sorrows and a fair degree of security, notwithstanding great harshness and even brutality, whereas the concentration camp was a particularly vicious death-cell. They shared a strong degree of authoritarianism, but so does the army or a revolutionary party, or even a family unit.

---

concentration camp analogy see the remarks of Daniel Boorstin as reported in the *Newberry Library Bulletin*, V (1958), 14–40 and Earle E. Thorpe, "Chattel Slavery & Concentration Camps," *Negro History Bulletin*, XXV (1962), 171–176. Unfortunately, Mr. Thorpe's thoughtful piece is marred by a clumsy discussion of the problem of wearing a mask before white men.

[57] Hannah Arendt, "Ideology and Terror: A Novel Form of Government," *Review of Politics*, XV (1953), 314. I am indebted to Professor Daniel Walden of the Pennsylvania State University for calling this illuminating article to my attention and for suggesting its relevance to the subject at hand.

With these criticisms of data we may turn to Elkin's discussion of personality theory. His use of Sullivan's theory of "significant others" breaks down because of his erroneous notion of the absolute power of the master. In theory the master's power over the slave in the United States was close to absolute; so in theory was the power of Louis XIV over the French. In practice, the plantation represented a series of compromises between whites and blacks. Elkins' inability to see the slaves as active forces capable of tempering the authority of the master leads him into a one-sided appraisal.[58]

According to Elkins, the Latin American slave could relate meaningfully to the friar on the slave ship; the confessor who made the plantation rounds; the zealous Jesuit who especially defended the sanctity of the family; the local magistrate who had to contend with the Crown's official protector of the slaves; and any informer who could expect to collect one-third of the fines. In general, it would not be unfair to say that, notwithstanding all these institutional niceties, the Latin American slave-owners, especially the Brazilian, ruled their plantations as despotically as any southerner. Priest, magistrate, and anyone careless enough to risk his life to play the informer came under the iron grip of the plantation owners' enormous local power.

Various other persons did affect meaningfully the lives of slaves in all systems. The plantation mistress often acted to soften her husband's rule. The overseer did not always precisely reflect the master's temperament and wishes, and slaves demonstrated great skill in playing the one against the other. The Negro driver often affected their lives more directly than anyone else and had considerable authority to make their lives easy or miserable. Slaves who found it difficult to adjust to a master's whims or who feared punishment often ran to some other planter in the neighborhood to ask for his intercession, which they received more often than not. Elkins ignores these and other people because they had no lawful right to intervene; but they did have the power of persuasion in a world of human beings with human reactions. To the vast majority of slaves in all systems, the power of the master approached the absolute and yet was tempered by many human relationships and sensibilities. To the extent that slavery, in all societies, restricted the number of "significant others," it may well have contributed toward the formation of a slavish personality, but Latin America differed from the South only in permitting a somewhat larger minority to transcend that effect.

Similar objections may be made with reference to the application of role theory. The Latin American slave could ordinarily no more act the part of a husband or father than could the southern. The typical field hand had roughly the same degree of prestige and authority in his own cabin in all societies. Legal right to property did not make most Latin

---

[58] For a perceptive and well-balanced discussion of this side of plantation life see Clement Eaton, *The Growth of Southern Civilization* (New York, 1961), p. 74 and *passim*.

American slaves property owners in any meaningful sense, and many southern slaves were de facto property owners of the same kind. The theoretical right of the one and the mere privilege of the other did not present a great practical difference, for the attitude of the master was decisive in both cases. For Tannenbaum's social analysis the significance of the difference stands; for Elkins' psychological analysis it does not.

The theory of personality that Elkins seems to slight, but uses to greatest advantage, is the Freudian, perhaps because it offers a simple direct insight quite apart from its more technical formulations. We do not need an elaborate psychological theory to help us understand the emergence of the slaveowner as a father figure. As the source of all privileges, gifts, and necessaries, he loomed as a great benefactor, even when he simultaneously functioned as a great oppressor. Slaves, forced into dependence on their master, viewed him with awe and identified their interests and even their wills with his. Elkins' analogy with concentration camp prisoners who began to imitate their SS guards indicates the extreme case of this tendency. All exploited classes manifest something of this tendency—the more servile the class the stronger the tendency. It is what many contemporary observers, including runaway slaves and abolitionists, meant when they spoke of the reduction of the slave to a groveling creature without initiative and a sense of self-reliance. Elkins, using Freudian insight, has transformed this observation into the politically relevant suggestion that the slave actually learned to see himself through his master's eyes.

Elkins has often been criticized for failing to realize that slaves usually acted as expected while they retained inner reservations, but he did recognize this possibility in his discussion of a "broad belt of indeterminacy" between playing a role and becoming the role you always play. The criticism seems to me to miss the point. The existence of such reservations might weaken the notion of total infantilization but would not touch the less extreme notion of a dependent, emasculated personality. The clever slave outwitted his master at least partly because he was supposed to. Masters enjoyed the game: it strengthened their sense of superiority, confirmed the slaves' dependence, and provided a sense of pride in having so clever a man-child. On the slave's side it made him a devilishly delightful fellow but hardly a man. The main point against Elkins here is the same as elsewhere—when he is sound he describes not a southern slave but a slave; not a distinctly southern Sambo personality but a slavish personality.[59]

Elkins' general argument contains a fundamental flaw, which, when uncovered, exposes all the empirical difficulties under review. In his model a regime of total power produces a Sambo personality. Confronted by the undeniable existence of exceptions, he pleads first things first and waives them aside as statistically insignificant. Even if we were to agree

---

[59] Brazilian slaves saw their masters as patriarchs and, in Freyre's words, "almighty figures." Freyre, *Mansions*, p. 234. See also Celso Furtado, *The Economic Growth of Brazil* (Berkeley, 1963), pp. 153–154.

that they were statistically insignificant, we are left with a serious problem. Elkins did not construct a model to determine probabilities; he constructed a deterministic model, which he cannot drop suddenly to suit his convenience. The notion of "total power" loses force and usefulness and indeed approaches absurdity in a world of probabilities and alternatives. If Elkins were to retreat from this notion and consequently from his determinism, he could not simply make an adjustment in his model; he would have to begin, as we must, from different premises, although without necessarily sacrificing his remarkable insights and suggestions. If the basic personality pattern arose from the nature of the regime, so did the deviant patterns. It would be absurd to argue that a regime could be sufficiently complex to generate two or more such patterns and yet sufficiently simple to generate them in mutual isolation. The regime threw up all the patterns at once, whatever the proportions, and the root of every deviation lay in the same social structure that gave us Sambo.

This range of patterns arose from the disparity between the plantations and farms, between resident owners and absentees, and above all between the foibles and sensibilities of one master and another. They arose, too, within every slaveholding unit from the impossibility of absolute power—from the qualities, perhaps inherited, of the particular personalities of slaves as individuals; from the inconsistencies in the human behavior of the severest masters; from the room that even a slave plantation provides for breathing, laughing, crying, and combining acquiescence and protest in a single thought, expression, and action. Even modern totalitarian regimes, self-consciously armed with unprecedented weapons of terror, must face that opposition inherent in the human spirit to which Miss Arendt draws attention. The freedom of man cannot be denied even by totalitarian rulers, "for this freedom—irrelevant and arbitrary as they may deem it—is identical with the fact that men are born and that therefore each of them *is* a new beginning, begins, in a sense, the world anew."[60] We need not pretend to understand adequately that remarkable process of spiritual regeneration which repeatedly unfolds before our eyes. The evidence extends throughout history, including the history of our own day; its special forms and content, not its existence, constitute our problem. Miss Arendt therefore concludes her analysis of terror wisely: "Every end in history necessarily contains a new beginning. . . . Beginning, before it becomes a historical event, is the supreme capacity of man; politically, it is identical with man's freedom. . . . This beginning is guaranteed by each new birth; it is indeed every man."[61]

Sambo himself had to be a product of a contradictory environment, all sides of which he necessarily internalized. Sambo, in short, was Sambo only up to the moment that the psychological balance was jarred from

---

[60] Arendt, *Review of Politics*, XV (1953), 312.

[61] *Ibid.*, 327.

within or without; he might then well have become Nat Turner, for every element antithetical to his being a Sambo resided in his nature. "Total power" and "Sambo" may serve a useful purpose in a theoretical model as a rough approximation to a complex reality, provided that we do not confuse the model with the reality itself. Neither slavery nor slaves can be treated as pure categories, free of the contradictions, tensions, and potentialities that characterize all human experience.

Elkins, in committing himself to these absolutist notions, overlooks the evidence from his own concentration camp analogy. Bettelheim notes that even the most accommodating, servile, and broken-spirited prisoners sometimes suddenly defied the Gestapo with great courage. Eugene Kogon devotes considerable space in his *Theory and Practice of Hell* to the development and maintenance of resistance within the camps.[62] In a similar way the most docile field slaves or the most trusted house slaves might, and often did, suddenly rise up in some act of unprecedented violence. This transformation will surprise us only if we confuse our theoretical model with the reality it ought to help us to understand.

Elkins has not described to us the personality of the southern slave, nor, by contrast, of the Latin American slave; he has instead demonstrated the limiting case of the slavish personality. Every slave system contained a powerful tendency to generate Sambos, but every system generated countervailing forces. Elkins, following Tannenbaum, might properly argue that differences in tradition, religion, and law guaranteed differences in the strength of those countervailing forces; he cannot prove and dare not assume that any system lacked them.

Elkins accounts for such forms of deviant behavior as lying, stealing, and shirking by absorbing them within the general framework of childish response. He is by no means completely wrong in doing so, for very often the form of a particular act of hostility degraded the slave as much as it irritated the master. Elkins' approach is not so much wrong as it is of limited usefulness. Once we pass beyond the insight that the form of rebelliousness might itself reveal accommodation, we cannot go much further. If all behavior short of armed revolt can be subsumed within the framework of childishness and dependence, then that formulation clearly embraces too much. Our historical problem is to explain how and under what conditions accommodation yields to resistance, and we therefore need a framework sufficiently flexible to permit distinctions between accommodating behavior that, however slightly, suggests a process of transformation into opposite qualities; such a framework must, moreover, be able to account for both tendencies within a single human being and even within a single act.

It has become something of a fashion in the adolescent recesses of our profession to bury troublesome authors and their work under a heap

---

[62] Bettelheim, *Journal of Abnormal and Social Psychology*, XXXVIII (1943), 451; Eugen Kogon, *The Theory and Practice of Hell* (New York, 1950), esp. Chs. XX, XXXI.

of carping general and specific complaints; it is no part of my purpose to join in the fun. Elkins' book has raised the study of southern slavery to a far higher level than ever before, and it has done so at a moment when the subject seemed about to be drowned in a sea of moral indignation. It has demonstrated forcefully the remarkable uses to which psychology can be put in historical inquiry. It has brought to the surface the relationship between the slave past and a wide range of current problems flowing from that past. These are extraordinary achievements. To advance in the direction Elkins has pointed out, however, we shall first have to abandon most of his ground. We cannot simply replace his psychological model with a better one; we must recognize that all psychological models may only be used suggestively for flashes of insight or as aids in forming hypotheses and that they cannot substitute for empirical investigation. As the distinguished anthropologist, Max Gluckman, has observed, respect for psychology as a discipline requiring a high degree of training in the acquisition and interpretation of data forces us to bypass psychological analyses whenever possible.[63] Or, to put it another way, if we are to profit fully from Elkins' boldness, we shall have to retreat from it and try to solve the problems he raises by the more orthodox procedures of historical research.

[63] Max Gluckman, *Order and Rebellion in Tribal Africa* (New York, 1963), pp. 2–3.

# 7

## SLAVERY
### David Brion Davis

O F ALL American institutions, Negro slavery has probably been the one most frequently compared with historical antecedents and foreign counterparts, and with the least benefit to systematic knowledge. Quite understandably, modern scholars have been so impressed by the long submission and degradation of southern Negroes, as well as by the extraordinary prevalence of racial prejudice in the United States, that they have often pictured American slavery as a system of unique and unmitigated severity that stands in marked contrast to other forms of servitude. Yet Thomas Jefferson could confidently assert that in Augustan Rome the condition of slaves was "much more deplorable than that of the blacks on the continent of America," and list barbarities and cruelties which were commonplace in Rome but presumably unknown in

Chapter 9 of *The Comparative Approach to American History*, edited by C. Vann Woodward, © 1968 by C. Vann Woodward, Basic Books, Inc. Publishers, New York.

Virginia. Apologists for American slavery were always fond of comparing the mildness of their own institution, supposedly evidenced by a rapidly increasing Negro population, with the harshness of slavery in the West Indies or ancient Rome, where a constant supply of fresh captives made up for an appalling mortality. Yet abolitionists were always inclined to argue that the slave system of their own country or empire was the worst in history. Foreign travelers were not only subject to nationalistic prejudice but tended to rank various slave systems on the basis of fortuitous impressions or the biased accounts of hospitable planters. When we recognize how often comparisons have been influenced by ulterior motives and have been directed to the fruitless question "Which nation's slavery was the worst?" we might conclude that the subject can most profitably be studied in geographical isolation.

Yet American slavery was a product of the African slave trade, which was itself an integral part of both European commercial expansion and New World colonization. Most of the components of the slave-trading and plantation systems were developed in the thirteenth and fourteenth centuries by Italian merchants who purchased Circassians, Tartars, and Georgians at commercial bases on the Black Sea and then transported them to markets in Egypt, Italy, and Spain. As early as 1300 the enterprising Italians were even working Negro slaves on sugar plantations in Cyprus. In the fifteenth century, when the Portuguese adopted similar practices in trading with West Africa, Negro slaves displaced the Moors and Russians as the lowest element in the labor force of Spain. Negroes were shipped to Hispaniola as early as 1502; and as the Spanish colonists gradually turned to the cultivation of sugar, the rising demand for labor became an enormous stimulus to the Portuguese African trade. By the seventeenth century the Atlantic slave trade had become a vast international enterprise as the Dutch, British, French, Danes, Swedes, and even Brandenburgers established forts and markets along the West African coast. On both sides of the Atlantic there was close contact between merchants, seamen, and planters of various nationalities. In addition to competing and fighting with one another, they borrowed techniques and customs, cooperated in smuggling, and gathered to buy slaves at such entrepôts as Curaçao. If the British planters of Barbados looked to Brazil as a model, Barbados itself provided the impulse for settling Carolina. There was, then, a high degree of institutional continuity which linked the European maritime powers in a common venture. A trade which involved six major nations and lasted for three centuries, which transported some to 10 to 15 million Africans to the New World, and which became a central part of international rivalry and the struggle for empire, cannot be considered as a mere chapter in the history of North America.

The unpleasant truth is that there could hardly have been successful colonization of the New World without Negro slaves, since there was no alternative source of labor to meet the needs required by the cultivation of sugar, rice, tobacco, and cotton, and since even the more diversified colonies were long dependent economically on the markets and earnings of the staple-producing regions. It must be emphasized that this common dependence on Negro slavery was never universally recognized or welcomed. From the first Spanish in Hispaniola to the British in Barbados and Virginia, colonists were slow and hesitant in committing themselves to a labor force of foreign captives. Among the frequent dreams of New World Utopias and second Edens, no one envisioned a model society of several thousand free Europeans overseeing the life and labor of several hundred thousand Negro slaves. From the beginning, racial antipathy was reinforced by the much stronger emotion of fear; and the dread of insurrection and racial war would always balance the desire for quick wealth through a reckless increase in slaves.

Nonetheless, from sixteenth-century Mexico to eighteenth-century Jamaica and South Carolina, colonial administrators were unable to maintain a reassuring ratio between white immigrants and Negro slaves. In regions where tropical or semitropical staples could be cultivated, it became clear that investment in slave labor was the key to expanded production and spectacular profit. The Negro slave played an indispensable role in the conquest and settlement of Latin America, and in the clearing and cultivation of virgin land from Trinidad to the lower Mississippi Valley and Texas. And as the possession of slaves became itself a symbol of affluence, prestige, and power, the demand for Negroes spread to urban and temperate zones. Important leaders in New England and French Canada seriously argued that only Negro slaves could meet the labor needs of their colonies. From 1732 to 1754 Negro slaves constituted more than 35 per cent of the immigrants entering New York City; by mid-century they were owned by about one-tenth of the householders of the province and accounted for 15 per cent of the total population. Meanwhile, the slave trade and American Negro slavery were sanctioned by treaties and the law of nations, by the acts and edicts of kings and parliaments, by the Spanish Council of the Indies and the great trading companies of England, Holland, and France, by the Catholic Church and the major Protestant denominations. All the colonies of the New World legalized the institution, and many competed with one another for a supply of labor that was never equal to the demand. For more than three centuries the Negro slave was deeply involved in imperial wars, revolutions, and wars of independence. Insofar as the Western Hemisphere has a common history, it must center on a common experience with Negro slavery.

But did slavery mean the same thing to the various colonists of the New World? The fact that Dutch slave traders imitated the Portuguese and that a Dutch ship brought the first Negroes to Virginia did not mean that a Negro's status would be the same in Virginia as in Brazil. In England, unlike Italy and the Iberian Peninsula, true slavery disappeared by the thirteenth century. On the other hand, English jurists perpetuated the legal concept of unlimited servitude, and English judges recognized the validity of enslaving and selling infidels. We still have much to learn about the character of servitude in the sixteenth century and the later evolution of slave status in the British, Dutch, and French colonies. In making future comparative studies it would be well to keep in mind two points which should prevent hasty generalizations. First, in many societies the slave has only gradually been differentiated from other kinds of unfree workers, and his status, rights, and obligations have been defined in practice before receiving legal recognition. Second, although the actual condition of slaves has varied greatly even within a single society, there has been a remarkable persistence and uniformity in the legal concept of the slave. Since this last point has often been disregarded in comparative approaches to American slavery, we shall elaborate on it here.

The status of slavery has always been surrounded with certain ambiguities that seem related to the institution's origins. To be enslaved as a result of capture in war or punishment for crime implied total subordination to coercive authority. Yet bondage for debt or as the result of self-sale suggested merely a reciprocal exchange of labor and obedience for sustenance and protection. When a bondwoman's offspring were claimed by her owner on the same basis as the natural increase of livestock, the status was assimilated to that of movable property. In societies where slaves have largely been recruited from the native poor and have performed no specialized economic function, as in ancient China, Egypt, and the Near East, the element of reciprocal rights and obligations has taken precedence over the elements of punishment and ownership. Nevertheless, the slave was legally defined as a thing not only in the Southern United States but in ancient Egypt, Babylonia, Greece, and Rome. And the Roman conception of the slave as at once a person and a piece of movable property prevailed in medieval France, Italy, and Spain; it was extended to Latin America and was incorporated in the Code Noir for the French colonies; and it reappeared in the laws and judicial decisions of British North America. A Virginia court merely affirmed the ancient Latin concept of chattel slavery when it ruled that "Slaves are not only property, but they are rational beings, and entitled to the humanity of the Court, when it can be exercised without invading the rights of property." And when an American master claimed the offspring of his female slaves or asserted his right to move, sell, trade, bequest, or give away his chattel property, he added nothing to a legal notion of slavery that had persisted in Europe for more than two thousand years.

The definition of the slave as chattel property implied a condition of rightlessness on the part of the slave. In neither Europe nor the Americas could a slave testify in court against a free person, institute a court action in his own behalf, make a legally binding will or contract, or own property. There were, to be sure, minor exceptions and variations. Slaves were sometimes allowed to testify in certain civil cases or give evidence against a master accused of treason. In North America at various times Negro bondsmen were permitted to plead benefit of clergy and to give evidence in capital cases involving other slaves. As in Rome and Latin America, they were accorded limited rights over personal property, including horses and cattle, and might act as a master's legal agent, though never with the freedom and complex prerogatives of the Roman slave. But what stands out above the exceptions and variations is the fact that from pre-Christian laws to the slave codes of the New World the bondsman had no civil capacities and was considered only as an extension of his master's legal personality. Even in Puritan Massachusetts slaves were, in the words of Cotton Mather, who was simply echoing Aristotle, "the *Animate, Separate, Active Instruments* of other men."

One of the few significant differences in the legal status of slaves was that bondsmen were denied legal marriage in ancient Rome and in Protestant America, whereas slave marriages were recognized in Carthage, Hellenistic Greece, and in Catholic Europe and America. Largely to prevent the sin of fornication, Catholic theologians even ruled that a slave might marry against his master's will. Yet according to St. Thomas Aquinas, slavery was an "impediment" to marriage, comparable to impotence, and a slave's first obligation must be to his master, not his spouse. If a master had a moral duty to try to preserve the integrity of slave families, he still had a legal claim to all slave children, and might of necessity divide husband from wife or children from parents. Since there is evidence that Latin American masters often did little to encourage or respect slave marriages, and that North American masters often recognized such marriages and tried to keep families intact, one may suspect that actual differences were more the result of individual personality and economic pressure than of legal and moral rights. The main point is that in no society have slaves had a legal claim to their wives and children.

Religious conversion has always complicated the question of a slave's status. The Muslims and ancient Hebrews drew a sharp distinction between enslaving infidels and temporarily holding servants of their own faith who had been deprived of freedom by economic necessity. Although the first Church Fathers ruled unmistakably that baptism should have no effect on the temporal status of slaves, medieval Christians showed an increasing reluctance to enslave their fellow Christians and came to think of perpetual bondage as a punishment suitable only for infidels. But the authorities who condemned the sale of Christians and yet preached slaving crusades against the infidels were ultimately faced with the problem of the baptized infidel. In 1366 the priors of Florence explained that it was valid to buy or sell slaves who had been baptized so long as they had originally come "from the land and race of the infidels." This was, in effect, the same test later applied in Virginia and other North American colonies. Baptism was to have no effect on a slave's status unless he had been a Christian in his native country. And if the Catholic colonists felt a much greater obligation to have their slaves baptized, North American laws encouraged conversion and recognized that the Negro had a soul that might be redeemed. After a century of inaction, the Protestant churches slowly began their work of spreading religion among the slaves, and by the mid-nineteenth century the proportion of converted Negroes was probably as large in parts of the United States as in Brazil. It is doubtful, however, whether the mass of slaves in any country ever enjoyed a meaningful religious life.

There was little that was distinctive in the police regulations and penal laws restricting the lives of North American slaves. Throughout the ages, and in virtually all parts of the Western Hemisphere, slaves were prohibited from carrying arms, traveling at night or without permission, and acting with disrespect toward a freeman. Fairly typical was a law of 1785 for Spanish Santo Domingo which ordered one hundred lashes and two years in jail for any Negro who raised his hand against a white man. The penalties for such crimes as theft and assault were everywhere more severe for slaves than for others. During the eighteenth century there was a tendency in most New World colonies to abandon the most sanguinary punishments, such as mutilation, dismemberment, and burning at the stake. Harsh restrictions and terrifying punishments persisted longest in the West Indies, where the disproportion of Negroes to whites was the greatest. But even in the West Indies the long-term trend was toward more humane punishment and an extension of the slave's legal protections.

It is misleading to say that Anglo-American law never recognized the Negro slave as a human personality whose rights to life, food, and shelter were protected by law. There was ample precedent for the 1846 ruling of a Kentucky judge that "A slave is not in the condition of a horse. . . . He is made after the image of the Creator. He has mental capacities, and an immortal principle in his nature. . . . The law . . . cannot extinguish his high born nature, nor deprive him of many rights which are inherent in man." Although a master might kill his slave with impunity in the ancient Near East, the Roman Republic, Saxon England, and under certain circumstances in the Iberian Peninsula and Latin America, and although in much of British America the murder of a slave was thought to merit only a modest fine, by the early nineteenth century the slave states of North America had put the killing or maiming of a Negro bondsman on the same level of criminality as the killing or maiming of a white man. In both the British Caribbean and the Southern states, courts sometimes held that slaves were protected by common law against such crimes as manslaughter or unprovoked battery. Georgia and North Carolina both held that slaves had a right to trial by jury, and North Carolina went so far as to recognize a slave's right to resist unprovoked attack. Of course it was one thing for American states to threaten punishment for cruelty to slaves, and to make masters legally obligated to give their bondsmen adequate food and shelter and to provide for their care in sickness and old age, and it was another matter to enforce such laws when Negroes were barred from testifying against white men. Nevertheless, one can plausibly argue that in terms of legal protections and physical welfare American slaves by the 1850's were as favorably treated as any bondsmen in history.

Yet one of the paradoxes of American slavery was that the laws protecting the physical welfare of slaves were accompanied by the severest restrictions on manumission. This brings us to the most important distinction between the legal status of slaves in British and Latin America. It should be stressed that taxes and other restrictions on manumission were common in antiquity, particularly in Rome and that freedom suffered from prejudice and legal disabilities even when the stigma of slavish origin was not associated with race. There were discriminatory freedmen's laws, for example, in medieval Spain and Italy, and in Latin America as well. But only in the Southern United States did legislators try to bar every route to emancipation and deprive masters of their traditional right to free individual slaves. It is true that thousands of American slaves were manumitted by their owners, many after buying their freedom in installments, as was far more common in Latin America. It is also true that in some areas of Latin America a slave had no more realistic chance of becoming free than did his brother in Mississippi. Nevertheless, one may conclude that slavery in North America was distinctive in its efforts to build ever higher barriers against manumission. And there is evidence that this had less to do with slavery as such than with social attitudes toward racial integration.

Although the questions are of compelling importance, we cannot begin to determine whether slavery was a source of racial prejudice or prejudice a source of slavery, nor can we explain why prejudice became more dominant in the United States than in other parts of the New World. One may briefly state the principal facts that are relevant to a comparative study of slavery. Without denying the significance of racial difference as an aggravation to American bondage, we may note that throughout history slaves have been said to be naturally inferior, lazy, cunning, thievish, lascivious, fawning, deceitful, and incapable of life's higher thoughts and emotions. When not differentiated by race, they have often been physically marked off by shaven heads, brands, tattoos, and collars. There is unmistakable evidence of racial prejudice in Italy and the Iberian Peninsula, where colored slaves generally suffered from various indignities and disabilities. In Latin America Negro bondsmen were long denied the privileges and protections of Indian workers. Nonetheless, while Latin America was by no means immune from racial prejudice, even against freemen of mixed blood, there was a gradual acceptance of racial intermixture and a willingness to accept each stage of dilution as a step toward whiteness. In the British colonies, although the first Negroes had an ill-defined status and worked side by side with white servants, there was never any tolerance of racial blending. White fathers seldom acknowledged their colored offspring, and a mulatto or quadroon was still legally classed as a Negro. These differences may have been related to religion, sexual mores, social stratification, or the proportion of white women in a colonial population. But whatever the reason, prejudice against Negroes seems to have grown in the United States with the advance of popular democracy. It can be argued that this had less to do with slavery than with the status of the free Negro in an unusually mobile and unstratified white society. In other words, differences in slave systems may not account for the fact that while the Negro in the United States today has far more economic and educational opportunities than the Negro in Latin America, he also suffers from more overt discrimination from whites who feel superior but are unsure of their own status.

By focusing thus far on the legal status of slaves, we have given an oversimplified picture of institutional homogeneity. In actuality, of course, American slavery took a great variety of forms that were largely the result of economic pressures and such derivative factors as the nature of employment, the number of slaves owned by a typical master, and the proportion of slaves in a given society. Thus we correctly categorize North American slavery as plantation and staple-crop slavery, but tend to forget that in 1820 Negro bondsmen constituted 20 per cent of the population of Southern cities and that in 1860 there were a half million slaves working in factories, on railroad construction, as stevedores, as lumberjacks, on steamboats, and in numerous other jobs unconnected with agriculture. As in ancient Athens and Rome, and as in Latin America, slaves in the Southern states were employed as valets, waiters, cooks, nurses, craftsmen, and prostitutes. In spite of these well-known facts, most comparisons of slavery in British and Latin America have assumed that the institutions were virtually monolithic. We still lack comparative studies of the domestic servant, the slave artisan, the rented worker, and the slave in manufacturing establishments.

It has been said that the latifundia of southern Italy and Sicily provided an ancient precedent for the gang labor, the rationalized system of production, and the absentee ownership of the Caribbean plantation. But one must be careful not to lump all plantation agriculture in an undifferentiated class. Since the production of sugar, for example, was a long and continuous process that could be ruined by a delay in cutting, milling, boiling, or curing, the rhythm of plantation life was probably much the same in parts of Brazil as in Jamaica and Louisiana. The cultivation of sugar and rice required heavy capital investment, and in the West Indies and South Carolina led to slave gangs of several hundred being divided for specialized tasks under constant surveillance. Slavery in colonial South Carolina, though less characterized by absentee ownership, had more in common with slavery in the West Indies than either had with the institution in Virginia and Maryland. But 1765 South Carolina's forty thousand whites were outnumbered by ninety thousand slaves; eight years late Jamaica's sixteen thousand whites kept uneasy watch over two hundred thousand slaves. In neither society could a field slave be in close or frequent contact with white men. In Virginia, on the other hand, the proportion of Negroes and whites was roughly equal, and the typical tobacco plantation employed less than twenty slaves. Unlike any of the previously mentioned staples, cotton did not require elaborate stages of preparation and processing, and could be probably grown on small-scale farms. It was thus not uncommon for the cotton farmer to own less than ten slaves and even to work beside them in the field. Even by 1860, after a long period of rising slave prices, nearly one-half of the Southern slaveholders owned less than five Negroes apiece; 72 per cent owned less than ten apiece and held approximately one-quarter of the entire number of American slaves.

Compared with the plantation agriculture of the West Indies and Brazil, the striking features of the American South were the wide dispersal of slave ownership and the relatively small units of production scattered over immense areas. This may have led to a greater variation and flexibility in the relationship between master and slaves, although we still lack comparative research on such vital questions as labor management, the social roles and subculture of Negroes, and the relation of plantation life to social structure. It seems plausible that if American Negroes sometimes benefited by a close relationship with white families, they were also denied the sense of massive solidarity that was probably essential for revolt. In the West Indies slaves not only had the opportunity to plan and organize revolts, but they were seldom tied by the close bonds of loyalty that led so many North American slaves to divulge plots before they were hardly formed.

This is not to suggest that North American slaves were less oppressed than those of other times and regions, but only that there were different forms of oppression. As comparative studies move ahead toward finer distinctions and a typology of slave systems, it is likely that less attention will be paid to legal status than to stages of economic development. It would be absurd to claim that all slave economies must pass through a pre-set cycle of boom and depression. Nevertheless, regardless of cultural differences and other variables, there are striking examples throughout the Americas of a pattern which began with an unmitigated drive for quick profit, a rapid expansion in slaves and land under cultivation, and a subsequent overproduction of staples. Whenever slaves were worked under boom conditions, as in the West Indies in the mid-eighteenth century and the Brazilian coffee plantations in the nineteenth, the institution was one of grinding attrition. A more relaxed paternalism tended to appear when prices had fallen, when there was little incentive to maximize production, and when planters in longer-settled regions looked to social and cultural distinctions to differentiate themselves from new generations of hard-driving speculators. Thus in the mid-nineteenth century there is evidence that in such states as Virginia and Maryland a more easy-going, paternalistic pattern of slavery was emerging, not unlike that of the depleted sugar plantations of Brazil. In Maryland and Delaware there was even a rapid decline in the proportion of slaves to freedmen, though this was partly a result of interstate migration. At the same time there was a heavy drain of slaves toward the expanding cotton areas of the Southwest, where the price of labor kept rising and slaves became more concentrated in the hands of a relatively few planters.

The question of stages of economic development is related to the much larger question of the place of slavery in the evolution of industrial capitalism. And here, though historians have long acknowledged the dependence of the world's cotton textile industry on the slave systems of North and South America, there is an astonishing lack of systematic and comparative analysis. The whole complex relationship between capitalism and slavery is still in the realm of suggestive speculation. Scholars still debate whether slavery was profitable and whether the forms it took in America can be termed capitalistic. We do not yet fully understand why so many areas where slavery flourished were stultified by soil depletion and a lack of capital formation, by an absence of internal markets, of urbanization, and of technological innovation. And finally, if we are really to comprehend the significance of slavery and the burdens it has entailed, comparative history must explain the great challenge posed to the institution by an emerging urban, bureaucratic, and capitalistic civilization, which led to a bitter conflict between England and her Caribbean colonies, to a sharp struggle between the Brazilian coastal cities and the interior valleys, and to an epic contest between the North and South in the United States.

# 8

## THE MEASURE OF BONDAGE IN THE SLAVE STATES
### Richard B. Morris

T HE more realistic and balanced portrayal of the economy of the Old South which has emerged from recent investigations has thrown the traditional image of the southern labor system sharply out of focus. Recognition of the role of the nonslaveholder and the small farmer and of the importance of food crops and grazing has served to place the plantation economy in proper perspective. Slavery, the paramount labor system in the production of money crops, has been shown to be far less consequential in other areas of the economy. Nevertheless, the "peculiar institution" holds tenaciously to its central place in southern labor history, a role grossly disproportionate to its numerical position.[1] While the spotlight has recently been played upon the yeoman farmer,[2] the

Richard B. Morris, "The Measure of Bondage in the Slave States," *Mississippi Valley Historical Review,* XLI (September 1954), pp. 219–249. Reprinted by permission of the publisher.

[1] Between 1790 and 1860 the ratio of whites to slaves in the South as a whole kept steadily at about two to one. At the height of the slavocracy in 1860 there were 3,953,760 slaves out of a total population in the slave states and the District of Columbia of 12,315,333. Ownership of slaves was confined to 384,884. On the other hand, there were a quarter of a million free Negroes in the slave states and several million "plain folk" who were not part of the plantation economy.

[2] Frank L. Owsley, *Plain Folk of the Old South* (Baton Rouge, 1949); Blanche H. Clark, *The Tennessee Yeomen, 1840–1860* (Nashville, 1942); Herbert Weaver, *Mississippi Farmers, 1850–1860* (Nashville, 1945); Harry L. Coles, Jr., "Some Notes on Slaveownership and Landownership in Louisiana, 1850–1860," *Journal of Southern History* (Baton Rouge), IX (August, 1943), 381–94.

problems of white labor, whether domiciled or migratory, of the tenant, the squatter, and the self-employed have been largely neglected. The conventional overemphasis upon agricultural slavery and upon operations in the great staple-producing areas has been at the expense of urban and industrial labor, both slave and free,[3] and of labor in the border states and in regions of a mixed economy. Historians of slavery, whether wearing the mantle of apologists or of critics, have often relied heavily on the slave codes without adequate verification by reference to court records and common usage. But perhaps as serious as these other traditional distortions of fact or emphasis has been the judgment of freedom and bondage by absolute standards when, in fact, a significant segment of the southern labor force of both races operated under varying degrees of compulsion, legal or economic, in a twilight zone of bondage.

It is the argument of this paper that while, technically, slavery in this country has been the status primarily reserved for persons of one race, actually mechanisms of compulsion were in operation in all three labor systems that functioned side by side—free white labor, slave labor, and bound labor, both white and Negro. That well-defined boundary line customarily drawn between slavery for Negroes and freedom for whites appears on close examination fuzzy and misleading. In fact, a portion of the laboring population of both races in the ante-bellum slave states dwelt in a shadowland enjoying a status neither fully slave nor entirely free. These compulsions, rooted in the nature of the cultivation of the great staples of the South, with their round of virtually continuous annual labor, were devised in early colonial times, took a variety of forms, but never disappeared completely. The indentured servitude of the colonial period was displaced in the years after the Revolution, not by free labor but by slave labor and tenancy. The Civil War failed to end compulsion, for through legal subterfuges labor contracts continued to be specifically performed during and after Reconstruction.

Before considering the varying degrees of bondage to which Negroes were subjected, it is necessary to see just what kind of freedom white labor in the slave states technically enjoyed before the Civil War. In many areas the whites worked under varying degrees of compulsion. Indentured servitude of the colonial pattern survived in the ante-bellum period, spreading from the older seaboard states to the newer states of the Southwest, where, in addition, peonage was introduced from Old Spanish and Mexican practices. These forms of compulsion under which white paupers, vagrants, debtors, and tenants worked out their obligations provided the framework for the neo-slavery which the Black Codes of Reconstruction fastened upon the former slaves. The virtual continuity of the institutions of compulsory labor from colonial times to very recent years is a phase of labor history that has been given far too little attention. To illustrate the continuity of white servitude, examples will be considered from some of the slave states.

---

[3] In 1850 some 400,000 slaves lived in urban communities.

The stress given by historians to the movement in the nineteenth century for the abolition of imprisonment for debt has obscured the persistence of debt bondage or peonage. Few of the slave states faced the issue as squarely as did Maryland. Indentured servitude, which was the dominant form of labor in the tobacco provinces in the seventeenth century, demonstrated amazing pertinacity in the face of large-scale importations of African slave labor and actually did not disappear as soon after independence as historians of labor would have us believe.[4] The time came, however, when it no longer was a practical system, as the directors of the Chesapeake and Ohio Canal Company learned in 1829. That company had engaged an agent to proceed to Wales to contract for laborers for canal construction work. The amount of $32 was to be charged against each laborer for passage and expenses, and the indenture of the laborer assigned by the agent to the company. Here was the old redemptioner system, which George Washington had futilely sought to utilize for the predecessor enterprise, the Potomac Company.[5] But laborers and management had quite different ideas about the sanctity of contract, and when the immigrants landed at Baltimore they promptly deserted the company's service for the Baltimore and Ohio Railroad, a ruthless competitor engaged in a characteristic piece of labor pirating. The canal company had the deserters committed to prison, and ordered that only those be released who would promise to return to work on the canal. While some made more favorable bargains and returned, those who remained in prison, shrewdly advised no doubt by the Baltimore and Ohio attorneys, sued out writs of habeas corpus in the Baltimore city court. The Chesapeake and Ohio was defended by William Wirt, who in many respects had a more thankless task on his hands on this occasion than in that summer in Richmond many years before when he had deflated the legend of that crackbrained romantic, Harman Blennerhassett. The arguments and decision were crucial to the survival of the redemptioner system in Maryland. The court ruled that the agreements made with the laborers "did not contemplate the relation of master and servant described by the act of 1715," which had laid down the basic principles of the white servitude system, not substantially modified since colonial times. The employer's only recourse, according to the court, was an action for damages. After the men had been discharged on habeas corpus, the company took out writs against them on their contracts. Again the reasoning was that they would be held to bail which they would not be able to raise, and hence would be left no alternatives but jail or work. But Wirt had the disagreeable duty of notifying his clients that the men could now evade jail by confessing judgments and being cleared under the insolvency laws. To save further costs the company finally dropped its suits.

[4] See John R. Commons and John B. Andrews, *Principles of Labor Legislation* (Rev. ed., New York, 1936), 321.

[5] *Proceedings of the President and Directors of the Potomac Company*, I, 1785–1807, pp. 7, 11, Department of Interior Archives (National Archives).

To the directors, the redemptioner "runaways" were considered "plagues," and henceforth they scrupulously avoided any such complicated arrangement.[6]

While the ruling of the Baltimore city court, made possible by the more liberal insolvency laws, doomed the redemptioner system in Maryland, it did not terminate the status of bondage and quasi-bondage for white labor. An examination of the Baltimore city jail records reveals that, while the great majority of labor absconders committed to jail prior to the Civil War were fugitive slaves, a substantial minority were "free" white laborers—apprentices, seamen, and wage workers. Absconding white servants and white apprentices continued to be held in jail subject to orders of their masters or to action of the court throughout the ante-bellum period. Indeed, emancipation had no immediate effect on the specific performance of contracts by the non-slave population. After the date when former slaves were enabled to secure their release on habeas corpus proceedings under the new constitution white apprentices were still committed to the Baltimore jail for absconding.[7]

In one occupation involuntary servitude, regardless of race, persisted long after the ante-bellum period. This was in maritime employment, where, traditionally labor contracts could be specifically enforced.[8] As a matter of fact, the jail population of all the chief ports, North as well as South, in ante-bellum days counted numberless deserting seamen.[9] Nor did emancipation and the Thirteenth Amendment terminate legal pressures for the specific performance of labor contracts. Absentee Negro "apprentices" (a subterfuge) and deserting seamen, white or Negro, were still forced to complete their contracts or remain in jail for an indeterminate period. In a sense, then, the labor of seamen was coerced labor like that of slaves, and it was not until 1915, when the La Follette Act of that year abolished imprisonment for deserting seamen, that mariners were at long last emancipated.

[6] Chesapeake and Ohio Canal Company Records, Proceedings of the Stockholders, Book A, 1828–1835; Proceedings of the Directors, Journal A, 1828–1829; Letters Received and Letters Sent, Letter Book A, 1828–1832, Department of Interior Archives. The directors considered a proposal to acquire 250 slaves, but finally turned it down, and then wrote to President Jackson, later to prove co-operative when the company had its most serious labor trouble, to use soldiers of the regular army on construction work.

[7] Caleb Winkfield (1865), Baltimore City Jail Records, Accommodation Docket, 1863–1893 (Maryland Hall of Records, Annapolis).

[8] See Richard B. Morris, Government and Labor in Early America (New York, 1946), 249 ff., 526, 527; also Robertson v. Baldwin, 165 U. S. 275, 287 (1897); Richard B. Morris, "Labor Controls in Maryland in the Nineteenth Century," Journal of Southern History, XIV (August, 1948), 393–95.

[9] See New Orleans Police Reports (1833), Third Municipal Police District (Microfilm, Butler Library, Columbia University); William H. Russell, My Diary North and South (Boston, 1863), 248. For typical instances where seamen were sent back to their ships to work off debts due boarding-house keepers, see New Orleans Daily Picayune, February 6, March 19, April 1, December 20, 1848; April 26, May 8, 24, June 4, November 9, 1849.

In general, it may be said that the position of white labor in the slave states showed little if any improvement in the ante-bellum period. The white worker was squeezed between the upper millstone of Negro labor competition and the nether millstone of foreign immigrant and northern labor, however transient. As labor controls tightened all along the line, many white workers suffered in fact a loss of their freedom of occupational choice and mobility, and in some areas failed to win recognition in law for their assumed right to take concerted action, a right which their northern brothers in a few states had acquired only after a bitter struggle. Forming an unskilled labor pool drawn upon for occupations considered too hazardous for Negro property, or used seasonally, as in the harvest when Negro labor was not available for hiring out, many white laborers stumbled into the quagmire of quasi-bondage.

Continuing into the ante-bellum period some of the labor controls of colonial times, the slave states bound out in involuntary apprenticeship white children who were pauper orphans, or whose parents were too poor to take care of them, illegitimate children over five likely to become chargeable to the parish, or other bastards who might become demoralized by their home environment. In some cases, as with the pauper apprenticeships of the Charleston commissioners of the poor house, who bound out orphans and paupers until eighteen or twenty-one years of age, there were usually no provisions for general education in the indentures.[10] In too many instances the apprenticeship of white children was merely a device for cheap labor exploitation.

While the apprenticeship of poor children could be defended as an educational and welfare device, enlightened Southerners were critical of the practice of binding out to labor adult white persons whose poverty or delinquencies brought them into conflict with the public authorities. South Carolinians, dissatisfied with the poorhouse system, were scarcely happier about turning again to what the Chester County grand jury in 1842 denounced as "the barbarous system of selling their paupers to the lowest bidder."[11]

The slave states did not hesitate to use compulsion in dealing with white vagrants or unemployed. In New Orleans the recorder's courts sentenced thousands of vagrants to the workhouse without proof, trial, or, in most cases, opportunity of appeal.[12] In fact, a New Orleans grand jury was impelled to protest against this failure to grant due process to those accused of vagrancy.[13] In South Carolina vagrants were sold at public

[10] Apprenticeship Indentures, Commissioners of the Poor House, Charleston (College of Charleston Library).

[11] Chester County (S. C.) Session Minutes, 1841–1845 (1842), 73 (Courthouse, Chester).

[12] New Orleans *Daily Picayune,* February 25, May 2, 1847.

[13] *Ibid.,* May 2, 1847.

vendue for terms ranging from six months to a year and a day.[14] The white workers at Gregg's mill at Graniteville were forced to agree that "all males over twelve years of age and not at school must be engaged in some useful employment as they will not be permitted to remain in idleness about the village."[15] In prosecuting for bastardy it was customary in some of the slave states to sell into servitude for a period of four years the putative father upon his defaulting on his duty to enter into recognizance to provide a stated maintenance for the illegitimate child until the age of twelve. The proceeds of this sale were applied to the child's upkeep. Despite the clear language of the South Carolina act of 1839 explicitly limiting such service to four years, the Barnwell County sessions court in 1843 sentenced one white malefactor to be sold for ten years.[16] The frequency of bastardy prosecutions in ante-bellum South Carolina sheds a pre-Kinseyan ray on nonmonagamous relationships and underscores the importance of the servitude penalty. It was not until 1847 that South Carolina repealed the four-year servitude term for defaulting fathers,[17] but in the neighboring state of North Carolina down until 1939 such fathers in default could still be bound out as apprentices at prices fixed by the court.[18]

Another form of compulsory labor in some southern states, though admittedly limited in scope, was road duty. While in many of the northern states road service by the eve of the Civil War had deteriorated into an assessment which could be worked out in some areas at a specified daily rate of pay or road tax, South Carolina stubbornly clung to impressment. This type of *corvée* has shown remarkable pertinacity, and in recent years the compulsory requirement that certain persons labor annually on the public highways has been held by the courts not to violate prohibitions against involuntary servitude.[19]

To sum up, the principal forms of coercive labor service to which the poor whites of the South were subject stemmed from peonage, a relationship based upon debt. In the slave state of Delaware, for example,

[14] Richard B. Morris, "White Bondage in Ante-Bellum South Carolina," *South Carolina Historical and Genealogical Magazine (Charleston)*, XLIX (October, 1948), 199 ff.

[15] Rules for Graniteville (Caroliniana Collection, University of South Carolina).

[16] Barnwell County Session Journal, 1841–1856 (1843), 37 (Courthouse, Barnwell).

[17] Henceforth, they were liable to execution as defendants convicted of misdemeanors then were. *South Carolina Acts of 1847* (Columbia, 1848), 436, 437.

[18] Apprenticeship was an alternative to twelve months in the house of correction. *North Carolina Code*, 1935, Sec. 276; eliminated in *North Carolina Code*, 1939, Sec. 276. For an instance long after the Civil War, see indenture of Charles Morphis, Orange County (N. C.) Court Book, No. 7 (1890), Southern History Collection (University of North Carolina Library).

[19] *In re* Dassler, 35 Kan. 678, 684, 12 Pacific 130 (1886); Dennis *v.* Simon, 51 Ohio State 233, 36 Northeastern 832 (1894); Butler *v.* Perry, 240 U. S. 328 (1916). In South Carolina those failing to pay the road commission tax are subject to a fine or imprisonment. *South Carolina Code*, 1952, Secs. 33–961 *passim*.

white debtors in the early part of the nineteenth century took advantage of the insolvency laws which authorized servitude as a legal alternative to imprisonment.[20] To satisfy judgments obtained by their creditors they would be sold off to labor service at public auction. But in 1827 a tricky modification of the law exempted white defaulting debtors and any females, white or Negro, from servitude, but by implication continued debt servitude for Negroes. While the convict lease system was still on the threshold of expansion in the slave states on the eve of the Civil War, [21] another system of penal servitude, quite separate and distinct, was still flourishing, its roots running deep into colonial soil. This was the colonial practice of imposing servitude upon convicted persons in satisfaction of monetary sums included in criminal sentences. In Delaware, where this system survived with vigor in ante-bellum days, seven-year servitude terms were authorized by act of 1826 for convicts who were unable to pay the restitution money adjudged by the court or the fine and costs. Between 1837 and 1839 white offenders were excepted from such sale into servitude, but were sentenced to prison terms instead; but for free Negro convicts compulsory servitude lasted until after the Civil War.[22] However, before these modifications of the law went into effect the orders reveal that in Kent County, for example, white convicts were sold for larceny and related felonies in a ratio of almost two and one-half to one to Negro offenders.[23] These servitude terms could be appreciable for the reason that a disproportionate share of service time was assigned to satisfy costs of trial and commitment as against time in lieu of restitution of the property stolen. Thus, sales of white servants for terms of seven years for the theft of a dollar or for a total judgment debt, including costs, of amounts like $12.50, were by no means infrequent. In the sentencing of white offenders in assault and battery cases there occurred some extraordinary instances of injustice. Seven-year terms were meted out for fines ranging from such nominal amounts as fifty cents to twenty dollars. The system demonstrated in emphatic terms the disproportion which trial fees and prison costs bore to the total judgment in criminal cases.

From this review of the forms of compulsion under which white paupers, vagrants, debtors, and convicted criminals in some of the slave states worked out their obligations, it should be apparent that they established precedents for the Black Codes of the Reconstruction period. This debt relationship was also the basis of traditional tenancy arrangements

[20] *Delaware Laws* (1797), I, 208 (1739); IV, 215 (1808).

[21] Fletcher M. Green (ed.), *Essays in Southern History Presented to J. G. de Roulhac Hamilton* (Chapel Hill, 1949), 113, 115; Blake McKelvey, *American Prisons: A Study in American Social History Prior to 1915* (Chicago, 1936), 172.

[22] See Richard B. Morris, "The Course of Peonage in a Slave State," *Political Science Quarterly* (New York), LXV (June, 1950), 245 ff.

[23] See Delaware Petitions of Servants and Slaves, 1779–1844 (Public Archives Commission, Dover).

which were not uncommon in Maryland and northern Virginia in colonial days and which expanded their grip on Maryland's Eastern Shore and in the valleys of East Tennessee in the ante-bellum period. Contemporaries considered rental terms exorbitant, for, as Edmund Ruffin remarked in South Carolina, they fell most heavily "on poor people who can neither buy nor move away."[24] The effect of white tenancy was to minimize mobility and freedom of occupational choice of the white tenant class.

White men were fettered in the slave states as well as Negroes. A proper question might be: How far did these legal compulsions hamper labor's freedom to bargain collectively and to organize? It is perhaps significant that no higher court in a slave state ever seems to have referred to the epoch-making decision of Chief Justice Lemuel Shaw in 1842, in effect legalizing concerted action by trade unions in Massachusetts (Commonwealth v. Hunt).[25] That does not mean that in the slave states the question was purely theoretical nor that white labor never sought to strike or bargain collectively. The record establishes a considerable degree of white labor militancy below the Mason and Dixon line. In the period of trade-union expansion that preceded the panic of 1837, concerted action by labor in the border states was not infrequently attended with riot and bloodshed. Most belligerent were the Irish construction laborers working on the railroads. When confronted by strikes of Irish labor the authorities almost invariably called out the troops, jailed the ringleaders, and counted upon the animosity of Yankee and German laborers to the Irish workmen to keep construction projects rolling.

But far more surprising than the existence of labor militancy in the northern tier of the slave states is the revelation of white labor insurgency in states like Virginia, South Carolina, and Louisiana, where white laborers as compared with slaves held an unfavorable and even degraded position. In the Southeast the chief strikes were on railroad and canal projects, and railroad officials considered "owning by purchase the labor necessary for service on the road" instead of allowing themselves "to continue to be exposed to all the hazards of hiring under the present system, and the chances of being raised upon in times of emergency."[26] The attitude of the public authorities as well as the vocally effective section of the community toward such strikes is fairly well exemplified by two contests between capital and labor—one in Virginia and the other in South Carolina.

[24] Lewis C. Gray, History of Agriculture in the Southern United States to 1860 (2 vols., Washington, 1933), I, 406; II, 646, 647.

[25] For two prosecutions of strikers for criminal conspiracy in a slave state, see Case of the Baltimore Cordwainers (1800–1806), John R. Commons et al. (eds.), Documentary History of American Labor (10 vols., Cleveland, 1910–1911), III, 249 (one of the 39 defendants was convicted), and Case of the Baltimore Weavers, ibid., IV, 269 (all acquitted by direction of the court).

[26] South Carolina Canal and Railroad Company, Third Annual Report, 1846, Franklin Institute, Journal (Philadelphia), Ser. III, Vol. XIV (July, 1847), 5. See also Directors of the Charleston and Hamburg Railroad, Annual Report, 1833.

The first strike took place at the Tredegar Iron Works in Richmond in 1847. The puddlers, their white helpers, the heaters, and the rollers demanded not only a wage increase but threatened not to return to work unless the Negroes recently employed were removed from the puddling furnace at the new mill and from the squeezer and rolls at the old mill. The entire Richmond press rallied behind the millowners. Said the *Times and Compiler:*

*The principle is advocated for the first time, we believe, in a slaveholding state, that the employer may be prevented from making use of slave labor. This principle strikes at the root of all the rights and privileges of the masters, and, if acknowledged, or permitted to gain a foothold, will soon wholly destroy the value of slave property.*

Were the right to take such strike action conceded "even for a moment," argued the *Daily Whig,* organ of big business, in the end "the entire control" would be "virtually transferred from the employers to the employees." The plant manager, Joseph R. Anderson, succeeded in breaking the strike by threatening the workers with prosecutions under the criminal conspiracy laws and by actually hailing the strike leaders before the mayor.[27] Tredegar continued to use Negro labor, and in the tobacco factories and the cotton mills of Richmond, white and Negro labor went on toiling side by side, not, however, without racial flare-ups.[28] But strikes for wages appear to have been tolerated in Richmond. Only where workers combined an attack on the use and value of slave property with an attempt to invade managerial prerogatives were they deemed to have exceeded the limits permitted white workers in that factory community.

Generally in the South, however, the courts were openly antagonistic to striking workers. When, in 1855, Irish construction hands sought to win a strike on the line of the North Eastern Railroad in the piney woods of South Carolina and resorted to demonstrations and militant picketing of nonstrikers, Judge Thomas J. Withers declared that such violence was "directed to an unlawful end." Individually each striker had the right, the judge conceded, to place his own value upon his labor, but an overt combination justified invoking the military arm. Withers denounced the Irish workers for the inclination "to make war upon the Negroes," and went so far as to assert that "slaves are, preeminently, our most valuable property—

[27] The comments from the *Times and Compiler* and from the *Daily Whig* both appeared in the issues of May 28, 1847. The court records are silent on the case, but, according to Anderson, "the prosecution was dismissed by the mayor upon the workmen disclaiming any purpose or design to commit an offence, avowing that they had not pledged themselves to one another." Tredegar Company Papers (Virginia State Library).

[28] For white and Negro labor side by side in the workshops of St. Louis, see Russell M. Nolen, "The Labor Movement in St. Louis Prior to the Civil War," *Missouri Historical Review* (Columbia), XXXIV (October, 1939), 34–35.

their rights center in the master, which he will vindicate to the bitter end." The Camden *Journal* added its approval and viewed the decision as applicable not only to conduct "by Pat in the ditch," but "to all persons who presume to make war upon our institutions."[29]

From the reaction of officialdom in most of the slave states, with the notable exception of Louisiana,[30] it would appear that strike action, like antislavery agitation, was an attack upon their "peculiar" institution. As long as Negro slave labor was available, the freedom of white workers to bargain collectively and take concerted action would be substantially curtailed. At the same time the marginal economic status of the white workers constantly kept them in jeopardy of coercive controls.

Alongside the legal and economic controls which measurably reduced the freedom of white workers in the slave states there operated a far more comprehensive set of controls for the Negro slave. The point should be made, however, that these controls were by no means uniform. In fact, the bondage under which slave labor operated varied considerably from region to region and from industry to industry. Court records, wills, deeds, manumission books, and newspapers, as well as plantation and business accounts, disclose, beneath a surface stereotype of conformity, great divergence in practice. The statutes or Black Codes constituted a façade behind which operated with little restraint the customs of the plantations, mines, or factories, the mores of town and country, and the personal whim of slaveowners, who might give lip service to the repressive codes and yet find it to their personal advantage to enlarge the amount of quasi-freedom granted their slaves.[31] On the other hand, greedy and sadistic employers might with considerable impunity choose to ignore even those minimum safeguards for the slave which the law laid down.

Despite various waves of repressive legislation, most formidable in the wake of the Nat Turner insurrection, many slaves continued to enjoy a considerable measure of nominal or quasi-freedom. The business of hiring set up one of these shadowland areas. Frederic Bancroft and other writers have stressed the exploitive aspects of the domestic slave mart,[32] while a few have recognized the upgrading and liberative possibilities inherent in hiring.[33] An examination of a large number of slave-hiring contracts reveals

[29] See Richard B. Morris, "Labor Militancy in the Old South," *Labor and Nation* (New York), IV (May–June, 1948), 35–36.

[30] While New Orleans was more tolerant of trade-union activity than perhaps any other city of the Lower South, strike demonstrations and picketing were not infrequently prosecuted under the riot act, New Orleans *Daily Picayune*, March 27, 1849; January 4, 10, February 23, 1850.

[31] See Charles S. Sydnor, "The Southerner and the Laws," *Journal of Southern History*, VI (February, 1940), 10.

[32] Frederic Bancroft, *Slave-Trading in the Old South* (Baltimore, 1931), 145–64.

[33] For example, Frederick Law Olmsted, *A Journey in the Seaboard Slave States* (New York, 1856), 102–103, 153 ff.

that many slave laborers were permitted to hold property, receive wages, make contracts, and assume supervisory responsibilities, and in addition possessed in fact some measure of mobility and occasionally a limited choice as to masters and occupations. To make the point in limited space, examples will be drawn chiefly from Virginia, where hiring arrangements may well have represented a more significant proportion of all slave-trading transactions than was the case in any other slave state. Virginia businessmen considered that slave hiring constituted healthy competition with white labor. Commenting on the high rates at which slaves were hired in January, 1857, one Richmond newspaper declared that a demand for higher rates on the part of slaveowners "would render white labor cheaper than Negro labor, and when the two interests are thus brought into competition, the owners of Negroes for hire will perceive the impolicy of attempting to exact an additional advance."[34] Hiring was particularly advantageous to the small entrepreneur who was enabled to invest his capital in plant and fixtures and not have it tied up indefinitely in labor.

In industry hired slaves were customarily reimbursed for services performed beyond an accepted minimum. For example, in the tobacco industry the Negro hireling generally received an incentive wage to stimulate production, a cash bonus for extra labor performed beyond the task assigned him or for overtime work. That the amount of these overwork payments was actually the result of bargaining between hirer and hireling is attested by contemporaries.[35] While no account books have been uncovered which would support the assertion of the Richmond *Daily Whig* of January, 1857, a period when hiring prices were at their peak, that tobacco hands in that city earned bonuses ranging from $8 to $12 a week,[36] the ledgers of Robert Leslie, a Scottish emigrant who established in 1818 one of the first tobacco factories in Petersburg, disclose monthly payments ranging from nominal sums under a dollar to amounts around $3 paid personally to hirelings for overwork.[37] Other evidence would put the top extra pay in Richmond in 1855 around $5,[38] a not insubstantial sum for a slave who, in most instances, had no housing, clothing, or food problems with which to concern himself. The manufacturers flirted with the idea of raising the standard tasks and thus eliminating overwork, but there is no evidence that they ever managed to break the long-standing custom of incentive wage payments.

[34] Richmond *Daily Whig*, January 8, 1857.

[35] See Richmond *Daily Dispatch*, December 18, 1856.

[36] Quoted in Richmond *Semi-Weekly Examiner*, January 27, 1857.

[37] Leslie Papers, Ledgers and Hiring Bonds, 1850–1852 (Duke University Library).

[38] Robert Russell, *North America: Its Agriculture and Climate* (Edinburgh, 1857), 152; an estimate substantiated by other observers. See Edward A. Wyatt, "The Rise of Industry in Ante-Bellum Petersburg," *William and Mary Quarterly* (Williamsburg), Ser. II, Vol. XII (January, 1937), 12.

Such overwork payments assume greater significance in the mining and metallurgical industries. Wages for extra work paid to slaves in the Richmond coal pits ran from $12 to $14 per annum.[39] William Weaver, the ironmaster and planter of Rockbridge and Botetourt counties, operated along similar lines. Overwork payments for slaves regularly appear in the ledgers of his enterprises, the Etna Furnace at Botetourt and the Buffalo Forge. Credits running as high as $30 were recorded for extra work in some cases. In addition, Sunday payments and night work swelled the income of these hirelings.[40] In practice the firm advanced cash, coffee, sugar, and sundries to the hired slaves, who generally wound up barely even or slightly in debt.[41]

For a realistic evaluation of such overwork payments to hirelings we should compare the net wages earned by slaves in the iron industry with the net earnings of free workers. White workers, who often labored side by side with Negro hands in the forges,[42] could be obtained in the 1850's for from $16 to $20, boarding themselves.[43] Like the Negro hirelings they too were debited for food, tobacco, shoes, and "sundries," and, in addition, had to maintain themselves out of wages. Case after case can be found in the ledgers where white workers found themselves hopelessly in debt to the company at the end of the year and were accordingly obliged to work for several more years to pay off their obligations.[44] Consider Jeremiah Brown's experience. After working a total of twenty-nine days and one night at the Graham Forge he was in debt for the sum of $3.18.[45] William Edmonds discovered that, after cutting a load of wood for which he was reimbursed thirty-eight cents and then working another three days for a total wage of $1.85, he still owed the forge $1.46.[46] Such experiences were typical of the ordinary white laborers, usually poor neighborhood farmhands living precariously on the brink of insolvency.[47] In fact as distinct from in law, the

---

[39] See McGraw Journal, 1834–1880 (University of Virginia Library).

[40] See Graham Slave Book, 1830–1831; Graham Furnace Negro Book, 1838, passim; Anderson Ledger, Negro Book, 1847–1849 (University of Virginia Library). For overwork payments by Jordan and Davis at Gibraltar Forge, see Jordan and Davis Papers, McCormick Historical Association (Microfilm, University of Texas Library).

[41] Buffalo Forge Negro Accounts, 1830–1841 (University of Virginia Library).

[42] See Etna Furnace Time Book, 1854–1857 (University of Virginia Library).

[43] Graham Forge Time Book (1855, 1856).

[44] See, for example, case of Jesse Williams, Graham Furnace Book No. 4, 1828–1830.

[45] Graham Forge Labourers Book K, 1850–1852.

[46] Graham Forge Hands Book No. 1, 1861–1862.

[47] The experience of the highly skilled iron worker and the supervisory employee was much more satisfactory, but their work was not comparable to that performed by slave labor.

poor white enjoyed no real economic advantage over Negro hired labor in the iron industry. His legal advantage was largely illusory.[48]

Aside from overwork payments, slaves hired to others occasionally received directly a portion of the hiring wages. For example, in 1843, Hugh Kelso directed in his will that "one third of the hires, that is of all the slaves belonging to my estate now or at any future period," should be paid to each slave annually, "in proportion to the sum each one shall earn."[49] John K. Poindexter provided that his slave, Aaron, was to be hired out "to whomsoever he might choose to live with" and that he was to receive "at the end of every year all the money arising from his hire."[50] A North Carolina court held that a weekly allowance of twenty-five cents to slaves hired out was the usual practice in Craven County and that this was sanctioned by public as well as private policy.[51]

At other times such wage payments appeared to operate as a disguised form of manumission.[52] A Georgia slave conveyance in 1838 provided that the vendee pay each slave "two dollars per month during their natural lives." The court held that this stipulation did not contravene the laws against manumission, and observed further that "it is the custom . . . to permit slaves to enjoy such little sums as are given to them, or as they may earn with the consent of their owners."[53]

With the enlargement of the quasi-freedom of hired Negroes came a corresponding increase in their mobility, even as compared with free Negroes, along with the right, negative if you will, to pick occupations and and employers. Masters were often reluctant to force slaves to work as hirelings in occupations they disliked or for masters whom they found uncongenial.[54] The Williamsburg *Gazette* advised masters that when making new hiring contracts at the beginning of the year they should not take their servants from employers who had treated them well, "even should the servants desire it," and cautioned them to discourage the practice of hirelings of changing "their place at the end of every year."[55] In negotiations

---

[48] The Etna Furnace went so far in 1854 as to withold 10 percent of the daily wages of one white worker until "the Rail Road is completed," with the proviso that "if he does not stay till the sd Road is finished he is to forfeit the same." Etna Furnace Time Book, 1854–1857.

[49] Mercer v. Kelso's Administrator, 4 Grattan (Va.) 106 (1847). See also Connor v. Trawick's Administrator, 37 Ala. 289 (1861); Joe v. Hart's Executors, 2 J. J. Marshall (Ky.) 349 (1829).

[50] Bailey v. Poindexter's Executor, 14 Grattan (Va.) 132, 133 (1858).

[51] Washington v. Emery, 4 Jones Equity (N. C.) 32, 37 (1858).

[52] Green v. Anderson, 38 Ga. 655 (1869).

[53] Spalding v. Grigg, 4 Ga. 75, 78, 93 (1848).

[54] Occasionally, where a hired girl ran from an employer who had severely disciplined her, the local courts respected her wishes. See, for example, Richmond *Daily Whig,* September 6, 1853.

[55] *Ibid.,* December 30, 1856.

for annual hirings between slaveowners and ironmasters there is considerable evidence to show that the wishes of the slave with reference to the
type of employment as well as the employer were taken into consideration
by humane and practical masters. One correspondent of John Jordan wrote
him that she was not willing for her "man," Phil, to work in the ore on
blowing rocks, "as he has been so much injuered by it, and he is very
dissatisfied at it."[56]

If it was difficult to eliminate the quasi-freedom enjoyed to some
extent by slaves hired to other employers, it was a far more formidable
task to restrain the mobility of slaves hired to themselves, to control their
earnings, separate property, or occupational choices. Despite legislation
directed against self-hiring in all of the slave states, there is no evidence that
there was any slackening of this trend.[57] As the practice of self-hiring bur-
geoned and the value of slaves mounted, courts and legislatures were
reluctant to enforce the sale and forfeiture provisions found, for example,
in early Virginia statutes. By reducing the fine to the nominal sum fixed by
the code of 1860, the Virginia legislature was yielding to economic and
social pressures. From a review of the prosecutions for self-hiring in the
hustings court of Richmond in the three decades before the Civil War, it
is evident that the largest number of prosecutions were in the early 1830s,
when fines ranging from $10 to $20 were imposed upon indulgent masters.
The $10 penalty paid by each of eleven Richmond masters in the year 1860
represented an amount too trivial to discourage the practice, especially
when one keeps in mind the rising price of slave hirings during this period.[58]
In 1850 the state of Georgia attempted to tax the quasi-free slaves out of
existence. A tax of $150 was imposed on "nominal slaves" and of $100 on
slaves "hiring their own time." These laws failed of enforcement, for, as the
comptroller pointed out the following year, "but two nominal slaves and
three slaves hiring their time have been returned this year, while there is
little doubt but that there are hundreds of nominal slaves in the state that
would pay the usual free Negro tax of $5 or a little more were they so
taxed."[59] Time after time South Carolina grand juries complained that the
laws against slaves hiring their own time were "grossly and habitually violated" and that stricter laws were needed.[60]

[56] Nancy M. Slater to John Jordan, January 18, 1831, Jordan and Irvine Papers, McCormick
Historical Association (Microfilm, University of Texas).

[57] See Richmond *Daily Whig,* September 28, October 5, November 24, 1853.

[58] Richmond Hustings Court Record, Books XI–XXIII (City Hall, Richmond).

[59] *Annual Report of the Comptroller for the State of Georgia to the Governor, 1851.* See
also Bagshaw v. Dorsett, Ga. Decisions 42, pt. 2 (1842).

[60] Sumter County (S. C.) General Session Journal, 1840–1853 (1849), 248 (Courthouse, Sumter); Edgefield County General Session Minutes, 1848–1868, p. 457 (Courthouse, Edgefield).
For the case of slave Hetty, allowed to hire her own time for nine years, see State v. Brown,
2 Speers (S. C.) 129 (1843). The courts held that self-hiring amounted to a condition of

Self-hiring was frequently a condition precedent to emancipation. One slave sale recorded in Alabama stipulated that the slave be allowed the proceeds of his labor and that he be manumitted upon payment of $1,250 and ten percent interest. In a decision on the eve of the Civil War the master in chancery ordered specific performance of the contract and, since manumission was not permissible in Alabama, provided that the slave be removed to a free state for that purpose. The appeals court, unimpressed by the logic of the decision, reversed the ruling.[61] But despite its illegality, self-hiring, if we are to judge from the volume of litigation, was as widespread in Alabama as in any other state of the Lower South.[62] Typical was the arrangement with a slave named Moses, whose mistress permitted him to labor in Mobile upon payment to her of stated wages and to retain all earnings in excess of that amount.[63]

In agricultural occupations, incentive wage payments—at times substantial—tied in with the task system are too familiar to require elaboration.[64] In much the same category are payments for Sunday and holiday work,[65] for ditching and leveeing, for ginning, pressing, and baling cotton, for special marketing tasks,[66] and Christmas gifts often related to productivity as well as good conduct.[67] Such extra earnings might at times run from $20 to $40 a year.[68] Louisiana went further than any other slave state in

---

emancipation in Mays v. Gillam, 2 Richardson (S. C.) 160 (1845); Rhame v. Ferguson and Dangerfield, Rice (S. C.) 196 (1839); Ford ex rel. Ferguson v. Dangerfield, 8 Richardson Equity (S. C.) 95 (1856). For North Carolina, see Kelly v. Bryan, 6 Iredell Equity (N. C.) 283 (1849). An indictment against Nat, a slave, for hiring his time in violation of law was reversed on jurisdictional grounds. Nat was engaged in running a boat carrying turpentine to and from Washington. A white man who hired Nat for three days testified that the slave told him that "he hired his time from his master; that he was to give his master $80 a year, and pay him quarterly." State v. Nat, a Slave, 13 Iredell (N. C.) 154 (1851).

[61] Evans v. Kittrell, 33 Ala. 449 (1859).

[62] As might be expected, the practice was even more extensive in the border states.

[63] Shanklin v. Johnson, 9 Ala. 271 (1846). Similarly in Knox v. Fair, 17 Ala. 503 (1850); Jones v. Nirdlinger, 20 Ala. 488 (1852); Stanley v. Nelson, 28 Ala. 514 (1856); Broadhead v. Jones, 39 Ala. 96 (1863); Donovan v. Pitcher, 53 Ala. 411 (1875).

[64] See, for example, Randolph Plantation Expense Books, 1847–1851, 1851–1863, Randolph Papers (Louisiana State University Library); Frederick L. Olmsted, Journey in the Back Country (New York, 1860), 5; Olmsted, Journey in the Seaboard Slave States, 439–43, 484, 682, 695.

[65] See Niblett v. White's Heirs, 7 La. 253 (1834); also Liddell Plantation Diary, 1841–1844; Ledger, 1850–1853 (Louisiana State University Library).

[66] Maverick v. Lewis and Gibbs, 3 McCord (S. C.) 211 (1825).

[67] One testator provided that his slaves were to receive Christmas gifts ranging from $5 to $20, "to each . . . according to their age, and faithful conduct." Stancell v. Kenan et al., 33 Ga. 56, 58 (1861).

[68] Liddell Diary and Ledgers; Randolph Plantation Expense Books, 1847–1851; after four years to "several hundred dollars." White v. Cline, 7 Jones (N. C.) 174, 175 (1859).

allotting the slave the proceeds of Sunday labor. In that state the colonial custom of allowing slaves to labor for themselves on Sunday and to dispose of their own time[69] carried down from the French into the American period. The Black Code in effect in the ante-bellum period specified that slaves were to be paid at the rate of fifty cents for Sunday work.[70]

While at law the acquisitions of the slave were the property of the master[71]—only Louisiana under civil law influence specifically recognized the slave's right to his earnings, or *peculium*[72]—in practice slaves were allowed their own patches.[73] Either they were permitted to market their own produce themselves or else the master handled the marketing and credited sales against advances for sundries he had laid out at the slave's request.[74] Masters even found it necessary at times to borrow corn from their own Negroes to feed their horses.[75]

While sale by slaves of their surplus food crops would normally not constitute serious competition to the planters, sale of money crops was quite a different story. In some areas planters permitted slaves to raise and market cotton for themselves.[76] So extensive was this practice and so serious

[69] See Loppinot v. Villeneuve (1774–1775), translation by Laura L. Porteous from the original MS. in Spanish Judicial Records of Louisiana (The Cabildo, New Orleans), *Louisiana Historical Quarterly* (New Orleans), XII (January, 1929, 40–120.

[70] Meinrad Greiner (comp.), *Louisiana Digest, 1804–1841* (New Orleans, 1841), 498, Art. 3363; U. B. Phillips (comp.), *The Revised Statutes of Louisiana* (New Orleans, 1856), 62, Sec. 86. This provision constituted an advance over Carondelet's Code, according to which the slaves were to have Sundays "except during harvest." The wage provision was upheld by the courts even against the master. Rice v. Cade et al., 10 La. 288 (1836). See also Niblett v. White's Heirs, 7 La. 253 (1834). For Sunday payments to slaves on a Louisiana plantation, see Liddell Plantation Diary, 1841–1844, "Negro Accounts" (1844); Ledger, 1852–1853; Ledger, 1855–1858, "Negro Accounts" (1856). Their pay varied with the difficulty of the task from fifteen cents to $1.25 a rod, with an average of 36 cents a rod in 1854, while white ditchers averaged $1 a rod. But it is likely that the latter, whose pay was subject to deductions for idleness and poor work, were called in for the most difficult ground.

[71] See, for example, Gist v. Toohey, 2 Richardson (S. C.) 424 (1846); Peay v. McEwen, 8 Richardson (S. C.) 31 (1854).

[72] Hardesty v. Wormley, 10 La. Annual Reports 239 (1855).

[73] See Herbert A. Keller (ed.), *Solon Robinson, Pioneer and Agriculturalist: Selected Writings* (2 vols. [*Indiana Historical Collections*, Vols. XXI-XXII], Indianapolis, 1936), II, 290–91, 295–96; Lawton v. Hunt et al., 4 Richardson Equity (S. C.) 233 (1852).

[74] See Heirs of Henderson v. Rost et al., 5 La. Annual Reports 441 (1850); Lawton v. Hunt et al., 4 Richardson Equity (S. C.) 233 (1852); Liddell Papers, Plantation Diary, 1841–1844; Ledger, 1850–1853; Randolph Expense Books, 1847–1851, 1853–1863.

[75] See Davis v. Whitridge, 2 Strobhart (S. C.) 232 (1848). For sales of land to a Negro slave, see Embry v. Morrison, 1 Tenn. Chancery 434 (1873). While the courts, especially toward the end of the ante-bellum period, were vigilant to curb indirect steps toward manumission, they did not interfere with the practice of making money payments to slaves or with the slave-patch arrangements.

[76] Sanders v. Devereaux, 25 Tex. Supplement 1 (1860).

a threat did it seem to pose to marginal farmers that a group of small planters in upcountry South Carolina were moved to petition the legislature in
1816 for relief. Their arguments testify to their sense of insecurity:

*Every measure that may lessen the dependence of a slave on his master
ought to be opposed as tending to dangerous consequences. The more
privileges a slave obtains the less depending he is on his master and the
greater nuisance he is likely to be to the public. In many parts of this dist-
trict Negroes have every other Saturday, keep horses, raise hogs, cultivate
for themselves everything for home consumption and for markets that their
masters do. But of all their privileges that of their making Cotton is the
most objectionable.*

Such a policy was calculated to encourage theft, they argued. But the legislature significantly declined to interfere at that time with an arrangement
that was obviously an incentive to labor on the better managed plantations.[77]

    Not only in fringe areas, in urban regions, and in the border states,[78]
but even on the great staple-producing plantations this trend toward enlarg-
ing the slave's area of free choice and property rights was increasing by the
eve of the Civil War, despite the fact that most southern states no longer
permitted emancipation and in the face of the avowed antagonism of state
legislatures to the subterfuges resorted to by the slaveowners and the courts
to circumvent the Black Codes. In fact the overlapping zone between nominal slaves who were quasi-free and free Negroes who were quasi-slave
was so considerable that the census returns for 1850 and 1860 for states
like Tennessee and the border areas must be accepted with healthy reservations.

    In marked contrast to this enlarged orbit of quasi-freedom for the
slave was the deteriorating position of the free Negro, who at times appears
to have retrograded to a state of servitude or quasi-slavery.[79] The free Negro's
status was not irrevocable. He could be reduced to servitude or even slavery
for the commission of various acts, and his mobility and freedom of occupational choice were severely limited. In towns like Richmond the registration papers of free Negroes were vigilantly checked. In the years before
the war this concern with the free Negro's movements greatly increased.
In 1851, for example, the Richmond hustings court issued new registers in

[77] Petitions, 1816 (South Carolina Historical Commission). A similar objection was voiced
by the *Southern Cultivator,* (Athens, Atlanta). Olmsted, *Journey in the Seaboard Slave States,*
350, 351. For a similar view, see Edwin A. Davis (ed.), *Plantation Life in the Florida Parishes
of Louisiana* (New York, 1943), 406–10.

[78] For the extent of nominal freedom in Tennessee, see J. Merton England, "The Free Negro
in Ante-Bellum Tennessee" (Ph.D. Dissertation, Vanderbilt University, 1941), 24.

[79] See John H. Franklin, "The Enslavement of Free Negroes in North Carolina," *Journal of
Negro History* (Washington), XXIX (October, 1944), 405 ff.

761 cases and jailed or hired out fifty-nine free Negroes for moving around town without proper papers. The whole registry system kept free Negroes in constant peril. In Maryland under statutes passed in 1854 and 1856 free Negroes bound to labor contracts could be returned to their employers by legal process, could be compelled to serve out the remainder of their terms, forfeit their wages for the time lost, and be liable for trial costs. Furthermore, the provision of the state constitution of 1864 abolishing slavery and involuntary servitude was held by the courts of that state not to be applicable to free Negroes lawfully apprenticed.[80]

In Delaware male free Negroes continued to be subjected to debt servitude throughout the ante-bellum period, and a law provided that idle and vagabond free Negroes and free mulattoes might be "compulsorily hired out to service" by a justice of the peace for the residue of the then current year. A law of 1851 provided that a free Negro coming into that state would be subject to a fine of $60, and, in the event of nonpayment and failure to leave the state in five days, would be sold out of the state to cover the fine and costs.[81] Long after white convicts ceased to be sold off for crimes against property and other offenses, free Negroes were customarily sold for seven-year terms. In fact this provision remained in force until 1867. It is apparent that Delaware's ante-bellum peonage practices substantially curtailed the free Negro's expectations of actual liberty.

Only five weeks before the firing on Fort Sumter the legislature of Delaware passed a statute which permitted imprisoned Negro debtors to make service contracts with their creditors to work off their indebtedness. For failure to do so, they could be sold off for a term not to exceed seven years. This special disability of Negroes to obtain release from imprisonment for debt unless they agreed to serve their creditors was re-enacted in subsequent nineteenth-century revisions of the Delaware laws, and was not repealed until 1915.[82] Despite the fact that the Thirteenth Amendment became part of the organic law of the land on December 18, 1865, the sale of free Negroes persisted beyond that date in Delaware, as is evidenced by broadsides of sheriffs' sales dated April, 1866.[83]

The trend toward upgrading slaves into a shadowland of quasi-freedom was actually offset by the deteriorating status of the free Negro. Any conclusion, then, that Negro slavery was evolving into a condition corresponding to the white servitude of the colonial period or that slavery was on its way out before the Civil War fails to take into account the increasing

---

[80] Morris, "Labor Controls in Maryland in the Nineteenth Century," *Journal of Southern History*, XIV (August, 1948), 392–93.

[81] See Morris, "The Course of Peonage in a Slave State," *Political Science Quarterly*, LXV (June, 1950), 244. For the attitude toward this act in the Lower South, see Holly Springs *Mississippi Palladium*, April 25, 1851.

[82] *Delaware Laws*, Revisions of 1915, p. 2037.

[83] Sheriff's Office Broadsides (Public Archives Commission, Dover).

hurdles which beset the free Negro and overstresses such aspects of free-dom as mobility, property rights, and occupational choice. Such freedoms, which have been the subject of this article, are all subordinate to the physical security of the person, the right to a normal family life, and to freedom from arbitrary government. Those who share the conviction that a free government is one where the deliberative forces prevail over the arbitrary will find this basic condition of independence largely absent in the slave states. With all due acknowledgement to the role that conscien-tious and fair-minded judges on some of the higher benches performed in placing due process above racial considerations, it is impossible to ignore the extent to which arbitrary rule and even lawlessness flourished in the South, how it was fed by perverted paternalism, by the psychological unbal-ance of the master-servant relationship, and by long-standing sexual tension between the races. These factors—aside from political considerations, capi-tal investment, and the fear inspired by the abolitionists and northern poli-ticians—would appear to rule out a peaceful solution of the problem of slavery.

In the last analysis the most cherished rights of personal security in the slave states were weakly buttressed for all labor, white or Negro. With-out such safeguards slave and "free Negro" managed to survive, but two thirds of that white population which was "free" in name never fully enjoyed the fruits of that freedom. At its best the institution of slavery was a sort of prolonged childhood without opportunity for maturation. It offered something analogous to the welfare security of the police state tempered by the sentimental and humanitarian standards prevailing in an anachronistic patriarchal system. At its worst it was far more incredible than even the most passionate abolitionist perceived. But the security and guardianship which the more favored slaves enjoyed were gains achieved at a cost of human aspiration, at the sacrifice of the right of Americans to hope for a better lot for their children than they themselves enjoyed. While slavery in America destroyed the institutional pattern of primitive life, it failed to substitute in its place a mode of life for the Negro that was truly creative. The legal and racial subordination implicit in the institution had a corrosive effect upon the Negro's personality. The impact of slavery upon the free white population was equally unfortunate. It seriously undermined the economic security of white labor in the slave states and left ugly scars upon the character and temperament of the ruling class.

Had slavery been only a matter of law, these evolutionary trends toward quasi-freedom which we have considered in some detail would have pointed toward a new and better status for the Negro. But slavery was above all a matter of race, and generations yet unborn at the time of the Civil War were to wrestle with that inscrutable problem without evolving a harmonious formula.

# 9

## DAY TO DAY RESISTANCE TO SLAVERY[1]
*Raymond A. and Alice M. Bauer*

THE tradition that has grown up about Negro slavery is that the slaves were docile, well adapted to slavery, and reasonably content with their lot. . . . The purpose of this paper is to study . . . the day to day resistance to slavery, since it is felt that such a study will throw some further light on the nature of the Negro's reaction to slavery. Our investigation has made it apparent that the Negroes not only were very discontented, but that they developed effective protest techniques in the form of indirect retaliation for their enslavement. Since this conclusion differs sharply from commonly accepted belief, it would perhaps be of value if a brief preliminary statement were made of how [a] belief so at variance with the available documentary materials could gain such acceptance.

The picture of the docile, contented Negro slave grew out of two lines of argument used in ante-bellum times. The pro-slavery faction contended that the slaves came of an inferior race, and that they were happy and contented in their subordinate position, and that the dancing and singing Negro exemplified their assumption. Abolitionists, on the other hand, tended to depict the Nego slave as a passive instrument, a good and faithful worker exploited and beaten by a cruel master. As one reads the controversial literature on the slavery question, it soon becomes apparent that both sides presented the Negro as a docile creature; one side because it wished to prove that he was contented, the other because it wished to prove that he was grossly mistreated. Both conceptions have persisted to the present time. Writers who romanticize the "Old South" idealize the condition of the slaves, and make of them happy, willing servitors, while those who are concerned with furthering the interests of the Negroes are careful to avoid mention of any aggressive tendencies which might be used as a pretext for further suppressing the Negroes.

Many travelers in the South have accepted the overt behavior of the slaves at its face value. The "yas suh, Cap'n," the smiling, bowing, and scraping of the Negroes have been taken as tokens of contentment. Redpath's conversations with slaves indicated how deep seated this behavior was.[2] This point of view, however, neglects the fact that the whites have

Raymond A. and Alice M. Bauer, "Day to Day Resistance to Slavery," *Journal of Negro History*, XXVII (October, 1942), pp. 388–419. © 1942 by the Association for the Study of Negro Life and History Inc.

[1] We wish to express our appreciation to Professor M. J. Herskovits, under whose direction this research has been carried on.

[2] Redpath, James, *The Roving Editor: or, Talks with Slaves in the Southern States,* New York, 1859.

always insisted on certain forms of behavior as a token of acceptance of inferior status by the Negro. The following quotation from Dollard is pertinent:

*"An informant already cited has referred to the Negro as a 'Dr. Jekyll and Mr. Hyde.' He was making an observation that is well understood among Negroes—that he has a kind of dual personality, two rôles, one that he is forced to play with white people and one the 'real Negro' as he appears in his dealings with his own people. What the white southern people see who 'know their Negroes' is the rôle that they have forced the Negro to accept, his caste role."[3]*

The conceptual framework within which this paper is written is that the Negro slaves were forced into certain outward forms of compliance to slavery; that, except for the few who were able to escape to the North, the Negroes had to accept the institution of slavery and make their adjustments to that institution. The patterns of adjustment which we have found operative are: slowing up of work, destruction of property, malingering and self-mutilation. . . .

The Negroes were well aware that the work they did benefited only the master. "The slaves work and the planter gets the benefit of it."[4] "The conversation among the slaves was that they worked hard and got no benefit, that the masters got it all."[5] It is thus not surprising that one finds many recurring comments that a slave did not do half a good day's work in a day. A northerner whom Lyell met in the South said:

*"Half the population of the south is employed in seeing that the other half do their work, and they who do work, accomplish half what they might do under a better system."[6]*

An English visitor, with a very strong pro-slavery bias corroborates this:

*"The amount of work expected of the field hand will not be more than one half of what would be demanded of a white man; and even that will not be properly done unless he be constantly overlooked."[7]*

Statements of other writers are to the same effect:

*"It is a common remark of those persons acquainted with slavelabour, that their proportion is as one to two. This is not too great an estimate in favour*

---

[3] Dollard, John, *Caste and Class in a Southern Town*, New Haven, 1937, pp. 255, 256.

[4] Wm. Brown, an escaped slave, in: Benjamin Drew, *The Refugee*, Boston, 1856, p. 281.

[5] Thomas Hedgebeth, a free Negro, in: Benjamin Drew, *The Refugee*, Boston, 1856, p. 276.

[6] Lyell, Sir Charles, *A Second Visit to the United States of America*, New York, 1849, II, 72.

[7] Ozanne, T. D., *The South as It Is*, London, 1863, pp. 165, 166.

*of the free-labourer; and the circumstances of their situation produce a still greater disparity."*[8]

"*A capitalist was having a building erected in Petersburg, and his slaves were employed in carrying up the brick and mortar for the masons on their heads: a Northerner, standing near, remarked to him that they moved so indolently that it seemed as if they were trying to see how long they could be in mounting the ladder without actually stopping. The builder started to reprove them, but after moving a step turned back and said: 'It would only make them move more slowly still when I am not looking at them, if I should hurry now. And what motive have they to do better? It's no concern of theirs how long the masons wait. I am sure if I was in their place, I shouldn't move as fast as they do.'"*[9]

A well-informed capitalist and slave-holder remarked,

"*In working niggers, we always calculate that they will not labor at all except to avoid punishment, and they will never do more than just enough to save themselves from being punished, and no amount of punishment will prevent their working carelessly or indifferently. It always seems on the plantations as if they took pains to break all the tools and spoil all the cattle that they possibly can, even when they know they'll be directly punished for it."*[10]

Just how much of this was due to indifference and how much due to deliberate slowing up is hard to determine. Both factors most probably entered. A worker who had to devote himself to a dull task from which he can hope to gain nothing by exercising initiative soon slips into such a frame of mind that he does nothing more than go through the motions. His chief concern is to escape from the realities of his task and put it in the back of his mind as much as possible.

There is, indeed, a strong possibility that this behavior was a form of indirect aggression. While such an hypothesis cannot be demonstrated on the basis of the available contemporary data, it is supported by Dollard's interpretation of similar behavior which he found in Southern towns.

"*If the reader has ever seen Stepin Fetchit in the movies, he can picture this type of character. Fetchit always plays the part of a well-accommodated lower-class Negro, whining, vacillating, shambling, stupid, and moved by very simple cravings. There is probably an element of resistance to white society in the shambling, sullenly slow pace of the Negro; it is the gesture*

---

[8] Anon., *An Inquiry Into the Condition and Prospects of the African Race*, Philadelphia, 1839, p. 83.

[9] Olmsted, F. L., *A Journey in the Seaboard Slave States*, New York, 1863, p. 210.

[10] *Ibid.*, p. 104.

*of a man who is forced to work for ends not his own and who expresses his reluctance to perform under these circumstances.'*[11]

Certainly description after description emphasizes the mechanical plodding of the slave workers:

"John Lamar wrote, 'My man Ned the carpenter is idle or nearly so at the plantation. He is fixing gates and, like the idle groom in Pickwick, trying to fool himself into the belief that he is doing something—He is an eye servant.' "[12]

"Those I saw at work appeared to me to move very slowly and awkwardly, as did those engaged in the stables. These also were very stupid and dilatory in executing any orders given them, so that Mr. C. would frequently take the duty off their hands into his own, rather than wait for them, or make them correct their blunders; they were much, in these respects, what our farmers call dumb Paddees—that is, Irishmen who do not readily understand the English language, and who are still weak and stiff from the effects of the emigrating voyage. At the entrance gate was a porter's lodge, and, as I approached I saw a black face peeping at me from it, but both when I entered and left, I was obliged to dismount and open the gate myself.

"Altogether, it struck me—slaves coming here as they naturally did in comparison with free laborers, as commonly employed on my own and my neighbors' farms, in exactly similar duties—that they must have been difficult to direct efficiently, and that it must be irksome and trying to one's patience, to have to superintend their labor."[13]

To what extent this reluctant labor was the rule may be appreciated when it is pointed out that a southern doctor classified it under the name *Dysaethesia Aethiopica* as a mental disease peculiar to Negroes. Olmsted quotes this Dr. Cartwright as follows:

" 'From the careless movements of the individual affected with this complaint, they are apt to do much mischief, which appears as if intentional, but it is mostly owing to the stupidness of mind and insensibility of the nerves induced by the disease. Thus, they break, waste, and destroy everything they handle—abuse horses and cattle—tear, burn, or rend their own clothing, and, paying no attention to the rights of property, steal others to replace what they have destroyed. They wander about at night, and keep in a half nodding state by day. They slight their work—cut up corn, cotton and tobacco, when hoeing it, as if for pure mischief. They raise disturbances with

[11] Dollard, *op. cit.*, p. 257.

[12] Phillips, U. B., *American Negro Slavery*, New York, 1918, p. 192.

[13] Olmsted, *op. cit.*, p. 11.

*their overseers, and among their fellow servants, without cause or motive, and seem to be insensible to pain when subjected to punishment.*

*" '. . . The term "rascality" given to this disease by overseers, is founded on an erroneous hypothesis, and leads to an incorrect empirical treatment, which seldom or never cures it.' '"*[14]

There are only two possible interpretations of the doctor's statement. Either the slaves were so extraordinarily lazy that they gave the appearance of being mentally diseased, or the doctor was describing cases of hebephrenic schizophrenia. Either situation is startling. The phenomenon was obviously widespread, and if it was actually a mental disease it certainly would indicate that Negroes did not become "easily adjusted to slavery."

Whatever the case, it is certain that the slaves consciously saved their energy. Olmsted, who always had his eye open for such incidents, reported:

*"The overseer rode among them, on a horse, carrying in his hand a raw-hide whip, constantly directing and encouraging them; but, as my companion and I, both, several times noticed, as often as he visited one line of the operations, the hands at the other end would discontinue their labor, until he turned to ride toward them again."*[15]

The few statements on this point we have by ex-slaves seem to indicate that the slaves as a group made a general policy of not letting the master get the upper hand.

*"I had become large and strong; and had begun to take pride in the fact that I could do as much hard work as some of the older men. There is much rivalry among slaves, at times, as to which can do the most work, and masters generally seek to promote such rivalry. But some of us were too wise to race with each other very long. Such racing, we had the sagacity to see, was not likely to pay. We had times out for measuring each other's strength, but we knew too much to keep up the competition so long as to produce an extraordinary day's work. We knew that if, by extraordinary exertion, a large quantity of work was done in one day, the fact, becoming known to the master, might lead him to require the same amount every day. This thought was enough to bring us to a dead halt whenever so much excited for the race."*[16]

Writer after writer, describing incidents in which slaves were compelled to assist in punishing other slaves, states that they did so with the greatest of reluctance.

[14] Olmsted, *op. cit.*, pp. 192, 193.

[15] *Ibid.*, p. 388.

[16] Douglass, Frederick, *Life and Times of Frederick Douglass*, p. 261.

"The hands stood still;—they knew Randall—and they knew him also take a powerful man, and were afraid to grapple with him. As soon as Cook had ordered the men to seize him, Randall turned to them, and said—'Boys, you all know me; you know that I can handle any three of you, and the man that lays hands on me shall die. This white man can't whip me himself, and therefore he has called you to help him.' The overseer was unable to prevail upon them to seize and secure Randall, and finally ordered them all to go to their work together."[17]

In some cases it was noted that the slave resisting punishment took pains not to treat his fellows with any more than the absolute minimum of violence.

With such demonstrations of solidarity among the slaves it is not surprising to find a slave telling of how he and his fellows "captured" the institution of the driver. The slave Solomon Northup was such a driver. His task was to whip the other slaves in order to make them work.

" 'Practice makes perfect,' truly; and during eight years' experience as a driver I learned to handle the whip with marvelous dexterity and precision, throwing the lash within a hair's breadth of the back, the ear, the nose without, however, touching either of them. If Epps was observed at a distance, or we had reason to apprehend he was sneaking somewhere in the vicinity, I would commence plying the lash vigorously, when, according to arrangement, they would squirm and screech as if in agony, although not one of them had in fact been grazed. Patsey would take occasion, if he made his appearance presently, to mumble in his hearing some complaints that Platt was whipping them the whole time, and Uncle Abram, with an appearance of honesty peculiar to himself would declare roundly I had just whipped them worse than General Jackson whipped the enemy at New Orleans."[18]

Williams, another slave whose task was to drive his fellows, said:

"He was at these periods terribly severe to his hands, and would order me to use up the cracker of my whip every day upon the poor creatures who were toiling in the field; and in order to satisfy him, I used to tear it off when returning home at night. He would then praise me for a good fellow and invite me to drink with him."[19]

The amount of slowing up of labor by the slaves must, in the aggregate, have caused a tremendous financial loss to plantation owners. The only way we have of estimating it quantitatively is through comparison of

[17] Brown, W. W., *Life of Williams Wells Brown, A Fugitive Slave,* Boston, 1848, p. 18. See also Williams, James, *Narratives of James Williams,* Boston, 1838, pp. 56, 62, 65.

[18] Northup, Solomon, *Twelve Years a Slave,* 1853, pp. 226, 227.

[19] Williams, James, *Narratives of James Williams,* Boston, 1838, p. 43.

the work done in different plantations and under different systems of labor. The statement is frequently made that production on a plantation varied more than 100% from time to time. Comparison in the output of slaves in different parts of the South also showed variations of over 100%. Most significant is the improvement in output obtained under the task, whereby the slaves were given a specific task to fulfill for their day's work, any time left over being their own. Olmsted gives us our best information on this point:

*"These tasks certainly would not be considered excessively hard by a northern laborer; and, in point of fact, the more industrious and active hands finished them often by two o'clock. I saw one or two leaving the field soon after one o'clock, several about two; and between three and four, I met a dozen women and several men coming home to their cabins, having finished their day's work.*

*"Under this 'Organization of Labor' most of the slaves work rapidly and well. In nearly all ordinary work, custom has settled the extent of the task, and it is difficult to increase it. The driver who marks it out, has to remain on the ground until it is finished, and has no interest in overmeasuring it; and if it should be systematically increased very much, there is danger of a general stampede to the swamp, a danger the slave can always hold before his master's cupidity."*[20]

*"It is the custom of tobacco manufacturers to hire slaves and free negroes at a certain rate of wages each year. A task of 45 pounds per day is given them to work up, and all they choose to do more than this, they are paid for—payment being made once a fortnight; and invariably this over-wages is used by the slave for himself, and is usually spent in drinking, licentiousness, and gambling. The man was grumbling that he had saved but $20 to spend at the holidays. One of the manufacturers offered to show me by his books, that nearly all gained by over-work $5 a month, many $20 and some as much as $28.*[21]

*"He (the speaker) was executor of an estate in which, among other negroes, there was one very smart man, who, he knew perfectly well, ought to be earning for the estate $150 a year, and who could if he chose, yet whose wages for a year being let out by the day or job, had amounted to but $18, while he had paid for medical attendance upon him $45."*[22]

The executor of the estate finally arranged for this man to work out his freedom, which he readily accomplished.

A quantitative estimate can be made from another situation which Olmsted observed. Rain during a previous day had made certain parts of the

[20] Olmsted, *op. cit.*, pp. 435, 436.

[21] *Ibid*, p. 103.

[22] *Ibid*, p. 103.

work more difficult than others. The slaves were therefore put on day work, since it would not be possible to lay out equitable tasks.

*"Ordinarily it is done by tasks—a certain number of the small divisions of the field being given to each hand to burn in a day; but owing to a more than usual amount of rain having fallen lately, and some other causes, making the work harder in some places than in others, the women were now working by the day, under the direction of a 'driver,' a negro man, who walked about among them, taking care they had left nothing unburned. Mr. X inspected the ground they had gone over, to see whether the driver had done his duty. It had been sufficiently well burned, but not more than a quarter as much ground had been gone over, he said, as was usually burned in tasked work,—and he thought they had been very lazy, and reprimanded them for it."*[23]

Most revealing of all is this statement:

*" 'Well, now, old man,' said I, 'you go and cut me two cords today!' 'Oh, massa! two cords! Nobody could do dat. Oh! massa, dat is too hard! Neber heard o' nobody's cuttin' more 'n a cord o' wood in a day, round heah. No nigger couldn't do it.' 'Well, old man, you have two cords of wood cut to-night or to-morrow morning you shall get two hundred lashes—that's all there is about it. So look sharp.' And he did it and ever since no negro ever cut less than two cords a day for me, though my neighbors never get but one cord. It was just so with a great many other things—mauling rails—I always have two hundred rails mauled in a day; just twice what it is the custom of the country to expect of a negro, and just twice as many as my negroes had been made to do before I managed them myself."*

*"These estimates, let it be recollected in conclusion, are all deliberately and carefully made by gentlemen of liberal education, who have had unusual facilities of observing both at the North and the South."*[24]

The slaves were well aware of their economic value, and used it to good advantage. The skilled laborers among the slaves knew their worth, and frequently rebelled against unsatisfactory work situations. Slaves who were hired out would run away from the masters who had hired them, and then either return home, or remain in hiding until they felt like returning to work.

*"The slave, if he is indisposed to work, and especially if he is not treated well, or does not like the master who has hired him, will sham sickness— even make himself sick or lame—that he need not work. But a more serious loss frequently arises, when the slave, thinking he is worked too hard, or*

[23] *Ibid,* p. 430.

[24] *Ibid,* p. 207.

being angered by punishment or unkind treatment, 'getting the sulks,' takes to 'the swamp,' and comes back when he has a mind to. Often this will not be till the year is up for which he is engaged, when he will return to his owner, who, glad to find his property safe, and that it has not died in the swamp, or gone to Canada, forgets to punish him, and immediately sends him for another year to a new master.

" 'But, meanwhile, how does the negro support life in the swamp?' I asked.

" 'Oh, he gets sheep and pigs and calves, and fowls and turkey; sometimes they will kill a small cow. We have often seen the fires, where they were cooking them, through the woods in the swamp yonder. If it is cold, he will crawl under a fodder stack, or go into the cabins with some of the other negroes, and in the same way, you see, he can get all the corn, or almost anything else he wants.

" 'He steals them from his master?'

" 'From anyone: frequently from me. I have had many a sheep taken by them.[25]

" 'It is a common thing, then?'

" 'Certainly it is, very common, and the loss is sometimes exceedingly provoking. One of my neighbors here was going to build, and hired two mechanics for a year. Juost as he was ready to put his house up, the two men, taking offense at something, both ran away, and did not come back at all, till their year was out, and then their owner immediately hired them out again to another man.' "[26]

One plantation overseer wrote to the plantation owner concerning a carpenter he had hired out to one G. Moore:

"Not long before Jim run away G More (sic.) wanted him to make some gates and I sent him theirselves (sic.) and he run away from him and cum home and then he left me withow (sic.) a cause."[27]

Even the threat of a whipping did not deter such slaves from running off for a time when they were displeased. The quotation from Olmsted below is typical of a constantly recurring pattern of statements:

"The manager told me that the people often ran away after they have been whipped or something else had happened to make them angry. They hide in the swamp and come into the cabins at night to get food. They seldom

---

[25] The speaker had freed his slaves.

[26] Olmsted, op. cit., pp. 100, 101.

[27] Bassett, J. S., The Southern Plantation Overseer as Revealed in His Letters, Northampton, Mass., 1925, p. 66.

remain away more than a fortnight and when they come in they are whipped."[28]

Some of the resistance took on the aspects of organized strikes:

"Occasionally, however, a squad would strike in a body as a protest against severities. An episode of this sort was recounted in a letter of a Georgia overseer to his absent employer: 'Sir: I write you a few lines in order to let you know that six of your hands has left the plantation—every man but Jack. They displeased me with their work and I give some of them a few lashes, Tom with the rest. On Wednesday morning they were missing. I think they are lying out until they can see you or your Uncle Jack.' The slaves could not negotiate directly at such a time, but while they lay in the woods they might make overtures to the overseer through slaves on a neighboring plantation as to terms upon which they would return to work, or they might await their master's posthaste arrival and appeal to him for a redress of grievances. Humble as their demeanor might be, their power of renewing the pressure by repeating their act could not be ignored."[29]

John Holmes, an escaped slave, told how he ran off and hid in the swamp after an overseer attempted to whip him.

"At last they told all the neighbors if I would come home, they wouldn't whip me. I was a great hand to work and made a great deal of money for our folks."[30]

The same overseer had further trouble with the slaves.

"She (a slave) was better with her fists, and beat him, but he was better at wrestling and threw her down. He then called the men to help him, but all hid from him in the brush where we were working.... Then (later) the calculation was to whip us every one, because we did not help the overseer.... That night every one of us went away into the woods.... We went back, but after a while (the overseer) came back too, and stayed the year out. He whipped the women but he did not whip the men, of fear they would run away."[31]

The indifference of the slaves to the welfare of the masters extended itself to a complete contempt for property values. The slaves were so careless with tools that they were equipped with special tools, and more clumsy than ordinary ones:

[28] Olmsted, F. L., A Journey in the Back Country, New York, 1863, p. 79.

[29] Phillips, U. B., American Negro Slavery, pp. 303, 304.

[30] Drew, B., The Refugee, p. 164.

[31] Ibid., p. 167.

"The 'nigger hoe' was first introduced into Virginia as a substitute for the plow, in breaking up the soil. The law fixes its weight at four pounds,—as heavy as the woodman's axe. It is still used, not only in Virginia, but in Georgia and the Carolinas. The planters tell us, as the reason for its use, that the negroes would break a Yankee hoe in pieces on the first root, or stone that might be in their way. An instructive commentary on the difference between free and slave labor!"[32]

"The absence of motive, and the consequent want of mental energy to give vigor to the arm of the slave is the source of another great drawback upon the usefulness of his labour. His implements or tools are at least one-third (in some instances more than twofold) heavier and stronger than the northern man's to counteract his want of skill and interest in his work. A Negro hoe or scythe would be a curiosity to a New England farmer."[33]

Not only tools but live stock suffered from the mistreatment by the slaves. Olmsted found not only the "nigger hoe" but even discovered that mules were substituted for horses because horses could not stand up under the treatment of the slaves.

. . . . "I am shown tools that no man in his senses, with us, would allow a laborer, to whom he was paying wages, to be encumbered with; and the excessive weight and clumsiness of which, I would judge, would make work at least ten percent greater than those ordinarily used with us. And I am assured that, in the careless and clumsy way they must be used by the slaves, anything lighter or less crude could not be furnished them with good economy, and that such tools as we constantly give our laborers and find profit in giving them, would not last out a day in a Virginia corn-field —much lighter and more free from stones though it be than ours.

"So, too, when I ask why mules are so universally substituted for horses on the farm, the first reason given, and confessedly the most con-clusive one, is, that horses cannot bear the treatment they always must get from negroes; horses are always soon foundered or crippled by them but mules will bear cudgeling, and lose a meal or two now and then, and not be materially injured, and they do not take cold or get sick if neglected or overworked. But I do not need to go further than to the window of the room in which I am writing, to see, at almost any time, treatment of cattle that would insure the immediate discharge of the driver, by almost any farmer owning them in the North."[34]

Redpath verifies Olmsted's statement—by telling how he saw slaves treat stock. It is important to note that Redpath was a strong abolitionist and most sympathetic toward the slaves.

[32] Parson, C. G., Inside View of Slavery, Boston, 1853, p. 94.

[33] Anon. An Inquiry Into the Condition and Prospects of the African Base, Philadelphia, 1839, p. 83.

[34] Olmsted, F. L., A Journey in the Seaboard Slave States, pp. 46, 47.

*"He rode the near horse, and held a heavy cowhide in his hand, with which from time to time he lashed the leaders, as barbarous drivers lash oxen when at work. Whenever we came to a hill, especially if it was very steep, he dismounted, lashed the horses with all his strength, varying his performances by picking up stones, none of them smaller than half a brick, and throwing them with all his force, at the horses' legs. He seldom missed.*

*"The wagon was laden with two tons of plaster in sacks.*

*"This is a fair specimen of the style in which Negroes treat stock."[35]*

The indifference to live-stock is well illustrated by an incident which Olmsted recounts:

*"I came, one afternoon, upon a herd of uncommonly fine cattle as they were being turned out of a field by a negro woman. She had given herself the trouble to let down but two of the seven bars of the fence, and they were obliged to leap over a barrier at least four feet high. Last of all came, very unwillingly, a handsome heifer, heavy with calf; the woman urged her with a cudgel and she jumped, but lodging on her belly, as I came up she lay bent, and, as it seemed, helplessly hung upon the top bar. . . . The woman struck her severely and with a painful effort she boggled over."[36]*

In the Sea Islands off the coast of Georgia, Kemble reported that the slaves started immense fires, destroying large sections of woods through careless or maliciousness.

*"The 'field hands' make fires to cook their midday food wherever they happen to be working, and sometimes through their careless neglect, but sometimes, too, undoubtedly on purpose, the woods are set fire to by these means. One benefit they consider . . . is the destruction of the dreaded rattlesnakes."[37]*

The slaves on Lewis' West Indies plantation let cattle get into one of his best cane-pieces because they neglected to guard them, being more interested in a dance which was going on. They were fully aware that the cattle were ruining the sugar cane, but kept right on singing and dancing. Lewis was able to get only a handful of house servants to drive the cattle out of the cane, and that not until the cane-piece was ruined.[38]

One tobacco planter complained that his slaves would cut the young plants indiscriminately unless they were watched. When it became late in

[35] Redpath, *op. cit.*, p. 241.

[36] Olmsted, F. L., *A Journey in the Back Country*, p. 227.

[37] Kemble, F. A., *Journal of a Residence on a Georgian Plantation in 1838–1839*, New York, 1863, p. 242.

[38] Lewis, M. G., *Journal of a West Indian Proprietor, 1815–1817*, London, 1929, p. 267.

the season and there was need of haste to avoid frost they would work only the thickest leaving the sparser ones untouched.[39] Another planter said that he could cultivate only the poorer grades of tobacco because the slaves would not give necessary attention to the finer sort of plants.[40] An English visitor said:

*"The kitchens and out-offices are always at the distance of several yards from the principal dwelling. This is done as well to guard against the house-Negroes through carelessness setting the houses on fire, for they generally sit over it half the night, as to keep out their noise." (sic.)*[41]

The full import of these practices strikes home fully only when they are read in the words of the original observers. Olmsted's comments, and the ease with which he found incidents to illustrate them, are most valuable. So important is his testimony that we must once more quote him at some length.

*"Incidents, trifling in themselves, constantly betray to a stranger the bad economy of using enslaved servants. The catastrophe of one such occurred since I began to write this letter. I ordered a fire to be made in my room, as I was going out this morning. On my return, I found a grand fire—the room door having been closed and locked upon it 'out of order.' Just now, while I was writing, down tumbled upon the floor, and rolled away close to the valance of the bed, half a hod-full of ignited coal, which had been so piled upon the diminutive grate, and left without a fender or any guard, that this result was almost inevitable. If I had not returned at the time I did, the house would have been fired."*[42]

*"On the rice plantation which I have particularly described, the slaves were, I judge, treated with at least as much discretion and judicious consideration of economy, consistently with humane regard to their health, comfort, and morals, as on any other in all the Slave States; yet I could not avoid observing—and I certainly took no pains to do so, nor were any special facilities offered me for it—repeated instances of that waste and misapplication of labor which it can never be possible to guard against, when the agents of industry are slaves. Many such evidences of waste it would not be easy to specify; and others, which remain in my memory after some weeks, do not adequately account for the general impression that all I saw gave me; but there were, for instance, under my observation gates left open and bars left down, against standing orders; rails removed from fences by the negroes (as was conjectured, to kindle their fires with,*

---

[39] Phillips, U. B., *Plantation and Frontier Documents, 1649–1863,* Cleveland, 1909, p. 34.

[40] Olmsted, F. L., *A Journey in the Seaboard Slave States,* p. 91.

[41] Hanson, C. W., *The Stranger in America,* London, 1807, p. 357.

[42] Olmsted, F. L., *A Journey in the Seaboard Slave States,* p. 145.

*mules lamed, and implements broken, by careless usage; a flat boat, carelessly secured, going adrift on the river; men ordered to cart rails for a new fence depositing them so that a double expense of labor would be required to lay them, more than would have needed if they had been placed, as they might have almost as easily been, by a slight exercise of forethought . . . making statements which their owner was obliged to receive as sufficient excuse, though, he told me, he felt assured they were false—all going to show habitual carelessness, indolence, and mere eyeservice."[43]*

But not only did the Negro slaves refuse to work, and not only did they destroy property, but they even made it impossible for planters to introduce new work techniques by feigning clumsiness. They prevented the introduction of the plow in this way on many plantations.[44] Olmsted here cites many instances. Lewis, quoted in *Plantation Documents*, found the same thing to be true in Jamaica.

*"It appears to me that nothing could afford so much relief to the negroes, under the existing system of Jamaica, as the substituting of labor of animals for that of slaves in agriculture wherever such a measure is practicable. On leaving the island, I impressed this wish of mine upon the mind of my agents with all my power; but the only result has been the creating a very considerable expense in the purchase of ploughs, oxen and farming implements; the awkwardness and still more the obstinacy of the few negroes, whose services were indispensable, was not to be overcome: they broke plough after plough, and ruined beast after beast, till the attempt was abandoned in despair."[45]*

Malingering was a well-known phenomenon throughout the slave states.[46] The purpose of feigning illness was generally to avoid work, although occasionally a slave who was being sold would feign a disability either to avoid being sold to an undesirable master, or to lower his purchase price so as to obtain revenge on a former master. The women

---

[43] *Ibid.,* p. 480.

[44] *Ibid.,* pp. 481–484.

[45] Phillips, U. B., *Plantation and Frontier Documents, 1694–1863,* p. 137.

[46] Since this paper was written a significant contribution has appeared which throws a new light on the subject of slave illness. (Felice Swados, "Negro Health on the Ante Bellum Plantations," *Bulletin of the History of Medicine,* vol. x, no. 3, October, 1941). Though Swados demonstrated that the rate of actual sickness among the Negroes was very high, she leaves some doubt as to what proportion of sickness was feigned. For instance, in a footnote (p. 472) she refers to Sydnor's compilations of the records of sickness on several plantations as indications of the extent of actual sickness, even going so far as to note that on one plantation most of the sickness occurred during the picking season. Sydnor, himself, indicates that he believes that these records demonstrate that a great deal of the sickness was feigned.

occasionally pretended to be pregnant, because pregnant women were given lighter work assignments and were allowed extra rations of food.

In a situation such as this in which physical disability was an advantage, one would expect much malingering. One might also expect to find functional mental disorders, hysterical disorders which would get one out of work. There is some evidence that many had such functional disorders.

"There are many complaints described in Dr. Cartwright's treatise, to which the Negroes, in slavery, seem to be peculiarly subject.

" 'Negro-consumption, a disease almost unknown to medical men of the Northern States and of Europe, is also sometimes fearfully prevalent among the slaves. 'It is of importance,' says the Doctor, to know the pathognomic signs in its early stages, not only in regard to its treatment but to detect impositions, as negroes, affllicted with this complaint are often for sale; the acceleration of the pulse, on exercise, incapacitates them for labor, as they quickly give out, and have to leave their work. This induces their owners to sell them, although they may not know the cause of their inability to labor. Many of the negroes brought South, for sale, are in the incipient stages of this disease; they are found to be inefficient laborers, and sold in consequence thereof. The effect of superstition—a firm belief that he is poisoned or conjured—upon the patient's mind, already in a morbid state (dyaesthesia), and his health affected from hard usage, overtasking or exposure, want of wholesome food, good clothing, warm, comfortable lodging, with the distressing idea (sometimes) that he is an object of hatred or dislike, both to his master or fellow-servants, and has no one to befriend him, tends directly to generate that erythism of mind which is the essential cause of negro consumption' " . . . 'Remedies should be assisted by removing the original cause[47] of the dissatisfaction or trouble of mind, and by using every means to make the patient comfortable, satisfied and happy.' "[48]

Of course it is impossible to determine the extent of these disorders. Assuming that Dr. Cartwright's assumption was correct, very few observers would be qualified to make an adequate diagnosis, and a very small proportion of these would be inclined to accept his interpretation. After all, functional disorders are in many cases almost impossible to tell from real disorders or from feigning, and since the behavior which Cartwright describes could very easily be interpreted on another, and easier, level by a less acute observer.

Of the extent to which illness was feigned there can, however, be little doubt. Some of the feigning was quite obvious, and one might wonder why such flagrant abuses were tolerated. The important thing to remember is that a slave was an important economic investment. Most slave owners sooner or later found out that it was more profitable to give the slave the benefit of the doubt. A sick slave driven to work might very well die.

[47] Cartwright's italics.

[48] Olmsted, F. L., A Journey in the Seaboard Slave States, p. 193.

*"But the same gentleman admitted that he had sometimes been mistaken and had made men go to work when they afterwards proved to be really ill; therefore, when one of his people told him he was not able to work, he usually thought, 'very likely he'll be all the better for a day's rest, whether he's really ill or not,' and would let him off without being very particular in his examination. Lately he had been getting a new overseer, and when he was engaging him he told him that this was his way. The observer replied, 'It's my way too, now; it didn't used to be, but I had a lesson. There was a nigger one day at Mr. ———'s who was sulky and complaining; he said he couldn't work. I looked at his tongue, and it was right clean, and I thought it was nothing but damned sulkiness so I paddled him, and made him go to work; but, two days after, he was under ground. He was a good eight hundred dollar nigger, and it was a lesson to me about taming possums, that I ain't going to forget in a hurry.' "*[49]

So one might find situations like this:

*"At one, which was evidently the 'sick house' or hospital, there were several negroes, of both sexes, wrapped in blankets, and reclining on the door steps or on the ground, basking in sunshine. Some of them looked ill, but all were chatting and laughing as I rode up to make inquiry."*[50]

The situation turned in on itself. The masters were always suspicious of the sick slaves, so that slaves who were moderately sick accentuated their symptoms in order to make out a convincing case.

*"It is said to be nearly as difficult to form a satisfactory diagnosis of negroes' disorders, as it is of infants', because their imagination of symptoms is so vivid, and because not the smallest reliance is to be placed on their accounts of what they have felt or done. If a man is really ill, he fears lest he should be thought to be simulating, and therefore exaggerates all his pains, and locates them in whatever he supposes to be the most vital parts of his system.*

*"Frequently the invalid slaves will neglect or refuse to use the remedies prescribed for their recovery. They will conceal pills, for instance, under their tongue, and declare they have swallowed them, when, from their producing no effect, it will be afterwards evident that they have not. This general custom I heard ascribed to habit acquired when they were not very disagreeably ill and were loth to be made quite well enough to have to go to work again."*[51]

[49] *Ibid.*, p. 189.

[50] *Ibid.*, pp. 416, 417.

[51] *Ibid.*, p. 187.

Fortunately in this field we have some quantitative estimates which enable us to appreciate fully the extent of these practices. Sydnor has digested the records of sickness on various plantations. From the Wheeles plantation records he found that of 1,429 working days 179 were lost on account of sickness, a ratio of almost one to seven. On the Bowles' plantation, in one year 159½ days were missed on account of sickness but only five days were on Sundays. This is a recurrent pattern, everybody sick on Saturday, and scarcely anybody sick on Sunday. On the Leigh plantation, where thirty persons were working there were 398 days of sickness. In examining this record Sydnor discovered that the rate of sickness was greatest at the times of the year when there was the most work to be done.[52] Olmsted says that he never visited a plantation on which twenty Negroes were employed where he did not find one or more not at work on some trivial pretext.[53]

Lewis' anecdote is typical:

*"On Saturday morning there were no fewer than forty-five persons (not including children) in the hospital; which makes nearly a fifth of my whole gang. Of these the medical people assured me that not above seven had anything whatever the matter with them. . . . And sure enough on Sunday morning they all walked away from the hospital to amuse themselves, except about seven or eight."*[54]

Sometimes the feigning did not work, as is shown by two incidents that Olmsted relates:

*A Mr. X asked if there were any sick people.*
*" 'Nobody, oney dat boy Sam, sar.'*
*" 'What Sam is that?'*
*" 'Dat little Sam, sar; Tom's Sue's Sam, sar.'*
*" 'What's the matter with him?'*
*" 'Don' spec der's nothing much de matter wid him nof, sar. He came in Sa'dy, complaining he had de stomach-ache, an' I give him some ile, sar, 'spec he mus' be well dis time, but he din go out dis mornin'.'*
*" 'Well, I see to him.*
*"Mr. X went to Tom's Sue's cabin, looked at the boy and concluded that he was well, though he lay abed, and pretended to cry with pain, ordered him to go out to work."*[55]

*A planter asked the nurse if anyone else was sick.*
*" 'Oney dat woman Caroline.'*

[52] Sydnor, C. S., *Slavery in Mississippi*, New York, 1933, pp. 45 ff.

[53] Olmsted, F. L., *A Journey in the Seaboard Slave States*, p. 187.

[54] Lewis, M. G., *Journal of a West Indian Proprietor, 1815–1817*, London, 1929, p. 168.

[55] Olmsted, F. L., *A Journey in the Seaboard Slave States*, pp. 423, 424.

" 'What do you think is the matter with her?'

" 'Well, I don't think there is anything de matter wid her, masser; I mus answer you for true, I don't tink anything de matter wid her, oney she's a little sore from dat whipping she got.' "

The manager found the woman groaning on a dirty bed and after examining her, scolded her and and sent her to work.[56]

The prevalence of malingering may be better appreciated when one realizes that despite the fact that Olmsted refers to it throughout four volumes of his works, in one place he has five whole pages of anecdotes concerning it.[57]

Pretending to be pregnant was a type of escape in a class by itself, since the fraud must inevitably have been discovered. This in itself may give us some insight into the Negroes' attitude toward the relative advantages of escaping work and of escaping punishment. Just as the slave who ran off into the woods for a temporary relief from work, the pseudo-pregnant woman must have realized in advance that she would inevitably be punished.

"I will tell you of a most comical account Mr. ———— has given me of the prolonged and still protracted pseudo-pregnancy of a woman called Markie, who for many more months than are generally required for the process of continuing the human species, pretended to be what the Germans pathetically and poetically call 'in good hope' and continued to reap increased rations as the reward of her expectation, till she finally had to disappoint the estate and receive a flogging.[58]

One woman sought to escape from the consequence of her fraud. The results were quite tragic:

"A young slave woman, Becky by name, had given pregnancy as the reason for a continued slackness in her work. Her master became skeptical and gave notice that she was to be examined and might expect the whip in case her excuse were not substantiated. Two days afterwards a Negro midwife announced that Becky's baby had been born; but at the same time a neighboring planter began search for a child nine months old which was missing from his quarter. This child was found in Becky's cabin, with its two teeth pulled and the tip of its navel cut off. It died; and Becky was convicted only of manslaughter."[59]

[56] Olmsted, F. L., A Journey in the Back Country, p. 77.

[57] Olmsted, F. L., A Journey in the Seaboard Slave States, pp. 187–191.

[58] Kemble, F. A., op. cit., p. 235.

[59] Phillips, U. B., American Negro Slavery, p. 436.

An outstanding example of malingering is given by Smedes, a writer who insisted so emphatically on the devotion of the slaves to their masters.

*"The cook's husband, who for years had looked on himself as nearly blind, and therefore unable to do more than work about her, and put her wood on the fire, sometimes cutting a stick or two, made no less than eighteen good crops for himself when the war was over. He was one of the best farmers in the country."*[60]

The most effective means of retaliation against an unpopular master which the slave had at his command was by feigning disability on the auction block. How often this was done we do not know, but Phillips accepts it as a recognized pattern.

*"Those on the block often times praised their own strength and talents, for it was a matter of pride to fetch high prices. On the other hand if a slave should bear a grudge against his seller, or should hope to be bought only by someone who would expect but light service he might pretend a disability though he had it not."*[61]

Coleman offers the same opinion:

*"Similar actions were not unknown in slave sales. Frequently on such occasions there is a strong indisposition in such creatures to be sold, and that by stratagem to avoid sale, they may frequently feign sickness, or magnify any particular complaint with which they are affected.*[62]

*As was customary at a public auction of slaves, the auctioneer announced that Mr. Anderson, the master, would give a bill of sale for his slave with the usual guarantee—'sound of mind and body and a slave for life.' While there began a lively bidding among the Negro traders, George suddenly assumed a strange appearance—his head was thrown back, his eyes rolled wildly, his body and limbs began to twitch and jerk in an unheard of manner.*
*" 'What's the matter with your boy, Mr. Anderson?' one of the traders asked the owner, who, astonished and puzzled, drew nearer the block. But Mr. Anderson did not answer the question. George was now foaming at the mouth, and the violent twitching and jerking increased precipitously.*
*" 'What's the matter with you, boy?' gruffly demanded the trader. 'O, I 'es fits I has!' exclaimed George, whereupon his body doubled up and rolled off the block.*

[60] Smedes, S., *Memorials of a Southern Planter*, Baltimore, 1887, p. 80.

[61] Phillips, U. B., *American Negro Slavery*, p. 199.

[62] Coleman, J. W., *Slavery Times in Kentucky*, Chapel Hill, N. C., 1940, p. 130.

"Of course the auction was hastily terminated. George was hustled off to jail, and a doctor sent for, but, after a careful examination, the medical man was somewhat mystified as to the slaves's actual condition. He advised the master to leave George in the jailer's custody for a while, promising to look in on him the next morning. Under his master's instruction, the wily slave was put to bed in the debtor's room, where he soon sank, apparently, into a sound sleep.

"Next morning when the jailer brought in breakfast, he found the bed empty. George was gone, and nothing was heard of him again until word came, several weeks later, that he was safe in Canada."[63]

Or, again, we read:

"A young girl, of twenty years or thereabouts, was the next commodity put up. Her right hand was entirely useless—'dead,' as she aptly called it. One finger had been cut off by a doctor, and the auctioneer stated that she herself chopped off the other finger—her forefinger—because it hurt her, and she thought that to cut it off would cure it.

" 'Didn't you cut your finger off?' asked a man, 'kase you was mad?'
She looked at him quietly, but with a glance of contempt, and said:
" 'No, you see it was a sort o' sore, and I thought it would be better to cut it off than be plagued with it.'

"Several persons around me expressed the opinion that she had done it willfully, to spite her master or mistress, or to keep her from being sold down South."[64]

Another instance is described as follows:

"As I came up, a second-rate plantation hand of the name of Noah, but whom the crier persisted in calling 'Noey,' was being offered, it being an administrator's sale. Noey, on mounting the steps, had assumed a most drooping aspect, hanging his head and affecting the feebleness of old age. He had probably hoped to have avoided sale by a dodge, which is very common in such cases. But the first bid—$1,000—startled him, and he looked eagerly to the quarter whence it proceeded. 'Never mind who he is, he has got the money. Now, gentlemen, just go on; who will say fifty.' And so the crier proceeds with his monotonous calling. 'I ain't worth all that, mass'r; I ain't much count no how,' cried Noey energetically to the first bidder. 'Yes you are, Noey—ah, $1,000, thank you, sir,' replies the crier."[65]

The strength of Negro resistance to slavery becomes apparent in the extent to which the slaves mutilated themselves in their efforts to escape

---

[63] *Ibid.,* pp. 129–130.

[64] Redpath, *op. cit.,* pp. 253–254.

[65] Pollard, E. A., *The Southern Spy,* Washington, 1859, pp. 13–14.

work. A girl on Lewis' plantation who had been injured tied pack thread around her wounds when they started to heal and then rubbed dirt in them. In her anxiety to avoid work she gave herself a very serious infection.[66] But this action was mild compared to that of others.

*"General Leslie Coombs, of Lexington, owned a man named Ennis, a house carpenter. He had bargained with a slave-trader to take him and carry him down the river. Ennis was determined not to go. He took a broadaxe and cut one hand off; then contrived to lift the axe, with his arm pressing it to his body, and let it fall upon the other, cutting off the ends of the fingers."[67]*

*" 'But some on 'em would rather be shot then be took, sir,' he added simply. "A farmer living near a swamp confirmed this account, and said he knew of three or four being shot on one day."[68]*

Planters had much trouble with slaves fresh from Africa, the new slaves committing suicide in great numbers. Ebo landing in the Sea Islands was the site of the mass suicide of Ebo slaves who simply walked in a body into the ocean and drowned themselves. A planter writing on the handling of slaves mentions the difficulty of adjusting the Africans to slavery. He advocates mixing them in with seasoned slaves.

*"It too often happens that poor masters, who have no other slaves or are too greedy, require hard labor of these fresh negroes, exhaust them quickly, lose them by sickness and more often by grief. Often they hasten their own death; some wound themselves, others stifle themselves by drawing in the tongue so as to close the breathing passage, others take poison, or flee and perish of misery and hunger."[69]*

The one problem of Negro resistance to slavery which is most enticing is that of the attitude of slave mothers toward their children. There are frequent references in the literature to Negro women who boasted about the number of "niggers they hade for the massah," but breeding was probably quite secondary to sex activity. It would be interesting to discover the motives behind this apparent pleasure in presenting babies to the master. Some of the women may have been sincere in their pride. What makes this problem peculiarly important is the presence of much indirect evidence that, the Negro mothers either had no affection for their children, or did not want them to be raised as slaves.

We know quite well that African Negroes are (at least reasonably)

[66] Lewis, *op. cit.,* p. 168.

[67] Clarke, *op. cit.,* p. 125.

[68] Olmsted, F. L., *A Journey in the Seaboard Slave States,* p. 160.

[69] Phillips, U. B., *Plantation and Frontier Documents,* II, p. 31.

able to take care of their children, and that the slave women efficiently tended the children of the plantation mistress. Yet one runs across comment after comment that the Negro mothers were ignorant, and careless, and did not know how to care for their own offspring. Typical of such statements is this:

*"The Negro mothers are often so ignorant and indolent, that they cannot be trusted to keep awake and administer medicine to their own children; so that the mistress has often to sit up all night with a sick Negro child."*[70]

Guion Johnson states that plantation owners in the Sea Islands offered the mothers rewards to take good care of their children. They were paid for those who survived the first year! This at least would indicate that there was something to be desired in their attitude toward their children.

Occasionally one runs across a reference to a slave mother killing her child, but the statements are almost invariably incomplete. For instance, Catterall[71] has a record of a trial, the details of which are: "The prisoner was indicted for murder of her own child," no more. Or a plantation overseer writes, "Elizabeth's child died last night. She smothered it somehow."[72] There is no indication as to whether or not the smothering was deliberate.

Several cases, where it was certain that parents killed their children to keep them from slavery, have been described. They are important enough to be given in detail.

*"Of all the cases of slave rendition, the saddest and probably the most circulated at the time was that of Margaret Garner. Winter was the best time for flight across the Ohio River, for when it was frozen over the difficulties of crossing were fewer. Simeon Garner, with his wife Margaret and two children, fled from slavery in Kentucky during the cold winter of 1856 and, after crossing the frozen stream at night, made their ways to the house of a free Negro in Cincinnati.*

*"Quickly tracing the fugitive Negroes to their hideout in Cincinnati, the armed pursuers, after some resistance, broke down the door and entered the house. There they found Margaret, the mother, who, preferring death to slavery for her children, had striven to take their lives, and one child lay dead on the floor. The case was immediately brought into court, where despite the efforts made by sympathetic whites, rendition was ordered. On their return to slavery, Margaret in despair attempted to drown herself and child by jumping into the river but even the deliverance of*

[70] Lyell, *op. cit.*, p. 264.

[71] Catterall, H. H., (ed.), *Judicial Cases Concerning American Slavery and the Negro*, Washington, D. C., 1926–1937, Vol. II, p. 59.

[72] Bassett, *op. cit.*, p. 59.

*death was denied her, for she was recovered and soon thereafter sold to a trader who took her to the cotton fields of the Far South.'*[73]

*"Not only were slaves known to take the lives of their masters or over-seers, but they were now and then charged with the murder of their own children, sometimes to prevent them from growing up in bondage. In Covington a father and mother, shut up in a slave baracoon and doomed to the southern market, 'when there was no eye to pity them and no arm to save,' did by mutual agreement 'send the souls of their children to Heaven rather than have them descend to the hell of slavery,' and then both parents committed suicide'*[74]

*" 'Take off your shoes, Sylva,' said Mrs. A., 'and let this gentleman see your feet.'*

*" 'I don't want to,' said Sylva.*

*" 'But I want you to,' said her mistress.*

*" 'I don't care if you do,' replied Sylva sullenly.*

*" 'You must,' said the mistress firmly.*

*"The fear of punishment impelled her to remove the shoes. Four toes on one foot, and two on the other were wanting! 'There!' said the mistress, 'my husband, who learned the blacksmith's trade for the purpose of teach-ing it to the slaves, to increase their market value, has, with his own hands, pounded off and wrung off all those toes, when insane with passion. And it was only last week that he thought Sylva was saucy to me, and he gave her thirty lashes with the horse whip. She was so old that I could not bear to see it, and I left the house.*

*" 'Sylva says,' Mrs. A. continued, 'that she has been the mother of thirteen children, every one of whom she has destroyed with her own hands, in their infancy, rather than have them suffer slavery'!'*[75]

The patterns of resistance to slavery studied in this paper are: (1) deliberate slowing up of work; (2) destruction of property, and indifferent work; (3) feigning illness and pregnancy; (4) injuring one's self; (5) suicide; (6) a possibility that a significant number of slave mothers killed their children.

The motivation behind these acts was undoubtedly complex. The most obvious of the motives was a desire to avoid work. It has been dem-onstrated that the slaves were acutely conscious of the fact that they had nothing to gain by hard work except in those instances where they were working under the task system. The destruction of property and the poor quality of the slaves' work was mainly due to their indifference to their tasks. There is enough evidence that they could, and did, work hard and well

---

[73] Coleman, J. W., *op. cit.,* p. 208.

[74] *Ibid.,* p. 269.

[75] Parson, C. G., *op. cit.,* p. 212.

when sufficiently motivated to refute any contention that the Negro slaves were congenitally poor workers.

Many of the slaves reacted to the institution of slavery in a far more drastic fashion than could be manifested by a mere desire to avoid work. Some of these slaves committed suicide; others killed members of their families, usually their children, in order that they might not grow up as slaves.

Possibly the most significant aspect of these patterns of resistance is the aggression against the white masters they imply. Unfortunately, however, though this aspect may be the most significant, it is the least subject to proof. On the plane of logic, there is every reason to believe that a people held in bondage would devise techniques such as have been described above as an indirect means of retaliation. The statement of Dollard, previously quoted, indicates that such techniques (slowness, inefficiency, etc.) are used at the present time as a means of indirect aggression.

The material presented here suggests the need for a reconsideration of the concept of the Negro's easy adjustment to slavery. He was not a cheerful, efficient worker, as has been assumed. Rather, he was frequently rebellious, and almost always sullen, as any person faced with a disagreeable situation from which he cannot escape will normally be. Nor, can the belief that racial inferiority is responsible for inefficient workmanship on his part be supported. For such deficiencies of his workmanship as he manifested, or, indeed, may still be manifested, are seen to be explainable in terms that are in no sense to be couched in the conventional mold of inherent racial differences.

# 10
## THE OLD ALLEGIANCE
### Willie Lee Rose

LAURA Towne stood on the veranda of Dr. Jenkins' plantation house on Station Creek and gazed across the salt flats to the distant point where the blue waters of Port Royal Sound narrow and flow past the straits of Bay Point and Hilton Head Island. It was here on this porch, the Negroes told her, that the St. Helena planters had converged on that Thursday back in November to watch the battle of Port Royal. They had hoped to see their sons and relatives in the Beaufort Volunteer Artillery drive off the invading fleet, but although they possibly

From *Rehearsal for Reconstruction: The Port Royal Experiment* by Willie Lee Rose, copyright © 1964, by the Bobbs-Merrill Company, Inc., reprinted by permission of the publishers.

had been too far away to hear the victorious strains of "Yankee Doodle," they had realized early in the afternoon that the forts were falling. Hastily mounting their horses, the planters had ridden away to spread the alarm.[1]

For the few confused hours that followed, the missionaries soon learned that every plantation had its own special story. A few planters had succeeded in quickly driving their slaves and livestock to the Beaufort ferry, but for every one who had succeeded in this, there were a dozen who failed. The Negroes too had heard the guns, and some had hidden in the swamps and in the fields, crouched low between the corn rows. Others had sensed their power for the first time and had stubbornly stood their ground before their masters, impervious to cajolery and threats that the Yankees would sell them to Cuba. Master Daniel Pope's seamstress, Susannah, told Laura Towne that she had asked her master when he urged and threatened, "Why should they [the Yankees] kill poor black folks who did no harm and could only be guided by white folks?"[2] The majority of the Negroes showed the shrewdness of a certain Dr. Sam's man Cupid, who recalled that his master had told his slaves to collect at a certain point so that "dey could jus' sweep us up in a heap, an' put us in de boat." The Negroes had taken to the woods instead. "Jus as if I was gwine to be sich a goat!" commented Cupid. Pompey of Coffin's Point informed Harriet Ware that some Negroes in his plantation would have been duped by the Cuba story but for the fact that the "poor whites" of Beaufort had made the slaves "sensible" to the fact that their own freedom was at stake in the conflict.[3]

Not every planter had even tried to remove his slaves. There were perhaps a few others who followed the course of Captain John Fripp of St. Helena Island. This remarkable man, who was at once one of the richest landowners in the district and a Union sympathizer, called his slaves together and explained the situation. He warned that they would probably starve if they followed him to the interior and advised them to hide until the Confederate soldiers had passed through the island. They should then keep together, work their provision crops as usual, and forget about the cotton. It was late in the day when Henry, the cook at Coffin Point, sounded the alarm on the northern end of St. Helena. He excitedly informed the overseer that he had better be off, for "all the Yankee ships were 'going in procession up to Beaufort, solemn as a funeral.'" The overseer left, but Henry did not.[4]

[1] Towne MS diary, November 12, 1862; J A J[ohnson's] account in Beaufort *Republican*, June 26, 1873. Johnson remembered hearing "Yankee Doodle" struck up as he and his fellow Confederate soldiers prepared to retreat from Bay Point.

[2] Rupert Sargent Holland (ed.), *Letters and Diary of Laura M. Towne* (Cambridge, 1912), p. 27; Towne MS diary, November 17, 1862; Elizabeth Ware Pearson (ed.), *Letters from Port Royal* (Boston, 1906), pp. 78–79, 127.

[3] Charlotte Forten, "Life on the Sea-Islands," *Atlantic Monthly*, XIII (May, 1864), 593; Pearson (ed.), *Letters*, p. 207.

[4] EP in *Second Series of Extracts from Letters Received* (Boston, 1862); Pearson (ed.), *Letters*, p. 127.

Henry had been wrong in thinking the gunboats were occupying Beaufort so promptly. After effecting a lodgment at Hilton Head and making a few tentative explorations, the Federal forces had waited patiently several days for some response to General T. W. Hunter's proclamation of assurance and protection to the citizens of the district. Had Du Pont's gunboats occupied Beaufort immediately, they would probably have intercepted almost the entire white population embarking for Charleston on a steamer that was docked conveniently at the town landing.[5] Such action would also have frustrated the enactment of a most instructive morality play on the true character of slavery. In the few days that elapsed before Federal authority was consolidated throughout the island region, the social and legal bindings of the peculiar institution unwound with the speed and ferocity of a coiled wire spring.

The sack of Beaufort was one event that the Negroes did not discuss with their new friends. The looting of the houses probably began with the motive of plunder, but in a short time crowds of field hands descended upon the town and took it apart, presumably for the satisfaction of doing it. Whatever manorial pride the field hands may have felt in the country estates of their late owners, it did not encompass the elegance of the family town houses. It is quite probable that most of these plantation Negroes had never been inside their masters' fine homes in Beaufort, but they were not intimidated. Over the protests of the house servants who had remained, they broke up furniture, loaded valuables onto boats to carry away, and helped themselves to the wine.[6] Thomas Elliott, who returned to his Beaufort house the day following the November 7 attack on the forts, reported that he discovered "Chloe, Stephens' wife, seated at Phoebe's piano playing away like the very Devil and two damsels upstairs dancing away famously. . . ." They were all plantation Negroes who had come into town. The house had little furniture left and had been "completely turned upside down and inside out. The organs in both churches were broken up," Elliott reported, "and the churches themselves robbed of many articles which were deposited there for safe keeping."[7]

The correspondent of the New York *Tribune* described the destruction that Du Pont and his landing party found when they went up to Beaufort on November 12. "We went through spacious houses where only a week ago families were living in luxury, and saw their costly furniture

---

[5] J A J[ohnson] in Beaufort *Republican,* June 23, 1873.

[6] Certain of the missionaries who arrived later than the first summer at Port Royal attributed the sack of the town to the soldiers, exculpating the Negroes. All the evidence of those on the spot at the time, including the whilom masters who were clandestinely roaming the region, said the field slaves did the damage. See the New York *Tribune,* November 20, 1861; Daniel Ammen, *The Atlantic Coast* (New York, 1898), pp. 33–34; Hazard Stevens, *Life of Isaac Ingalls Stevens,* II, 354–355.

[7] Thomas R. S. Elliott to his mother, Monday night [November 11, 1861), Elliott-Gonzales MSS.

despoiled; books and papers smashed; pianos on the sidewalk, feather beds ripped open, and even the filth of the Negroes lying in parlors and bedchambers." The destruction had been "wanton," and much of it could have served "no purposes of plunder" but only a "malicious love of mischief gratified."[8] Nothing that happened illustrated better the frustrated hostilities of generations than the desecration of the stylish houses in the east end of town.

Commodore Du Pont was saddened by what he saw but at the same time remembered with contempt how South Carolina fire-eaters had said their own slaves "would drive out the Yankees." They had known very little, reflected the Commodore, "of the relations existing between master and servant. Oh my! It was with difficulty they could get away [with] a household domestic—the field hands remained to a man . . . and immediately commenced plundering until we stopped them."[9]

Du Pont heard other, darker things as well. The planters and overseers were in some cases shooting down rebellious slaves who would not leave the plantations with them.[10] In a panic to retrieve the most portable part of his evaporating fortunes, each planter had, in his own way, borne witness by action to his private conception of chattel slavery. For every man like Captain John Fripp, who thought first of his slaves as people, there was another who thought of them first as property. During the revolutionary days before the Federal pickets were posted over the islands, numerous planters concluded that there was yet time to evacuate Negroes and burn their cotton. When Thomas R. S. Elliott returned to his plantation and found the Negroes idle, he attempted to force them away with him. He was unsuccessful and commented grimly, "I think we will have to make a terrible example of many of them." Although Elliott's meaning is not precise, it is clear that many "terrible examples" were made.[11]

William Elliott had once written, in a candid defense of slavery, that masters were usually kind and that slavery served the interests of civilization. "Against *insubordination alone,* we are severe."[12] That was precisely what the masters had been obliged to deal with when the islands were invaded. The only eye-witnesses of these atrocities were the Negroes themselves, but their accounts were complete in many cases with names and places and were sufficient to convince the naval officers who questioned

---

[8] New York *Tribune,* November 20, 1861.

[9] Samuel Francis Du Pont to Henry Winter Davis, December 9, [18]61, Samuel Francis Du Pont MSS, Eleutherian Mills Historical Library, Greenville, Wilmington, Delaware.

[10] *Ibid.*

[11] Thos. R. S. Elliott to his mother, Monday night [November 11, 1861], Elliott-Gonzales MSS.

[12] Lewis Pinckney Jones, "Carolinians and Cubans: The Elliotts and Gonzales, Their Work and Their Writings" (unpublished doctoral dissertation, University of North Carolina, 1952), Part I, p. 14.

them. Commodore Du Pont was horrified to hear from an army officer, whose information had come "from reliable testimony," of recalcitrant slaves being burned to death in their cotton-houses. George W. Smalley, the correspondent of the New York *Tribune,* concluded that "the horrible fact stands out with appalling clearness and certainty that the murder of slaves who cannot be compelled to follow their masters is a deliberate and relentless purpose." His informants too gave names and places. A responsible Negro named Will Capers told Laura Towne that he had known of thirty Negroes who were shot for resistance.[13]

In the early days at Port Royal the missionaries heard many such stories. When all possible allowance is made for exaggeration, understandable mistakes, and even for the possibility that Negroes met death by accident while hiding in burning cotton-houses, the sheer weight of the evidence leads to the belief that many white men were willing to go to extreme lengths to retrieve their human property. James Petigru, following the Port Royal story from Charleston, heard of a planter who had burned all the buildings on his plantation, including all stores of corn and cotton, "and by so doing compelled his negroes to follow him, as they were on an island without food and shelter."[14]

The masters' problems were by no means over if they succeeded in recovering their slave property. Petigru wrote, "They have to find new homes, and provide for their people for a whole year, while the abandonment of their crops just harvested leaves them penniless." For men in the Confederate army, obliged to conduct these affairs through their wives and overseers, the problem was acute. Sometimes, when hiring out failed and there were no funds to meet financial pressures, the sale of slaves was the only answer.[15]

Masters who owned slaves on the periphery of the territory held by the Union forces were faced with the possible loss of all their slaves through running away. John Berkeley Grimball, who owned slaves and plantations in Beaufort and Colleton Districts, recorded in his diary for the early days of March in 1862 the gradual depopulation of his estates. The forty-eight slaves who stayed, including the old and sick, had their reward at the end of the season in being sold for the round figure of $820 each.[16] Some masters relied upon severe punishment to discourage running away. When Ralph Elliott frustrated the escape of his father's slaves from Oak Lawn, he had two of the leaders sold in Charleston, and "the others were punished by

[13] Du Pont to Henry Winter Davis, December 9, [18]61, Du Pont MSS; New York *Tribune,* December 7, 1861; Holland (ed.), *Towne,* p. 27.

[14] James Petigru Carson, *Life, Letters and Speeches of James Louis Petigru* (Washington, D. C., 1920), p. 414.

[15] *Ibid.,* p. 416; John Jenkins to his wife, Marcy, January 1, 1863, and April 10, 1863, John Jenkins MSS, South Caroliniana Library, Columbia, South Carolina.

[16] John Berkeley Grimball MS diary, March 3, 8, 14, 25, 1862; December 17, 1862, Grimball MSS, Southern Historical Collection, Chapel Hill.

whips and hand-cuffing." Every night they were chained and watched while Elliott waited for the danger to pass.[17]

But the danger did not pass. To William Elliott the Negroes seemed "utterly demoralized" by Yankee propaganda. The missionaries saw it differently. The streams of Negroes were coming out of the interior as a result of their total dissatisfaction with the "patriarchal institution." Generations of servitude had not stamped out of these people the desire to do as they pleased, although any real understanding of the responsibilities of freedom must have been, for most of them, very remote. E. L. Pierce wrote, in a moment of insight, that "the slave is unknown to all, even to himself, while the bondage lasts." Not even the keenest outside observer, "much less the master can measure the capacities and possibilities of the slave, until the slave himself is transmuted to a man."[18]

He might have added that the moment of freedom revealed the essence of ownership as well. The barbaric behavior of certain of the masters was probably no surprise to the Negroes who had been their slaves. A slave's life was one long lesson in accommodation to his master, and the slaves *did* recognize their own economic value. The missionaries, on the other hand, demonstrated occasionally a real sense of shock at the more severe aspects of the slave system as it was exercised in the old Sea Island region. There were plantations where nearly every Negro's back showed the marks of whipping, and the testimony of the Negroes against certain of the old owners was remarkably consistent. Occasionally, the discovery of a revealing letter in the correspondence of the vanished white people bolstered the verdict of the Negroes. The missionaries heard again and again the same condemnation of certain cruel men and virtually unanimous praise of others.[19]

The Negroes of the islands, wrote Edward Pierce, "had become an abject race, more docile and submissive than those of any other locality." Nowhere else had "the deterioration from their native manhood been carried so far. . . ." Pierce was by no means alone in this conclusion, for all the missionaries were struck with certain childish qualities manifested by many of the Negroes.[20] Elizabeth Botume described a class of young adults:

*They rolled up their eyes and scratched their heads when puzzled, and every line in their faces was in motion. If any one missed a word, or gave a wrong answer, he looked very grave. But whenever a correct answer was given, especially if it seemed difficult, they laughed aloud, and reeled about,*

[17] William Elliott to his son, William Elliott, August 25, 1862, Elliott-Gonzales MSS.

[18] Pierce, "The Freedmen at Port Royal," *Atlantic Monthly,* XII (September, 1863), 301.

[19] Towne MS diary, May 23, June 13, 16, 1862; Pearson (ed.), *Letters,* pp. 31, 79, 206; William F. Allen MS diary, January 11, 1864, pp. 90–91, typescript copy.

[20] Pierce, "The Freedmen at Port Royal," *Atlantic Monthly,* XII (September, 1863), 300.

*hitting each other with their elbows. Such "guffaws" could not be tolerated in regular school hours. They joked each other like children; but, unlike them, they took all good-naturedly.*[21]

A superintendent concluded that the Negroes were entirely dependent, lacking in initiative, and that they needed "the positive ordering that a child of five or ten years of age requires." The sum of these observations added up to a picture of the personality known in American literature as "Sambo," the plantation slave, "docile but irresponsible, loyal but lazy, humble but chronically given to lying and stealing."[22]

But it is well to remember that although "Sambo" finds many illustrations in the observations of the teachers on the islands, he remains a *statistical* concept, and the record contains as many stories of protest, disloyalty to the late masters, and manly independence as of servile acquiescence. The extent to which the personality of the common field hand had been fundamentally altered by the experience of slavery finds a good test in his response to the opportunities offered by the new order inaugurated in the wake of the Northern occupation. The first reaction can be found in the large numbers of slaves willing to risk severe punishment and even death by running away from their masters. The wild sacking of Beaufort and the plantation houses and the complete destruction of the cotton gins show a bitter and long dammed-up hostility that, if perhaps childish in its discharge, is yet remarkably similar to the venting of spleen demonstrable among more "civilized" peoples. Other and more positive tests as to the fundamental damage to the slaves' personality would be provided as time went on in the success, or lack thereof, of the missionaries' labors to make the people self-reliant.

A more probable and immediate explanation of the obsequious and infantile behavior of the majority of slaves who demonstrated childish traits is that playing "Sambo" had its rewards and that failing to play him incurred many risks. That the role could be one of conscious hypocrisy is illustrated by the case of Elijah Green. This ancient veteran of slavery remembered with rancor, many long years after his freedom came, having been obliged to give an affectionate endorsement of the new brides and grooms who joined his master's family, whether he liked them or not.[23]

The main effect of slavery was a thick residue of accumulated habits and responses that a slave child learned early in life. It was a culture, in short, that invested its members with a number of character traits useful in slavery but unbecoming in free men. The extent to which these traits developed in an individual slave depended in part upon the class to which he belonged. It has been a general assumption that more enlightenment and

[21] Elizabeth Hyde Botume, *First Days Among the Contrabands* (Boston, 1893), p. 96.

[22] Holland (ed.), *Towne*, p. 9; Elkins, *Slavery, A Problem in American Institutional and Intellectual Life* (Chicago, 1959), p. 82.

[23] Slave Narrative Collection, XIV, Part II, 198, in Rare Book Room, Library of Congress.

self-respect were to be found among house servants and the Negroes of the towns than among field slaves. The common corollary, however, that these "Swonga" people, as they were denominated by the field hands, also possessed a greater spirit of *independence* is, at the very least, a debatable point. They had merely absorbed more of the white man's culture, and they paid for it in daily contacts with the "superior" beings whose very presence was a reminder of their own inferior status. Sometimes the loyalty of a well-treated house servant could make war on the very notion of independence. There is considerable evidence to support the idea that, while the Swonga people had perhaps more self-esteem and were better dressed, the field hands had more self-reliance. It would be hard to conceive of a more independent spirit than that shown by the six strapping sons of "Mom Peg." They had all been field slaves, and they defied an overseer to whip them. When one brother was threatened, all took to the woods in a body and had to be guaranteed immunity before returning. Described as "tall and handsome," the brothers held "high rank in church and council" and were to enjoy a bright future in freedom. On the other hand, Laura Towne met two women in Beaufort, formerly house servants, who assured her that they would not have run away from their masters except for their desire not to be separated from their kin. But they were already feeling nostalgic for the old ways, with the coming of April, for in the spring they had always come to Beaufort with their masters' families and had had "such gay times." They hoped the teachers would not go away, for it "seemed like they couldn't be happy widout white ladies 'roun.'"[24]

The story of Lydia Smalls is most instructive. When she was a girl, her mistress had taken her away from field work on the Ashdale plantation on Ladies Island and had brought her to Beaufort, where she became a trusted house servant. When Lydia's own son was growing up as a pampered pet in the Prince Street house of their master, Henry McKee, Lydia was afraid he did not realize the meaning of slavery or the full indignity of his position. Ever a rebel in her heart, Lydia forced her son to watch a slave being whipped in the yard of the Beaufort jail. Then young Robert went himself to stay for a time at the Ashdale plantation. He had seen the seemingly dull and cringing plantation people every week when he had come with his master to bring their rations. He never understood much about them, however, until the day he stayed and his master rode away. The apathetic people suddenly found the spirit to grumble and complain heartily about their diet. It was on the plantation that Robert Smalls first heard about Frederick Douglass and decided that he too would become a free man.[25]

For many a servant, a close personal tie with a good master or mis-

---

[24] Holland (ed.), *Towne*, p. 225; Towne MS diary, April 17, 1862.

[25] Dorothy Sterling, *Captain of the Planter, The Story of Robert Smalls* (New York, 1958), pp. 16, 24, 29–31. Written in a style to appeal to youthful readers, this biography of a prominent Negro leader in South Carolina Reconstruction politics is based upon sound research and is factual in essential details.

tress could go a long way toward reconciliation to a dependent condition. "Henry," formerly cook for Mrs. Thomas Aston Coffin, spoke affectionately of his former mistress to Harriet Ware and readily seized upon Miss Ware's offer to write to Mrs. Coffin for him. He had hesitated to make the request himself for fear "they wouldn't think it right to have anything to do with the old people—'but she's a Nort' lady, you know, Ma'am,'" he said to Miss Ware, "'a beautiful lady, I would serve her all my life.'" When Thomas Chaplin's slave "Anthony" died, Chaplin wrote, perhaps a little self-consciously, "he is regretted by many—white and black—I miss him more than I would any other negro that I own," and added, "Peace be to his soul."[26]

Anthony had belonged, as a "driver," to the uppermost rank of plantation life. These foremen and the skilled laborers enjoyed an even more exalted position than the house servants. The driver held the most responsible position a slave could occupy. His job included maintaining order in the quarters as well as calling the Negroes to work, assigning the daily tasks, and seeing that the work was well done. That the driver was sometimes a cruel despot, as he was frequently portrayed in abolition literature, is undeniable; but there is little evidence in the Sea Island story to indicate that he was commonly such. If the driver developed a fine knowledge of farming and enjoyed his master's confidence over a period of years, their relationship could become one of mutual esteem and friendly respect, contrasting most favorably with the often unstable and transient connections between plantation owners and their overseers.

Isaac Stephens, "master servant" to William Elliott, was able to keep his master informed of the condition of the crops on Elliott's numerous estates while the latter was on extended trips from home. He had been certain enough of his own standing to pass judgment on the relative qualities of the white overseers at the several plantations and to exchange social information with his master about the family at home:

*Old Mistress and Miss Mary are quite well. I was quite sorry that some of my young mistress and masters wear [sic] not in Beaufort to enjoy some of the fine dinners and Tea partys [sic] old Mistress has been giving for her grandchildren. . . .*

*Master will be so kind as to give my love to my wife—all her friends are well—and say howdey to her and myself just like an old Buck—hearty and prime. . . .*[27]

---

[26] Pearson (ed.), *Letters*, pp. 206–207; Chaplin MS diary, May 5, 1850.

[27] Isaac Stephens to William Elliott, October 22, 1849, Elliott-Gonzales MSS. Another revealing letter in the same collection is that of "Jacob" to Elliott, July 3, 1860, showing that Jacob was carrying on the farming operations, borrowing necessary supplies on his master's credit, asking Elliott's advice, and requesting the assistance of a carpenter. Of all the evangels, Philbrick alone gave the "drivers" a poor rating on intelligence and responsibility. See his letter to Atkinson, June 15, 1863, Atkinson MSS. On a number of Sea Island plantations the drivers served as de facto overseers, for the planters seem to have disre-

There must have been few Negroes on the islands who had enjoyed so relaxed a relationship with their masters, or who had had such opportunities to develop judgment and leadership. The evangels could count on these few, however, to provide an example for the rest in making an adaptation to freedom.

There had even been a few opportunities for slaves to develop special talents outside the economic hierarchy of the plantation. Religious leaders enjoyed special standing with their fellows, and women sometimes achieved status as midwives. For all the slaves there was a small economic venture open in the raising of poultry and a little garden crop, or perhaps a pig. The surplus was sold to the master for cash; occasionally, it was sold outside the plantation by the slave himself. Although a statute against trading with slaves existed, it was usually ignored.[28] Outside these limited interests, there was nothing for most slaves but the dull routine of the cotton field. The real trouble with slavery as a "school" for anything was that the institution provided so few directions in which to grow and so much necessity to conform.

The Negro child on a large Sea Island plantation began learning how to be a slave almost from the moment of birth. In view of the generally acknowledged impact of early childhood experiences upon personality, the restrictions of a slave's childhood may go further than institutions or laws to explain certain of "Sambo's" failings. When the slave mother emerged from her confinement and returned to the field at the end of the third or fourth week, she saw her baby in the day only long enough for feeding and had very little time for the affectionate caressing so important for the development of the child's personality and security.[29] On the other hand, the mother herself could not experience the happiest aspects of motherhood when the child was merely an additional drain upon a tired body. The missionaries frequently observed that numbers of mothers on the great plantations appeared to demonstrate very little affection for their offspring. Arthur Sumner complained that the children "are invariably spoken to in harsh and peremptory tones" by adult Negroes and were "whipped unmercifully for the least offence." A stern system called for stern discipline, and an old Negro woman asked Elizabeth Botume "What the Lord Almighty make trees for if they ain't fur lick boy chillen?" Toys were little known, and

---

garded freely the statute stipulating the residence of a white person on plantations of more than ten working slaves. See Lorenzo Dow Turner, *Africanisms in the Gullah Dialect* (Chicago, 1949), p. 4; Slave Narrative Collection, XIV, Part II, 88.

[28] Guion Griffis Johnson, *A Social History of the Sea Islands* (Chapel Hill, 1930), p. 86; H. M. Henry, *The Police Control of the Slave in South Carolina* (Emory, Virginia, 1914), p. 80; Richard Fuller and Francis Wayland, *Domestic Slavery Considered as a Scriptural Institution* (New York, 1845), p. 151.

[29] Frances Anne Kemble, *Journal of a Residence* on a Georgian Plantation in 1838–1839 (London, 1863), p. 220; "Pat has baby [and] will be out on Monday as it's a month old today." Fripp MS diary, June 13, 1857; Towne MS diary, August 25, 1863.

games usually took the form of fighting and wrestling in lieu of more constructive play. But the numbers of tender stories of maternal love show that,
even among the victims of such a severe regimen, the human instincts
served to soften the general harshness of the lives of children.[30]

When the mother returned to the field the child usually went, on the
large Sea Island plantations, to a nursery, where he joined numbers of other
children under the supervision of superannuated "Maumas" or grannies.
Frederika Bremer pronounced this system "repulsive." She had seen "sometimes as many as sixty or seventy or even more [small children] together,
and their guardians were a couple of old Negro witches who with a rod of
reeds kept rule over these poor little black lambs, who with an unmistakable
expression of fear and horror shrunk back whenever the threatening witches
came forth, flourishing their rods." Aunt Jane Grant recalled in her old age
some vivid details of her childhood in Beaufort. The little children of her
establishment were cared for by an old mauma who fed them thus: "Dey'd
clean off a place on de ground near de washpot where dey cooked de peas,
clean it off real clean, den pile de peas out dere on de ground for us to eat."[31]

For fortunate slave children there came a time when they might, as
the chosen playmates of the master's children, be able to take a part in the
free country life about them. Sometimes the white parents objected that
"the little negroes are ruining the children," but sooner or later the democracy of childhood broke down parental resolutions. Mrs. Thomas Chaplin
might complain of the "badness" little Jack was teaching her son Ernest,
but shortly she would see the two riding off on the same horse to gather
wild plums or mulberries. The slave child's formal education would consist
of learning the catechism, on plantations where that was deemed important,
and he was instructed that his duty to his master was faithful work and that
he was responsible to God for a good performance.[32] An important lesson
most small slaves learned early was their relation to the white race in general and to the master in particular. Little Jane, of the Robert Oswald household, learned it the day she objected to calling her mistress's small son
"Marse" and was sent around to Wilcox's store for a cowhide switch.[33]

The plantation child quickly grasped other things also. He learned

---

[30] Arthur Sumner to Nina Hartshorn, July 9, 1863, Arthur Sumner MSS; Botume, *First Days*,
pp. 257, 253; EHP in *Third Series of Extracts from Letters* (Boston, 1863); Towne MS diary,
April 5, 1864. Despite commenting upon severe discipline, Miss Botume thought that with
Negro mothers the "maternal feeling was intensified." See her *First Days*, p. 163.

[31] Frederika Bremer, *Homes of the New World; Impressions of America* (New York, 1854),
II, 449; Slave Narrative Collection, XIV, Part II, 179.

[32] Chaplin MS diary, May 10, 1854; Nehemiah Adams, *A South Side View of Slavery* (Boston,
1854), p. 85; Fripp MS diary, March 3, 1857; Rebecca Grant recalled that the children were
given Sabbath School lessons every Sunday morning on the porch of the master's house,
where they were taught the catechism and "to be faithful to the missus and Marsa's work
like you would do your heavenly Father's work." Slave Narrative Collection, XIV, Part II, 185.

[33] *Ibid.*, p. 179.

how the slave enjoys life a little more at his master's expense. Thomas Chaplin wrote with some sense of resignation:

*More robery* [sic].—*discovered that my little rascal William, who I had minding the crows off the watermellons* [sic] *had been the worst crow himself, and does the thing quite sistematically* [sic]. *He turns over a mellon, cuts a hole on the under side large enough to admit his hand, eats out the inside, when he finds a ripe one, then turns the mellon back again, not breaking it off the vine, there it lays, looking as sound as ever. No one would suppose it hollow. In picking some—we found no less than 23 or 4 in this fix. Cunning, very.*[34]

It is not surprising that the missionaries should have found the former slaves irresponsible. At no point in his passage to adulthood did the slave youth have the experience of learning to accept responsibility. The peculiar circumstances of his life became most apparent at the time of marriage. Nehemiah Adams was usually blind to the worst aspects of slave life, but even he saw clearly that slavery was inimical to the family as an institution, and he wrote particularly of "the annihilation . . . of the father in the domestic relations of the slaves. . . ." The master supplied the necessaries of life, and what else there was to receive was far more likely to be in the power of the wife to dispense than in that of her husband. The cabin was regarded as hers, and the small poultry and garden operations were usually her primary responsibility. She converted the yard goods into clothing for herself and her family and did the cooking. Even the children were acknowledged to be the mother's and were usually known by her name, as in the case of "Binah's Toby," or "Moll's Judy."[35] Unless he had a friendly alliance with some good-natured woman, the male slave did without many conveniences. Laura Towne commented drily that the liberated Negro men were better satisfied about being released from domestic tyranny than about any other aspect of their freedom. It is worth mentioning that the family picture under slavery was actually a reinforcement of the West African family pattern, arising, as it had there, from the polygynous household. The individual wives in the African community no doubt had to bow to the will of the husband; but within her own hut, and to her own children, the mother had been the omnipotent reality. Rivalry for preferences and honors to her children had provided the African woman with political outlets not unknown in the courts of Europe.[36]

Despite the legal and social obstacles, marriage had a reasonable chance of lasting if it was honored and respected by the owners of the principals. Thomas B. Chaplin complained of the "tomfoolery" of his wife,

[34] Chaplin MS diary, July 10, 1854.

[35] Adams, *South-Side View,* p. 85; Elkins, *Slavery,* p. 130; Johnson, *Social History,* p. 137.

[36] Melville J. Herskovits, *The Myth of the Negro Past* (Boston, 1958), pp. 64–65.

who took care to make a special occasion of the double wedding of her two maids, "Eliza" and "Nelly." The girls were married by "Robert," the spiritual leader of the plantation, and the party was provided with "a grand supper." "They had out," Chaplin complained, "my crockery—Tables, chairs, candle-sticks, and I suppose everything else they wanted." Then there was some of Chaplin's "good liquor made into a bowl of punch" for the guests. Twenty-seven years later, Chaplin penciled into the margin of his diary that the two girls were still alive, well, and still married to "the very same husbands." Many owners did not devote this interest to their slave marriages, but some element of formality was usually present.[37] Without legal protection, however, marriages suffered real stress under the conditions of slavery, which often promoted transient unions and easy partings. The religious leaders among the slaves complained often of unchastity and tried, sometimes without good effect, to bring moral suasion to the aid of family stability.[38] An understanding of this situation requires only the remembrance that the social and legal forces at work to bind together unhappy nineteenth-century white couples were largely inoperative with the slaves. One major problem for the evangels would clearly be to strengthen the Negro family, encouraging the fathers to assume hitherto unknown responsibilities.

So many of the faults of the slave had been perversions of laudable impulses, impulses of protest; those who learned them best frequently comprised the most spirited people on a plantation. Even Master Chaplin had a species of respect for his small slave who had thought of a smart way to steal watermelons. Grown slaves learned how to gain a little time for themselves by idling or pretending illness, and as often as not the matter simply had to be faced with resignation. "Jim and Judge both lying up today," complained their master, "they will have their time out."[39]

When a man carried protest to the passionate length of running away, he had to be prepared for extreme punishment. Sweet must have been the knowledge to a "prime" runaway, even while reflecting on the bitter cost, that he was depriving his master of a week's hard work in the cotton field. Overt rebellion indeed existed, but it was for the few. Most slaves had learned to accept their condition, as one evangel said, just as "sand receives the cannon-ball, neither casting it off nor being shattered by it."[40] For the majority, the humdrum and safe satisfactions of a well-timed

---

[37] Chaplin MS diary, December 26, 1849. Chaplin's subsequent notation in pencil is dated "Christmas, 1876." This slave wedding no doubt formed a part of the holiday celebration on the Chaplin plantation; Olmsted, *Seaboard Slave States*, p. 449.

[38] Adams, *South-Side View*, p. 88. See Kemble, *Journal*, p. 263, for indictment of complaisance of masters and overseers toward promiscuity among slaves.

[39] Chaplin MS diary, May 21, 1857; see also entries May 10 and July 9, 1850.

[40] [Gannett and Hale], "The Freedmen at Port Royal," *North American Review*, CI (July, 1865), 7. For runaways and their punishments, see Chaplin MS diary, November 27, 1853; David Gavin MS diary, July 4, 1857; Towne MS diary, June 13, 1845.

lie, petty theft, or feigned illness had seemed the appropriate defenses of reasonable beings. This mood permeates a folk story that was long told on St. Helena, of an old slave who had never worked in his life because his master was convinced he was a cripple. His master caught him one day, however, strumming his banjo to the words:

> I was fooling my master seventy-two years,
> And I'm fooling him now.

The enraged master prepared to whip the old man, but the timely magic of a "Negro doctor" intervened. "When his master started to whip him, none of the licks touch: And he had freedom."[41]

Frederika Bremer wrote after her visit to the Sea Islands just before the war that she had not found a single plantation where the master was able to advance the social well-being of the slaves. Even the efforts of progressive men who tried to institute some means of self-regulation among the slaves had merely achieved a superior form of discipline. She concluded somberly, "In the darkness of slavery I have sought for the moment of freedom with faith and hope in the genius of America. It is no fault of mine that I have found the darkness so great and the work of light as yet so feeble in the slave states."[42]

There was hardly a plantation that had not a harsh old tale of abuse, and on many the abject fear the slaves had of all white men said all that needed to be told. In the final analysis, however, it was the institution in all its aspects, knowing and foolish, kind and cruel, that had created the prevailing problems confronting Gideon's Band: an exaggerated attitude of dependency; a weak sense of family; an inevitable tendency toward the classic faults of the slave—lying, theft, and irresponsibility. As one Gideonite clearly saw, the barbarism of exceptional slave masters did not really signify much in the total picture. "The real wrong in slavery did not affect the body; but it was a curse to the soul and mind of the slave. The aim of the master was to keep down every principle of manhood and growth, and this held for good and bad planters alike, and was the natural growth of slavery itself."[43] And that was why, despite the moving and testimonial exceptions of strength and character found among the slaves, the larger number of the liberated Negroes of the islands constituted, according to Gannett, "a race of stunted, misshapen children, writhing from the grasp of that people, which, in so many respects, is foremost of the age."[44]

[41] Elsie Clews Parsons, *Folk-Lore of the Sea Islands, South Carolina* ("Memoirs of the American Folk-Lore Society," XVI [Cambridge, 1923], 62).

[42] Bremer, *Homes of the New World,* II, 492.

[43] Clipping from the Bristol [England] *Post,* October 23, 1865, in the Gannett MSS, Box XXVIII. The quotation is from a speech Gannett made in Bristol after the war.

[44] [Gannett and Hale], "The Freedmen at Port Royal," *North American Review,* CI (July, 1865), 1.

## SUGGESTIONS FOR
## FURTHER READING

**B** ECAUSE of its sympathy for the antebellum South and its racist assumptions, the best way to begin understanding southern slavery is by reading *Ulrich B. Phillips, *American Negro Slavery* (New York, 1918). The revision of Phillips' work began with Richard Hofstadter, "Ulrich B. Phillips and the Plantation Legend," *Journal of Negro History,* XXXIX (April 1944). As noted in the introduction to this chapter Phillips' views of slavery have been the starting point for Kenneth M. Stampp, *The Peculiar Institution: Slavery in the Ante-bellum South* (New York, 1956); *Stanley M. Elkins, *Slavery, A Problem in American Institutional and Intellectual Life* (2d rev. ed.; Chicago, 1968), and *Eugene D. Genovese, *The Political Economy of Slavery: Studies in the Economy and Society of the Slave South* (New York, 1965). The Genovese article reprinted here appears in *Civil War History,* XIII (December 1967) with other articles on the Elkins thesis by Aline Kraditor, Christopher Lasch, and George Frederickson; a forthcoming book edited by Ann J. Lane will include still other discussions of the Elkins thesis with a response by him. An evaluation of Genovese's support of Phillips' work, by Elkins, Stampp, and David Potter, is in *Agricultural History,* XLI (October 1967).

Among the many state studies of slavery, the most informative are *Charles S. Sydnor, *Slavery in Mississippi* (New York, 1933) and Chase C. Mooney, *Slavery in Tennessee* (Bloomington, Ind., 1957). Even more specialized, and thereby avoiding some of the dangers of excessive generalization is Edward W. Phifer, "Slavery in Microcosm: Burke County, North Carolina," *Journal of Southern History,* XXVIII (May 1962). Ideological justifications for slavery and racism are explored in *William R. Stanton, *The Leopard's Spots: Scientific Attitudes Toward Race in America, 1815–1859* (Chicago, 1959) and Walter Fisher, "Physicians and Slavery in the Antebellum *Southern Medical Journal,"* *Journal of the History of Medicine and Allied Science,* XXIII (1968).

The most detailed study of slave resistance is *Herbert Aptheker, *American Negro Slave Revolts* (New York, 1943); it has been severely criticized by Genovese and defended by its author in *Studies on the Left,* VI (November–December 1966). The excerpt from Rose's book and the Bauers' article, selections 8 and 9, should be supplemented by Marion D. de B. Kilson, "Toward Freedom: An Analysis of Slave Revolts in the United States," *Phylon,* XXV (Summer 1964). The causes and effects of specific slave revolts are analyzed in Richard C. Wade, "The Vesey Plot: A Reconsideration," *Journal of Southern History,* XXX (May 1964); *William W. Freehling, *Prelude to Civil War: The Nullification Crisis in South Carolina, 1816–1830* (New York, 1966); and F. Roy Johnson, *The Nat Turner Insurrection* (Murfreesboro, N. C., 1966).

The pioneering study of comparative slavery is *Frank Tannenbaum, *Slave and Citizen: The Negro in the Americas* (New York, 1946). The Tannenbaum–Elkins thesis is challenged in Arnold A. Sio, "Interpretations of Slavery," *Comparative Studies in Society and History,* VII (April 1965) and Marvin Harris, *Patterns of Race in the Americas* (New York, 1964). *David Brion Davis, *The Problem of Slavery in Western Culture* (Ithaca, N. Y., 1966) further criticizes this thesis and analyzes slavery from antiquity to the end of the eighteenth century; it also con-

* An asterisk indicates that the book is available in paperback.

tains the best bibliography on comparative slavery. The thesis is defended in Herbert S. Klein, *Slavery in the Americas: A Comparative Study of Cuba and Virginia* (Chicago, 1967). West Indian slavery is described in Elsa V. Goveia, *Slave Society in the British Leeward Islands at the End of the Eighteenth Century* (New Haven, Conn., 1965). Valuable sources of material on South American slavery for comparison with North American slavery are Gilberto Freyre, *The Masters and the Slaves: A Study in the Development of Brazilian Civilization* (New York, 1946); C. R. Boxer, *Race Relations in the Portuguese Colonial Empire, 1415–1825* (Oxford, 1963); his *The Golden Age of Brazil, 1690–1750* (Berkeley, Calif., 1962); and *Stanley J. Stein, *Vassouras: A Brazilian Coffee County, 1850–1890* (Cambridge, Mass., 1957). Summarizing many of the conflicting views about North and South American slavery is Carl N. Degler, "Slavery in Brazil and the United States: An Essay in Comparative History," *American Historical Review*, LXXV (April 1970).

Sources of narratives by slaves are described in Norman R. Yetman, "The Background of the Slave Narrative Collection," *American Quarterly*, XIX (Fall 1967). A biography of the most renowned fugitive slave is *Benjamin Quarles, *Frederick Douglass* (Washington, D.C. 1948). Douglass' own autobiography appears in innumerable reprints. Among the most revealing fugitive-slave accounts are *Benjamin Drew (ed.), *A North-side View of Slavery* (Reading, Mass., 1969); *An Autobiography of The Reverend Josiah Henson* (Reading, Mass., 1969); *Austin Steward: Twenty-Two Years a Slave and Forty Years a Freeman* (Reading, Mass., 1969); and *The Narrative of William Wells Brown: A Fugitive Slave* (Reading, Mass., 1969). The historic value of slave songs is described in *Miles Mark Fisher, *Negro Slave Songs in the United States* (New York, 1953).

# &CHAPTER FOUR&
# Free Men in a Slave Nation

&S OUTHERN slavery obviously was an essential factor in shaping white-black relations before the Civil War and has remained a fundamental part of the black heritage, but it also is imperative to examine the antebellum legacy of freedom. How free black men thought and acted and how they were treated by whites may be just as important as the behavior of slaves and slaveowners. Slave docility and resistance reveal much about American slavery but not very much about the relationship of free black men to each other or to slaves. How they responded to their free status and how they related to whites were as revealing as slave behavior. And although there were free black men living in the slave South, the status of free northern Afro-Americans was more significant for future race relations. How northern whites dealt with free blacks during the antebellum era becomes especially crucial in seeking to understand how they subsequently acted toward emancipated slaves and the entire issue of black freedom during and after Reconstruction.

Significantly, the most prominent black historians usually have written about free black men, not about slaves. This can be explained, perhaps, by their desire to destroy the widespread myth that all Afro-Americans were descended from slaves and thus were unaccustomed to the responsibilities of freedom. The black heritage has deep roots in freedom and has expressed itself by the action of free black men. In selection 11 John Hope Franklin, the most prominent present-day Afro-American historian, writes about the life of free black people in antebellum North Carolina where slavery never attained the importance it did in many other southern states. He discusses the presence of a nonslave black yeomanry with legal rights to possess land and personal property. Readers should especially note his disclosure that "at no time during the antebellum period were free Negroes in North Carolina without slaves."

Closely associated with the study of slavery has been the belief that an elaborate network of white northern sympathizers assisted great numbers of slaves to escape to freedom in the North and Canada. Most Americans, both in the North and South, believed in the extensiveness of this Underground Railroad to the point that the Fugitive Slave Act became a major part of the Compromise of 1850. Fiercely disagreeing on the desirability of the act, they did agree that it would eliminate the opportunity for many thousands of slaves to escape from bondage. Larry Gara, in selection 12, challenges the existence of an Underground Railroad as it was pictured in the antebellum era and in subsequent times. Gara, among other things, has uncovered the role of northern black men aiding escaping fugitives and thereby reveals their active response to the plight of the slaves. Readers should think about why North and South accepted the myth of the Underground Railroad and why the myth has remained unchallenged for so long.

Slaves who succeeded in escaping to the North soon learned that freedom was not synonomous with equality. Fearing an increase in their black population, many northern states closest to the South legislated to prohibit or discourage the influx of black people. From 1820 to the Civil War every new state constitution restricted black suffrage. Ironically, as suffrage was extended for white men in the 1820s, many black citizens were disenfranchised. Some 93 percent of the northern black population as of 1840 resided in states where suffrage was prohibited to them or had special requirements. Five states prevented court testimony by black men in cases involving whites. Only in Massachusetts could they serve as jurors. Segregated public schools existed in almost all states. These conditions and the continuation of slavery in the South provided the impetus for black political action and militancy in the North.

The wide variety of tactics used to seek changes in the racial status quo are analyzed in selections 13 and 14 by Howard H. Bell and Benjamin Quarles. Black responses to antislavery political parties and to the radical Garrisonian allegiance to a nonviolent and nonpolitical antislavery movement reveal dilemmas for black activism. Advocacy of black emigration from the United States by Henry Highland Garnet and Martin Delany exemplified the pessimism of some free Afro-American leaders who believed that neither the North nor the South would ever become a congenial place for their people to live. Readers should give special attention to the relationship of free black activists to their white allies and to the problems of working with integrated organizations.

# 11

## THE FREE NEGRO IN THE ECONOMIC LIFE OF ANTE-BELLUM NORTH CAROLINA
### John Hope Franklin

IN a state that was as decidedly rural as ante-bellum North Carolina, and where the majority of the free Negroes lived in the rural areas,[1] it was only natural that most of them made their living from the soil. The majority of the free Negro apprentices were bound out to learn the trade of a farmer, and upon reaching manhood they expected to pursue this occupation.[2] Since, moreover, it was extremely difficult for free Negroes to secure training in the skilled trades, many who may have had the inclination were forced into other fields. They *had* to make a living. Tradition and their meager training compelled the majority of the free Negroes to seek their living from the soil.

North Carolina was never one of the chief slaveholding states. In numbers, its slaves were fewer than those of her neighbor states of Virginia, South Carolina, and Georgia.[3] As a matter of fact, sixty-seven percent of the slaveholding families held fewer than ten slaves in 1860, while seventy-two percent of North Carolina's families held no slaves at all.[4] This suggests that in a state where the plantation system was only fairly well entrenched, the supply of slave labor was definitely limited. The farm labor in North Carolina was done not only by the slave but, in some areas, by the members of the white farming family, by white farm laborers, and by free Negro farm laborers.[5] In finding this work opportunity, the free Negro was extremely fortunate, and his labor was not as frequently rejected as it was in the more skilled occupations. Naturally there were objections to his presence on plantations where there were slaves, but these objections were more likely to be raised to the hiring of free Negroes on the neighbor's plantation than

John Hope Franklin, "The Free Negro in the Economic Life of Ante-Bellum North Carolina," *North Carolina Historical Review*, XIX (October 1942), pp. 359–375. Reprinted by permission of the publisher.

[1] Only 3,197, or scarcely ten percent, of the free Negroes lived in towns in 1860. Census Office, *The Population in 1860*, pp. 350–359.

[2] See the occupations of free Negro apprentices in the unpublished population schedules for the census of 1860. (Unless otherwise indicated, all manuscripts cited in this article are in the archives of the North Carolina Historical Commission, Raleigh.)

[3] Census Office, *Population in 1860*, pp. 214, 452, 518.

[4] Guion G. Johnson, *Ante-Bellum North Carolina*, p. 468 ff.

[5] In describing the small farmer (white) in ante-bellum North Carolina, Dr. Guion Johnson refers to this group as the largest single class of whites in the state, and continues, "Their farms were small, and they cultivated their own land with the assistance of their families and an occasional hired hand or slave." Johnson, *Ante-Bellum North Carolina*, p. 65.

on one's own. Though there may have been fears that the free Negro's presence on a slave plantation might cause insolence among the slaves as well as inspire desires of freedom among them, this did not prevent the white slaveholders from hiring free Negroes to perform some of the tasks from time to time.[6]

There was, moreover, an opportunity for the free Negro to secure seasonal work on the farms of North Carolinians who had no slaves at all. The yeoman frequently harbored violent antipathies for the slave system and would refuse to hire slave labor even when it was available. He was more likely to look for assistance, during rush seasons, among the poor landless whites or among the free Negroes. The large number of free Negro farm laborers in counties where there was little or no slaveholding seems to support this point of view. In Cabarrus County, for example, where the slave population was small, there were fourteen free Negro farm laborers in 1860 and only four free Negro farmers.[7]

Naturally there were more free Negro farm hands in counties where the free Negro population was large. These counties, incidentally, also had a large slave population. As field hands, drivers, and all-around laborers, free Negroes found work opportunities on the largest of plantations. It was not unusual for free Negroes to live on slave plantations and to participate in the life there. Some of them had slave wives or husbands, and the benevolent master frequently permitted them to live there together, hiring the services of the free person.[8] Thomas Newton of Craven County secured his freedom from his master, Benjamin Woods, and by continuing to work for him Newton was able to purchase his wife, who had been a slave on the same plantation.[9]

Of course the number of free Negro farm laborers varied from county to county. The number to be found in any particular county depended not only upon the scarcity or abundance of farm labor, slave or free, and the attitude of the whites toward free Negro labor, but also upon the mobility of the landless free Negro population. It was extremely difficult for free Negroes, although without the trappings which usually tie people to a particular location, to move from one place to another. The reluctance of the

[6] See the unpublished population schedules for the census of 1860. Many free Negro farm laborers were listed as living with white families. This is all the more remarkable in view of the fact that, in such instances, the white farmer was responsible for all the debts and obligations that were incurred by the free Negro.

[7] See the unpublished population schedules for the census of 1860. It is quite likely, moreover, that many of the free Negroes who gave their occupation as "common laborer" found work on the farms and may have been, more properly, "farm hands."

[8] See, for example, the unpublished population schedules for the census of 1860 (Wake County). It seems that such a practice was quite inconsistent with the point of view that the presence of free Negroes among slaves "contributes to excite and cherish a spirit of discontent and disorder among the slaves." Petition of the citizens of New Bern to the General assembly, December, 1831. MS. in the Legislative Papers for 1831–1832.

[9] Minutes of the Court of Pleas and Quarter Sessions for Craven County, March, 1811.

authorities to grant passes permitting free Negroes to move about[10] and the impecunious state of a majority of the free Negroes made it quite difficult for free Negro farm laborers to migrate even to the adjoining county. It was possible, therefore, for a newly freed Negro to live and die in an area that was least suited for his advancement.

With these facts in mind, it is interesting to observe the location of the bulk of the free Negro farm hands in ante-bellum North Carolina. Of the 1,746 free Negro farm hands in the state in 1860, more than one thousand were located in the seven eastern counties which constituted the stronghold of the slave system.[11] Halifax County alone had 384 free Negro farm hands, while Pasquotank County had 284. Thirty-one counties were without any free Negro farm hands at all, while 700 were scattered among the remaining forty-eight counties.[12]

A more interesting group of free Negroes who made their living from the soil were those who either rented land or owned land and planted their own crops. They may properly be called the free Negro yeomanry. It was possible for a free Negro to obtain permission from a white landowner to live on the latter's land and to cultivate a portion of it and share in the returns from his labor. This, however, was looked upon with disfavor, and white owners of land were discouraged in the practice. A law of 1827 required each white person to list all free Negroes living on his land and to be responsible for the taxes which might be levied on such free Negroes.[13] Free Negro tenants who showed a disposition to work and to shoulder their responsibilities could still convince landowners that they would not be a burden to them. The tax lists of various counties and the census reports bear witness to the fact that there were free Negro tenants on the lands of white persons down to the end of that period. In the tax list for Beaufort County in 1850, for example, A. Eborn, a free Negro, was listed as the tenant of John Cutter, white. One wealthy white farmer, R. H. Reddick of Lower Broad Creek, had fourteen free Negro tenants on his land and was responsible for $143.93 in taxes for them. In the same list, F. Hackey, a free Negro, was the tenant of Samuel Swan, white.[14] At the end of the period, despite the financial risks on the part of white land-

---

[10] After 1831 free Negroes desiring to go to other counties had to receive a license from the clerk of the Court of Pleas and Quarter Sessions of the county in which they resided. Laws, 1831–1832, p. 11.

[11] The seven counties were Granville, Halifax, Hertford, Northampton, Pasquotank, Perquimans, and Sampson.

[12] This information was taken from the unpublished population schedules for the census of 1860. Most of the counties with no free Negro farmhands were located in the western part of the state.

[13] Laws, 1827–1828, p. 21.

[14] MS in the County Records for Beaufort County, 1850 (Beaufort County Courthouse, Washington, N. C.).

owners, many free Negro tenants were still living on the land of white landowners.[15]

That the number of free Negroes who owned their farms was considerable can be seen in the real property columns of the unpublished population schedules of the census returns. Many of these individuals, like John Stanly of New Bern, had started with small holdings, and by thrift and business acumen had accumulated sizable holdings. They usually engaged in tobacco and cotton farming and marketed their crops in much the same way that other farmers in the state marketed theirs. By far the majority of the property owned by free Negroes was in the rural areas and was, of course, in the possession of free Negro farmers.

The free Negro farmer was generally in better circumstances than free Negroes in other areas of economic activity. In 1860 there were 1,047 free Negroes who gave their occupation as farmers. Of this number, approximately fifty percent possessed some real property. In some cases they did not own an amount sufficient for their purposes, but the figures seem to suggest that the free Negro was becoming a landowner. David Reynolds, a farmer of Halifax County, owned $3,000 worth of real property in 1860. J. A. Collins of Hyde County had $1,000 worth of real property at the same time. The well known Thomas Blacknall of Franklin County owned $6,000 worth of land. Of the fifty-three Negroes with property valued at more than $2,500 each in 1860, thirty-one were farmers.[16]

In North Carolina the free Negroes who made their living from the soil numbered approximately three thousand. Doubtless this number could be augmented considerably when one takes into account the number of minors and housewives who assisted their fathers, brothers, and husbands in the fields. That they constituted the most important element in the economic life of the free Negro in ante-bellum North Carolina in terms of numbers and holdings is clearly shown by the facts. For the most part they went their way unnoticed. The disproportionate part of the stage occupied by the free Negroes in other pursuits was the result of the focus of light thrown upon them in the more thickly settled communities. Meanwhile the free Negro farmer, living in the inarticulate and relatively sparsely settled countryside, steadily rose in economic independence and, consequently, in the respect—somewhat disquieted, perhaps—of his fellows.

At no time during the period before the Civil War was the free Negro's right to own real property questioned. He enjoyed all the protection in the matter of acquisition, transfer, devise, and descent that other citizens of North Carolina enjoyed. The records of the county courts indicate that free Negroes used them regularly for the purpose of recording changes in ownership of real and personal property. The following record is typical of many that were found in the minutes of the county court: "A deed from

[15] See the unpublished population schedules for the census of 1860.

[16] Unpublished population schedules for the census of 1860.

Ezra F. Holmes to Southey Kease (free Negro) was proved in open court by the oath of William T. Bryan a witness thereto ordered to be registered.'"[17]

Having once acquired land, the free Negro could be fairly certain that the courts would protect him during his period of possession. In 1838 Benjamin Curry, a free Negro of Guilford County, was driven off the property which he had owned for twelve years. Of the four white men charged with dispossessing Curry, one claimed that the free Negro had sold him his house, land, and five slave children, and that the transaction had been executed in a deed of trust between the two parties. At the trial the solicitor for the state objected to the deed as evidence, contending that it was a slick piece of extortion and that the free Negro did not intend to give up his land. The lower court convicted the defendants of having "riotously and routously" assembled to disturb the peace of the state and with force of arms trespassed upon the property of the free Negro.

The defendants appealed the case to the Supreme Court. After making a thorough review of the facts in the case and after listening to lengthy arguments from both sides, Judge Gaston, speaking for the Court, said:

*We are of the opinion that there was no error in the conviction of which the defendant complains. In cases where the law gives to the judges a discretion over the quantum of punishment, they may, with propriety, suspend the sentence [In this case, the principal defendant had received a fine of $100.] for the avowed purpose of affording the convicted an opportunity to make restitution to the person peculiarly aggrieved by his offense.*

*The judgment against the defendant is, therefore, reversed, and this opinion is to be certified to the Superior Court—for the County of Guilford, with directions to award sentence of fine or of fine and imprisonment against the defendant agreeably thereto and to the laws of the state.*[18]

The leniency of Judge Gaston was inspired by the defendant's having already restored the property to the free Negro. Though there was a reversal of the conviction, the case remains significant in that the Supreme Court went on record as being vigorously opposed to the abridgment of property rights even in the case of a free Negro.[19]

Free Negroes could sell or transfer their land at will as long at it was for a legal consideration. In 1833, for example, Benjamin Neale of Craven County sold one hundred acres of land, and the following indenture makes known the transaction:

---

[17] Minutes of the Court of Pleas and Quarter Sessions for Beaufort County, December, 1843 (Beaufort County Courthouse, Washington, N. C.).

[18] State v. John H. Bennett, 20 N. C., p. 135 ff.

[19] See also the case of State v. Emory, 51 N.C., p. 142, in which the Supreme Court held that a free Negro could not be forcibly ejected from the possession of a house.

*February 4, 1833*
*State of N.C.*
*County of Craven*
    *Be it known that Benjamin Neale (coloured man) for and in considera-
tion of the sum of fifty dollars to me paid in hand by William B. Masters of
the same State and County aforesaid, have bargained sold enfeoffed and
confirmed unto the same Wm. B. Masters his heirs and assigns forever a
certain parcel of land. . . . [A description of the land is given.] The said
Benjamin Neale purchased of Thomas Cooke dec. containing by estimation
one hundred acres be the same more or less. To have and to hold the said
piece or parcel of land with all the woods ways waters and every other
appurtenances thereunto belonging against the lawful claims of all and
every other person.*

*Benjamin   Neale*[20]

    The right of a free Negro to sell his property was confirmed by the
Supreme Court in a decision of 1843. A white man, Pearson, rented a small
tract of land for one year to Elijah Powell, a free Negro, who promised to
give him one-half of the corn crop. The Justice of the Peace gave Pearson
permission to sell Powell's crop. Powell asked that the sale be postponed
until after the corn was gathered. When the corn was sold, one Hare
objected, saying that he had already bought half of the crop from Powell.
Pearson denied that Powell could sell his share, contending that he was
only a servant. The Nash Superior Court said that Powell was a tenant and
could therefore dispose of his property as he pleased. In upholding this
view, the Supreme Court, through Judge Daniel, said:

*Even if Powell was a servant, the division had given him a share which all
would have to admit. The corn had been placed in the defendant's barn
upon the naked bailment for safe-keeping. The sale of it and the demand
by the purchaser put an end to the bailment.*[21]

    It was not at all unusual for free Negroes to direct the disposition of
their property through wills. Upon the death of the testator, the will was
recorded in the minutes of the county court and an executor was appointed
by the court. The minutes of the Beaufort County Court for 1843 give a
typical example:

*State of North Carolina*
*Beaufort County*
    *A paper writing purporting to be the last will and testament of John
Hambleton deceased (free Negro) was duly proved in open court to be the*

[20] MS in the James W. Bryan Papers (University of North Carolina Library, Chapel Hill, N. C.).
See also the deed from John and Rebecca Hambleton, free Negroes, to Churchill Moore, in
the Minutes of the Court of Pleas and Quarter Sessions for Beaufort County, December,
1842 (Beaufort County Courthouse, Washington, N. C.).

[21] Hare v. Pearson, 26 N. C., p. 62.

*last will and testament of said John Hambleton and duly executed so as to*
*pass seal on personal estate by the oath of John W. Latham the subscribing*
*witness thereto and ordered to be recorded and Edward Hyman the Executor*
*named therein was qualified as Executor.*[22]

An interesting case involving the will of a free Negro woman was
that of the aged Mary Green of Wilmington, who left all of her property
to a white attorney. She looked to him not only for counsel, the records
showed, but also for protection and occasionally for small sums of money.
In addition to these favors, he also collected rent on the property that had
been accumulated by the testator's free Negro husband. The only relative,
a niece, had received a house and lot from her aunt before she died. Upon
the advice of the free Negro husband, all the property was left to the white
attorney. The niece went into court and contended that her aunt had been
under "undue influence" and sought to have the will invalidated. Upon
losing the case in the New Hanover Superior Court, the niece appealed to
the Supreme Court. In upholding the decision of the lower court, Judge
Manly said,

*It seems that the legatee [Joshua Wright] and the decedent [Mary Green]*
*stood in relation of client and attorney patron and dependent, and the court*
*below—informs the jury that persons bearing these relations are to be sus-*
*pected and scrutinized more closely and carefully than dealings between*
*others. These relations, as facts pertinent to the issue—were submitted to*
*the jury with proper instructions. That was all, we think, the court was*
*authorized to do by the law of the land.*
    *We concur with the court below that undue influence must be*
*fraudulent and controlling and must be shown to the satisfaction of a jury,*
*in a court of law, upon an issue of devisavit vel nom.*[23]

Free Negroes, as other individuals, sometimes had difficulty in establishing their rightful claim to property left to them in a will. If, however,
their freedom could be established and if the circumstances under which
the will was made were valid, the free Negro could secure the necessary
protection in the courts of the state. In 1851, one Benjamin Dicken of
Edgecombe County died. His will directed his executor to free all of his
slaves and send them to some free state and divide $12,000 among them.
All except one woman, who died soon after, left the state. Her daughter,

---

[22] Minutes of the Court of Pleas and Quarter Sessions of Beaufort County, June, 1843
(Beaufort County Courthouse, Washington, N. C.). Free Negroes were sometimes appointed
executors, as in the case of Southey Keis, of Beaufort County, who in March, 1856, appeared
in court and qualified as the executor of the estate of Mary Keis. Minutes of the Court of
Pleas and Quarter Sessions of Beaufort County, March, 1856 (Beaufort County Courthouse,
Washington, N. C.).

[23] Wright v. Howe, 20 N. C., 318.

who had gone to Canada, claimed her mother's share of the estate for her and the other children. The executor claimed that the mother had not complied with the stipulation of the will since she had not left the state and therefore, that her heirs could claim no part of the money intended for her. Judge Pearson, of the Supreme Court, said that the removing of the Negroes was not a condition precedent to emancipation, but a condition subsequent, "by the non-performance of which they may forfeit their newly acquired freedom." The Judge was satisfied that the deceased free Negro woman had good intentions:

1.   We are satisfied that Mariah the mother of the plaintiff at the time of her death—was to all intents and purposes, a free woman, and had the capacity to take property and transmit it by succession to her personal representative.
2.   We are also satisfied that the children of Mariah were entitled to call upon her administrator to make distribution among them, as her next of kin—and we think it clear that all of her children are to be considered distributees.[24]

In one case several technicalities arose which made it difficult for a free Negro devisee to retain the town property that had been left her by a wealthy white man of Tarboro. In his will he said: "I give and devise to Mary Ann Jones, a free colored woman of the town of Tarboro and to her heirs and assigns forever, the lot of ground and house thereon erected on which she now lives." Since two lots belonging to the testator were adjacent, the executor interpreted the will literally and proceeded to take possession of the lot next to the one on which the devisee's house stood. Before his death, the testator had fenced in both lots together, and the free Negro woman used both lots for a garden and for other purposes. In 1860 Judge Manly of the Supreme Court awarded both lots to the estate of the free Negro woman—by that time deceased. He took the point of view that the gift to the free Negro woman "is not confined to the fifty yards square called a lot in the plan of the town, but extends at least to the lands enclosed and used in connection with the house." In the will the testator used the word "lot" to mean "parcel" or "piece."[25]

Perhaps the most interesting case of the period involving the inheritance of property by free Negroes arose in 1857. While a slave, a certain Miles married another slave. Afterward he was freed and subsequently purchased his wife. They had one child; then the wife was set free, and they had several other children. After this wife died, Miles married a free Negro woman by whom he had three children. When he died intestate, in 1857, a contest arose between the two sets of children over the division of the property. The children by the first wife claimed tenancy in common with

[24] Alvany, a free woman of color, v. Powell, 54 N. C., p. 34.

[25] Done on the demise of Mary Ann Jones v. Norfleet, 20, N. C., p. 365. A plan of the lots was included in the report of the court.

the children by the second wife. When the case came before the Supreme Court, that body denied that the children by the first wife had any valid claims:

*A slave cannot make a contract. Therefore, he cannot marry legally. Marriage is based upon contract. Consequently, the relation of "man and wife" cannot exist among slaves. Neither the first nor the others of the children by the first wife were legitimate. The parties after being freed ought to have married according to law; it is the misfortune of their children that they neglected or refused to do so, for no court can avert the consequences.*[26]

The possession of slaves by free Negroes was the only type of personal property holding that was ever questioned during the ante-bellum period. There may not have been much objection to the ownership of one's own family by a free Negro; but when one undertook to acquire slaves to improve his economic status, there were those who looked upon it as a dangerous trend, the legality of which was seriously questioned. If the free Negro was not a full citizen, could he enjoy the same privileges of ownership and the protection of certain types of property that other citizens enjoyed? Around this question revolved a great deal of discussion at the beginning of the militant period of the anti-slavery movement.[27]

When a slave was found guilty of concealing a slave on board a vessel, in violation of the act of 1825, it was contended by his owner that the prisoner, a slave, was not a person or mariner within the meaning of the act and that Green, the owner of the concealed slave, was a mulatto and hence not a citizen of the state and could not own slaves. The decision of the Supreme Court, handed down in 1833 by Judge Daniel, established once and for all the rights of the free Negro in the matter of the ownership of slaves. He said:

*By the laws of this State, a free man of color may own land and hold lands and personal property including slaves. Without therefore stopping to inquire into the extent of the political rights and privileges of a free man of color, I am very well satisfied from the words of the act of the General Assembly that the Legislature meant to protect the slave property of every person who by the laws of the State are entitled to hold such property. I am, therefore, of the opinion that the owner is a citizen within the meaning of the Act of Assembly, and it appearing he was a mulatto is not a reason to grant a new trial to the person who concealed his slave.*[28]

[26] Done on the demise of Frances Howard v. Sarah Howard, 51 N. C., p. 238 ff.

[27] Since the possession of slaves enhanced one's social position in the community, the whites may well have objected to the ownership of slaves by free Negroes on the grounds that it would tend to upset the social structure—or that by such possession the free Negroes might begin to feel that they had "arrived" socially.

[28] State v. Edmund, a slave, 15 N. C., p. 278.

The decision of Judge Daniel in this case remained the accepted point of view until the very end of the period. When the hostility between the sections was developing into open conflict, the free Negro in the South witnessed an almost complete abrogation of his rights. One of the most significant laws passed during the momentous session of the legislature in 1860–1861 was the "Act to prevent free Negroes from having the control of slaves." While it did not affect a large number of free Negroes within the state,[29] it showed the extent to which the North Carolina solons were willing to go in order to combat the forces that were striking at the heart of their long-cherished system. Among other things, the law provided:

*That no free Negro, or free person of color, shall be permitted or allowed to buy, purchase, or hire for any length of time any slave or slaves, or to have any slave or slaves bound as apprentice or apprentices to him, her or them, or in any other wise to have the control, management or services of any slave or slaves, under the penalty of one hundred dollars for each offence, and shall further be guilty of a misdemeanor, and liable to indictment for the same.*

Another section of the law provided that free Negroes already in the possession of slave property would not be affected by the enactment.[30]

Despite the innumerable obstacles that stood in the way of the accumulation of property by free Negroes, several amassed a considerable amount of property during their lifetime. The life of Julius Melbourn is about as interesting as one can find in the period. Born a slave in 1790 on a plantation near Raleigh, he was bought, at five years of age, by the wealthy widow of a British army official, who lived in Raleigh. When her only son was slain in a duel—said to have been fought because of some derogatory remarks concerning his mother having reared Melbourn as a gentleman—the slave was emancipated and made the sole heir to the estate of $20,000. By the time Melbourn was twenty-five years old his estate was worth about $30,000. By careful saving and shrewd investment, he was soon worth $50,000. When he decided that he could not live and die in a country "where the laws sustained and justified such disregard to individual rights and tolerated such inhumanity," as was manifested in the treatment of free Negroes, he sailed for England, where he spent the remainder of his life. That he was still wealthy is attested by the fact that he set up his son in a $20,000 mercantile business in London.[31]

Most of the free Negroes who owned property were possessors of small estates worth a few hundred dollars or less. These individuals, more-

[29] The number of free Negroes who owned slaves was steadily decreasing. See below.

[30] *Laws,* 1860–1861, p. 69.

[31] Julius Melbourn, *Life and Opinions of Julius Melbourn, passim.*

over, comprised only a small percentage of the total free Negro population. The great majority of free Negroes in North Carolina were, during the entire period, without any property whatsoever. At the end of the period, only 3,659, or slightly more than ten percent, owned any property. Of this number, only 1,211 owned any real estate. In few counties did more than ten percent of the free Negroes own property. Craven County, with 1,332 free Negroes in 1860, had only 179 free Negro property owners. Cabarrus County, with 115 free Negroes, had twelve free Negro owners of property. Halifax County, with its 2,452 free Negroes, however, had 463 free Negroes who owned property.[32] In 1860 the following free Negroes had property valued at $2,500 or more:[33]

Free Negroes having property valued at more than $2,500

| Name | Occupation | Value | Name | Occupation | Value |
|------|-----------|-------|------|-----------|-------|
| Alee, M. | Baker | $2,750 | Knight, J. | Confection | $5,903 |
| Alston, O. | Farmer | 17,644 | Lan'ton, D. | Carpenter | 2,500 |
| Bell, H. | | 14,000 | Lewis, W. | Farmer | 2,750 |
| Bethel, J. | Barber | 3,550 | Locklier | Farmer | 5,200 |
| Blacknall, T. | Farmer | 7,300 | Mangum, L. | Farmer | 20,816 |
| Bryan, C. | Farmer | 2,535 | Martin, W. | Farmer | 2,500 |
| Burchett, J. | Farmer | 2,500 | Men'hall | Farmer | 3,197 |
| Butch, H. | Farm Hand | 3,450 | Michael, S. | Farmer | 5,000 |
| Collins, J. | Farmer | 9,000 | Miller, E. | Wheelwright | 8,150 |
| Corn, D. | Farmer | 5,250 | Moore, D. | Barber | 4,400 |
| Corn, N. | Farmer | 2,800 | Norris, A. | Carpenter | 3,000 |
| Cuff, N. | Farmer | 3,475 | Ox'dine, J. | Farmer | 9,825 |
| Day, T. | Cab. Maker | 4,000 | Picar, E. | | 2,500 |
| Dial, G. | Farmer | 4,900 | Piles, A. | Clerk | 5,000 |
| Erwin, J. | Musician | 3,100 | Reed, W. | Farmer | 3,300 |
| Evans, E. | Farmer | 11,830 | Revel, E. | Farmer | 4,826 |
| Evans, W. | Farmer | 3,932 | Reynolds | Farmer | 4,000 |
| Freeman, J. | Farmer | 20,300 | Sampson, J. | Carpenter | 36,000 |
| Graham, J. | Farmer | 2,800 | Scott, A. | Farmer | 3,766 |
| Green, M. | Farmer | 2,600 | Silvester | Farmer | 2,670 |
| Guy, W. | Farmer | 2,695 | Smith, N. | Farmer | 2,500 |
| Hites, E. | Carpenter | 4,000 | Stanly, C. | Dress Maker | 4,000 |
| Howard, J. | | 2,500 | Steward, W. | Farmer | 3,000 |
| Jacobs, J. | Farmer | 3,712 | Taboon, A. | Farm Hand | 5,554 |
| Jones, M. | Housekeeper | 5,500 | Webb, S. | Farmer | 2,810 |
| Jones, T. | | 6,700 | Winn, C. | Blacksmith | 2,800 |
| Jordan, J. | Farmer | 4,700 | | | |

While this table does not represent the average holdings of the free Negro in ante-bellum North Carolina, it suggests that there was a number of indi-

[32] Unpublished population schedules for the census of 1860.

[33] These statistics were compiled from the unpublished population schedules for the census of 1860.

vidual cases in which free Negroes rose to a position of economic independence, despite obstacles.

In six counties in 1860 free Negroes owned no real estate.[34] While each county listed some personal property held by free Negroes, eight counties listed only one such person each.[35] Perhaps nothing is a more striking commentary on the plight of the free Negro in North Carolina than his inability to acquire property, both real and personal.

A study of the value of the property which free Negroes did possess will shed further light on the economic status of the free Negro in antebellum North Carolina. Of course it is difficult for one living in the fifth decade of the twentieth century to appreciate the figures which reveal the value of property owned by free Negroes in, say, 1860. Land values were so much lower at the time that it was quite possible for an individual with one hundred dollars worth of real property to have an adequate amount for farming purposes, and with a few hundred dollars he could erect a house that would be about as modern as the age could provide. There was a likelihood, however, that the land of the free Negro would be the least desirable in a given area. Since the majority of free Negroes were small farmers, they faced the same difficulty that other North Carolina yeomen faced: that of trying to obtain satisfactory property in the same market where the more resourceful plantation owner was making his purchases. It is a point of interest, therefore, that some free Negroes, like John C. Stanly of New Bern and James D. Sampson of New Hanover, were able to acquire some of the most desirable land in their respective communities.

On the whole, a larger number of free Negroes possessed some type of personal property, ranging from silver watches to farming tools. Thus, in the larger number of counties, the value of personal property was higher than the value of real property. But the poverty of the free Negro group can be seen clearly through this study of the value of the property of the group. They possessed an aggregate wealth of $1,045,643. (See table below.) When one considers that more than 30,000 people had to share in this wealth of slightly more than one million dollars, the realization of their plight is inescapable. The per capita wealth of the free Negroes of North Carolina was only $34 in 1860. Thousands of these were landless and without any kind of property. Even when one ascertains the per capita wealth of the free Negro property owners, the picture remains gloomy, for they had a per capita wealth of $287. It must be remembered that fifty-three were worth more than $2,500, while several were worth more than $15,000.[36]

---

[34] They were Alleghany, Davie, Harnett, Haywood, Jackson, and Madison. Interestingly enough, none of these counties was in the eastern part of the state.

[35] They were Catawba, Haywood, Henderson, Hyde, Jackson, Martin, McDowell, and Rutherford.

[36] Unpublished population schedules for the census of 1860.

The following table shows the value of real and personal property of free Negroes in 1860.[37]

One area in which considerable interest has always been manifested is the ownership of slaves by free Negroes. At no time during the ante-

## Aggregate value of property owned by free Negroes

| County | Real | Personal | County | Real | Personal |
|--------|------|----------|--------|------|----------|
| Alamance | $13,500 | $7,415 | Jackson | | $125 |
| Alexander | 500 | 390 | Johnston | $4,060 | 4,853 |
| Alleghany | | 600 | Jones | 1,500 | 1,875 |
| Anson | 3,798 | 7,660 | Lenoir | 625 | 2,250 |
| Ashe | 2,200 | 2,495 | Lincoln | 100 | 270 |
| Beaufort | 12,410 | 6,960 | Macon | 4,050 | 5,100 |
| Bertie | 1,280 | 3,615 | Madison | | 615 |
| Bladen | 6,289 | 5,112 | Martin | 5,549 | 1,200 |
| Brunswick | 6,487 | 6,239 | McDowell | 4,000 | 1,000 |
| Buncombe | 3,540 | 3,184 | Mecklenburg | 8,875 | 3,720 |
| Burke | 200 | 785 | Montgomery | 362 | 1,285 |
| Cabarrus | 1,072 | 2,050 | Moore | 550 | 1,975 |
| Caldwell | 1,295 | 1,284 | Nash | 8,939 | 10,889 |
| Camden | 1,000 | 768 | New Hanover | 37,720 | 35,060 |
| Carteret | 3,150 | 950 | Northampton | 12,824 | 15,359 |
| Caswell | 4,208 | 5,530 | Onslow | 1,735 | 3,475 |
| Catawba | 50 | 75 | Orange | 2,800 | 13,375 |
| Chatham | 1,680 | 2,960 | Pasquotank | 20,440 | 22,195 |
| Cherokee | 350 | 515 | Perquimans | 5,000 | 8,601 |
| Chowan | 3,600 | 2,793 | Person | 5,180 | 3,080 |
| Cleveland | 3,150 | 4,652 | Pitt | 2,100 | 5,560 |
| Columbus | 9,135 | 8,990 | Polk | 700 | 1,446 |
| Craven | 29,865 | 21,137 | Randolph | 5,290 | 8,745 |
| Cumberland | 11,500 | 7,722 | Richmond | 10,750 | 20,930 |
| Currituck | 1,270 | 1,745 | Robeson | 37,555 | 42,159 |
| Davidson | 1,200 | 1,428 | Rockingham | 2,750 | 1,900 |
| Davie | | 1,040 | Rowan | 1,300 | 970 |
| Duplin | 3,360 | 3,777 | Rutherford | 225 | 100 |
| Edgecombe | 7,100 | 10,350 | Sampson | 10,014 | 4,742 |
| Forsyth | 1,530 | 1,665 | Stanly | 950 | 835 |
| Franklin | 6,535 | 6,013 | Stokes | 325 | 550 |
| Gaston | 2,700 | 2,300 | Surry | 925 | 1,144 |
| Gates | 5,125 | 18,755 | Tyrrel | 725 | 1,615 |
| Granville | 15,987 | 13,845 | Union | 300 | 975 |
| Greene | 2,475 | 2,920 | Wake | 22,204 | 45,362 |
| Guilford | 5,425 | 13,445 | Warren | 9,931 | 13,935 |
| Halifax | 30,948 | 42,778 | Washington | 5,843 | 5,077 |
| Harnett | | 375 | Watauga | 475 | 595 |
| Haywood | | 75 | Wayne | 13,380 | 9,900 |
| Henderson | 150 | 100 | Wilkes | 2,710 | 3,835 |
| Hertford | 15,482 | 16,624 | Wilson | 4,984 | 3,999 |
| Hyde | 1,000 | 8,000 | Yadkin | 840 | 2,912 |
| Iredell | 330 | 150 | Yancey | 1,525 | 1,803 |

[37] These statistics were compiled from the unpublished population schedules for the census of 1860.

bellum period were free Negroes in North Carolina without some slaves. The motives for such ownership were perhaps varied, as in other groups. Without a doubt there were those who possessed slaves for the purpose of advancing their economic well-being. With such a view in mind, these free Negro slaveholders were more interested in making their farms or carpenter shops "pay" than they were in treating their slaves humanely. The enterprising free Negro owners of slaves can usually be identified because of their extensive holdings of real and personal property and because of their inactivity in the manumission movement. For thirty years Thomas Day, the free Negro cabinet maker of Milton, used slaves to help him in his business. In 1830, he had two;[38] by 1860 he had three.[39] For thirty years Thomas Blacknall of Franklin County kept slaves, though the number fell from seven to three between 1830 and 1860.[40] It seems clear that these enterprising free Negroes were at least as deeply interested in the labor of their slaves as they were in their comfort.

It seems that by far the larger portion of free Negro owners of slaves were possessors of this human chattel for benevolent reasons. There are numerous examples of free Negroes having purchased relatives or friends to ease their lot. Many of them manumitted such slaves,[41] while others held title to slaves who were virtually free. An examination of the slaveholding by free Negroes seems to bear out this point. Slave Richard Gaston ran away from his master and remained in the woods until his free Negro wife had saved the necessary funds for his purchase.[42] Lila Abshur continued to hold title to her father when the legislature acted unfavorably on her petition to emancipate him.[43] While John C. Stanly undoubtedly held some slaves with the view to increasing his wealth,[44] he held others purely out of benevolence.[45]

The fluctuation in the number of free Negro owners of slaves during the period under observation is an interesting development. At the time of the taking of the first census in 1790, twenty-five free Negroes in eleven counties owned seventy-three slaves.[46] In 1830 the number of free Negro

[38] C. G. Woodson, *Free Negro Owners of Slaves in 1830,* p. 24.

[39] Unpublished population schedules for the census of 1860.

[40] Woodson, *Free Negro Owners,* p. 25 and the unpublished population schedules for the census of 1860.

[41] See the Minutes of the Court of Pleas and Quarter Sessions of Craven County, March, 1811. These records show that Thomas Newton, a free Negro, liberated his slave wife.

[42] C. D. Wilson, "Negroes Who Owned Slaves," *Popular Science Monthly,* LXXXI, p. 485.

[43] MS. in the Legislative Papers for 1856.

[44] In 1830 he held eighteen slaves. Woodson, *Free Negro Owners,* p. 24.

[45] In 1815 Stanly emancipated a slave woman and her five children, as well as a slave man. Minutes of the Court of Pleas and Quarter Sessions of Craven County, March, June, 1815.

[46] Census Office, *Heads of Families in the United States in 1790,* passim.

slaveholders had increased to 191, distributed in thirty-seven counties, while their human chattel numbered 620.[47] Interestingly enough, by 1860 there were only eight free Negro owners of slaves, the latter numbering only twenty-five.[48]

Several observations can now be made. In the first place, the number of slaves held by free Negroes was usually small. Notable exceptions are the eleven slaves held by Samuel Johnston of Bertie County in 1790;[49] the forty-four slaves each owned by Gooden Bowen of Bladen County and John Walker of New Hanover County in 1830; and the twenty-four slaves owned by John Crichlon of Martin County in 1830.[50] Free Negroes usually held one, two, or three slaves; and the petitions of free Negroes to manumit relatives suggest that a sizable number of slaves had been acquired as a result of benevolence.

In the second place, the increase in the number of free Negroes with an accompanying increase in economic independence on the part of some caused a larger number of Negro slaves to be acquired by free Negroes. No doubt, moreover, there was some effort to conform to the pattern established by the dominant slaveholding group within the state in the effort to elevate themselves to a position of respect and privilege. Thus by 1830 more than 600 slaves were held by free Negroes. Finally, the remarkable decline both in the number of free Negro slaveowners and in the number of slaves held toward the end of the period suggests the increasing economic and political difficulty that the free Negro was encountering. Many of those slaves held in 1830 had been manumitted according to the plans of the free Negro owners. Other slaves had been lost in the maze of the economic setbacks that many free Negroes were experiencing.[51] Perhaps also the fervor to acquire slave relatives and set them free was waning, as the free Negro himself began to doubt the blessings of freedom.[52] Thus even before it became illegal for free Negroes to acquire slaves—in 1861—the group had ceased to make such acquisitions. In this case the enactment made legally impossible that which the free Negro had already ceased to do.

Surrounded on all sides by a legal system which denied them the

---

[47] Woodson, *Free Negro Owners*, pp. 24–26, and the unpublished population schedule for the census of 1830.

[48] The list was compiled by the writer from the unpublished population schedules for the census of 1860.

[49] *State Records*, XXVI, 278.

[50] Woodson, *Free Negro Owners*, pp. 24–25.

[51] In such cases the free Negro was losing his slaves in much the same way that the white slaveholder was losing his. By 1860 the rate of increase of slaves in North Carolina was noticeably declining. Taylor, *Slaveholding, passim*.

[52] By 1858 free Negroes had begun to send petitions to the General Assembly asking to be reenslaved. See the MSS. in the Legislative Papers for 1858, 1859, and 1860.

opportunity to seek a livelihood where they could and by a hostile community that often made them as unwelcome as a contagious disease, the
free Negroes tried to find their place in the economic life of ante-bellum
North Carolina. If they were "idle, thievish, roguish, and indolent"—a
sweeping generalization that can reasonably be doubted—they merely
reflected the restraints and stigma that society had placed upon them, and
their reactions were no more than natural. In view of the circumstances,
it is not surprising that they were not a more powerful economic force than
they were. The amazing thing is that under such adverse circumstances
they were able to acquire more than a million dollars worth of property
by the end of the period and to have possessed several hundred slaves
during the seventy-year period ending in 1860.

# 12

## THE UNDERGROUND RAILROAD: LEGEND OR REALITY?
*Larry Gara*

F EW stories in our national history are more familiar to Americans
than those of the underground railroad with its legendary heroes.
Generations of youngsters have thrilled to the account of Eliza
Harris eluding the slave-catchers and their bloodhounds by leaping from
ice cake to ice cake on the thawing Ohio River, and to her later adventures
as a passenger on the underground line. Along with Paul Bunyan and Mike
Fink, Eliza and some of the underground railroad conductors have become
figures of American folklore. Much of the underground railroad story has
been handed down by oral tradition with its inevitable mixture of fact,
fancy, and exaggeration. Writers of popular accounts and local histories,
journalists, antiquarians and scholars have all been influenced by the legend
and have repeated some of its unproved assertions in their writings.

Like most legends, that of the underground railroad is vague and
indistinct. However, in the minds of many people there is an image of
the mysterious institution with which they associate certain general char-

Larry Gara, "The Underground Railroad: Legend or Reality?" *Proceedings of the American
Philosophical Society*, CV (June 1961), pp. 334–339. Reprinted by permission of the publisher and the author.

[1] The author is indebted to the Research Committee of the American Philosophical Society
for a grant from its Penrose Fund which made possible an extensive research trip to gather
material for this study. This article partially summarizes the findings presented in a book-
length study entitled *The Liberty Line: The Legend of the Underground Railroad* (Lexington,
Kentucky, 1961).

acteristics. One of these is the existence of a highly organized network of underground railroad lines, with stations literally dotting the North and penetrating into the South. In the popular mind, at least, a board of directors managed the road's affairs and gave it the benefit of centralized control.[2] The author of a semi-fictional account claimed that for more than twenty years the underground railroad "extended its great trunk lines across all the northern states from Mason and Dixon's line and the Ohio River to the Queen's Dominion, and its ramifications far into the southern states."[3]

Another characteristic of the legendary underground railroad was secrecy. According to a 1936 newspaper account, it was "the most successful secret organization that ever existed in this country."[4] In the legend most of the fugitive slaves, like Eliza, are only a jump or two ahead of their would-be captors, but the adroit conductors outwit the slave-catchers through the use of secret code signals and numerous hiding places. They had, said a popular book on the subject, "false closets through trap doors in kitchens or parlors, false cupboards over brick ovens, sliding panels by fireplaces where wood was stowed, secret rooms without windows."[5] There is also a persistent belief that the need for secrecy led to the destruction of all the records and documents concerning the work of the underground. Publicly, "there was no Underground Railroad," said a student of the Pennsylvania branch. "Had the existence of it even been suspected, the Government or the kidnappers would have wiped it out."[6]

In the context of the popular legend the underground railroad was a very busy enterprise, running its numerous trains nearly every night. There is a distinct impression of an extremely heavy traffic on the underground line. A Pennsylvania newspaper story of underground railroad activity in the state commented, "Thousands of slaves passed through these stations for thirty years."[7] When a writer recently sent out a questionnaire requesting several hundred people to guess at the number of slaves who ran away from the South between 1851 and 1860, the average answer was two

[2] For an excellent example of the use of this concept in fiction, see Stern, Philip Van Doren, *The drums of morning,* 325–432, New York, Doubleday, 1942.

[3] Johnson, Homer U., *From Dixie to Canada: romances and realities of the underground railroad,* 12–13, Orwell, Ohio, H. U. Johnson, and Buffalo, C. W. Moulton, 1894.

[4] Clipping from the *Cincinnati Enquirer,* March 8, 1936, in the Wilbur H. Siebert Papers in the Ohio Historical Society. (All Siebert Papers hereafter cited are in the Ohio Historical Society.)

[5] Buckmaster, Henrietta, *Let my people go: the story of the underground railroad and the growth of the abolition movement,* 199, Boston, Beacon, 1959.

[6] William Hutchinson Smith to Wilbur H. Siebert, December 28, 1933, in the Siebert Papers.

[7] Clipping from the *Upper Darby News,* August 5, 1954, in the Chester County (Pa.) Historical Society.

hundred and seventy thousand, or twenty-seven thousand each year. Several answered a million.[8]

In the romanticized legend it is the abolitionist, or underground railroad conductor, who stands in the spotlight. He is the hero. The operators of the underground railroad, as described in a recent book, lived in a time that called for greatness, "and they had the greatness within them."[9] They were willing to risk all for the cause they served. The stereotype of the heroic abolitionist is matched by that of the ignorant and helpless fugitive. Although the fugitives of the legend are determined to be free, they lack the necessary knowledge and skill to reach the Promised Land without the assistance of the underground transportation system.

The legend of the underground railroad is a combination of fact and fancy. Many of the stories handed down by word of mouth had a factual basis, but frequent repetition has led to exaggeration and sometimes, in the annals of local history, fantasy has become fact. Far too much of the underground railroad's history rests upon the reminiscences of aged abolitionists written many years after the events had transpired, and after their cause had become respectable. The underground railroad of historical reality existed, but it was markedly different from the institution of the popular legend.

There was no nationwide conspiracy to spirit fugitive slaves to Canada. It was largely a matter of sheltering and assisting fugitives who had already escaped. Abolitionists held different opinions concerning the importance of underground railroad activity. Only a very few of them approved of enticing slaves from their masters or taking them from the southern states. Some thought that such activity was unethical and most believed that it was unwise. Even the extremist Oberlin anti-slavery reformers refused to sanction the program of three of their group who ventured into the South to guide slaves to freedom. Members of the Philadelphia Vigilance Committee also disapproved of sending agents south to assist slaves to run away, although in a few instances they did abet such escapes from southern bondage.[10]

When abolitionists provided assistance to the absconding slaves in the form of food and other necessities, temporary lodging, and transportation, it was often on a haphazard basis. Some abolitionists who took a special interest in this phase of anti-slavery activity organized underground railroad work in certain local areas, but at no time did such efforts become centralized. Levi Coffin, for example, introduced a semblance of order into the underground railroad efforts in the parts of Indiana and Ohio where

[8] Furnas, J. C., *Goodbye to Uncle Tom,* 239, New York, Sloane, 1956.

[9] Breyfogle, William, *Make free: the story of the underground railroad,* 35, Philadelphia, Lippincott, 1958.

[10] Report of an interview between Wilbur H. Siebert and James H. Fairchild, August 3, 1892 in the Siebert Papers; Still, William, *The underground rail road,* 177, Philadelphia, Porter and Coates, 1872.

he lived.[11] Similarly, Thomas Garrett took the initiative in the Wilmington-Philadelphia area, where he had the active cooperation of a group of militant anti-slavery Quakers in Delaware and neighboring counties of Pennsylvania and of the Philadelphia Vigilance Committee.[12]

The vigilance committees, organized in a number of northern cities, assumed special responsibility for giving assistance to the bondsmen fleeing from slavery. Those committees which were founded before the passage of the Fugitive Slave Law of 1850 were sometimes brought into being by free Negroes who, in certain communities like New York City, worked wholly on their own, without ties to any abolitionist society. The New York committee reported in 1837 that it had protected 335 persons from slavery. David Ruggles was the competent and energetic Negro secretary of the New York committee. In 1845 a group of New England Negroes formed a Freedom Association with the object of extending "a helping hand to all who may bid adieu to whips and chains, and by the welcome light of the North Star, reach a haven where they can be protected from the grasp of the manstealer."[13]

After 1850 the abolitionists created a number of new vigilance committees. Among the best known were those of Philadelphia, Syracuse and Boston. Their object was to give aid to the fugitives, to protect free Negroes from kidnappers and to obstruct the Fugitive Slave Law. Those committees would have been unnecessary had there been in operation a centralized network of underground railroad stations. The rescue of alleged fugitives from slave-catchers or from officers of the law provided exciting diversion for a number of the vigilance committees. One of the most famous rescues was that of the slave William Henry, or "Jerry," in Syracuse in 1851. Celebrating the anniversary of the Jerry Rescue became a regular event with the abolitionists and provided effective propaganda for the anti-slavery cause. An announcement of one such celebration said that the rescue had been "the heroism of the Right" which "stirred the hearts, and quickened the pulse, of the Friends of Freedom throughout America."[14]

Although most abolitionists used the fugitive issue for propaganda purposes not all of them took an active part in the underground railroad. Some even questioned the validity of such work. The major objective of the abolition movement was to end slavery rather than to assist a few fugitives to escape from it. Abolitionists made a distinction between the two efforts and they deplored any tendency of the lesser cause to divert energy

---

[11] Coffin, Levi, *Reminiscences of Levi Coffin, the reputed president of the underground railroad . . .*, *passim*, Cincinnati, R. Clarke and Co., 1880 (hereafter cited as *Reminiscences*).

[12] Drake, Thomas E., Thomas Garrett, Quaker abolitionist, in *Friends in Wilmington, 1738–1938*, 75–86, Wilmington, Del., n.d.

[13] Aptheker, Herbert, ed., *A documentary history of the Negro people in the United States*, 162–163, 253–254, New York, Citadel, 1951.

[14] New York *National Anti-Slavery Standard*, September 16, 1852.

and attention from the greater. Mrs. Sarah Otis Ernst of Cincinnati, for example, feared that the abolitionists' "energies and funds would be so frittered" away by such things as a colored orphan asylum and the running off of fugitives that they would have no means left for their "higher and more important work."[15] For the abolitionists the propaganda aspects of the fugitive issue were even more important than the fate of an individual fugitive. In 1850 a Chicago abolitionist newspaper suggested that it might be "expedient for some fugitives to suffer martyrdom . . . and consent to return awhile to slavery as propagandists of liberty, and as a standing appeal to the humanity of the North."[16]

Those abolitionists who emphasized working with the fugitive slaves often carried on their underground railroad activity with very little attempt at secrecy. Levi Coffin recalled that slave-catchers frequented Cincinnati but that none ever bothered him, even though his reputation as an underground railroad conductor was no secret to anyone in the area.[17] Thomas Garrett openly boasted of the large number of fugitive slaves he had helped to freedom.[18] Although anyone who refused to obey the Fugitive Slave Law was legally liable for punishment, the government seldom prosecuted violators. In 1853 an anti-slavery newspaper in Ohio commented, "not even one of the thousands who have refused obedience to this law, has yet been condemned."[19] Actually, there were probably fewer than a dozen prosecutions under the act during its fourteen-year existence, although in most of those cases there were a number of defendants.

Moderation also characterized the use of the law to return individuals to slavery. Only fifty alleged slaves had been arrested by the spring of 1853 when the Massachusetts Anti-Slavery Society commented in its annual report that the law "was but an electioneering trick, not designed nor expected to be of material advantage to the Slaveholders."[20] Not all the runaway slaves were pursued, and very few were pursued by their masters. The expense involved in tracking down a fugitive slave was often greater than the value of one known to be addicted to running away. A few dramatic incidents involving slaves who had been pursued have given a false impression of pursuit as a common occurrence.

The abolitionists sometimes advertised their underground railroad services in newspapers. As early as 1844 the Chicago *Western Citizen* published a cartoon captioned "Liberty Line" which pictured the underground

[15] Mrs. Sarah Otis Ernst to Miss Weston, February 6, 1852, in the Weston Papers in the Boston Public Library.

[16] Chicago *Western Citizen*, November 5, 1850.

[17] Coffin, *Reminiscences*, 118.

[18] Boston *Liberator*, May 22, 1857.

[19] Salem, Ohio, *Anti-Slavery Bugle*, March 19, 1853.

[20] *Twenty-first annual report presented to the Massachusetts Anti-Slavery Society by its board of managers, January 26, 1853*, 43, Boston, 1853.

train chugging its way to Canada with a full cargo of jubilant fugitive slaves. Under the drawing was a humorous description of the "improved and splendid Locomotives" and "best style" passenger accommodations for those "who may wish to improve their health or circumstances, by a northern tour."[21] This was only one example of a number of similar notices. In 1856 a Syracuse paper carried an item telling of eight fugitives who passed through on their way to Canada. The Reverend J. W. Loguen, a former slave, was a key person in the Syracuse Vigilance Committee. "Brother Loguen," said the article, "talks of keeping a Hotel Register, after the manner of aristocratic establishments, for the purpose of recording the names of his guests, and having them published."[22]

There was a great deal of underground railroad material in the anti-slavery press. Abolitionist editors reported all stories of slaves escapes that came to their attention. On occasion they notified the slaves' owners that their chattels had crossed the border into Canada where they were safe from all fugitive slave laws. In March of 1856 the New York *National Anti-Slavery Standard* reprinted an advertisement from a Richmond paper offering rewards for the return of Henry and Tazewell. The *Standard's* editor commented that the owners could save themselves the expense of further advertisement. "Tazewell and Henry," he wrote, "both passed over 'tother side of Jordan,' one day last week, 'shouting happy.' "[23] In reporting such stories the reformer editors seldom distinguished between fugitives who had received assistance from the abolitionists and those who had accomplished their flight wholly on their own resources.

The publication of underground railroad stories was of no practical benefit to the fugitive slaves, and neither were the pronouncements of the anti-slavery politicians. The anti-slavery faction in Congress found the fugitive slave issue an especially useful one. The passage of the Fugitive Slave Law of 1850 brought forth a flood of speeches. Anti-slavery congressmen used the unpopular law to arouse pride in the North's free institutions, to criticize the South's violation of civil liberties, to challenge the power of southern leadership and to attempt to strike fear into the hearts of the slaveholders. They used strong language in condemning the legislation. "In the long catalogue of public crimes among civilized nations, there is none more cruel and barbarous than the fugitive slave law . . ." said Wisconsin's Representative Charles Durkee. Congressman A. P. Haskell of New York maintained that the law had "no parallel for its monstrosity since the time that the English wrested Magna-Charta from their monarch, . . ."[24]

In 1852 Congressman Joshua R. Giddings of Ohio assured his col-

---

[21] Chicago *Western Citizen*, July 18, 1844.

[22] New York *National Anti-Slavery Standard*, July 5, 1856, quoting the *Syracuse Journal*.

[23] New York *National Anti-Slavery Standard*, March 29, 1856.

[24] *Congressional Globe*, 32 Congress, 1 session, appendix, 886, August 6, 1852, and 585, May 17, 1852.

leagues who talked of enforcing the Fugitive Slave Law that *"it cannot be done."*[25] In 1860 New York's Congressman Charles B. Sedgwick said, "It must have been expected that so infamous a law would have been evaded by underground railroads, and by all other honorable methods." He denied that there was any difference of opinion on the issue in the North. "All parties wink at its evasion," he commented, "and all sympathy is with the fugitive."[26]

Repetition of such material helped to create a false impression concerning the number of passengers on the underground railroad. Complaints of southerners about extensive losses suffered by their constituents because of the abolitionist underground railroad strengthened the impression. Southern spokesmen tended to take the propaganda statements of the abolitionists and the anti-slavery politicians at face value. Extremist defenders of southern rights found underground railroad rumors valuable for their criticism of the North. Delegates to the Nashville Convention of 1850 listed among their grievances against the northern people the forming of organizations "to carry off slaves from the South," and protecting them from recapture.[27] Early in 1861 Tennessee's Governor Isham G. Harris charged that northern opponents of slavery had "run off slave property by means of the 'under-ground railroad,' amounting in value to millions of dollars."[28] Such statements could not be proved; like the propaganda barrage of the abolitionists, they were meant to sway men's minds, not to provide them with accurate information.

Many years later those abolitionists who wrote reminiscent accounts of their underground railroad service added immeasurably to the legend of the mysterious road. The aged crusaders wrote of the stirring times when they alone had opposed the minions of slavery. With the emancipation of the slaves their cause had triumphed and the abolitionists became the heroes of their own thrilling narratives.[29] One of them wrote, "Considering the kind of labor performed, the expense incurred and the danger involved, one must be impressed with the unselfish devotion to principle of the men

[25] *Congressional Globe,* 32 Congress, 1 session, appendix, 740, June 23, 1852.

[26] *Congressional Globe,* 36 Congress, 1 session, appendix, 179, March 26, 1860.

[27] Resolutions and address of the Nashville Convention, in the New York *National Anti-Slavery Standard,* June 27, 1850.

[28] *Message of His Excellency Isham G. Harris, to the General Assembly of Tennessee, in extra session, January 7th, 1861,* 8, Nashville, 1861.

[29] Autobiographical accounts of underground railroad conductors include: Coffin, *Reminiscences;* Fairbank, Calvin, *Rev. Calvin Fairbank during slavery times,* Chicago, Patriotic Publishing Co., 1890; Butler, Marvin Benjamin, *My story of the Civil War and the underground railroad,* Huntington, Ind., United Brethren Publishing Establishment, 1914; Cockrum, William Monroe, *History of the underground railroad as is was conducted by the Anti-Slavery League,* Oakland City, Ind., Press of J. W. Cockrum Printing Co., 1915; and Pettit, Eber M., *Sketches in the history of the underground railroad . . . ,* Fredonia, N. Y., W. McKinstry and Son, 1879.

and women thus engaged."[30] Another said that he "had no apology to make for his book." He thought it right "that the young people should know how things were carried on during the fifties by the pro-slavery people who had control of the government."[31]

The reminiscers seldom included statistics but in retrospect their underground railroad became greatly magnified, both in terms of the number of slaves they had assisted and in terms of the importance of that service to the fugitive slaves. It was a matter of distance lending enchantment to the view, as one of them admitted.[32] Yet the underground railroad epoch, as seen from the perspective of the abolitionists, is basically the one which has found popular acceptance. It has been repeated in newspaper articles, local histories, works of fiction, and even in some reference works and scholarly monographs.

Usually there was a grain of truth in the underground railroad stories. They are exaggerated rather than wholly false accounts. Because of the romantic nature of the material it easily lent itself to exaggeration. In some localities, at certain times, the underground railroad was a flourishing institution. In 1856 J. Miller McKim of the Philadelphia Vigilance Committee wrote an Irish friend, "The 'Underground' is becoming a great institution. We had 25 arrivals last week, all within the space of 48 hours."[33] Such a dramatic event made a lasting impression on the abolitionists and those who read about their exploits. Yet, even for the active Philadelphia committee, it was an unusual amount of business. When William Still published his documentary account of his eight years of service with the committee he listed only about eight hundred fugitives who had used its facilities.[34]

Actual figures of underground railroad traffic are difficult to compile. Scholars have mistrusted the census statistics which indicate that about a thousand slaves a year escaped from the South, even though some contemporaries, including some of the abolitionists, accepted those figures as substantially correct. For example, Gamaliel Bailey, editor of the abolitionist newspaper The National Era, cited the census of 1850 as proof "that the number of fugitive slaves in the North has been greatly exaggerated."[35]

Certainly a very small percentage of the millions of slaves in the South escaped or attempted to escape to the North or to Canada. Temporary running away was much more common and should not be confused with escape from slavery. When slaves disappeared, those responsible for finding them seldom assumed that they had fled to the North. The run-

[30] Butler, My Story of the Civil War and the underground railroad, 180.

[31] Cockrum, History of the underground railroad, foreword v.

[32] Sloane, Rush R., The underground railroad of the firelands, The Firelands Pioneer, new ser. 5: 35, 1888.

[33] J. Miller McKim to Richard D. Webb, April 4, 1856, in the Garrison Papers in the Boston Public Library.

[34] Still, The underground rail road, passim.

[35] Washington, The National Era, June 19, 1851.

aways often returned voluntarily after hiding out for a time in the woods, in a nearby swamp or at a neighboring plantation. In truth, the great majority of slaves had no alternative but to accept their situation. They had practically no accurate information about other parts of the country. Furthermore, the status of free Negroes, both in the North and the South, was probably not attractive enough to inspire the average slave to undertake the highly dangerous plunge for freedom. The slaves who ran away permanently were unusual individuals, either constitutionally incapable of adjustment to the slave system or so sensitive and intelligent as to make the break regardless of the heavy odds against them.

The slaves who absconded from bondage were generally self-reliant individuals who planned and carried out their own escapes. Some literally walked away from slavery, traveling by night and hiding and resting by day. Many slaves knew about the north star and they also obtained directions from other slaves, free Negroes and sympathetic southern whites. One group of fugitives from Virginia traveled only at night for three weeks before they reached Pennsylvania.[36] A fugitive slave from Tennessee journeyed five weeks to reach Michigan.[37] Some made good their escape from the deep South, alone and unaided.

Slaves heading north often took advantage of available water transportation. Steamships running from southern ports sometimes carried fugitive slaves, either as stowaways or as passengers hidden with the consent of the ship captain or crew members. Despite the risks involved, some ship captains made extra money carrying such cargo. They were not necessarily abolitionists, but were willing to carry whatever kind of freight would bring them the best profit.[38]

Some of the escaping slaves devised ingenious methods to implement their desire to reach free soil. Mulattoes often passed as white travelers. Fugitives sometimes posed as free Negroes, carrying forged free papers to prove their status should it become necessary. The famous ex-slave Frederick Douglass used a sailor's free papers in his flight from Maryland. Disguises were common. Men posed as women, and women as men. When William and Ellen Craft escaped from Georgia, Ellen, who was nearly white, posed as an ailing planter and William as his trusted servant. They traveled by train and had little difficulty along the way.[39] Henry "Box" Brown was only the most famous of a number of individuals who escaped or attempted to escape by having themselves crated and shipped to the North.[40]

When the fugitives did somehow find themselves on the underground railroad it was usually only after they had already completed the most

[36] Smedley, Robert C., *History of the underground railroad in Chester and the neighboring counties of Pennsylvania*, 228, Lancaster, Pa., Office of the Journal, 1883.

[37] Haviland, Mrs. Laura Smith, *A woman's life-work*, 213, Chicago, 1889.

[38] Still, *The underground rail road*, 74–75, 166, 263.

[39] Still, *The underground rail road*, 368–377; *Running a thousand miles for freedom; or the escape of William and Ellen Craft from slavery*, London, 1860.

[40] Stearns, Charles, *Narrative of Henry Box Brown*, . . . , 59–62, Boston, 1849.

difficult and dangerous stretch of their journey without such assistance. One fugitive from Virginia located the underground railroad in Ohio after getting that far by himself.[41] Another, from Nashville, Tennessee, reached Ottawa, Illinois before contacting an abolitionist who helped him get to Chicago.[42] Still another arrived in New York after a three-week ordeal of "sleeping in the woods and caves by day and traveling at night."[43] The assistance given these fugitive slaves by the abolitionists was helpful but not necessarily essential for the success of their flight from slavery.

The fugitives themselves deserve more recognition than they have received in the popular legend of the underground railroad with its emphasis on the abolitionists and their role in the exciting drama. The legend has contributed to the popular idea that large numbers of slaves traveled to freedom on the underground line, and it has presented later generations with a distorted view of the workings of the underground railroad itself. Based partly on the writings of aged participants, the legend of the underground railroad has been further entrenched in the popular mind by the addition of countless local folk tales and unproved traditions. Elements of it have been repeated by some scholars as well as popular writers and journalists. Yet the over-simplified picture of the past as presented in legendary accounts should not be accepted as history. The actual history of the institution is much more complex and even more interesting than the legend itself.

[41] New York *National Anti-Slavery Standard,* February 3, 1853, quoting the New York *Tribune.*

[42] Drew, Benjamin, *The refugee: or, the narratives of fugitive slaves in Canada,* 314–320, Boston, J. P. Jewett; New York, Sheldon, Lamport and Blakeman, 1856.

[43] Boston *Liberator,* December 2, 1859, citing the *Taunton* (Mass.) *Republican.*

# 13

## EXPRESSIONS OF NEGRO MILITANCY IN THE NORTH, 1840–1860
*Howard H. Bell*

THE use of physical violence in securing the liberty of the enslaved had been frowned upon by the abolitionist leaders in the 1830's, and Negro sentiment in the North seems generally to have been in accord with that view. But "moral suasion" had failed to

Howard H. Bell, "Expressions of Negro Militancy in the North, 1840–1860," *Journal of Negro History,* XLV (January 1960), pp. 11–20. © 1960 by the Association for the Study of Negro Life and History Inc.

secure the freedom of those in bondage and moral suasionists had stood helplessly by while escaped slaves were returned to captivity. Consequently many Negroes, by 1840, were moving slowly away from Garrisonian leadership. Many began associating with Liberty Party adherents and came shortly to advocate the viewpoints of that party as opposed to the moral suasionism of the Garrisonians. Meantime, they assumed, gradually but surely, a more militant attitude toward the government which allowed members of their race to be held in servitude.

This new militancy had its basis in the Negro's re-evaluation of his own importance, first as an individual, and second, as a force to be reckoned with in the changing American scene. The attention received as a result of the first national conventions of the 1830's led many Negroes to recognize that they had a voice to which the ear of the nation was attuned, but that attention also engendered a new self-confidence and with that self-confidence there came the feeling that they must speak for themselves—that they must fight their own battles. Philip A. Bell put this new attitude into telling words:

*It matters not what our friends may do; they may make OUR CAUSE their perpetual theme . . . yet all will be of no avail, so far as we, ourselves, are personally interested without our thinking and acting, as a body, for ourselves.*[1]

Three years later the young men of New York carried Bell's philosophy a logical step further when they declared: "If we act with our white friends . . . the words we utter will be considered theirs, or their echo. That will be the general impression, the voice of the majority only will be heard, theirs only be considered."[2] Thus it was that the new Negro leadership of New York—and of other areas, especially those west of the Hudson River—began grappling with their own problems in their own way and in their own conventions. In local meetings, in state and national conventions composed of ministers, editors, barbers, carpenters, doctors, bricklayers, politicians, and members of other professions, Negroes met to discuss the problems which were especially important to them. Sometimes they numbered scarcely a score of delegates, sometimes they numbered over 100, but their discussion of education, temperance, politics, labor, suffrage, moral reform and other matters tended to keep alive the hope for a better day. But delay in the fulfillment of that hope caused the voice of the nation's greatest minority to assume a new militancy in the early 1840's.

The opening speech at the Buffalo National Convention of 1843 gave voice to this militancy in the statement: "We love our country, we love our

---

[1] *The Weekly Advocate* (New York), January 21, 1837.

[2] *National Anti-Slavery Standard* (New York), July 16, 1840.

fellow-citizens—but *we love our liberty more.*"[3] The convention continued by condemning as "Synagogues of Satan" those churches which refused to take a stand against slavery and prejudice.[4] This attack on the fence-straddling churches was more or less expected, but a provocative speech by Henry Highland Garnet took the convention by surprise. Addressing himself to the American slave population he admonished them that it was better to to "die *immediately* than live slaves" and that "there is not much hope of Redemption without the shedding of blood."[5]

Garnet's speech was suppressed by the convention, but he repeated its main ideas at the next national convention at Troy, New York in 1847,[6] and published it the following year. By that time (1848–1849) Garnet was not alone in upholding violence in freeing the slaves. A Boston meeting, in spite of opposition from loyal Garrisonians, paid deference in 1848 to the idea that the individual had the right to defend himself against being returned to bondage, even if he had to shed blood in so doing.[7] Maine and New Hampshire Negroes meeting at Portland, Maine, in September, 1849, debated seriously whether they were not duty-bound to give physical aid to any insurrectionary movement of slaves,[8] and throughout the North the attitude of Negro leaders was much the same. A meeting at Oberlin, Ohio, recorded a resolution encouraging slaves to come north to a land of liberty.[9] At about the same time a mass meeting at the City Hall in Detroit, Michigan, passed a resolution declaring it their intention to defend their freedom with their lives if necessary.[10] A group at Hanover, Ohio, although they went on record as opposed to bloodshed, were nevertheless in favor of trampling under foot any law "that conflicts with reason, liberty,

[3] *Minutes of the National Convention of Colored Citizens: Held at Buffalo, on the 15th, 16th, 17th, 18th and 19th of August, 1843, For the Purpose of Considering Their Moral and Political Condition as American Citizens* (New York: Piercy & Reed, printers, 1843), p. 5.

[4] *Ibid.*, p. 15.

[5] Henry Highland Garnet, *An Address to the Slaves of the United States of America (Rejected by the National Convention of 1843)*, as printed in David Walker's *Walker's Appeal, in Four Articles, Together with a Preamble, to the Colored Citizens of the World, but in Particular, and Very Expressly to Those of the United States of America. Written in Boston, in the State of Massachusetts, Sept[ember] 28, 1829.* (2nd ed., with corrections, etc.; n.p., 1830), p. 94. In this case Garnet's *Address* was merely added to Walker's *Appeal*, using consecutive pagination, or both articles were printed together in 1848, using the 1830 edition of the *Appeal*.

[6] *The Liberator* (Boston), November 19, 1847.

[7] *Ibid.*, February 18, 1848.

[8] *Minutes of the Eighth Anniversary of Maine and New Hampshire Historical & Agricultural Society, Held in the Colored Congregational Church[,] Portland, September 4th, 5th, and 6th, 1849* (Portland, [Maine]: A. Shirley & Son, 1849), p. 8.

[9] *The Liberator*, March 2, 1849; *The Pennsylvania Freeman* (Philadelphia), March 15, 1849.

[10] *The Liberator*, March 9, 1849.

and justice, either North or South."[11] And, at a state convention held at Columbus, Ohio, in January, 1849, a resolution was passed authorizing the purchase and gratuitous distribution of 500 copies of David Walker's *Appeal* and Garnet's *Address* to the slaves.[12] In so doing the convention was officially promoting two of the most radical works published by Negroes in the past decades—and the people were now ready to listen.

By 1850 the efforts of Northern and Southern leaders to save the Union by compromise was resting ill with the Negro population, for it was their rights and privileges which were being jeopardized, their bodies which were being endangered, and their souls which were being sacrificed on the altar of expediency. Accordingly, when their protests went unheeded and the stringent Fugitive Slave Law of 1850 went into effect, the voice of the Negro assumed an even more militant tone as he stated his right to full citizenship under the Constitution. In conversation and speeches, in letters and editorials, Negroes outspokenly condemned the Fugitive Slave Law and its concomitants. And during the succeeding decade they turned more and more to working out their own destiny—either in the land to which their forefathers had been unwillingly transplanted, or in some area beyond the borders of that land where the discriminatory laws passed by the Caucasian majority would no longer cast their blight.

As early as April, 1850, Boston leaders, anticipating a more stringent fugitive slave law, were committing themselves to such protection "as the God of nature bestows upon us,"[13] and Henry Bibb, an escaped slave, was proclaiming that "when we have crossed Mason and Dixon's line, a portion of our rights have been restored to us, namely, the right of self-defense."[14]

By August 21, 1850, when the provisions of the Fugitive Slave Law were before the public, a convention of fugitive slaves at Casenovia, New York, declared their sympathy for those still in bondage and urged them to abscond with the fastest horse from the stables of their respective masters. They urged the fleeing slave also to arm himself and to use those arms even to the point of taking the life of his pursuer if necessary.[15] The convention address, though denying that the group was actually promoting violence, still reminded those in slavery that if Americans of 1776 had cause to revolt against England, then the American slave of 1850 had more than ample reason for resort to arms.[16]

[11] *Anti-Slavery Bugle* (Salem, Ohio), May 18, 1849.

[12] *Minutes and Address of the State Convention of the Colored Citizens of Ohio, Convened at Columbus, January 10th, 11th, 12th, & 13th, 1849* (Oberlin: from J. M. Fitch's Power Press, 1849), p. 18.

[13] *The Liberator*, April 5, 1850.

[14] *Ibid.*, April 12, 1850.

[15] *The Pennsylvania Freeman*, August 29, 1850.

[16] *The North Star* (Rochester), September 5, 1850.

Two days before the Casenovia convention, Cleveland Negroes declared their firm belief "that slaves owe no service nor obedience to their masters" and that "we will protect them [fleeing slaves] from recapture, whether the kidnapper comes to us as an officer of the government, or otherwise."[17]

Chicago Negroes recognized publicly the necessity for self-defense; they pledged mutual support in case of need; they accepted the possible necessity of shedding human blood in defense of their rights. Then, in ironic vein, they quoted the language of the Fugitive Slave Bill: "All good citizens are hereby requested to aid and assist us in the execution of our intentions."[18] New York leaders declared adhesion to the Virginia motto: "Resistance to tyranny is obedience to God."[19] And a group at Portland, Maine, warned their "fellow citizens" that since they had been deprived of legal protection they would "protect our right to freedom at whatever cost."[20]

Within a few months the state conventions began to take a hand in the universal condemnation of the Fugitive Slave Bill. At Columbus in January, 1851, Ohio Negroes declared that "if we have no protection [under the Fugitive Slave Bill], we owe no allegiance, the amount of allegiance, according to the arrangement of nations, being graduated by the rights guaranteed, and the protection afforded."[21]

New York leaders, meeting in state convention at Albany in July, 1851, passed a series of resolutions hammering home the idea that the laws of tyrants and of God were incompatible and that they chose to obey God. Furthermore, they found the law to be in violation of the Declaration of Independence and the Constitution of the United States.[22]

A similar reasoning was expounded in a county convention at Gallipolis, Ohio, in October, 1851,[23] and at the Ohio state convention in Cincinnati, January, 1852. At Cincinnati the group resolved that "in guarding our liberty, we will use the mildest means in our judgment, adequate to the end."[24] And when they met in state convention at Cleveland in the fall,

---

[17] The Daily True Democrat (Cleveland), September 30, 1850.

[18] Western Citizen (Chicago), October 8, 1850; Chicago Daily Journal, October 3, 1850.

[19] National Anti-Slavery Standard, October 10, 1850.

[20] The Liberator, September 20, 1850.

[21] Minutes of the State Convention of the Colored Citizens of Ohio, Convened at Columbus, Jan[uary] 15th, 16th, 17th, and 18th, 1851 ([n.p.]: E. Glover, 1851), p. 6. (Copy at Huntington Library).

[22] Proceedings of the State Convention of Colored People, Held at Albany, New-York, on the 22d, 23d, and 24th of July, 1851 (Albany: Charles Van Benthuysen, 1851), pp. 29–30.

[23] Frederick Douglass' Paper (Rochester), January 1, 1851 [1852].

[24] Proceedings of the Convention of the Colored Freemen of Ohio, Held in Cincinnati, January 14, 15, 16, 17, and 19, [1852] (Cincinnati: printed by Dumas and Lawyer, 1852), p. 7.

Ohioans considered a resolution which held that:

*The only way to mitigate the evils of the Fugitive Slave Law is for each . . . to enforce for himself . . . the right to life, liberty and pursuit of happiness, and in no case to deal more mildly with the robber of the body than with the high-wayman or the assassin.*[25]

Even some ministers were shaken out of their usual reticence toward the mixing of politics or social reform with religion. At a New York convention of the African Methodist Episcopal Zion Church in May, 1852, ministers passed anti-Fugitive Slave Law resolutions. And when some of their number suggested a resolution favoring Christian love and sympathy for the perpetrators of the law, they were hooted down. In fact, some went so far as to indicate that they would rather pray for the damnation of such individuals, and that "they would rather give them powder and shot than gospel."[26]

Meantime the retreat to Canada had been in progress for several decades. That area had long been considered primarily an asylum for the escaped slave, but after the passage of the Fugitive Slave Law the appeal to the free Negro was equally great. Two escaped slaves, Henry Bibb and Samuel R. Ward, established newspapers in Canada early in the decade and used those organs to invite others to come. As early as 1851, Bibb's *Voice of the Fugitive* was the means of calling a "North American Convention" at Toronto. Bibb not only urged the slave to flee to Canada, he also condoned the killing of the pursuer in self-defense; and the convention was in accord with his views.[27] Two years later a Canadian convention at Amherstburgh held that the United States Negro owed nothing to his country by way of loyalty, and that he had better come to Canada. In the eyes of the Canadian Negro, those who refused to cross the border to a land of freedom were playing with revolution at home.[28]

This invitation to come to Canada encouraged an incipient emigration movement, and as talk of emigration increased, so did the feeling of resentment against the land that refused to give the Negro the rights of full citizenship. One man, grown weary of the prejudice and inequality which he faced in the United States, unburdened himself in spirited language:

*I owe it [the United States] no allegiance because it refuses to protect me . . . I can hate this government without being disloyal, because it has*

[25] *Anti-Slavery Bugle,* September 18, 1852, from *The Daily True Democrat.*

[26] *Frederick Douglass' Paper,* June 10, 1852.

[27] *Voice of the Fugitive* (Sandwich and Windsor, Canada), October 22, 1851.

[28] *Minutes and Proceedings of the General Convention for the Improvement of the Colored Inhabitants of Canada, Held by Adjournments in Amherstburgh, C[anada] W[est] June 16th and 17th, 1853* (Windsor, C[anada] W[est]: Bibb and Holly, 1853), p. 12.

*stricken down my manhood and treated me as a saleable commodity. I can join a foreign enemy and fight against it, without being a traitor, because it treats me as an ALIEN and a STRANGER, and I am free to avow that should such contingency arise I should not hesitate to take any advantage in order to procure indemnity for the future.*[29]

Philadelphia, though not particularly known for its militancy, was moved to protest that "Those who, without crimes, are outlawed by any Government, can owe no allegiance to its enactments."[30] In New York the moderate James McCune Smith wrote to a friend of a new abolition society which, in contrast to the Garrisonian interpretation, was designed "to abolish slavery by means of the Constitution; or OTHERWISE. The last two words I squeezed into the preliminary Resolution: and should there be any quarrel in the future as to the meaning of them, I mean *fight*."[31]

As the decade progressed and the plight of the Negro went from bad to worse, the men of Ohio spoke out in strong denunciation of the inequalities in rights and privileges to which they were constantly subjected:

*If we are deprived of education, of equal political privileges, still subjected to the same depressing influences under which we now suffer, the natural consequences will follow; and the State, for her planting of injustice, will reap her harvest of sorrow and crime. She will contain within her limits a discontented population—dissatisfied, estranged—ready to welcome any revolution or invasion as a relief. . . .*[82]

In Illinois, Frederick Douglass, on a speaking tour in 1853, is reported to have advocated killing slavecatchers if necessary for the preservation of the liberty of escaped slaves.[33] Three years later the Illinois State Convention, mindful that their group had neither suffrage, equal education facilities, nor a guarantee of a fair jury trial, declared "that to tax us while we are not allowed to be represented, is but to enact, upon a grander scale,

[29] [H. Ford Douglass], *Speech of H. Ford Douglass, in Reply to Mr. J. M. Langston Before the Emigration Convention, at Cleveland, Ohio Delivered on the Evening of the 27th of August, 1854* (Chicago: printed by Wm. H. Worrell, 1854), pp. 11–12. The National Emigration Convention was held August 24-26, 1854, and Douglass's speech seems to have been given on one of those days, rather than on the 27th of August as the above title would indicate. See *Proceedings of the National Emigration Convention of Colored People: Held at Cleveland, Ohio, on Thursday, Friday and Saturday, the 24th, 25th and 26th of August, 1854. With a Reference Page of Contents* (Pittsburgh: printed by A. A. Anderson, 1854), p. 13.

[30] *Anti-Slavery Bugle*, June 24, 1854.

[31] James McCune Smith to Gerrit Smith, March 1, 31 [addition to original letter on March 31], 1855, in Gerrit Smith Miller Collection, Syracuse University.

[32] *Proceedings of the State Convention of Colored Men, Held in the City of Columbus, Ohio, Jan[uary] 16th, 17th, & 18th, 1856* ([n.p., n.d.]; no title page), p. 6.

[33] *The Chicago Tribune*, October 17, 1853, from *Freeport (Illinois) Daily Bulletin*.

the outrages that forced our Revolutionary Fathers to treat King George to a continental tea party in *Boston Harbor*."[34] This same convention spoke of "neither asking nor giving quarter, spurning all compromises," and it refused to change the wording to a more moderate expression.[35]

In California the state convention of 1856 listened to W. H. Newby as he challenged a proposed resolution to "hail with delight its [the nation's] onward progress,"[36] and as he declared that he would welcome a foreign army if it would bring freedom to his people.[37] Though the convention did not support Newby in his most radical statements, it did vote down the contested resolution, thereby not only refusing its sanction to a clause designed to be complimentary to the United States government, but also expressing, by implication, its animosity toward that government.

By 1857 Ohio Negroes were warning the government that "if you have a right to tax us for the benefit of the state . . . we have a right to demand of you protection, and if you deny us our plea, we say to you 'fie upon your law.' "[38] The Dred Scott Decision merely added fuel to the flames of Negro discontent. In New York the decision was condemned as the most infamous act in history,[39] while Ohioans declared that "we trample the Fugitive Slave Law and the dicta of the Dred Scott decision beneath our feet, as huge outrages, not only upon the Declaration of Independence and Constitution of the United States, but upon humanity itself."[40] Discouraged by the continued chain of events working to their disadvantage, prominent leaders in Ohio who had previously cautioned moderation now turned to advocating militant action. Among them were John M. Langston and William H. Day, who favored resort to arms in defiance of the Fugitive Slave Law and the Dred Scott Decision;[41] and Peter H. Clark, who expressed himself as both willing and ready to start grabbing for his rights instead of petitioning.[42]

---

[34] *Proceedings of the State Convention of Colored Citizens of the State of Illinois, Held in the City of Alton, Nov[ember] 13th, 14th and 15th, 1856* (Chicago: Hays and Thompson, 1856), pp. 6–7.

[35] *Ibid.*, p. 8.

[36] *Proceedings of the Second Annual Convention of the Colored Citizens of the State of California. Held in the City of Sacramento, Dec[ember] 9th, 10th, 11th, and 12th [1856]* (San Francisco: J. H. Udell and W. Randall, 1856), p. 13.

[37] *Ibid.*, p. 14.

[38] *Proceedings of the State Convention of Colored Men of the State of Ohio, Held in the City of Columbus, January 21st, 22d, & 23d, 1857* (Columbus: John Geary & Son, 1857), p. 17.

[39] *The Troy Daily Times*, September, 1858.

[40] *Proceedings of a Convention of the Colored Men of Ohio. Held in the City of Cincinnati, on the 23d, 24th and 26th Days of November, 1858* (Cincinnati: Moore, Wilstach, Keys & Co[mpany], 1858), pp. 15–16. Hereafter cited as *Ohio State Convention, 1858*.

[41] *Ibid.*, p. 17.

[42] *The Liberator*, December 3, 1858.

As the discontent increased, the incipient emigration movement began once more to claim the imagination of the Negro. A regular correspondent from San Francisco spoke of a Negro nationality and of a land where that nationality might develop.[43] In Ohio E. P. Walker spoke in favor of the idea that the land of coffee, sugar and cotton belonged to the colored race, and that they should congregate in that area.[44] While emigration to Canada continued, Martin R. Delany and Henry Highland Garnet were, by the close of the decade, heading rival emigration organizations interested in Africa and many Negroes were looking to Haiti as the land of promise.

In final analysis, there was ample reason for the growing militancy of a self-respecting minority. The decade of the 1850's opened with the passage of the Fugitive Slave Law—a law which tightened the yoke of slavery more firmly upon the Southern Negro, and which made even the life of the free Negro of the North insecure. America's program of "Manifest Destiny" was not conducive to quieting the fears of Negroes looking for security, even in areas beyond the borders of the United States. Nor was the Kansas-Nebraska Act or the Dred Scott Decision designed to make their place in America secure. Expatriation and re-enslavement laws added to the problems of the free Negro in the South, while the immigrants from Europe were displacing Negro labor in the North. Even the election of the first Republican in 1860 gave no reassurance to Negroes in America, for Mr. Lincoln had expressed himself as more interested in the preservation of the Union than in the freeing of the slaves. And he might well have added that he would not be pushed hurriedly into demanding equality for the free Negro.

Faced with these unfavorable conditions, the Negro acted accordingly. There was seldom a state or national convention during the decade of the 1850's which failed to emphasize the position of the Negro community in its demand for the elimination of slavery and for equality before the law. Twice during the decade the Negro's desire to be free from his second-class citizenship had caused so much interest in emigration that established leaders were hard pressed to devise a program to counteract that interest. And the program which these leaders devised, though opposed to emigration, was, nevertheless, similarly militant in spirit and motivated by the same desire—a desire for the recognition of the value of each person as a human being worthy of the consideration and respect of his peers.

[43] *The Weekly Anglo-African* (New York), November 26, 1859.

[44] *Ohio State Convention, 1858*, pp. 11–12.

# 14

## THE POLITICS OF FREEDOM
*Benjamin Quarles*

❧ T HE right to vote never loomed so large to Negroes as in the two decades before the Civil War. Through political action slavery might be rooted out and equal justice brought into play. A Negro electorate could give needed support to antislavery men and measures in Congress. Fairer treatment of the Negro could be gotten locally if white legislators had to reckon with a colored constituency.

But the Negro who wished to vote faced a sea of troubles. The great friend of the colored man, William Lloyd Garrison, decried politics, holding that the Constitution was proslavery and that all who took an oath of office to support it were ridden with the virus. But Garrison's theories of non-voting and disunion were maintained by only a handful of Negro leaders. Robert Purvis held fast to the Garrisonian viewpoints, crying in May 1857 that the United States government was "one of the badest, meanest, most atrocious despotisms that ever saw the face of the sun." During the same month, Charles Lenox Remond, in a debate with Frederick Douglass at Shiloh Church in New York, argued that the Constitution was proslavery. But in 1848 Remond had temporarily abandoned his nonvoting stance when he cast a ballot for Stephen C. Phillips, Free Soil candidate for governor, justifying his action on the grounds that Phillips had favored larger appro-priations for Negro schools.[1]

It the great majority of Negroes could not support Garrison's views on politics, they could sympathize with his single-minded devotion to the principle of nonvoting. But what left them unsympathetic and stirred up was the lukewarm reaction toward Negro suffrage that characterized the majority of the voting abolitionists. Ahead of their times in some important respects, the abolitionists nonetheless were in the main much like other Americans of their day when it came to political equality for the Negro. The freedom of the slave, yes. But to stand at the polls on a par with the black man, this was another matter. The friends of the colored people took part in antislavery work as a matter of duty, wrote the San Francisco cor-respondent of *Frederick Douglass' Weekly,* but they were no more likely to believe that Negroes were naturally equal to whites than they were to believe that chalk was cheese.[2] Many white abolitionists shared the com-mon belief that political equality would lead inevitably to social equality, something for which they were not ready.

Benjamin Quarles, *Black Abolitionists* (New York: Oxford University Press, 1969), pp. 168–177, 180–190, 195–196. Reprinted by permission of the publisher.

[1] *Standard,* May 23, 1857. *Ibid.* May 30, 1857. *Ibid.* June 7, 1849.

[2] *Douglass' Paper,* June 15, 1855.

Another discouragement for the vote-minded Negro was the legal barrier. By 1860 equal suffrage existed only in New England, excluding Connecticut. In the remaining states the Negro was barred outright from the polls or, as in New York, faced with a property requirement.[3] Colored men found their exclusion particularly galling since it came during a period in which voting rights were being expanded. In many states the political disfranchisement of the black man took place almost simultaneously with the removal of all barriers for white men.

This conferring of the ballot upon the white workingman brought a special problem to the Negro, for it added to the electorate a class which opposed his advancement. The white mechanics and workers in the North feared the Negro as a labor competitor, and this fear was well known to politicians. Increasingly, therefore, the voteless black man became a whipping-boy for office-seekers pandering to race prejudice. In 1855 a Negro San Franciscan likened the colored people of California to a beast of burden by which political demagogues rode into power.[4]

Participation in political life would not be easy for Negroes—this they knew. But the outlook was not wholly bleak. The colored people would have to bear the brunt of the battle themselves, but they knew there were some whites, men of influence if small in number, upon whom they could count. And, best of all, politics and political parties were in a state of flux after 1840, and out of the new equilibrium might come a new niche for the Negro. "Amid the confusion of parties and the death struggle of old political dynasties," wrote J. W. Loguen to Frederick Douglass in the spring of 1855, "we cannot fail to accomplish much with proper exertion."[5]

The Negro seeking to strike at slavery through political action operated on both state and national levels. He had to win the ballot in his own commonwealth and then to support the political party best serving his interests in the Congress and, if possible, at the White House. It was the first of these steps that was crucial and difficult—to wipe out the states' legal requirement that the ballot be conferred upon whites only, or that Negroes meet special qualifications.

Negroes in New York had faced this "strings attached" problem since 1821, when a state constitutional convention decreed that before a Negro could vote he had to own $250 worth of landed property. The convention, and subsequently the voters, ignored a petition of protest from fifty

[3] For Negro disfranchisement see Charles H. Wesley, *Neglected History* (Wilberforce, Ohio, 1965), 41–77; Litwack, *North of Slavery*, and the pioneer study, still useful, Emil Olbrich, *The Development of Sentiment on Negro Suffrage to 1860* (Madison, Wis., 1912); hereafter cited as *Negro Suffrage*.

[4] *Douglass' Paper*, May 4, 1855.

[5] Loguen to Douglass, Apr. 9, 1855, *Douglass' Paper*, Apr. 20, 1855.

Negroes, twenty of whom could write their own names. In 1826 the state legislature added to the vexation of the Negroes by voting to retain the property proviso.

With the rise of the militant abolitionist movement the colo ed people throughout the state initiated a drumfire against the restriction. In February 1837 the Negroes of New York City, led by such abolitionist figures as Philip A. Bell, Samuel E. Cornish, Thomas Downing, Thomas L. Jennings, Thomas Van Rensselaer, and Henry Sipkins, held a meeting at which they drafted a petition to the state legislature to remove the Negro suffrage restriction. After the meeting the petition was kept at Phoenix Hall for three days in order to run up the number of signatures. At the end of this period of grace the document bore 620 names, 365 of them in the signers' own handwriting, one of which read, "Independence Roberts, born on 4th of July, 1776, in Philadelphia." Placed in a double envelope, the petition was taken to Albany by a special messenger and delivered in person to the mail guard at the state house. Reaching the legislature at the same time were similar petitions from Negroes in Oswego and Genessee counties and Albany.[6]

The legislature proved unresponsive, thus bringing upon itself the condemnation of a monster meeting of Negro young men in New York City on August 21, 1837, with speeches by Timothy Seaman, John Zuille, Henry Highland Garnet, and George T. Downing. The meeting authorized Charles B. Ray and Philip A. Bell to visit Negroes throughout the state urging them to deluge the legislature with petitions to abrogate the property requirement for Negro voting.[7]

The silence of the legislature did not crush the Negroes, since they had decided that if one petition failed, another would be presented. This drafting of petition after petition was the avowed object of the Association for the Political Improvement of the People of Color, formed in New York in July 1838. Two months later the association sent a supply of blank petitions to Utica for distribution at the New York State Anti-Slavery Society. With young Alexander Crummell as one of the secretaries at the Utica meeting and Thomas S. Wright as one of the featured speakers, the association felt that the petitions would not lack signers. In the following year the association held an August 1 meeting in New York City, at which petitions were circulated before and after the oration by Alexander Crummell.[8]

In the summer of 1840 the Negroes held a statewide convention at Albany, based on the proposition that "political disfranchisement is becoming more and more odious." With Austin Steward as president and William H. Topp, Charles L. Reason, and H. H. Garnet as secretaries, the convention drew up an address to the colored people of the common-

[6] Colored American, Mar. 11, 1837, and Philanthropist, Mar. 31, 1837.

[7] Colored American, Sept. 2, 1837, and Emancipator, Sept. 7, 1837.

[8] Colored American, July 4, 1838. Ibid. Oct. 6, 1838. Ibid. Aug. 17, 1839.

wealth calling upon them to press for the ballot: "Let every man send in his remonstrance. Let petitions be scattered in every quarter."[9]

But if the colored people were aroused, the white voters of the state were indifferent, making no effort to remove the property proviso for Negroes. With the emergence of the Liberty party in the 1840's it was inevitable that the equal suffrage issue would come before the constitutional convention of 1846. This body referred the question to the electorate, with results that were hardly surprising. In November 1846 the property qualification for Negroes was retained by a vote of 224,000 to 85,000. It is to be noted that in addition to the race and color factor the Negro's political inclinations entered into this lob-sided tally. Negroes were Whiggish or Liberty party-ish and hence could hardly expect Democrats to vote for a measure that would add to the political strength of their opponents.

The pattern in New York did not change for the remainder of the prewar period, with Negroes pressing without success for equal suffrage. At a state convention held in Troy in September 1855 the delegates condemned political discrimination and proceeded to organize the New York State Suffrage Association. Stephen Myers was appointed lobbyist at Albany. In this capacity he attended the sessions of the legislature, buttonholing most of its members. In February 1856 Myers reported that two-thirds of the lawmakers were favorable to extending the franchise.[10] But either this figure was inflated, or a number of men changed their minds.

Four years later, during another presidential year, the issue was still high on the agenda of the New York Negroes. The state suffrage association was now joined by a number of local groups, including the New York County Suffrage Committee, the Brooklyn Elective Franchise Club, the Albany County Suffrage Club, and the Elective Franchise Club of Ithaca. By September 1860 there were forty-eight local suffrage clubs in New York City and eighteen in Brooklyn. But again the voters turned down the equal suffrage proposal. The negative vote was smaller in percentage than in 1846, but there was no ambiguity as to the result, 337,900 to 197,000. Sorrowfully the members of the state suffrage committee might have read again one of the lines appearing in a pre-election circular they had issued: "Our white countrymen do not know us. They are strangers to our characters, ignorant of our capacity, oblivious to our history and progress, and are misinformed as to the principles and ideas that control and guide us, as a people."[11]

The Negro in Pennsylvania had to undergo a political shock even greater than that of his fellows in New York. Down to 1838 many Negroes had voted in Pennsylvania, but this privilege was abrogated in that year

[9] *Emancipator*, Dec. 31, 1840.

[10] *Douglass' Paper*, Sept. 14, 1855. *Ibid.* Feb. 22, 1856.

[11] *The Suffrage Question in Relation to Colored Voters in the State of New York* (no place or date, but undoubtedly New York, 1860), 2.

when a constitutional convention added the word "white" to the suffrage requirement. During the extended debate the convention had received a number of petitions on the issue, two from groups of Negroes in Philadelphia and Luzerne calling for impartial suffrage.[12]

While the new constitution was before the voters the Negroes drew up a lengthy protest, an "Appeal of Forty Thousand Citizens Threatened With Disfranchisement, to the People of Pennsylvania." Largely the work of Robert Purvis, it told of the role of the Negro in the history of the state and described his progress and his present condition. It bore an abolitionist flavor:

*We freely acknowledge our brotherhood to the slave, and our interest in his welfare. Is this a crime for which we should be ignominiously punished? The very fact that we are deeply interested in our kindred in bonds shows that we are the right sort of stuff to make good citizens. Were we not so, we should better deserve a lodging in your pentitentiaries than a franchise at your polls.[13]*

Despite its erudition and its eloquence, the appeal did not change many minds. The anti-abolitionist outbreak at Pennsylvania Hall in May 1838, although not the work of the reformers, brought about an increase in sentiment against Negro voting. Hence, in October the new constitution disfranchising the colored man won decisive approval at the polls. The Negroes were dismayed, their mood deepened by the story of a white boy who seized the marbles of a colored boy, telling him, "You have no rights now."[14]

During the 1840's Pennsylvania Negroes kept the suffrage issue alive through county and state conventions. One of the latter, meeting at Harrisburg in December 1848, asked the white voters to petition the legislature, adding somewhat plaintively that "our petitions can only reach the Humanity of the Legislator, while yours will instruct him in a course of action." At the annual meetings of the Pennsylvania Anti-Slavery Society, Negro participants such as Purvis, Remond, J. J. G. Bias, and Thomas Van Rensselaer, invariably got in a word condemning the disfranchisement of the blacks. The Negro protest was also expressed in petitions and memorials sent to the state legislature, the number totaling eighty-one from 1839 to 1851.[15]

---

[12] Olbrich, *Negro Suffrage*, 53.

[13] *Appeal of Forty Thousand Citizens Threatened with Disfranchisement, to the People of Pennsylvania* (Phila., 1838), 18.

[14] Joseph B. Braithwaite, ed., *Memoirs of Joseph John Guerney* (Phila., 1854), 131.

[15] *Minutes of the State Convention of Colored Citizens of Pennsylvania, Convened at Harrisburg, December 13 and 14, 1848* (Phila., 1849), 10. Edward R. Turner, *The Negro in Pennsylvania, 1619–1861* (Washington, D. C., 1911), 191, n. 81.

The unresponsiveness of the state legislature led Philadelphia Negroes to take the unusual step in 1855 of sending a petition on a state issue to Congress. This "Memorial of Thirty Thousand Disfranchised Citizens of Philadelphia to the Honorable Senate and House of Representatives" was a recital of the Negro's record of patriotism and good citizenship, his ownership of property, and his payment of taxes. But this appeal to the national legislature brought results as barren as those sent previously to the state capital at Harrisburg. Nearly twenty years of such legislative indifference had a dispiriting effect on some Negroes. At Philadelphia during the winter of 1856–57 two public meetings on equal suffrage drew small audiences of some forty each.[16]

In New Jersey and Connecticut Negroes held state conventions to obtain the suffrage. Such meetings followed a familiar pattern—the drafting of a document which listed the grievances of the Negroes, affirmed their right to vote, through residence, military service, or taxpaying, and appealed to the white electorate's sense of fair play. The result was negative in both states although in New Jersey the Judiciary Committee of the lower house brought out a favorable report.[17]

In the Midwest the Negro protest against political discrimination was voiced in Illinois, Iowa, Michigan, and Wisconsin. In Illinois the call to a state convention of colored citizens to be held at Alton in November 1856 stated the key issue in the opening sentence—"First: We complain of being taxed without the right to vote." In Ohio with its large black population the outcries were louder and more sustained than elsewhere in the region. Ohio Negroes held seven state conventions in the decade before the Civil War, six of them at Columbus and one at Cincinnati. One of the Columbus meetings was held in the legislative hall, the assembly having graciously granted the request by the Negroes.[18]

The most prominent of the participants in the Ohio conventions was J. Mercer Langston, offspring of a wealthy Virginia planter, graduate of Oberlin, and a practicing lawyer, having passed the state bar in 1850. Langston was a member of a small committee selected at the convention of 1851 to visit Governor Reuben Wood seeking his support in removing the Negro's political disability. The state convention of 1854 selected Langston to draw up an equal suffrage petition to the legislature. Langston's memorial was read at the state senate meeting on April 14, those who listened not finding it unworthy of their attention. In 1856 the State Central Committee of Colored People of Ohio appointed Langston as lecturer and

[16] Memorial of Thirty Thousand Disfranchised Citizens of Philadelphia to the Honorable Senate and House of Representatives (Phila., 1855). W. Still to Provincial Freeman, Mar. 15, 1857, in Provincial Freeman, Mar. 28, 1857.

[17] Marion T. Wright, "Negro Suffrage in New Jersey, 1776–1875," Journal of Negro History, Apr. 1948 (XXXIII), 191.

[18] Proceedings of the State Convention of Colored Citizens of the State of Illinois, Held in the City of Alton, November 13, 14, 15, 1856 (Chicago, 1856), 3. Bugle, Jan. 19, 1850.

agent to canvass the state in the interest of Negro suffrage, not only speaking but taking up collections and soliciting donations in the committee's name.[19]

But the idea of the black man as a voter was slow in winning converts. In 1849 Negroes had finally won the right to testify against whites in legal proceedings. But if Ohioans were ready for a measure of equality in the courts this was not the case at the polls.

To Negroes west of the Mississippi this issue of testifying against whites took priority even over the privilege of voting. In California the law depriving the Negro of his oath in court was the major topic to come before the statewide Negro conventions held in 1855, 1856, and 1857. At the first gathering, held in Sacramento, the forty-seven delegates from ten counties drafted an address to the people of the state clearly setting forth the problem: "You have enacted a law excluding our testimony in the courts of justice in this State, in cases of proceedings in wherein white persons are parties, thus openly encouraging and countenancing the vicious and dishonest to take advantage of us."[20]

The California petitioners were heartened by a message from Philadelphia Negroes who commended "their brethren on the Pacific coast" for their noble struggle for the rights of man. White Californians did not view the petition in quite this cosmic light. Like the people in the other nonslave states, Californians feared that the removal of restrictions on Negroes might lead to an increase in their numbers. In California, however, the already racially mixed population made it more difficult to discriminate against the Negro.[21] Hence in 1861 the law barring Negro testimony was repealed. But California was not ready to revise its policy of white manhood suffrage, its Negro voting restrictions remaining on the statute books until the Fifteenth Amendment in 1870. And, except for Wisconsin, this would be the case in all the other states where such restrictions existed.

The denial of the right to vote was discouraging to black abolitionists. Most of them, however, took an optimistic, long-range point of view. Jacob C. White, speaking at the closing exercises of the Philadelphia colored high school in May 1855, at which the governor of the state was the honored guest, stressed the point that although Negroes were "not recognized in the political arrangements of the Commonwealth," they were preparing themselves for a future day when citizenship in America would be based on manhood and not on color. . . .[22]

---

[19] Bugle, Feb. 22, 1851. The Langston memorial is carried in Douglass' Paper, June 16, 1854. Ibid. July 25, 1856.

[20] Proceedings of the First State Convention of the Colored Citizens of the State of California (Sacramento, 1855), 27.

[21] Douglass' Paper, Dec. 7, 1855. Eugene H. Berwanger, "The 'Black Law' Question in Ante-Bellum California," Journal of the West, Apr. 1967 (VI), 218.

[22] Still to Mary Ann Shadd, May 30, 1855, in Provincial Freeman, June 9, 1855.

Woman suffrage, white or black, was not achieved in ante-bellum America and Negro manhood suffrage was limited. But Negro abolitionists maintained their interest in politics, realizing its importance in a country in which the voice of the people was deified. And in this popular chorus the voice of the Negro was not completely stilled. In some states the colored man could vote and join political parties, and in all states he could exercise the right of petition.

The Negro's role as a voter and party-worker was strongest in New England and New York. The Negroes in Massachusetts had been politically active since the emergence of the new abolitionists. A group of colored Bostonians attended a legislative hearing at the state house in March 1838 at which five white abolitionists, including Angelina Grimké, testified against slavery and on behalf of the free Negro. At a meeting held shortly thereafter, the Boston Negroes commended the state-house sergeant at arms for treating them courteously, and thanked their white friends who testified at the hearing. Four years later another breakthrough took place when Charles Lenox Remond appeared before a Massachusetts House of Representatives committee to protest against jimcrow on the railroads and steamboats. In his remarks Remond referred to the "elective franchise," saying that if the Negroes in Massachusetts had it he saw no reason why it should be denied in other states. A year later the Negroes of Boston petitioned the legislature to prohibit segregation in public transportation and repeal the law against intermarriage.[23]

At New Bedford the Negroes had a meeting in October 1839 pledging themselves to vote for no official, from governor down, who was not in favor of immediate abolition. A committee of eighty-three was appointed to visit the candidates for public office, putting to them a series of questions, of which the first two are typical: "Is Liberty the will of the Creator? Does Congress have the power to abolish slavery in the District of Columbia, and should such power be immediately exercised?"[24]

In Rhode Island the Negroes managed to retain equal suffrage despite an effort in 1841 to push through a new constitution which eliminated the Negro voter. Supported by resident Negroes like Alexander Crummell, a team of white abolitionists along with Frederick Douglass journeyed to the state late in 1841. The abolitionists and black supporters held a series of meetings, some of them broken up by mobs opposed to "nigger voting."[25] The constitution adopted in 1843, however, had no race or other qualification for voting. Negroes increasingly voted throughout the state, but, topped by the nearly four hundred other registrants in Providence, their numbers were not large enough to win concessions from the political parties.

It was in New York State that political activity among Negroes reached

---

[23] *Liberator*, Mar. 30, 1838. *Ibid*. Feb 25, 1842. *Ibid*. Feb. 10, 1843.

[24] *Ibid*. Nov. 1, 1839.

[25] *Standard*, Dec. 23, 1841.

its peak, many of them being able to meet the property requirement. These qualified colored men were not likely to spurn a privilege like the ballot, particularly with the Negro press spurring them on. *Rights of All* urged its readers to get out and vote, admonishing them to make their choices carefully: "Set an example for the whites, who are already, too many of them, politically half crazy." Another editor advised unpropertied Negroes to save the money they spent on "perishable finery" at the clothing store in order to accumulate enough to enable them to go to the polls.[26]

The number of Negroes eligible to vote is not easy to determine. In New York City the figure reached 250 in 1838. Six years later there was a 1000 total for the state. In 1846 abolitionist Gerrit Smith set aside 120,000 acres for colored men (drunkards excluded), one of his purposes being the increase in the number of black voters. The Smith grantees eventually totaled 1985. By 1850 the list of qualified colored voters had risen to 1200 for New York City and environs. And whatever the figures they do not tell the whole story. Many Negroes followed the advice given by suffrage-seeking organizations: If denied the right to vote yourself, try to influence others to cast their ballots for the right candidates.[27]

Negroes eligible to vote needed no exhortation to exercise it. An organization calling itself the Colored Freeholders of the City and County of New York met periodically after 1838. At their first meeting, held in Philomathian Hall on October 29, 1838, they drafted two resolutions against slavery and one in support of Luther Bradish for lieutenant governor. Bradish had gone on record as favoring equal suffrage and passage of a law granting a jury trial to alleged fugitives. The public official that won the greatest admiration of the colored voter was Governor William H. Seward. A group of Negroes meeting in Union Hall in December 1842 sent him an address praising his antislavery stance—his refusal to render fugitives, his approval of the act establishing trial by jury in runaway slave cases, and the repeal of the nine months' residence law permitting slavery. In a gracious responding letter, Seward expressed his gratitude for the tribute.[28]

After 1840 the attention of the politically minded New York Negro was drawn to the new political parties that took an antislavery posture. Interest in these new alignments was felt no less by Negroes throughout the North. Hence while focusing attention on the relationship between Empire State Negroes and the new parties, it would be well on occasion to touch upon the wider scene.

---

[26] *Rights of All*, Oct. 16, 1829. *Human Rights*, in *Herald of Freedom*, Dec. 22, 1838.

[27] *Herald of Freedom*, Dec. 22, 1838. Olbrich, *Negro Suffrage*, 72. *An Address to the Three Thousand Colored Citizens of New York Who are the Owners of One Hundred and Twenty Thousand Acres of Land in the State of New York, Given Them by Gerrit Smith, Esquire, September 1, 1846* (New York, 1846). *Standard*, Nov. 8, 1849. *Douglass' Monthly*, Oct. 1860.

[28] *Colored American*, Nov. 3, 1838. *Standard*, Jan. 26, 1843.

The first of these new political groups bore a magic name to Negroes, the Liberty party. Founded in 1839 this body reflected the belief that the existing parties, Whigs and Democrats, could never strike a strong blow at slavery because their memberships counted hundred of thousands of slave-owners. Hence only a new party could really push for measures repealing the fugitive slave laws, striking at slavery in the District of Columbia, prohibiting the domestic slave trade and excluding slavery from the territories. By 1839 most abolitionists west of Massachusetts were ready for independent political action. In April of the following year the new party selected James G. Birney and Thomas Earle, both active abolitionists, as its candidates for president and vice president.

One of the earliest responses to the new party's nominees came from a group of Albany Negroes meeting at the Baptist Church late in April, with Benjamin Paul in the chair. After the standard denunciation of the property qualification for Negro voting in New York, the group called upon all colored voters to sustain Birney and Earle in the coming election. The convention urged Negroes throughout the North to be politically active so as to "hasten the consummation of our disenthralment from partial and actual bondage." The new party won the enthusiastic support of *The Colored American,* which generally furnished an accurate barometer of Negro thought.[29]

In the presidential election, Birney polled barely seven thousand votes, but his followers were not to be discouraged. Six months after the election the party's central nominating committee met in New York to select the standard-bearers for the 1844 campaign. The committee members included Theodore S. Wright, John J. Zuille, and Charles B. Ray. Among Negroes the most ardent of the early Liberty party men was Henry Highland Garnet. At the convention of the Massachusetts branch of the party, which was held in Boston in February 1842, Garnet delivered one of the major addresses. A defense of the principles and goals of the new party, Garnet's speech was enthusiastically received, the Faneuil Hall audience constantly interrupting him with laughter, applause, and cries of "hear, hear." The delegates also listened to a plea for money from Lunsford Lane, raising $33 to help him purchase a member of his family.[30]

Garnet took his Liberty party advocacy to the national convention of colored men held at Buffalo in August 1843. His resolution endorsing the new party was supported by Theodore S. Wright, Charles B. Ray, and nearly fifty others. With only seven dissenting votes the delegates gave their blessing to the Liberty party, a circumstance that Garnet reported with pride at the national meeting of the party held two weeks later in the same city.

At this Buffalo convention of the Liberty party three Negroes took a prominent part. Garnet delivered an address on a resolution he had proposed affirming that the new party was the only one in the country that

[29] *Emancipator,* May 15, 1840. *Colored American,* May 23, 1840.

[30] *Emancipator and Free American,* Mar. 4, 1842.

represented the true spirit of liberty. Samuel Ringgold Ward opened one of the sessions with prayer and also delivered a formal address, and Charles B. Ray served as one of the convention secretaries. Two of the party planks referred to the colored man, one extending a cordial welcome to him to join the party and another condemning racial discrimination as a relic of slavery.

Garnet and Henry Bibb took the field for the Liberty party in the election of 1844, the latter speaking mainly in Michigan. The party polled some sixty-two thousand votes, which was a considerable improvement over the results of the preceding presidential campaign. But Theodore S. Wright found reason for vexation because many Negroes still clung to the old patries.[31]

Support for the Liberty party of both Negroes and whites declined after the peak year of 1844. By the time of the next presidential campaign the party had split into two factions. But the greatest reason for its declining fortunes was the emergence in 1848 of a new party, the Free Soilers. This party, too, owed its existence to the slavery issue. Democrats and Whigs who opposed the extension of slavery in the territories met in Buffalo in the summer of 1848 and organized a new party with the proclaimed goals of free soil, free speech, free labor, and free men.

The question facing the Negro voter in 1848 was whether to support the badly enfeebled Liberty party or the seemingly vigorous Free Soilers. The latter had chosen as its standard-bearer Martin Van Buren, a former president of whom Negroes had no fond memories. In his inaugural address eleven years earlier, he had announced his opposition to the abolition of slavery in the District of Columbia and his intention not to interfere with slavery wherever it existed. Samuel R. Ward took a strong stand against the Van Buren-led Free Soil party, but the great majority of Negroes took a half-a-loaf attitude, believing that it would be wiser to support the party that had a chance to win.

In New York the Free Soilers won more support from Negroes than any of the rival parties. They did much better in Massachusetts, where some communities voted the ticket almost unanimously. This was not the case, however, in Rhode Island. Here the Whigs issued a pamphlet reminding the Negro that it was they who had fought six years earlier to retain his right to vote.[32] Such peculiar and local considerations operated against the Free Soilers in more than one state, thus contributing to its failure to carry a single one of them and to elect only five men to Congress.

The elections of 1848, while hardly cheering to Negroes, had demonstrated that the old parties were splitting. This circumstance was viewed by the more optimistic as a proof of the progress of the abolitionist crusade. And despite their outcome, the elections had whetted the Negro's interest in politics and his desire to be a participant in its processes. This interest

[31] Wright to Joshua Leavitt, Oct. 19, 1844, in *Emancipator*, Oct. 30, 1844.

[32] *North Star*, Nov. 24, 1848.

tended to remain largely in the Free Soilers. This party numbered such friends of the colored people as Joshua Giddings, Salmon P. Chase of Ohio, and Charles Sumner, Henry Wilson, and Charles Francis Adams of Massachusetts. In Ohio it was the Free Soil party that championed Negro suffrage, and in Massachusetts it was Free Soil men who had successfully battled to remove discrimination in the marriage laws, in transportation, and in the public schools.

Negroes attended the national convention of the Free Soil party in August 1852 at Pittsburgh, held to select presidential candidates. The speaker drawing the loudest applause was Frederick Douglass, even though he emphasized that slavery should be exterminated rather than merely contained, as the Free Soilers advocated. Their party platform did not go that far, and it was silent as to the discriminations against the free Negro. But for national office the convention selected two men highly regarded by the colored people, John P. Hale and George W. Julian.

In the closing weeks of the campaign Free Soil Negroes throughout New England held a series of rallies in Boston, all characterized, according to William C. Nell, by great enthusiasm. At these gatherings such political figures as Hale, Sumner, Giddings, and Horace Mann were praised, and the two old parties were condemned. The speakers, including J. C. Beman of Connecticut and William J. Watkins and Jermain W. Loguen of New York, called upon the colored voter to sustain Free-Soilery and thereby advance the antislavery cause.[33]

A handful of Negroes, and not many more whites, remained with the Liberty party, headed by Gerrit Smith, the reformer-philanthropist. Smith, campaigning for Congress, won a seat, but on a local issue unrelated to slavery. Otherwise the elections brought little cheer to Negroes and abolitionists, the Free Soil vote being smaller than that of 1848.

Antislavery political parties, however, were far from having run their course, the greatest one of all coming into existence in 1854. In that year the Kansas-Nebraska Act, opening the door to slavery in territory where it had been prohibited since 1820, created a deep resentment in the North. "This Nebraska business is the great smasher in Syracuse, as elsewhere," wrote J. W. Loguen to Frederick Douglass, adding that the atrocious villainy of the author of the bill, Stephen A. Douglas, was doing a fine work for the slave, "but no thanks to him." A group of Philadelphia Negroes, headed by James McCrummell, held a meeting condemning the act on the grounds that slavery could not be legalized, and praising the congressmen who voted against it, Seward, Chase, Sumner, Giddings, Gerrit Smith, and Benjamin F. Wade.[34]

Negroes were not the only ones bitterly opposing the measure. Its passage prompted "Conscience" Whigs and antislavery Democrats to join with the Free Soilers to form a new party, the Republicans. Its ranks grew

[33] *Liberator*, Dec. 10, 1852.

[34] Loguen to Douglass, Mar. 7, 1854, in *Douglass' Paper*, Apr. 14, 1854. *Ibid.* Apr. 7, 1854.

rapidly, spurred by the news of the bloody conflicts that accompanied the opening of Kansas.

Negroes as a whole hailed this newer and stronger party committed to the containment of slavery. But there were a few dozen colored voters who, like the Liberty party to which they belonged, refused fellowship with the Republicans. With a stubbornness almost unparalleled in politics, the Liberty party would not take itself out of existence. Despite its microscopic vote in 1852 the party scheduled two conventions in New York in 1853, the second of them at Canastota in October, with Jermain W. Loguen presiding.[35] A year later at Syracuse, thirty Liberty party diehards, among them Frederick Douglass, went through the ritual of nominating a candidate for governor and declaring that it was the right and duty of the federal government to do away with slavery.

The coming of the Republicans did force the Liberty party people to make one change, that of experimenting with a new name. The Radical Abolition party was organized in June 1855 at Syracuse, with J. McCune Smith as the presiding officer at the three-day convention. The party platform was indicated in the title of a lengthy statement drafted by the delegates, an "Exposition of the Constitutional Duty of the Federal Government to Abolish Slavery." The Radical Abolitionists held two subsequent conventions, one in Boston in October 1855 and the other at Syracuse in May 1856. Four Negro leaders took part in these gatherings, Smith, Douglass, Amos Beman, and J. W. Loguen.

The mass of Negro voters, however, made no effort to join the Radical party, despite its name. They felt that its chances of success were remote to the point of fantasy, a prediction that proved all too true. This attitude of "why waste your vote" even affected Frederick Douglass, who in mid-August 1856 announced that he was switching his support to the Republicans. Like the great majority of Americans, white or black, Douglass wanted his vote to count for something more than the affirmation of an abstract principle, however noble. Compromise was unavoidable if a political party hoped to attract enough voters to win at the polls. Negroes soothed their consciences by reasoning that the Republican party had a chance to win, that its victory would prevent any extension of slavery into the territories, and that such a policy of containment would cause slavery to die out for lack of breathing space.

The Republicans looked less drab to the Negro when contrasted with the only major alternative party, the Democrats. A group of Ohio Negroes meeting early in 1856 voiced its support of the Republicans because the opposing party was "the black-hearted apostle of American Slavery." Later in the year, Henry Highland Garnet took the same position in urging New York State's six thousand black voters to come out for the Republicans. Of all the things he hated to see, said Garnet, the worst was a black Democrat, although he had to admit that there were some colored men who were

[35] Pennsylvania Freeman, Oct. 13, 1853.

"so ignorant and misguided as to favor these avowed supporters of the enslavement of their race."[36] Negro support of the new party became even more solid after its opponents dubbed its followers as "Black Republicans."

Whatever one party might call another, the key issue in the election was slavery in the territories. The Republicans lost at the polls, but their candidate, John C. Frémont, did amass a popular vote of 1,340,000 as against James Buchanan's 1,838,000. Such a large vote for the candidate of a party only two years old certainly augured a promising future, an optimism shared by the Negroes.

Essentially their policy was a continuing attack on the Democrats. At a convention of Negroes in Troy in September 1858, the fifty-five delegates avowed that they were Radical abolitionists at heart but that their strong desire to defeat the Democrats would lead them to throw their support to the Republicans. The convention appointed William J. Watkins as a traveling solicitor to drum up Republican votes. A month later Watkins went to Cincinnati to attend the state convention of colored men. Here at Union Baptist Church he added his voice to that of John Mercer Langston and others to the effect that the Democratic party must be destroyed. Support for the Republicans, while strong, did not meet with the same unanimity, Peter H. Clark asserting that the rights of the Negro were no safer with the Republicans than with the Democrats.[37]

Negroes in the Northeast, like those in Ohio and New York, gave their support to the Republicans. A convention of New England Negroes meeting at Tremont Temple on August 1, 1859, with George T. Downing in the chair, gave its endorsement to the new party. The delegates voted, however, to press the Republicans to give their support to the black man's struggle for the right to vote. By so doing, they pointed out, the party would deserve the support of all who favored the cause of freedom.[38]

By election time in 1860 the Negro vote was almost solidly Republican. Their only possible rivals for black ballots, the Radical Abolitionists, were weaker, if possible, than in 1856. And, as in that year, the Republicans, although making no effort to win the colored vote, were attacked by the Democrats as being "nigger worshipers." Negroes, if only to strike back, almost had to support the Republicans. Thus did the colored man ally himself with a party that was not as much a workingman's party as the Democrats were. But he could scarcely join a party that villified him.

The victory of the Republicans in 1860 heartened the Negroes and the voting abolitionists. There was, however, a sense of frustration over the decisive defeat, previously noted, of the equal suffrage amendment in New York. "We were overshadowed and smothered by the Presidential struggle

[36] *Pro. of State Con. of Colored Men . . . 1856*, 2. *Douglass' Paper*, Oct. 3, 1856.

[37] *Standard*, Oct. 9, 1858. *Proceedings of a Convention of the Colored Men of Ohio, Held in Cincinnati, November 23, 24, 25, 26, 1858*, passim.

[38] *Weekly Anglo-African*, Aug. 6, 1859.

—over laid by Abraham Lincoln and Hannibal Hamlin," wrote Frederick Douglass. "The black baby of Negro Suffrage was thought too ugly to exhibit on so grand an occasion."[39] Hence, while the elections of 1860 were more favorable for the antislavery crusaders than in any preceding quadrennial campaign, it was evident that racial discrimination and its sustaining base of slavery still exerted a formidable influence. . . .

To the various state legislatures in the North came petitions from Negro residents. As a rule these memorials dealt with discriminatory measures, impending or already enacted, against colored people. These petitions had one other thing in common—their instigators were almost invariably active abolitionists. For example, the eleven-page memorial sent to the Pennsylvania assembly in March 1832, protesting against a proposed bill severely limiting Negro migration to Pennsylvania, was planned at a meeting at which James C. McCrummell was chairman and Jacob C. White was secretary. The petition was worded by three men of equal reputation as black abolitionists—James Forten, Robert Purvis, and William Whipper.

In their petitions to state legislatures, then, Negroes were not addressing themselves solely to local or internal grievances. They were at the same time leveling their pieces at much bigger game—the jungle king of slavery.

Abolitionists found that political activity brought some gains. But it had its limitations. Petitions were of little good unless they were followed up. Voting for a winning candidate did not ensure the desired legislation. And even the law itself, particularly a new law, often turned out to be less binding than social and economic pressures. These strong pressures came to the fore in American life with a compelling urgency in the 1850s. And, with a twist that was not wholly surprising, they made their debut with a law relating to fugitive slaves.

[39] *Douglass' Monthly,* Dec. 1860.

## SUGGESTIONS FOR FURTHER READING

**A**MONG the accounts of free Afro-Americans in the South are John Hope Franklin, *The Free Negro in North Carolina, 1790–1860* (Chapel Hill, 1943); *Luther P. Jackson, *Free Negro Labor and Property Holding in Virginia, 1830–1860* (New York, 1942); and Carter G. Woodson, *Free Negro Owners of Slaves in the United States in 1830* (Washington, D.C., 1925). For discussions of black men in various occupations, see Philip Durham, "The Negro

* An asterisk indicates that the book is available in paperback.

Cowboy," *American Quarterly*, VII (Fall 1955); *John H. Russell, *The Free Negro in Virginia, 1619–1865* (Baltimore, Md., 1913); and Charles S. Sydnor, "The Free Negro in Mississippi before the Civil War," *American Historical Review*, XXXII (July 1927).

The most informative survey of the status of northern black men is *Leon Litwack, *North of Slavery, The Negro in the Free States, 1790–1860* (Chicago, 1961). Louis Ruchames, "Jim Crow Railroads in Massachusetts," *American Quarterly*, VIII (Spring 1956); Eugene H. Berwanger, *The Frontier Against Slavery: Western Anti-Negro Prejudice and the Slavery Extension Controversy* (Urbana, Ill., 1967); and Lorman Ratner, *Powder Keg: Northern Opposition to the Anti-Slavery Movement* (New York, 1968) unveil the northern counterpart to southern racism. Topical studies of the black man's status are Robert Ernst, "The Economic Status of New York City Negroes, 1850–1863," *Negro History Bulletin*, XII (March 1949); Carter G. Woodson, *The Education of the Negro Prior to 1861* (New York, 1915); and by the same author, *The History of the Negro Church* (Washington, D.C., 1921).

*Larry Gara, *The Liberty Line: The Legend of the Underground Railroad* (Lexington, Ky., 1961) analyzes the relationship between free black men and fugitive slaves. *Benjamin Quarles, *Black Abolitionists* excerpted in this chapter, can be supplemented by his biography of Frederick Douglass; by Ray A. Billington, "James Forten: Forgotten Abolitionist," *Negro History Bulletin*, XIII (November 1949); and William M. Brewer, "John B. Russwurm," *Journal of Negro History*, XIII (October 1928). The relationship between black and white abolitionists is analyzed in Leon Litwack, "The Abolitionist Dilemma: The Antislavery Movement and the Northern Negro," *New England Quarterly*, XXXIV (March 1961) and in William H. and Jane H. Pease, "Antislavery Ambivalence: Immediatism, Expediency, Race," *American Quarterly*, XVII (Winter 1965). Biographies of white abolitionists which heavily emphasize black-white alliances are Bertram Wyatt-Brown, *Louis Tappan and the Evangelical War Against Slavery* (Cleveland, Ill., 1969) and *Tilden G. Edelstein, *Strange Enthusiasm: A Life of Thomas Wentworth Higginson* (New Haven, Conn., 1968). The most comprehensive survey of the antislavery movement is *Louis Filler, *The Crusade Against Slavery* (New York, 1960). *Eric Foner, *Free Soil, Free Labor, Free Men* (New York, 1970) and Larry Gara, "Slavery and the Slave Power: A Crucial Distinction," *Civil War History*, XV (March 1969) relate white politics to antislavery action.

Black attitudes toward colonization in other countries are discussed in Hollis R. Lynch, "Pan-Negro Nationalism in the New World, Before 1862," *Boston University Papers on Africa*, II (Boston, Mass., 1966); and by Lynch in *Edward Wilmot Blyden: Pan-Negro Patriot 1832–1912* (New York, 1967); and also, James M. McPherson, "Abolitionists and Negro Opposition to Colonization During the Civil War," *Phylon*, XXVI (Summer 1965). The standard work on colonization has been P. J. Staudenraus, *The African Colonization Movement, 1816–1865* (New York, 1961).

* An asterisk indicates that the book is available in paperback.

# ❧ CHAPTER FIVE ❧

# Emancipation and Freedom

❧ W ARS and revolutions often bring results different from those intended by their leaders and participants. The contending forces are swept along by surrounding events to such a degree that the expected achievements are seldom realized. The American Civil War, which many historians have viewed as both war and revolution, dramatically illustrates this phenomenon. When the war began, the North was committed to defeating secession and preserving the Union—not ending slavery. Pressured, however, by black and white abolitionists and the necessities of war, the sympathetic Abraham Lincoln slowly moved the North to a policy of emancipation accompanied by the extensive use of black troops in the Union army. By the end of the war some 200,000 black men (or 12 percent of the total northern army) were in uniform and had participated in well over 450 battles. Free northern Afro-Americans and slaves liberated by the invading army joined the Union ranks and lost their lives in a higher proportion than their white comrades. Black contributions to the northern victory had a major effect in shaping attitudes about the postwar reconstruction. There was a widespread feeling of indebtedness to black men but significant differences as to how the Union's debt should be paid.

The South, when the war began, counted on the loyalty of its black population and expected to maintain plantation slavery by achieving independence from the North. Black laborers and artisans, free and slave, performed crucial tasks for the embattled Confederacy as iron workers, miners, railroad hands, cooks, teamsters, ambulance drivers, and fortification laborers. At the same time that their white masters served in the army, most slaves continued working on plantations. While northern black men were an essential element in the Union war effort, southern black men helped keep the Confederacy alive in the face of the northern war strategy of attrition. But black men also fled the South in sufficient numbers to damage industrial war production and deserted their masters' plantations at an enormous rate once the approach of Union troops provided the realistic opportunity for freedom. Only in the last days of the war, when it was too late, did the Confederacy risk enlisting its black population as combat troops. This pragmatic ambivalence between white and black southerners—not deep loyalty or widespread defiance—would continue to characterize southern black attitudes during Reconstruction.

Economically devastated by the war and shorn of slavery by the Thirteenth Amendment, the South was left with the revolutionary result of four million newly emancipated Afro-Americans in its midst. To the victorious and weary North fell the responsibility of helping to protect these freedmen. The most burdensome hardships, however, were shouldered by southern black men. Without jobs, funds, education, or the rights of citizens, the freedmen faced a precarious future.

Joel Williamson, in selection 15, shows the difficulties and dilemmas confronting the freedmen. Their responses to their new freedom, to their old masters, and to the prospect of remaining in the South are essential elements in postwar Reconstruction. Readers should recall the earlier excerpt from Willie Lee Rose's work when considering the relevance of the slavery legacy to the freedmen. How were they affected by their past experience in the South?

The North had won the Civil War because of its superior resources and dogged persistence through four agonizing years of conflict. August Meier, in selection 16, surveys the recent historical writings on black Reconstruction. Previous historians have emphasized and deplored the radical nature of the victor's race policy, while recent historians like Joel Williamson conclude that Reconstruction was a "period of unequalled progress" for Afro-Americans. Meier, on the other hand, argues that Reconstruction "was really not a genuine revolution, not even an abortive one." Readers should judge the soundness of these competing views. And the emphasis by some historians upon the importance of land to the freedman should be compared to the view expressed by still other historians who suggest that much of the available land could not have been profitably farmed in small units. Antebellum racial attitudes and laissez-faire social policies of the national government also should be recalled when seeking to understand the limits of the North's Reconstruction commitment to the freedmen and the latters' quest for political and economic independence.

# 15

## THE MEANING OF FREEDOM
*Joel Williamson*

**F**REEDOM was a nominal legacy of the war, yet telling the slave that he was free did not make him so. Ultimately, the Negro had to establish his freedom by some deliberate, conscious act entirely his own, or he would remain a slave in fact, if not in name. Emancipation simply gave him that choice. With near unanimity, Negroes in South Carolina chose liberty.

In the spring of 1865, the news of emancipation and the close of the war filtered slowly into the hinterland of South Carolina. In mid-May, the commanding general of the Department of the South, Q. A. Gillmore, issued a proclamation declaring that governmental policy would soon be made known. "It is deemed sufficient, meanwhile," he said, "to announce that the people of the black race are free citizens of the United States, that it is the fixed intention of a wise and beneficent government to protect them in the enjoyment of their freedom and the fruits of their industry. . . ."[1] Upon hearing of the order, a few masters formally released their slaves. Francis W. Pickens, for instance, the secession governor of the state and an extensive planter on the Savannah River in Edgefield District, heard of the order on May 23, and on the same day he called his slaves together, acknowledged their emancipation, and contracted to pay them for their labor during the remainder of the year.[2] Most slaveholders were not so forehanded, releasing their slaves only after occupation forces arrived from the coastal area late in May and subsequently. Even after the occupation was completed, a few masters, particularly among those living in the uplands in the extreme western portion of the state, stubbornly refused to recognize the new status of their Negro laborers. Under these circumstances, many Negroes became certain of their emancipation only by traveling to the lower districts with the men who still acted as their masters. A resident of Pendleton, visiting Columbia late in June with a neighbor and the neighbor's slave, noted with alarm that Toney, the slave, had "shown symptoms of demoralization since his arrival here." Apparently observing the presence of Union troops in the city and the formal recognition of emancipation generally accorded to the Negroes there, Toney "got somewhat excited and talked of making a 'bargain' when he returned to Pendleton." "No Negro is improved by a visit to Columbia,"

Joel Williamson, *After Slavery: The Negro in South Carolina During Reconstruction, 1861–1877* (Chapel Hill: University of North Carolina Press, 1965), pp. 32–55, 63. Reprinted by permission of the publisher.

[1] General Orders No. 63, Department of the South, reprinted in the *New York Times*, May 23, 1865, p. 1.

[2] MS Contract, May 23, 1865, Francis W. Pickens Papers.

the Carolinian concluded, "& a visit to Charleston is his certain destruction."[3]

By whatever means the Negro learned of emancipation, the most obvious method of affirming his freedom was simply to desert the site of his slavery and the presence of his master. Patience Johnson, an ex-slave on a Laurens District plantation, must have expressed the sentiment of many freedmen when she answered a request by her mistress that she remain in her usual place and work for wages. "No, Miss," she declined, "I must go, if I stay here I'll never know I am free."[4]

Contrary to tradition, however, the typical slave upon hearing of emancipation did not shout with delight, throw his hat into the air, gather the few possessions he claimed, and run pellmell for Charleston. The great majority received the news quietly and began to make deliberate preparations to terminate their slavery definitely by some overt act. Representative of the reaction of the freedmen in the lower and middle districts was that of the Negroes on the Elmore plantation near Columbia. On May 24, as the secret channels of slave communication crackled with rumors of emancipation, an impatient field hand named Caleb ran away. On May 27, Union forces occupied Columbia. "We told the negroes they were free on the 30th"; noted young Grace Elmore, "they waited patiently and respectably." Nevertheless, the freedmen initiated arrangements for separation. "Philis, Jane and Nelly volunteered to finish Albert's shirts before they left and to give good warning before they left," Grace reported, while Jack, the driver, "will stay till the crops are done." Not all of the freedmen were as explicit in stating their plans. "Old Mary, the nurse, took the news quietly on Sat evening; said that none could be happy without prayer, and Monday by day light she took herself off, leaving the poor baby without a nurse."[5]

In the upcountry, the same pattern prevailed. In Spartanburg District, David Golightly Harris first heard of Gillmore's emancipation order on June 5, but made no mention of the news to his slaves. On the same day, however, and apparently before Harris himself had heard of the order, York, one of his field hands, "disappeared." The remainder said "nothing on the subject" and continued to "work as usual." Desertion on neighboring plantations became increasingly frequent, and, in early July, another of Harris' slaves, Old Will, disappeared, "to try to enjoy the freedom the Yankey's have promised the negroes." By late July, it was rumored that some masters in the neighborhood were recognizing formally the freedom of their laborers. Finally, in mid-August, occupation forces stationed in Spartanburg ordered masters to explicitly inform the Negroes of their freedom. On August 15, most did so. When Harris made the announce-

---

[3] J. K. Robinson to "Mrs. Smythe," June 28, 1865, A. T. Smythe Letters.

[4] William Watts Ball, *The State That Forgot: South Carolina's Surrender to Democracy* (Indianapolis, 1932), p. 128.

[5] Grace B. Elmore MS Diary, entries for May 24, 30, 1865.

ment to his slaves, only one, Ann, left immediately, while "the others wisely concluded they would remain until New Years day."[6]

Desertion was a common means by which the ex-slave asserted his freedom; yet variations in the time and spirit of the desertion yield interesting insights into the Negro's attitudes toward his new status. Generally, freedmen who as slaves had labored as domestics, mechanics, and in the extractive industries departed at the first reasonably convenient opportunity. In doing so, they typically exhibited some degree of malice toward their recent owners. On the other hand, those who had labored in the fields generally finished the year in their accustomed places, and when they left seldom departed with expressions of ill will toward their late masters.

It is astonishing that among the servant or domestic class (where slave labor was reputedly least arduous and relations with the master most intimate and satisfactory), defection was almost complete. Correspondence and diaries of the period are replete with instances in which the master or mistress declared "all of our servants have departed."[7] The disintegration of the household staff of the Holmes residence in Camden was typical of the process in the larger houses. None of the dozen adult slaves on the staff departed with General Sherman, but two were lost to Potter's raiders in April. Early in May, two maids were discharged for insubordination, even though the mistress of the household persisted in her refusal to recognize the freedom of those who remained. Later in the same month, an occupation force arrived in the village, and the mistress told the servants of the emancipation order but refused to release them "because it was not at all certain that they would be freed." By mid-June, Isaac, Marcus, Mary (with her two children), and Catherine had, nevertheless, deserted the household without warning. The mistress became fearful that Chloe, eminently necessary to the house as cook and queen-pin of the serving staff, might go the same way. After a conversation in which the mistress presumed to explain President Johnson's position as implying that the slaves were not really free, she implored the cook "not to sneak away at night as the others had done, disgracing themselves by running away, as she had never done." Chloe agreed to stay, "but if she could she would like to go to Charleston in the autumn when the railroad was finished." Having won one battle, however, another was immediately lost. On the same day, Ann, the laundress, "poor deluded fool, informed mother she could not wash any longer, nor would she remain to finish the ironing . . . and off she went." By late August, even the "faithful" Chloe had left "after two days notice,"

[6] David Golightly Harris MS Farm Journal, entries for June 5, 6, 14, July 6, 24, 25, August 14, 15, 16, 1865.

[7] For instances, see: G. E. Manigault to his cousin, May 22, 1865, Heyward-Ferguson Papers; "R. R. E." (probably Ralph Elliott) to a friend, July 11, 1865, Habersham Elliott Papers; Meta Grimball MS Diary, entry for "February," 1865; Grace B. Elmore MS Diary, *passim*.

and without waiting for the repair of the railroad. Thereafter, hired servants came and went at a rapid rate, and when they departed they usually did so in a cloud of irritation. "We have had a constant ebb and flow of servants," wrote Emma Holmes on October 1, "some staying only a few days, others a few hours, some thoroughly incompetent, others though satisfactory to us preferring plantation life." What was true in the Holmes household was true of their neighbors. "In every direction we hear of families being left without a single servant, or, those who stay doing almost nothing," reported Emma. "All have turned fool together."[8]

In the face of wholesale desertions the more pretentious white families were forced to resort to extremes. Many came to rely entirely upon the service of Negro children. "Our servants here behaved very badly & have all left us, with little exception," quipped one Camden resident in August. "Two of Patty's children are now waiting upon us, little William & Veny."[9] The vacuum in domestic labor, however, was most generally filled by the white ladies of the household. A gentleman refugee in the upcountry, noting the widespread desertion by domestics, was "struck by the cheerful & smiling manner" in which the ladies assured him that "It's a great relief to get rid of the horrid negroes."[10] In May, Emma Holmes had expressed the same spirit of independence. ". . . the servants find we are by no means entirely dependent on them," she wrote with a literary toss of her head. Yet, by mid-August, cheerful independence had soured into galling resentment. After a long day of arduous household labor, Emma complained, "but I dont like cooking or washing, even the doing up of muslins is great annoyance to me and I do miss the having all ready prepared to my hand." In late August, there was only fatigue. "I am very weary," she confessed, "standing up washing all the breakfast and dinner china, bowls, kettles, pans, silver, etc.—a most miscellaneous list of duties, leaving no time for reading or exercise."[11]

The frequency with which domestics deserted their masters discredits the myth of the "faithful old family servant" (the ex-slave) loyally cleaving to his master through the pinching years of Reconstruction. Most of the "faithful few" were literally old, or else very young, or infirm, or encumbered by family arrangements which made desertion impossible. James Hemphill, a wealthy lawyer and politician residing in Chester, indicated that faithfulness among this class of freedmen could be something less than a blessing—a feeling many of his contemporaries shared. "My crowd of darkies is rapidly decreasing," he reported to his brother in September, 1865. "Almost two weeks ago, my cook departed with her

<hr>

[8] Emma E. Holmes MS Diary, entries for "End of May," July 15, 26, August 22, 25, October 1, 1865.

[9] Martin S. Wilkins to J. Berkeley Grimball, August 5, 1865, J. B. Grimball Papers.

[10] "R. R. E." (probably Ralph Elliott) to a friend, July 11, 1865, Habersham Elliott Papers.

[11] Holmes Diary, entries for "End of May," August 14, 25, 1865.

child. Last week, our house girl left, and this morning, another girl, lately employed in the culinary department, vacated. We still have six big and little—one old, three children, one man sick, so that you may perceive there are mouths and backs enough, but the labor is very deficient."[12] Three days previously, a former slaveholder in Abbeville District verbalized the same complaint. Of his fifteen slaves, only three remained, "one woman and her two children," who, he lamented, were "in place of a benefit . . . a heavy expense to me for their bread and clothing."[13]

Doubtless, some servants did remain with their late masters from motives of genuine loyalty and contentment. A Charlestonian wrote in September, 1866, that his "old" coachman and the coachman's wife held steadfast in their devotion to him all during the war and afterward.[14] Such instances were rare, however, and became increasingly so as Reconstruction progressed. An instance of real, but not unlimited, faithfulness was provided by Patty, a Negro woman who had served the John Berkeley Grimball family for thirty-six years before emancipation, fleeing with them during the war from the coast to Greenville and remaining with them after emancipation. In the first disordered months of peace, she had taken out articles to sell and brought back food for the family, stubbornly refusing to take anything for herself. In January, 1866, when finally she did leave to join her son and husband in the lowcountry, she washed all the clothes, gave the young ladies of the house presents, and left two of her younger children to wait on the family.[15]

In spite of obvious and often painful realities, the myth of the "faithful old family servant" persisted both North and South and even grew in the years following Reconstruction. In 1881, John W. De Forest, a Connecticut Yankee who had been a Freedmen's Bureau officer in South Carolina and who certainly knew better, published a remarkably successful novel set in postwar Charleston. Among the host of noble stereotypes who crowded its pages were the "high bred," proud, but impoverished young "Miss Virginia Beaufort" of the Carolina aristocracy and her old crone of a servant, Maume Chloe, "the last faithful remnant of the feminine property of the Beauforts," who, of course, played her role to perfection and lived happily ever after.[16] Most Northerners were probably relieved to find that they had left their erstwhile charges in such good hands; but in the South the myth had a rather more tragic aspect. Living in a world they never made, life for Southerners was somehow eased by this small fiction which evoked a pleasurable image of the better world they had aspired to build. This was possibly what a lady of Charleston was saying in 1873 when she

[12] James Hemphill to W. R. Hemphill, September 11, 1865, Hemphill Papers.

[13] William Hill to his brother, September 8, 1865, William Hill Papers.

[14] Anonymous letter, September 2, 1866, Wilmot S. Holmes Collection.

[15] Meta Grimball MS Diary, entry for February 20, 1866.

[16] John W. De Forest, *The Bloody Chasm* (New York, 1881), p. 29, *et seq.*

wrote to a friend upon the death of an elderly woman servant who had been her slave. "I feel a link has been broken, an occasion lamented," she sadly declared, "a really burial of what can never take place again."[17] And it could not, if, indeed, it ever had.

Mechanics and laborers outside of agriculture (in lumbering, mining, turpentine, and other industries) were as quick as domestics to leave their masters. Even where they did not desert their late owners, there was often a disposition to do so. In July, 1865, E. J. Parker, engaged in the turpentine business in the deep piney woods of Williamsburg District, despaired of inducing his former slaves to continue laboring for him even for wages. "I do not believe we shall hire our own negroes to work," he wrote to his partner; "it would be much better if we could hire other negroes. They would work much better." By late September, he had persuaded most of his late bondsmen to contract; but the conflict in their minds between economic necessity and their desire to be free of their recent master was evident. "They signed it with grate reluctance," Parker reported. "And Isaac Reid would not do it and had to take him to Kingstree. He cut up all sorts of Shines. Said he would suffer to be Shot down before he would sign it. That he did not intend to do anything for any man he had been under all his life."[18]

The liberty of freedmen engaged in agriculture to leave their former masters was restricted by the insistence of the occupation forces and the Freedmen's Bureau that plantation owners and laborers contract to harvest and divide the 1865 crop before parting. Many who did not contract found it convenient, nevertheless, to complete the agricultural season. But even as they worked they eagerly anticipated the New Year and the Christmas holidays that preceded it as a kind of second emancipation. Augustine Smythe, managing his mother-in-law's plantation, Lang Syne, near Fort Motte in Orangeburg District, described the expectancy among his laborers early in December. "The poor negro," he wrote to his mother, "besotted with ignorance, & so full of freedom, looking forward to January as to some day of Jubilee approaching, with all the difficulties & dangers of a free man's life to encounter, & none of the experience or sense necessary to enable him successfully to battle with them, thinking only that freedom confers the privilege of going where & doing as they please, work when they wish, or stop if they feel disposed, & yet be fed, supported & cared for by his Master, lazy, trifling, impertinent! Mother, they are awful!"[19]

Christmas Day, 1865, saw many South Carolina plantations entirely deserted by their Negro populations. Smythe's plantation was thus abandoned, and, in Spartanburg District, David Golightly Harris recorded in his journal that all of his "negroes leave to day, to hunt themselves a new

[17] Eliza T. Holmes to Mary B. Chesnut, April 8, 1873, Williams-Chesnut-Manning Papers.

[18] E. J. Parker to D. W. Jordan, July 24, September 29, 1865, D. W. Jordan Papers.

[19] To his mother, December 12, 1865, A. T. Smythe Letters.

home, while we will be left to wait upon ourselves."[20] After visiting the plantation of a relative on February 9, 1866, the Reverend John Hamilton Cornish reported that, "Not one of their Negroes is with them, all have left."[21] Like many domestics, most of those field hands who remained on the plantations were very old, very young, ill, or encumbered. The mistress of the Ball plantation in Laurens District recalled at the turn of the century that at the end of 1865 "many of the negroes sought employment on other places, but the least desirable stayed with us, for they could not easily find new homes and we could not deny them shelter."[22]

This pattern was broken only on the very large plantations. Here, apparently, many freedmen deliberately chose to remain on the "home place."[23]

The inclination of domestics, mechanics, and laborers in the extractive industries and on relatively small plantations to leave their masters at the first reasonable opportunity while agriculturalists on the larger plantations remained suggests that desertion correlated very closely with the degree of proximity that had existed between the slave and his owner and, further, that the freedman was much more interested in leaving behind the personal reminders of slavery than he was the physical.

In South Carolina, the mass movement among the Negro population was not the "aimless," endless, far-flung wandering so often described. Freedmen most often left their homes to separate themselves distinctly from slavery, but their destination was nearly always fixed by economic design or necessity. Most migrants resettled themselves within a matter of days or weeks and within a few miles of the place which, as slaves, they had called home. "In almost every yard," wrote Emma Holmes in June, 1865, "servants are leaving but going to wait on other people for food merely, sometimes with the promise of clothing."[24] Many former domestics went into the fields to labor, and, conversely, a few agricultural laborers entered household service. For instance, in February, 1866, the Grimballs hired Josey, one of their ex-field hands, and Amy, his wife, and their daughter, Delia, to replace the "faithful" Patty.[25] Also, Northerners on the Sea

---

[20] Louisa Smythe to her aunt, December 21, 1865; A. T. Smythe to his mother, January 13, 1865; A. T. Smythe Letters; Harris Farm Journal, entry for December 25, 1865.

[21] Cornish, Diary, entry for February 9, 1866.

[22] Ball, *The State That Forgot,* p. 128.

[23] Contracts for 1865 and 1866 on the Robert N. Hemphill plantation in Chester District, the MacFarland plantations in Kershaw, the H. L. Pinckney plantation in Sumter, and Mulberry on the lower Cooper River indicate that a high proportion of former slaves remained in their places.

[24] Diary, entry for June 15, 1865.

[25] Meta Grimball, MS Diary, entry for February 20, 1866.

Islands, during and after the war, frequently drew their servants from among the plantation hands.

Large numbers of agricultural laborers left their native plantations during the Christmas season to camp in a neighboring village while they searched for an employer. Employment, however, was not always easily found. David Golightly Harris, visiting Spartanburg on New Year's Day, 1866, "saw many negroes *enjoying* their *freedom* by walking about the streets & looking much out of sorts. . . . Ask who you may 'What are you going to do,' & their universal answer is 'I don't know.' "[26] Augustine Smythe found much the same conditions prevailing in the vicinity of Fort Motte in Orangeburg District. "There is considerable trouble & moving among the negroes," he reported. "They are just like a swarm of bees all buzzing about & not knowing where to settle."[27]

Having proved their freedom by leaving their former masters, many Negroes, apparently, were soon willing to return to them. By late September, two out of the three servants who had deserted James Hemphill's Chester household had returned; and Cuffee, a domestic in the residence of John Richardson Cheeves (a son of Langdon Cheeves) in Abbeville, returned to his usual labors in October, 1865, after having savored both freedom and hunger downriver in Savannah.[28] A large number of agricultural laborers also returned to their native plantations after a short stay abroad. In mid-January, the wife of the manager of Lang Syne in Orangeburg District jested that "fifteen turkeys 'nebber come home,' " indirectly indicating that more than half of the laboring force had again settled in their places on the home plantation. Frequently, agricultural laborers returned to remain against the wishes of the owners. The manager of Lang Syne reported that one Negro woman had returned and asked to be hired. He refused but she declined to leave and secreted herself in one of the outbuildings. Several days later, she appealed over the manager's head to the owner of the plantation to order her acceptance and was again refused. Finally, the manager "walked her off," but later suspected that she was still hiding in one of the Negro houses.[29] A small planter in Union District cried out in anguish early in 1866 when some of his slaves, being discharged, returned against his wishes and persisted in going into the fields and laboring alongside those he had agreed to employ.[30]

Apparently, many freedmen were driven to return to their old places by economic necessity. Isabella A. Soustan, a Negro woman who had some-

---

[26] Farm Journal, entry for January 1, 1866.

[27] To his mother, January 13, 1865, A. T. Smythe Letters.

[28] James Hemphill to W. R. Hemphill, September 26, 1865, Hemphill Papers; Rebecca Cheeves to J. R. Cheeves, October 24, 1865, R. S. Cheeves Papers.

[29] Louisa Smythe to her mother-in-law, January 15, 1866; A. T. Smythe to his brother, December 5, 1865, A. T. Smythe Papers.

[30] Robert N. Gage to his sister, January 31, 1868, James M. Gage Papers.

how found freedom in a place called Liberty, North Carolina, in July, 1865, expressed her thoughts on the dilemma that many ex-slaves faced in their first year of emancipation. "I have the honor to appeal to you one more for assistance, Master," she petitioned her recent owner. "I am cramped hear nearly to death and no one ceares for me heare, and I want you if you pleas Sir, to send for me." Some few freedmen were willing to exchange liberty for security. "I don't care if I am free," concluded Isabella, "I had rather live with you, I was as free while with you as I wanted to be."[31] Yet, even those who did return soon found that freedom bore no necessary relationship to geography.

While migrants were motivated by combinations of many desires, much of their behavior is explained by their love of the homeplace—the "old range" as they themselves rather warmly termed it. White contemporaries, perhaps obsessed with the idea that theirs was a white man's land, never fully appreciated the fact that Negroes, too, were strongly devoted to the soil upon which they had been born and labored. "The aged freedwomen, and many also of the aged freedmen," reported a Bureau officer, "had the bump of locality like old cats." Similarly, a local official of the state, frustrated in his attempts to resettle Negroes on public lands in Georgetown County, found this sentiment a serious deterrent. "Local attachment, you know, has always been a ruling passion with the agricultural classes of our people," he explained to his superior.[32] Thus, ironically, the Negro frequently moved to get away from his late master, but he almost always moved to settle in the very locale where he had served in bondage.

The desire to return to the "old range" was particularly evident in the coastal areas in the year following the war. On the one hand, very nearly all the Negroes who had fled to the islands during the conflict returned to the mainland within the first two or three years of peace.[33] On the other hand, thousands of Negroes who had been taken inland by their masters during the war returned to the coast. In the months following emancipation, the stream of coastward migration was continuous, but as the upland farming season closed in October and November, 1865, the flow swelled into a flood. By December, it was estimated that Negroes were passing through Columbia at the rate of a thousand a month.[34] In January, the migration reached its crest and declined to a trickle by late

[31] To her late master (probably George C. Taylor), July 10, 1865, George Coffin Taylor Collection.

[32] James H. Croushore and David Morris Potter (eds.), *John William De Forest, A Union Officer in the Reconstruction* (New Haven, 1948), p. 36; *Reports and Resolutions of the General Assembly of the State of South Carolina* (1871–1872), p. 369. Cited hereinafter as *Reports and Resolutions*.

[33] For one example, the return of the freedmen to John Berkeley Grimball's Grove plantation, *see* John Berkeley Grimball MS Diary, entry for March 9, 1866, *et seq.*

[34] *The Nation*, I, No. 26 (December 28, 1865), 813.

February when the new planting season was underway.[35] Doubtless, it was the return of these freedmen to their coastal haunts that led Northern observers, virtually all of whom felt compelled to make the pilgrimage from Charleston to Columbia to see the ruins, to exaggerate the volume of Negro movement throughout the state and to conclude that the migrants were bound for Charleston simply because there "freedom was free-er." Later writers accepted and perpetuated these erroneous impressions.

Many of the coastward migrants moved with assurance of employment upon arriving at their destinations.[36] Many also returned without such guarantees, but with the aid of the Bureau and promises that work could be found in their native communities. Whatever their prospects, the road of the migrant freedman was never easy, and the obstacles they overcame to return home suggest the great strength of the pull of place upon them. From deep in the interior, many of them trudged along the ribbons of mud called roads to the fire-gutted city of Columbia. Riding with the driver in the "boot" of a westbound stagecoach one clear, cold December morning in 1865, one Northern traveler counted within a distance of eight miles thirty-nine Negroes walking toward Columbia. All were underclothed, miserable, and tired in appearance, carrying their possessions in bundles on their backs. One middle-aged Negro woman, he noted, was carrying a bundle on her head and a baby on her back. At the same time she was leading a little girl by the hand, while a small boy followed behind. As they passed, the driver shouted down to her, "Goin' down to Columby after you 'free, be ye? Well, go on.'"[37] From Columbia, they plodded some 100 miles along the line of the railroad to Charleston. There, while awaiting transportation to the homeplace by Bureau steamer, they took refuge in the deserted houses of their masters or in the burned-out buildings of the lower district.[38] In January, 1866, a Northern correspondent saw fifteen hundred of them camped on the waterfront, wretched and pitiable, some living in the open coal sheds along the wharves. As he walked among them, they cooked and ate their breakfasts around smoky fires, amidst "tubs, pails, pots and kettles, sacks, beds, barrels tied up in blankets, boxes, baskets, [and] bundles," while "hens were scratching, pigs squealing, cocks crowing, and starved puppies whining." An old woman belonging to a group bound for Colleton District catalogued their miseries. "De jew and de air hackles we more'n anyting," she declared. "De rain beats on we, and de sun shines we out. My chil'n so hungry dey can't hole up. De

[35] Croushore and Potter, A Union Officer, p. 36, fn.

[36] The Nation, I, No. 26 (December 28, 1865), 812. Specific arrangements of this nature are also mentioned in F. H. Spawn to T. R. S. Elliott, December 12, 1865, T. R. S. Elliott Papers; John Colcock to James Gregorie, Gregorie-Elliott Papers; The Nation, II, No. 27 (January 4, 1866), 14.

[37] Ibid.

[38] Martin S. Wilkins to J. B. Grimball, August 5, 1865, John Berkeley Grimball Papers; John Berkeley Grimball MS Diary, various entries, 1865 and 1866.

Guv'ment, he han't gib we nottin'. Said dey would put we on Board Saturday. Some libs and some dies. If dey libs dey libs, and if dey dies dey
dies."[39] After such Odysseys, one can readily believe those early returnees
who told a northern teacher on Edisto Island in June, 1865, that they were
"glad to get back to their old homes."[40]

Some freedmen, cut loose from their moorings by war and emancipation, continued to drift wherever the winds and currents of chance
carried them; yet, by the spring of 1866, the great mass of Negroes in
South Carolina had come again to settle upon the "Old range."

In the first weeks of emancipation, many (perhaps most) freedmen
interpreted their liberty as a temporary release from labor. "Already in
the neighborhood they have refused to work & c," wrote Augustine Smythe
in June, 1865, speaking of the vicinity of Fort Motte. The difficulty, he
thought, lay in the presence of Northerners in the state. "Here we are having Yankee, Yankee, Yankee, White Yankee and nigger Yankee, till we are
more disgusted with them than ever."[41] Early in July, an elderly planter living
near Walterboro noted the prevalence of much the same sentiment.
". . . negroes generally very idle," he observed, "wandering about the country enjoying their freedom, tho to my mind wonderfully civil, under the
circumstances."[42]

Yet, the mass of Negroes did not equate freedom with permanent
idleness. In fact, they wanted to work, but only for themselves and at
their own discretion. Almost universally, they showed an aversion to
cultivating the great staple—cotton, and a willingness to grow food crops
sufficient for themselves and their families. In March, 1865, for instance,
the mistress of a Christ Church plantation, along with one of her neighbors,
gave her slaves freedom to work or not as they pleased. "In every place
they have gone to work planting for themselves on their usual places," she
reported, meaning that the Negroes were cultivating the garden plots
allowed them as slaves.[43] The average freedman expected to work for his
own subsistence, but he wanted to choose the time and place of that

[39] J[ohn] T[ownsend] Trowbridge, The South, a tour of its Battle Fields and Ruined Cities,
a journey through the desoluted States, and talks with the people, etc. (Hartford, 1866),
pp. 537–38.

[40] Mary Ames, From a New England Woman's Diary in Dixie in 1865 (Springfield, 1906),
p. 63.

[41] To his aunts, June 11, 1865, A. T. Smythe Letters.

[42] John W. Rutledge to Benjamin F. Perry, July 9, 1865, B. F. Perry Papers. As one might
expect, the close of the argricultural season at the end of the year brought another period
of general idleness. A Charlestonian wrote to his daughter early in January, 1866, that "in
the plantations in general they refuse to work and some are insolent and obstinate . . ."
N. R. Middleton to his daughter, January 10, 1866, N. R. Middleton Papers.

[43] "Mother" to her son (probably Wilmot G. De Saussure), March 31, 1865, H. W. and
W. G. De Saussure Papers.

labor. Late in May, 1865, Grace B. Elmore, living in her mother's house near Columbia, interviewed Philis, her maid, on the subject. Asked if she liked the idea of freedom, Philis answered "yes, tho she had always been treated with perfect kindness and could complain of nothing in her lot, but she had heard a woman who had bought her freedom from kind indulgent owners, say it was a very sweet thing to be able to do as she chose, to sit and do nothing, to work if she desired, or to go out as she liked and ask nobody's permission, and that was just her feeling." Even so, Grace was assured, "Philis says she expects to work."[44]

When arrangements were satisfactory, the great mass of Negroes exhibited an eagerness to labor. Indeed, enforced idleness made the Negro agrarian uneasy. "We wants to git away to work on our own hook," explained a migrant waiting on a Charleston wharf for a steamer to return him to his home plantation. "It's not a good time at all here. We does nothing but suffer from smoke and ketch cold. We want to begin de planting business."[45] By the early spring of 1866, most Negro farmers had done precisely that.

Apparently, Negroes labored less arduously in freedom than they had in slavery. To many whites, the slowdown seemed a stoppage. During the hot, dry summer of 1865, when the woods were in danger of bursting into flames, a planter near Grahamville complained to the Bureau officer that "my negroes in the fairest weather refuse to go out to work at all, to save my place from danger of fire." A flagrant show of ingratitude, he thought, "as this was their old home, to which they said they were anxious to move, it seems now to avoid work altogether." However, he admitted, "they did do some work."[46] Similarly, the lessee of a lowcountry tract declared in early August that his plantation was "litterly taurn up" since "under the present labour system but little is done & what is done is badly done, it being impossible to get work done as it aught to be."[47] Planters above the fall line were also distressed. In Chester, James Hemphill lamented in September, "there is a general indisposition to labor, both among whites and blacks, and nothing is more needed than steady hard labor at present";[48] and an Abbeville resident declared, "the negro is so indolent and lazy that he is incapable of any exertion to better his circumstances."[49] A freedman's version was expressed on August 13, 1865, at Lewisfield, a small station on the North Eastern Railroad some forty miles

[44] Diary, entry for May 24, 1865.

[45] Trowbridge, The South, p. 537.

[46] Anonymous to B. F. Perry, n.d. (probably July, 1865), B. F. Perry Papers, quoting the author's letter to the local Bureau agent.

[47] W. W. Bateman to J. L. Manning, August 2, 1865, Williams-Chesnut-Manning Papers.

[48] To W. R. Hemphill, September 11, 1865, Hemphill Papers.

[49] William Hill to his brother, September 8, 1865, William Hill Papers.

from Charleston. There a Negro "asked the Yankee officer if they would be expected to do as *much* work as formerly. He replied certainly. Upon which the freedman said they did not intend to do any such thing."[50]

Of course, there were freedmen who lost the habit of labor during the transition from slavery to freedom. These tended to collect in the larger cities, on abandoned plantations, and, occasionally, on the farm of some larcenous poor white. Finding his former slaves encamped in his Charleston house late in the summer of 1865, one island planter "made arrangements to take his people back to Hilton Head and provision them, but only Anthony would then agree to go."[51] In time, however, the military and the Bureau were successful in clearing idlers from the population centers. More frightening to the whites than urban idlers were those in the country. Early in September, 1865, a planter near Georgetown complained to the absentee owner of a neighboring plantation that it was "being rapidly filled up by vagabond negroes from all parts of the country who go there when they please and are fast destroying what you left of a settlement. They are thus become a perfect nuisance to the neighbourhood and harbor for all the thieves and scamps who wont work."[52]

Idleness of this hardened sort soon dwindled to negligible proportions. Much of the continued malingering was apparently a manifestation of the Negro's dissatisfaction with his rewards under the new system, a sort of unorganized slowdown by which he fought his employer or prospective employer. Idleness, of course, had been a normal part of slavery, and it was no less evident among the whites than Negroes. Sundays, Christmas, and New Year's Day were customarily holidays from labor for both races and remained so. Further, agrarian communities normally recognized the laying-by season in the early summer and the end of the harvest season in the fall and winter as periods of reduced labor, celebrations and idleness. It is not surprising that the Negro in freedom continued to recognize them as such, and to relish them all the more.

Desertion, migration, and idleness were temporary as mass phenomena among the Negro population in postwar South Carolina. Much more lasting was the universal tendency among freedmen to identify their freedom with liberty to ignore the infinite minor regulations that had been imposed upon them as slaves. They assumed new forms of dress, kept dogs and guns, hunted, and they traveled about without passes. Many refused to yield the sidewalks to the white gentry, omitted the slave-period obeisances, and rode horses or mules or in carriages in the presence of white pedestrians. They conversed in public and in secret with any number of other Negroes and entered into associations for a variety of purposes.

[50] E. P. Millikey to R. H. Gourdin, August 14, 1865, R. H. Gourdin Papers.

[51] Martin S. Wilkins to J. B. Grimball, August 5, 1865, J. B. Grimball Papers.

[52] Charles Alston, Jr., to D. W. Jordan, September 1, 1865, D. W. Jordan Papers.

The master class, exasperated and outraged by the assertiveness of the freedmen, was particularly alert in noting and meticulously recording this metamorphosis of their erstwhile bondsmen. In Camden, early in April, 1865, Emma Holmes, attending services in the Methodist Church where the Negroes sat in the galleries, was incensed at the Negro women who wore "round hats, gloves and even lace veils, the men alone looking respectable."[53] A white resident returning to Charleston in June of the same year was appalled by "Negroes shoving white person[s] . . . [off] the walk. Negro women dressed in the most outré style, all with veils and parasols for which they have an especial fancy. Riding on horseback with negro soldiers and in carriages."[54] At the same time, a planter on the lower Cooper River complained that the Negroes would not stay out of Charleston, where they "claim they are free," and the women are frequently seen "with blue & pink veils, etc." The same planter was mortified while hunting in the swamps with a group of white gentlemen to encounter suddenly a number of Negro men engaged in the same entertainment, armed with shotguns and following the hounds like ebony images of their white superiors.[55]

To the freedman, his new liberty conveyed the right to assemble in public, to speak, and to celebrate—the cause most often and extravagantly celebrated being freedom itself. Celebrations occurred frequently, on plantations, in villages and towns, and pre-eminently in Charleston. The Negro community in Charleston was large, wealthy, well informed, and organized. Zion Church, having been established by the Presbyterians before the war primarily for the accommodation of their Negro members and having a seating capacity of two thousand, logically became the focal point of organized activity among the Negroes and their Northern friends.

Perhaps one of the most impressive parades ever seen in Charleston was staged by the Negro community on March 29, 1865, scarcely a month after the occupation of the city. The marchers began assembling at noon and a procession of about four thousand was soon formed. It was led by two Negro marshals on horseback. Among the marchers were fifty butchers carrying knives and preceded by a display of a large porker. Then followed a band and the Twenty-first United States Colored Troops (the Third South Carolina Volunteers), a company of school boys, and a car of Liberty carrying thirteen young girls representing the original thirteen states (which were cheered enthusiastically). The main body of the parade consisted of eighteen hundred school children with their teachers. The trades were represented by tailors carrying shears, coopers with hoops, blacksmiths, painters, carpenters, wheelwrights, barbers, and others. Eight companies of firemen wearing red shirts paraded with their equipment. Also in the procession was a cart bearing a mock auction block. While a boy rang

[53] Diary, entry for April 2, 1865.

[54] H. W. Ravenel to A. L. Taveau, June 27, 1865, A. L. Taveau Papers.

[55] [—.—.] Deas to his daughter, July —, 1865, [—.—.] Deas Papers.

a bell, an auctioneer extolled the salability of two Negro women seated on the block with their children standing around them. The cart carried a sign: "A number of Negroes for sale." A long rope was tied to the cart and a number of men were tied to the rope. Another cart bore a coffin displaying the signs: "Slavery is dead," "Who owns him, No one," and "Sumter dug his grave on the 13th of April 1861." The cart was followed by mourners in black. Then came fifty sailors, a company of wood sawyers, the newspaper carriers, and several clubs and associations. The procession was three miles long and wound through the streets below the Citadel. The Negroes, both participants and spectators, were "wild with enthusiasm," reported one observer. "Good order and appreciation of freedom were evident."[56]

As the war drew to a close other mass meetings of Negroes followed in rapid succession. On April 5, while Potter was making a sortie from Georgetown, the Negroes of Charleston met in Zion Church and passed resolutions thanking the army for their liberation.[57] Fort Sumter, already reduced to rubble by artillery fire, might well have sunk beneath the waters under the sheer weight of victorious abolitionists who flocked from the North to stand upon its ruins. On April 14, Robert Anderson himself returned to raise the flag over the ruins. Before the ceremonies began Robert Smalls brought the *Planter* alongside and set ashore more than three thousand Negroes from the city. Remaining aboard to watch the proceedings from the quarterdeck was the son of Denmark Vesey, the man who thirty-three years before had shocked the state—and, indeed, the South—with the threat of mass insurrection. "As the old silken bunting winged itself to its long-deserted staff, thousands of shouts, and prayers fervent and deep, accompanying, greeted its reappearance." And then the speeches began. "I have been a friend of the South," declared William Lloyd Garrison, and Henry Ward Beecher, Theodore Tilton, Henry Wilson, Joshua Leavitt, William D. Kelley, Joseph Holt, and George Thompson applauded.[58]

Other Negro communities were not long in following the example of Charleston. The editor of the *New York Times* praised the stand of the Negroes of Columbia in refusing to abandon plans to celebrate Independence Day in 1865 despite the protests of the whites. "They may not get the vote or court rights in this way," asserted the editor, "but there are a hundred petty regulations of the slave period which they can break to exert their influence. It is good that the white become accustomed to negro meetings."[59] In the village of Aiken on the Fourth, the Reverend Cornish observed

---

[56] *New York Times,* April 4, 1865, p. 9.

[57] *Ibid.,* April 11, 1865, p. 5.

[58] *Ibid.,* April 23, 1865, p. 2; Rollin, *Life and Public Services of Martin R. Delany,* pp. 193–95.

[59] July 2, 1865, p. 4.

that "the Negroes had a Pic Nic—somewhere, & a prayer meeting & a dance at the Hotel Headquarters."[60] Even in the remote hamlet of Spartanburg, scarcely a month after most of the slaves had been formally released by their masters, David Golightly Harris noted that "the negroes had a jubilee . . . at the village, the yankeys and the negroes going hand in hand."[61] Throughout Reconstruction, the Negroes made New Year's Day and Independence Day their special holidays and devoted them to the celebration of emancipation and union, concepts which were inseparably intertwined in their minds. On these days, even in the smallest villages, the Negro community usually staged some sort of jubilee.[62]

These celebrations were significant as assertions of freedom, but they were also important in other ways. They obviously gave the Negro population a feeling of unity and an awareness of the power that unity bestowed. Further, they pushed forth leaders from among their own numbers who, in time, would translate that power into political realities.

Freedmen often interpreted their liberty as a license to express candidly, either by words or deeds, their true feelings toward the whites in general and their late masters in particular.

Many Negroes continued to show the same respect and cordiality toward individual whites which they had exhibited in slavery. "I have been very agreeably disappointed in the behavior of the negroes," wrote a young planter visiting Charleston in August, 1865. "They are as civil & humble as ever. All I met greeted me enthusiastically as 'Mass Gus.' "[63] In September, another visiting native white concurred. "The negroes behave admirably," he reported to his wife, "when you consider the ordeal of temptation & teaching they have passed through."[64] And an elderly Charlestonian observed, "The negroes about town behave as far as I see extremely well. I have met with nothing but respect and good-will from them . . ."[65] On the plantations, returning masters sometimes encountered the same response. "I met with universal politeness from our former slaves," wrote a Beaufort District planter after a visit to the family plantations in December, 1865. "They were glad to see me & inquired after all the family."[66]

Yet, while many Negroes manifested cordial feelings toward the whites, others exhibited insolence and insubordination. As the war drew to

[60] Cornish, Diary, entry for July 4, 1865.

[61] Farm Journal, entry for September 23, 1865.

[62] The *Intelligencer* (Anderson), July 7, 1870, reported celebrations of Independence Day occurring in seven upcountry villages and in Columbia in that year. The *Charleston Daily Republican*, July 7, 8, 13, 1870, recorded the same pattern in the lowcountry.

[63] A. T. Smythe to his wife, August 19, 1865, A. T. Smythe Letters.

[64] Ellison Capers to his wife, September 10, 1865, Ellison Capers Papers.

[65] N. R. Middleton to his daughter, January 10, 1866, N. R. Middleton Papers.

[66] "R. S. E." to his sister, December 19, 1865, Elliott-Gonzales Papers.

a close, and before emancipation became a certainty, such displays often served as a device by which Negroes tested their freedom. "There is quite a difference of manner among the Negroes," Grace B. Elmore noted in Richland shortly after Sherman's passage, "but I think it proceeds from an uncertainty as to what their condition will be. They do not know if they are free or not and their manner is a sort of feeler by which they will find out how far they can go." Grace's brother, fresh from a visit to slave-rich lower Richland District, "found quite a spirit of insubordination among the negroes who supposed they were free, but they are gradually discovering a Yankee army passing through the county and telling them they are free is not sufficient to make it a fact."[67] As emancipation became assured many ex-slaves took obvious pleasure in expressing heretofore concealed feelings of animosity toward their recent owners. In June, 1865, Edward, personal servant to Henry W. Ravenel, accompanied his master from their refuge in Greenville to Columbia. There Edward obtained permission from Ravenel to find his wife, and was given five of the master's last nine dollars to enable him to follow Ravenel to Charleston. Ravenel proceeded to Charleston where Edward subsequently appeared, but "was excessively insolent— told the Servant in the yard that he had no further use for me and that he had been left in Columbia to starve." The indignant Ravenel concluded: "So much for the fidelity of indulged servants."[68] Even more blatant was the insubordination of a "so-called" servant who, when ordered by her Charleston mistress to scour some pots and kettles, replied: "You betta do it yourself, Ain't you smarter an me? You think you is——Wy you no scour for you-self."[69] Not all freedmen were so vociferous; many were content simply to ignore their late masters. "Rosetta, Lizzie's maid, passed me today when I was coming from Church without speaking to me," wrote one aristocrat to his wife. "She was really elegantly dressed, in King Street style."[70]

A very few Negroes believed that freedom warranted the exercise of vengeance upon the whites—that theft, arson, and violence even to the extremity of homicide were justifiable retributions for their bondage. This sentiment was particularly apparent in areas subjected to Union raids and it persisted through the summer and fall of 1865. After Sherman had passed through Camden, a serious case of arson was narrowly averted, and "many other attempts at setting fire were discovered either just in time, or after some damage had been done—both in Camden and the surrounding country—keeping everyone in a constant state of anxiety and alarm."[71] In several communities, disturbances reached the proportions of insurrections. In March, in the vicinity of Christ Church on the lower Cooper River, an

---

[67] Diary, entry for March 4, 1865.

[68] To A. L. Taveau, June 27, 1865, A. L. Taveau Papers.

[69] Louisa McCord to A. T. Smythe, August 27, 1867, A. T. Smythe Letters.

[70] Ellison Capers to his wife, September 10, 1865, Ellison Capers Papers.

[71] Holmes, Diary, entry for March 27, 1865.

area which lay between the Union lines and Confederate pickets, the mistress of a plantation reported: "A band of armed negro men, principally from one of the neighboring plantations, until put to flight by Confederate Scouts, did without any authority for what they did, arming & marching about the country, stopping people on the highway with guns pointed at their heads, suddenly surrounding a man on his own plantation attending to his own affairs, going to peoples homes at night threatening them & in one instance I hear firing on the man who came out to see what the noise was about . . ." Another planter "was threatened with having his house burned and himself shot if he tried to save a single piece of furniture."[72] The relief afforded by Confederate cavalry in this area was only temporary. In mid-July, a Cooper River planter complained that in Christ Church and St. Thomas Parishes and on the river, in general, the Negroes claimed everything and, in some cases, had driven away the owners. Five or six Negroes had come to three plantations—Richmond, Basis, and Kensington—and encouraged the freedmen to seize everything for themselves. "Insubordination & insolence," he concluded, were frequently observed.[73] Other low-country communities witnessed similar scenes. Near Plantersville in Georgetown District, a Union raid in March, 1865, released a large number of Negro slaves who were "indulging in the free use of wine & liquors obtained from the houses of former masters," and "preparing themselves for the commission of crime," "or worse, might break into open insurrection at any time."[74] "During the stay and after the departure of Genl Potters army," a group of Pineville planters complained in September, 1865, "the negroes evinced treachery and vindictiveness—illustrated by robbery, plundering, false accusation and insolence, in the three weeks after the departure of said army, by an open outbreak in arms—taking possession [sic] of and patroling this village night and day, threatening the lives of men and the chastity of women, & finally firing upon Confederate Scouts by whom they were dispersed."[75] During the same period on the mainland in the vicinity of Beaufort, a planter complained that robbery and theft were committed wholesale by the Negroes "& no redress given"; while "Mr. Chavis & others, as you are aware has been compelled with his Family to fly his home, from vagrant negroes, returned from the Islands, chiefly." Such was the case, he averred, "every where where officers of Colored troops have had jurisdiction any length of time."[76]

---

[72] "Mother" to her son (probably Wilmot G. De Saussure), March 31, 1865, H. W. and W. G. De Saussure Papers.

[73] [—.—.]Deas to his daughter, July—and 15, 1865, [—.—.] Deas Papers.

[74] MS Petition from the citizens of Plantersville to the Naval Commander in Georgetown, March 10, 1865, Sparkman Family Papers.

[75] Petition of several planters of Pineville to the area commander, September 11, 1865, Trenholm Papers.

[76] Anonymous to B. F. Perry, n.d. (probably July, 1865), B. F. Perry Papers.

Notwithstanding the charges of the whites that Negro soldiers often instigated such disorders, the occupation rapidly established comparative peace. It is true, nevertheless, that the Negro population was most restless in those areas occupied by Negro troops—an area which included the low-country from Georgetown to Savannah and, roughly, the southern half of the state from the sea to the mountains. The effect of the Negro military on the population of Aiken, as seen through the diary of the Reverend Cornish, presents a good case study. In June, 1865, the village was occupied by a detachment of the Thirty-third United States Colored Troops (the First South).[77] On Sunday, June 18, about twenty Negro soldiers entered the Baptist Church with the apparent intention of attending services. They were ordered by the white ushers to find places in the galleries. As some of the soldiers began to ascend the stairs, one of their number ordered them to halt, and the whole group attempted to take seats on the main floor. When some of the white men rose and blocked their way, the soldiers flourished their bayonets and began to curse. Finally, they were allowed to seat themselves below, but the church closed that evening. Monday morning, Cornish's serving woman, Phobe, used "intemperate" language in addressing the Reverend, and, upon being reproved, continued the abuse. When asked whose servant she was, Phobe answered, "My own servant." She was then told to recant or leave. She left. On the same morning, a Mr. Wood "was badly beaten by the 'Black and Blues,' " as the Negro soldiers were called. The beating brought the inspector general from Augusta, but on Saturday, August 5, there was another such "disturbance."[78]

It is difficult to distinguish fact from fiction in the disordered first weeks that followed the war; but the rumor circuit buzzed with tales of whites murdered by Negroes, usually their ex-slaves. Emma E. Holmes reported that William Prioleau returned to his lowcountry plantation after the Union forces had passed and spent the night, "but never woke again. His throat was cut from ear to ear." Another planter reported killed was William Allen, "who was chopped to pieces in his barn," as Emma graphically related.[79] A less impressionable recorder wrote from Walterboro early in July that "several citizens about Ashepoo & Combahee, eight or nine, have been murdered by negroes." Much of this lawlessness he blamed on the presence of Negro troops. "We have had them here and tho the officers & men behave as well as I had expected the soldiers (black) made great mischief among servants generally and plantation negroes particularly," he declared. "Things were bad before, but their influence made them infinitely worse."[80]

The great mass of Negroes in South Carolina at the end of the Civil

[77] Higginson, *Army Life in a Black Regiment,* p. 265.

[78] Cornish, Diary, entries for June 18 through August 5, 1865.

[79] Diary, entries for "End of May," June 15, 1865.

[80] J. W. Rutledge to "Colonel," July 9, 1865, B. F. Perry Papers.

War hoped and expected that freedom meant that each would soon be settled upon his own plot of earth. Indeed, to the Negro agrarian freedom without land was incomprehensible. "Gib us our own land and we take care ourselves," a Union officer quoted as the sentiment of the mass of country Negroes in the spring of 1865, "but widout land, de ole massas can hire us or starve us, as dey please."[81] The desire for land touched all classes of former slaves. "She also said," wrote a young mistress late in May, paraphrasing the words of her maid, that "the commonest and most universal view was that each man would have his farm and stock and plenty to eat & drink and so pass through life."[82] The prevalence of this roseate view of the future among freedmen was confirmed by Mary Boykin Chesnut of Kershaw District, wife of a Confederate senator and general, and herself heiress to three generations of cotton culture, who reported that the Negroes "declare that they are to be given lands and mules by those blessed Yankees."[83] Similarly, a Northern correspondent, arriving in Orangeburg after a trip through the lowcountry, declared that the desire for land was active and widespread among the Negroes. "Some of the best regiments have white soldiers who tell the negroes they are the rightful owners of the land, that they should refuse to work or go to the islands to get lands."[84]

"Forty acres and a mule," that delightful bit of myopic mythology so often ascribed to the newly freed in the Reconstruction Period, at least in South Carolina during the spring and summer of 1865, represented far more than the chimerical rantings of ignorant darkies, irresponsible soldiers, and radical politicians. On the contrary, it symbolized rather precisely the policy to which the government had already given and was giving mass application in the Sea Islands. Hardly had the troops landed, in November, 1861, before liberal Northerners arrived to begin a series of ambitious experiments in the reconstruction of Southern society. One of these experiments included the redistribution of large landed estates to the Negroes. By the spring of 1865, this program was well underway, and after August any well-informed, intelligent observer in South Carolina would have concluded, as did the Negroes, that some considerable degree of permanent land division was highly probable. . . .

Thus, even in the early days of freedom, former slaves with amazing unanimity revealed—by mass desertion, migration, idleness, by the breaching of the infinite minor regulations of slavery, by a new candor in relationships with whites, and by their ambition to acquire land—a determination to put an end to their slavery. It is true that the Negro's freedom was still severely circumscribed a year after emancipation, and his experi-

---

[81] Reid, *After the War*, p. 59.

[82] Elmore, Diary, entry for May 24, 1865.

[83] Isabella D. Martin and Myrta Lockett Avary (eds.), *A Diary from Dixie, as written by Mary Boykin Chesnut* (New York, 1905), p. 396.

[84] *The Nation*, I, No. 4 (July 27, 1865), 106.

ence during the whole term of Reconstruction could hardly be described as a success story. Yet, the Negro did not, upon emancipation, immediately jump a quick half-step forward and halt. In the favorable atmosphere generated by his political ascendency during Reconstruction, freedom for the Negro in South Carolina was a growing thing, flowering in areas political historians have often neglected. The growth was, in part, the result of cultivation by alien hands; but it was also the result of forces operating within the organism itself. The gains won during these early years enabled the Negro community to continue to move forward in vital areas of human endeavor in the post-Reconstruction period while, ironically, its political freedom was rapidly dwindling to virtual extinction. In this sense, far from being the disaster so often described, Reconstruction was for the Negroes of South Carolina a period of unequaled progress.

# 16

## NEGROES IN THE FIRST AND SECOND
## RECONSTRUCTIONS OF THE SOUTH
*August Meier*

"REVOLUTIONS never go backwards": so declared the editors of the first Negro daily newspaper, the New Orleans *Tribune,* late in 1864.[1] Northern troops had occupied the city and much of Louisiana as early as 1862, and the *Tribune* insisted that the logical second step, after crushing the slaveholders' rebellion, was that the national government divide their plantations among the freedmen. Washington failed to act upon this proposal, and seventy years later W. E. B. Du Bois, in assessing the reconstruction experience, perceived it as a revolution that had indeed gone backwards. It had gone backwards, he held, mainly because Congress had failed to press forward to the logical corollary of its reconstruction program; the distribution of the former slaveowners' lands among the Negroes.[2] More recently, Willie Lee Rose, though starting from a different philosophy of history, arrived at rather similar conclusions. In her volume on the South Carolina Sea Island Negroes during the Civil War she

August Meier, "Negroes in the First and Second Reconstructions of the South," *Civil War History,* XIII (June, 1967), pp. 114–130. Reprinted by permission of the publisher.

[1] New Orleans *Tribune,* Nov. 29, 1864. This paper was one of a series read at Roosevelt University in the fall of 1965, marking the centennial of reconstruction.

[2] W. E. B. Du Bois, *Black Reconstruction* (New York, 1935).

describes how the military authorities divided many of the Sea Island plantations among the freedmen. President Andrew Johnson, however, returned
the lands to the former owners, and Congress failed to intervene. Mrs. Rose
pithily sums up this sequence of events by entitling the last chapter of her
book "Revolutions May Go Backwards."[3] Nevertheless, in the face of such
distinguished scholarly opinion, I would like to suggest that what occurred
during reconstruction was really not a genuine revolution, not even an
abortive one.

Consider the following example. In Georgia, in April, 1868, slightly
a year after the passage of the Reconstruction Act of 1867, a constitution
drawn up under the procedures required by Congress was ratified by the
voters, and new officials were elected. The process of reconstruction was
supposedly completed when, in July, the legislature ratified the Fourteenth
Amendment, and military authority was withdrawn. The new state government, however, was no genuinely "radical" regime. Just six weeks later the
legislature expelled its Negro members, on the grounds that Negroes,
though guaranteed the right to vote, had not been specifically made eligible
for office.[4]

Before they departed, one of the Negro representatives, Henry M.
Turner, a minister of the African Methodist Episcopal Church, and formerly
a Civil War chaplain and Freedmen's Bureau agent, delivered a ringing,
sarcastic speech, defiantly expressing his vision of a democratic America.
He would not, he said, behave as some of his thirty-one colored colleagues
had, and attempt to retain his seat by appealing to the magnanimity of the
white legislators. He would not, "fawn or cringe before any party nor stoop
to beg them for my rights," like "slaves begging under the lash. I am here to
defend my rights, and to hurl thunderbolts at the men who would dare
to cross the threshold of my manhood. . . . I was not aware that there was
in the character of the [Anglo-Saxon] race so much cowardice, . . . pusilla-
nimity . . . [and] treachery." It was the Negroes who had "set the ball of
loyalty rolling in the State of Georgia . . . and [yet] there are persons in this
legislature, today, who are ready to spit their poison in my face, while they
themselves . . . opposed the ratification of the Constitution. *They* question
my right to a seat in this body."

Then, in rhetoric typical of the era, Turner stated the Negro's claims.

*The great question is this. Am I a man? If I am such, I claim the rights of a
man. Am I not a man because I happen to be of darker hue than honorable
gentlemen around me? . . . Why, sir, though we are not white, we have*

[3] Willie Lee Rose, *Rehearsal for Reconstruction: The Port Royal Experiment* (Indianapolis, 1964).

[4] Ethel Maude Christler, "The Participation of Negroes in the Government of Georgia, 1867–1870" (M.A. thesis, Atlanta University, 1932), *passim,* is the best general treatment. See also C. Mildred Thompson, *Reconstruction in Georgia, Economic, Political and Social* (New York, 1915), chaps. vii, viii, and x.

*accomplished much. We have pioneered civilization here; we have built up your country; we have worked in your fields, and garnered your harvest, for two hundred and fifty years. And what do we ask of you in return . . .? Do we ask retaliation? We ask it not. . . . but we ask you now for our RIGHTS. It is extraordinary that a race such as yours, professing gallantry, and chivalry, and education and superiority, living in a land where ringing chimes call child and sire to the Church of God—a land . . . where courts of justice are presumed to exist . . . can make war upon the poor defenseless black man. . . .*

*You may expel us, gentlemen, but I firmly believe that you will someday repent it. The black man cannot protect a country, if the country doesn't protect him; and if, tomorrow, a war should arise, I would not raise a musket to defend a country where my manhood is denied . . . . You may expel us . . .; but while you do it remember that there is a just God in Heaven, whose All-Seeing Eye beholds alike the acts of the oppressor and the oppressed, and who, despite the machinations of the wicked, never fails to vindicate the cause of justice.*[5]

The events just described epitomize two things: the aspirations and hopes of Negroes on the one hand; and the superficial character of the reconstruction process on the other. Pressure from Congress and the state supreme court did later secure a reversal of the ban on Negro legislators, and one Georgia Negro, Jefferson Long, sat in Congress for a term. Nevertheless, southern whites actually dominated the state's government, and by 1872 the Redeemers, or Democrats, had returned to power. Thus the period of so-called Radical or Black reconstruction can scarcely be said to have existed in Georgia; and what happened in that state can hardly be called a revolution, even a revolution that later went backwards. Most writers on the history of Negroes during reconstruction have dwelt upon developments in South Carolina, Louisiana, and Mississippi, where Negroes formed a majority of the population and therefore held more high offices than elsewhere. What happened in Georgia was, however, a good deal more typical of what happened in most of the southern states during reconstruction.

The failure of congressional reconstruction, the return of the southern states to white hegemony, and the subordination and oppression of the black man were due not only to southern white recalcitrance, but equally as much to northern indifference and to the limitations in congressional policy. Northern indifference to the Negro's welfare and the consequent inadequacies of Congress' program were deeply rooted in the historical racism of the American public. They were thus fundamentally a continuation of a cultural tradition that had not only permitted existence of slavery in the South, but had relegated free Negroes to second-class citizenship in the North.

[5] Henry M. Turner, *Speech on the Eligibility of Colored Men to Seats in the Georgia Legislature . . . September 3, 1868* (Augusta, 1868), *passim*.

In the opening months of the Civil War, for example, Negroes and the small band of white abolitionists had been far in advance of northern opinion in regarding the war as fundamentally a struggle for the emancipation of the slaves. From the day of the firing on Fort Sumter, Negroes had envisioned the situation as an irrepressible moral conflict between slavery and liberty, and a war for the rights of man in fulfillment of the genius of the American democratic faith. However, the President, the Congress and most of the nation at first regarded the war simply as a campaign to preserve the Union, and only slowly and reluctantly, and as a result of the exigencies of a prolonged and difficult military conflict, did the Federal government come to emancipate the slaves and enlist Negroes in the armed forces.[6] Moreover, the vast majority of northerners continued to resist the idea that Negroes should be accorded the rights of citizens. In 1863, at the thirtieth anniversary convention of the founding of the American Anti-Slavery Society, Frederick Douglass excoriated those abolitionists who felt that their work was accomplished when the slaves were freed. Negroes, along with a handful of white abolitionists, formed the vanguard of those who insisted that with emancipation the struggle for Negro freedom had only begun. To Negroes the issues were moral ones, based upon the promise of American life, upon the assumptions of the American faith that were rooted in the Declaration of Independence and the ethics of Christianity. As a conclave of Pennsylvania leaders declared in 1868: "It is America that you have to civilize, to Christianize, and compel to accept and practically apply to all men, without distinctions of color or race, the glorious principles and precepts laid down in her immortal Declaration of Independence."[7]

Long before the war had ended, northern Negro leaders had spelled out the specific program they deemed essential for the creation of a truly democratic America. In October, 1864, the race's most prominent men met in Syracuse, New York, to organize an Equal Rights League that would agitate for citizenship rights and racial equality. At that time the slaves had not yet been freed in the loyal Border States, and most of the northern states prohibited Negroes from voting, from testifying against whites in court, from serving on juries, and in some cases from attending public schools (even segregated schools). The convention delegates were critical of the fact that most northern states still refused to accord Negroes the ballot, and they even denounced the Republican party for being arrayed with the proslavery Democratic party in its support of racial prejudice. Their two chief demands were abolition and political equality. As Douglass pointed out in an address before the Massachusetts Anti-Slavery Society a few months later, Negroes wanted the suffrage . . .

[6] James M. McPherson, *The Negro's Civil War* (New York, 1965), chaps. ii and iii; McPherson, *The Struggle for Equality: Abolitionists and the Negro in Civil War and Reconstruction* (Princeton, 1964), chap. iii.

[7] *Proceedings of the American Anti-Slavery Society at its Third Decade . . . December 3, 4, 5, 1863* (New York, 1864), pp. 110–118; *Proceedings of the Fourth Annual Meeting of the Pennsylvania State Equal Rights League . . . 1868* (Philadelphia, 1868), p. 35.

*because it is our* right, *first of all. No class of men can, without insulting their own nature, be content with any deprivation of their rights. Again, I want the elective franchise . . . because ours is a peculiar government, based upon a peculiar idea, and that idea is universal suffrage. If I were in a monarchical . . . or aristocratic government, where the few ruled and the many were subject, there would be no special stigma resting upon me because I did not exercise the elective franchise . . ., but here, where universal suffrage . . . is the fundamental idea of the Government, to rule us out is to make us an exception, to brand us with the stigma of inferiority, and to invite to our heads the missiles of those about us. . . .*[8]

Douglass and other Negro leaders, while addressing the nation on matters of abolition and citizenship, advocated also a program of economic and moral improvement to be undertaken by Negroes themselves. The Syracuse convention exhorted the freedmen "to shape their course toward frugality, the accumulation of property, and above all, to leave untried no amount of effort and self-denial to acquire knowledge, and to secure a vigorous moral and religious growth." To men of the nineteenth century thrift and industry and the acquisition of property—especially land—were essential parts of the good life, along with citizenship rights. Moreover, a common school education was almost a *sine qua non* for securing a comfortable livelihood. It cannot be overemphasized that along with agitation for political and civil rights, Negro leaders stressed the cultivation of middle-class morality, the pursuit of education, and the acquisition of property. To use the phraseology of the time, these things, like the ballot, were regarded as essential for elevating the race and securing its inclusion in the "body politic."

Southern Negroes espoused the same program, and in some respects were more radical than the northern ministers, editors and artisan-businessmen who predominated at Negro conventions. Representative of the point of view of articulate southern Negroes was the New Orleans *Tribune,* which in 1864 and 1865 prefigured the outlook of most Negro spokesmen during the decade after the war. This journal denounced Lincoln's plan of reconstruction and endorsed that of the congressional Radicals. Only through congressional reconstruction would Negroes "secure the full enjoyment of our rights—not as a matter of gratuitous or benevolent grant, revocable at will—but as an embodiment of the principles set forth in the Declaration of Independence."[9] Highest among these rights was that of the franchise, for it was the only means by which Negroes could protect themselves from civil and economic discrimination.[10] To those who argued that a time of preparation should elapse before the ex-slaves were enfran-

---

[8] *Proceedings of the National Convention of Colored Men . . . 1864* (Boston, 1864); Frederick Douglass, "What the Black Man Wants," in William D. Kelley, Wendell Phillips and Frederick Douglass, *The Equality of all Men Before the Law* (Boston, 1865), pp. 36–37.

[9] New Orleans *Tribune,* Jan. 3, 1865.

[10] *Ibid.,* Aug. 5, 1865; Sept. 13, 1864.

chised, the *Tribune* replied: "We do not know of a single reform, in the whole course of history, that was brought about by gradual and systematic preparation. In fact, how is preparation practicable without the free exercise of the right contended for . . .? Could the white man of America be prepared to the general exercise of the franchise, unless by going to the polls and voting?" Given the opportunity, the freedmen would show a comprehension of "their own interests" and a "Devotion to the Union" that should justify their immediate enfranchisement.[11]

The *Tribune* also gave pointed attention to the question of segregation. It opposed a bill introduced in the legislature, providing for separate schools,[12] and it continually protested against the system of "star cars" for Negroes in the city until the military authorities ordered the provisional governor to end this example of discrimination.[13] The editors regarded segregation as silly, since it was due to the white man's lust that miscegenation had proceeded to the point where "it would be a pretty hard thing to find a pure . . . Negro in the whole city of New Orleans, where seventy thousand persons of African descent are now residing."[14]

The journal devoted much space to economic matters, especially to the conditions under which the former slaves labored on the plantations. On this subject the *Tribune* went far beyond the thinking of most northern Negro leaders at this time, and beyond the thinking of many southern leaders as well. The editors boldly advocated what only the most radical of the Republicans and abolitionists were thinking of—the destruction of the plantation system. It criticized the United States government for not immediately confiscating and dividing the lands of the rebellious planters into five-acre lots, to be assigned to the "tillers of the soil" at a nominal price, so that the freedmen would be "thoroughly imbued with that . . . praiseworthy 'Yankee' idea, *that every man should own the land he tills, and head and hands he works with.*"[15] In calling for these steps the editors hoped to accomplish a democratic revolution in the South against the power of the antebellum slaveowning aristocracy: "The division of the lands is the only means by which a new, industrious and loyal population may be made to settle in the South. Large estates will always be in the hands of an aristocracy. Small estates are the real element of democracy."[16]

Broadly speaking, the Negro elite stressed above all the importance of the franchise and civil rights. Next in order of importance, in the thinking of most of them, was the value of at least a common school education for

[11] *Ibid.*, May 4, 1865.

[12] *Ibid.*, July 26, Dec. 24, 1864; Feb. 17, 1865.

[13] *Ibid.*, Feb. 28, May 21, Aug. 10, 1865.

[14] *Ibid.*, Aug. 15, 1865.

[15] *Ibid.*, Sept. 10, Sept. 24, 1864.

[16] *Ibid.*, Sept. 15, 1865.

the masses of the race. Finally, they were concerned with the economic problems of the freedmen. Most of them urged the masses to work hard, save their money, and acquire property; but some at least advocated a radical expropriation of the slaveowners' plantations and the creation, under Federal benevolence, of a numerous landowning yeoman peasantry. Such a policy would not only provide Negroes with an economic opportunity, but would supply the foundation for loyal and democratic governments in the southern states.

On the other hand, the evidence indicates that the masses had a scale of priorities that was precisely the opposite of that of the elite. Their primary interest was in land ownership. Close to this in importance for them was education. Though politics was of somewhat lesser value in their thinking, enfranchisement did initiate enthusiastic political participation on the part of the freedmen. Like the elite Negroes they displayed a profound awareness of the importance of political activity in American culture. The same is true of their interest in education. Old and young flocked to the schools opened by the northern missionaries and the Freedmen's Bureau. Especially notable were the freedmen's own efforts at self-help in education, establishing schools, hiring teachers, and erecting buildings.

Most of all, like oppressed peasants the world over, the freedmen wanted land. As Vernon Lane Wharton put it in his study of Negroes in Mississippi after the Civil War: "Their very lives were entwined with the land and its cultivation; they lived in a society where respectability was based on ownership of the soil; and to them to be free was to farm their own ground."[17] When President Andrew Johnson restored the Sea Island plantations to their former owners, he sent General O. O. Howard, head of the Freedmen's Bureau, to Edisto Island to inform the freedmen of his decision. The Negroes who crowded the church at which Howard spoke were disappointed and angry, and shouted "No, no!" to his remarks. Howard later recorded in his autobiography that one man called out from the gallery: "Why, General Howard, why do you take away our lands? You take them from us who have always been true, always true to the Government! You give them to our all-time enemies! That is not right!" The committee selected by the freedmen to meet with the representatives of the planters in order to arrange the details of the transfer of property informed Howard that they would not work for their old masters under overseers, though they were willing to rent the land if ownership was ruled out. The planters, however, were not interested in this kind of arrangement and after a series of indignation meetings the freedmen wrote a final appeal to the President. They insisted that it was "very oppressing . . . [that] wee freemen should work for wages for our former oners." They felt it was unfair for the President to expect the freedmen to ask "for bread or shelter or Comfortable for his wife and children" from men whom they had fought against "upon the feal of battle." They had, they said, no confidence in their former

[17] Vernon Lane Wharton, *The Negro in Mississippi, 1865–1890* (Chapel Hill, 1947), p. 59.

masters, one of whom had declared he would refuse to sell land to freedmen, even at $100 an acre. Johnson, of course, remained unmoved, and in the end the Negroes had to capitulate.[18]

A significant number of the freedmen attempted to buy their own farms, even in the face of white reluctance to sell land to them. Travelers from the North, Freedmen's Bureau agents and missionaries reported enthusiastically upon evidence of progress in this direction. A New England cotton planter on the Sea Islands reported the case of "a black Yankee . . . [with] the energy" and eye "for his own advantage of a born New Englander." His industry and sharp dealing had put him ahead of the other on the plantation, though half of them had fenced in their own gardens and were raising vegetables for the Hilton Head market.

*Linus in his half-acre has quite a little farmyard besides. With poultry-houses, pig-pens, and corn-houses, the array is very imposing. He has even a stable, for he made out some title to a horse, which was allowed; and then he begged a pair of wheels and makes a cart for his work; and not to leave the luxuries behind, he next rigs up a kind of sulky and bows to the white men from his carriage. As he keeps his table in corresponding style . . . the establishment is rather expensive. So, to provide the means, he has three permanent irons in the fire, his cotton, his Hilton Head express, and his seines. . . . While other families "carry" from three to seven acres of cotton, Linus says he must have fourteen. . . . With a large boat which he owns, he usually makes weekly trips to Hilton Head, twenty miles distant, carrying passengers, produce and fish. . . . I presume his savings since . . . the capture of the island amount to four or five hundred dollars. He is all ready to buy land, and I expect to see him in ten years a tolerably rich man.*[19]

Only a few with exceptional ability or luck were able to become permanent and substantial landowners. The plantation system remained intact. In fact, it may even have increased in extent. It simply changed its form. Instead of slavery, the characteristic labor arrangement became that known as sharecropping.

By the last quarter of the nineteenth century sharecropping, in combination with the crop-lien system, had become a system of gross exploitation, which reached its most extreme form in debt peonage. Here was a system in which the Negro tenant was almost at the complete mercy of the white planter. Yet, in its origins at least the sharecropping system was not something that was simply forced upon Negroes, but was in part a result of the freedmen's desire for independence, freedom and economic advancement. Much research on this subject remains to be done before the origins of sharecropping during the reconstruction period will be fully

---

[18] Rose, *Rehearsal for Reconstruction*, pp. 353–355.

[19] Elizabeth Ware Pearson (ed.), *Letters from Port Royal* (Boston, 1906), p. 37.

understood but recent studies suggest that what likely happened followed the general pattern outlined below.[20]

After the emancipation of the slaves and the close of the Civil War, planters generally attempted to employ Negroes as wage laborers with annual contracts. Under these contracts the freedmen were worked in gangs as they had been under slavery. In order to enforce the contractual obligation, it was common for planters to hold back part of the pay until the end of the cotton harvest. Such a system, characterized by gang labor and with its powers of coercion lodged in the planter's hands, smacked altogether too much of slavery and Negroes resisted working under it. Universally the freedmen wanted to own their own land; where this was not possible they preferred to rent land for cash if they could. But, as in the case of the Sea Islands, planters resisted such an arrangement because it did not give them as much control over the labor force as they desired. The sharecropping system thus seems to have emerged, in large part, as a sort of compromise. Under it, the tenants had their own plots, organized their own time, and were not subject to the *direct* discipline of the planters. On the other hand the system was beneficial to the planter in that it encouraged the tenant to stay on the land until the crop was harvested, and encouraged him to work hard since he kept a share of the crop. Nevertheless, as late as the 1880's it was common for planters in certain areas to complain about the sharecropping system.

Rudimentary sharecropping arrangements had appeared even before the close of the Civil War, but they received considerable impetus from the encouragement of the Freedmen's Bureau during the late 1860's. Negroes were never satisfied with the system; they always aspired to become cash renters or landowners. Moreover, what started out as a concession to the freedmen's desire for independence, quite rapidly became a system of racial repression.

The responsibility for the unsatisfactory resolution of the land question did not rest entirely with the southern whites. In large part it rested upon the actions of the northern whites. Despite the talk of confiscation, most political leaders—even many of the Radical Republicans and abolitionists—had too strong a sense of the importance of property rights to espouse confiscation of anyone's estates—even those of the rebels. In the end it was Congress and the Republicans as much as President Johnson who betrayed the freedmen on this crucial matter. The proposal was entirely too revolutionary for nineteenth-century America. The Republican leaders and the upper- and middle-class white abolitionists were for the most part simply too conservative to accept confiscation with equanimity. In fact, in their thinking, the right of an individual to his personal freedom and to his

---

[20] The ideas developed in the following discussion owe a good deal to material in Martin Abbott, "Free Land, Free Labor, and the Freedmen's Bureau," *Agricultural History*, XXX (1956), pp. 150–156; and Joel Williamson, *After Slavery: The Negro in South Carolina During Reconstruction, 1861–1877*, chaps. iii and v.

property were two closely interrelated rights, both of them founded in the values of individualism. For a similar reason there was a lack of unity among the friends of the freedmen regarding the degree to which the government should practice a paternalistic benevolence in uplifting the ex-slaves. Many thought that government assistance to the freedmen in the form of granting them land would discourage the individual initiative and independence which they hoped the freedmen, crushed down under slavery, would quickly develop.[21]

In some ways the land issue was the central or crucial issue in reconstruction as far as Negroes were concerned. As the New Orleans *Tribune* suggested, and as students as diverse as W. E. B. Du Bois and Gunnar Myrdal have maintained more recently,[22] it can be argued that the failure to confiscate the large estates and redistribute them in small plots among the freedmen, doomed Congress' plans for political reconstruction to failure and the black men to generations of oppression. Viewed more broadly, the North's failure to grapple seriously with the land question was simply part and parcel of the whole pattern of northern indifference to the status of Negroes in American society. To put the matter baldly, most of the people in a position of political influence were not really interested in the Negroes' welfare. Only a handful of Radical Republicans had any sincere desire to make Negroes full citizens. Citizenship rights and the franchise were provided almost as a by-product of political squabbling in Washington. The civil rights bills and the Fourteenth and Fifteenth Amendments were passed reluctantly, and only as the result of long battles and many compromises. Recent research suggests that they would not have been passed at all if President Johnson and the Democrats had acted skillfully instead of pushing the moderate Republicans into accepting the proposals of the Radicals. Negro suffrage resulted mainly from the desire to protect southern white unionists and from northern fears about the disloyalty of the ex-rebels.[23]

Moreover, as noted above, at the end of the Civil War Negroes did not enjoy equal rights, even in a legal sense, in most of the North. The states of the Old Northwest rejected efforts to enfranchise Negroes within their borders, and outside of New England and New York Negroes did not obtain the franchise until after the passage of the Fifteenth Amendment. And because the Fifteenth Amendment was rejected by a number of northern states, it was ratified only with the votes of the reconstructed southern states. Jim Crow practices existed in most of the Old Northwest and the

[21] For a suggestive discussion see Kenneth Stampp, *The Era of Reconstruction* (New York, 1965), pp. 28–30.

[22] Du Bois, *Black Reconstruction, passim;* Gunnar Myrdal, *An American Dilemma* (New York, 1944), I, 224–227.

[23] I have been greatly stimulated by Eric L. McKitrick, *Andrew Johnson and Reconstruction* (Chicago, 1960); LaWanda and John H. Cox, *Politics, Principle, and Prejudice, 1865–1866* (New York, 1963), and Stampp, *The Era of Reconstruction,* though none of these authors would necessarily fully agree with conclusions stated here and elsewhere in this paper.

Middle Atlantic states. In Pennsylvania, for example, only a long fight led by Negro abolitionists finally secured a state law against segregation in public conveyances in 1867; and not until 1881 was school segregation abolished in that state.[24] The Fourteenth Amendment, now interpreted as making segregation unconstitutional, was actually extremely vague on the matter of Negro rights. For most congressmen, even the Radicals, granting protection to life, liberty and property, and equality before the law, meant nothing more than the right to own and dispose of property, to sue and be sued, and to testify in courts. It apparently did not imply desegregation of transportation and public accommodations—a lack rectified only with the passage, after several years' arduous agitation, of Sumner's Supplementary Civil Rights Act in 1875. This law, unfortunately, for the most part went unenforced. The Fourteenth Amendment certainly did not encompass the idea of school desegregation. All these things, however, have been read into the amendment by the Supreme Court during the last twenty years.

Whether one accepts the older view that politicians and capitalists desirous of continued Republican ascendancy brought about Negro enfranchisement in order to protect their interests, or whether one accepts the newer view that Negroes received suffrage and citizenship rights as a sort of by-product of the political factionalism in Washington and the self-defeating tactics of Johnson and the northern Democrats, one thing emerges quite clearly—responsible whites in positions of influence were simply not listening to the Negroes. Negroes received their rights in the South for a few brief years during reconstruction not because of the brilliantly worded resolutions, addresses and petitions of the Negro conventions and orators, or because of the deep-rooted desires of the mass of freedmen for economic independence and dignity, but because of the activities of the northern whites, to whom the welfare of the Negroes was usually an incidental or secondary issue. What was true for the Republicans was also true in modified form for the abolitionists. James McPherson, in his recent volume, *The Struggle for Equality,* makes a good case for attributing at least a part of the development of congressional sentiment for Negro rights to the agitation of some of the old abolitionists who felt that their work was not done with the emancipation of the slaves. Yet even the abolitionists were divided, many of them asserting that once emancipated the southern freedman should be left to help themselves. Others, like the great orator, Wendell Phillips, and certain of the northern school teachers who went south after the war and made the education of the freedmen their life work, were sincerely interested in bringing citizenship rights and real equality for the Negroes. Even these idealists often had an unconscious paternalism about them. They sincerely believed in racial equality, but they also believed that they knew what was best for the Negroes. Willie Lee Rose

[24] Leslie H. Fishel, Jr., "Northern Prejudice and Negro Suffrage, 1865–1870," *Journal of Negro History,* XXXIX (1954), 8–26; McPherson, *Negro's Civil War,* pp. 255–261; McPherson, *Struggle for Equality,* chap. x.

records the shock that some of the white missionaries on the Sea Islands received when Negroes wanted to make their own decisions.[25]

There is little evidence that such people listened, at least very much, to what the Negroes were saying. Rather, their views in favor of citizenship rights and, in some cases, of land for the Negroes, were not a response to Negro demands, but grew out of their own philanthropic ideals. McPherson carefully records the influence of Negro abolitionists upon the white abolitionists during the Civil War and reconstruction. But from reading his book it is clear that the only Negro whom the white abolitionists really listened to in this period was Frederick Douglass, a figure so Olympian that he commanded respect; and it does not appear that they listened even to him very much.

The granting of citizenship rights and the vote to Negroes came about not because of what the Negroes were articulating, but because of what whites, for their own various reasons, decided to do about the Negroes. Even the most advanced and liberal journals did not deem it worth their while to report what Negroes themselves were thinking and doing about their status and their future. Since the white abolitionists and Radical Republicans were not, for the most part, genuinely committed to a belief in the essential human dignity of Negroes—much as many of them verbally protested that they did—it was easy for many of them to become disillusioned with reconstruction, to accept the southern viewpoint about corruption and black power and to wash their hands of the whole problem. This was even true of many who had once been enthusiastic about guaranteeing Negroes their citizenship rights.

It is thus clear how it was that Turner and his colored colleagues were so easily expelled from the Georgia legislature, and how it was that even though they were readmitted the following year, Georgia returned to the hands of the white supremacists in 1872. It also should be clear why Congress was really ineffective in dealing with the violence perpetrated by the Ku Klux Klan and other terrorist organizations, and why it was that, one after the other, the southern states were all permitted to return to white supremacy. The fact is that neither the North as a whole, nor Congress, nor even the majority of the white abolitionists were sufficiently concerned about Negroes to protect the citizenship rights which they had guaranteed them.

These attitudes, characteristic even of the Negroes' friends, afford some insight into the role which Negroes played in southern politics during the era of congressional or black reconstruction. We can spell out the numbers and names of prominent Negro officeholders, and at first glance the list is impressive. Two Negroes, Alonzo J. Ransier and Richard H. Gleaves, served as lieutenant-governor in South Carolina; three, Oscar J. Dunn, C. C. Antoine, and P. B. S. Pinchback, held this office in Louisiana, and Pinchback served briefly as acting governor; and one, A. K. Davis, was

---

[25] McPherson, *Struggle for Equality, passim;* Rose, *Rehearsal for Reconstruction,* p. 369.

lieutenant-governor in Mississippi. South Carolina and Mississippi had Negro speakers of the house—Robert B. Elliott and Samuel J. Lee in South Carolina, and John R. Lynch in Mississippi. William J. Whipper was an associate justice of the supreme court of South Carolina. James J. Hill served as secretary of state in Mississippi; Francis L. Cardozo held both that post and that of state treasurer in South Carolina; and Jonathan C. Gibbs was first secretary of state and superintendent of education in Florida. Three other states also had Negro superintendents of education: Mississippi, Louisiana, and Arkansas. On the national level Mississippi sent two Negroes to the Senate—Blanche K. Bruce and Hiram R. Revels; and seven states elected Negroes to the House of Representatives during reconstruction.

No one has really yet investigated the question: exactly how did the Negro politicians function in the southern reconstruction governments?[26] Probably, just as their numbers were small in proportion to the number of Negroes in the southern states, so their influence was less than their abilities or numbers warranted. After all, even the white abolitionists, the most equalitarian group in American society, did not permit their Negro colleagues in the movement to play a significant leadership role. Douglass, the only Negro of real influence in the movement, had to establish himself as an independent force outside of the two major antislavery societies. It is therefore most unlikely that the mixed bag of northerners and southerners, idealists, opportunists and adventurers that composed the southern Republican party were willing to accord Negroes a vital role.

Only three states, South Carolina, Louisiana, and Alabama, sent more than one Negro to the national House of Representatives; four others—Georgia, Mississippi, Florida, and Louisiana—were represented by one each; while three southern states—Virginia, Arkansas, and Texas—sent no Negroes at all to Congress during reconstruction. Moreover, outside of Florida, where Gibbs was superintendent of education, only Arkansas and the three states with a Negro majority in their population selected Negroes for prominent state-wide office. Even taking these three states—Mississippi, Louisiana, and South Carolina —we find that never was a Negro elected governor; that Negroes were unable to send one of their number to the United States Senate from either Louisiana or South Carolina, despite efforts to do so; and that only one of the states, South Carolina, had a Negro on its supreme court. And only in South Carolina did Negroes form a majority in the constitutional convention or even for a brief period in one house of the state legislature.

We know practically nothing of the interaction among the Negro and white politicians, but it would appear that to a remarkable extent office-holding at the highest levels tended to be a symbolic function. Each of the three states with a Negro majority had Negro lieutenant-governors—a purely honorific post. The two Negroes who served in the United States

---

[26] For a thoughtful discussion of the Negro political leaders during reconstruction see John Hope Franklin, *Reconstruction: After the Civil War* (Chicago, 1961), pp. 86–92, 133–138.

Senate were both moderates. Revels, the first one, voted Democratic consistently after reconstruction, while the other, Bruce, became a large plantation owner. In post-reconstruction Mississippi, the Bruce-Hill-Lynch triumvirate, which dominated the state's Republican party, cooperated closely with the Democrats, making a deal known as fusion, whereby a few posts would go to Negroes in those sections of the state where they were in a heavy majority, though most of the posts and all the important ones remained in white hands. A similar arrangement obtained in the black counties of coastal South Carolina.[27]

The power of the Negro politicians in these states is revealed by what happened to the school system. A nonsegregated school system was an important issue raised in a number of the state constitutional conventions. But only South Carolina and Louisiana provided for mixed schools in their constitutions. Even in these two states, in fact, the schools were administered so that there was practically no integration. Only the New Orleans school system and the University of South Carolina were integrated.[28] Neither on this issue nor on land reform were the Negro politicians able to deliver—any more than they were able to control a fair proportion of the offices.

The foregoing should not be taken as suggesting that Negro politicians were powerless. They were not. In Florida, for example, Negroes exercised a balance of power between two white factions, and under the astute leadership of the state superintendent of education, Jonathan C. Gibbs, were able to obtain certain concessions and keep Florida in the ranks of the Radical states until 1877. In Louisiana and South Carolina the Negro majorities among the voters did exercise some power, and certain individuals, such as Robert Brown Elliott and Francis L. Cardozo, seem to have been men with a measure of influence. But not only was their influence far less than the prosouthern historians have insisted, but it was also considerably less than their numbers, education, and ability warranted. Neither southern white opportunists, nor paternalistically benevolent northern whites, were inclined to accord positions of real power to Negroes.[29]

If the states with Negro majorities experienced a relative lack of political power on the part of Negroes, it is clear why in other states Negro officeholders had even less of a role, beyond the symbolic one. Effective power stayed in the hands of the whites in all the southern states. Much of the responsibility for this situation rests with the Republicans in Congress.

As the North, the Republicans, and many of the abolitionists deserted and betrayed the southern Negroes, the visions of the equal rights conven-

[27] Wharton, *Negro in Mississippi*, pp. 202–203; George B. Tindall, *South Carolina Negroes, 1877–1900* (Columbia, S.C., 1952), pp. 62–64.

[28] Louis R. Harlan, "Segregation in New Orleans Public Schools During Reconstruction," *American Historical Review*, LXVII (1962), pp. 663–675; Williamson, *After Slavery*, pp. 219–223, 232.

[29] For a sharply contrasting view see Williamson, *After Slavery*, chaps. xii and xiii.

tions of the 1860's and the hopes of the rural black masses remained only hopes. Sharecropping and peonage, mob violence and disfranchisement became the order of the day. By 1877 southern Negroes were left with only the shreds of their status during the apogee of congressional reconstruction. And even these shreds were destroyed in the wave of proscriptive legislation passed at the turn of the century. Meanwhile, the Supreme Court turned the Fourteenth Amendment upside down. In 1883 it held the Civil Rights Act of 1875 unconstitutional, and thirteen years later, in 1896, it enunciated the separate-but-equal doctrine, justifying state laws requiring segregation. And two years after that, in 1898, it sustained the provisions of the Mississippi constitution of 1890 with its subterfuges that effectively emasculated the Fifteenth Amendment.

Yet these two amendments, passed during the first reconstruction, are the constitutional basis of the new or second reconstruction of the present decade. First of all they were the foundation for the NAACP court victories which, starting in 1915, had by the 1950's so undermined the legal underpinnings of the southern race system that they produced a revolution of expectations among Negroes. And that revolution in expectations is at the bottom of the civil rights revolution of the 1960's. Secondly, it is largely in these reconstruction amendments that the legislative and executive branches have found constitutional sanction for increasing federal intervention in the South.

Although tactics differ markedly from those employed during the first reconstruction, Negro demands today are remarkably similar to those made a hundred years ago—civil rights, the franchise, and economic opportunity. Like prominent Negroes then, civil rights leaders today are concerned with more than constitutional rights; and, quite remarkably, in both cases there is the conviction that the Federal government should undertake the responsibility of providing special assistance to the Negro to compensate for the past. Yet there is a striking difference in the dynamics of the two situations. A hundred years ago whites were not listening to what Negroes were saying. But in the 1960's Negroes, rather than whites, furnish the impetus for social change.

A century ago, as in our own day, something of a moral revolution was going on in the conscience of white America, a revolution forced by the slavery question. It is true that the causes behind that moral revolution were not themselves entirely moral. For one thing they were largely military. Northerners who expected a short war were shocked by military defeat into advocating the destruction of the slave system; and this very practical and *amoral* consideration blended inextricably with, and gave enormous stimulus to fervently moral antislavery doctrines. For the first time white northerners generally became convinced that slavery was a moral evil that had to be swept away; that the Civil War was God's punishment upon a transgressing nation that had condoned slavery for so long. But few came to believe that Negroes were inherently equal to whites.

In the 1960's again military exigencies have played their role in changing the moral climate—the country's leading role in world affairs, the Cold War, and the crucial position of colored nations in the international power system. Yet unquestionably more and more white Americans have become aware that Negroes have aspirations that should be respected. This new awareness has been manifested not only in the increasing concern for equal rights but also in the way in which whites have been paying attention to what Negroes are saying and doing.

Will the new reconstruction prove as temporary and evanescent as the old? The history of the first reconstruction suggests that revolutions—if indeed there was a revolution—can go backwards; that the white majority may grow disillusioned or just weary of idealism.[30] On the other hand, the recent changes in the attitudes of white Americans appear more deeply rooted than those of a hundred years ago. For one thing changing racial views are part of a long-term trend  rooted in the New Deal period, in the moral sensitivities aroused as a result of the struggle with racist Nazi Germany, and the postwar international pressures. Moreover for the past couple of decades the northern Negro vote has been a decisive factor in many elections, and the weight of increasing numbers of registered Negro voters in the South will be felt, the current "white backlash" notwithstanding.[31]

Reforms can be reversed; revolutions may indeed go backwards. It is conceivable that the new reconstruction will be undone as was the old. Certainly, at best it will be accomplished in a halting and spasmodic manner, and every advance will be the fruit of costly and hard-fought struggles, involving compromises and even reverses along the way. Nevertheless, if one may hazard a prediction, the increasing sensitivity of whites to the Negroes' needs and demands—a growing concern for Negroes as *persons* as contrasted to concern about the *institution* of slavery—suggest that the new reconstruction is more likely to prove to be a permanent one.

[30] For sensitive discussion of such trends see C. Vann Woodward, "What Happened to the Civil Rights Movement?" *Harper's Magazine* (Jan., 1967), pp. 29–37.

[31] See, for example, Reese Cleghorn and Pat Watters, "The Impact of Negro Votes on Southern Politics," *The Reporter* (Jan. 26, 1867), pp. 24–25, 31–32.

## SUGGESTIONS FOR FURTHER READING

THE most informative study of abolitionist efforts to commit the Union to a policy of emancipation and to the mustering of black troops is *James M. McPherson, The Struggle for Equality: Abolitionists and the Negro in the Civil War and Reconstruction* (Princeton, N. J., 1964). An astute study

* An asterisk indicates that the book is in paperback.

of related administrative military policies is Fred A. Shannon, "The Federal Government and the Negro Soldier, 1861–1865," *The Journal of Negro History*, XI (October 1926). Benjamin Quarles, *Lincoln and the Negro* (New York, 1962) and Hans L. Trefousse, *The Radical Republicans: Lincoln's Vanguard for Racial Justice* (New York, 1969) sketch the relationship of Lincoln with antislavery politicians and agitators regarding emancipation. *John Hope Franklin, *The Emancipation Proclamation* (New York, 1963) judiciously defends the document's importance. The best study of the military behavior of black men is Dudley T. Cornish, *The Sable Arm: Negro Troops in the Union Army, 1861–1865* (New York, 1956). Other helpful accounts are *Benjamin Quarles, *The Negro in the Civil War* (Boston, 1953); Herbert Aptheker, "Negro Casualties in the Civil War," *Journal of Negro History* XXXII (January 1947); Bell I. Wiley, "Billy Yank and the Black Folk," *Journal of Negro History*, XXXVI (January 1951). The northern racist atmosphere during the Civil War is described in V. Jacques Voegeli, *Free But Not Equal: The Midwestern Negro During the Civil War* (Chicago, 1967); *Forrest G. Wood, *Black Scare: The Racist Response to Emancipation and Reconstruction* (Berkeley, Calif., 1968); and Williston H. Lofton, "Northern Labor and the Negro During the Civil War," *Journal of Negro History*, XXXIV (July 1949). *Bell I. Wiley, *Southern Negroes, 1861–1865* (New Haven, Conn., 1938); Harrison A. Trexler, "The Opposition of Planters to the Employment of Slaves as Laborers by the Confederacy," *Mississippi Valley Historical Review*, XXVII (September 1940); Charles H. Wesley, "The Employment of Negroes as Soldiers in the Confederate Army, *Journal of Negro History*, IV (July 1919); and Nathaniel Stephenson, "The Question of Arming the Slaves," *American Historical Review*, XVIII (January 1913) provide the Confederate context.

*W. E. B. Du Bois, *Black Reconstruction in America* (New York, 1935) is the earliest and most comprehensive study of the subject. A model account of black-white relations is *Willie Lee Rose, *Rehearsal for Reconstruction: The Port Royal Experiment* (Indianapolis, Ind., 1964). The most important government organization for black men is incisively analyzed in George R. Bentley, *A History of the Freedmen's Bureau* (Philadelphia, 1955); Martin Abbot, *The Freedmen's Bureau in South Carolina, 1865–1872* (Chapel Hill, N. C., 1967); and *William S. McFeely, *Yankee Stepfather: General O. O. Howard and the Freedmen* (New Haven, Conn., 1968). Martin Abbot, "Free Land, Free Labor and the Freedmen's Bureau," *Agricultural History*, XXX (April 1956); and LaWanda Cox, "The Promise of Land for the Freedmen," *Mississippi Valley Historical Review*, XLV (December 1968) treat that important Reconstruction question. *William Gillette, *The Right to Vote: Politics and the Passage of the Fifteenth Amendment* (2d ed.; Baltimore, Md., 1969) contradicts the views about enfranchising the freedmen found in LaWanda and John Cox, "Negro Suffrage and Republican Politics," *Journal of Southern History*, XXVIII (August 1967). The best account of a white carpetbagger's relationship with the freedmen is Otto H. Olsen, *Carpetbagger's Crusade: The Life of Albion Winegar Tourgée* (Baltimore, Md., 1965). *Otis Singletary, *The Negro Militia and Reconstruction* (Austin, Tex., 1957); and Samuel D. Smith, *The Negro in Congress, 1870–1901* (Chapel Hill, N. C., 1940) acutely treat some of the results of black Reconstruction.

Excellent state studies of Reconstruction are Joel Williamson, *After Slavery, the Negro in South Carolina During Reconstruction, 1861–1877* (Chapel Hill, N. C., 1965); Vernon Wharton, *The Negro in Mississippi, 1865–1890* (Chapel Hill, N. C.,

* An asterisk indicates that the book is in paperback.

1947); A. A. Taylor, *The Negro in the Reconstruction of Virginia* (Washington, D.C., 1926); Luther P. Jackson, *Negro Officeholders in Virginia, 1865–1895* (Norfolk, Va., 1945); and Joe M. Richardson, *The Negro in the Reconstruction of Florida, 1865–1877* (Tallahassee, 1965).

The role of organized southern resistance to black Reconstruction can be found in Stanley F. Horn, *Invisible Empire: The Story of the Ku Klux Klan, 1866–1871* (Boston, 1939); William P. Randel, *The Ku Klux Klan: A Century of Infamy* (New York, 1965); and Otto H. Olsen, "The Ku Klux Klan: A Study in Reconstruction Politics and Propaganda," *North Carolina Historical Review,* XXXIX (Summer 1962). Patrick W. Riddleberger, "The Radical Abandonment of the Negro During Reconstruction," *Journal of Negro History,* XLV (April 1960), and Richard O. Curry, "The Abolitionists and Reconstruction," *Journal of Southern History,* XXXIV (November 1968) should be contrasted with James M. McPherson, "Abolitionists and the Civil Rights Act of 1875," *Journal of American History,* LII (December 1965); and his "Coercion or Conciliation? Abolitionists Debate President Hayes's Southern Policy," *New England Quarterly,* XXXIX (March 1966). *C. Vann Woodward, "Equality: America's Deferred Commitment," *The Burden of Southern History* (rev. ed.; Baton Rouge, La., 1968) and his "Seeds of Failure in Radical Race Policy," in Harold Hyman (ed.), *New Frontiers of the American Reconstruction* (Urbana, Ill., 1966) are pertinent to the issue of racial policy. Revealing specialized studies of Reconstruction politics and Afro-Americans are in Richard O. Curry (ed.), *Radicalism, Racism, and Party Realignment: The Border States During Reconstruction* (Baltimore, 1969).

August Meier suggests areas in black Reconstruction still needing research in his essay in Hyman's *New Frontiers of the American Reconstruction.* James G. Randall and David Donald, *The Civil War and Reconstruction* (rev. ed.; New York, 1969) provides the most helpful bibliography for the entire era from 1850 to 1880.

* An asterisk indicates that the book is available in paperback.

# &CHAPTER SIX&

# The Withdrawal from Reconstruction

**T**HE limited gains that Afro-Americans achieved during Reconstruction were gradually eroded in the three decades following the so-called Compromise of 1877. Segregation spread from a few areas such as schools and hospitals until it permeated almost every aspect of southern life. Southern states moved in the direction of erecting a legal system that made black men's access to the ballot box extremely difficult if not impossible.

Segregation and disfranchisement, however, were not new creatures created by Southerners in the post-Reconstruction period. Rudimentary forms of segregation existed in the cities of the slave South. Even during the Reconstruction era there were instances of separate public facilities for black and white. In the antebellum North, law and custom imposed a second-class position upon the majority of blacks. Most northern states either barred blacks from the polling booth or demanded that they fulfill conditions not required of whites. Many urban blacks found transportation and school systems segregated. A number of northern states enacted laws that prevented blacks from bringing suit against whites or being witnesses in cases involving whites. The roots of the Jim Crow system that was to evolve between the end of Reconstruction and the opening decade of the twentieth century, then, were present in the antebellum North. Despite these precedents, as of 1877 southern race relations lacked what C. Vann Woodward has called the "rigid uniformity that was to come toward the end of the century."[1] More and more often the force of law would give moral and legal justification to segregation.

In selection 17, John Hope Franklin describes the process by which southern states disfranchised Afro-Americans. Beginning with Mississippi in 1890, state after state in the South enacted laws that virtually closed the ballot box to blacks. Franklin discusses the techniques of disfranchisement and the forces accounting for such actions. He especially emphasizes the relationship between the race issue and the struggle between conservatives and agrarian radicals for economic reform in the South. After reading Franklin's article think about why the radical agrarians turned from cooperation with black farmers and agreed to their disfranchisement. Consider what motivated conservatives to join with radicals in depriving Afro-Americans of the vote.

The drive to strip blacks of many of the rights gained during Reconstruction was not a sectional issue but a national one. Franklin alludes to the Republican party's re-examination of its southern policy. An increasing number of Republicans in the post-Reconstruction period questioned the wisdom of building a southern wing of the party based upon that section's Afro-American electorate. Concluding that this plan had failed and that conflict over the race issue had resulted in an unstable environment for business investment, these men advanced proposals for a basically white Republican organization. Those Republicans who urged their party to continue in its appeal for black support dwindled in both numbers and influence as the period progressed. By the 1890s the failure of the latter group became apparent as lily white Republicanism spread throughout the South.

Americans also became tired of the controversy surrounding the issues of Reconstruction. In the desire to heal the wounds of past sectional conflict, the black man was the loser. The negative attitude most white Americans held toward people of different color around the world and a large portion of the scientific knowledge of the day re-enforced earlier views of the black man's inferiority. The Social Darwinist position, which gained wide credence in the late nineteenth century, considered the Afro-American a lesser species. The literature of the period —whether the paternalistic racism of Joel Chandler Harris's Uncle Remus or the vitriolic racism of Charles Carrol's The Negro A Beast—pictured the Negro as innately inferior to the white man. Even former defenders of black people's desire for equality, such as the Nation magazine, now accepted the presumptions underlying these writings and at the very least acquiesced in the drive to place the Afro-American in a second-class position.

It is against this background that Barton J. Bernstein, in selection 18, analyzes the Supreme Court's "separate but equal" ruling in Plessy v. Ferguson. A Court composed of a northern majority proceeded from the assumption that blacks were not the equal of whites. Accordingly, Bernstein maintains, the Court wrote the "prevailing social science 'truths' into law." Its pronouncement that laws cannot alter social prejudices or bring about social equality reflected William Graham Sumner's contention that one cannot legislate folkways. Bernstein points out that the Court neither disregarded the prevailing attitudes toward race nor looked only to the law. Its rationale included the dominant attitudes of the period

[1] C. Vann Woodward, The Strange Career of Jim Crow (2d rev. ed.; New York, 1966), p. 33.

and it not only justified segregation in public facilities but declared unconstitutional the Civil Rights Act of 1875.

Selection 19 by George B. Tindall deals with South Carolina blacks engaged in farming. He reviews the different methods of farm labor as well as the events giving rise to them. While farm tenancy became a firmly established system of agricultural labor in the late nineteenth century, Tindall presents evidence that it existed during Reconstruction. For the freedmen, the crop-lien and sharecropper systems were not as objectionable in their earlier years as they were to be later. "What started out as a concession to the freedmen's desire for independence," August Meier noted in selection 16, "quite rapidly became a system of racial repression."

In light of Tindall's essay and the other articles in this and the chapter devoted to Reconstruction, the reader should evaluate the relationship between the southern black's decline in status following the Compromise of 1877 and the failure of Congress to enact a comprehensive land reform program during the Reconstruction period. As Frederick Douglass remarked in 1880: "To the freedmen was given the machinery of liberty, but there was denied to them the steam to put it in motion."

# 17

## "LEGAL" DISFRANCHISEMENT OF THE NEGRO
John Hope Franklin

IN 1890 some Southern whites were celebrating what may well be described as an uneasy victory over the individuals and groups that favored the enfranchisement of the Negro. Many Negroes had, of course, retired from politics. Some had retreated at the point of the guns of white supremacists, while others had found it impossible to cope with the economic pressures, fantastic obstacles at polling places, and a variety of petty "legal" nuisances. Even with the sharp decline of Negro participation in politics, there was hardly justification for Henry W. Grady's claim in 1889 that the Negro, "as a political force has dropped out of consideration."[1] In a moving tribute to him at the time of his death one writer credited Grady, the "Spokesman of the New South," with "literally loving a nation into peace."[2] In his claim regarding the ineffectiveness of the Negro as a political

John Hope Franklin, " 'Legal' Disfranchisement of the Negro," *Journal of Negro Education,* XXVI (Summer 1957), 241–248. Reprinted by permission of the publisher and the author.

[1] Henry W. Grady, *The New South,* New York, 1912, p. 244.

[2] Atlanta *Constitution,* December 27, 1889, quoted in Raymond B. Nixon, *Henry W. Grady: Spokesman of the New South,* New York, 1943, p. 331.

force Grady was literally *wishing* the Negro "as a political force" out of the picture.

The situation at the end of the eighties required more than wishing, however. Negroes were still voting in many parts of the South. Between 1876 and 1890 their voting strength had been cut in some Southern states by as much as one-half, but it had not been completely wiped out anywhere.[3] Negro voters remained so considerable in some areas, especially in the Black Belt districts, that they posed a real problem for white candidates for public office who vied with each other for Negro support; and it was not unheard-of that a white candidate for one office had to join forces with a Negro candidate for another office in order to be certain of victory. It was this situation that made it possible for Negroes to continue to hold office during the eighties. In Mississippi there were seven Negroes in the legislature in 1888.[4] In the same year there were eight Negroes in the Virginia General Assembly.[5] They held numerous minor offices in many parts of the South; and in 1890 there were three Negroes in the federal Congress.[6] These conditions merely increased the anxiety of the Gradys who wanted to be rid of the Negro factor in politics.

Other factors added to the obvious anxiety of whites regarding the role of Negroes in Southern politics. In 1889 the Republicans not only inaugurated a President but regained control of both house of the Congress. In an early message to the Congress President Harrison called for a law providing for federal intervention to police elections.[7] Henry Cabot Lodge had advocated such a law for several years, and it was the growing sentiment favoring such legislation that impelled Henry W. Grady to go to Boston in December, 1889, to speak against it in his last public address.[8] If the federal government was to offer its strength to protect the remaining Negroes who were exercising the franchise and holding office, there was a real danger that the Negro would become an even more important factor in Southern politics. All the favorite arguments against federal intervention were advanced.[9] Ever-present was the claim of corruption and venality. The Negro, himself an active corrupting element during Reconstruction, had become, after the "overthrow," an irresistible temptation to the white man

[3] Wm. A. Dunning, "The Undoing of Reconstruction," *The Atlantic Monthly,* LXXXVIII (October, 1901), p. 437. See, also, Kirk H. Porter, *A History of Suffrage in the United States,* Chicago, 1918, pp. 191–227.

[4] Vernon Lane Wharton, *The Negro in Mississippi, 1865–1890,* Chapel Hill, 1947, p. 202.

[5] Luther Porter Jackson, *Negro Office-Holders in Virginia, 1865–1895,* Norfolk, 1945, pp. 1–43.

[6] Samuel D. Smith, *The Negro in Congress, 1870–1901,* Chapel Hill, 1940, p. 6.

[7] James P. Richardson, *A Compilation of the Messages and Papers of the Presidents,* vol. IX, p. 56.

[8] Nixon, *op. cit.,* p. 317.

[9] See, for example, Grady's speech in Boston, December 12, 1889, entitled, "The Race Problem in the South," in Grady, *op cit.,* p. 244 ff.

to corrupt himself by buying the Negro's vote in order to make him "safe."[10]

As if the anxieties created by these conditions were not enough, there were others that were caused by the most distressing developments of an entirely different kind. The position of the Southern farmer in the eighties had steadily deteriorated. The small group of well-to-do planters and business men at the top, whose political strength had increased, were growing stronger as a result of their association with Northern industrialists and financiers. As the South became industrialized the merchant and industrialist ascended the economic and political ladder and moved toward a position of dominance. At times they merged their interests and identity with the planter who could offer them social position if nothing else. The economic changes did not substantially improve conditions among either the masses of Southern whites or the Negroes. Most of them remained agricultural workers, and the long years of depression in the areas of cotton production following the panic of 1873 caused suffering that bred unrest.[11] The dissatisfaction that transcended racial lines tempted Negroes and whites to join forces to seek through political action some relief from their ills.

The radical agrarian movement in the South attracted discontented elements of both races, who maintained separate organizations. At the same time they achieved a wide area of agreement as far as goals were concerned. Many of these goals were to be reached through the candidates who sought public office under the banner of the Populist party or some coalition of radical agrarian groups with one of the regular parties. Even as these biracial combinations developed, they had within them the seeds of their own destruction. The whites involved in such combinations were largely the upland yeomen and landless element whose antagonisms toward the Negro went back to the antebellum period and whose association with Negroes, even for the common good, was of the most tenuous and indefinite nature. They needed only to have their confidence shaken or their racial antipathies aroused to cause them not only to desert their Negro allies but to turn against them with great vehemence.

The successes of the early agrarian efforts were impressive. In 1888 Negroes and whites considered the question of promoting a strike for higher wages among the cotton pickers.[12] Within a matter of months they were organizing for political purposes. In the last decade they achieved a surprising degree of success in certain areas of the South such as Georgia, Virginia, and North Carolina. The conservative element in the South had reason to be apprehensive. They denounced Populism as radical, fanatical, and unAmerican; they seized every opportunity to undermine this frightening turn of events.

[10] C. Van Woodward, *Origins of the New South, 1877–1913*, Baton Rouge, 1951, p. 326 ff.

[11] Francis B. Simkins, *A History of the South*, New York, 1953, p. 349 ff.

[12] John Hope Franklin, *From Slavery to Freedom: A History of American Negroes*, New York, 1956, p. 331.

President Harrison's call in 1889 for the enactment of legislation for the federal control of elections gave the conservative South its first real opportunity to undermine the biracial political movement. When Henry Cabot Lodge introduced such a bill in June, 1890, the Southern whites began to call for a closing of the ranks. They recalled the "horrors" of reconstruction days and declared they would never tolerate such treatment again. They implored the dissident whites to return to the party of their fathers and uphold the honor of the South. And even as Populists began to bid for power they began to suffer from the defections of those who were easily persuaded to return to the fold.

Convinced that more effective disfranchisement of the Negro was needed to remove him completely as a voter and as an issue in elections, Southern whites decided to write Negro disfranchisement into the constitutions of their states. This would make it possible for whites to divide on the basis of issues, would reduce corruption by eliminating the temptation of rival white candidates to purchase Negro votes, would eliminate the disproportionate influence of white politicians in "corrupt" black counties, and would prevent the rise of Negroes as social and economic competitors with the whites. The time was at hand, therefore, to disfranchise the Negro by "legal, constitutional" means, without seeming to violate the Fifteenth Amendment to the Federal Constitution.

In 1890 it was Mississippi that took the initiative by calling a convention to do what various segments of the state's population had been discussing since 1877.[13] Oddly enough, some of the most liberal elements in the state, such as the Farmers Alliance, favored the convention, while many conservatives opposed it on the grounds that racial peace had been achieved and well enough should be let alone! Regardless of motives of those who supported the calling of the convention, it is clear that the majority of the delegates who assembled were primarily interested in devising some scheme of insuring white supremacy.

At the Mississippi convention the delegates from white counties were suspicious of most disfranchisement proposals. They were fearful that the proposed measures would operate against many of their white constituents. Finally, the leaders from the black counties were able to enlist their support for measures designed merely to eliminate the Negro voter. Thus, the Constitution was amended to grant the franchise only to those who met the state residence requirement of two years, who were free from criminal records, who had paid the poll tax of two dollars per year, and who could read or understand any section of the state constitution.[14] While the "understanding clause" was, on the face of it, applicable to whites and blacks alike and could be used to disfranchise one group or the other, it was clear that in practice it was intended to enfranchise illiterate whites.

---

[13] Albert D. Kirwan, *Revolt of the Rednecks, Mississippi Politics: 1876–1925*, Lexington, 1951, p. 60.

[14] Mississippi Constitution, 1890, Sects. 241, 243, 244, 249, 251.

Negroes were to be disfranchised by the literacy clause. The intentions of the framers were made clear by President S. S. Calhoon on the closing day of the convention.[15] Even the United States Supreme Court, although feeling helpless—or disinclined—to do anything about it, took cognizance of the framers' intentions when it said that the provisions "swept the horizons of expediency to find a way around the Negro amendments to the Federal Constitution."[16]

Southerners in other states viewed the developments in Mississippi with admiration and wondered if they could do as well. In the same year Tennessee took one feeble step by instituting a poll tax requirement, the example for which was actually set by Florida in 1889, while Arkansas followed suit in 1893.[17] Meanwhile, Virginia and Georgia tightened their election laws in 1893 and 1894.[18] In some instances they were administered so as to eliminate potential Negro voters from the polls.

South Carolina was the only other state that took the drastic step of constitutional disfranchisement of the Negro before the collapse of Populism. In September, 1895, the "people of South Carolina assembled in convention for the third time since the Civil War to make a fundamental law."[19] They had lived under the "Radical" Resconstruction Constitution for twenty-seven years, and in an unguarded moment some would admit that it was an excellent document. But Negroes had participated in its construction and, worse still, under it some Negroes continued to enjoy the franchise, despite the numerous election laws the state had enacted to obstruct them. In order to write a fundamental law that would disfranchise all Negroes and, at the same time, permit every white person however ignorant or poor, to vote, Ben Tillman left his seat in the United States Senate to serve as chairman of the convention's suffrage committee. By cajoling, persuading, and threatening Tillman steered through the convention a provision designed to achieve these ends.

Like the Mississippi provision, the South Carolina constitution set up a residence requirement of two years, required the payment of a poll tax, and excluded persons, who were invariably convicted Negroes, of a specified list of crimes. Up to January 1, 1898, any man who fulfilled these requirements and who could read or understand the constitution was to be a voter for life. After that date, any person who fulfilled the requirements or who paid taxes on $300 worth of property could become a voter.[20]

[15] *Journal of the Proceedings of the Constitutional Convention of the State of Mississippi . . . . 1890,* Jackson, 1890, p. 700 ff.

[16] *Williams* v. *Mississippi,* 170 U.S. 213.

[17] V. O. Key, *Southern Politics in State and Nation,* New York, 1949, p. 578 ff.

[18] Woodward, *New South,* p. 275.

[19] Francis B. Simkins, *Pitchfork Ben Tillman, South Carolinian,* Baton Rouge, 1944, p. 291.

[20] Constitution of the State of South Carolina, 1895, Article II.

Once again, in order to circumvent the Fifteenth Amendment, registration and election officials were to be left free to discriminate against prospective Negro voters and show partiality for whites.[21]

The hesitation that other Southern states had in coming to grips with the question of the Negro voter seemed to disappear as they became deeply involved with radical agrarianism in the mid-nineties. While they were afraid to call constitutional conventions as long as Populism was at high tide, lest the mischievous radicals do more harm than good, they became determined to do so at the first opportunity. Gradually, however, the corner was turned. White Populists began to buy the conservative argument that the elimination of the Negro from voting was a healthy step toward strengthening the two-party system and opening the door for constructive reform. Thus, reaction conspired with reform to accelerate the disfranchisement of the Negro toward the end of the century.

There were always those who feared that the literacy and understanding tests would, in the hands of scrupulous registrars, operate to disfranchise some whites and, thus, go beyond the real intentions of the disfranchising conventions. Some, moreover, hoped that the disfranchisement measures would remove some of the more undesirable whites as well as all the Negroes from the lists of eligible voters.[22] It was Louisiana that sought to guard against such a deplorable eventuality. When that state revised its constitution in 1898 it followed the pattern set by Mississippi and Louisiana as far as residence, literacy, and understanding of the constitution were concerned. It went one step further, however, by granting the franchise to any one who, lacking the educational and property qualifications, was eligible to vote on January 1, 1867, or who was the son or grandson of a person eligible to vote on that date. The right to register under the "grandfather clause" had to be exercised by September 1, 1898.[23] Louisiana thereby embraced a measure that Tillman's South Carolina had rejected because of doubtful constitutionality. In 1910 the young state of Oklahoma was to follow this lead and precipitate the controversy that led to the outlawing of the grandfather clause.[24]

Thus, before the beginning of the twentieth century the basic techniques by which Negroes were to be "legally" disfranchised had been developed. In subsequent years no significant modifications were made to the methods that had been introduced by Mississippi, South Carolina, and Louisiana. The states that changed the suffrage provisions of their constitutions in the early years of the new century were content merely to refine the methods of the pioneers. But they left no doubt that they were as determined as their predecessors to destroy every vestige of political power

---

[21] Simkins, *Ben Tillman,* p. 299 ff.

[22] See Key, *op. cit.,* p. 542.

[23] Constitution of Louisiana, 1897, Article 197.

[24] Guinn and Beal v. United States, 238 U. S. 347.

in the hands of the Negroes. And they seemed even less fearful of running afoul of the Fifteenth Amendment. In North Carolina the bitter campaigns of 1898 and 1900 were fought on a pledge to remove Negroes from politics. In the latter year the victors fulfilled their promise by introducing into the constitution a reading and writing qualification for voting and a temporary grandfather clause to accommodate illiterate whites.[25]

In 1901 the Alabama convention did a good deal of "refining of" the suffrage provisions of its constitution. It experienced difficulty in developing a "scheme pure and simple" which would "let every white man vote and prevent any Negro from voting." Too many Negroes were prompt in paying their taxes for the whites to rely solely on a poll tax. Too many Negroes could establish the identity of their white ancestors to rely solely on the grandfather clause. The fact that one-half of the Negro electorate could read and write cast doubt on the efficacy of a literacy test.[26] The confused delegates finally set up literacy poll tax and property tests as the principal requirements and placed their real hopes in the hands of election registrars who were given wide discretionary powers.[27]

The Virginia convention, extending from the early summer of 1901 into the winter of 1902, was protracted largely because of the many disagreements regarding the most effective way to disfranchise Negroes. There seemed to be no controversy over the main purpose of the convention. It was aptly put by Carter Glass when he said, "Discrimination! Why that is precisely what we propose; that, exactly, is what this convention was elected for—to discriminate to the very extremity of permissible action under the limitations of the Federal Constitution, with a view to the elimination of every Negro voter who can be gotten rid of, legally, without materially impairing the numerical strength of the white electorate."[28] None disagreed with the aims of Glass, but there was great difficulty in arriving at a satisfactory formula by which these aims were to be realized. After much heated debate the delegates finally agreed on literacy, property, and poll tax tests and a proposal to enfranchise any man or the son of any man who had seen service in the Confederate or United States forces or in the state militia.[29]

For a time it appeared as though Georgia would not join the movement to disfranchise the Negro legally. Some Georgians doubted that the white public would support a disfranchising scheme, believing that the long-established poll tax, combined with time-honored "informal" methods, had all but completed the disfranchisement of Negroes. But it was the

[25] William Alexander Mabry, " 'White Supremacy' and the North Carolina Suffrage Amendment," North Carolina Historical Review, 13: 5–6, January, 1936, pp. 5–6.

[26] Paul Lewinson, Race, Class, and Party, New York, 1932, p. 84.

[27] Constitution of Alabama, 1901, Article VIII.

[28] Quoted in Lewinson, op. cit., p. 86.

[29] Constitution of Virginia, 1902, Article II.

use and manipulation of the Negro electorate that finally inspired reformers to advocate the legal disfranchisement of Negroes. Led by Tom Watson, the agrarians who had formerly supported universal suffrage, began a vigorous campaign for disfranchisement by 1906. They were fearful that the conservatives would enlist Negro voters in their fight against legislation designed to control railroads, corporations, and other "enemies" of the people. Consequently, the agrarians campaigned and won in 1906 on a platform that demanded the disfranchisement of the Negro. Two years later a new constitution went into effect that contained the conventional educational and property tests.[30]

By 1910 the white supremacists could rest much more comfortably than they did in 1890. Every former Confederate state had strengthened its stand against Negro voting by "legally" disfranchising Negroes. There seemed to be nothing that anyone could do about it. The one Negro delegate in the Mississippi convention and the six in the South Carolina gathering were helpless. There were no Negroes in the conventions of the other states. Outsiders, such as Booker Washington, had no more effect in their requests for moderation and justice than the friends of Negro suffrage who sat in the conventions. And, except in the case of Alabama, the new constitutions were not submitted to the people of the several states.[31] In the very manner in which they ignored the pleas of interested victims and in which they brushed aside the apprehensions of the "legitimate" electorate, the revisionists displayed their grim determination to drive the Negro from politics.

It is, of course, difficult to measure the success of the new machinery in achieving white supremacy at the Southern polls. In every Southern state the number of Negroes who could qualify to vote under the new constitutions sharply declined.[32] One cannot be certain, however, that "legal" disfranchisement accomplished the neat trick of driving the Negro from the Southern polling places. As V. O. Key has observed, "Law often merely records not what is to be but what is, and ensures that what is will continue to be."[33] Certainly the confusion created by the agrarian unrest, the suppression of the Populist revolt, and the persistence of Negro voting stimulated the fight against Negro voting. Legal disfranchisement crystallized and gave formal expression to this fight. But all these developments were occurring at the same time that another technique, extralegal and presumably not in violation of the Fifteenth Amendment, was developing. This was the white primary. In the long run it was, perhaps, to be

---

[30] C. Vann Woodward, *Tom Watson, Agrarian Rebel,* New York, 1938, p. 385 and Alex M. Arnett, *Populist Movement in Georgia,* New York, 1923, pp. 220–221.

[31] In North Carolina the suffrage amendment was passed by the legislature and ratified by the people in August, 1900.

[32] Woodward, *New South,* p. 342 ff.

[33] Key, *op. cit.,* p. 535.

more effective than the legal machinery in keeping Negroes from voting. Whatever the effective techniques were, it was "legal" disfranchisement that gave the entire trend respectability and maintained in the South the fiction that it was not running over the Federal constitution but living under it.

# 18

## PLESSY V. FERGUSON:
## CONSERVATIVE SOCIOLOGICAL JURISPRUDENCE
Barton J. Bernstein

> "The felt necessities of the time, the prevalent moral and political theories, intuitions of public policy, avowed or unconscious, even the prejudices which judges share with their fellow-men, have had a good deal more to do than the syllogism in determining the rules by which men should be governed."
>
> OLIVER WENDELL HOLMES, THE COMMON LAW

**F**OR fifty-eight years *Plessy v. Ferguson*,[1] the federal source of the "separate but equal" doctrine, had escaped judicial challenge. When the 1954 Supreme Court in effect overruled the *Plessy* doctrine in the *Segregation Cases*,[2] the Warren tribunal's decision was attacked as sociological jurisprudence.[3] Implicit in this criticism was

---

Barton J. Bernstein, "Plessy v. Ferguson: Conservative Sociological Jurisprudence," *Journal of Negro History*, XLVIII (July 1963), 196–205. Reprinted by permission of the *Journal of Negro History*.

[1] 163 U.S. 537 (1896).

[2] *Brown et al. v. Board of Education et al.*, 347 U.S. 483, has since been called the *Segregation Cases*. Since only in a case identical in material facts to *Plessy v. Ferguson*, a transportation case, could the Supreme Court overrule *Plessy*. The overruling did not occur until such a transportation case came before the Warren court. *Gayle v. Browder*, 352 U.S. 903 (1956).

[3] In *Brown* the court had announced that "we cannot turn the clock back to 1868 when the Amendment [Fourteenth] was adopted, or even to 1896 when *Plessy v. Ferguson* was written. We must consider public education in the light of its full development and its present place in the American life throughout the nation." The court did not seek to erect an impressive legal argument, buttressed by case law, to overturn *Plessy*. Case law was deemed inapplicable, and the history of the original meaning of the Fourteenth Amendment was judged "inconclusive." The high court cited sociologcial and psychological studies

an assumption that *Plessy* was free of social theory and allegedly based upon the more solid grounds of precedent and constitutional law.

However, recent studies of the tangled history of the Fourteenth Amendment establish that the Amendment did not require the Supreme Court's decision in *Plessy*.[4] And a careful examination of the case law cited by the *Plessy* court reveals that only through distortion could these cases have been used to support the court's holding.[5] In view of this research the court's opinion merits analysis to determine whether social theories shaped the "separate but equal" position.

I

Homer Plessy, part Negro, had been arrested in Louisiana where he had violated the state law requiring separate accommodations for the races in intrastate travel. Plessy's contention that the Louisiana statute was unconstitutional was rejected by the state court and appealed to the United States Supreme Court. With only Justice John Marshall Harlan dissenting, the Supreme Court held that the state law was a reasonable exercise of the state police power and therefore constitutional.

Before the Supreme Court, counsel for Plessy had attacked the segregation provision as unreasonable. In an argument which Harlan adopted in his dissent, the counsel had argued that a decision against Plessy and for segregation would authorize the states to require separate cars for people with different colors of hair, aliens, or Catholics or Protestants, or to require colored people to walk on one side of the street and white people on the other side, or to demand that white men's homes be painted white and black men's homes black. These analogies were close enough

---

to establish that separate educational facilities cannot be equal; the "separate but equal" doctrine was self-contradictory.

Criticism of the *Segregation Cases* as sociological jurisprudence has been based on three propositions: the Fourteenth Amendment was not intended to prohibit Jim Crow education, and the framers' intent should be followed; the court should have followed the precedent, *Plessy*, and later segregation cases whose broad holdings could be interpreted as Supreme Court approval of "separate but equal"; and social theories should not be the basis for a legal decision.

[4] John Frank and Robert Munro, "The Original Understanding of 'Equal Protection of the Laws'," *Columbia Law Review*, L, No. 1 (January, 1950), 131; Jacobus Ten Broek, *The Antislavery Origins of the Fourteenth Amendment* (Cal., 1951); Howard Graham, "The Anti-Slavery Backgrounds of the Fourteenth Amendment," *Wisconsin Law Review*, 1950, No. 3 (May, 1950), No. 4 (July, 1950), 479, 610; Alfred Kelly, "The Fourteenth Amendment Reconsidered," *Michigan Law Review*, LIV, No. 8 (June, 1956), 1049; Robert Harris, *The Quest for Equality* (Louisiana St. Univ., 1960); and Jack Greenberg, *Race Relations and American Law* (Columbia, 1959).

[5] Bernstein, "Case Law in *Plessy v. Ferguson*," *Jour. Negro Hist.* XLVII, No. 3 (July, 1962), 192–198.

to the case at bar to compel the court to distinguish these fact situations and justify its reasoning in *Plessy*.[6]

Judge Henry Billings Brown, writing the court's opinion, replied that "every exercise of the police power must be reasonable, and extend only to such laws as are enacted in good faith for the promotion of the public good, and not for the annoyance or oppression of a particular class." He relied upon two arguments to establish the contention that the Louisiana statute was a reasonable exercise of the state police power. Each revealed that sociological and psychological theories controlled the court's decision.

First, Brown maintained that the Louisiana act was not designed as an "annoyance or oppression" and should not have been so considered. He contended that laws requiring racial segregation did not "necessarily imply the inferiority of one race to the other." The underlying fallacy of the plaintiff's argument was "the assumption that enforced separation of the two races stamps the colored race with a badge of inferiority." Such reasoning, Brown explained, would mean that if a Negro legislature separated whites, the whites would feel inferior. He concluded that they would not.[7]

Harlan might have attacked Brown's analogy. Or the dissent might have noted that the court avoided relevant facts: the white race outnumbered the Negro in the nation; Negroes had only recently been freed from servitude and awarded legal equality; their alleged inferiority was attested to by a host of pseudo-scientific theories. Harlan, however, simply asserted that candor demanded recognition "that the statute in question had its origin in the purpose . . . to exclude colored people from the coaches" of white people. The Louisiana statute, he maintained, was designed as an annoyance and intended as oppression. "The brand of servitude and degradation" was placed upon a large class of fellow citizens. Harlan concluded: "The thin disguise of equal accommodations for passengers . . . will not mislead anyone, nor atone for the wrong this day done."[8] Harlan's statement about the law's purpose leads to the conclusion that the Louisiana act was unreasonable—by Brown's criteria.

Brown's second argument wrote conservative theory and the prevailing social science "truths" into law. The court explained that the standard of reasonableness is determined "with reference to the established usages, customs, and traditions of the people." This is the underlying social doctrine upon which the case is erected. Law is reasonable when it follows custom. The court implied that law is unreasonable when it violates custom or tradition or seeks to change the folkways of the people. Judge Brown denied that "social prejudices may be overcome by legislation. . . . 'This end can neither be accomplished nor promoted by laws

[6] S. F. Phillips and F. D. McKenney, *Brief for Plaintiff in Error in Plessy v. Ferguson,* 13.

[7] 163 U.S. 537 at 551.

[8] 163 U.S. 537 at 562, 3.

which conflict with the general sentiment of the community upon whom they are designed to operate.' " Brown concluded that "legislation is power-less to eradicate racial instincts. . . . If one race be inferior to the other socially, the Constitution of the United States cannot put them upon the same plane."[9]

The court believed that it was only within the duty and capacity of government to guarantee the races equal civil and political rights, and that state laws requiring racial segregation did not constitute a violation of these rights. Brown considered Jim Crow laws an abridgement of social equality.[10] Social equality could not be legislated, and the court approved that it should not be legislated. "If the two races are to meet upon terms of social equality," the court concluded, "it must be the result of natural affinities, a mutual appreciation of each other's merits and a voluntary consent of individuals."[11]

## II

At least four questionable factual allegations or dubious legal and scientific theories were employed by the court to justify the legislation of prejudice: racial segregation is a custom or tradition; law is reasonable when it follows custom and unreasonable when it does not adhere to custom; a contrary decision in Plessy would have meant the enforcement of social equality; and law cannot "eradicate [the] racial instincts." Each of these reflects the underlying theories and prejudices upon which the decision rests.

Contrary to the Plessy court's contention, segregation in transporta-tion was not consistent with custom or tradition. Racial segregation in the Old South had been unknown.[12] The system of slavery would have been

[9] 163 U.S. 537 at 550, 1. The quote within the quote is persuasive authority from People v. Gallagher, 93 N.Y. 438 at 448 (1883). Earlier in the Plessy opinion the Supreme Court had recognized that Negroes were considered inferior. Brown had written: "the reputation of belonging to the dominant race, in this instance the white race, is property, in the same sense that a right of action, or of inheritance is property. . . . If he be a white man assigned to a colored coach he may have his action for damages against the company for being deprived of his so-called property. Upon the other hand, if he be called a colored man [and he is]. . . , he has been deprived of no property since he is not lawfully entitled to the reputation of being a white man." 163 U.S. 537 at 545.

[10] John Marshall Harlan contended that the issue was a violation of a civil right, not a social right. A railroad, he reasoned, was a public highway, and all rights pertaining to its use were consequently civil rights.

[11] 163 U.S. 537 at 551.

[12] Speaking about the Old South, W.E.B. Du Bois later noted, the two races sometimes "lived in the same house, shared in the family life, often attended the same church, and talked and conversed with each other." The Souls of Black Folks (McClure, 1903), 184.

virtually inoperative had Jim Crow prevailed.[13] Nor did Jim Crow spontaneously arise after the war. Negroes and whites frequently shared the same coaches; although sometimes the freedmen were barred from the first-class cars, the races did share the same second-class coaches. A South Carolinian remarked in 1877 that Negroes in his state "were permitted to, and frequently do ride in first-class railway and street cars." At first this had caused trouble, but it was then "so common as hardly to provoke remark."[14] One reporter observed that Negroes rode "exactly as white people . . . and in the same cars" in Virginia.[15] When the *Plessy* court judged it custom, Jim Crow transportation was but a recent Southern creation. By 1896 only eight Southern states had such laws, and seven of the statutes were less than eight years old.[16] These regulations were frequently the enactment of codes of recent practice. The caste system was not yet a custom or tradition; it was a new pattern. Institutionalized prejudice had not hardened; that was the promise of *Plessy v. Ferguson*. By its decision the Supreme Court constitutionalized the state enactment of race prejudice.

Laws severely violating custom and tradition are usually unenforceable and may therefore be judged unreasonable. This proposition does not, however, mean that custom must be reflected in law. Customs can exist independently of law, and custom is not violated if it is not enacted in law. If the *Plessy* court had declared the Louisiana statute unconstitutional, custom would not have been violated. The court was right in stating that social equality cannot be enforced, because social relations constitute an area of free selection, and when human relations are legislated by government, they cease to be social and are transformed into political relations.

But if the court had decided that the law was unconstitutional, it would not have been enforcing social equality. The court's illogical predictions to the contrary, enforced commingling of the races would not have occurred. The practices of railroads and the social habits of passengers would not have been immediately affected. The prevailing policy would have been maintained: where informal segregation existed, it would have remained; where commingling occurred, it would have continued. However, the court's decision that "separate but equal" facilities were constitutional did enforce political inequality. Those of each race who were in

---

[13] Three southern states—Florida and Mississippi in 1865, and Texas in 1866—did enact Jim Crow transportation laws. The last of these was repealed in 1873. Franklin Johnson, *The Development of State Legislation Concerning the Free Negro* (Arbor, 1918), 13–16.

[14] Belton O'Neall Townsend, "South Carolina Society," *Atlantic Monthly*, XXXIX (June, 1877), 676.

[15] George Cable, *Silent South* (New York, 1885), 85–6, quoted by C. Vann Woodward, *Origins of the New South, 1877–1913* (Vol. IX, *A History of the South*, Louisiana St. Univ., 1951), 210.

[16] See Johnson, *op. cit.*, 15, 54, 62–207, and Gilbert Stephenson, *Race Discrimination in American Law* (New York, 1910), 216–217.

the habit of mingling with members of the other were denied this right by law.

The court argued that social attitudes cannot be shaped by law.[17] While this was poor history, it was consistent with the popular sociology which emerged after the Civil War. All good Spencerians—most sociologists—agreed that society, the organism of evolution, could not be refashioned by legislation. William Graham Sumner explained that "legislation cannot makes mores" and stateways cannot change folkways. Franklin Henry Giddings, Columbia University's counterpart of Sumner, had emphasized "consciousness of kind," a new guise for the "racial instincts" concept, to explain segregation. The implication in *Plessy* was that this social custom, the desire for racially segregated facilities, was grounded in "race instincts." These instincts were unchangeable before man-made law.[18]

The vague theory of "racial instincts," requiring the separation of the races, provided the "scientific" means for justifying the Southern system of white superiority which had been threatened by the abolition of slavery. One Southerner succinctly stated the new ideology as scientific fact: "there is an instinct, ineradicable and positive, that will keep the races apart."[19] Inferiority of the Negro was an article of Southern faith to which many clung. To yield their position of superiority and accept the Negro as an equal would have overturned the habits nurtured by many decades of slavery. However, only some Southern whites felt threatened by the rising status of Negroes. It was the lower class white who demanded Jim Crow laws when the Negro competed with him for subsistence wages.[20] White superiority could be guaranteed by this new enforced relationship between whites and blacks. For the poor white, caste would protect class. Jim Crow was designed as an "annoying oppression," contrary to the *Plessy* opinion. Separation of the two races would constitute a constant and visible affirmation of the continuing inferiority of blacks to whites.

[17] The Massachusetts high court in *Roberts v. City of Boston,* 59 Mass. (5 Cush) 198 (1849), the source of the "separate but equal" doctrine, had stated that race prejudice "is not created by law, and probably cannot be changed by law."

[18] It is to be noted that the court did not tilt against anti-miscegenation laws. Obviously if a "racial instinct" required segregation, such laws were unnecessary; by instinct everyone would refrain from interracial marriage.

[19] Quoted by Paul Buck, *The Road to Reunion, 1865–1900* (Vintage, 1959), 299, from Joel Chandler Harris, *Life, Writings, and Speeches of Henry W. Grady* (New York, 1890), 289ff.

[20] Woodward speaks of this process as "one of the paradoxes of Southern history that political democracy for the white man and racial discrimination for the black were often products of the same dynamics." Negroes understood that economic pressures were creating the pressures for Jim Crow. "It took a lot of ritual and Jim Crow to bolster the creed of white supremacy in the bosom of a white man working for black man's wages. . . . A North Carolina Negro wrote: 'The best people in the South do not demand this separate car business . . . and, when they do, it is only to cater to those of their race who, in order to get a big man's smile, will elevate them to place and power.'" Quoted by Woodward, *op. cit.,* 211, from Editorial, *Southland* (Salisbury, N.C.), 1 (1890), 166–167.

Out of earlier American doubts and theories a new doctrine had arisen to justify segregation. It merged the discoveries of older thought and the contemporary science.[21] "Racial instinct" and white supremacy were intertwined theories promoted by the Frenchman, Joseph Gobineau,[22] who had not awaited the appearance of Darwinism. Shortly after Gobineau, "survival of the fittest," the popular catchword summary of Darwin's theory of organic evolution, was invoked to establish white superiority over the Negro. Biologists and anthropologists readily confirmed Negro inferiority. The Negro's skull was weighed and his brain measured. Elaborate scientific studies were said to demonstrate that in brain size, pelvic expanse, and a great variety of physiological and psychological traits Negroes were inferior to whites. Comparative disease rates and criminality percentages, always favorable to the whites, "scientifically" established this superiority. It was demonstrated ·hat the Negro's intelligence did not control his actions.[23] Studies showed that he was "light-hearted and carefree," seldom allowing "responsibility to weigh on his mind."[24] Obviously whites were more mature and civilized; they had advanced higher on the evolutionary scale. The Negro's inferiority made him a child while the white was an adult. Some racists sought to modify this bastard offspring of Darwinism by accenting the supremacy of the Anglo-Saxon or Aryan, terms more specific in the categories they excluded than those included. A German strain of racism, born in Romanticism and carried to America by German seminar-trained students, advanced this theory.[25] Either explicitly or implicitly, the Negro was always relegated to hopeless inferiority by the scientific "truths."

[21] See William Stanton, The Leopard's Spots (Univ. of Chicago, 1960); Oscar Handlin, Race and Nationality in American Life (Little, Brown, 1957), cc. 1–4; William Jenkins, Pro-Slavery Thought (Univ. of N. C., 1935); Charles Wesley, "Negro Inferiority in American Thought," Jour. Negro Hist., XXV, No. 4 (Oct., 1940), 540; and Leon Litwack, North of Slavery (Univ. of Chi., 1961).

[22] In his Essai sur l'inegalite des races humaines (1853), he had demonstrated the alleged superiority of the white race over other races, and Aryans over other whites. A translation of his work appeared in America in 1856, with some notes by an admirer, Moral and Intellectual Diversity of the Races . . . with an Analytic Introduction and Copious Historical Notes, by H. Hotz to which is Added an Appeal Concerning a Summary of the Latest Scientific Facts Bearing Upon the Question of Unity or Plurality of Species, by J. C. Nott (1856). For a brief discussion of Gobineau, see Handlin, op. cit., c. 4, and Jacques Barzun, Race: A Study in Modern Superstition (Meuten, 1938).

[23] Tests measuring the speed of mental reactions showed that the Negro reacted more rapidly than the white. From this it was concluded that intelligence did not control the black man's actions; actually he was close to the savage. R.M. Burke, "Reaction Time with Reference to Race," Psychological Review, 11 (1895), 474.

[24] Charles Johnson and Horace Bond, "Investigation of Racial Differences Prior to 1910," Jour. Negro Ed., 111, No. 3 (July, 1934), 337.

[25] The late nineteenth century germ theory of politics, promoted by Herbert Baxter Adams and John Burgess, the dominant intellectual figures at Johns Hopkins and Columbia, respectively, provided respectable garb for racism. Richard Hofstadter, Social Darwinism in American Thought (Boston, 1959), c. 9.

The influence of these ideas was apparent in *Plessy v. Ferguson,* and probably reflected the dominant thoughts and fears of an uneasy American society. At the same time sectional tensions were being eliminated at the price of abandoning the Negro. The Negro was sacrificed "on the altar of reconciliation, peace and prosperity." The Supreme Court had anticipated this movement in earlier decisions. Southern writers had contributed their efforts. Thomas Nelson Page, Joel Chandler Harris, and their associates in the South, with the aid of Northern editors and publishing houses, had created an image of a friendly South where the child-like Negroes loved the white folks.[26] Northerners seeking sectional reconciliation with the South put the "bloody shirt" in their trunks and were mouthing the shibboleths of white supremacy and Negro inferiority.[27] Most Northerners who advocated Negro rights embraced a philosophy of segregation and wanted to improve the black man's status within this framework. The aggressive Negro leadership of Frederick Douglass had been replaced by a new movement more concerned about Negro advancement than integration. The year before the *Plessy* decision became the law of the land, Douglass had died and Booker T. Washington, the spearhead of the new order, delivered the famous Atlanta address calling for a program of racial coexistence grounded in racial separation: "The opportunity to earn a dollar in a factory just now is worth infinitely more than an opportunity to spend a dollar in an opera-house."[28] Social advancement, it was hoped, would occur within the context of segregation.

### III

While the most respected Negro leader was counselling patience and gradual progress through economic advancement, the Supreme Court, in constitutionalizing racial separation, had condemned the Negro to an inferiority confirmed by the legal recognition of contemporary biological and social science "truths." By not acknowledging that social attitudes could be shaped by law, the court assured that Jim Crow would become

---

[26] See Buck, *op. cit.,* for a discussion of sectional reconciliation, particularly the literature of the period.

[27] C. Vann Woodward, *The Strange Career of Jim Crow* (Oxford, 1955), 52–53. Such expressions frequently appeared in *Nation, Harper's Weekly, North American Review,* and *Atlantic Monthly* of the period. Illustrative of the change in Northern attitudes is the case of Thomas Wentworth Higginson. As a young man he had led a mob to free a fugitive slave from jail, and in the Civil War he had commanded a regiment of Negro troops. Thirty years after Appomattox he shed tears as he read of the death of a slave owner in a popular story. Buck, *op. cit.,* 244. Also see Vincent De Santis, *Republicans Face the Southern Question* (Johns Hopkins, 1959), and Stanley Hirshson, *Farewell to the Bloody Shirt* (Univ. of Indiana, 1962).

[28] In the same address he explained, "The wisest among my race understand that the agitation of questions of social equality is the extremist folly. . . ." *Up From Slavery* (Doubleday, 1901), 223–224.

custom and treatment of Negroes as second-class citizens habit.[29] The seeds of race hatred were sown. It was Harlan, the constant champion of Negro rights, who predicted that the decision would stimulate "aggressions, more or less brutal or irritating, upon the admitted rights of colored citizens." "What," he added, "can more certainly arouse race hatred?"[30]

[29] A half century later the brief submitted for the Negro children in *Brown v. Board of Education* surveyed the success of the *Plessy* decision: "Without the 'constitutional' sanction which *Plessy v. Ferguson* affords, racial segregation could not have become entrenched in the South. . . . The doctrine of *Plessy v. Ferguson* was essential to the successful maintenance of a racial caste system in the United States." Herbert Hill, et al., *Brief for Appellants in Brown v. Board of Education et al.*, 62.

[30] Harlan concluded: "State enactments, regulating the enjoyment of civil rights, upon the basis of race, and cunningly devised to defeat legitimate results of war, under the pretense of recognizing equality or rights, can have no other result than to render permanent peace impossible, and to keep alive the conflict of the races, the continuance of which must do harm to all concerned." 163 U.S. 537 at 560–561.

# 19

## SOUTH CAROLINA NEGROES IN AGRICULTURE, 1877–1900
### George B. Tindall

T HE precedent established in ante-bellum experimentation with white tenant farming was rapidly spread after the Civil War both among the freedmen and the poor whites, owing its rapid spread, though not its origin, to the necessity for other systems of tenure and labor after the abolition of slavery. Negro farm laborers, desirous of independence from the ante-bellum gang system and unable to secure the ownership of land, found in various forms of tenancy and sharecropping the most satisfactory available compromise between their wishes and the desire of the whites to maintain close supervision over the labor force.[1]

By 1880 the system had been widely accepted by both whites and Negroes in the Piedmont region as the proper solution to their problems.

Reprinted from *South Carolina Negroes, 1877–1900*, by George Brown Tindall, by permission of the University of South Carolina Press. Copyright © 1952 by the University of South Carolina Press. Pp. 96–101, 103–114.

[1] For a discussion of ante-bellum tenancy, see Marjorie Mendenhall. "The Rise of Southern Tenancy," *Yale Review*, XXVII (September, 1937), 110–29.

At first, the freedmen formed an agricultural proletariat, having nothing to offer but their labor. The landlord furnished the land, shelter, rations, seed, tools, stock, and stock-feed, and took one-half of the crop. This system prevailed widely in 1880, although in some sections of the Piedmont, notably Greenville, Fairfield, and Spartanburg counties, the landlord took two-thirds of the crop, leaving only one-third to the laborer. A more favorable arrangement was sometimes reached under which laborers rented the land for a share of the crop, for a specified amount of the crop, or even for cash, and furnished their own supplies. Where the arrangement was for a share of the crop the landlord's portion usually amounted to one-third or one-fourth.[2] Cash rental, of course, varied from place to place, depending upon the value of the land, but in 1880 it generally ranged between $3 and $5 per acre.[3]

In the lower portions of the state a somewhat different plan prevailed, involving a sharing of the land rather than of the crop. Here the compromise of Negro laborers with white landlords brought about a system that more nearly resembled the ante-bellum gang system. Under an early version of this plan the laborer worked under supervision and in return received a house, rations, three acres of land separate from the plantation, and a mule and plow every other Saturday to work it, with $16 in cash at the end of the year. But in 1867 a number of laborers proposed to work only four days, feed themselves, and take double the land and mule work.[4] In 1879 it was reported in Kershaw County that most of the labor contracts took this form.[5] With the passage of years variations on the system required laborers to work from two to five days a week with various amounts of land and other perquisites in return.[6]

On the sea islands south of Charleston the "two day" variant became widely established.[7] Under this system on Edisto Island the Negro laborer was furnished with five to seven acres of land, a house, and the privilege of using the wood on his place. In return he promised to give two days of work each week, usually performed Monday and Tuesday, and the rest of the week he had to work his own crop. In a survey made during 1880 it was reported that the laborer was expected to work two "tasks," or half an acre a day (in some places an acre a day), so that during the week he

[2] State Board of Agriculture of South Carolina, *South Carolina Resources and Population. Institutions and Industries* (Charleston, 1883), pp. 155–56. Hereinafter cited as *Handbook of 1883.*

[3] *Ibid.,* pp. 156–57.

[4] *Ibid.,* p. 83.

[5] Columbia *Daily Register,* January 28, 1879.

[6] *Handbook of 1883,* pp. 83–84.

[7] For an example of a "two day" contract, see contract dated January 10, 1880, in James B. and R. B. Heyward Papers, Southern Historical Collection, University of North Carolina.

cultivated one or two acres for the landlord.[8] A reporter for the Charleston *News and Courier* said that he "should think the negroes would be very well satisfied, as I have seen them returning from the fields having accomplished their day's work by 9 o'clock in the morning. The head of the family puts his wife and children to work, and accomplishes in three hours what it would take him all day to do."[9]

Wage labor was the least popular system with Negro workers because of the lack of independence that it entailed, but it was widely lauded by the white planters because it permitted them to exercise a close control not only over the laborer but over methods of cultivation. Wages for this type of labor fluctuated between forty and seventy-five cents a day. This was in addition to shelter, fuel, and board, which usually consisted of a ration of three pounds of bacon and one pack of grits a week.[10] But in particularly bad times wages sank to lower levels. Around Jamison in 1894 they were generally thirty cents a day. . . ."[11]

Wages, however, were sometimes better on paper than in reality. Despite state legislation passed in 1872 to force employers to pay plantation laborers in currency, the laborer frequently received payment in scrip redeemable at some definite or indefinite future date or valid only in the plantation stores. A loophole in the law permitted payment in scrip where there was specific provision for it in the labor contract,[12] but it seems unlikely that it was always necessary to utilize this loophole in order to evade the intent of the law. Sometimes payment took the form of credits in the books of the plantation store. Thus the family of Duncan Dixon . . . took its week's wages for cotton picking in the form of merchandise. The system of payment in scrip was especially prevalent on rice plantations.

The state's one Negro congressman, Thomas E. Miller, in 1891 presented a number of plantation checks for publication in the *Congressional Record*. One read "Due the bearer 25 CENTS For plantation work, Payable March 1, 1889. A. M. MANIGAULT. Jan. 1, 1885." Another check was good

---

[8] The Charleston *News and Courier,* April 22, 1880, carries a lengthy survey by J. K. Blackman of conditions on John's, James, Wadmalaw, and Edisto islands, the major sea islands to the south of Charleston; *see also* Harry Hammond, "Cotton Production," *Census* (1880), VI, 60–61.

[9] Charleston *News and Courier,* April 22, 1880.

[10] *Ibid.; Handbook of 1883,* pp. 29, 65, 83, 98, 164. The state commissioner of agriculture reported in 1885 an average wage for male farm laborers of $0.45 per day, $8.72 per month, and $90.75 per year with board. "Annual Report of the Commissioner of Agriculture of the State of South Carolina, 1885," *Reports and Resolutions* (1885), II, 105; *see also* William C. and E. T. Coker, "Day Labor Account Book for 1880," South Caroliniana Library, University of South Carolina, which shows daily wages of forty to seventy-five cents for various jobs.

[11] Charleston *News and Courier,* November 25, 1894, quoting O. F. Gundby in New York *Evening Post.*

[12] *Statutes at Large,* XV, 216.

for "$2 TWO DOLLARS $2 For labor under contract," with no specified date of payment. Other checks were inscribed "Good for 25 TWENTY-FIVE CENTS 25 In trade," "Eldorado Plantation, 25 CENTS In merchandise," and "PALO ALTO STORE. Due the bearer in trade 25 CTS. J. & S. C. DOSS."[13] "No one knows but God," said Miller, "how many heartaches and disappointments these promises to pay have caused the innocent holders, for in many cases the employers failed long before the time of their redemption, and left the laborer poor indeed, with no possession other than the remembrance of how he toiled and how magnificently his master entertained upon the fruit of his labor."[14]

The general desire of Negro farmers to become independent landowners has already been noted. However, after the early days of Reconstruction there was little active attention given in government policy to the possibility of establishing the freedmen as landowners. During the Civil War, in the area of Port Royal and St. Helena Islands, a quantity of land had been confiscated in default of a special direct tax levied by Congress and sold to Northerners and Negroes. The number of purchasers was 2,300 and the amount sold was 23,844 acres.[15] Much of this land remained in the hands of Negroes after the war, and was tenaciously held by them, so that as late as the 1930's St. Helena Island constituted a unique society of "black yeomanry" that attracted the special attention and study of sociologists.[16]

In January, 1865, General William T. Sherman issued his famous Field Order No. 15, setting aside the sea islands from Charleston south and the rice plantations for thirty miles inland for the exclusive use of Negroes, but this measure was undone four months later by President Johnson.[17] Lengthy discussion of the land question in the Radical constitutional convention in 1868 culminated in the authorization of a land commission, which was later established by the legislature with authority to issue bonds to the amount of $900,000 to purchase lands for sale in small plots to settlers.[18] This, however, was of scant significance in view of the fact that the total agricultural property in the state was valued at $59,535,219 in

[13] *Congressional Record, XXII* (51st Congress, 2d Session), pp. 2695–96.

[14] *Ibid.,* p. 2694.

[15] *Handbook of 1883,* p. 431; Charleston *News and Courier,* December 26, 1888, quoting Thomas D. Howard, "The Freedman's Paradise," *Unitarian Review,* n. d.

[16] Thomas Jackson Woofter, *Black Yeomanry* (New York, 1930); Guion Griffis Johnson, *A Social History of the Sea Islands, with Special Reference to St. Helena Island, South Carolina* (Chapel Hill, 1930); Guy Benton Johnson, *Folk Culture on St. Helena Island, South Carolina* (Chapel Hill, 1930).

[17] Francis B. Simkins and Robert H. Woody, *South Carolina During Reconstruction* (Chapel Hill, 1930), pp. 28–32.

[18] A. A. Taylor, *The Negro in South Carolina During the Reconstruction* (Washington, D. C., 1924), pp. 133–34, 164–65.

1870,[19] and much of the money available to the land commission was reported to have been frittered away by corruption.[20] . . .

A comparison of the amount of land sold under the provisions of the wartime confiscation with the statistics of Negro land ownership in the area of Beaufort in 1876 shows that the greater amount of acreage was obtained by Negroes through their own efforts. In the remainder of the state this was universally the means whereby Negro farmers came into possession of the land. Faced by an economic situation in which the whites were dominant, many of them nevertheless succeeded remarkably in realizing the goal of home ownership set by editor William Holloway of Charleston, who advised his Negro readers: "Nothing can be accomplished, by waiting for somebody to do something for you, or for some political change to effect a benefit in your behalf. The wiser plan is to get to work yourself, and see that your affairs are put in shape for any circumstances that may arise. . . . Nothing is more important than getting a home. . . ."[21]

By 1880 a small minority of Negro farmers were reported as owning their homes or farms. In Greenville County sixteen per cent owned either house or land. In Spartanburg, Fairfield, Chester, and Laurens the proportion was estimated as five per cent. In Newberry, York, and Abbeville, the number was negligible.[22] In the Upper Pine Belt, about five per cent were reported as owners in Aiken County, and from three to five per cent in Marlboro and Marion. [23] In the Lower Pine Belt county of Colleton, only about two per cent owned land or houses.[24] . . .

Independent merchants who frequently doubled as planters and landlords were the sources of supplies and rations for the rural populace. Plantation stores were prevalent especially where the gang system was established. Through the plantation stores the landlords supplied laborers who had been promised rations under sharecropping or land sharing contracts, and sold to those who had cash or had been credited with wages on the books or in scrip. The plantation Negroes sometimes brought supplies for a week at one time, but enjoyed livening up their uneventful lives by crowding into the stores each night to buy daily supplies.[25]

Country stores independent of plantations were more numerous, supplying Negroes who owned their farms or who had tenant contracts under which they furnished their own supplies and rations, and providing the supplies for landlords who had agreed to "stand for" the tenants. Almost invariably the merchants were forced to advance their merchandise on a promise of future payment, and always in such cases they assumed

[19] *Census* (1890), V, 94.

[20] Taylor, *The Negro in South Carolina During the Reconstruction*, pp. 54–55.

[21] Charleston *New Era*, April 7, 1883.

[22] *Handbook of 1883*, p. 155.

[23] *Ibid.*, pp. 84–85.

[24] *Ibid.*, p. 59.

[25] Duncan C. Heyward, *Seed from Madagascar* (Chapel Hill, 1937), p. 183.

a lien on the crop to be produced by the person receiving the merchandise. Because of the great risk involved, the lack of competition, and the complete dependence of the farmers on them, the merchants charged from twenty-five to a hundred per cent markup or interest on supplies furnished on promise of future payment.[26]

It was reported in 1880 that in the Piedmont region, "The system of credits and advances prevails to a large extent, consuming from one-third to three-fifths of the crop before it is harvested." In eleven counties of the Piedmont that year the number of liens nearly equalled the number of farms.[27] An anonymous letter in the Columbia *Daily Register* in 1881 indicated the severe incidence of markups and interest by suggesting that the usury law be amended to permit loans at twelve per cent instead of seven, a limit which made cash credit unavailable. Farmers could then supply their needs more cheaply with cash and landlords could supply their tenants at the relatively low rate of twenty-five per cent in order to lessen their burden![28]

The lien system also served to ensnare the farmers and croppers into growing a continuous round of cotton. The merchant who took a lien demanded a cash crop on which he could realize quickly if he had to foreclose.

Despite the evils and frequent denunciations of the system, Negro tenants and owners who were able to supply themselves through it sometimes found kind words for a scheme that freed them to a degree from control by landlords. "Their consolation," said a white editor, "and it is fallacious, is that they are perfectly free from control by any one, and while the lien law will give them credit, they will continue to live under this foolish delusion."[29]

Robert Simmons, a Negro farmer of Berkeley County, remarked in the state senate that "He had been poor and had been forced to mortgage his crops to get supplies, but by good management had accumulated property and become so well off that at present he could afford to make advances himself to his poorer neighbors."[30] Without the lien system, said Simmons, he would have been forced to give up farming. Mat Garrett, a Negro farmer of Greenville County, also demonstrated the way in which good use might be made of the lien system. In 1879 he rented a small farm and went into debt for both guano and supplies. The first year he made enough surplus to buy a mule and to pay all of his expenses for the following year, except for guano. By late summer of 1882 he estimated his prospective crop as thirteen bales of cotton, two hundred and fifty bushels of

[26] Columbia *Daily Register,* December 9, 1881.

[27] *Handbook of 1883,* p. 154.

[28] Columbia *Daily Register,* December 9, 1881.

[29] Columbia *Daily Register,* December 5, 1877, quoting the *Keowee Courier.*

[30] Columbia *Daily Register,* December 16, 1884.

corn, one hundred pounds of tobacco, and forty or fifty bushels of peas. In the spring he had harvested twenty-five bushels of wheat. He and his wife alone had accomplished this without going into debt after the first two years. They still had on hand enough corn and bacon to supply them for the remainder of the year and enough hogs to supply the next year's bacon.[31]

But for the less able and less fortunate contemporaries of Robert Simmons and Mat Garrett the picture was not so bright. Under the furnishing system the Negro tenants generally turned their crops over at the end of the year to the party advancing to them, and after paying their debts, received the balance, if any. The family of William Pickens, living at the foothills of the mountains, found that "It always took the whole of what was earned to pay for the scant 'rations' that were advanced to the family, and at settlement time there would be a margin of debt to keep the family perennially bound to a virtual owner." This family managed to escape virtual serfdom because a man in Pendleton who ran a bar and hotel was willing to pay off the margin of debt and move the family to town in order to have the father become a man of all work and the mother a cook. "They went," said Pickens, "as one instinctively moves from a greater toward a lesser pain."[32]

But the greater pain of perennial indebtedness was inescapable for most, and the whole system was an invitation to the practice of deceit and fraud by sharp-dealing merchants. A white observer said: "The entire earnings of these people, pass through the hands of local white traders, and are greatly reduced in the process. To these traders they look for every class of goods for use or adornment which they need or do not need, from a pin to coffin; from a pound of bacon to the decision of a personal quarrel. . . . The goods which they purchase are usually of coarse quality and low grade, but they do not buy them at correspondingly low prices. The profits charged on goods are far higher than they ought to be in a healthy business. . . ." He concluded that "the worst foe of the struggling negro race is the cunning white man of low tone, be he trader or politician. He is the vampire who sucks and never sates. . . . Thus there is possible a species of free slavery, this slavery of free ignorance to designing wit, cunning and greed."[33]

Of 4,645 stores in the state in 1880 Negroes owned only 49. They operated 25 in the coastal region, 5 in the Lower Pine Belt, 16 in the Upper Pine Belt, and 3 in the Piedmont.[34] At the end of the century only 457

[31] Greenville *Enterprise and Mountaineer*, August 30, 1882.

[32] William Pickens, *Bursting Bonds* (Boston, 1923) p. 13.

[33] Isaac D. Seabrook, "Before and After, or, The Relation of the Races in the South" (unpublished manuscript in South Caroliniana Library, University of South Carolina, 1895), Chapter III, p. 16.

[34] *Handbook of 1883*, p. 661.

Negroes listed themselves with census enumerators as merchants and dealers, some of whom were probably clerks and many of whom were located in the towns.[35] Here and there affluent Negroes like Robert Simmons of Berkeley County and John Thorne of Edisto Island, were in a position to make advances to their colored neighbors, but on the whole the rural Negroes were dependent upon the economically dominant whites. "As the negro establishes no supply stores of his own," a white commented in 1895, "and waives all competition he is compelled to accept the salesman's dictum."[36]

The lien system had grown up without plan and probably with little realization that it was to become a permanent system of agricultural credit. In the first years after the war the planters found it impossible to offer any other security for advances than anticipated crops, for land was too cheap to be acceptable security. The General Assembly in 1866 gave legal recognition to this system. Persons making advances became entitled to a lien on the crop in preference of all other liens, provided a contract were made in writing by the parties to the agreement and duly registered in the county courthouse.[37]

The lien law of 1866 was retained on the statute books by the Radical Republicans, with the addition of a clause that gave the laborer, whether working on shares or for wages, a prior lien on the crop.[38] While that addition was left on the statute books by the Democrats, it was obviously difficult for impoverished laborers to enforce their rights, and this legislation was rendered less and less meaningful by changes enacted in subsequent Democratic legislatures.

Bourbon legislators shifted the emphasis toward the expansion of the legal privileges of the landlord. Grievances of landlords against merchants found frequent expression in the press and in the legislature long before Ben Tillman organized his movement of agrarian protest. One objection was that the lien system encouraged the small time poor white and Negro tenant "to squat on poor ridges and set themselves up as farmers, with a bull yearling and a scooter plow, a side of bacon and a few sacks of guano as supplies."[39] In short, advances by merchants made it more difficult for landlords to secure labor on their own terms.

However, no one seemed able to offer a workable substitute for the

[35] Bureau of the Census, *Negroes in the United States* (Washington, 1904), pp. 184–87.

[36] Seabrook, "Before and After," Chapter III, p. 16.

[37] *Statutes at Large*, XIII, 366$^{12}$–366$^{13}$.

[38] *Revised Statutes of the State of South Carolina* (Columbia, 1873), pp. 557–58. Hereinafter cited as *Revised Statutes* (1873).

[39] Columbia *Daily Register*, December 5, 1877, quoting *Keowee Courier; ibid.,* December 14, 1881, quoting letter dated October 5, 1881, from J. B. Humbert, Tumbling Shoals, to Charleston *News and Courier; ibid.,* December 24, 1881, letter dated December 19, 1881, from James R. Magill, Russell Place, Kershaw County.

lien system. The first Democratic legislature, in its special session of 1877, boldly resolved the issue by repealing the legislation guaranteeing merchants' liens, effective January 1, 1878.[40] This move was supported by Negro Republican Hastings Gantt of Beaufort County, who was happy to find the legislature "now disposed to protect the farmers and make them stand on their own responsibility, and learn how to make and to keep what they make. It is our duty to make such laws as to bring our people up to a sense that they must take care of themselves, and not take what they make to the stores and sacrifice it there. The sooner they understand how to get along without this lien law the better." His colleague, Thomas Hamilton, a Negro from the same county, protested. The farmers, he recognized, would require credit in some form, and the proposal to throw them on their own resources was no adequate solution to their needs, for their resources were entirely too scant. Nevertheless, most of the Negro representatives followed Gantt's lead and voted for the repeal proposition.[41]

By the following March, three months after the effectiveness of the repeal, the spring credit situation had become so stringent that the General Assembly reenacted the merchants' lien legislation in precisely the same language. This was intended to be only a temporary expedient, but in December, 1878, the legislation was once again made permanent.[42] Repeal was an inadequate solution in the absence of other sources of agricultural credit, but it was again and again to find advocates among exasperated farmers.[43]

Liens for the landlord on the crops raised on his rented lands had been added to the merchants' and laborers' liens by the Republican legislature in 1874. Under that legislation it was provided that the land, whether rented for cash or on shares ". . . shall be deemed and taken to be an advance for agricultural purposes." Upon reducing the condition of this "advance" of land to writing and properly recording it, the landowner was entitled to a lien "in preference to all other liens existing or otherwise, to an amount not exceeding one-third of the entire crop. . . ."[44]

The Democrats, in connection with their reenactment of the merchants' lien law in 1878, strengthened the landlord's liens so that they should be valid over one-third of the crops grown on his land without recording or filing. A lien over more than one-third of the crop, forbidden under Republican legislation, now became permissible if it were reduced to writing and properly filed in the court house.[45] In December, 1878, after

[40] *Statutes at Large,* XVI, 265.

[41] Columbia *Daily Register,* May 13, 1877; *House Journal* (1877, special session), p. 98.

[42] *Statutes at Large,* XVI, 410–11, 713–14.

[43] See debates in the legislature as reported in Columbia *Daily Register,* December 9, 10, 1881, and December 16, 1884.

[44] *Statutes at Large,* XV, 788, 844.

[45] *Ibid.,* XVI, 410–11.

the Democrats had secured nearly complete domination of the legislature, the legislation was further strengthened by a clause providing that "the landlord shall have a lien on all the crop raised by the tenant for all advances made by the landlord during the year."[46]

With these changes, strengthening the hold of the landlord over crops grown on his lands, the lien laws assumed permanent shape. In all their essentials the laws had been enacted before the overthrow of the Radical Republicans, and what had started as a temporary expedient to meet the lack of capital immediately after the war, had become the permanent credit system of agriculture. Sporadic opposition to a system that upheld "the thriftless, idle, worthless class,"[47] the merchants, continued to be voiced by the landlord class, which was influential in the Democratic party, and efforts were made again in 1881 and 1884 to repeal the merchants' liens, but they were unsuccessful. In the only available record vote, the three Negro members of the state senate in 1884 all voted with the majority against the repeal of merchants' liens.[48]

The only major legislation with regard to agricultural liens after 1878 was passed in 1884 and 1885. The legislation of 1884 provided for the enforcement of landlords' and merchants' liens less than $100 by constables or sheriffs, who were authorized to seize crops upon the issuance of warrants from trial justices.[49] The act of 1885 clarified earlier legislation by giving priority to the liens in inverse order to the time of their enactment; first priority to the landlord's lien for rent, second priority to the laborer's, and third priority to all other liens. This act also reaffirmed the validity of the landlord's contract "whether the same be in writing or verbal."[50]

Labor contract laws were a related field of legislation pertinent to the status of Negro agricultural laborers. In this field, too, it is significant to find that the Reconstruction legislation was essentially conservative in nature. All labor contracts, under the Republican law, had to be witnessed by one or more disinterested persons, and upon the request of either party, had to be executed before a trial justice, whose duty it was to read the contract and explain its contents to the interested parties. Such contracts, it was provided, "shall clearly set forth the conditions upon which the laborer or laborers engaged to work, embracing the length of time, the amount of money to be paid, and when; if it be on shares of crops, what portion of the crop or crops." Wherever labor was performed on shares, the division should be made by a mutually acceptable third party or by the

---

[46] *Ibid.,* pp. 743–44.

[47] Columbia *Daily Register,* December 9, 1881.

[48] *Senate Journal* (1884), p. 212.

[49] *Statutes at Large,* XVIII, 751–52.

[50] *Ibid.,* XIX, 146.

trial justice nearest resident. Punishment was provided for either party's attempting to practice fraud or to remove the crop surreptitiously. It is significant, however, that if the landlord, his agent, or the "disinterested party" were guilty of fraud, the punishment was specifically limited, whereas for the laborer it was not defined. The landlord or his agent was liable to a fine of from $50 to $500; the disinterested party to a similar fine, or imprisonment of one month to a year; the laborer was "liable to fine and imprisonment, according to the gravity of the offence, upon proof to conviction before a Trial Justice, or a Court of competent jurisdiction."[51]

One of the most oppressive features of labor contract legislation was that which permitted verbal contracts. Agreements between landowner and tenant for periods of less than one year could be made orally under legislation in effect before the end of the Reconstruction period, and this legislation was preserved jealously as an excellent means of labor control.[52] After 1878 it was possible for the landlord to secure a lien over the entire crop by an oral contract.

Among the landlords an attempt to entice away laborers to work on another farm or in another state was a cardinal sin. In addition to extensive use of the power of social pressure to maintain the adherence of laborers to their masters, increasingly stringent legislation was employed. In 1880 it was made a misdemeanor for any person to "entice or persuade, by any means whatsoever, any tenant or tenants, servant, or servants, laborer or laborers under contract with another . . . to violate such contract," or even to hire such a person, knowing him to be under contract to another.[53]

In 1889, after the state Supreme Court had invalidated the old Republican legislation providing unequal punishments for persons guilty of fraud in violation of contracts, the Democratic legislature passed a new act which lessened considerably the punishment of landlords and their agents, and provided specifically the same punishment for laborers—a fine of $5 to $100 or imprisonment for ten to thirty days.[54]

The incidence of such laws, of course, fell heavily on the Negro laborer with the instruments of enforcement altogether under the control of the whites. In 1891 Thomas E. Miller complained that his people had ". . . struggled in a land where they receive little assistance from the courts and where the juries are systematically formed to oppress them; where they work often on the promise to pay; where they receive no protection from the labor law. . . ."[55] The use to which the verbal contract was put by white masters is indicated in the complaint that

[51] *Revised Statutes* (1873), pp. 490–92.

[52] *Ibid.*, p. 433.

[53] *Statutes at Large*, XVII, 423.

[54] *Ibid.*, XX, 381–82.

[55] *Congressional Record*, XXII (51st Congress, 2d Session), 2693.

*In my State, if the employer states verbally that the unpaid laborer of his plantation contracted to work for the year no other farmer dares employ the man if he attempts to break the contract rather than work for nothing: for down there it is a misdemeanor so to do, the penalty is heavy, and the farmer who employs the unpaid, starving laborer of his neighbor is the victim of the court.*[56]

But in 1897, still not satisfied with its farm labor legislation, the General Assembly enacted a law to provide punishment for the laborer who had received advances in money or supplies and afterward failed to perform "the reasonable service required of him by the terms of the said contract." Such persons were liable to imprisonment of twenty to thirty days or fines of $25 to $100.[57]

Actual enforcement of the 1889 and 1897 legislation against the violation of contract by laborers, however, was seldom necessary, and the mere threat of its use or mere knowledge of its existence was sufficient to keep Negro laborers in virtual bondage. This legislation, together with the permissible verbal contract, made it possible for an unscrupulous landlord to utilize the laws to keep his laborers in a state of perpetual peonage. When a group of Negro laborers at the Loudon Place in Marlboro County struck in 1898, the white owner simply had six of the "ring-leaders" arrested and placed in jail. At the trial, all of them "realized their condition, expressed a willingness to resume work and behave themselves," and were allowed to do so after paying all costs. A few days later it was reported that "Everything on 'Loudon' is quiet and everybody is at work."[58]

The legislature had, however, overreached itself in the headlong rush toward reaction and this legislation was declared void when a *habeas corpus* case was brought by Jack Hollman in the state Supreme Court in 1907. Justice C. A. Woods in a unanimous decision held the law to be unconstitutional and void on the ground that it required involuntary servitude. "It is nothing in support of the statute," said Justice Woods, ". . . that it enforces involuntary servitude on account of a debt by the compulsion of a statute providing for indictment and imprisonment for quitting such service, rather than allowing the employer to compel it under a guard. In contemplation of the law the compulsion to such service by the fear of punishment under a criminal statute is more powerful than any guard which the employer could station."[59]

But such legislation, even though declared unconstitutional, reveals the drift of white attitudes and the climate of opinion in which Negro laborers had to work. The trial justices, or magistrates, with whom the laborer

[56] *Ibid.*

[57] *Statutes at Large*, XXII, 457.

[58] Charleston *News and Courier*, October 5, 1898.

[59] *Ex Parte Hollman*, 79 S. C. Reports 22.

was more apt to deal than with the courts, did not always demonstrate the judicial temper shown by the Supreme Court in 1907. One Negro spoke of trial justices as men "whose judgment and decisions the 'Boss' influences as I would the movements of a devoted dog."[60]

[60] New York *Age*, May 16, 1885.

## SUGGESTIONS FOR FURTHER READING

**&G**OOD introductions to the discriminatory practices of this era are Gilbert T. Stephenson, *Race Distinctions in American Law* (New York, 1910); *Paul Lewinson, *Race, Class and Party: A History of Negro Suffrage and White Politics in the South* (New York, 1932); *C. Vann Woodward, *The Strange Career of Jim Crow* (2d rev. ed.; New York, 1965); and John Hope Franklin, "Jim Crow Goes to School: The Genesis of Legal Segregation in Southern Schools," *South Atlantic Quarterly,* LVIII (Spring 1959). For state studies on this topic as well as on the economic status of southern blacks, see *Vernon L. Wharton, *The Negro in Mississippi, 1865–1890* (Chapel Hill, N.C., 1947); *George B. Tindall, *South Carolina Negroes, 1877–1900* (Columbia, S.C., 1952); Charles E. Wynes, *Race Relations in Virginia, 1870–1902* (Charlottesville, Va., 1961); Frenise A. Logan, *The Negro in North Carolina, 1876–1894* (Chapel Hill, N.C., 1964); and Clarence Bacote, "Some Aspects of Negro Life in Georgia, 1880–1908," *Journal of Negro History,* XLIII (July 1958). A model study is *Louis R. Harlan, *Separate and Unequal: Public School Campaigns and Racism in the Southern Seaboard States, 1901–1915* (Chapel Hill, N.C., 1958).

The relationship of blacks to the agrarian reform movement is discussed in *C. Vann Woodward, *Origins of the New South, 1877–1913* (Baton Rouge, La., 1951); Helen G. Edmonds, *The Negro and Fusion Politics in North Carolina, 1894–1901* (Chapel Hill, N.C., 1951); and Jack Abramowitz, "The Negro in the Populist Movement," *Journal of Negro History,* XXXVIII (July 1953). Differing perspectives on the attitudes of participants in the Progressive movement toward black Americans are advanced by Woodward, *Origins of the New South,* chapter XIV; Dewey W. Grantham, Jr., "The Progressive Movement and the Negro," *South Atlantic Quarterly,* LIV (October 1955); and Gilbert Osofsky, "Progressivism and the Negro: New York, 1900–1915," *American Quarterly,* XVI (Summer 1964).

Discussions of the antecedents of post-Reconstruction discriminatory practices are covered in *Leon F. Litwack, *North of Slavery: The Negro in the Free States, 1790–1860* (Chicago, 1961); *Richard Wade, *Slavery in the Cities: The South* (New York, 1964); and *Joel Williamson, *After Slavery: The Negro in South Carolina During Reconstruction, 1861–1877* (Chapel Hill, N.C., 1965). Important studies of the ideological basis of anti-Negro practices are *William Stanton, *The Leopard's Spots: Scientific Attitudes Toward Race in America, 1815–1859* (Chicago, 1960); *Thomas Gossett, *Race: The History of An Idea* (New York, 1965); *Idus

* An asterisk indicates that the book is available in paperback.

Newby, *Jim Crow's Defense: Anti-Negro Thought in America, 1900–1930* (Baton Rouge, La., 1965); and G. G. Johnson, "The Ideology of White Supremacy," in Fletcher M. Green (ed.), *Essays in Southern History* (Chapel Hill, N.C., 1949). Two books that deal with white attitudes, both northern and southern, in this period are *Paul Buck, *The Road to Reunion* (Boston, 1937) and *Rayford Logan, *The Betrayal of the Negro* (paperback title; New York, 1965).

The Republican party's policy toward the blacks and the South is brought down to the 1890s in Vincent P. De Santis, *Republicans Face the Southern Question* (Baltimore, Md., 1959) and *Stanley P. Hirshon, *Farewell to the Bloody Shirt* (Bloomington, Ind., 1962). Among the essays on the political parties and black Americans in the early 1900s are August Meier, "The Negro and the Democratic Party, 1875–1915," *Phylon*, XVII (Summer 1956); Seth M. Scheiner, "President Theodore Roosevelt and the Negro, 1901–1908," *Journal of Negro History*, XLVII (July 1962); Emma Lou Thornbrough, "The Brownsville Episode and the Negro Vote," *Mississippi Valley Historical Review*, XLIV (December 1957); Arthur S. Link, "The Negro as a Factor in the Campaign of 1912," *Journal of Negro History*, XXXII (January 1947); and Nancy J. Weiss, "The Negro and the New Freedom: Fighting Wilsonian Segregation," *Political Science Quarterly*, LXXXIV (March 1968).

For black attitudes and actions during this period, see *August Meier, *Negro Thought* (Ann Arbor, Mich., 1963); Leslie H. Fishel, "The Negro in Northern Politics, 1870–1900," *Mississippi Valley Historical Review*, XLII (December 1955); Clarence Bacote, "Negro Proscriptions, Protests and Proposed Solutions in Georgia, 1880–1908," *Journal of Southern History*, XXV (November 1959); and works listed under the suggestions for further reading in the next chapter.

Discussions of Supreme Court decisions in this era are included in Robert J. Harris, *The Quest for Equality* (Baton Rouge, La., 1960); *Loren Miller, *The Petitioners: The Story of the Supreme Court of the United States and the Negro* (New York, 1966); and *Monroe Berger, *Equality by Statute* (rev. ed.; New York, 1967).

---

* An asterisk indicates that the book is available in paperback.

# CHAPTER SEVEN
# Black Reaction to Jim Crow

T OGETHER with the laws and practices that undermined the rights of blacks in the late nineteenth century, there was a decline in militancy among Afro-Americans. Gaining ascendancy were those blacks who de-emphasized protest and underscored the internal development of the black community. The chief spokesman for this position, the accommodationist, was Booker T. Washington. Widely applauded for his philosophy in many circles, both white and black, Washington was not free from criticism. Opponents condemned Washington and the accommodationists for diverting the attention of blacks from the major reason for their second-class status—discrimination by whites. In the first decade of the twentieth century, W. E. B. Du Bois emerged as the leading voice in the protest camp. The expanded activities and attempts at organization by the protesters and sympathetic whites culminated in the creation of the National Association for the Advancement of Colored People at the close of the decade.

August Meier in two chapters from his pioneering study, *Negro Thought in America,* analyzes the philosophies of Washington and Du Bois. Meier sees two main themes in Negro thought: One stressing race pride, racial solidarity, self-help, and economic development; a second focusing on civil rights, political activity, and immediate integration. Black leaders enunciated in varying degree elements in both of these positions—the ethnocentric and integrationist. Meier shows that Washington despite his advice to fellow Afro-Americans to avoid agitation on civil rights issues, participated in politics and worked behind the scenes to frustrate discriminatory legislation and practices. And Washington considered his program for the internal development of the black community not an end in itself, but the wisest course toward attaining equality with whites. Despite this, white America took the Tuskegee educator's means to be his ends.

Scholars have often cast Du Bois as the antithesis of Washington. Beginning his career as a supporter of Washington, Du Bois announced his independence with the publication of his *The Souls of Black Folk* in 1903. He rebuked Washington for placing upon Negroes the responsibility for their second-class position. Du Bois put a higher premium than Booker Washington upon protest, the vote, and immediate integration. But there is more to Du Bois's philosophy than recitation of these points. In his study, Meier avoids a simplistic interpretation of Du Bois. Like Washington, Du Bois espoused race pride and economic cooperation. Washington, in turn, wanted blacks to attain the equal rights accentuated in Du Bois's program. Consider the following questions after you read the selection. Do these apparent inconsistencies reduce the ideological gap between the two men? Are their differences more ones of degree or strategy than basic philosophical disagreement? To be more specific: Did Washington comprehend or advocate the cultural pluralism so important to Du Bois? How significant are the differences in their programs for black economic development?

In assessing the views of Du Bois and Washington the reader should pay particular attention to Meier's emphasis on the "ethnic dualism" in black thought. Both camps, as noted above, called for economic development, race pride, and equal rights. Very often one shifted gears and advanced ideas associated with the other. Meier finds this ambivalence most apparent in Du Bois, "the epitome of the paradoxes in American Negro thought." In Du Bois's own words: "One feels his twoness—an American, a Negro, two souls, two thoughts, two unreconciled strivings, two warring ideals in one dark body. . . . The history of the American Negro is the history of this strife,—this longing to attain self-conscious manhood, to merge his double self into a better and truer self."*

A framework for the examination of the accommodationist and protest positions is provided in selection 21, Emma Lou Thornbrough's article on the Afro-American League. The League was the idea of the leading black newspaper editor in the late nineteenth and early twentieth century, T. Thomas Fortune. His initial program, presented in 1887 and 1890, contained striking similarities to that propounded by the NAACP in 1910. In the 1890s, Fortune became an ally, if an erratic one, of Washington. The League (which had changed its name to the Afro-American Council) became involved in the struggle between Washington and his opponents. As Miss Thornbrough observes: its history "was inextricably linked with the fight over Washington as a race leader." Her study of the Afro-American League appears to lend support to Meier's thesis on the ethnic ambivalence in Negro thought. In his analysis of the selections that follow in this volume, the reader should keep in mind the arguments of Meier and Thornbrough.

---

* Quoted in August Meier, *Negro Thought in America, 1880–1915* (Ann Arbor, Mich., 1963), p. 190.

# 20

WASHINGTON AND DU BOIS
*August Meier*

## BOOKER T. WASHINGTON:
## AN INTERPRETATION

B OOKER T. Washington had assiduously cultivated a good press and from time to time had received the attention accorded leaders who were, as the phrase went, "succeeding." Yet it was with relative suddenness that he emerged at the Atlanta Exposition in September 1895 as a figure of national reputation and the acknowledged leader of Negroes in America.

To Washington the solution of the race problem lay essentially in an application of the gospel of wealth, and he opened and closed his address that memorable afternoon with references to material prosperity. He urged Negroes to stay in the South, since when it came to business, pure and simple, it was in the South that the Negro was given a man's chance. Whites were urged to lend a helping hand in the uplifting of the Negroes in order to further the prosperity and well-being of their region. Coupled with this appeal to the self-interest of the white South was a conciliatory phraseology and a criticism of Negroes. Washington deprecated politics and the Reconstruction experience. He criticized Negroes for forgetting that the masses of the race were to live by the production of their hands and for permitting their grievances to overshadow their opportunities. He grew lyrical in reciting the loyalty and fidelity of Negroes—"the most patient, faithful, law-abiding and unresentful people that the world had seen." He denied any interest in social equality when he said: "In all things that are purely social we can be as separate as the five fingers, yet one as the hand in all things essential to mutual progress." In conclusion he asked for justice and an elimination of sectional differences and racial animosities, which, combined with material prosperity would usher in a new era for "our beloved South."[1]

Washington's emphasis upon economic prosperity was the hallmark of the age. The pledges of loyalty to the South and the identification of Negro uplift with the cause of the New South satisfied the "better class" of Southern whites and Northern investors; the generalities about justice to

From August Meier, *Negro Thought in America, 1880–1915: Racial Ideologies in the Age of Booker T. Washington* (Ann Arbor: The University of Michigan Press, 1963), pp. 100–114, 116–118, 190–206. Copyright © 1963 by The University of Michigan Press.

Except where otherwise noted, all works cited in this chapter are by BTW, and all citations to correspondence are to the BTW Papers.

[1] *Address . . . Delivered at the Opening of the Cotton States and International Exposition, 1895* (no imprint, n.d.), 6–11.

the Negro, of interracial co-operation in things essential to mutual progress, coupled with a denial of interest in social equality, encompassed a wide range of views that could be satisfied by ambiguous phraseology. Washington's generalized references to justice and progress and uplift soothed the pallid consciences of the dominant groups in the nation and at the same time allowed the white South to assume that justice could be achieved without granting Negroes political and civil rights. Yet a careful reading of the address indicates that it could also be interpreted as including ultimate goals more advanced than white Southerners could possibly support. Negroes must begin at the bottom, but surely Washington believed that eventually they would arrive at the top. Most Negroes interpreted social equality as meaning simply intimate social relationships which they did not desire, though most whites interpreted it as meaning the abolition of segregation. Even though Washington said that "it is important and right that all privileges of the law be ours; but it is vastly more important that we be prepared for the exercise of these privileges," and that "the opportunity to earn a dollar in a factory just now is worth infinitely more than the opportunity to spend a dollar in an opera house," his Negro supporters emphasized the future implications of his remarks, and his statement that "no race that has anything to contribute to the markets of the world is long in any degree ostracized." Unlike Negroes, the dominant whites were impressed by his conciliatory phraseology, confused his means for his ends, and were satisfied with the immediate program that he enunciated.

Washington captured his audience and assured his ascendancy primarily because his ideas accorded with the climate of opinion at the time. His association with industrial education, his emphasis upon the economic, and his conciliatory approach were undoubtedly important reasons why he was selected to speak on this prominent occasion. As Charles S. Johnson has suggested, Washington was effectively manipulating the symbols and myths dear to the majority of Americans.[2] It cannot be overemphasized that Washington's philosophy represents in large measure the basic tendencies of Negro thought in the period under consideration. Armstrong at Hampton had expressed the identical program as a ground of compromise between the white North, the white South, and the Negro. Indeed, it is clear that the chief source of Washington's philosophy was his experience at Hampton Institute, for he unmistakably bore the stamp of its founder.

How much the youthful Washington was shaped by his Hampton experience it is hard to say. He later recounted his strenuous efforts to obtain an education while working in the salt and coal mines at Malden, West Virginia, his lessons of cleanliness, thoroughness, and honesty as the servant of the wife of Yankee General Lewis Ruffner, and his bold trip, largely on foot, of five hundred miles from his home to Hampton. These were all evidences of the self-reliant personality that was his. Consequently,

---

[2] Johnson, "The Social Philosophy of Booker T. Washington," 1940, MS lent to the author by the late Dr. Johnson.

Yankee, Puritan, industrious Hampton and this ambitious and industrious youth of sixteen, who presented himself at its doors in the fall of 1872, clicked from the first. "At Hampton," he wrote later, "I found the opportunities . . . to learn thrift, economy and push. I was surrounded by an atmosphere of business, Christian influences, and the spirit of self-help, that seemed to have awakened every faculty in me."[3]

Armstrong was undoubtedly the most influential person in Washington's life, and his viewpoint contained the major ingredients of Washington's philosophy. Yet Washington was not fully committed to the Hampton idea when he left the school in 1875. He taught for two years in his home town in West Virginia, attended briefly the liberal arts Wayman Seminary in Washington, toyed with the idea of a political career, and started the study of law. Like the majority of his future students he at no time seriously considered practicing a trade for a livelihood. All questions were settled, however, when he was asked to return to Hampton to teach in 1879. Then, in 1881 Washington set forth to establish his own school at Tuskegee, Alabama, on the meager appropriations that resulted —paradoxically enough—from a political deal on the part of an ex-Confederate colonel who solicited Negro votes by promising to introduce a bill for a Negro industrial school in the legislature.[4] From then until 1895 Washington was engaged in building the school—a story of trial and success in the best Hampton tradition.

In discussing Washington's ideology it will be necessary to examine both his overtly expressed philosophy of accommodation and his covertly conducted attack on racial discrimination. His conciliatory approach was an important factor in his achieving eminence, and his continued ascendancy in Negro affairs, due as it was to the support of dominant white elements, depended upon his playing this tactful role to the fullest extent. Yet his very prominence brought him into situations that led to secret activities that directly contradicted the ideology he officially espoused.

In comparison with other figures in this study, Washington's expressed ideology remained remarkably consistent throughout his public life.[5] There appear to have been no significant changes in his publicly stated outlook except for a somewhat more accommodating attitude after 1895 than

---

[3] *Future of the American Negro* (Boston, 1899), 107. Biographical details are supplied in *Up From Slavery* (New York, 1901), and in the more revealing *Story of My Life and Work* (Naperville, 1900).

[4] Emmett J. Scott and Lyman B. Stowe, *Booker T. Washington: Builder of a Civilization* (New York, 1916), 3–4.

[5] The following discussion of Booker T. Washington's philosophy is based chiefly on *Up From Slavery, Future of the American Negro, My Larger Education* (New York, 1911), *The Case of the Negro* (Tuskegee, 1902), *Sowing and Reaping* (Boston, 1900), and *Selected Speeches of Booker T. Washington*, ed. by E. Davidson Washington (New York, 1932). Also utilized were a number of his other books, pamphlets, and articles in both Negro and white magazines, the clipping books in the BTW Papers, and materials at the Department of Records and Research, Tuskegee Institute.

before, and except for a growing emphasis upon racial solidarity and economic chauvinism after the turn of the century. Through the years he was conciliatory in manner toward the white South, emphasized the ordinary economic and moral virtues, claimed that he regarded political and civil rights as secondary and ultimate rather than as primary and immediate aims, held up Negro moral and economic progress to public view, even while criticizing the weaknesses of Negroes and insisting that they should shoulder much of the blame for their status and the primary responsibility for their own advancement, and optimistically insisted that race relations were improving.

The central theme in Washington's philosophy was that through thrift, industry, and Christian character Negroes would eventually attain their constitutional rights. To Washington it seemed but proper that Negroes would have to measure up to American standards of morality and material prosperity if they were to succeed in the Social Darwinist race of life. Just as the individual who succeeds can do something that the world wants done well, so with a race. Things would be on a different footing if it became common to associate the possession of wealth with a black skin. "It is not within the province of human nature that the man who is intelligent and virtuous, and owns and cultivates the best farm in his county, shall very long be denied the proper respect and consideration."[6]

Consequently Negroes, he felt, must learn trades in order to compete with whites. He blamed Negroes for neglecting skills acquired under slavery, for the loss of what had been practically a monopoly of the skilled labor in the South at the close of the Civil War. He feared that unless industrial schools filled the breach, the next twenty years would witness the economic demise of the Negro. He was often critical of higher education. He never tired of retelling the anecdotes about the rosewood piano in the tumble-down cabin, or about the young man he found sitting in an unkempt cabin, studying from a French grammar. He denied that he intended to minimize the value of higher education, and his own children in fact enjoyed its advantages, but practical education, he believed, should come first in the rise of a people toward civilization. Occasionally, he praised higher education, but he often cited cases of college graduates who were accomplishing nothing, and once at least he referred to "the college bacillus."[7]

Fundamentally, Washington did not think in terms of a subordinate place in the American economy for Negroes. Though his language was ambiguous, he thought in terms of developing a substantial propertied class of landowners and businessmen. There was, as he often put it, a great need for "captains of industry." He felt a deep sympathy with the wealthy, and he preferred to talk most of all to audiences of businessmen who, he

---

[6] *Future of the American Negro,* 176.

[7] "A University Education for Negroes," *Independent,* LXVIII (March 24, 1910), 613–18; "What I am Trying to Do," *World's Work,* XXVII (Nov., 1913), 103.

found, were quick to grasp what he was saying. In all this he was thoroughly in accord with the New South philosophy. He praised Robert C. Ogden of Wanamaker's (a trustee of Tuskegee and Hampton and chairman of the General Education Board) and H. H. Rogers, the Standard Oil and railroad magnate, as men whose interest in uplifting the Negro was partly motivated by their desire to develop one of the neglected resources of the South.[8]

Part of Washington's outlook toward capital and the New South was his antagonistic attitude toward labor unions. He recollected that before the days of strikes in the West Virginia coal mines where he had worked, he had known miners with considerable sums in the bank, "but as soon as the professional labor agitators got control, the savings of even the more thrifty ones began disappearing." To some extent, he felt, the loss of the Negro's hold on the skilled trades was due to the unions. He boasted that Negro labor was, if fairly treated, "the best free labor in the world," not given to striking. Later, writing in the *Atlantic Monthly* in 1913, Washington, though still basically hostile, appeared somewhat more favorable toward unions. He admitted that there were cases in which labor unions had used their influence on behalf of Negroes even in the South, and he knew of instances in which Negroes had taken a leading part in the work of their unions. Nevertheless, he felt that unions would cease to discriminate only to the extent that they feared Negro strikebreakers.[9]

Exceedingly important in Washington's outlook was an emphasis on agriculture and rural landownership that has ordinarily been overlooked. He constantly deprecated migration to cities where, he said, the Negro was at his worst and insisted that Negroes should stay on the farmlands of the South. Since all peoples who had gained wealth and recognition had come up from the soil, agriculture should be the chief occupation of Negroes, who should be encouraged to own and cultivate the soil. While he called Negroes the best labor for Southern farms, he optimistically looked forward to an independent yeomanry, respected in their communities.

Also associated with Washington's middle-class and Social Darwinist philosophy were the ideas of the value of struggle in achieving success, of self-help, and of "taking advantage of disadvantages." As he put it, "No race of people ever got upon its feet without severe and constant struggle, often in the face of the greatest disappointment."[10] He turned misfortune into good fortune, and middle-class rationalization of the strenuous life into an accommodating rationalization of the Negro's status. Paradoxical as it might seem, the difficulties facing the Negro had on the whole helped him more than they had hindered him, for under pressure the Negro had put

[8] *My Larger Education*, 72–73, 76–77.

[9] *Up From Slavery*, 68–69; "The Best Free Labor in the World," *Southern State Farm Magazine* (Jan., 1898), 496–98 (clipping in BTW Papers); "The Negro and the Labor Unions," *Atlantic Monthly*, CXI (June, 1913), 756–67.

[10] *The Case of the Negro*, 2.

forth more energy which, constructively channeled, had been of untold value.

While whites had some responsibility, the most important part in the Negro's progress was to be played by the Negro himself; the race's future recognition lay within its own hands. On the negative side this emphasis on self-help involved a tendency to blame Negroes for their condition. Washington constantly criticized them for seeking higher rather than practical education, for their loss of places in the skilled trades, for their lack of morality and economic virtues, and for their tendency toward agitation and complaint. But in its positive aspects this emphasis involved race pride and solidarity. Negroes should be proud of their history and their great men. For a race to grow strong and powerful it must honor its heroes. Negroes should not expect any great success until they learned to imitate the Jews, who through unity and faith in themselves were becoming more and more influential. He showed considerable pride in the all-Negro communities. At times he espoused a high degree of racial solidarity and economic nationalism. On one occasion he declared: "We are a nation within a nation." While Negroes should be the last to draw the color line, at the same time they should see to it that "in every wise and legitimate way our people are taught to patronise racial enterprises."[11]

If emphasis upon racial pride and self-help through economic and moral development formed one side of Washington's thinking, another was his insistence that interracial harmony and white good will were prerequisite to the Negro's advancement. In appealing to whites Washington spoke in both moral and practical terms. Southern whites should aid Negroes out of economic self-interest and should act justly since to do less would corrupt their moral fiber. Washington constantly reiterated his love for the South, his faith in the Southern white man's sense of justice, his belief that the South afforded Negroes more economic opportunity than the North. In 1912, answering the question "Is the Negro Having a Fair Chance?" he did go so far as to admit the existence of the standard grievances, but declared that nowhere were there ten million black people who had greater opportunities or were making greater progress than the Negroes of the South; nowhere had any race "had the assistance, the direction, and the sympathy of another race in all its efforts to rise to such an extent as the Negro in the United States." Washington devoted one whole book, *The Man Farthest Down* (1912), to the thesis that American Negroes were better off than the depressed classes in Europe. In general, Washington appealed to the highest sentiments and motives of the whites and brushed lightly over their prejudices and injustices in an attempt to create the favorable sentiment without which Negro progress was doomed. He frequently referred to the friendship Southern whites exhibited toward Negroes and constantly cited examples of harmonious relations between the races. At a time when Mississippi was notorious for "whitecapping"

[11] Detroit *Leader,* Sept. 8, 1911 (in BTW Clipping Books).

(the attacking of business establishments owned by prosperous Negroes who were then run out of town), he opined that "there, more than anywhere else, the colored people seem to have discovered that, in gaining habits of thrift and industry, in getting property, and in making themselves useful, there is a door of hope open for them which the South has no disposition to close." He was incurably optimistic in his utterances—as he said, "We owe it not only to ourselves, but to our children, to look always upon the bright side of life."[12]

Washington constantly deprecated protest and agitation. Leading virtuous, respectable lives and acquiring wealth would advance the race more than any number of books and speeches. Speaking at the Afro-American Council in July 1903 he urged patience and optimism:

*In the long run it is the race or individual that exercises the most patience, forbearance, and self-control in the midst of trying conditions that wins . . . the respect of the world. . . . We have a right in a conservative and sensible manner to enter our complaints, but we shall make a fatal error if we yield to the temptation of believing that mere opposition to our wrongs . . . will take the place of progressive, constructive action. . . . Let us not forget to lay the greatest stress upon the opportunities open to us, especially here in the South, for constructive growth in labor, in business and education. . . . An inch of progress is worth more than a yard of complaint.*[13]

While Washington never changed his basic ideology, before 1895 he tended to be more frank, though always tactful, regarding the Negro's goals. In 1894, for example, he admitted that conventions and organizations whose aims were to redress certain grievances were "right and proper," though they should not be the chief reliance of the race, and went on to declare that if his approach did not in time bring every political and civil right then everything, even the teaching of Christ, was false. As conditions grew worse Washington became more rather than less conciliatory. The outstanding exception to his general policy was his address at the Jubilee celebration held in Chicago after the Spanish-American War, where with President McKinley in the audience, he made one of his famous *faux pas*. Reviewing the valorous deeds of Negroes in the military history of the United States, especially in the recent war, he contended that a race that was thus willing to die for its country should be given the highest opportunity to live for its country. Americans had won every conflict in which they had been engaged, "except the effort to conquer ourselves in the blotting out of racial prejudice. . . . Until we thus conquer ourselves I make no empty statement when I say that we shall have a cancer gnawing at the heart of

---

[12] "Is the Negro Having a Fair Chance?" *Century*, LXXXV (Nov., 1912), 50–55, 46; *My Larger Education*, 189, 197–98; "Fundamental Needs for the Progress of the Race" (1904, MS at Tuskegee Institute Department of Records and Research).

[13] *Selected Speeches* . . . , 94–95, 98.

this republic that shall some day prove to be as dangerous as an attack from an army without or within." This statement aroused considerable ire in the Southern press, and Washington characteristically qualified his remarks. He explained that he seldom referred to prejudice because it was something to be lived down rather than talked down, but since that meeting symbolized the end of sectional feelings he had thought it an appropriate time to ask for "the blotting out of racial prejudice as far as possible in 'business and civil relations.' "[14]

On the three major issues of segregation, lynching, and the franchise, the Tuskegeean expressed himself with characteristic circumspection. Prior to the Atlanta address he had made it clear that he opposed segregation in transportation. Speaking in 1884 he had said that "the Governor of Alabama would probably count it no disgrace to ride in the same railroad coach with a colored man." As late as 1894 he urged Negroes to follow the example of Atlanta citizens who had boycotted the newly segregated streetcars and predicted that such economic pressures would make it respectable for both races to ride in the railway coach as well. But after 1895 he held that separate but equal facilities would be satisfactory. As he once put it: "All . . . parts of the world have their own peculiar customs and prejudices. For that reason it is a part of common-sense to respect them."[15] And he did respect the customs of other parts of the world. He accepted President Roosevelt's dinner invitation in 1901 after careful consideration. He was on intimate terms with distinguished philanthropists and was entertained in circles in the North and abroad that few white Southerners could have entered. Yet he declared that the objection to the Jim Crow car was "not the separation, but the inadequacy of the accommodations." Again, speaking in 1914 on the matter of municipal segregation ordinances, Washington stirred up a hornet's nest of criticism by remarking: "Let us, in the future, spend less time talking about the part of the city that we cannot live in, and more time in making the part of the city that we can live in beautiful and attractive." Yet in a posthumously published account of "My View of Segregation Laws" Washington—or his ghostwriter—tactfully gave his reasons for condemning them, and in a most unusual concluding statement openly declared that segregation was "ill-advised" because it was unjust and all thoughtful Negros resented injustice. There was no case of segregation, he said, that had not widened the breach between the two races. That Negroes did not constantly express their embitterment, he added, was not proof that they did not feel it.[16]

[14] "Taking Advantage of Our Disadvantages," A.M.E. Review, XX (April, 1894), 480; Story of My Life and Work, 265–66, 274–76.

[15] Selected Speeches . . . , 2–3; "Taking Advantage of Our Disadvantages," 480; My Larger Education, 178.

[16] "Is the Negro Having a Fair Chance?" 51; Report of the Fifteenth Annual Convention of the National Negro Business League . . . 1914 (no imprint [1914]), 82; "My View of Segregation Laws," New Republic, V (Dec. 4, 1915), 113–14.

Even on lynching Washington expressed himself rarely, but when he did his statements received considerable attention. He generally emphasized the harm lynching did to the whites—to their moral fiber, to economic conditions, and to the reputation of the South—and at the same time counseled Negroes to cultivate industry and cease the idleness that led to crime. Yet he could be forthright in his condemnation of mob violence. "Within the last forthnight," he said in a statement issued to the press in 1904,

*three members of my race have been burned at the stake; one of them was a woman. No one . . . was charged with any crime even remotely connected with the abuse of a white woman. . . . Two of them occurred on Sunday afternoon in sight of a Christian church. . . . The custom of burning human beings has become so common as scarcely to excite interest. . . . There is no shadow of excuse for departure from legal methods in the cases of individuals accused of murder.*[17]

Ordinarily, Washington did not discuss politics, but there were occasions when he did admit that "I do not favor the Negro's giving up anything which is fundamental and which has been guaranteed to him by the Constitution. . . . It is not best for him to relinquish his rights; nor would his doing so be best for the Southern white man." He was critical of Reconstruction, when Negroes had started at the top instead of the bottom, in the senate instead of at the plow, and had been the unwitting instruments of corrupt carpet-bagger politicians. "In a word, too much stress had been placed upon the mere matter of voting and holding political office rather than upon the preparation for the highest citizenship." Washington's solution to the question of political rights was suffrage restriction applied to both races—a notion that had been growing in popularity since about 1890. "The permanent cure for our present evils will come through a property and educational test for voting that shall apply honestly and fairly to both races." In a letter to the Louisiana Constitutional Convention of 1898 he outlined his views. He was, he said, no politician, but had always advised Negroes to acquire property, intelligence, and character as the basis of good citizenship, rather than to engage in political agitation. He agreed that franchise restrictions were necessary to rid the South of ignorant and corrupt government, but suggested that no state could pass a law that would permit an ignorant white man to vote and disfranchise ignorant Negroes "without dwarfing for all time the morals of the white man in the South." In 1899, in referring to the disfranchisement bill before the Georgia legislature, he had forcefully declared that its object was to disfranchise the Negroes. Yet three years later he became notorious for his defense of the disfranchisement constitutions: "Every revised constitution throughout the Southern States has put a premium upon intelligence,

[17] *Recorder*, March 17, 1904.

ownership of property, thrift and character," he wrote in a general letter to the press.[18] But his hope that these qualifications would be equitably applied remained unfulfilled, and after 1905 Washington no longer rationalized about the disfranchisement constitutions, as he had done, but simply held that the acquisition of character, wealth, and education would break down racial discrimination.

All in all, in viewing Washington's philosophy, one is most impressed by his accommodating approach. By carefully selected ambiguities in language, by mentioning political and civil rights but seldom and then only in tactful and vague terms, he effectively masked the ultimate implications of his philosophy. For this reason his philosophy must be viewed as an accommodating one in the context of Southern race relations. In the context of the Negro thinking of the period, perhaps the most significant thing in his philosophy was his emphasis upon self-help and social solidarity.

In certain quarters Washington did not like to be considered an extreme accommodator. Writing to Francis J. Garrison of the New York Evening *Post* in 1899 he said that he hesitated to appear on the same platform with W. H. Councill, who "has the reputation of simply toadying to the Southern white people." In a letter to the noted author and lawyer, Charles W. Chesnutt, he denied that he was interested only in education and property, and he enclosed two recent statements he had made on the franchise and lynching. True, he spoke only when he thought it would be effective, rather than agitating all the time, but "I cannot understand what you or others want me to do that I have left undone." He conceded that agitation had its place; justice he believed would be attained both through education and agitation. "You will assist in bringing it about in your way and those of us who are laboring in the South will do something to bring it about in our way."[19]

Although overtly Washington minimized the importance of the franchise and civil rights, covertly he was deeply involved in political affairs and in efforts to prevent disfranchisement and other forms of discrimination.

For example, he lobbied against the Hardwick disfranchisement bill in Georgia in 1899. While his public ambiguities permitted Southern whites to think that he accepted disfranchisement if they chose to, through the same ambiguities and by private communications Washington tried to keep Negroes thinking otherwise. In 1903 when the Atlanta editor Clark Howell implied that Washington opposed Negro officeholding, he did not openly contradict him, but asked T. Thomas Fortune to editorialize in the *Age* that Howell had no grounds for placing Washington in such a position, for it was "well understood that he, while from the first deprecating the

---

[18] *Future of the American Negro*, 141, 13, 153; *An Open Letter to the Louisiana Constitutional Convention, Feb. 19, 1898* (no imprint [1900?]), 1–2; interview reprinted from Atlanta *Constitution*, ———, 1899 in *ibid.*, 6; *Gazette*, Dec. 20, 1902.

[19] BTW to Garrison, Sept. 23, 1899, in F. J. Garrison Papers; BTW to Chesnutt, July 7, 1903.

Negro's making political agitation and office-holding the most prominent and fundamental part of his career, has not gone any farther."[20] Again, while Washington opposed proposals to enforce the representation provisions of the fourteenth amendment (because he felt that the South would accept reduction in representation and thus stamp disfranchisement with the seal of constitutionality), he was secretly engaged in attacking the disfranchisement constitutions by court action. As early as 1900 he was asking certain philanthropists for money to fight the electoral provisions of the Louisiana constitution. Subsequently, he worked secretly through the financial secretary of the Afro-American Council's legal bureau, personally spending a great deal of money and energy fighting the Louisiana test case.[21] At the time of the Alabama Constitutional Convention in 1901 he used his influence with important whites in an attempt to prevent discriminatory provisions that would apply to Negroes only.[22] He was later deeply involved in testing the Alabama disfranchisement laws in the federal courts in 1903 and 1904. So circumspect was he in this instance that his secretary, Emmett J. Scott, and the New York lawyer Wilford Smith corresponded about the cases under pseudonyms and represented the sums involved in code. Washington was also interested in efforts to prevent or undermine disfranchisement in other states. For example, in Maryland, where disfranchisement later failed, he had a Catholic lawyer, F. L. McGhee of St. Paul, approach the Catholic hierarchy in an attempt to secure its opposition to disfranchisement and urged the Episcopal divine George Freeman Bragg of Baltimore to use his influence among important whites.[23] Washington contributed money generously to the test cases and other efforts, though, except in the border states, they were unsuccessful. In 1903 and 1904 he personally "spent at least four thousand dollars in cash, out of my own pocket . . . in advancing the rights of the black man."[24]

Washington's political involvement went even deeper. Although he always discreetly denied any interest in politics, he was engaged in patronage distribution under Roosevelt and Taft, in fighting the lily-white Republicans, and in getting out the Negro vote for the Republicans at national

[20] BTW to Garrison, Nov. 28, 1899 in Garrison Papers; BTW to T. Thomas Fortune, Nov. 10, 1899, June 23, 1903.

[21] BTW to Garrison, Feb. 27, and March 11, 1900, Garrison Papers; Jesse Lawson to BTW, March 29, June 26, July 30, Oct. 2, Dec. 30, 1901; April 30, June 24, 1902; BTW to Lawson, Dec. 11, 1903. On BTW's opposition to reduced representation for Southern states, see BTW to R. C. Ogden, May 15, 1903; BTW to W. H. Baldwin, March 4, 1904.

[22] E.g., Correspondence with A. D. Wimbs, 1901.

[23] Correspondence of Wilford Smith (alias J. C. May) and Emmett J. Scott (alias R. C. Black) 1903 and 1904; F. L. McGhee to BTW, Jan. 12, 1904; BTW to George F. Bragg, March 10, 1904. For fuller documentation of this and other points made in this section see August Meier, "Toward a Reinterpretation of Booker T. Washington," *JSH*, XXIII (May, 1957), 220–27.

[24] BTW to J. W. E. Bowen, Dec. 27, 1904.

elections. He might say that he disliked the atmosphere at Washington because it was impossible to build up a race whose leaders were spending most of their time and energy in trying to get into or stay in office,[25] but under Roosevelt he became the arbiter of Negro appointments to federal office. Roosevelt started consulting Washington almost as soon as he took office, and later claimed that Washington had approved of his policy of appointing fewer but better-qualified Negroes.[26] Numerous politicians old and new were soon writing to Tuskegee for favors, and in a few cases Roosevelt consulted Washington in regard to white candidates.[27] Ex-Congressman George H. White unsuccessfully appealed to Washington after the White House indicated that "a letter from you would greatly strengthen my chances." Scott reported that the President's assertion to one office seeker that he would consider him only with Washington's endorsement, had "scared these old fellows as they never have been scared before." Washington had at his disposal a number of collectorships of ports and internal revenue, receiverships of public monies in the land office, and several diplomatic posts, as well as the positions of auditor of the Navy, register of the Treasury and recorder of the deeds. As Roosevelt wrote to a friend in 1903, his Negro appointees "were all recommended to me by Booker T. Washington."[28] Furthermore, Roosevelt sought Washington's advice on presidential speeches and messages to Congress and consulted him on most matters concerning the Negro. Every four years also Washington took charge of the Negro end of the Republican presidential campaign.[29]

If Washington reaped the rewards of politics, he also experienced its vicissitudes. From the start he was fighting a desperate but losing battle against the lily-white Republicans. His correspondence teems with material on the struggle, especially in Louisiana and Alabama, and in other states as well. As he wrote to Walter L. Cohen of the New Orleans land office on October 5, 1905: "What I have attempted in Louisiana I have attempted to do in nearly every one of the Southern States, as you and others are in a position to know, and but for my action, as feeble as it was, the colored

[25] My Larger Education, 159.

[26] See especially Roosevelt to BTW, Sept. 14, Dec. 12, 1901; and Roosevelt to James Ford Rhodes, Dec. 15, 1905, in Elting E. Morison, ed., The Letters of Theodore Roosevelt (Cambridge, 1951–54), IV, 1072; Roosevelt to Richard Watson Gilder, Nov. 16, 1908, in Roosevelt Papers, Library of Congress.

[27] Samuel R. Spencer, Jr., Booker T. Washington and the Negro's Place in American Life (Boston, 1955), 136, 138; two letters of BTW to Roosevelt dated Nov. 4, 1902; Roosevelt to John Graham Brooks, Nov. 13, 1908, in Roosevelt Papers.

[28] White to BTW, Oct. 7, 1901; Scott to BTW, July 2, 1902; Roosevelt to Silas McBee, Feb. 3, 1903, in Morison, Letters of Theodore Roosevelt, III, 419.

[29] The correspondence concerning Washington's political activities during the Roosevelt and Taft administrations is enormous. See especially correspondence with Roosevelt, James R. Clarkson, George Cortelyou, William Loeb, and Charles W. Anderson during Roosevelt's presidency, and with Taft, C. D. Norton, C. D. Hilles, and Anderson during Taft's

people would have been completely overthrown and the Lily Whites would have been in complete control in nearly every Southern State." Later, troubles came thick and fast after Taft's inauguration. The new president appointed fewer Negroes to office and did not consult Washington as much as Roosevelt had done. Not until 1911, after desperate efforts at convincing the administration of the need for some decent plums in order to retain the Negro vote, was it finally arranged to make a few significant appointments, most notably that of W. H. Lewis as assistant attorney general—the highest position held by a Negro in the federal government up to that time.

In areas other than politics Washington also played an active behind-the-scenes role. On the Seth Carter (Texas) and Dan Rogers (Alabama) cases involving discrimination in the matter of representation on juries, Washington worked closely with the lawyer Wilford Smith and contributed liberally to their financing.[30] He was interested in preventing Negro tenants who had accidentally or in ignorance violated their contracts from being sentenced to the chain gang.[31] He was concerned in the Alonzo Bailey Peonage Case, and when the Supreme Court declared peonage illegal, confided to friends that he and his associates had been working at the case for over two years, securing the free services of some of the best lawyers in Montgomery and the assistance of other leading white people. Yet Washington characteristically interceded to reduce the sentence of the convicted man, who was soon released.[32]

Of special interest are Washington's efforts against railroad segregation. At Washington's suggestion Giles B. Jackson of Richmond undertook the legal fight against the Jim Crow Law in Virginia in 1901.[33] When Tennessee in 1903 in effect prohibited Pullman accommodations for Negroes by requiring that such facilities be entirely separate, he stepped into the breach. He worked closely with Napier in Nashville and enlisted the aid of Atlanta leaders like W. E. B. Du Bois. This group, however, did not succeed in discussing the matter with Pullman Company president Robert Todd Lincoln, in spite of the intercession of another railroad leader, William H. Baldwin, president of the Long Island Railroad, an important figure in the Pennsylvania and Southern systems, and Washington's closest white friend. And, though Washington wanted to start a suit, the Nashville people failed to act.[34] Again, in 1906, employing the Howard University Professor Kelly

[30] E.g., J. C. May to R. C. Black, July 15, 1903; BTW to Smith, Feb. 2, March 3, 1904; Smith to BTW, Feb. 4, 1904.

[31] BTW to Villard, Sept. 7, 1908; Villard to BTW, Sept. 8, 1908.

[32] BTW to Anderson, Jan. 6, 1911; BTW to R. W. Thompson, Jan. 7, 1911; BTW to Hilles, ——, 1911; Crisis, II (Aug., 1911), 139.

[33] Jackson to BTW, Jan. 24, 1901.

[34] Napier to BTW, Oct. 28, Dec. 11, 1903; BTW to Napier, Nov. 2, 1903; BTW to Lawson, Nov. 5, 1903; BTW to Du Bois, Dec. 14, 1903, Feb. 27, June 4, 1904; Baldwin to BTW, Jan. 7, 1904.

Miller and the Boston lawyer Archibald W. Grimké as intermediaries, Washington discreetly supplied funds to pay ex-Senator Henry W. Blair of New Hampshire to lobby against the Warner-Foraker Amendment to the Hepburn Railway Act.[35] This amendment, by requiring equality of accommodations in interstate travel, would have impliedly condoned segregation throughout the country, under the separate-but-equal doctrine. The amendment was defeated, but whether due to Blair's lobbying or to the protests of Negro organizations is hard to say.

Thus, in spite of his accommodating tone and his verbal emphasis upon economy as the solution to the race problem, Washington was surreptitiously engaged in undermining the American race system by a direct attack upon disfranchisement and segregation, and in spite of his strictures against political activity he was a powerful politician in his own right. . . .

Thus, although Washington held to full citizenship rights and integration as his objective, he masked this goal beneath an approach that satisfied influential elements that were either indifferent or hostile to its fulfillment. He was not the first to combine a constructive, even militant emphasis upon self-help, racial co-operation and economic development with a conciliatory, ingratiating, and accommodating approach to the white South. But his name is the one most indissolubly linked with this combination. He was, as one of his followers put it, attempting to bring the wooden horse within the walls of Troy.

Washington apparently really believed that in the face of an economic and moral development that assimilated Negroes to American middle-class standards, prejudice would diminish and the barriers of discrimination would crumble. He emphasized duties rather than rights; the Negro's faults rather than his grievances; his opportunities rather than his difficulties. He stressed means rather than ends. He was optimistic rather than pessimistic. He stressed economics above politics, industrial above liberal education, self-help above dependence on the national government. He taught that rural life was superior to urban life. He professed a deep love for the South and a profound faith in the goodness of the Southern whites—at least of the "better class." He appealed more to the self-interest of the whites—their economic and moral good—than to their sense of justice.

The ambiguities in Washington's philosophy were vital to his success. Negroes who supported him looked to his tactfully, usually vaguely worded expressions on ultimate goals. Conservative Southerners were attracted by his seeming acceptance of disfranchisement and segregation, and by his flattery. Industrialists and philanthropists appreciated his petit bourgeois outlook. Washington's skillful manipulation of popular symbols and myths like the gospel of wealth and the doctrines of Social Darwinism enhanced his effectiveness. Terms like "social equality," "civil relations,"

[35] Miller to BTW, May 22, 1906; Grimké to BTW, May 25, June 10, 1906; BTW to Grimké, June 2, 4, 10, 1906; Scott to Thompson, June 5, 1906.

"constitutional rights," "Christian character," "industrial education," and "justice" were capable of a wide variety of interpretations. The Supreme Court, for example, did not appear to think that the fourteenth and fifteenth amendments prohibited segregation and the use of various subterfuges that effected disfranchisement. Washington shrewdly used these ambiguities, and they were an important source both of his popularity and of the acrimonious discussion over his policy that occupied Negroes for many years.

Washington did not appeal to all groups. Extremists among white Southerners liked him no more than did the Negro "radicals." Men such as Governor Vardaman of Mississippi and the author Thomas Dixon, who feared any Negro advancement, opposed the Tuskegeean's program of elevation and uplift. Washington basically appealed to conservative, propertied elements both North and South. His stress upon the economic rather than the political was parallel to the New South philosophy of emphasizing industry rather than politics as a way of advancing the South in the councils of the nation. Yet he also capitalized on the myth of the small farmer, and the romantic agrarian traditions of the South. His call for a justly applied property and educational test that would disfranchise ignorant and poor Negroes and whites alike, and enfranchise the propertied, taxpaying, conservative Negroes, met the approval of important elements in the Black Belt plantation and urban areas of the South, who had no more love for the "poor whites" than Washington did. Again, Washington espoused a Social Darwinism of competition between individuals and races of uplifting backward races, that was congenial to his age. He conveniently put Negro equality off into a hazy future that did not disturb the "practical" and prejudiced men of his generation. At the same time, by blaming Negroes for their condition, by calling them a backward race, by asserting that an era of justice would ultimately be ushered in, by flattering the whites for what little they had done for Negroes, he palliated any pangs of conscience that the whites might have had.

His program also appealed to a substantial group of Negroes—to those Negroes who were coming to count for most—in large part to a rising middle class. In fact, stress upon economics as an indirect route to the solution of the race problem, interest in industrial education, the appeal to race pride and solidarity, and denial of any interest in social equality were all ideas that had become dominant in the Negro community. The older upper-class Negroes in certain Northern centers, who had their economic and sometimes their social roots in the white communities, were less sympathetic to Washington. But to self-made middle-class Negroes, and to lower middle-class Negroes on the make, to the leaders and supporters of Negro fraternal enterprises, to businessmen who depended on the Negro community for their livelihood, Washington's message seemed common sense. Interestingly enough, this group, especially in the North, did not always express Washington's conciliatory tone, but assumed that Washington was using it to placate the white South.

To what extent Washington directly influenced Negro thought is difficult to evaluate. Washington was acceptable to Negroes partly because of the prestige and power he held among whites, and partly because his views—except for his conciliatory phraseology—were dominant in the Negro community throughout the country, and his accommodating approach was general throughout the South. Then, too, his Negro supporters read a great deal into his generalizations about eventual justice and constitutional rights. The fact that Negroes tended to see in his words what they already believed would appear to minimize his direct influence. Yet his prestige, the teachers sent out by Tuskegee and her daughter schools, and the widespread publicity generated by the National Negro Business League of which Washington was the founder and president, undoubtedly had a significant impact on Negro thought, reinforcing tendencies already in the foreground.

### THE PARADOX OF W. E. B. DU BOIS[36]

If, of the great trio of Negro leaders, Frederick Douglass best expressed the aspirations toward full citizenship and assimilation, and Booker T. Washington the interest in economic advancement, it was Du Bois who most explicitly revealed the impact of oppression and of the American creed in creating ambivalent loyalties toward race and nation in the minds of American Negroes. As Du Bois said in 1897:

*One feels his two-ness—an American, a Negro, two souls, two thoughts, two unreconciled strivings, two warring ideals in one dark body. . . .*

*The history of the American Negro is the history of this strife,—this longing to attain self-conscious manhood, to merge his double self into a better and truer self. . . . He would not Africanize America for America has too much to teach the world and Africa. He would not bleach the Negro soul in a flood of white Americanism, for he knows that Negro blood has a message for the world. He simply wishes to make it possible for a man to be both a Negro and an American, without being cursed and spit upon. . . .*

More than any other figure Du Bois made explicit this ambivalence—an ambivalence that is perhaps the central motif in his ideological biography. Even Du Bois has described himself as integrally a part of European civilization, and "yet, more significant, one of its rejected parts; one who expressed in life and action and made vocal to many, a single whirlpool of social entanglement and inner psychological paradox."[37]

[36] All works cited are by Du Bois unless otherwise stated. The Du Bois Papers have been closed to scholars for some years. All references to letters to and from Du Bois and all references to manuscript materials by Du Bois are to the notes on these materials made by Francis L. Broderick and placed on file at the Schomburg Collection of the New York Public Library.

[37] "Strivings of the Negro People," *Atlantic Monthly*, LXXX (Aug., 1897), 194; *Dusk of Dawn* (New York, 1940), 2.

A proud and sensitive youth reared in a western Massachusetts town, Du Bois had occasion to know the sting of prejudice and early realized that "I was different from others; or like, mayhap in heart and life and longing, but shut out from their world by a vast veil." Subsequently he therefore found the segregated community of Fisk University, which he attended from 1885 to 1888, an enriching experience. Though he yearned for the full recognition of his American citizenship, he was also, he later recollected, "thrilled and moved to tears," and recognized "something inherently and deeply my own" as a result of his association there with a "closed racial group with rites and loyalties, with a history and a corporate future, with an art and a philosophy." By the time he received his A.B. from Fisk and entered Harvard as a Junior in 1888, "the theory of race separation was quite in my blood," and the lack of social acceptance he experienced at Harvard, he recalled later, did not disturb him. Yet it certainly was his sensitivity to discrimination that led him at this time to view Negroes as a "nation"—Americans, but rejected in the land of their birth.[38]

Meanwhile, Du Bois had been expressing himself on other subjects. As a correspondent for Fortune's New York *Globe* during the early 1880's and as editor of the Fisk *Herald,* he displayed an interest in industriousness and ambition. Furthermore, as a student at Fisk and at Harvard—where he received his Ph.D. in 1895—and as a professor at Wilberforce University (1894–96), Du Bois proved more than willing to meet Southern whites half way. He told both Fisk students and his white associates in the Tennessee prohibitionist movement that the interests of the two races were essentially the same. To his Fisk audience he proposed the admittedly unorthodox idea that Negroes should divide their vote in order not to exacerbate race relations. He assured Southern whites that they could depend on the friendship of Negroes if only the whites would grant them citizenship rights and adequate educational facilities. Since the Negro's condition was such as to encourage prejudice, for their part Negroes must stress duties as well as rights, and work for their own advancement. At both Harvard and Wilberforce he could, in a single speech, lash out at America's immoral and unAmerican treatment of Negroes (and at Harvard suggest that Negroes would revolt if other means failed) and at the same time adopt a conciliatory position. Since Negroes had not yet achieved what it took the Anglo-Saxons a millennium to do, they were not yet equipped to vote. What he objected to was not the disfranchisement of the Negro masses, but of intelligent, law-abiding Negroes; and what he advocated was a franchise limitation fairly applied to both races along with adequate educational opportunities for all. In 1891 it was even reported in the *Age* that Du Bois had asserted that the whole idea underlying the Lodge Elections Bill was wrong, for it was proposed on the assumption that

---

[38] "Strivings of the Negro People," 194–95; "Public Rhetoricals," Fisk University, MS [1885–88]; *Dusk of Dawn,* 23–24, 101, 36; "A Vacation Unique," MS, 1889; "What Will the Negro Do?" MS, 1889.

*law can accomplish anything. . . . We must ever keep before us the fact that
the South has some excuse for its present attitude. We must remember that
a good many of our people . . . are not fit for the responsibility of republican
government. When you have the right sort of black voters you will need no
election laws. The battle of my people must be a moral one, not a legal or
physical one.*[39]

It was no wonder then that after Washington's address Du Bois wrote the
*Age* suggesting "that here might be the basis of a real settlement between
whites and blacks."[40]

Meanwhile, Du Bois was formulating his notion of leadership by a
college-educated elite, which he regarded as necessary for the advancement of any group. In 1891 he deplored the South's effort to make common
and industrial schools rather than colleges the basis of its educational system. For only a liberally educated white leadership could perceive that,
despite the justification for overthrowing the Reconstruction governments,
to permanently disfranchise the working class of a society in the process of
rapid industrialization would, as socialists from Lassalle to Hindman had
said, result in economic ruin. And only a liberal higher education could
create an intelligent Negro leadership. Thus, while still a student at Harvard,
Du Bois had suggested his theory of the talented tenth, foreshadowed his
later concern with the working class, and adumbrated the thesis he later
stressed so much—that without political rights Negroes, primarily a working
group, could not secure economic opportunity. Furthermore, it should be
noted that his educational views were not unrelated to his ethnocentric
feelings. As he said at Wilberforce, the educated elite had a glorious opportunity to guide the race by reshaping its own ideals in order to provide the
masses with appropriate goals and lift them to civilization.[41]

After two years at Wilberforce, Du Bois accepted a one-year research
appointment at the University of Pennsylvania. Then in 1897 he became
professor of sociology at Atlanta University, where he remained until 1910,
teaching and editing the annual Atlanta University Studies on the American
Negro.

At no time in his life did Du Bois place greater and more consistent
stress upon self-help and racial solidarity than during the last four years of
the century. Like many of his contemporaries he fused this emphasis with
one on economic advancement; and like a few of them he synthesized it
with his educational program for the talented tenth. To Du Bois in fact,
the race prejudice which isolated the Negro group and threw upon it "the

[39] New York *Globe*, e.g., Sept. 8, 1883; Fisk *Herald*, V (Dec., 1887), 8 and V (March, 1888),
8–9; "Political Serfdom," MS, 1887; "An Open Letter to the Southern People," MS, 1888
[?]; "What Will the Negro Do?"; "Harvard and the South," MS, 1891; "The Afro-Americans,"
MS [1894–96]; *Age*, June 13, 1891.

[40] *Dusk of Dawn*, 85. Unfortunately the files of the *Age* are not available for the early 1890's.

[41] "Harvard and the South"; "The Afro-American"; "The True Meaning of a University,"
MS, 1894.

responsibility of evolving its own methods and organs of civilization" made the stimulation of group co-operation "the central serious problem."[42]

It was his appointment to the University of Pennsylvania that provided Du Bois with his first opportunity to begin a scientific study of the race problem. He had long awaited such an opportunity because he believed that presentation of the facts derived from scientific investigation would go a long way toward solving the race problem. The resulting monograph, *The Philadelphia Negro*, leaned toward the blame-the-Negro, self-help point of view. Yet Du Bois did describe what it meant to be snubbed in employment and in social intercourse, and he judged that the Negro's participation in politics had been, in net effect, beneficial to the city and to the Negro himself. Above all, he felt that Negroes must uplift themselves, and by racial co-operation open enterprises that would provide employment and training in trades and commerce. Whites had their duty to help but society had too many problems "for it lightly to shoulder all the burdens of a less advanced people." Negroes ought to constantly register strong protests against prejudice and injustice, but they should do so because these things hindered them in their own attempt to elevate the race. And this attempt, Du Bois held, must be marked by vigorous and persistent efforts directed toward lessening crime and toward inculcating self-respect, the dignity of labor, and the virtues of truth, honesty, and charity.[43]

Like Washington, then, Du Bois combined an enthusiasm for racial solidarity with one for economic development and the middle-class virtues. In fact, he regarded a college education as "one of the best preparations for a broad business life" and for the making of "captains of industry." Likening Negroes to other nationalities, he chided them for being ashamed of themselves, and held that such success as had been achieved by other nations no larger in population than the American Negroes could be accomplished only through a badly needed co-operation and unity. In view of the poverty of the Negro and the economic spirit of the age, it was most important to achieve success in business. Because of race prejudice the major opportunity for such achievement lay in commercial activity based on Negroes pooling their earnings and pushing forward as a group. Though their collective capital be small, thrift and industry could succeed even under the handicaps of prejudice. Under the circumstances a penny savings bank would be more helpful than the vote. Negroes should patronize and invest their money in Negro-owned enterprises, even at a personal sacrifice. For "we must cooperate or we are lost. Ten million people who join in intelligent self-help can never be long ignored or mistreated."[44]

[42] *Some Efforts of American Negroes For Their Own Social Betterment* (AUP No. 3, 1898), 43.

[43] *The Philadelphia Negro* (Philadelphia, 1899), 325, 388–91, chap. xvii, and *passim*.

[44] "Careers Open to College-Bred Negroes," in Du Bois and H. H. Proctor, *Two Addresses* (Nashville, 1898), 7, 12; "The Meaning of Business," MS, 1898; quotation at end of paragraph is from resolutions of the Fourth Atlanta University Conference, *The Negro in Business* (AUP No. 4, 1899), 50.

It should be noted, of course, that Du Bois did not, during the *fin de siècle* years, give up all interest in political rights, though like the majority of articulate Southern Negroes of the day he was willing to compromise on the matter. He was among those who in 1899 petitioned the Georgia legislature not to pass the Hardwick disfranchisement bill, though like Booker T. Washington he was willing to accept an educational and/or property qualification as long as free school facilities were open to all.[45]

During this period Du Bois was more emphatic than at any other time about the value of racial integrity. Speaking on "The Conservation of Races" in 1897 he asserted that there existed subtle psychic differences, which had definitely divided men into races. Like his racist contemporaries, he was certain of the universality of "the race spirit," which he regarded as "the greatest invention for human progress." Each race had a special ideal— the English individualism, the German philosophy and science, and so forth. Therefore, "only Negroes bound and welded together, Negroes inspired by one vast ideal, can work out in its fullness the great message we have for humanity." To those who argued that their only hope lay in amalgamating with the rest of the American population, he admitted that Negroes faced a "puzzling dilemma." Every thoughtful Negro had at some time asked himself whether he was an American, or a Negro, or if he could be both; whether by striving as a Negro he was not perpetuating the very gulf that divided the two races, or whether Negroes "have in America a distinct mission as a race." Du Bois' answer was what is now called cultural pluralism. Negroes were American by birth, in language, in political ideas, and in religion. But any further than this, their Americanism did not go. Since they had given America its only native music and folk stories, "its only touch of pathos and humor amid it mad money-getting plutocracy," it was the Negroes' duty to maintain "our physical power, our intellectual endowment, our spiritual ideas; as a race, we must strive by race organizations, by race solidarity, by race unity to the realization of the broader humanity which freely recognizes differences in men, but sternly deprecates inequalities in their opportunity of development." To this end, separate racial educational, business, and cultural institutions were necessary. Despised and oppressed, the Negroes' only means of advancement was a belief in their own great destiny. No people that wished to be something other than itself "ever wrote its name in history; it must be inspired with the Divine faith of our black mothers, that out of the blood and dust of battles will march a victorious host, a mighty nation, a peculiar people, to speak to the nations of the earth a Divine truth that should make them free." Washington, it should be pointed out, while advocating race pride and race integrity, did not glory so much in the idea of a distinctive Negro culture (though he was always proud of the spirituals or "plantation melo-

---

[45] Du Bois and others, *Memorial to the Legislature of Georgia Upon the Hardwick Bill,* Pamphlet, 1899, Du Bois Papers; "The Suffrage Fight in Georgia," *Independent,* LX (Nov. 30, 1899), 3226–28.

dies"). Nor did he exhibit Du Bois' sense of identification with Africans, evident in Du Bois' advocacy of "pan-Negroism" in this same address.[46]

During the last years of the century Du Bois developed his educational theories at considerable length, attempting to construct "A Rational System of Negro Education" by reconciling the two widely diverging tendencies of the day—training for making a living and training for living a broad life. All agreed, he said, on the necessity of universal common school training, and on the contribution Hampton, Tuskegee, and the Slater Fund had made in stressing the building of an economic foundation, the freedmen's primary concern. But unfortunately only three or four schools made broad culture their chief aim. Du Bois criticized the talk of rosewood pianos in dingy cabins, of ignorant farmers, of college graduates without employment, though he agreed that more stress had been placed on college training than the economic condition of the race warranted. But the vogue for industrial education had become so great that the colleges were hard-pressed for funds. This was particularly deplorable because the isolation of the Negro community demanded the creation of an indigenous leadership of college-trained captains of industry and scholars, who would advance the masses economically and culturally, and who could view the race problem from a broad perspective.[47]

There were remarkable similarities between Du Bois and Washington during the late 1890's—a period when more Negro leaders than at any other time adopted a conciliatory tactic. Both tended to blame Negroes largely for their condition, and both placed more emphasis on self-help and duties than on rights. Both placed economic advancement before universal manhood suffrage, and both were willing to accept franchise restrictions based not on race but on education and/or property qualifications equitably applied. Both stressed racial solidarity and economic co-operation. Du Bois was, however, more outspoken about injustices, and he differed sharply with Washington in his espousal of the cause of higher education.

The years from 1901 to 1903 were years of transition in Du Bois' philosophy, years in which he grew more critical of industrial education and more alarmed over disfranchisement. Writing in 1901 he engaged in sharp protest against the Southern race system, even while recognizing that Negroes must adjust to it. He denied that the "many delicate differences in race psychology" excused oppression. He complained of the economic discrimination that retarded the development of a substantial landowning and artisan class. He bemoaned the lack of contact between the races that increased prejudice by preventing the best classes of both

[46] *The Conservation of Races* (American Negro Academy, Occasional Papers No. 2, 1897), 7, 9–13. Nor was Du Bois averse to a considerable number of American Negroes migrating to Africa, uniting for the uplift and economic development of the continent. See "Possibility of Emigration to Congo Free State," Memorial to Paul Hegeman, Belgian Consul-General to the United States [1895–97].

[47] "A Rational System of Negro Education," MS [1897–1900]; Du Bois, ed., *The College-Bred Negro* (AUP No. 5, 1900), 29.

races from knowing each other. Yet he felt that, since Negroes must accept segregation, the road to uplift and economic improvement lay in the development of college-educated leaders: "Black captains of industry and missionaries of culture" who with their knowledge of modern civilization could uplift Negro communities "by forms of precept and example, deep sympathy and the inspiration of common kindred and ideals." But while Negroes would have to temporarily acquiesce in segregation, they could not acquiesce in disfranchisement. Du Bois did not object to "legitimate efforts to purge the ballot of ignorance, pauperism and crime," and he conceded that it was "sometimes best that a partially developed people should be ruled by the best of their stronger and better neighbors for their own good," until they were ready to stand on their own feet. But since the dominant opinion of the South openly asserted that the purpose of the disfranchisement laws was the complete exclusion of Negroes from politics, the ballot was absolutely necessary for the Negro's safety and welfare. Moreover, as European experience had demonstrated, workers under modern industrial conditions needed the vote in order to protect themselves; Negroes, laboring under racial discrimination, needed it even more.[48]

Du Bois developed further his educational views and the theme of the talented tenth. He agreed that it was most important to train Negroes to work, and he conceded that industrial schools would play an important role in achieving this end. He also approved of the compromise function of industrial education, which had brought together races and sections; and although industrial education would not solve the problem he asserted that "it does mean that its settlement can be auspiciously begun." Yet he had come to criticize the overinsistence of industrial schools upon the practical, the unfortunate opposition of their advocates toward colleges, the fact that industrial schools were preparing their students in obsolete crafts, and the fact that they produced few actual artisans. Du Bois defended Negro colleges from charges that they had erred in training school teachers and professional men before turning to industrial training. He pointed out that historically the European university had preceded the common school, and that out of the liberal arts institutions came the backbone of the teaching force of the Negro common schools and of industrial schools like Tuskegee, where almost half of the executive council and a majority of the heads of departments were college graduates. All races, he held, had been civilized by their exceptional men; "the problem of education, then, among Negroes, must first of all deal with the Talented Tenth."[49]

It is evident that Washington and Du Bois had come to disagree not only in their educational philosophy, but also on the fundamental question

---

[48] "The Relations of the Negroes to the Whites of the South" (Annals of the American Academy of Political and Social Science, XVIII, July, 1901), 121–33; "The Case for the Negro," MS, 1901.

[49] "The Talented Tenth," in BTW and others, The Negro Problem (New York, 1903), 60–61; The Negro Artisan (AUP No. 7, 1902), 81; "Of the Training of Black Men," Atlantic Monthly, XC (Sept., 1902), 291; "The Talented Tenth," 45, 33–34.

of the immediate importance of the ballot. By 1903 Du Bois was not only pleading for higher education, but had begun to criticize the work of the industrial schools. Both men spoke of captains of industry, but where the Tuskegeean emphasized economic skills, the Atlanta educator stressed a high grade of culture. And unlike Washington, Du Bois had come to believe that educational and property qualifications for voting would not be equitably applied. True, Du Bois never gave up his belief that, in the face of white prejudice and discrimination group solidarity was necessary, especially in economic matters. But all that really remained to make the two men irreconcilable ideological opponents was for Du Bois to advocate the importance of protest rather than accommodation. This he did in his opening attack on Washington in 1903.

During the 1890's Washington and Du Bois had been cordial in their relationships. Upon returning to the United States from Germany in 1894 Du Bois accepted a position at Wilberforce, having had to turn down a somewhat later offer from Tuskegee. Again in 1896, 1899, and as late as 1902 Du Bois seriously considered invitations to Tuskegee.[50] In his correspondence with Washington, through his articles and speeches, and by attending the Hampton and Tuskegee Conferences he exhibited his sympathetic interest in Washington's work. He had, it is true, mildly criticized the Tuskegeean in an article in 1901. In it he said that some of the most prominent men of the race regarded the Hampton-Tuskegee approach as only a partial approach to the race problem, in that they stressed the highest aspirations of the race, advocated college education, and believed that Negroes should enjoy suffrage equally with whites. But as late as July 1902 the *Guardian* denounced Du Bois for siding with Washington at the St. Paul meeting of the Afro-American Council. "Like all the others who are trying to get into the bandwagon of the Tuskegeean, he is no longer to be relied upon," declared the editor, Monroe Trotter.[51]

Kelly Miller has asserted that Trotter wove a "subtle net" around Du Bois and captured him for the radical cause. It would be difficult to test the truth of this statement. Certain it is, however, that by January 1903 Trotter was praising Du Bois as a brilliant leader who, despite temptations, "has never in public utterance or in written article, betrayed his race in its contest for equal opportunity and equal rights." Du Bois himself has recalled that he was gradually growing more disturbed after 1900—less by the ideological difference between him and Washington (which he remembered as mainly one of emphasis) than by the immense power over political appointments, over philanthropic largess, and over the press wielded by what Du Bois has labeled the "Tuskegee Machine." Du Bois found Wash-

[50] Samuel R. Spencer, Jr., *Booker T. Washington and the Negro's Place in American Life* (Boston, 1955), 146, 148–49.

[51] "The Evolution of Negro Leadership," *The Dial*, XXXI (July, 1901), 54 (an article which anticipated in several significant respects Du Bois' discussion in "Of Booker T. Washington and Others"); *Guardian*, July 27, 1902.

ington's influence over the press especially deplorable, in view of the Tuskegeean's soft-pedaling of agitation on segregation and disfranchisement.[52] Yet whatever his actual motivation for criticizing Washington, his first public statement on the matter was confined to ideological issues.

This statement was Du Bois' famous essay, "Of Booker T. Washington and Others," in *Souls of Black Folk,* published in the spring of 1903. "Easily the most striking thing," began Du Bois, "in the history of the American Negro since 1876 is the ascendancy of Mr. Booker T. Washington." Others had failed in establishing a compromise between the North, the South, and the Negroes. But Washington, coming with a simple though not entirely original program of industrial education, conciliation of the South, and acceptance of disfranchisement and segregation, had succeeded. For with "singular insight" he had grasped the spirit of the age—"the spirit and thought of triumphant commercialism."

Du Bois went on to criticize the Tuskegeean because his policy "practically accepted the alleged inferiority of the Negro," allowed economic concerns to dominate over the higher aims of life, and preached a "submission to prejudice." Although Washington had made some statements about lynching and the franchise, generally his speeches purveyed the "dangerous half-truths" that the Negro's lowly condition justified the South's attitude and that the Negro's elevation must depend chiefly on his own efforts. Du Bois perceived paradoxes in Washington's attempt to make Negro workers businessmen and property owners when it was impossible for workers to defend themselves without the ballot; in his preaching self-respect while counseling accommodation to discrimination and in his advocacy of industrial and common schools while depreciating the colleges that supplied the teachers. Furthermore, Washington's propaganda had undoubtedly hastened the disfranchisement, the increased segregation, and the decreased philanthropic concern for higher education that accompanied his ascendancy.

Washington's popularity with whites, Du Bois held, had led Negroes to accept his leadership, and criticism of the Tuskegeean had disappeared. The time was ripe therefore for thinking Negroes to undertake their responsibility to the masses by speaking out. In addition to the few who dared to openly oppose Washington, Du Bois thought that men like Archibald and Francis J. Grimké, Kelly Miller, and J. W. E. Bowen could not remain silent much longer. Such men honored Washington for his conciliatory attitude, and they realized that the condition of the masses of the race was responsible for much of the discrimination against it. But they also knew that prejudice was more often a cause than a result of the Negro's degradation; that justice could not be achieved through "indiscriminate flattery"; that Negroes could not gain their rights by voluntarily throwing them away, or obtain respect by constantly belittling themselves; and that, on the con-

[52] Miller, *Race Adjustment* (3d ed.; New York, 1909), 14; *Guardian,* Jan. 10, 1903; *Dusk of Dawn,* 70–77.

trary, Negroes must speak out constantly against oppression and discrimination.

Du Bois had indeed moved away from his conciliatory ideology of the 1890's. Yet attempts at co-operation between him and Washington were not quite at an end. In the summer of 1903 Du Bois spoke at Tuskegee. The two men also continued their collaboration—begun in 1902—in an effort to prevent the exclusion of Negroes from Pullman cars. Nevertheless, after the "Boston Riot" Du Bois was—with reservations—lining up with Trotter. He did not, he said, agree with Trotter's intemperate tactics, but he admired his integrity and purpose, which were especially needed in view of Washington's backward steps.[53] The Carnegie Hall Meeting of January 1904 and Du Bois' appointment to the Committee of Twelve temporarily restored an uneasy working relationship between him and Washington, but he soon resigned from the Committee and in 1905 was chiefly responsible for inaugurating the Niagara Movement. Meanwhile, he has recollected, he found it increasingly difficult to obtain funds for his work at Atlanta, experienced criticism in the Negro press, and in other ways "felt the implacability of the Tuskegee Machine."[54] He was one of the most active members of the Conference on the Negro in 1909, and when the N.A.A.C.P. was organized in 1910 he became director of publicity and research and editor of the *Crisis*.

Thus by 1905 Du Bois had definitely come to the parting of the ways with Washington. And it is in the Niagara Movement manifestoes and in the pages of the *Horizon* and *Crisis* that one can best observe Du Bois as the consistent agitator, the ardent and brilliant fighter for integration and citizenship rights. For example, he insisted that disfranchisement retarded the economic development of the Negro because the voteless could not protect their property rights. He cited cases of persecution of prosperous Negroes as evidence that Washington's program would not obtain the respect of the white man and the rights of citizenship.[55] In a typical editorial he pointed out that in spite of Washington's conciliatory policy conditions had grown worse. True, as Washington said, Negroes had continued to accumulate property and education, but how Washington could assert that discrimination and prejudice were decreasing was incomprehensible to Du Bois. Horrible as race prejudice was, it could be fought if faced frankly. But "if we continually dodge and cloud the issue, and say the half truth because the whole stings and shames . . . we invite catastrophe." Elsewhere he insisted that opportunism was a dangerous policy that gave moral support to the race's enemies, and he denounced the stress on sycophancy, selfishness, mediocrity, and servility at the expense of the best education,

[53] Spencer, *Booker T. Washington*, 157; on Pullman Car matter see pp. 305–306 above; Du Bois to Clement Morgan, Oct. 19, 1903, and Du Bois to George Foster Peabody, Dec. 28, 1903.

[54] *Dusk of Dawn*, 82–83, 86, 95. On embarrassment Du Bois' stand caused Atlanta University, see Horace Bumstead to Du Bois, Dec. 5, 1903 and Jan. 26, 1905.

[55] E.g., *Crisis*, VII (Feb., 1914), 189–90; I (Dec., 1910), 27.

the highest ideals, and self-respect.[56] Naturally he criticized industrial schools. On one occasion he attacked Hampton for its opposition to the work of the Negro colleges, and described it as "a center of that underground and silent intrigue which is determined to perpetuate the American Negro as a docile peasant," lacking political rights and social status. Du Bois was unequivocal in his stand on segregation. He scathingly denounced the separate-but-equal doctrine: "Separate schools for Whites and Blacks, and separate cars for Whites and Blacks are not equal, can not be made equal, and . . . are not intended to be equal." He charged that what the South wanted was not mere separation but subordination, and insisted that no "square deal" was possible as long as segregation existed. And unlike Washington he opposed a colored Episcopal bishop to work only among Negroes, even though this would have elevated a Negro to a high church office.[57]

It is evident from a reading of Du Bois' less publicized scholarly and nonpolemical statements that throughout these years he still maintained his interest in racial solidarity and self-help, in the group economy, and in the American Negro's ties to Africa. On occasion he was most explicit about his concept of economic nationalism. Just as a country can by tariffs build up its separate economy to the point where it can compete in international trade, so the Negro should create a group economy that would "so break the force of race prejudice that his right and ability to enter the national economy are assured." His enthusiasm for the group economy was indeed at times interpreted as implying a favorable attitude toward segregation, and in an exchange of letters on the subject with the editor of the Boston Transcript, Du Bois was finally prompted to declare that while opposed to physical separation he was prepared to accept for some time to come a "spiritual" separation in economic life that would involve Negroes trading only among themselves. True, he shifted his support from the creation of captains of industry who would exploit the Negro proletariat to the building up of a consumers' and producers' co-operative movement among Negroes. But inevitably he had to reconcile his espousal of a group economy with his demands for full integration. In 1913, replying to a communication which claimed it was hard to meet the argument that segregation forced Negroes to develop themselves, Du Bois agreed that undoubtedly thousands of Negro businesses, including the Crisis, had developed because of discrimination, capitalizing, in a sense, on race prejudice. But this did not make discrimination a "veiled blessing." While Negro enterprises had done creditable work under the circumstances, and although Negroes must make the best of segregation, turning even its disadvantages to their advantage, they "must never forget that none of its possible advantages can

---

[56] *Crisis*, II (June, 1911), 63–64; "The Forward Movement," MS, 1910.

[57] *Crisis*, XVI (Nov., 1917), 11; *Horizon*, II (Oct., 1907), 16; *Crisis*, I (Feb., 1911), 20–21; *Horizon*, II (Oct., 1907), 7–8.

offset its miserable evils, or replace the opportunity . . . of free men in a free world."[58]

A similar paradox was involved in Du Bois' stand on intermarriage. Writing in the *Independent* in 1910 he held that a person had the right to choose his spouse, that the prohibition of intermarriage was not justified when it arbitrarily limited friendships, and that where satisfactory conditions prevailed, race mixture had often produced gifted and desirable stocks and individuals, such as the Egyptians, and Hamilton, Pushkin, Douglass, and Dumas. He believed, however, that for the present widespread intermarriage would be "a social calamity by reason of the wide cultural, ethical and traditional differences" between the races, and predicted that if Negroes were accorded their rights and thus encouraged to build up their racial self-respect, the two races would continue to exist as distinct entities, perhaps forever, and this not "at the behest of any one race which recently arrogantly assumed the heritage of the earth, but for the highest upbuilding of all peoples in their great ideal of human brotherhood."[59]

Nor was Du Bois consistent in his views on race differences. Earlier, while never accepting any idea of Negro inferiority, he had referred to Negroes as a backward, childlike, undeveloped race, and he had accepted the idea of inherent racial differences. But in March 1908 he attacked the "glib" Darwinist interpretations about undeveloped races and the survival of the fittest. After the Universal Races Congress in London in 1911 Du Bois enthusiastically reported its conclusion that there was no proven connection between race and mental or cultural characteristics. Yet in 1913 he harked back to the idea of inherent racial differences and described the Negro as primarily an artist, possessing a "sensuous nature . . . the only race which has held at bay the life destroying forces of the tropics," gaining thereby an unusual aesthetic sensitivity. This quality explained the artistic achievements of the Egyptians and the Ommiads, the literature of Pushkin, the bronze work of Benin, and the "only real American music."[60]

As a matter of fact Du Bois maintained his strong feeling of identification with other colored peoples, especially Africans. At one time he was secretary of a company which aimed to participate in the economic advancement of East Africa. Years before Melville J. Herskovits cited anthropological evidence for African origins of the culture of American Negroes,

[58] *Negro American Artisan* (AUP No. 17, 1913), 128–29; E. H. Clement to Du Bois [Dec.? 1907], Dec. 18, 1907, and Du Bois to Clement, Dec. 10 and 30, 1907; *Economic Co-Operation among Negro Americans* (AUP No. 12, 1907), 12; *Crisis*, XV (Nov., 1917), 9; *Crisis*, V (Jan., 1913), 184–86.

[59] "The Marrying of Black Folk," *Independent*, LXIX (Oct. 13, 1910), 812–13.

[60] *Philadelphia Negro*, 359: "Relations of Negroes to the Whites of the South," 121–22; *The Souls of Black Folk* (Chicago, 1903), 50; *Horizon*, III (March, 1908), 5–6; *Crisis*, II (Aug., 1911), 157–58; "The Negro in Literature and Art," in *The Negro's Progress in Fifty Years* (Annals of the American Academy of Political and Social Science, XXXIX [Sept., 1913]), 233–37.

Du Bois held that their religious life and institutions, family life, burial and beneficial societies, the roots of economic co-operation, and the skill of Negro artisans all had their origins in Africa. Finally, *The Negro,* published in 1915, dealt with Negro history from ancient Egypt to the United States and was especially notable for its discussion of the history and culture of West Africa. In it he also adopted the Italian anthropologist Giuseppe Sergi's thesis that an ancient rather dark-skinned race spawned all of the ancient Mediterranean civilizations. Moreover, he predicted the emergence of a pan-African movement, uniting Negroes everywhere, and a growing unity of the darker races against the intolerable treatment accorded them by the white man. Since the colored races were in a majority, the future world would probably be what colored men make it, and "in the character of the Negro race is the best and greatest hope. For in its normal condition it is at once the strongest and gentlest of the races of men."[61]

A new theme in the pages of the *Horizon* and *Crisis* was Du Bois' interest in the labor movement and in socialism. At one time he had viewed the white working class as the Negro's "bitterest opponent." By 1904 he had come to believe that economic discrimination was in large part the cause of the race problem, and to feel sympathetic toward the socialist movement. Three years later, he was writing favorably of the socialists in the *Horizon.* Elsewhere he advised the socialists that their movement could not succeed unless it included the Negro workers, and wrote that it was simply a matter of time before white and black workers would see their common economic cause against the exploiting capitalists. Though in 1908 Du Bois did not vote for the socialists because they had no chance of winning, in 1911 he joined the party. In a Marxist exegesis in the concluding pages of *The Negro,* Du Bois viewed both American Negroes and Africans, both the white workers and the colored races, as exploited by white capital which employed the notion of race differences as a rationalization of exploitation, segregation, and subordination. And he predicted that the exploited of all races would unite and overthrow white capital, their common oppressor.[62]

Du Bois' espousal of the cause of labor was so deep-seated that he had the *Crisis* printed by members of a union that did not admit Negroes, and in its pages he welcomed the rare signs that white and Negro workers might be getting together. In this regard he was certainly ahead of his time,

[61] Circular of African Development Company, March 1, 1902; Melville J. Herskovits, *Myth of the Negro Past* (New York, 1941); *The Negro Church* (AUP No. 6, 1903), 5–6; *The Negro American Artisan,* 24; *The Negro American Family* (AUP No. 13, 1908), 10–17; *Economic Co-Operation Among Negro Americans,* 12–14; *The Negro* (New York, 1915), chap. ii, 241–242; Sergi, *The Mediterranean Race* (London, 1901).

[62] *The Negro Artisan,* 25; Du Bois to I. M. Rubinow, No. 17, 1904; *Horizon,* I (Feb., 1907), 7–8; "A Field for Socialists," MS [1907–9]; "The Economic Revolution in the South," in BTW and Du Bois, *The Negro in the South* (Philadelphia, 1907), 116; Du Bois to Mr. Owens, April 17, 1908; Elliott Rudwick to author, July 17, 1954; *The Negro,* 238–41. Note also his Marxist, economic interpretation in his first novel, *The Quest of the Silver Fleece,* 1911.

and even he finally expressed discouragement after the 1917 East St. Louis riot in which unionists played such a striking role.[63] Thus Du Bois' attempts to woo union labor had succeeded no better than his related attempt to woo the Democratic party. . . . But Du Bois never gave up his vision of a union of white and black workers creating a society of economic and racial justice. He had in fact shifted from pinning his faith on the intellectuals or talented tenth of professional and business men to pinning it on the actions of the black working classes, though quite likely they were to be led, as has been suggested, by a talented-tenth intelligentsia.[64]

In W. E. B. Du Bois then, the most distinguished Negro intellectual in the age of Booker T. Washington, we find explicity stated most of the threads of Negro thought at that time. On the one hand he had a mystic sense of race and of the mission of the Negro, which made him sympathetic toward ideas of racial pride and solidarity as sentiments useful for racial uplift. On the other hand he held explicitly and constantly, especially after 1901, to the ideal of waging a struggle for full acceptance in American society. While at times he seemed to view segregated institutions as good in themselves, actually he regarded them as second-best instruments in the struggle for advancement and citizenship rights. He envisaged not amalgamation but cultural pluralism as the goal. He was inconsistent on the question of innate race differences, but he never admitted that Negroes were inferior. Above all he insisted that Negroes wanted to be both Negroes and Americans, maintaining their racial integrity while associating on the freest terms with all American citizens, participating in American culture in its broadest sense, and contributing to it in fullest freedom.

It is notable that though Du Bois expressed the views held by most of the articulate Negroes of the age of Booker T. Washington, both in his stress on racial solidarity and economic co-operation and in his demand for full citizenship rights, nevertheless he frequently found himself in the minority. Few articulate Negroes exhibited the same extent of political independence; not many Northern Negroes agreed with his accommodating tactic of the late nineteenth century; relatively few championed the cause of liberal education as enthusiastically as he did; few either dared or cared to follow him in the extent to which he championed the protest movement during the first years of the twentieth century; and few embraced socialism or the cause of the black workers and interracial working-class solidarity. It is important to note, however, that many times people, who at heart agreed with his point of view, were not courageous enough to flout the power structure both within and outside of the Negro community as he did.

Of the great trio of Negro leaders, Douglass was the orator, Du Bois the polished writer, and Washington the practical man of affairs. Like Douglass, Du Bois has been known primarily as a protest leader, though he

---

[63] *Crisis,* XVI (1918), 216–17.

[64] Elliott Rudwick to author, Nov. 14, 1955.

was not as consistent in this role as Douglass. Like Douglass, too, he exhibited a marked oscillation in his ideologies—in fact his was more marked than that of Douglass. Like Douglass he clearly stated the ultimate goals which Washington obscured. Yet Du Bois displayed more of a sense of racial solidarity than Douglass usually did. Nor did he envisage the degree of amalgamation and the loss of racial consciousness that Douglass regarded as the *summum bonum*. On the contrary he, like Washington, emphasized race pride and solidarity and economic chauvinism, though after 1905 he no longer championed support of the individualist entrepreneur but favored instead a co-operative economy. Where Washington wanted to make Negroes entrepreneurs and captains of industry in accordance with the American economic dream (a dream shared with less emphasis by Douglass), Du Bois stressed the role of the college-educated elite and later developed a vision of a world largely dominated by the colored races which would combine with the white workers in overthrowing the domination of white capital and thus secure social justice under socialism. All three emphasized the moral values in American culture and the necessity of justice for the Negro if the promise of American life were to be fulfilled. But of the three men it was Douglass who was pre-eminently the moralist, while Washington and Du Bois expressed sharply divergent economic interpretations. Where Douglass and Washington were primarily petit-bourgeois in their outlook, Du Bois played the role of the Marxist intelligentsia. Where the interest of Douglass and Washington in Africa was largely perfunctory, Du Bois exhibited a deep sense of racial identity with Africans. Above all, though only Douglass favored amalgamation, all three had as their goal the integration of Negroes into American society.

Scholar and prophet; mystic and materialist; ardent agitator for political rights and propagandist for economic co-operation; one who espoused an economic interpretation of politics and yet emphasized the necessity of political rights for economic advancement; one who denounced segregation and called for integration into American society in accordance with the principles of human brotherhood and the ideals of democracy, and at the same time one who favored the maintenance of racial solidarity and integrity and a feeling of identity with Negroes elsewhere in the world; an equalitarian who apparently believed in innate racial differences; a Marxist who was fundamentally a middle-class intellectual, Du Bois becomes the epitome of the paradoxes in American Negro thought. In fact, despite his early tendencies toward an accommodating viewpoint, and despite his strong sense of race solidarity and integrity, Du Bois expressed more effectively than any of his contemporaries the protest tendency in Negro thought, and the desire for citizenship rights and integration into American society.

# 21

## THE NATIONAL AFRO-AMERICAN LEAGUE, 1887–1908
*Emma Lou Thornbrough*

TODAY, almost a century after the abolition of slavery in the United States, the fight to secure equal civil and political rights for Negroes continues. For half a century the most conspicuous part in the fight has been played by the National Association for the Advancement of Colored People, but it was not the first organization with this objective. In the latter part of the nineteenth century there were several unsuccessful and almost forgotten attempts at permanent organizations to fight against racial discrimination. Of these the most important was the National Afro-American League, which was later revived as the National Afro-American Council. So completely has this organization been forgotten that the best general history of the Negro in the United States does not even mention it, but speaks of the Niagara Movement, founded in 1905, as "the first organized attempt to raise the Negro protest against the great reaction after the Reconstruction."[1]

The dominant figure in the Afro-American League was T. Thomas Fortune, editor of the New York *Age,* who was regarded by his contemporaries as the most able Negro journalist of his day. Although he made his reputation in the North, Fortune knew from personal experience what it was to be a Negro in the South during the Reconstruction and post-Reconstruction era. Born a slave in 1856, he saw the Ku Klux Klan in action as a boy in Marianna, Florida, the scene of some of its worst outrages. With little formal education, but with practical knowledge of the printer's trade, Fortune came to New York in 1879. Soon after his arrival he became part owner and editor of his own newspaper, the *Globe,* which later became the *Freeman,* and finally the *Age.* The reputation of the *Age* as the best Negro paper of its day rested principally on the editorial page, which was an expression of Fortune's views and personality. His editorials, sometimes bitter, sometimes sardonically humorous, in their denunciation of all forms of racial discrimination, attracted comment in the white press in both the North and the South.[2]

Emma Lou Thornbrough, "The National Afro-American League, 1887–1908," *Journal of Southern History,* XXVII (November 1961), 494–512. Copyright © 1961 by the Southern Historical Association. Reprinted by permission of the Managing Editor.

[1] John Hope Franklin, *From Slavery to Freedom; a History of American Negroes* (2nd ed., New York, 1956), 438. See also Elliott M. Rudwick, "The Niagara Movement," *Journal of Negro History,* XLII (July 1957), 177.

[2] There is a short sketch of Fortune's career in Cyrus Field Adams, "Timothy Thomas Fortune: Journalist, Author, Lecturer, Agitator," *Colored American Magazine,* IV (January–February 1902), 224–28. During the nineties Fortune wrote regularly for the New York *Sun.* He later contributed editorials to the Boston *Transcript.*

In 1887, just ten years after the end of Reconstruction, Fortune called upon Negroes to form an organization to fight for the rights denied them. The legal status of Negroes was not yet as degraded as it was to become in a few years, but the guarantees of the Fourteenth and Fifteenth amendments were already being widely ignored in the South, and in the North there was generally acquiescence in this state of affairs. In an editorial in the *Freeman* of May 28, 1887, Fortune said,

*We think that it has been thoroughly demonstrated that the white papers of this country have determined to leave the colored man to fight his own battles. . . . There is no dodging the issue; we have got to take hold of this problem ourselves, and make so much noise that all the world shall know the wrongs we suffer and our determination to right these wrongs.*

He called for the organization of the National Afro-American League and listed six principal grievances which the organization should combat. First on the list he put the suppression of voting rights in the South, which, he said, had the effect of denying Negroes a voice in the government in the very states in which they were most numerous. Second he attacked "the universal and lamentable reign of lynch and mob law," which was all the more outrageous because it existed in states where the lawmaking and law enforcing machinery were in the hands of the persons who resorted to these lawless methods. The third grievance was the inequities in the distribution of funds between white and colored schools. The fourth was "the odious and demoralizing penitentiary system of the South, with its chain gangs, convict leases, and indiscriminate mixing of males and females." Fifth was the "tyranny" practiced by Southern railroads, which denied equal rights to colored passengers and permitted white passengers to subject them to indignities. Sixth, and last, was the denial of accommodations to Negroes in such places as hotels and theaters.[3]

Except for the last, all of the grievances were either peculiar to the Southern states or were more aggravated in that region than in the North. Because the most serious injustices were found in the South and because the bulk of the Negro population lived there, Fortune felt that the stronghold of the organization should be in the South, while in the North its principal function would be to arouse public opinion and to exert political pressure. He recognized the peculiar difficulties to be faced in setting up such an organization where freedom of speech and assembly on the part of Negroes were curtailed. He admitted that Southern members might be subjected to personal danger. He even intimated that the use of force might be necessary under some circumstances when he said,

[3] New York *Freeman*, June 4, 1887; T. Thomas Fortune, *Black and White: Land, Labor, and Politics in the South* (New York, 1884), 70. See also Fortune, "Who Are We? Afro-Americans, Colored People, or Negroes?" *Voice of the Negro*, III (March 1906), 194–98. Although Fortune had written on the injustice and extravagance of the separate school systems, he did not propose to use the League in fighting school segregation.

*We propose to accomplish our purpose by the peaceful methods of agita-tation, through the ballot and the courts, but if others use the weapons of violence to combat our peaceful arguments it is not for us to run away from violence.*

Later, realizing that his advocacy of violence would probably prove fatal to the cause he was trying to promote, Fortune retreated. In an article explaining the constitution which he proposed for the League, he explained that the purpose should be "to secure the ends desired through peaceable and lawful means" and that members who engaged in acts of violence might be expelled.[4]

A large part of the Negro press in both the North and the South as well as a few prominent individuals at once gave enthusiastic support to the League idea. From Tuskegee Institute in Alabama, youthful and still relatively unknown Booker T. Washington wrote, "Push the battle to the gate. Let there be no hold-up until a League shall be found in every vil-lage."[5] But other Southern Negroes warned of the dangers and practical difficulties involved in attempting such a movement in the South. A Negro member of the Florida legislature, T. V. Gibbs, explained his reasons for doubting the success of the proposed League. First of all, he said, in the places where the need for such an organization was most acute, colored people would be too ignorant and too dependent to maintain it. Because of his economic dependency a Negro was unable to stand on an equal footing with the "land owning, contract making, figuring white man." He summed up the situation by saying, "The whites have money, arms, educa-tion, the courts and the machinery of government—the colored people have none of them." He admitted that from a Northern standpoint his position would probably seem "weak and pusillanimous," but, he insisted, "facts are facts, and he is not a wise man who does not heed their deduc-tions."[6]

A few white journals in the South took notice of Fortune's proposal. The Charleston, South Carolina, *News and Courier* warned,

*The colored people it is certain, have nothing whatever to gain by organiza-tion in the race or color line. This merely strengthens racial divisions . . . and strengthens the very groups who are strongest in their opposition to the very rights which Negroes are demanding.*

The Atlanta *Constitution* declared, "There is no conceivable direction in which an organization can do the Negro race any good, and it might do

[4] New York *Freeman*, June 4, September 10, 1887.

[5] *Ibid.*, June 18, 1887.

[6] *Ibid.*, July 23, 1887. The Jacksonville, Florida, *Southern Leader* called Fortune's proposal a "wild scheme, and one that would result in more harm than good" and warned that the League "would intensify rather than allay race troubles in the South." Quoted in New York *Freeman*, June 25, 1887.

great harm." In the North, in *Harper's Weekly,* George William Curtis gave qualified approval to the League idea, but pointed out that lawsuits, which would have to be the chief weapon of the organization, would require money. Failure to raise the necessary funds would do further harm to the reputation of Negroes by furnishing evidence of their alleged lack of practical ability.[7]

Fortune's plan was to organize local and state leagues before attempting to effect a national organization. In the months following his initial proposal, local leagues of varying size and strength were formed—in New England, Pennsylvania, New York, Illinois, Minnesota, and even in distant San Francisco. In the South organizations were attempted in Virginia, Texas, North Carolina, Tennessee, and Georgia.[8] In January 1890, one hundred forty-one delegates from twenty-three states assembled in Chicago to form a permanent national organization. As might have been expected, the largest numbers were from states in the Chicago area, but somehow seven persons from Georgia managed to attend, and South Carolina, North Carolina, Texas, Tennessee, and Virginia were also represented. It was an all-Negro meeting. No effort had been made to invite interested white persons. A few whites, among them the novelist Albion W. Tourgée, sent messages of good will, but even such expressions were viewed with suspicion by some of the delegates, who were convinced that white men interested themselves in the affairs of Negroes only to dominate them.[9]

Fortune as temporary chairman of the convention made a long, earnest, and carefully prepared address in which he reviewed earlier examples of man's long fight against tyranny and oppression and called upon his listeners to continue the struggle in behalf of members of their race in America. He cried,

*We have been patient so long that many believe that we are incapable of resenting insult, outrage and wrong; we have so long accepted uncomplainingly all the injustice and cowardice and insolence heaped upon us, that many imagine that we are compelled to submit and have not the manhood necessary to resent such conduct.*

He ended on a solemn note:

*As the agitation which culminated in the abolition of African slavery in this country covered a period of fifty years, so may we expect that before the rights conferred upon us by the war amendments are fully conceded, a full century will have passed away. We have undertaken no child's play. We*

[7] Charleston *News and Courier,* quoted in New York *Freeman,* October 8, 1887; Atlanta *Constitution,* quoted in the New York *Freeman,* July 23, 1887; *Harper's Weekly,* XXXI (October 1, 1887), 703.

[8] New York *Freeman,* September 10, October 8, 1887; New York *Age,* October 5, 12, 1889.

[9] *Ibid.,* January 25, February 1, 1890; Indianapolis *Freeman,* February 1, 1890.

*have undertaken a serious work which will tax and exhaust the best intelligence of the race for the next century.*[10]

The convention adopted a constitution along the lines which Fortune recommended. It declared that the objects of the League should be attained "by the creation of a healthy public opinion through the medium of the press and the pulpit, public meetings and addresses, and by appealing to the courts of law for redress of all denial of legal rights." One article stated that the League was a nonpartisan body and provided that any officer of the League who was elected or appointed to a political post must resign his League office. Fortune insisted that the organization must refrain from identifying itself in any way with partisan politics in order to prevent it from being used as a mere adjunct of the Republican party as most earlier Negro organizations had been. His insistence upon this point undoubtedly was the reason that few prominent Negro politicians supported the League and one of the reasons why the League did not attract a greater following.[11]

In electing a president the convention passed over Fortune, probably because some of the delegates feared that he was too militant and because they considered him a political maverick, and chose instead a Southern Negro, Joseph C. Price, president of Livingston College in North Carolina. William A. Pledger of Georgia became vice-president, and Fortune secretary.[12]

The proceedings of the convention received some attention in the Northern press, not all of it favorable. Among the Chicago papers the *Tribune* spoke disparagingly of Fortune's address as an "oily harangue" and characterized him as "a tricky New York coon" who was playing the part of "a Democratic decoy duck." A St. Louis paper insisted that the convention did not represent "the decent Negroes of the South." It considered the Southern Negro a useful member of society, but a Northern Negro, like Fortune, who called himself an "Afro-American," it considered a "ridiculous blatherskite." The *Nation* accused the convention of seeking "class legislation" and expressed the opinion that such gatherings as the one in Chicago only strengthened the growing resentment against Negroes. On the other hand the New York *Sun*, speaking of the League, said, "The attempt may not succeed, but the object is entirely legitimate and respectable. The colored citizens are only exercising their rights as citizens to organize, agitate, cooperate."[13]

[10] Fortune, "Why We Organize a National Afro-American League," *Afro-American Budget*, I (February 1890), 231, 240.

[11] *Ibid.,* 240; Indianapolis *Freeman*, January 18, 1890; Indianapolis *World*, January 25, 1890. At the second national convention the constitution was amended to allow the League to take any political action which was regarded as being for the good of the race, and the ban on political office holding by League officers was also dropped. New York *Age*, July 25, 1891.

[12] Indianapolis *Freeman*, February 1, 1890; Indianapolis *World*, January 25, 1890.
[13] Chicago *Tribune*, St. Louis *Republic*, New York *Sun*, quoted in New York *Age*, February 8, 1890; *Nation*, L (February 13, 1890), 123.

In spite of the fact that the Chicago meeting appeared to be a success, the League lacked vitality and failed to attract mass support. At a second national meeting held in Knoxville in 1891, only a handful of delegates showed up. Those who came paid their own expenses because the local leagues lacked funds. Fortune was elected president of the languishing organization, but he was unable to carry out any part of the program he had envisaged when he first proposed the League.[14] He had pinned his hopes upon a test case to attract attention and win support for the League, but all of his efforts in this direction were frustrated. Serious consideration was given to instituting a case after a member of the Afro-American League who was traveling by railroad in Tennessee was compelled to leave a Pullman car and ride in the Jim Crow coach. But plans for the suit were dropped because the League treasury was empty, and, as Fortune pointed out, it was "tomfoolery" for a group without funds to try to sue a railroad.[15]

In August 1893 Fortune announced that the League was defunct because of lack of funds, lack of mass support, and lack of support from race leaders. He declared himself thoroughly discouraged and disillusioned and expressed the opinion that the attempt to organize the League had been premature.[16] But as the condition of Southern Negroes continued to worsen, as lynchings increased and the disfranchisement movement gained strength, there were calls for a revival of the League. At a meeting in Rochester, New York, in September 1898, it was agreed to reconstitute the organization and to adopt a statement of objectives almost identical with the original platform of the League.[17] The revised organization, which took the same name of National Afro-American Council, included in its membership most of the prominent Negroes of the day and received much more attention in the white press than had the League, but its achievements were few, and, like the League, it failed to win a following among the Negro masses.

During this second phase three men were dominant. The ostensible leaders were Fortune and Alexander Walters, a bishop of the African Methodist Episcopal Zion Church, who had been active in the Afro-American League in New York City, and who took the initiative in calling the meeting in Rochester. Between them the two men held the presidency

[14] New York *Age,* July 25, 1891.

[15] *Ibid.,* August 8, September 5, 19, 1891. At an informal meeting with Fortune and the Rev. W. H. Heard, the man who had been evicted from the Pullman car, representatives of the Pullman Company agreed to discharge the offending Pullman conductor and reimburse Heard for the price of his ticket. *Ibid.,* September 19, October 3, 10, 1891.

[16] Washington *Bee,* August 19, 1893; Indianapolis *World,* August 26, 1893; New York *Sun,* May 17, 1897.

[17] Alexander Walters, *My Life and Work* (New York, 1917), 98–102; Indianapolis *Freeman,* September 3, 1898; New York *Sun,* September 15–16, 1898; Mrs. N. F. Mosell, "The National Afro-American Council," *Colored American Magazine,* III (August 1901), 291–95; Washington *Evening Star,* December 29, 1898.

and the chairmanship of the executive committee during almost the entire history of the Council.[18] In the background loomed the enigmatic figure of Booker T. Washington, who since 1895 had been acclaimed by the white press as a kind of official leader and spokesman for the entire Negro population. Washington held no office in the Council and only occasionally attended meetings, but his influence was great and pervasive. The fact that the Council was identified with him was the reason some Negroes supported it and accounted in part for the publicity which the Council received. On the other hand there were Negroes who held aloof and attacked the Council because of hostility to Washington.

To most of his contemporaries Washington was the symbol of the conservative, compromising, conciliatory approach to race problems. In his published writings and utterances he gave priority to economic progress and self-help as means for improving the status of Negroes. He deprecated emphasis upon political activity and made statements which could be interpreted as indicating acquiescence in disfranchisement. Behind the scenes he worked secretly against segregation, disfranchisement, and the Lily White movement, and was himself to become a powerful figure in the administration of Theodore Roosevelt. These particular activities were so carefully concealed that only a few persons were aware of them, and Washington was constantly under attack by Negro intellectuals who accused him of a willingness to betray his race and a willingness to accept second-class citizenship for Southern Negroes. Washington himself sedulously sought to silence or discredit his critics and to preserve a façade of racial solidarity and unanimous support for his leadership.[19] The history of the Afro-American Council, which Washington sought to dominate, was inextricably linked with the fight over Washington as race leader. Almost every convention of the Council became a battleground between supporters and opponents of the Tuskegee Wizard with the result that other issues tended to be obscured or confused.

Throughout the history of the Council, Washington and Fortune, who had become friends soon after Washington went to Tuskegee, were on terms of intimacy. In spite of marked differences in temperament and personality there was a strong bond of mutual admiration and affection between the two men, and for years Fortune was one of Washington's

[18] After Fortune refused to accept the presidency of the Council at the Rochester meeting, Walters was elected. Washington *Colored American,* September 24, October 1, 1898. Walters held the presidency for seven terms.

[19] August Meier, "Toward a Reinterpretation of Booker T. Washington," *Journal of Southern History,* XXIII (May 1957), 220–27. My own research in the Booker T. Washington Papers (Division of Manuscripts, Library of Congress) leads me to the same conclusions as those of Meier. For Washington's efforts to influence the Negro press and his efforts to conceal these efforts, see Meier, "Booker T. Washington and the Negro Press: With Special References to the *Colored American Magazine,*" *Journal of Negro History,* XXXVIII (January 1953), 67–90, and Emma L. Thornbrough, "More Light on Booker T. Washington and the New York Age," *ibid.,* XLIII (January 1958), 34–49.

closest confidants. Although Fortune was by nature militant and impatient with compromise, he felt that he and Washington were in agreement as to ultimate objectives and admitted that residence in the South imposed peculiar restraints upon Washington.[20] In later years the friendship of the two was punctuated by violent quarrels behind the scenes, but publicly they continued to co-operate and Fortune continued to defend Washington against his critics. Because of his support of Washington, Fortune, who a few years earlier had been the symbol of aggressive, militant race leadership, came increasingly under attack by Negro intellectuals and the anti-Washington press which labeled him as Washington's subservient tool. Washington's relations with Bishop Walters were never as close as they were with Fortune. At times Walters appeared to waver and to move in the direction of the anti-Washington group, but for the most part he co-operated with the Tuskegeean and helped to promote the appearance of racial solidarity under Washington's leadership.

Washington's critics were openly active at the second national convention of the Afro-American Council, which met in Chicago in August 1899. One whole session was consumed in debating resolutions condemning him, none of which was adopted. W. E. B. Du Bois of Atlanta University, later to become one of Washington's leading opponents, took an active part in the convention but was careful to dissociate himself from the anti-Washington group. He told newspaper reporters that attacks upon Washington did not represent the true spirit of the convention and that he personally would be "very sorry if it went out into the world that this convention had said anything detrimental to one of the greatest men of our race."[21]

In 1900 Washington was accused of attempting to undercut the Afro-American Council by calling a meeting in Boston to organize the National Negro Business League just prior to the date on which the Council convention was to meet in Indianapolis. The Chicago *Conservator*, one of his staunchest critics, declared that Washington, "instead of going to Indianapolis and helping Prof. Du Bois and the Council," had called an "opposition meeting" which would be injurious to the Council. It concluded, "It looks like Mr. Washington is determined to help no movement he does not inaugurate."[22]

Whatever Washington's misgivings about the Council may have been in 1900, two years later his influence there was clearly in the ascendancy. At the convention in St. Paul in 1902, the first he attended, a slate of officers

[20] The voluminous correspondence between Fortune and Washington in the Washington Papers furnishes abundant evidence as to the intimacy of their relationship. See the Boston *Globe*, January 14, 1899, for an interview with Fortune in which he compared Washington's approach to the race problem with his own.

[21] Undated clipping from Springfield *Republican* in Washington Papers; Chicago *Tribune*, August 20, 1899.

[22] Chicago *Conservator*, quoted in Indianapolis *Freeman*, July 14, 1900.

friendly to him was elected, with Fortune made president. In a letter to Washington, his private secretary gloated over the discomfiture of Du Bois and Ida Wells Barnett at their inability to control the convention. He exulted,

*It is not hard for you to understand that we control the Council now. . . . It was wonderful to see how completely your personality dominated every-thing at St. Paul.*[23]

Negro newspapers opposed to Washington were less pleased. The Negro *Guardian*, organ of Washington's most vitriolic critic, Harvard gradu-ate Monroe Trotter, declared that Fortune would be president in name only—that the real power would be wielded by Washington.

*It is well known* [the Guardian *asserted*], *that Fortune is only a "me too" to whatever Washington aspires to do.*

*These two men have long since formed themselves into one twain in their dealings with the Negro race, Fortune furnishing whatever brain the combination needs, and Washington the boodle.*[24]

At the 1903 convention in Louisville where Fortune was re-elected, Trotter made a bitter attack upon Washington from the floor but was shouted down when he tried to introduce a series of resolutions against the Tuskegeean. Meanwhile Du Bois, whom Trotter had criticized after the 1902 convention for not challenging Washington, had by now openly aligned himself with Washington's critics.[25]

While leaders fought among themselves for control of the Afro-American Council, the rank and file of the Negro population remained

[23] Scott to Washington, July 17, 1902, in Washington Papers. At this meeting Scott replaced W. E. B. Du Bois as head of the business bureau of the Council. Ida Wells had attended the Knoxville meeting of the Afro-American League in 1891. In 1898 (after her marriage to Ferdinand Barnett) she participated in the Rochester meeting of the Council and served as secretary of the Council until 1902. She was later one of the six Negroes who signed the call for the formation of the NAACP.

[24] Boston *Guardian*, quoted in Washington *Bee*, July 26, 1902. The *Bee* said of the Council convention: "The 'Wizard of Tuskegee' was there. . . . His satellites were in the saddle. . . . They trotted and pranced as he pulled the reins and his ticket was elected and his namby-pamby policy . . . was incorporated into the address, which was nothing more than a pronouncement of his nibs, the boss of Negro beggars." For an account of Trotter see Charles W. Puttkamer and Ruth Worthy, "William Monroe Trotter, 1872–1934," *Journal of Negro History*, XLIII (October 1958), 298–316.

[25] Louisville *Herald*, July 4, 1903; Louisville *Evening Post*, July 3, 1903; Francis L. Broderick, *W. E. B. Du Bois, Negro Leader in a Time of Crisis* (Stanford, Calif., 1959), 68–72. A few weeks later when Washington and Fortune were in Boston to address a gathering Trotter created such a disturbance that the meeting was disrupted. Trotter was arrested for disturb-ing the peace and sentenced to a month in jail. The anti-Washington press made a martyr of Trotter as the result of his arrest. Boston *Transcript*, July 31, 1903; Boston *Globe*, July 31, 1903; Washington *Bee*, August 8, 1903; New York *Age*, November 5, 1903.

indifferent. The Council was having little more success than the earlier League in attracting members. Few of the local councils were active or had any real vitality, and none of them gave more than nominal financial support to the national organization. Early in 1904 Fortune went on a lecture tour in New York State and the Middle West for the purpose of organizing local councils and raising funds. He returned thoroughly discouraged, having spent on his personal expenses fifty dollars more than he was able to raise for the Council. Soon afterwards he resigned from the presidency of the Council, partly because of his discouragement over the apathy of the masses, partly as the result of one of his bitter, periodic quarrels with Washington. In his letter of resignation he declared that race leaders had done what they could, "with small response from the masses of the race, to stem the fearful tide of civil and political and material degradation of the race to a condition of pariahs in the citizenship of the Republic." Of himself he said,

*I have grown old and impoverished in the lone struggle, and I must now take heed to my age and precarious health and devote my time and energies to repairing my personal fortunes in the interest of my immediate family.*[26]

Torn as it was by internal dissension and, more important, lacking adequate financial support, the Council made little progress in carrying forward the fight for racial equality. Every convention adopted resolutions embodying very much the same list of grievances against which Fortune had complained when he first called for the organization of the Afro-American League. At the top of the list was usually the denial of voting rights to Negroes. For example, the address to the nation adopted at the first convention of the Council in 1898 called attention to the persistent attempts to eliminate the Negro from politics in the South and declared,

*We are not to be eliminated. Suffrage is a federal guarantee and not a privilege to be conferred or withheld by the States. We contend for the principle of manhood suffrage as the most effective safeguard of citizenship.*[27]

But members of the Council disagreed among themselves as to the best method of implementing this declaration. One group insisted that the most effective way of forcing Southern states to permit Negroes to vote was to enforce the clause in the Fourteenth Amendment which provided for reduction of representation in the House of Representatives and in the Electoral College for states which limited the voting rights of citizens over twenty-one. Fortune was strongly opposed to this approach. He insisted

[26] Fortune to Scott, January 13, 21, 1904, in Washington Papers; Indianapolis *Freeman*, January 30, 1904; New York *Age*, October 25, 1905; Fortune, "The Quick and the Dead," *A.M.E. Review*, XXI (April 1916), 248–49.

[27] Washington *Evening Star*, December 31, 1898.

that for the Council to endorse reduction of representation would give the impression that they acquiesced in disfranchisement and would give color to the idea that a state could legally disfranchise part of its citizens. Both Walters and Washington were won over to Fortune's position, and Washington in turn persuaded President Theodore Roosevelt not to recommend reduction of Southern representation.[28] But Washington and Fortune were not always in complete agreement as to the position which the Council should take with regard to suffrage. Washington at various times indicated that he was not opposed to literacy and property requirements for voting if applied in the same way to both blacks and whites and not used merely for the purpose of disfranchising Negroes while permitting the illiterate and propertyless whites to vote. Doubtless as the result of Washington's influence the address adopted in 1898, mentioned above, while endorsing the principle of manhood suffrage, stated that the Council was not opposed to "legitimate restrictions of the suffrage," provided they applied to citizens of all states.[29] In an editorial in the Age just before the Louisville convention of the Council in 1903, Fortune asserted that he and Washington differed on the suffrage question and denied that he had ever been in agreement with accepting educational or property requirements. He declared that the right of voting was fundamental to citizenship and that it should be protected by the federal government and that control of federal elections should be taken away from the states. He prepared an address for delivery in Louisville in which he said that all the wrongs which Negroes suffered grew out of the abridgment of voting rights. The text of the speech appeared in the Louisville newspapers, but apparently it was not actually delivered. Washington's critics insisted that the speech had been suppressed at his orders.[30] On the floor of the convention Washington once more reiterated that he had no objection to the disfranchisement of the ignorant Negro, "provided the same class of the other race is similarly dealt with," but he admitted that the purpose of suffrage measures recently adopted in the South was primarily to disfranchise Negroes.[31]

[28] Fortune to Washington, February 20, 1900; Washington to Fortune, November 22, 1902; John E. Milholland to Washington, January 17, 1905, in Washington Papers; Washington Evening Star, December 30, 1898; New York Age, January 4, 1900, December 29, 1904, January 26, 1905.

[29] Washington Evening Star, December 31, 1898. Washington's views were set forth in a letter which he addressed to the Louisiana Convention in 1898 when it was considering the voting question. He said: "The negro agrees with you that it is necessary for the salvation of the South that restrictions be put upon the ballot. . . . The negro does not object to an educational or property test, but let the law be so clear that no one clothed with State authority will be tempted to perjure and degrade himself by putting one interpretation upon it for the white man and another for the black man. . . ." New Orleans Times Democrat, February 21, 1898.

[30] New York Age, July 2, 1903; Louisville Herald, July 2, 1903; Washington Bee, July 11, 1903; Boston Guardian, July 11, 1903.

[31] Louisville Herald, July 4, 1903.

In spite of the restraining influence which he seems to have exercised in the matter of Fortune's speech and other public pronouncements made in the name of the Council, behind the scenes Washington lent his support to efforts to initiate test cases against disfranchisement. As early as January 1899, he and Fortune were discussing the possibility of a test of the Louisiana suffrage law of 1898. It was decided that the Afro-American Council of New Orleans should institute a case with the sympathy of the national organization. The services of a group of Negro lawyers were enlisted to prepare a case. Part of the money for the lawyers' fees was furnished by the Council, part of it from Washington's personal funds, and the remainder by white philanthropists to whom Washington appealed. Much time and a considerable sum of money were expended, but the case never actually materialized. Fortune laid the blame for the failure upon the New Orleans attorneys.[32]

The Council took partial credit for bringing to trial a case testing the Alabama voter registration law. The case grew out of the refusal of the registrars of Montgomery County to enroll Negro voters. One of the Negroes sought a court order to compel the officers to register him. When the lower court refused to issue the order, its decision was appealed and reached the United States Supreme Court in 1903. Wilford Smith, who had the distinction of being the only Negro lawyer who had won a case before that court, was employed to prepare the case. The Supreme Court upheld the refusal of the lower court to grant the order. Justice Oliver Wendell Holmes, who wrote the opinion, argued that the wrong complained of was political in nature and hence the remedy for it must be sought through legislation and not through the courts. In the light of this decision Wilford Smith expressed doubt as to whether it would ever be possible to bring a case resulting in a decision which would cause the Fifteenth Amendment to be enforced in a practical way. He was convinced that the most effective way of insuring voting rights would be a federal registration law.[33]

After Fortune's resignation as president in 1904 the Afro-American Council languished, but it was revived in 1905 by a call from Bishop Walters. The call for a revived Council came just after W. E. B. Du Bois and a group of anti-Washington intellectuals launched the Niagara Movement as a militant organization to fight for racial equality. The platform of the new group, including demands for suffrage and civil rights and economic betterment for Negroes, Fortune accused Du Bois of stealing from the declaration of principles which he had framed for the Afro-American League in 1890. Washington, alarmed by the challenge to his leadership which the Niagara Movement represented, sought to undermine

---

[32] Fortune to Washington, December 30, 1899, June 4, 21, 27, July 22, 1901, August 4, 1902, in Washington Papers; Indianapolis *Freeman*, December 29, 1900, July 6, 1901; New York *Age*, October 25, 1906; Meier, "Toward a Reinterpretation of Booker T. Washington," 221.

[33] *Giles* v. *Harris*, 189 U.S. 475 (1903); Meier, "Toward a Reinterpretation of Booker T. Washington," 222; New York *Age*, October 11, 1906.

the new organization by planting spies in its ranks, influencing the Negro press against it, and by persuading white philanthropists not to support it.[34]

Newspapers opposed to Washington interpreted the move to revive the Afro-American Council solely as an effort to counteract the Niagara Movement and declared that the Council was dead.[35] But in spite of its allegedly moribund condition the Council held the largest and most ambitious convention in its history in New York City in 1906. Booker T. Washington, who privately expressed the hope that the convention would adopt a conservative platform, was much in evidence. He gave a characteristic speech in which he condemned inflammatory statements by Northern Negroes and stressed racial harmony, but the general tone of the convention was militant and uncompromising. An innovation was the participation of several white speakers. Among them was Oswald Garrison Villard, later to issue the call resulting in the formation of the National Association for the Advancement of Colored People, who spoke at Washington's invitation. Another was John E. Milholland, president of the Constitutional League, who was to become a vice-president of the NAACP. In spite of previous failures plans were laid to raise funds to continue the fight in the courts against disfranchisement.[36]

The ambitious plans discussed in New York failed to materialize. The Council continued to exist but was little more than a name. In the months following the New York meeting Washington apparently lost interest in the Council. He and Walters, who continued to serve as Council president, did not quarrel openly, but it was evident that Washington's influence over Walters and the Council had waned.[37] Walters made some efforts at rapprochement with the Niagara group. There were newspaper reports that some of the Niagara men were present at the convention of the Afro-American Council in Baltimore in June 1907, and that most of the delegates to the convention "denounced Booker T. Washington as a Judas to his

---

[34] New York Age, July 27, 1905, February 8, 1906; Broderick, W. E. B. Du Bois, 75 ff.; Rudwick, "Niagara Movement," 181–87.

[35] According to the Chicago Conservator no Council meeting would have been called in 1905 if it had not been for the Niagara Movement. Unidentified and undated clipping in Washington Papers.

[36] New York Times, October 10, 1906; New York Press, October 11, 1906; New York Age, October 11, 1906; Washington Post, October 12, 1906; Indianapolis Freeman, November 3, 1906.

[37] President Theodore Roosevelt's action in discharging three companies of Negro troops from the United States Army following disorders at Brownsville, Texas, played a part in bringing about the split between Washington and Walters. Although Washington did not approve of Roosevelt's action, he tried to quiet protests against it. On the other hand Walters and almost all other Negro leaders openly condemned the discharge. The National Afro-American Council employed legal counsel to protect the rights of the discharged troops. Emma Lou Thornbrough, "The Brownsville Episode and the Negro Vote," Mississippi Valley Historical Review, XLIV (December 1957), 473–77, 482; Indianapolis Freeman, December 1, 8, 1906; Cleveland Gazette, December 1, 1906; New York Age, January 17, 1907.

race."[38] By 1908 Bishop Walters had joined the Niagara Movement, and in the political campaign of that year made common cause with Washington's arch enemy, Monroe Trotter, in an unsuccessful effort to swing the Negro vote away from Taft, whom Washington supported.[39] But by this time it was evident that the Niagara Movement had little prospect of becoming an effective force. Du Bois himself admitted that there was less enthusiasm for the movement than there had been at the time of its founding.[40]

In 1909 a group of white persons took the initiative in the formation of the National Association for the Advancement of Colored People. Among the six Negroes who joined in signing the call for the new organization were Bishop Walters, as president of the National Afro-American Council, and Du Bois from the Niagara Movement. At the national conference on the Negro which met in New York City in 1909 and took the preliminary steps in the establishment of the NAACP, resolutions reminiscent of the statements formed by Fortune in 1887 and 1890 were adopted. They demanded:

*(1)   That the Constitution be strictly enforced and the civil rights guaranteed under the Fourteenth Amendment be secured impartially to all.*
*(2)   That there be equal educational opportunities for all . . . , and that public school expenditure be the same for the Negro and the white child.*
*(3)   That in accordance with the Fifteenth Amendment the right of the Negro to the ballot on the same terms as other citizens be recognized in every part of the country.*

Booker T. Washington's name was conspicuously absent from the list of Negroes who participated in the formation of the NAACP. In fact, he tried to undermine the new group.[41] Nor did Fortune have any part in its formation. In 1907 he had suffered a nervous collapse, which was followed by years of mental and physical illness, and he became an almost forgotten figure. But the program of the NAACP, both in its objectives and methods, was essentially the program which Fortune had conceived for the Afro-American League twenty years earlier.[42]

[38] Baltimore *Sun*, June 29, 1907; Baltimore *American*, July 1, 1907. In the New York *Age*, July 18, 1907, Walters denied that there had been any criticism of Washington at the Baltimore meeting.

[39] Herbert Aptheker (ed.), *A Documentary History of the Negro People in the United States* (New York, 1951), 915; Indianapolis *Freeman*, February 22, April 18, 1908.

[40] Rudwick, "The Niagara Movement," 191; Broderick, *W. E. B. Du Bois*, 77–79.

[41] Aptheker (ed.), *Documentary History,* 915; August Meier, "Booker T. Washington and the Rise of the N.A.A.C.P.," *Crisis*, LXI (February 1954), 69–76.

[42] Fortune, who was a victim of alcoholism, lost control of the *Age* in 1907 and became an almost forgotten figure. He lived until 1928, long enough to see some of the early victories of the NAACP.

## SUGGESTIONS FOR
## FURTHER READING

THE single most important study of black thought from Reconstruction to Washington's death in 1915 is *August Meier, *Negro Thought in America, 1880–1915* (Ann Arbor, Mich., 1963). A less successful examination on the same subject, but one that brings the story down to the 1960s is *S. P. Fullinwider, *The Mind and Mood of Black America* (Homewood, Ill., 1969).

A definitive biography of Booker T. Washington has not been published. A brief and laudatory volume is *Samuel R. Spencer, Jr., *Booker T. Washington and the Negro's Place in American Life* (Boston, 1955). Insights into Washington's ideas and activities can be gained from Meier, *Negro Thought;* *Hugh Hawkins (ed.), *Booker T. Washington and His Critics* (Boston, 1955); and from his own writings, for example, *Up From Slavery* (New York, 1901). Louis Harlan, who is editing the Washington papers and writing a study of Washington, has written two interesting essays "Booker T. Washington and the White Man's Burden," *American Historical Review*, LXXI (January 1966) and "Booker T. Washington and the National Negro Business League," in *William G. Shade and Roy C. Herrenkohl (eds.), *Seven on Black* (Philadelphia, 1969).

There are two biographies of Du Bois: *Francis L. Broderick, *W. E. B. Du Bois: Negro Leader in Time of Crisis* (Stanford, Calif., 1959) and *Elliott M. Rudwick, *W. E. B. Du Bois: A Study in Minority Group Leadership* (Philadelphia, 1960). One should also consult Du Bois's early statement of his philosophy, *The Souls of Black Folk* (Chicago, 1903) and his "tentative" autobiography, *Dusk of Dawn* (New York, 1940).

Black protest and organizational activities in the late nineteenth and early twentieth centuries are treated in August Meier and Elliott M. Rudwick, "The Boycott Movement Against Jim Crow Streetcars in the South, 1900–1906," *Journal of American History*, LV (March 1969); Elliott M. Rudwick, "The Niagara Movement," *Journal of Negro History*, XLII (July 1957); Charles Flint Kellogg, *NAACP: A History, 1909–1920* (Baltimore, Md., 1967); and Avrah Strickland, *History of the Chicago Urban League* (Urbana, Ill., 1966).

---

* An asterisk indicates that the book is available in paperback.

# &CHAPTER EIGHT&
# The Black Ghetto

&I N the twentieth century the United States was transformed from a rural into an urban nation. Blacks and whites turned to the city for homes, jobs, and more exciting ways of life. Urban America emerged as the focal point of society and the home of more and more Americans. A bare majority lived in cities in 1920 (51 percent); however, by 1966 some 64 percent of the population resided in urban areas. Black Americans gravitated to cities in large numbers. Though only 19.8 percent lived in cities in 1890, 34 percent did so in 1920 and 70 percent in 1960.

Black settlement in cities has extended to all sections of the nation. In the South, which is the least urbanized region, black urbanites comprised more than one-half (58 percent) of that area's total black population in 1960. Afro-Americans residing in northern and western states have concentrated in cities to an even greater extent and over a longer period of time. As early as 1890 when only 15 percent of southern blacks made their homes in cities, approximately 60 percent of those blacks living in the North and West were classified as urbanites. In the years that followed black residence in cities increased. According to the 1960 census, 95 percent of nonsouthern black Americans resided in urban centers.

Migration from the South is the single most important factor accounting for the growth in the northern and western black population. Beginning in the

1890s blacks deserted the South in substantial numbers. It was not until World War I that white America became aware of this exodus. In the decade from 1910 to 1920 the net migration of blacks from the South was about 450,000. Since 1920 black migration northward, except for the 1930s, has assumed even greater proportions—ranging from approximately 750,000 for the ten-year period between 1920 and 1930 to almost 1,500,000 in the decade between 1950 and 1960.

What accounts for this mass migration of blacks? In selection 22, Louise P. Kennedy in a passage from her study *The Negro Peasant Turns Cityward* focuses on migration during the World War I period and the 1920s. She separates the reasons for black migration into two broad classifications—"pushes" (propelling forces) and "pulls" (attracting forces). Under these categories she includes economic developments, discrimination in the South, natural catastrophies, the use of propaganda to attract blacks to the North, and the effects of World War I. Of particular interest is her assertion that discrimination and mob violence served as "occasional strengthening and accompanying" causes rather than primary motives for the Afro-American outflow from the South.

Upon arriving in the northern city, the newcomer sought a place to live. He usually settled in or on the fringes of the black ghetto. As a result existing black neighborhoods increased in density and size. St. Clair Drake and Horace Cayton in selection 23 devote a portion of their *Black Metropolis* to tracing the evolution of the Chicago black ghetto. Contrary to some impressions, the "Black Belt" existed before the Great Migration of World War I. And Drake and Cayton attribute the major responsibility for its emergence to white attitudes and actions.

Hostile Chicago whites resorted to a diversity of techniques, including in some cases violence, to discourage Afro-Americans from moving into their neighborhoods. Drake and Cayton relate these devices, the antiblack attitudes of many Chicago whites, and the housing shortage, to the violent actions that culminated in the riot of 1919.

Drake and Cayton also concentrate on living conditions in the Chicago black ghetto from the early 1900s to the mid-1940s. It is the too often familiar picture of overcrowding, inadequate municipal services, high sickness and death rates, landlord neglect of housing, and the low economic level of the ghetto majority. Since Drake and Cayton published their findings in 1945, as Karl E. and Alma F. Taeuber's essay makes clear, ghettoization of Chicago blacks has persisted. To facilitate their analysis of racial and ethnic residential patterns in Chicago between 1930 and 1960, the Taeubers employ a "segregation index." Their research leads them to conclude that segregation is far greater among blacks than other ethnic groups. Where residential separation has declined for European immigrants and their descendants, the degree of Afro-American segregation from other groups has remained virtually constant. Even more recent arrivals in Chicago, Puerto Ricans and Mexicans, are less segregated than Afro-Americans.

Finally, the Taeuber's investigation of the reasons for the high segregation rate challenges some long held assumptions about the Afro-American experience in America. They question the beliefs that a high segregation rate for blacks results from their desire to live together and their low socioeconomic status.

# 22

## THE NEGRO PEASANT TURNS CITYWARD
*Louise P. Kennedy*

**T** HE chief factor in producing recent mass movements of southern Negroes to northern cities has been the general economic situation in the North, which furnished an unexpected and irresistible opportunity for colored laborers. Previous to the World War immigrant workmen from Europe had kept pace with the demand for labor in the various industries. Northern Negroes had been largely confined to the fields of domestic and personal service, only a small proportion being found in the manufacturing and mechanical industries. With the beginning of the World War there came an extraordinary expansion of industry in the United States due to European demands for war materials and supplies. The entrance of our own country into the war resulted in further increased industrial activity; new factories sprang up and old ones enlarged their facilities; labor was needed in the shipyards, in the mines, in transportation, and in all the varied industrial pursuits directly or indirectly affected by a state of war.

Along with this increased call for labor of all kinds, there came a marked decrease in the supply of available workers. One of the first effects of the war was the cutting off of immigration from Europe, as is shown by the following table:[1]

| Year | Volume of Immigration | Year | Volume of Immigration |
|------|-----------------------|------|-----------------------|
| 1913 | 1,197,892 | 1916 | 298,826 |
| 1914 | 1,218,480 | 1917 | 295,403 |
| 1915 | 326,700 | 1918 | 110,618 |

At the same time, some of the foreign laborers returned to Europe to join the armies of their native country. Upon the entrance of the United States into the war this shortage of laborers was further intensified by the withdrawal of men from industrial pursuits into military and naval service. Immediately, the workmen who remained had an opportunity to go into the higher paid and more skilled positions, thus creating a particularly urgent demand for unskilled labor. Even after the close of the war and the return of the soldiers to peaceful pursuits, the need for colored laborers continued to exist due to the passage of the 1921 immigration law and

From Louise P. Kennedy, *The Negro Peasant Turns Cityward: Effects of Recent Migrations to Northern Centers* (New York: Columbia University Press, 1930), pp. 42–55. Reprinted by permission of the publisher.

[1] Annual Reports of the Commissioner General of Immigration.

particularly to the law of 1924, which permitted an annual immigration quota of only two per cent of each national group as it existed numerically in this country in 1890.[2] By reducing the supply of immigrant labor this whole situation diminished the strength of the group which had so successfully excluded the Negro from industry and furnished him with an unprecedented opportunity in the northern labor market, an opportunity which involved an increase in the amount of employment available and in the variety of occupations open to him.

Higher wages also formed part of this irresistible call to northern industry, for wages in general throughout the North were materially greater than in the South. To the poorly-paid southern farm hands the wages paid by northern industries—and paid in cold cash by the week or month instead of in store credit once a year—seemed fabulous sums promising speedy wealth and success. In the majority of cases they were too ignorant to comprehend that these unheard-of money wages might be largely offset by increased cost of living; consequently, they responded to the difference as if the northern wage scale represented an actual rather than, perhaps, a nominal increase in real wages. As it happened, they were frequently justified in this attitude, for so great was the wage increase that, in many cases, even the exceedingly higher cost of rent, food and clothing did not prevent some improvement in their general economic condition.

This unprecedented economic opportunity in the North exerted the "pull" upon southern Negroes. At the same time, the agricultural situation and prevailing low wages in the South acted as a "push" that made response to the "pull" inevitable. The share-tenancy mode of farming characteristic of the South usually involves crop liens and an unsound credit system which often prevented the Negro tenants from making an economic profit from a year's work.

The characteristic feature of share tenancy is that the owner furnishes not only the land but also part, or all, of the necessary capital and equipment, receiving in return a portion of the crop commensurate with the amount of capital he has expended. The Negro tenant, on the other hand, provides the necessary labor and, at times, part of the equipment, obtaining his compensation in the form of a share of the product at the final crop settlement. The form of share-tenancy varies not only in the relative proportions of the crop received by the owner and tenant and the extent to which the landlord furnishes the tools, work animals, fertilizer, seed, etc., but also in the amount of supervision exerted by the owner over the tenant. This ranges from the absolute dependence of the tenant who provides only his labor and is practically a wage earner working under closest supervision and direction, to the one who furnishes most of his equipment and works largely on his own initiative. The rent form of tenancy also shows

[2] Exceptions were made, in that countries situated in either North or South America were not subjected to the quota principle.

variations, having, in particular, different modes of payment; the tenant may agree to pay a cash rent or a stipulated amount of cotton per acre, or part cash and part produce.

Since Negro tenants usually have little or no capital with which to pay rent and provide the necessities of life while they wait for the maturing, harvesting and selling of their crop—which is usually the single crop, cotton—a system has developed whereby the colored farmers obtain their food, clothing and other essentials by long-time payments, either directly from the landlord, or in cases where the planter is unable or does not wish to furnish these necessities, from the local merchants, the owner securing a lien on the crop for the rent and whatever supplies he advances and the merchant securing another lien to cover his investments. One of the results of this crop-lien system has been the tendency of many planters or store keepers to charge exorbitant prices for the supplies, which the Negro tenant obtains on time instead of with cash. The creditor, whether merchant or landowner, takes considerable risk in investing large sums of capital on the security only of a cotton crop, and necessarily feels justified in protecting himself by charging more than the current cash prices. This whole system of tenancy with its concomitant evils of long-time credit and crop liens has provided splendid opportunities for unscrupulous planters and store keepers to exploit the ignorant and illiterate Negroes. In many cases the white men have taken advantage of these opportunities and have seen to it that the colored farmer has little to show for his year's work, though there are, of course, innumerable instances of white owners who have dealt honestly and kindly with their tenants and have tried to encourage them in habits of thrift and industry. However, the tenancy system has frequently resulted in much dissatisfaction with the final crop settlements, at which time the crop is shared between tenant and owner, and from the tenant's portion is deducted the payment for all advances. The Negroes complain that they are often cheated out of their share of the crop, are charged unfair prices, and are obliged to pay for articles they never bought. As Woofter points out,[3] "Some of these complaints are justified and some arise from the fact that the tenants are illiterate and keep no accurate accounts, and hence are uninformed as to their true financial status at the end of the crop year." As a further consequence of these mortgages and high prices, the Negro often finds himself in debt year after year and has little prospect of ever getting on his feet financially.

In recent decades the troubles inherent in the tenancy system have been intensified by the ravages of the boll weevil, which had appeared in the southwest corner of the southern states long before the war period, and had been persistently spreading north and east. By 1915 and 1916 the pest had reached Georgia and South Carolina, so that crop failures and agricultural depression were widespread throughout the cotton belt of the

[3] [Thomas Jackson Woofter, Jr., *Basis of Racial Adjustment* (New York: Ginn & Co., 1925), p. 48.]

South. The economic demoralization which resulted from this spread of
the boll weevil was further aggravated in 1916 by a series of heavy rain-
falls and floods, which in themselves did a great deal of damage and at the
same time made more difficult the fight against the boll weevil, which
thrives in rainy seasons.

Southern plantation owners have tended to produce only one principal crop, and in the sections where cotton is the chief interest this constant shortage or complete failure in cotton production was, and is,
disastrous. Discouraged by the weevil invasion, many planters have given
up the struggle and turned to other crops, such as corn, oats, sweet pota-
toes, peanuts and various food products, and have also frequently introduced new farm machinery to plant and cultivate them. For the most part,
these new crops have required fewer laborers than did the production
of cotton, and many Negro farm hands have been thrown out of work as a
result of this change in agricultural products and methods of farming.
Furthermore, since the farming experience of these colored workers has
been practically confined to the raising of cotton, their ignorance and lack
of training have handicapped the Negroes in their ability to cope with the
changing agricultural situation.

Moreover, the plantation owners have often found it difficult to
obtain loans from the banks during periods of agricultural depression and
in many cases have been without means of making the customary advances
of supplies, being obliged by their financial losses to cut down their labor
force and their farming operations. This, of course, has increased both the
deplorable financial condition of the Negroes and the amount of unemployment that had already been aggravated by the boll weevil and changing farming methods.

The factor of low wages has also been a serious phase of the Negro's
economic situation in the South, for throughout the southern states wages
for all classes have been lower than in the North. The earnings of farm
laborers, particularly, have frequently not been sufficient to provide an
adequate living.

At the time when southern Negroes were first widely afforded opportunity of employment in northern industries they were struggling in the
South with the tenancy system, crop failures, the invasion of the boll weevil,
changing methods of farming and low wages. All of these factors combined
to form an economic situation from which they were glad to escape. Since
those days the economic factors in both North and South have continued
to operate as motives of migration but in a less striking and more stable
form. There is not the acute demand for colored labor in northern industries that there was at the time of the war but Negroes continue to find
positions which promise more economic success than can be attained on
southern farms with their low wages and frequently unsatisfactory tenancy
system. The boll weevil persists in spreading disaster and confusion in the
agricultural life of the South, with the result that colored tenants move on
to newer lands in the southwest and to the cities of the South and North.

## SOCIAL CAUSES

While economic conditions, North and South, have been largely responsible for the mass movements of Negroes which have occurred since
the beginning of the war, at the same time certain social factors in
the South contributed to the restlessness and dissatisfaction of the Negroes
and to their eagerness to leave when the opportunity arose. Southern
colored people have constantly listed among their reasons for migrating the
discrimination and injustice to which they were subjected in the South.

One of the complaints of the Negroes is that they have been denied
participation in the political life of southern states and have been practically
disfranchised by such state legislative action as the "Grandfather clauses,"
educational tests, and property or poll taxes, or by the functioning of the
direct primary, from which Negroes are excluded in some states and which
is usually equivalent to an election. To some Negroes the right to vote is
a coveted privilege, any curtailment of which is considered an injustice,
and among migrants who have flocked into the northern cities during the
last fifteen years the inability to vote has frequently been given as one of
the reasons for leaving the South.

Further, the Negro complains of his widespread insecurity of life
and property in the South, which results in his social and economic as well
as political intimidation. Although the number of lynchings of Negroes has
decreased encouragingly in the last decade, yet the fact that in 1928 ten
Negroes[4] were murdered by mobs shows that there is still a basis for those
complaints of insecurity which are raised by the colored people. However,
recent statistical analyses of the relation between lynching and migration
reveal the necessity of caution in attributing too much importance to mob
violence as a motivating factor in recent Negro movements. It has been
shown, for instance, that: (1) The number of Negroes actually increased in
some counties in which lynchings occurred; (2) counties in which Negro
population decreased show a similar decrease in white population; and
(3) it even happens that a county with several lynchings in its history may
show an increase of Negroes but a decrease of whites.[5] In regard to both
political discrimination and mob violence it is well to realize[6]

*That lynching for the past twenty-five years has been slowly but surely
decreasing and disfranchisement is no new thing but has been an accomplished fact for more than forty years, . . . (so) that whatever grievance of
this nature the Negro may have against the South, he has at least, no new*

[4] [*World Almanac*, 1930, p. 402; cf. "Lynching Industry—1919," *Crisis*, XIX (Feb., 1920), 183–
86.]

[5] [Charles S. Johnson, "How the Negro Fits in Northern Industries," *Industrial Psychology*,
I (June, 1926), 403 and "How Much is the Migration a Flight from Persecution?", *Opportunity*, I (Sept., 1923), 272–74.]

[6] [W. O. Scroggs, "Interstate Migration of Negro Population," *Journal of Political Economy*,
XXV (Dec., 1917), 1041.]

*complaint and therefore no stronger reason for migrating on this account in 1917 than he has had for several decades.*

While it is undoubtedly true that in numerous instances lynching and other forms of outrage have prompted Negroes to move, yet rationalization of motives is a peculiar tendency of human nature and such a widely discussed evil as lynching might easily be accepted and given as a primary cause in cases where other factors were more fundamental. It seems probable that, like political discrimination, mob violence has exerted an influence upon Negro migration but has acted as an occasional strengthening and accompanying cause rather than as a fundamental and generally prevalent motive.

Racial discrimination in the carrying out of civic laws is another form of injustice of which Negroes complain perhaps even more than they decry mob violence, since this phase of inequality occurs more widely and constantly. Aspects of legal discrimination which are most generally alleged to be motivating factors in the Negroes' discontent are included in such contentions as that laws are unequally enforced, that discrimination is shown by officers of the law in making arrests, and that injustice is practiced in court procedure. Colored people in the South maintain that as a result of these tendencies, they are subject to hasty arrests without sufficient evidence, they are more easily convicted and are given longer and more severe sentences, and their value as witnesses and jurymen is not considered equal to that of the white man.

Lack of adequate educational facilities in the South forms one of the most generally listed reasons for those feelings of discrimination and discontent which have led many Negroes to change their place of residence. The basis of the southern educational situation is to be found in the double school system required by state constitutions and statutes, whereby the two races are segregated in separate schools. The injustice of which the Negroes complain is not so much the fact of separation as it is the discrimination shown in these separate buildings. Negro schools do not receive their proportionate share of state school funds, so that the physical equipment which can be provided, such as buildings, seating arrangements, blackboards, maps, etc., is far from adequate, and the salaries are so low that only teachers with meager training and ability can be secured. Furthermore, the lack of funds frequently necessitates a school year of only three or five months instead of the customary nine. In every way Negro children in the South are handicapped by the meager educational facilities which are available for them.

Another form of social discrimination which affects Negroes of any age or walk in life is the practice, found throughout the South, of separating the two races in residential sections, public conveyances and public gatherings. The chief complaint of the Negroes in this regard is that the provisions for their accommodation under this policy of segregation are invariably inferior to those made for white people. Residential areas allotted to the colored population in towns and cities are generally in the most undesirable sections and are frequently without such necessities and civic improvements as pavements, sewers, lighting and sanitary provisions. In traveling, too, Negroes are often given poor and inadequate accommodations even though they pay the same prices as do the whites. On railroad trains they are forced to ride in coaches set apart for their use and are usually unable to obtain places in sleeping or dining cars. As a general rule, the coaches given over to Negroes are crowded and unsanitary. On street cars, in theaters, in stores and in places of public gatherings of all sorts, the separate accommodations provided for them are likely to be inferior and unpleasant. At times, too, Negroes assert that in the general contacts between the two races they are subjected to embarrassments, humiliations and insults which are degrading to their self-respect and are subversive of their rights as citizens.

Thus the colored people of the South have complained of political disfranchisement, of the constant menace of mob violence and lynching, of inadequate educational facilities for their children, of legal discriminations, of "Jim Crow" segregation in transportation and public places, and of humiliations and embarrassments suffered in their contacts with white people. The extent to which this social situation has contributed to actual removal from the South varies with different individuals but in many cases it has been an influential factor in producing a determination to migrate. However, during the migrations of the last decade and a half, social conditions have tended to act as secondary and contributing causes of the movements rather than as a primary influence. When an appraisal and examination of their economic status had once been started, so that the feeling of unrest and discontent became more conscious and verbal, social factors readily furnished additional reasons for dissatisfaction and strengthened the desire to take advantage of the economic opportunities that were opening up in northern cities.

### SOCIO-PSYCHOLOGICAL CAUSES

Other factors have also played a part in producing these movements. The Negro's knowledge of the possibilities of migration and his attitude toward it are inevitably influenced by his personal relations with others and by the activities of the social group of which he is a member. Conversations with those already moving North, published discussions and appeals, and the general atmosphere of unrest which existed in many parts of the South, all exerted an effect upon the phenomenon of migration. During the first year or two of the European War the direct appeal of labor agents from the North was responsible for the migration of numbers of colored laborers, but the activities of these agents were soon limited, as many southern states attempted by legislative action to prevent them from soliciting labor for northern industries. However, this did not mean a cessation in appeals to migrate, for around 1916 to 1918 the Negro press was constantly urging colored people to leave the land of oppression and discrimination and fly to the freedom and equality which awaited them in the North. Probably the most influential of the Negro newspapers was the Chicago *Defender,* published in the North yet read widely in the South. This paper is said to have increased its circulation from 10,000 to 93,000 during the years of the war migration. By the use of glaring headlines and sensational articles it carried on a definite propaganda of migration which had an incalculable effect upon southern Negroes. It not only printed direct appeals to them to come North but gave much space to news items, anecdotes and poems which created the impression of a general mass movement and effort to escape from a life of bondage and oppression in the South. By constantly making the Negroes conscious of their "wrongs" and holding up before them the golden opportunities of the North and the example of their fellowmen, this newspaper and others like it crystallized the more underlying economic and social causes of discontent into immediate motives for migration.

After the migration had once started, one of the strongest incentives to its spread was the pressure exerted by the return of migrants for visits, by letters from migrants already established in the North, and by the general public opinion which prevailed in the South. When Negroes came back to visit their former homes, their tales of financial success and social freedom and their display of clothes and money as proof of their prosperity tended to encourage others to follow. Furthermore, as soon as a Negro had received employment in some northern city, he usually wrote to friends and relatives who remained behind, and urged them to join him. Like the Negro press and the return visits of migrants, these letters served to make southern Negroes aware of northern opportunities and conscious of their social and economic deprivations in the South, thus increasing their restlessness and discontent until the point of actual migration was reached. The extent to which such letters augmented migration cannot be estimated accurately but various investigations furnish ground for believing that this factor was highly important.

When the movement of colored people had once assumed noticeable proportions in any community, in itself it served as a cause of further migration. Throughout the South the departure of Negroes, newspaper propaganda, offers made by labor agents and letters from migrants, all started a wave of discussion. The economic and social conditions surrounding Negroes in the South and the opportunities in other regions became the absorbing topic of conversation in the churches, on the streets, in the stores and social gatherings, and wherever groups of colored people congregated. This constant discussion of migration fanned the smoldering restlessness into general awareness of the discriminations endured by southern Negroes and into acute discontent with the existing situation. Likewise, it induced a social pressure which stimulated further movements by suggestion and imitation, until in some communities the departure of colored people from the South assumed the appearance of an hysterical stampede.

Credulity was rife, caution and reason were thrown to the winds, and many Negroes sold or gave away their household goods, left their work and homes and followed their friends and neighbors, sometimes not even knowing where or why they were going. The wildest sort of rumors sprang from nowhere apparently and were given full credence, causing migrants to follow the crowd on the flimsiest pretexts. A type of rumor most frequently circulated and believed was the report that on certain dates excursions would be made up to go North; and this setting of a definite date for "The Great Northern Drive" proved an irresistible attraction to many Negroes. Stimulated by discussion, by the suggestions of those around them, by the fear of being left alone and by rumors and alluring tales, many of the migrants were caught up in the wave of enthusiasm and could not resist the impulse to leave.

On the whole, however, such socio-psychological causes of migration tended to be immediate rather than underlying, fundamental motives and were more effective after the movement had begun. Some of these have died out during the last fifteen years and no longer serve as potent causal factors. After the first excitement subsided and the fact of migration became a matter of course, there was less hysteria, wild rumor, and emotional discussion of the subject. On the other hand, such factors as letters of migrants probably increased in effectiveness when the Negroes became adjusted to northern living and working conditions and had opportunity to find jobs and shelter for their friends and relatives. Since that first mass movement to the North, the emotional element has diminished, so that there has been a practical disappearance of some of the motivating forces and a quiet and less spectacular persistence of others.

# 23

## BLACK BELT—BLACK GHETTO
*St. Clair Drake and Horace Cayton*

THE strongest visual evidence of a color-line in midwest metropolis is the existence of a Black Belt. Of the city's 337,000 Negroes, over ninety out of every hundred live in areas predominantly Negro.

It is not unusual for a language, nationality, or racial group to begin life in the city as a "colony." The distinctive thing about the Black Belt is

From *Black Metropolis*, copyright, 1945, by St. Clair Drake and Horace Cayton. Reprinted by permission of Harcourt, Brace & Jovanovich, Inc. Pp. 174–180, 198–213.

that while other such "colonies" tend to break up with the passage of time, the Negro area becomes increasingly more concentrated. By 1940, this area in Chicago had virtually ceased to expand in size, but new migrants to the city were pouring into it, and very few Negroes were trickling out into other parts of the city.

The persistence of a Black Belt, whose inhabitants can neither scatter as individuals nor expand as a group, is no accident. It is primarily the result of white people's attitudes toward having Negroes as neighbors. Because some white Chicagoans do not wish colored neighbors, formal and informal social controls are used to isolate the latter within congested all-Negro neighborhoods.

The native-born, middle-class, white population is the group that sets the standards by which various people are designated as desirable or undesirable. The attitudes of this middle-class group are probably decisive in restricting Negroes and other groups to special areas of the city. These attitudes become translated into economic terms, and though the kinds of people the white middle class desires as neighbors do not affect property values adversely, their dislike and fear of other groups is reflected by a decline in the sales value of residential property when such people begin to penetrate a neighborhood. In Midwest Metropolis, such ethnic groups as the English, Germans, Scotch, Irish, and Scandinavians have little adverse effect on property values. Northern Italians are considered less desirable, followed by Bohemians and Czechs, Poles, Lithuanians, Greeks, and Russian Jews of the lower class. Southern Italians, along with Negroes and Mexicans, are at the bottom of the scale of middle-class white "desirability."[1]

The areas in which these groups are concentrated become stigmatized as "slum neighborhoods," and there is a tendency to blame the group for the condition of the area. One factor that complicates this whole matter of land-values—for the areas in question *are* predominantly slums—is the fact that "the undesirable" groups usually inherit sections of the city that the older, more well-to-do inhabitants have abandoned and thus "the undesirable racial factor is so merged with other unattractive features, such as proximity to factories, poor transportation, old and obsolete buildings, poor street improvements, and the presence of criminal or vice elements, that the separate effect of race cannot be disentangled."[2]

Given the definition of an area and the people in it as "undesirable," the expansion of the area will be resisted. If, however, individuals within it are able to change the telltale marks of poverty, name, foreign language, or

[1] Most social-distance scales indicate that native-born Americans tend to arrange people in a rank-order of desirability as neighbors which places Northern Europeans at the top, and Negroes, Mexicans, and similar colored groups near the bottom.

[2] The scale of "desirability" of various ethnic groups, as well as this estimate of the influence of the racial factor on property and land values, is from Homer Hoyt, *One Hundred Years of Land Values in Chicago*, University of Chicago, 1933, p. 317.

distinctive customs, they may move out and lose themselves in middle-class, native-born white neighborhoods. This, Negroes wearing the badge of color, cannot do. Negro areas must either expand as parts of a constantly growing Black Belt, or stagnate as deteriorating slums.

### EVOLUTION OF A BLACK BELT

The Negro area of Midwest Metropolis has been expanding for almost a hundred years—sometimes slowly, sometimes rapidly; occasionally with serious disturbances, but usually as a peaceful process. The expansion has taken two forms—a gradual filtering-in of Negroes among the white population, and mass invasion. Before the Great Migration, the usual process of filtering-in seems to have been one in which a few Negroes would move out of the Negro colony into surrounding areas. As others followed them, small nuclei of Negroes were formed. Then, when the proportion of Negroes to whites became large, the white population would move, leaving the areas all-Negro.

Before the Great Migration, over half of the Negro population lived outside of the then small Black Belt.[3] Some of these were servants living near the white families for whom they worked. Others were families who had bought property on the outskirts of a city that eventually grew out to meet them. Still others were moderately prosperous people following the general residential trend away from the center of the city.

Old Settlers have a tendency to romanticize this period, but it is evident from their comments that sporadic, unorganized resistance to Negro neighbors was sometimes encountered. One woman, referring to her experience in the Eighties, indicates that antagonism toward Negroes was strong enough to permit a person to annoy a neighbor by renting a house to a Negro:

*"There has always been race prejudice here, but not so strong as it is now. The owner of this house was a German and he was mad at his neighbor. He was tickled to death to rent it to colored, just in order to spite Mrs. Richmond. Later I bought the house."*

Occasionally a light-skinned Negro would move into a neighborhood and it might be some time before he was "discovered." One very light Negro, reporting such an episode, said:

*"In 1904 or 1905, I moved in here. I bought in 1907. There were white neighbors on both sides at first. I rented the house the first time I moved*

---

[3] In 1910 there were no communities in which Negroes were over sixty-one percent of the population. More than two-thirds of the Negroes lived in areas less than fifty percent Negro, and a third lived in areas less than ten percent Negro. By 1920, eighty-seven percent of the Negroes lived in areas over half Negro in composition. A decade later ninety percent were in districts of fifty percent or more Negro concentration. Almost two-thirds (sixty-three percent) lived where the concentration was from ninety to ninety-nine percent Negro!

in it. *The man I rented the house from talked to me about the place, and rented it to me, and he thought I was a white man. The neighbors made complaints about it. He said, 'The man has a lease and he'll keep it until it is up.' After the lease was up, I bought the house for a price reasonable at that time. The fellow was a Scotchman.*"

The experiences of individual Negroes during this filtering-in process depended on many factors, including the social-class and ethnic composition of the area, as well as the class and skin-color of the Negro. When only a few Negroes were involved, and they were of equivalent social status to the whites, or when the whites were of lower class position than the colored people, initial hostility usually gave way to tolerance or even friendliness. But when large numbers of Negroes followed, antagonisms were aroused, and eventually the white population would move away. Old Settlers frequently refer to the relative ease with which they made adjustments, once they had filtered into some types of white neighborhoods. The following two statements summarize the experiences of scores of pre-migration Negro families. One woman states:

"*I came to Chicago in 1903. I lived on Lincoln Street—there were foreigners there. My children used to go to white kids' parties, for where we lived there was nothing much but foreigners. There was only one other colored family in that block. The white people never used to call my children names.*"

Another woman suggested that while relations between children and adults in such areas were often friendly, the social barrier stiffened during the critical adolescent period:

"*I was raised on the Near North Side and at that time we were the only Negro family over there. I didn't know so much about color until I was about eleven or twelve years old. In fact, I hadn't given it a second thought. My playmates were all white. I used to go to their parties and they would come to mine; but after I was old enough to go into high school, that was where the trouble started. I never did have any serious trouble, but it wasn't so pleasant as it had been when I was a child.*"

This woman also blamed an increase in the *number* of Negroes for changes in white neighborhood sentiment:

"*As long as there was just one colored family over there it was all right, but after the neighborhood began to have an increase in the number of colored families, the children started to making trouble among themselves, and, of course, that brought the older people into it.*"

Concurrently with the filtering-in process, the Black Belt itself was expanding in these pre-Migration years. As whites moved out of areas adjacent to the Black Belt to seek better homes farther from the center of the city, Negroes moved in. So long as Negroes were but a minute percentage of the population, they were easily accommodated. It was only after 1915, when 65,000 migrants came into the city within five years, that resistance became organized. Negro migrants were then compelled to spill over the margins of the Black Belt, and their search for homes in other parts of the city was eventually interpreted as a "mass invasion." Yet even the Negroes who streamed into the city during the first three years of the Great Migration had little difficulty in renting or buying property near the small Black Belt, for middle-class white residents were abandoning these areas. Real-estate agents and property owners of both races promoted the expansion of the Black Belt, and there was little friction.

But when the United States entered the World War in 1917 building operations were suspended and a housing shortage quickly resulted. Property owners' associations began to talk of re-establishing neighborhoods adjacent to the Black Belt as exclusively white. This meant that the Negroes who had already moved in must be forced out if possible, and that no others must be allowed to enter. Before the housing shortage, these adjacent white communities had been willing to absorb a few Negroes and then to relinquish the community to them as they became too numerous. Now they were disposed to stay and fight.

Several property owners' associations which had been originally organized for neighborhood improvement, now began to focus their attention upon keeping out Negroes. They sponsored numerous mass meetings to arouse the citizens to the peril of "invasion." They published scathing denunciations of Negroes branding them arrogant, ignorant, diseased, bumptious, destructive of property and generally undesirable. A wave of violence flared up and between July, 1917, and March, 1921, fifty-eight homes were bombed—an average of one every twenty days. Two Negroes were killed, a number of white and colored persons were injured, and property damage amounted to over a hundred thousand dollars. The victims of the bombings were Negro families that had moved into white neighborhoods, as well as Negro and white real-estate men who sold or rented property to them. Feeling was particularly strong against real-estate men who were suspected of renting to one or two Negroes in a block in order to frighten the white residents away so that the realtors could move Negroes in at higher rents.

The most widely publicized bombing case was that of Jesse Binga, the Negro banker and real-estate dealer. . . . Binga was of relatively high social and economic status, and could hardly be accused of not knowing how to care for property. In fact, the property owners' associations attacked him precisely because he *did* represent a higher-status Negro. When he bought a home in a white middle-class area, the *Property Owners' Journal* denounced him for having "wormed his way into a white neighborhood," characterizing him as one of the "misleaders of the Negro, those flamboyant, noisy, witless individuals, who by power of superior gall and gumption have blustered their way into positions of prominence amongst their people."[4] Since verbal threats failed to dislodge him, bombs were tried. These also failed.

The property owners' association never admitted complicity in these bombings, and responsibility was never definitely placed by the police. Indeed, individual groups of property owners warned against violence, one such group declaring that the *moral* onus rested on the associations if the bombings continued, even though the associations were not actively involved.

By 1925, the wave of bombings had ceased. Since that time the major device for controlling the expansion of the Negro community has been the restrictive covenant—an agreement between property owners within a certain district not to rent or sell to Negroes. Although their constitutionality is being questioned, the covenants have been recognized as legal by the courts, and property owners' associations continue to use the pressure of public opinion to secure signatures from white owners who may be reluctant to enter into them.

As early as January, 1902, the Chicago *Tribune* reported[5] under the caption, "United Action Keeps Negroes Out of 57 Homes," that

*The Chicago Real Estate Board extended felicitations to the Grand Boulevard branch of the Kenwood and Hyde Park Property Owners' Associations yesterday, when the association proclaimed that in sixty days it had forestalled Negro occupancy of fifty-seven houses south of Thirty-ninth Street.*

In May of the following year, the same paper noted that the Chicago Real Estate Board was as ready to penalize those who sold to Negroes as to felicitate those who would not:[6]

*Immediate expulsion from the Chicago Real Estate Board will be the penalty paid by any member who sells a Negro property in a block where there are only white owners. This was voted unanimously at a meeting of the board yesterday, following an appeal by Col. V—— H. S——, a former president of the organization, that the board take a definite stand on the Negro question. He called the Chicago Real Estate Board cowardly, and declared it had always sidestepped the issue. His motion followed a plea by the Grand Boulevard Property Owners' Association for co-operation of the realtors in settling the property ownership problem. . . .*

[4] Quoted in Chicago Commission on Race Relations, *The Negro in Chicago* (Chicago, 1922), p. 12.

[5] Chicago *Tribune,* January 10, 1920.

[6] *Ibid.,* May 21, 1921.

## BLACK BELT—BLACK GHETTO

The deep-seated feeling that Negroes are, in the final analysis, some-how fundamentally different from Poles, Italians, Greeks, and other white ethnic groups finds its expression in the persistence of a Black Belt. Mid-west Metropolis seems to say: "Negroes have a right to live in the city, to compete for certain jobs, to vote, to use public accommodations—but they should have a community of their own. Perhaps they should not be segre-gated by law, but the city should make sure that most of them remain within a Black Belt." As we have suggested previously, Negroes do not accept this definition of their "place," and while it is probably true that, if allowed free choice, the great majority would live as a compact unit for many years to come, they believe that *enforced* segregation is unjust. They do not always clearly see the full implications and consequences of resi-dential segregation, but they are generally resentful. A sampling of com-ments made at a time when discussion was widespread about restrictive covenants in Hyde Park will reveal the nature of this resentment. Thus, one prominent Old Settler, the daughter of a German father and a Negro mother, was vitriolic in her denunciation of residential segregation:

*"I don't think we would need any housing projects on the South Side if Chicago wasn't so full of this silly old race prejudice. We ought to be able to live anywhere in the city we want to. What the government should do, or somebody with money, is to fight these restrictive covenants and let our people move where they want to. It's a dirty shame that all types of foreign-ers can move anywhere in the city they want to, and a colored man who has been a soldier and a citizen for his country can live only in a Black Belt. What's the use of fighting for a country that treats you that way?"*

A colored "wringer man" in a laundry came to Chicago in 1921 because he had heard of "the good wages and grand opportunities." Now, having become well-adjusted, he resents residential segregation:

*"Residential segregation is a big mistake. When I came here, there were white and colored living in the same neighborhood and the people seemed to understand each other. But since this neighborhood is colored only, everything is different. There are less jobs, and the neighborhood is not kept as clean as it used to be. I cannot offer any way to break down segregation. When I was married, I tried to rent houses out of the district, and the real-estate agents wouldn't rent to me. Yes, if Negroes can get houses in Hyde Park, or anywhere else, they ought to take them—for the housing condition for colored on the South Side is rotten."*

Another laborer from Georgia who has been in the city nearly thirty years was also heated in his denunciation:

*"Racial segregation is rotten. When white and colored both lived in this section, the rents were not so high and there seemed to be a better understanding. I have often wondered if segregation has not had a lot to do with the lack of employment, for there are certain white people that try to prove that all Negroes are bad. When they come over here, they go to the worst part of the section to prove their point."*

Somewhat more moderate in his disapproval is a colored chauffeur who came to Chicago in 1912 as a Pullman porter:

*"Racial segregation is something that I am not sure is a blessing. The housing proposition is serious, for the rents are very high, and the houses are not kept up as they are in white neighborhoods. On the other hand, if we were scattered among the white people there would be far less work, for by being close together we get a lot of work from the stores owned by white people that are doing business in our neighborhood. I have thought of ways to break down this segregation, but when I think that anything you do makes you a lawbreaker, you then cease to fight individuals, for then it becomes a war with the law. Remember that the police, the judges, and the strongest lawyer groups are all white and they stick together. I have seen one case of a fight between the police and the colored citizens and know that it was far from being an equal fight."*

Many other Negroes, however, express a willingness to risk trouble in attacking this form of segregation. A skilled worker, a respectable church member, was very emphatic on this point:

*"Hyde Park is no more than any other place in Chicago. The Negroes ought to move into Hyde Park or any other park they want to move into. I don't know of anything on earth that would keep me out of Hyde Park if I really wanted to move into it. Personally, I don't care anything about the good-will of white people if it means keeping me and my people down or in restricted neighborhoods."*

A minority defends the existence of enforced residential segregation. This is done not on principle, but as a matter of expediency, or for fear of racial clashes, or because such persons feel that the time to attack segregation has not yet come. Thus, a colored waiter who blames most of the discrimination against Negroes on the Great Migration, partly defends segregation:

*"I myself believe segregation is good, for if the white and colored lived together there would be fights constantly. About the only business benefit we derive from a Black Belt region is from a political standpoint, for there are a lot of people working that have gotten their appointments from their*

*power as a voting factor. I think segregation is caused by the Negro's failure to try to get out of the district. In fact, I have never tried to live out of the district. There is no reason—I just have not thought of it."*

Occasionally the opinion is expressed that Negroes are not "ready" to move into better neighborhoods, that they must first prove their worth by making the Black Belt a cleaner, more orderly, better-kept area. Thus one man states:

*"Our duty to ourselves and to those with whom we come in contact is to show the world that we are an advanced people, that we are law-abiding and respectable and that we are able to care for the property we control or occupy. You can bet your bottom dollar that when we do this, we will be welcome wherever we care to live."*

This theory that individual Negroes must wait until the whole group improves itself before they can get out of the Black Belt is not at all popular with ambitious Negroes.

Most Chicago Negroes feel that the right to rent or buy a house offered to the public should be inalienable. Yet Negro businessmen and politicians will sometimes state privately that they prefer keeping the Negro population concentrated. During a campaign against restrictive covenants, one prominent Negro leader confided to an interviewer:

*"Sure, I'm against covenants. They are criminal. But I don't want Negroes moving all over town. I just want to add little pieces to the Black Belt. I'd never get re-elected if Negroes were all scattered about. The white people wouldn't vote for me."*

Most Negroes probably have a similar goal—the establishment of the *right* to move where they wish, but the preservation of some sort of large Negro community by voluntary choice. But they wish a community much larger than the eight square miles upon which Black Metropolis now stands.

At one session of the Mayor's Conference on Race Relations in 1944, the Chairman of the Chicago Housing Authority stated[7] of the Black Belt that

*"In 1939 there was an excess population of 87,300 persons, measured by citywide standards of density. Since then an estimated 60,000 or more persons have moved into the area to accentuate an already bad condition.*

*"The race relations problem of Chicago revolves itself around the question of living space for Negro citizens. A major revision in public opinion on race relations must be effected before private or public agencies can make any substantial contribution to the solution of this problem."*

[7] Mayor's Conference on Race Relations, *City Planning in Race Relations*, p. 21.

Negro newspapers and civic leaders unanimously oppose enforced residential segregation and bitterly attack the forces that have created an overcrowded Black Belt. To them, the area is a Black Ghetto, and they insist that "new areas should be opened to break the iron ring which now restricts most Negro families to intolerable, unsanitary conditions. Restrictive-covenant agreements and the iron ring creating a Negro ghetto must be smashed."[8]

Even the Chairman of the Mayor's Committee accepted the characterization of the Black Belt as a "ghetto," and there was general agreement among the participants in the Mayor's Conference in 1944 that most of the social problems within the Black Belt were fundamentally related to the operation of restrictive covenants. (Only the spokesman for the Chicago Real Estate Board disagreed.[9]) The conference listed among the "ghetto conditions" high sickness and death rates;[10] a heavy relief load during the Depression; inadequate recreational facilities; lack of building repairs; neglect of garbage disposal and street cleaning; overcrowded schools;[11] high

[8] Chicago *Defender*, July 22, 1944.

[9] The real-estate interests in Midwest Metropolis insist that a general scarcity of houses is the primary problem, and that, if there were enough houses or a building program in process, middle-class white families would move away from areas close to the Black Belt and Negroes could then take over the abandoned houses. They blame New Deal restrictions and the Federal housing program for the housing shortage, charging that private capital has been made reluctant to invest. The Chicago Real Estate Board refuses, unequivocally, to sanction the abolition of restrictive covenants. Yet plenty of houses would not solve the basic question of the *quality* of housing available for Negro occupancy. Negroes would still be concentrated in areas of the city that have begun to deteriorate.

[10] In 1925, Chicago had the lowest death rate for any American city of 1,000,000 and over, but the Negro death rate was twice that for whites. (H. L. Harris, Jr., "Negro Mortality Rates in Chicago," *Social Service Review*, v. 1, no. 1, 1927.) The average standard death rate for the years 1928–1932 was 9.2 for native-whites, 10.4 for foreign-whites, and 20.0 for Negroes. (Elaine Ogden, *Chicago Negro Community*, WPA, 1939, p. 201.) Differences in infant mortality are reflected in the fact that three Negro babies die before their first birthday to every two white babies. Social disorganization in the Black Ghetto is reflected in deaths from homicide—six Negroes die from violent assaults for every white person who is killed.

The striking differentials in morbidity rates are those for tuberculosis . . . and venereal diseases. The Negro tuberculosis rate is five times the white rate and the venereal disease rate is reported as twenty-five times that for whites. Both diseases are closely related to a low material standard of living and widespread ignorance of hygiene. *It should be borne in mind, however, that we are dealing with rates, not absolute numbers.* The actual number of Negroes who have venereal disease does not warrant the common belief that "the Negro race is eaten up with syphilis and gonorrhea." About seventy-five venereal disease cases were reported among every 1000 Negroes in 1942, and three among whites.

[11] Civic leaders are most bitter about the double- and triple-shift schools in the Black Belt. In 1938, thirteen of the fifteen schools running on "shifts" were in Negro neighborhoods. Pupils spent half of the day in school and were "on the streets" for the rest of the day. In 1944, the School Board alleged that this system had been abolished, but Negro leaders disputed the claim. The Board of Education consistently refused to give the authors any data on overcrowding in the schools. A building program has been projected which may relieve the situation in the future.

rates of crime and juvenile delinquency; and rough treatment by the police.

The ghetto characteristics of the Black Belt are related, in the first instance, to the poverty of its people. Here, the proportion of families on relief during the Depression was the highest for the entire city. . . . The restricted economic base of the community was also evident in the high proportion of women doing domestic service. As a low-income area, the community was unable to maintain a high material standard of living. This poverty was aggravated by the housing problem which caused overcrowding. Given these factors, and the lack of widespread health education among Negroes, it is not surprising that the tuberculosis death rate is five times higher than it is for whites, and that the Negro areas have the highest sickness and death rates from tuberculosis. Chicago has the highest Negro death rate from tuberculosis of any metropolitan city in the United States.[12]

The Black Ghetto also suffers from a type of social disorganization which is reflected in high illegitimacy and juvenile delinquency rates[13] and a high incidence of insanity. . . .

Restrictions upon free competition for housing, and the inability of the Black Belt to expand fast enough to accommodate the Negro population, have resulted in such a state of congestion that Negroes are living 90,000 to the square mile as compared with 20,000 to the square mile in adjacent white apartment-house areas. Since they entered the city last and are a low-income group, Negroes, in the aggregate, have inherited the worst sections of Midwest Metropolis. They have been able to "take over" some fairly decent housing in neighborhoods that were being abandoned by white residents, but these were no longer prized as residential neigh-

---

[12] These high tuberculosis morbidity and mortality rates among Negroes may reflect the fact that Negroes as a recently urbanized group have not developed immunity to the disease. But the wide differentials also reflect the well-known fact that the care of tuberculosis demands bed rest with plenty of nutritious food. (Rates from Dorothy J. Liveright, "Tuberculosis Mortality Among Residents of 92 Cities of 100,000 or More Population: United States, 1939–41," U. S. Public Health Reports, July 21, 1944, pp. 942–955.)

| Cities of one million and Over Population | Tuberculosis Death Rates: 1939–41 | |
|---|---|---|
| | For Whites | For Negroes |
| Chicago, Illinois | 45.4 | 250.1 |
| New York, New York | 40.4 | 213.0 |
| Philadelphia, Pennsylvania | 44.3 | 203.5 |
| Detroit, Michigan | 36.5 | 189.0 |
| Los Angeles, California | 49.7 | 137.3 |

[13] In 1944, the Superintendent of the State Training School for Girls at Geneva, Ill., reported that Negro girls made up thirty-six percent of all girls at the institution. Frazier has noted a steady rise between 1919 and 1930 in the proportion of Negro boys brought before the juvenile court. In the latter year 21.7 percent of the boys brought before the court were Negroes.

borhoods. Negroes have thus become congested in undesirable residential areas.

Over half of Black Metropolis lies in that area which the city planners and real-estate interests have designated as "blighted." The "blighted areas" have come into being as a part of the process of uncontrolled city growth, for as Midwest Metropolis has grown, spontaneously and in response to economic utility, its center has become a citadel of imposing office buildings surrounded by an ever-widening belt of slums. As the city expands, this slum land becomes valuable as the site of future wholesale establishments, warehouses, transportation terminals, and light industries. No one wishes to invest in new housing upon these potentially valuable spots. Housing already there is allowed to deteriorate and is then torn down. From the standpoint of residential desirability, this entire area is "blighted."

The superficial observer believes that these areas are "blighted" because large numbers of Negroes and Jews, Italians and Mexicans, homeless men and "vice" gravitate there. But real-estate boards, city planners, and ecologists know that the Negro, the foreign-born, the transients, pimps, and prostitutes are located there because the area has already been written off as blighted. The city's outcasts of every type have no choice but to huddle together where nobody else wants to live and where rents are relatively low.

Black Metropolis has become a seemingly permanent enclave within the city's blighted area. The impecunious immigrant, once he gets on his feet, may—as we have mentioned several times––move into an area of second-settlement. Even the vice-lord or gangster, after he makes his pile, may lose himself in a respectable neighborhood. Negroes, regardless of their affluence or respectability, wear the badge of color. They are expected to stay in the Black Belt.

During the last twenty years the Negro's demand for housing has always exceeded the supply. The rental value of residential property in the Black Belt is thus abnormally high. The speculative value of the land on which the property stands is also high, and—even more than the restriction of supply—this has a tendency to drive rents up. A prominent real-estate operator, during the Depression, said frankly to a Negro social worker: "There are two ways to handle residential property in the Black Belt. Figure on amortizing the investment in twenty years and scale the rent accordingly. Plan to amortize your investment in ten years and double the rent. If this section is doomed for residential purposes anyhow, the latter is a better business practice for us." Houses in Black Metropolis pay off now. The land they occupy will do so in the future.

Midwest Metropolis does not intend to keep on growing haphazardly. City planners and the larger real-estate interests hope some day to control its growth, and Chicago's master plan calls for the eventual reclamation of the inner city, with a garden belt of privately financed, medium-rental apartments replacing the slums. Here, it is hoped, members of the new middle class will make their homes, close to the Loop where they work, and well within the city limits. The blighted areas will thus be reclaimed. Low-cost housing nearer steel mills and industrial plants in the suburbs will be constructed (also, for the most part, with private funds) to attract the skilled and semi-skilled workers. But some question marks remain.

"What," asked an official of a Negro civic agency, "do the Chicago Real Estate Board, and the city, plan to do with the Negroes who now live in the blighted areas? Will restrictive covenants be relaxed so they, too, can move to the suburbs and near-suburbs?" This was during the Depression, when Negro labor was not in demand, and the answer of a member of the Real Estate Board was crisp: "We have no plans for them. Perhaps they can return to the South."

The realtor's remark reflected the rather general antagonism of Chicago taxpayers toward the 40,000 Negroes who migrated to Black Metropolis during the Depression. There was a tendency during this period to feel that Midwest Metropolis had no responsibilities toward an unwanted population which was crowding into the already saturated Black Belt. Vacancy rates for the entire city were low, and no new areas of occupancy were opened to Negroes until near the eve of the Second World War, when one square mile was added to Black Metropolis. It is ironic that the lone Federal housing project within the Black Belt actually displaced sixteen more families than it accommodated. The Second World War brought 60,000 more Negroes to the city—this time a welcome addition to the labor market. Over 1,500 units of war housing were made available, but at least 10,000 more were needed. Wartime controls froze Black Belt rents at their already high levels, and overcrowding mounted to an almost intolerable point.

Some private real-estate groups have become interested in the possibilities of investing in Negro housing, but the question still remains: "Where shall it be situated?"

Negro civic leaders in Chicago were quite pleased when Newton Farr, a former president of the National Association of Real Estate Boards and one of Chicago's most intransigent defenders of restrictive covenants, conducted a survey of "hundreds of the best posted real estate men in eighteen large cities" on their opinion of Negroes as renters and potential home owners. The questions and replies are summarized below:[14]

*(1)   Does the Negro make a good home buyer and carry through his purchase to completion? . . . . . . 17 of the 18 cities reported YES.*

*(2)   Does he take as good care of property as other tenants of a comparable status? . . . . . . 11 of the 18 cities reported YES.*

*(3)   Do you know of any reason why insurance companies should not purchase mortgages on property occupied by Negroes? . . . . . . 14 of the 18 cities reported NO.*

[14] The quoted material and summary are from the New York *Herald Tribune,* November 19, 1944.

*(4) Do you think there is a good opportunity for realtors in the Negro housing field in your city? . . . . . . 12 of the 18 cities reported YES.*

*To a double-barreled question, "Is the Negro good pay as a tenant or are more frequent collections necessary and losses greater?" six cities said the Negro tenant is "good pay," seven said "no," and two reported conflicting experiences. On the second half of the question ten cities reported more frequent collections are necessary, while two disclaimed this.*

*A majority of cities commented that Negroes maintain neatness and repairs on new property as well as whites, but underscored that relatively few properties in good condition are sold to Negroes.*

Some weeks later, Newton Farr, as determined as ever to "hold the line," reiterated to Negro leaders that he was interested in providing *Negro* housing, not in mixing whites and Negroes within neighborhoods. He felt that *Negro* housing might be a paying investment in the post-War world, but segregation must be maintained.

The city faces a dilemma—a sort of social paralysis. Midwest Metropolis doesn't want to let Negroes stay where they are, and it doesn't want them to scatter freely about the city. It doesn't want to rebuild the inner city to house them, nor does it wish to provide homes elsewhere. And all the time Black Metropolis—a big, stubborn, eight-square-mile fact crammed with over 300,000 people—grows more and more congested.[15]

These Negroes, upon whom the city depends for much of its unskilled and semi-skilled labor and for a large part of its domestic service, continue to pile up upon one another within these congested areas. As they do so, morbidity and morality rates rise out of all proportion to those in the rest of the city. Crime and juvenile delinquency rates, too, indicate that serious maladjustments are present in the Black Belt. Black Metropolis acquires the

[15] The Chicago Plan Commission has divided all residential areas into five types, as of 1942, and made plans for the future status of each. Thus, "blighted and near blighted" areas are to be eliminated, becoming *rebuilt* areas; "conservation" areas are those which will, in the future, become *ripe for rebuilding;* those which are, at present, "stable" are expected to become *conservation* property; present areas of "arrested" or "progressive" development and "new growth" will some day be *stable.* "Vacant" areas will gradually become ripe for *new growth.*

Two-thirds of the main Black Belt area has been classified as "blighted" or "near-blighted" and a third as "conservation" property.

Of the 250,000 people in the Black Belt, the Commission estimated that at least 87,000 persons should be moved out in order to thin the population down to the optimum in conservation areas and to a level of health and decency upon rebuilding the blighted areas with a combination of walk-up apartments and row-houses. At least 16,000 should move even if three-story walk-up apartments replaced all the present housing in the blighted areas.

The Commission favored intensive new building within two small Negro communities outside of the Black Belt and the creation of a new segregated community on the edge of the city limits. These three Jim-Crow communities could accommodate 30,000 or 40,000 people from the main Black Belt.

(Cf. booklet *Design for Public Improvements,* by the Chicago Plan Commission and mimeographed memorandum, "Population in South Side Negro Areas.")

reputation of being a "slum area," and the bare statistical record and surface impressions seem convincing evidence that Negroes make undesirable neighbors. This estimate of Negroes is reinforced deliberately by the real-estate interests and incidentally by the press and radio. Rumor and chance impressions further confirm the reputation of Black Metropolis as a "rough" neighborhood.

During the fifteen years between the Great Migration and the Depression, the Black Belt gained the reputation of being a colorful community, "wide-open" and rough. It was also considered "easy picking" for the Republican machine. Yet most of the city paid little attention to Black Metropolis for ten years after the Race Riot of 1919, except during the excitement of an election campaign or an occasional "vice crusade." Its immediate neighbors, however, feared it because it was steadily expanding and pressing upon them.

The Depression made the entire city conscious of Black Metropolis. In the first place, the area became the scene of the eviction riots and the "Spend Your Money Where You Can Work" Campaign. Then it reversed its political tradition of fifteen years and went Democratic. Throughout the Depression period Black Metropolis was good copy for the white press. The Chicago *Tribune,* for instance, professing alarm at the high proportion of Negroes on the WPA, occasionally made snide comments on the waste of the taxpayers' money. The militant demands which Negroes raised for better housing and more relief were sometimes hysterically interpreted as evidence that Black Metropolis was turning "Red," and on at least one occasion a Hearst paper headlined a revolution in progress. (The incident was merely a tenant strike in a single building.) All the daily papers rediscovered the presence of a widespread gambling syndicate, and devoted columns to the life and works of Negro racketeers. Though the *Times,* a liberal tabloid, tried to be helpful and ran several feature stories with appropriate pictures emphasizing the dirt and squalor and ramshackle housing in the area, it rounded off the series with a sensational exposé of Black Belt "rackets."

Whenever an institution in the Negro community launched a drive for funds, the evidences of community disorganization were emphasized in the press in order to stimulate charity. On one occasion, a city-wide drive against syphilis involved the uncritical publication of statistics and maps which suggested the Black Belt was a "cesspool of disease" (the actual words of one newspaper).[16] Such publicity helped to fix the reputation of Midwest Metropolis during the Depression. A new liberal daily, the *Sun,*

---

[16] Negro civic leaders are very ambivalent about the matter of publicizing health statistics on Negro communities. They point out that persons unfamiliar with statistics confuse high *proportions* with high *absolute* figures. For instance, only five Negroes in a 100 may have syphilis, but if the fact is publicized that the Negro *rate* is forty times that for white people, the public will begin to view every Negro as a potential paretic. Yet, in order to focus the attention of the larger white world upon the Negro's plight, it is necessary to emphasize poverty and disorganization, to display the sores of Black Metropolis like a beggar seeking

appearing in 1941, inaugurated a less sensational approach to Black Belt problems, but the reputation of the area was already fixed.

The existence of these conditions has become a convenient rationalization for keeping Negroes segregated. The University of Chicago (with properties tangential to the Black Belt), neighborhood property owners' associations all around it, and the Chicago Real Estate Board have visualized restrictive covenants as a permanent *cordon sanitaire*.

Community leaders in Black Metropolis, as well as professional and businessmen generally, are worried about the area's reputation in the larger white world—a world which identifies each of them with the Black Ghetto. Throughout 1938, one Negro weekly newspaper ran a symposium, "Is the South Side Doomed?", encouraging discussion of community improvement. The series of articles revealed general agreement on the necessity for abolishing restrictive covenants if doom was to be averted. Community leaders devote much of their time and attention to petition, protest, and legal action designed to abolish restrictive covenants. (They have been doing this for twenty years, without success.) While aware of the economic and social forces which create the ghetto, they also cling tenaciously to the possibility of reducing life within the area to order and neatness. This hope has resulted in "clean-up campaigns," drives for increased police protection and health facilities, and the constant stimulation of community morale. These efforts are frustrated, however, by the necessity for trying to improve living conditions within an area too small to accommodate the population, given the present amount and quality of housing.

As it becomes increasingly crowded—and "blighted"—Black Metropolis's reputation becomes ever more unsavory. The city assumes that *any* Negroes who move *anywhere* will become a focal point for another little Black Belt with a similar reputation. To allow the Black Belt to disintegrate

---

alms. One civic leader pointed out that this approach sometimes boomerangs and quoted the words of an industrialist that he had approached about hiring some Negroes: "Mr. Smith was over here recently soliciting money for that Negro hospital. He showed me a lot of charts and graphs on tuberculosis and syphilis. I can't put your people in my factory using the same rest-rooms and cafeterias that the other workers use."

The following sampling of editorial appeals in daily papers during a money-raising drive for a hospital in Black Metropolis suggests the manner in which the white public's fears are aroused and the unsavory reputation of Black Metropolis reinforced, in order to stimulate charity. The editorials of three daily newspapers, in addition to presenting factual material, stressed the imminence of some disaster originating in the Black Belt. The *Times* stated: "We must at once remedy our dereliction or, with the growing consciousness of the Negro of his political and collective power, find it remedied in ways we may not care for." (June 26, 1938.) The *Daily News* suggested that "protection of health in the Negro area means health protection to every citizen of Chicago. . . . Quite aside from the humanitarian reasons, the rest of Chicago cannot afford to let this institution stop or even to curtail its activities." (July 5, 1938.) According to the *Tribune*, "Failure to raise the money will mean a vast amount of needless suffering and it may not be confined to the Negroes." (July 8, 1938.)

would scatter the Negro population. To allow it to expand will tread on the toes of vested interests, large and small, in the contiguous areas. To let it remain the same size means the continuous worsening of slum conditions there. To renovate it requires capital, but this is a poor investment. It is better business to hold the land for future business structures, or for the long-talked-of rebuilding of the Black Belt as a white office-workers' neighborhood. The real-estate interests consistently oppose public housing within the Black Belt, which would drive rents down and interfere with the ultimate plan to make the Black Belt middle-class and white.

The Race Relations Director of the regional office of the Federal Housing Authority suggested to the Mayor's Committee in 1944 that it "request the Real Estate Board, the Chamber of Commerce, the banks, the City Plan Commission, the Chicago Housing Authority, Chicago Housing Council, and labor organizations to develop a program to house the citizens of Chicago, including Negro families of the South Side, in the immediate postwar period. Request them to join with efforts to abolish restrictive covenants. Point out to them that the abolition of restrictive covenants will not involve the influx of any large number of Negro families to any predominantly white neighborhood, any more than free access to the purchase of automobiles will encourage all Negroes to purchase Cadillac or Ford cars. Request these groups to support public housing for the rental market which cannot be served by private enterprise."[17]

The Mayor's Committee itself went on record as being opposed to restrictive covenants and pledged to "continue to work earnestly with other effective agencies to rid the city of arbitrary restrictions on the living space of any group." The Committee chairman stated: "No people can live decently unless they can live freely. The ghetto is a feature of medieval Europe that has no place in America. . . . At present Negroes are confined to restricted areas with bad houses and exorbitant rents. They are confined to these districts by an atmosphere of prejudice and specifically by conspiracies known as restrictive covenants. This Committee has by formal vote declared itself categorically opposed to restrictions of race, creed, or color on the place where any of Chicago's citizens may live." Black Metropolis, remembering similar statements twenty years before by another Commission on Race Relations, remains skeptical.

On June 23, 1945, the *Defender* published an editorial, *DANGER: DYNAMITE AT LARGE*, which said, in part:

*Hate-crazed incendiaries carrying the faggots of intolerance have in the past several months attacked some 30 homes occupied by Negroes on the fringes of the black belt, solely because these colored citizens have desperately crossed the unwritten boundary in their search for a hovel to live in. Buildings have been set afire, bombed, stoned and razed. Their occupants have been shot and slugged.*

[17] *City Planning in Race Relations,* p. 60.

*To date the Chicago Police Department has done virtually nothing to apprehend the guilty.*

*With the hot summer days ahead, there is dire danger in continued inaction.*

*Today racial dynamite is scattered about the South side. It needs but a spark to explode.*

The *Defender* spoke scornfully of "studies and surveys . . . promises and pledges."[18] It demanded that the City suspend restrictive covenants by a war emergency order and "post full and complete police protection" for Negroes moving into houses.

The inhabitants of the Black Ghetto grow restless in their frustration, penned in, isolated, overcrowded. During a depression or a war (the periods covered by this account), the consciousness of their exclusion and subordination is tremendously heightened. Within this spatial and social framework morale tends to be low and tempers taut. Anti-Semitic sentiments are latent. Demands for the economic and political control of the Black Belt arise. Resentments assume various organizational forms. The people marshal their economic and political power and make demands for improvements within the Black Belt and for its ultimate dissolution as an enforced state of existence. For, while it is conceivable that many Negroes would prefer to live in an all-Negro community, they resent being forced to live there.

[18] After declaring its opposition to restrictive covenants, the Mayor's Committee seemed to avoid any further discussion of the abolition of covenants. Evidently the Committee soon realized that it had no power or authority to attack them legally and was hesitant to antagonize the political machine and powerful real estate interests. As in other fields when up against entrenched interests, the Mayor's Committee found itself powerless to act and seemingly reluctant to continue any agitation.

# 24

## THE NEGRO AS AN IMMIGRANT GROUP: RECENT TRENDS IN RACIAL AND ETHNIC SEGREGATION IN CHICAGO
*Karl E. and Alma F. Taeuber*

DURING the last half of the nineteenth century and the early decades of the twentieth, millions of immigrants from Europe entered the United States. Many of these immigrants settled initially in ethnic colonies in large northern cities and found jobs as unskilled

Paper No. 15 in the series, "Comparative Urban Research," was issued from the Population Research and Training Center, University of Chicago, under a grant from the Ford Founda-

laborers in burgeoning mass-production industries. With the onset of World War I in Europe, and with the passage of restrictive legislation in the United States in the early 1920s, the period of massive overseas migration came to an end. At the same time, however, there developed a large-scale migration of Negroes from the South to the same large northern industrial cities. Like the immigrants from abroad, the Negro migrants to northern cities filled the lowest occupational niches and rapidly developed highly segregated patterns of residence within the central cities.

In view of many obvious similarities between the Negro migrants and the various immigrant groups preceding them, it has been suggested that northern urban Negroes are but the latest of the immigrant groups, undergoing much the same processes of adaptation to city life and of assimilation into the general social structure as the European groups preceding them.[1] The persistence of Negroes as a residentially segregated and underprivileged group at the lowest levels of socioeconomic status, however, is frequently interpreted in terms of distinctive aspects of the Negro experience, particularly their historical position in American society.[2]

The question of whether or not a northern urban Negro population can fruitfully be viewed as an immigrant population, comparable to European immigrant populations of earlier decades with respect to the nature and speed of assimilation, will be explored on the basis of data permitting analysis of recent trends in racial and ethnic segregation in Chicago.

The processes by which various immigrant groups have been absorbed into American society are complex and have been studied from a variety of viewpoints. Unfortunately there is no sociological consensus on a definition of assimilation and there is nothing approaching a definitive study of the processes of assimilation for any one immigrant group. It is beyond the scope of our task here to attempt to provide such a definition. We feel that a distinctively sociological approach to the topic must view assimilation as a process of dispersion of members of the group throughout the social structure. Cultural and psychological processes, we feel, should not be incorporated into a sociological definition, although their relationship to institutional dispersion should, of course, be retained as one focus of research on assimilation.

---

tion. A preliminary version of this paper was read at the 1962 annual meetings of the American Statistical Association. We appreciate the reactions of Stanley Lieberson, Judah Matras, and Margaret G. Reid to that version.

Karl E. and Alma F. Taeuber, "The Negro as an Immigrant Group: Recent Trends in Racial and Ethnic Segregation in Chicago," *American Journal of Sociology*, LXIX (January 1964), 374–382. Reprinted with the permission of The University of Chicago Press.

[1] Philip M. Hauser, "On the Impact of Urbanism on Social Organization, Human Nature and the Political Order," *Confluence*, VII (Spring, 1958), 65. Elsewhere Hauser has expressed a more cautious view, emphasizing the lack of definitive knowledge; see his *Population Perspectives* (New Brunswick, N. J.: Rutgers University Press, 1960), p. 129.

[2] D. J. Bogue, "Chicago's Growing Population Problem," *Commerce*, LIX (July, 1962), 31.

For our purposes, it will suffice to have a working definition of the process of assimilation considerably less sophisticated than that required for a general sociological theory. Accepting the view that both immigrant groups and Negro migrants originally settled in segregated patterns in central areas of cities and ranked very low in terms of socioeconomic measures, assimilation then consisted in large part of a process of social and economic advancement on the part of the original members of the group and their descendants, along with a decreasing residential concentration in ethnic colonies. Our concern with diminishing residential segregation as a necessary concomitant of the assimilation process derives from Myrdal's discussion of the "mechanical" importance of residential segregation in facilitating other forms of segregation and discrimination, and Hawley's discussion of the impact of spatial patterns on race relations.[3] Our concern with socioeconomic advance reflects the initially low status of the groups with which we are concerned, whereas a more general treatment would need to reckon with the unusually high status of some immigrant stocks, as well as with other aspects of social status and institutional dispersion than those for which we have data.

The data in Table 1 illustrate for selected immigrant groups the patterns of socioeconomic advance and residential dispersion from highly segregated ethnic colonies. For each of the larger ethnic groups, data for 1950 show the average standing on three measures of socioeconomic status, standardized for age, of the first generation (the foreign-born white, FBW) and the second generation (native white of foreign or mixed parentage, NWFMP). The nationality groups are split into "old," "new," and "newer" groups in an extension of the traditional system. On the average, comparing within the first or within the second generation, the "old" immigrant groups are the best off on these measures, the "new" groups are intermediate, and the "newer" groups are the worst off. It cannot be determined from these data to what extent the old immigrants are better off by virtue of their longer average length of residence in the United States, or to what extent they may have been better off at their time of immigration than the newer immigrants were at the time of their move.

Comparisons between the first and second generations might appear to be a more direct means for assessing the extent of socioeconomic advance, particularly since the emphasis in the literature on assimilation is on intergenerational processes rather than simply on processes of upward mobility through time in the status of the original immigrants. Comparisons of corresponding status measures for the first and second generations in Table 1 reveal, in general, the expected pattern of intergenerational advance. Data such as these, however, do not refer directly to a specific set of immigrant parents and their native-born children and must be interpreted with

---

[3] Gunnar Myrdal, *An American Dilemma* (New York: Harper & Row, 1944), I, 618; Amos H. Hawley, "Dispersion versus Segregation: Apropos of a Solution of Race Problems," *Papers of the Michigan Academy of Science, Arts, and Letters,* XXX (1944), 667–74.

great caution.[4] For instance, it would be unwarranted on the basis of these data to assume that descendants of German immigrants are not as well off as their parents in terms of education. It is more credible that recent immigrants from Germany, under our immigration laws, include a large proportion of persons of high socioeconomic status.

Measures of the changing residential patterns of the immigrant groups are given in columns 7–9 of Table 1. The measure, an index of residential segregation between the total foreign stock (FBW+NWFMP) of each nationality and the total native whites of native parentage (NWNP) assumes a value of 100 for maximum residential segregation and a value of 0 if the residential distributions are identical.[5] The indexes were computed from the distribution of each group among the seventy-five community areas of the city of Chicago for 1930 (the last previous census year that included information on the total foreign stock) and 1960. The degree of residential segregation from the native population is highest for the "newer" immigrants and lowest for the "old" immigrants. Between 1930 and 1960, most of the ethnic groups became less segregated from the native population. Only for England, Ireland, and Sweden did the indexes fail to decline, and these were already at relatively low levels.[6]

This general approach to the measurement or assimilation of immigrant groups has been pursued for a number of cities and longer time periods by Lieberson. He found a remarkably persistent and consistent association through time between residential desegregation of an ethnic group and increasing socioeconomic similarity to native whites, and cross-sectionally between the position of each group as compared to others on measures of residential segregation and its relative levels on status measures.[7]

The index of residential segregation between Negroes and NWNP for 1930 was eighty-four, and for 1960, eighty-two. These values are higher than any of those for specific immigrant stocks. Furthermore, each of the immigrant stocks was highly segregated from Negroes in 1930 and 1960. There is relatively little intermixture of Negro residences with those of any group of whites. Even the "newer" immigrant groups, the Puerto Ricans and Mexicans, are not joining or replacing Negroes in established Negro areas but are moving into separate ethnic colonies of their own at the

[4] For an enumeration of some of the difficulties see C. A. Price and J. Zubrzycki, "The Use of Inter-marriage Statistics as an Index of Assimilation," *Population Studies*, XVI (July, 1962), 58–69.

[5] The index of residential segregation is an index of dissimilarity between the residential distributions of each group. For further discussion, see Otis Dudley Duncan and Beverly Duncan, "A Methodological Analysis of Segregation Indexes," *American Sociological Review*, XX (April, 1955), 210–17.

[6] For a more detailed discussion of these patterns using data for 1930 and 1950, see Otis Dudley Duncan and Stanley Lieberson, "Ethnic Segregation and Assimilation," *American Journal of Sociology*, LXIV (January, 1959), 364–74.

[7] Stanley Lieberson, *Ethnic Patterns in American Cities* (New York: Free Press, 1963).

Table 1 Selected characteristics (age-standardized) of foreign-born and native ethnic populations in 1950, and indexes of residential segregation of selected groups of foreign stock from native whites of native parentage, 1930 and 1960, Chicago[a]

| Country of origin | Percent highschool graduates (males age 25 and over) | | Percent with income above $3,000 (persons with income) | | Percent with white-collar jobs (employed males) | | Index of residential segregation (compared with NWNP) | | |
| --- | --- | --- | --- | --- | --- | --- | --- | --- | --- |
| | FBW | NWFMP | FBW | NWFMP | FBW | NWFMP | 1930 | 1960 | Change |
| "Old" immigrant groups: | | | | | | | | | |
| England and Wales | 45 | 50 | 53 | 58 | 49 | 51 | 11 | 18 | + 7 |
| Ireland | 24 | 47 | 47 | 56 | 22 | 47 | 23 | 31 | + 8 |
| Norway | 31 | 47 | 54 | 57 | 24 | 51 | 44 | 37 | − 7 |
| Sweden | 25 | 48 | 59 | 60 | 23 | 51 | 26 | 30 | + 4 |
| Germany | 37 | 34 | 53 | 55 | 34 | 42 | 22 | 19 | − 3 |
| "New" immigrant groups: | | | | | | | | | |
| Austria | 29 | 40 | 54 | 57 | 33 | 44 | 30 | 16 | −14 |
| Czechoslovakia | 25 | 33 | 44 | 54 | 22 | 36 | 59 | 37 | −22 |
| Italy | 15 | 27 | 47 | 53 | 24 | 37 | 52 | 32 | −20 |
| Poland | 18 | 25 | 42 | 49 | 25 | 30 | 63 | 38 | −25 |
| U.S.S.R. | 35 | 60 | 60 | 69 | 59 | 74 | 51 | 44 | − 7 |
| "Newer" immigrant groups: | | | | | | | | | |
| Mexico | 14 | 16 | 38 | 29 | 8 | 13 | 71 | 54 | −17 |
| Puerto Rico[b] | 13 | 29 | 16 | 37 | 22 | 36 | † | 67 | b |

[a] Data for 1930 and 1950 refer to foreign white stock (foreign-born plus native of foreign or mixed parentage); data for 1960 refer to total foreign stock. Abbreviations used are FBW for foreign-born white, NWFMP for native white of foreign or mixed parentage, and NWNP for native white of native parentage. The three socioeconomic characteristics refer to the Standard Metropolitan Area population, while the segregation indexes are based on community areas within the city. Age-standardization was by the direct method, using age groups 25–44 and 45 and over, with the Standard Metropolitan Area age composition as a standard.

[b] Socioeconomic characteristics for Puerto Rican population refer to total United States; Puerto Rican population by community areas for Chicago available for 1960 only.

Source: Characteristics from U. S. Bureau of the Census, U. S. Census of Population: 1950, Vol. IV, Special Reports, Pt. 3, chap. A, "Nativity and Parentage," and chap. D, "Puerto Ricans in Continental United States," Distributions of population by community areas for 1930 and 1960 from data on file at Chicago Community Inventory, University of Chicago.

periphery of Negro areas. Negroes clearly occupy a distinctive position as the most residentially segregated of the principal migrant groups. The separation of Negroes from all groups of whites is sharper than any of the patterns of residential segregation between ethnic groups or between socioeconomic groups within the white population.[8] Apparently this pattern has developed during the last few decades. Lieberson has demonstrated that, although prior to the great Negro migrations of World War I there were instances of immigrant stocks being more segregated from native whites than were Negroes, since 1920 there has been a general tendency for Negro residential segregation to be highest.[9]

Data pertaining specifically to the comparison between whites and non-whites (ninety-seven percent of Chicago's non-whites are Negroes) on

Table 2 Selected socioeconomic characteristics (unstandardized) of whites and non-whites, Chicago, 1940, 1950, and 1960

| Characteristic | Non-white | White |
|---|---|---|
| Residential segregation index, whites vs. Negroes:[a] | | |
| 1930 | 85 | |
| 1940 | 85 | |
| 1950 | 79 | |
| 1960 | 83 | |
| Percent high school graduates, ages 25+: | | |
| 1940 | 16 | 25 |
| 1950 | 25 | 37 |
| 1960 | 29 | 37 |
| Percent white-collar, male: | | |
| 1940 | 17 | 40 |
| 1950 | 17 | 41 |
| 1960 | 21 | 40 |
| Percent home-owners: | | |
| 1940 | 7 | 26 |
| 1950 | 12 | 33 |
| 1960 | 16 | 39 |
| Percent multiple-person households with 1.01 or more persons per room: | | |
| 1940 | 41 | 17 |
| 1950 | 46 | 14 |
| 1960 | 34 | 10 |

[a] These values differ slightly from those cited in the text for Negroes as compared to native whites of native parentage.
Source: Data for 1940 from the 1940 Census Tract Bulletin for Chicago; for 1950 from Philip M. Hauser and Evelyn M. Kitagawa (eds.), Local Community Fact Book for Chicago, 1950 (Chicago: Chicago Community Inventory, 1953); and for 1960 from the 1960 Census Tract Bulletin for Chicago.

[8] For a discussion of class residential segregation in Chicago see Otis Dudley Duncan and Beverly Duncan, "Residential Distribution and Occupational Stratification," American Journal of Sociology, LX (March, 1955), 493–503.

[9] Lieberson, op. cit., pp. 120–132.

measures of socioeconomic status and of residential segregation are presented in Table 2. For each of four measures reflecting socioeconomic status, there was improvement in the status of the non-white population between 1940 and 1960. (For whites, improving status would be more clearly evident if the data referred to the entire metropolitan area rather than just the city of Chicago.) The indexes of residential segregation between whites and Negroes, in the top panel of the table, show minor fluctuations around an extremely high level and give no indication of the decline anticipated on the basis of the socioeconomic advancement of the Negro population. That this is not an atypical finding is indicated by reference to other data showing a long term historical trend toward increasing residential segregation between whites and non-whites. Increasing racial residential segregation was evident in most large cities of the United States between 1940 and 1950, while during the 1950s, southern cities continued to increase in segregation and northern cities generally registered modest declines.[10]

In broad perspective, the historical trend toward improving socioeconomic status of immigrant groups has gone hand in hand with decreasing residential segregation. In contrast, Negro residential segregation from whites has increased steadily over past decades until it has reached universally high levels in cities throughout the United States, despite advances in the socioeconomic status of Negroes.

We have been unable to locate any data permitting a comparison between Negroes long resident in Chicago, or born and raised in the North, and Negroes with lesser periods of residence in the city. Thus we are not able to make even the crude intergenerational comparisons for Negroes that are possible for the immigrant groups. The only analysis of this type possible with census data is a comparison between recent migrants and the rest of the population, and the only published data are residential distributions, with no socioeconomic characteristics. For 1960, with the seventy-five community areas of Chicago as units, the index of residential segregation between non-whites resident in the metropolitan area five years or more and native whites of native parents is 80.5. Comparing non-whites with less than five years' residence in the metropolitan area and NWNP, the index was 81.0. Comparing the recent in-migrants with the non-whites who were resident in the metropolitan area five years or more, the index was thirteen. Thus the recent non-white in-migrants are distributed differently from the rest of the non-white population, but each group is highly segregated from the native whites. Unfortunately, these results cannot be readily interpreted in terms of the general assimilation and dispersion processes under consideration. Possibly there are trends toward socioeconomic advancement and residential dispersion on the part of "second generation"

[10] Karl E. Taeuber, "Negro Residential Segregation, 1940–1960: Changing Trends in the Large Cities of the United States" (paper read at the Annual Meetings of the American Sociological Association, 1962).

Negroes in Chicago that are confounded in the data for the total Negro population.

Decreasing residential concentration of immigrant groups occurred despite the efforts of many nationality organizations to maintain the ethnic colonies.[11] Few Negro organizations have been as explicitly segregationist. In some immigrant groups, many members were dispersing from the ethnic colonies even while large-scale immigration of that group was still under way. For every immigrant group, diminishing residential segregation has been evident since the cessation of large-scale immigration. For Negroes, however, residential segregation has increased since the first period of large-scale immigration to northern cities, and this increase in residential segregation continued during the late 1920s and 1930s when the volume of migration was at a low level. These observations tend to discredit the argument that a major barrier to residential dispersion of the Negro population of Chicago is its continuing rapid increase. However, the size of the Negro population and the magnitude of its annual increase are larger than for any single ethnic group in the past, and comparisons with smaller groups are not completely convincing. That rapid increase of Negro population does not necessarily lead to increasing residential segregation was demonstrated directly in the intercity comparative study previously cited. There was no definite relationship between increase in Negro population and increase in the value of the segregation index. Indeed, during the 1950–1960 decade, there appeared to be a slight relationship in the opposite direction.[12]

More significant in accounting for the divergent trends in residential segregation may be the different urban contexts in which the immigrant and Negro populations found themselves. Comparing the residential locations of Italian-born and Polish-born in Chicago in 1899 and in 1920, Wallace observed:

it can be seen that the areas of greatest dispersion, low proportion, and presumably of "second" settlement for many immigrants were those which were not settled at all in 1899.

The implication of this fact is that the so-called "assimilation" process was not reflected by the geographic dispersion of the immigrant populations into "cosmopolitan American areas." The dispersal was more directly related to an increase in housing alternatives as the city grew at the periphery.[13]

By the time the Negro concentrations were forming near the central areas of Chicago, the city was built up and the urbanized area extended well beyond the present boundaries. Residential alternatives at a price Negroes

[11] David A. Wallace, "Residential Concentration of Negroes in Chicago" (unpublished Ph.D. dissertation, Harvard University, 1953).

[12] Taeuber, op. cit.

[13] Wallace, op. cit., p. 205.

could afford and located sufficiently close in to permit inexpensive commuting were no longer available.

It has been suggested that considerable time is required for Negroes to make the transition from a "primitive folk culture" to "urbanism as a way of life."[14] Several types of data indicate that large and increasing proportions of the Negro urban population are city-born and raised. For instance, there is a rapidly decreasing color differential in the percentage of the Chicago population born in the state of Illinois. In 1960, forty-four percent of the native-born, non-white residents of Chicago were born in Illinois, as contrasted to sixty-six percent of the white population.[15] National estimates for 1958 showed that of all males aged 45–64 living in metropolitan places of 500,000 or more population, sixty-five percent of the non-whites, as compared to seventy-seven percent of the whites, had lived in this size city for twenty years or longer.[16] Estimates of the components of growth of the non-white population of Chicago indicate that between 1950 and 1960 natural increase was as important as net immigration, and that natural increase will in the future account for rapidly increasing proportions of the growth of the non-white population.[17]

Unfortunately there is inadequate knowledge of the specific length of time under specified conditions for the required cultural transformation to occur. Wallace's observations indicate a significant degree of dispersal over time among first-generation immigrants. Such processes are more often conceived as primarily intergenerational. That many of the "first generation" Negro migrants to northern cities have lived there for twenty years or more and that in the younger adult ages there are sizable numbers of "second-generation" urban Negroes suggest that there has been ample time for any necessary adjustment to urban living, at least for large proportions of the Negro population. It is also clear that if northern Negroes remain inadequately educated for urban living and fail to participate fully in the urban economy, the "primitive folk culture" of the South can less and less be assigned responsibility, and northern cities will be suffering from the neglect of their own human resources.

The "visibility" of Negroes due to skin color and other features which make the large majority of second-, third-, and later-generation descendants readily identifiable as Negroes is often cited as a basic factor in accounting for the distinctive position of Negroes in our society. It is

---

[14] Philip M. Hauser, "The Challenge of Metropolitan Growth," *Urban Land*, XVII (December, 1958), 5.

[15] Data from U. S. Bureau of the Census, *U. S. Census of Population, 1960: General Social and Economic Characteristics, Illinois*. Final Report PC(1)–15C, Tables 72 and 77.

[16] Karl E. Taeuber, "Duration-of-Residence Analysis of Internal Migration in the United States," *Milbank Memorial Fund Quarterly*, XXXIX (January, 1961), Table 3.

[17] D. J. Bogue and D. P. Dandekar, *Population Trends and Prospects for the Chicago-Northwestern Indiana Consolidated Metropolitan Area: 1960 to 1990* (Chicago: Population Research and Training Center, University of Chicago, 1962).

exceedingly difficult to assess the significance of visibility. There is no other group that is strictly comparable to Negroes regarding every factor except visibility. It is not completely irrelevant, however, to note that non-white skin color, by itself, is not an insurmountable handicap in our society. The socioeconomic status of the Japanese population of Chicago in 1950 substantially exceeded that of the Negro population; and their residential segregation from whites, although high, was considerably lower than that between Negroes and whites.[18] Unfortunately there are no trend data available on the characteristics of the Japanese in Chicago. A more appropriate Japanese population for comparison, however, is the much larger one in the San Francisco area. A recent study there affirmed that "ethnic colonies of Japanese are gone or rapidly going" and documented their rapid socioeconomic advance.[19]

In the traditional immigrant pattern, the more recent immigrants displaced the older groups at the bottom socioeconomic levels. How do the Negroes compare with the other "newer" immigrant groups, the Mexicans and the Puerto Ricans? The limited data now available suggest that the Negroes may soon be left alone at the bottom of the social and economic scale. We have already noted (from data in Table 1) that the "newer" groups were, in 1950, of very low status compared to the other immigrant groups, and that their residential segregation from the native whites of native parentage was the highest of all the immigrant groups. For 1960, data on distribution within Chicago of persons born in Puerto Rico are available separately from data on those persons born in the United States of Puerto Rican parentage. Thus it is possible to compute indexes of residential segregation for first- and second-generation Puerto Ricans. For Chicago in 1960, these index values were 68.4 for the first generation and 64.9 for the second generation, indicating that residential dispersion has already begun for the Puerto Ricans. This difference actually understates the amount of dispersion, since the second generation consists in large proportion of children still living with their first-generation parents.

Selected socioeconomic measures for the Puerto Rican and the non-white populations of Chicago in 1960 are shown in Table 3. On every measure, the Puerto Rican population is less well off—it is less educated, has lower income, is more crowded, is less likely to own homes, is less well housed, and lives in older buildings. Yet the index of residential segregation (computed with respect to NWNP) for Puerto Ricans is sixty-seven as compared with eighty-two for Negroes.

Up to now we have been making comparisons between Negroes and immigrant groups, demonstrating that residential dispersion has not

---

[18] Although the maximum value of the residential segregation index is less than 100 for ethnic groups of small size, this is not sufficient to vitiate the Negro-Japanese comparison.

[19] Harry H. L. Kitano, "Housing of Japanese-Americans in the San Francisco Bay Area," in Nathan Glazer and Davis McEntire (eds.), *Studies in Housing and Minority Groups* (Berkeley, Calif.: University of California Press, 1960), p. 184.

Table 3 *Selected socioeconomic characteristics (unstandardized) of Puerto Ricans and non-whites, Chicago, 1960*

| Characteristic | Non-white | Puerto Rican |
|---|---|---|
| Residential segregation vs. whites | 83 | 67 |
| Percent high school graduates, total | 29 | 11 |
| Median family income | $4,742 | $4,161 |
| Percent families earning <$3,000 | 28 | 27 |
| Percent families earning >$10,000 | 9 | 4 |
| Percent home-owners | 16 | 6 |
| Percent substandard dwellings | 26 | 33 |
| Percent 1.01 or more persons per room | 34 | 52 |
| Percent housing units built since 1940 | 12 | 6 |
| Median gross rent | $88 | $79 |
| Median number of rooms | 3.9 | 3.7 |
| Median number of persons | 3.0 | 4.0 |

Source: Data are from the 1960 Census Tract Bulletin for Chicago.

accompanied socioeconomic advance by Negroes in the way it did for immigrant groups. Economic status and expenditure for housing, however, are clearly correlated, and there is also a correlation between economic status and residential segregation. By virtue of variations in the type, age, and quality of housing, and in the patterns of residential choice by persons of varying socioeconomic status, the subareas of a city are differentiated in terms of the average status of their residents. Since Negroes are of much lower average status than whites, they would be expected to be disproportionately represented in low-status residential areas. In fact, an extreme position regarding the relationships between patterns of socioeconomic residential segregation and racial residential segregation would attribute all of the latter to the former. Such a position is sometimes offered as a counterargument to charges of racial discrimination against the real estate business. To the extent that this position is correct, it might be expected that future economic advances on the part of the Negro population should be translated into decreased residential segregation.

The task of partialing out a component of racial segregation due to economic factors involves some difficult methodological problems, and no method is entirely satisfactory.[20] Our approach utilizes indirect standardization of available census data. Let us delineate the status of a residential area in terms of, say, the income distribution of its residents. Specifically, consider for each community area of Chicago the number of families with incomes below $1,000, from $1,000–1,999, from $2,000–2,999, and so forth. For the city as a whole in 1960, forty-four percent of all families with an income below $1,000 were non-white, as were forty-four percent of families with incomes from $1,000–1,999, and forty percent of families with incomes from $2,000–2,999. For each community area, we can apply these

[20] A general discussion of this problem can be found in the section on explanation of areal variation in Otis Dudley Duncan, Ray P. Cuzzort, and Beverly Duncan, *Statistical Geography* (New York: Free Press, 1961).

city-wide percentages to the observed income distribution to obtain the number of non-white families expected if income alone determined the residential locations of whites and non-whites.

By the method of indirect standardization just outlined, we obtain an expected number of non-white and white families for each of the seventy-five community areas. We can then compute an index of residential segregation between expected numbers of non-white and white families. This index can be regarded as the amount of racial residential segregation attributable to patterns of residential differentiation of income groups. For 1950, the index of residential segregation between the numbers of whites and non-whites expected on the basis of income was eleven, as compared with the actual segregation index of seventy-nine. As a rough measure, then, we can attribute 11/79, or fourteen percent, of the observed racial residential segregation in Chicago in 1950 to income differentials between whites and non-whites. For 1960, the corresponding values are ten for the expected index, eighty-three for the observed index, and twelve percent for the racial segregation attributable to income differentials.

In a recent study of the relationships between housing consumption and income, Reid has demonstrated many pitfalls in the uncritical use of income distributions in the analysis of housing patterns.[21] We have therefore repeated the above analyses, using distributions by major occupational groups and distributions by educational attainment. For 1960, the index of residential segregation computed from the numbers of whites and non-whites expected on the basis of patterns of occupational differentiation is nine, and that expected on the basis of patterns of educational differentiation is three. The results using income distributions are thus supported by the results from other measures of socioeconomic status, and the conclusion seems clear that patterns of socioeconomic differentiation of residential areas can account for only a small proportion of observed racial residential segregation.

Reid demonstrated that differences between whites and non-whites in observed patterns of housing consumption are largely attributable to income differentials between whites and non-whites. Our analysis suggests that residential segregation cannot be attributed to these differentials. Apparently the economic structure of the housing market for whites is similar to that for non-whites, even though non-whites are excluded from a large share of the housing supply for which their economic circumstances would allow them to compete.

The judicious conclusion from our review of a variety of pieces of data is that we simply do not yet know enough about immigrant assimilation processes and any corresponding processes among Negro migrants to northern cities to be able to compare the two. We believe that this very lack of knowledge makes questionable any attempt to reason from presumed patterns of assimilation among immigrants in the past to current

[21] Margaret G. Reid, *Housing and Income* (Chicago: University of Chicago Press, 1962).

racial problems in northern cities. Furthermore, such evidence as we could compile indicates that it is more likely to be misleading than instructive to make such comparisons.

Our definition of assimilation as involving socioeconomic advancement and residential dispersion is simple, and greater differences between groups would appear were a more complex definition adopted. Restriction of portions of the analysis to the city of Chicago had little effect on the measures for non-whites, but probably led to an understatement of the degree of assimilation of the immigrant stocks insofar as higher-status members of these groups have moved to the suburbs. The segregation indexes probably overstate somewhat the residential isolation of small groups, such as particular immigrant stocks, as compared with large groups such as total native whites of native parents. Taking account of any of these limitations in our data would tend to increase the differences between Negroes and immigrant groups. Even so, our data showed that second-generation persons from several countries are of higher socioeconomic status than the total native whites of native parentage. Relatively few Negroes in Chicago have white-collar jobs or incomes above the median level for whites, and yet there are large numbers of adult Negroes who were born in the city. Basic differences between the Negroes and the immigrant groups seems to us implicit in the failure of residential desegregation to occur for Negroes while it has continued for the immigrant groups.

In view of the fundamental impact of residential segregation on extralegal segregation of schools, hospitals, parks, stores, and numerous other facilities, the failure of residential dispersion to occur strikes us as an especially serious social problem. Socioeconomic advance and residential dispersion occurred simultaneously for the various immigrant groups. It is apparent that the continued residential segregation of the Negro population is an impediment to the continued "assimilation" of Negroes into full and equal participation in the economy and the society at large.

## SUGGESTIONS FOR FURTHER READING

S TUDIES of black migration to the North and the cities that supplement Louise P. Kennedy, *The Negro Peasant Turns Cityward* are *Emmett J. Scott, *Negro Migration During the War* (New York, 1920); *Arna Bontemps and Jack Conroy, *Anyplace But Here* (paperback title; New York, 1966); Lynn T. Smith, "The Redistribution of the Negro Population of the United States, 1910–1960," *Journal of Negro History*, LI (July 1966); and Reynolds Farley, "The

* An asterisk indicates that the book is available in paperback.

Urbanization of Negroes in the United States," *Journal of Social History,* I (Spring 1968). An interesting analysis of the five-year period from 1955 to 1960 is given in Karl E. and Alma F. Taeuber, "The Changing Character of Negro Migration," *American Journal of Sociology,* LXX (January 1965).

For the historical background of the ghetto, the reader should consult *W. E. B. Du Bois, *The Philadelphia Negro* (Philadelphia, 1897); *Seth M. Scheiner, *Negro Mecca: A History of the Negro in New York City, 1865–1920* (New York, 1965); *Gilbert Osofsky, *Harlem: The Making of a Ghetto, 1890–1930* (New York, 1966); *St. Clair Drake and Horace Cayton, *Black Metropolis* (New York, 1945); *Allan H. Spear, *Black Chicago: The Making of a Negro Ghetto, 1890–1920* (Chicago, 1967); and *Constance Green, *The Secret City: A History of Race Relations in the Nation's Capital* (Princeton, N.J., 1967). An investigation of a particular group of migrants was made by *Clyde V. Kiser, *Sea Island to City: A Study of St. Helena Islanders in Harlem and Other Urban Centers* (New York, 1932).

There is need for studies of the relationship between the urbanization process and institutions of the black community. A number of works have examined certain institutions. For the church, see Benjamin E. Mays and Joseph Nicholson, *The Negro Church* (New York, 1933); Arthur Huff Fauset, *Black Gods of the Metropolis: Negro Religious Cults of the Urban North* (Philadelphia, 1944); *E. Franklin Frazier, *The Negro Church in America* (New York, 1963); and Seth M. Scheiner, "The Negro Church and the Northern City, 1890–1930," in *William G. Shade and Roy C. Herrenkohl (eds.), *Seven on Black* (Philadelphia, 1969). For the family, see *E. Franklin Frazier, *The Negro Family in the United States* (rev. ed.; Chicago, 1966); *Lee Rainwater and William Yancey (eds.), *The Moynihan Report* (Boston, 1967); and *Andrew Billingsley, *Black Families in White America* (Englewood Cliffs, N.J., 1968). For politics, see *Harold F. Gosnell, *Negro Politicians: The Rise of Negro Politics in Chicago* (Chicago, 1935) and *James Q. Wilson, *Negro Politics* (Glencoe, Ill., 1960). For the relationship between urbanization and class structure, see *E. Franklin Frazier, *Black Bourgeoisie* (Glencoe, Ill., 1957); G. Franklin Edwards, *The Negro Professional Class* (Glencoe, Ill., 1959); August Meier and David Lewis, "History of the Negro Upper Class in Atlanta, Georgia, 1880–1958," *Journal of Negro Education,* XXVIII (Spring 1959); and Nicholas Babchuk and Ralph V. Thompson, "The Voluntary Associations of Negroes," *American Sociological Review,* XXVII (October 1962).

In recent years scholars have devoted substantial time to investigating residential patterns and living conditions in the ghetto. For the former, and to some extent the latter, the following are very useful: Otis and Beverly Duncan, *The Negro Population of Chicago* (Chicago, 1957); Stanley Lieberson, *Ethnic Patterns in American Cities* (New York, 1963); *Karl E. and Alma F. Taeuber, *Negroes in Cities* (Chicago, 1965); Leo F. Schnore, "Social Class Segregation Among Non-whites in Metropolitan Centers," *Demography,* II (1965); and Nathan Kantrowitz, "Ethnic and Racial Segregation in the New York Metropolis, 1960," *American Journal of Sociology,* LXXIV (May 1969). Life in the ghetto is perceptively dealt with in *Kenneth Clark, *Dark Ghetto* (New York, 1965). An earlier work but still useful is Robert C. Weaver, *The Negro Ghetto* (New York, 1948). Also valuable is Richard L. Morrill, "The Negro Ghetto: Problems and Alternatives," *Geographical Review,* LV (July 1965).

---

* An asterisk indicates that the book is available in paperback.

# ❧CHAPTER NINE ☙
# The Militant Twenties

**❧ "I** , MYSELF, is anxious to leave this part of the country and be where a negro man can appreshate beaing a man. . . ."* For the Alabama black who expressed these feelings in a letter to the Chicago *Defender* in 1917 and the multitude of blacks who held similar sentiments, the North seemed to hold out the opportunity for a new life. It was the promised land. Feelings of optimism among blacks were further encouraged by World War I propaganda that spoke of making "the world safe for democracy." Yet it was a guarded optimism. It is a "bit of high-sounding phraseology," wrote the Afro-American author, musical composer, social critic, and race leader, James Weldon Johnson, but those who are mouthing it "are advertising the article, making it a household word."

The dream was tarnished by events in the immediate postwar period. Riots directed against blacks during and after the war (particularly the more than twenty-five in the last half of 1919), the lynching of black soldiers still in uniform, discrimination in employment, and substandard living conditions in northern ghettos led to disillusionment. But disillusionment did not mean suffering in silence; nor did it stem the tide of migration northward.

There were various forms of protest in the 1920s. Urbanization stimulated both ethnocentric and integrationist tendencies. Calls for internal development, racial solidarity, and the abolition of discriminatory practices increased. The NAACP pursued actions in the courts against violations of the Fourteenth and Fifteenth Amendments. Socialists such as A. Philip Randolph and Chandler Owen condemned capitalistic exploitation of the working class and the NAACP's alleged middle-class bias. The writings of the "New Negro" stressed pride in black culture and to some extent criticized discrimination. Marcus Garvey turned to Africa as an escape from the racism in American society. And some blacks retaliated against white violence in a few white-initiated riots.

The rising militancy among many blacks in the 1920s led to the designation "New Negro." Following trends in evidence before World War I, the New Negro was not only more impatient with discriminatory practices but took special pride in his color and culture. "We younger Negro artists who create," wrote Langston Hughes of his fellow artists of the Negro Renaissance, "now intend to express our individual dark-skinned selves without fear or shame."

In selection 25, Wayne Cooper concentrates on one participant in the Negro Renaissance, Claude McKay. Poet and novelist, McKay emphasized race consciousness, expressed disillusionment with both capitalism and Western civilization, and urged blacks to fight against discriminatory practices. In his poems and novels, as Cooper notes, McKay spoke positively of the Afro-American's folk culture and placed his faith in the Negro masses. His writings sought to make black respectable. McKay also shared the Lost Generation's alienation from society. Many white writers and artists joined McKay in glorifying the black folk culture, but their perspective appears to have been different. Consider how the white intellectual's conception of the black and black culture in the 1920s differed from those of McKay and other Afro-American artists.

Edmund David Cronon notes in selection 26 that the forces which gave rise to the Negro Renaissance also contributed to the Garvey movement's appeal. Like McKay and other black writers of the 1920s, Garvey encouraged pride in color and heritage, called for racial solidarity, and implored blacks to determine their own destiny. Garvey and the New Negro, though, did not develop their ideas in a vacuum. They drew upon earlier traditions in the Afro-American experience. Years before Garvey arrived in the United States, as noted in earlier selections, other blacks had espoused his dream of establishing a nation of black Americans in Africa, his proposals for a separate black economy, and his view of the black man's cultural heritage. The economic program of Garveyism, for example, contained striking similarities to Booker T. Washington's philosophy. Washington's *Up From Slavery* made a profound impression upon Garvey. Both men reflected the ethnocentric tradition that August Meier referred to earlier in this volume. One can find striking parallels in their ideology. To what extent was Garvey's program, like that of Washington's, an accommodation to racism in American society? The reader should compare Cronon's analysis of Garvey with Meier's examination of Washington and Du Bois.

In contrast to Washington and the New Negro of the twenties, it appears that Garvey had a wide appeal among lower-class blacks. Despite their use of themes based on the life of the black masses, it is unlikely that the writers of the Negro Renaissance gained the enthusiastic and extensive acceptance among lower-class blacks that Garvey did. Garvey represented far more directly the frustrations experienced by the urban black masses. "Black nationalism has its roots in . . . urban tensions and in the hopeless frustration which the Negroes experience in trying to identify themselves and their aspirations with white society."[1] Cronon explores the techniques employed by Garvey to give those at the bottom of the economic ladder a sense of involvement in his movement.

Cronon considers Garvey's call for a return to Africa counterproductive. The New Negro and most black Americans rejected a mass exodus to Africa. Their emphasis on race pride and self-help was directed to resolving Du Bois's dilemma of being both a Negro and American. The reader should consider the following questions. Did Garvey want all black Americans to relocate in Africa? Or did he visualize a powerful African nation as a lever for improving the position of blacks in the United States? Should not the Garvey movement be evaluated in terms of the black experience in America rather than the success or failure of its back-to-Africa program and its various business ventures?

[1] E. U. Essien-Udom, *Black Nationalism: A Search for an Identity in America* (Chicago, 1962), p. 23.

# 25

## CLAUDE McKAY AND THE NEW NEGRO OF THE 1920's
### Wayne Cooper

A S used in the 1920's, the term "New Negro" referred to more than the writers then active in the Negro Renaissance. The New Negro also included the Negro masses and especially the young. "For the younger generation," Alain Locke wrote in 1925, "is vibrant with a new psychology."[1] This new spirit he described as basically a renewal of "self-respect and self-dependence."[2]

The new confidence which characterized Negroes in the twenties resulted from many forces. Prior to World War I, militant new leaders had arisen. By demanding immediately full civil liberties and an end to segregation, men such as W. E. B. Du Bois had inspired a greater self-assertiveness in their people. World War I and the resulting mass migration of Negroes to the urban North further disrupted old patterns of life and created new hopes, as well as new problems. The fight for democracy abroad led to greater expectations at home. The bloody race riots of 1919 did not kill these hopes, although the remarkable popularity of Marcus

Wayne Cooper, "Claude McKay and the New Negro of the 1920's," *Phylon*, XXV (Fall 1964), 297–306. Reprinted by permission of *Phylon*.

[1] Alain Locke (ed.), *The New Negro* (New York, 1925), p. 3.

[2] *Ibid.,* p. 4.

Garvey and his black nationalism indicated the Negro masses could not forever contain their frustrated aspirations.[3] As the Negro people entered the twenties, the "promised land" of the old spirituals still seemed far away. But their new militancy demonstrated that the long journey down the bitter desert years of history had strengthened, not weakened, their determination to reach the good life ahead.

That sudden flowering in literature called the Negro Renaissance gave voice to the new spirit awakening in Negroes in the twenties.[4] In addition, the Negro Renaissance became a part of the general revolt by the writers of the decade against the gross materialism and outmoded moral values of America's new industrial society. Negro writers found new strength in their own folk culture. As Robert Bone has written, "The Negro Renaissance was essentially a period of self-discovery, marked by a sudden growth of interest in things Negro."[5]

Of all the Renaissance writers, Claude McKay was one of the first to express the spirit of the New Negro.[6] His first American poems appeared in 1917. Before the decade of the Negro Renaissance had begun, he was already winning recognition as an exciting new voice in Negro literature.[7] A brief examination of his early career will perhaps reveal more clearly some of the important characteristics of the New Negro of the 1920's.

Claude McKay was born September 15, 1889, on the British West Indian island of Jamaica. There he grew to manhood. In 1912, at the age of twenty-three, he came to the United States to study agriculture at Tuskegee Institute. In Jamaica, McKay had already established a local reputation as a poet, having produced before he left two volumes of dialect poetry, Song of Jamaica and Constab Ballads.[8]

These volumes revealed McKay to be a sensitive, intelligent observer of Jamaican life. Of black peasant origin himself, he used the English dialect of rural Jamaica to record lyrically the life of his people. In evaluating McKay's Jamaican verse, Jean Wagner has recently written:

Here, we are far from the dialect of the Dunbar school, inherited from the whites, who had forged it in order to perpetuate the stereotype of Negro

---

[3] Two recent general discussions of the New Negro of the twenties are found in Robert A. Bone, The Negro Novel in America (New Haven, 1958), pp. 51–107; and Jean Wagner, Les Poetes Negres des États-Unis (Paris: Librairie Istra, 1963), pp. 161–207.

[4] Wagner, op. cit., p. 161.

[5] Bone, op. cit., p. 62.

[6] Wagner, op. cit., p. 211.

[7] McKay first became widely known after the appearance of his poem, "If We Must Die," in The Liberator (July, 1919), 20–21.

[8] Claude McKay, Songs of Jamaica (Kingston: Aston W. Gardner and Co., 1912); Constab Ballads (London, 1912).

*inferiority, and at best fix them in their role of buffoons charged with diverting the white race. . . .*[9] *All things being equal, McKay's portrait of the Jamaican peasant is in substance that of the peasant the world over. Profoundly attached to the earth, he works the soil with a knowledge gained from age long habit; although a hard worker, the Jamaican, like his counterpart the world over, is condemned to exploitation.*[10]

On the eve of his departure to the United States, McKay appeared to be an ambitious, talented young man with a fine future in Jamaica. In his poetry he had closely identified himself with its people. He had also revealed a deeply sensitive, independent spirit, keenly responsive to the good and evil in both man and nature.

Like many before him, however, he was strongly attracted to the United States. Years later, he wrote that America then seemed to him, "a new land to which all people who had youth and a youthful mind turned. Surely there would be opportunity in this land, even for a Negro."[11] Although far from naïve, McKay had never experienced firsthand American racial prejudice, and he seemed to have been totally unprepared for its vicious effects.

His initiation into the realities of Negro American life must certainly have been a swift one. Landing in Charleston, South Carolina, in the summer of 1912, he proceeded to Alabama's Tuskegee Institute. In 1918, McKay recorded in *Pearson's Magazine* his first reaction to Southern racial prejudice.

*It was the first time I had ever come face to face with such manifest, implacable hate of my race, and my feelings were indescribable. At first I was horrified; my spirit revolted against the ignoble cruelty and blindness of it all. . . . Then I found myself hating in return, but this feeling could not last long for to hate is to be miserable.*[12]

Accompanying this statement were several poems, which, McKay said, had been written during his first year in America. "I sent them so that you may see what my state of mind was at the time."[13] Among them was one of his most eloquent polemics—"To the White Fiends." This poem shows a personality unaccustomed to servility and murderously aroused against the brutish debasement of Southern prejudice. If the poet could not

[9] Wagner, *op. cit.,* p. 219.

[10] *Ibid.,* p. 220.

[11] McKay, *My Green Hills of Jamaica* (Unpublished mss. in the Schomburg Collection, New York Public Library), p. 80, written in the mid-1940s.

[12] *Pearson's Magazine* (September, 1918), 275.

[13] *Ibid.*

physically defeat it, he, nevertheless, could throw a revealing light on its moral inferiority. . . .

Soon tiring of what he described as "the semi-military, machine-like existence"[14] at Tuskegee, McKay transferred to Kansas State College, where he remained until 1914. In that year he was given several thousand dollars by an English friend.[15] Having decided his future lay in writing, not agricultural science, he took the money and went to New York City.

Once there, literary success did not come quickly. In fact, during his first year in New York, little time seems to have been devoted to writing. As he described it, through "high-living" and "bad investments" he soon managed to lose all his money.[16] His marriage to a Jamaican girl shortly after his arrival in New York lasted almost as briefly as his money.[17] "My wife," McKay wrote in 1918, "wearied of the life [in New York] in six months and went back to Jamaica."[18] McKay himself made a different decision. "I hated to go back after having failed at nearly everything so I just stayed here and worked—porter . . . janitor . . . waiter—anything that came handy."[19]

He also wrote, "If I would not," he said, "graduate as a bachelor of arts, I would graduate as a poet."[20] Within two years, Waldo Frank and James Oppenheim accepted for *Seven Arts Magazine* two of his sonnets, "The Harlem Dancer" and "Invocation."[21] A year later he was discovered by Frank Harris, who brought him to public notice again in *Pearson's Magazine*. Shortly afterwards, McKay met Max Eastman and his sister, Crystal. A life-long friendship resulted.

At the time, Max Eastman was editor of *The Liberator,* then America's most openly Marxist literary magazine.[22] Through the *Liberator,* McKay quickly became identified with the radical-bohemian set in Greenwich Village. In 1919, Eastman and his staff were eagerly praising the young communist government of Russia, violently denouncing the repressive post-war hysteria at home, and writing stories and poems that ranged from fighting proletariat propaganda to tender pieces of home and mother. Few maga-

[14] *Ibid.*

[15] Letter from McKay to James Weldon Johnson, March 10, 1928, in the McKay folder of Johnson Correspondence (James Weldon Johnson Collection, Yale University Library).

[16] Countee Cullen (ed.), *Caroling Dusk, An Anthology of Verse by Negro Poets* (New York, 1927), p. 82.

[17] Marriage certificate in the McKay Papers (Yale University Library).

[18] *Pearson's Magazine* (September, 1918), 276.

[19] *Ibid.*

[20] McKay, *A Long Way From Home* (New York, 1937), p. 4.

[21] Wagner, *op. cit.,* p. 215.

[22] For a good discussion of *The Liberator* and its origins see, Daniel Aaron, *Writers on the Left, Episodes in American Literary Communism* (New York, 1961), pp. 5–108.

zines, then or now, could match the *Liberator* in enthusiasm. Despite its flamboyancy, however, it was rich in talents. "On the surface," Robert Aaron has written, "*The Liberator* reflected the aimless, pointless life of the village." Yet, as Aaron pointed out, after World War I, it displayed a "toughness and militancy in its social attitudes,"[23] which belied its bohemian character.

Into such an atmosphere McKay fitted well. Eastman has described him then as a very black, handsome, high-spirited young man, with peculiar, arched eyebrows which gave him a perpetually quizzical expression.[24] Another old radical, Joseph Freeman, remembered also in his autobiography McKay's charm and wit.[25]

If McKay was sometimes given to abandoned gaiety, in the summer of 1919 he had good reason to exhibit a greater seriousness, as well as toughness. 1919 was the year of the Great Red Scare, one desperate phase of the effort to return to pre-war "normalcy." For Negroes, the year turned into a nightmare of bloody riots and violent death.[26] From June until January there occurred no less than twenty-five riots in major urban centers throughout the country.[27] The Chicago riot of July was the worst. When it was over, authorities counted 38 Negroes and whites dead, over 520 injured, and 1,000 families homeless.[28] Like all Negroes, McKay felt the emotional effects of such battles.

In the July issue of the *Liberator*[29] there appeared, along with six other poems, his now famous "If We Must Die." Today, it is the one poem by which McKay is most widely known. "If We Must Die" was a desperate shout of defiance; almost, it seemed a statement of tragic hopelessness. At the same time, it loudly proclaimed that in Negroes the spirit of human courage remained fully alive. . . .

After his appearance in *The Liberator*, McKay entered more fully into the literary world. His career through the twenties reads, in fact, like a romance of the decade itself. Through the generosity of friends, he went to England in late 1919 and stayed for more than a year, working part of the time for Sylvia Pankhurst's socialist paper, *The Workers' Dreadnought*. While there his third book of poems, *Spring in New Hampshire*, appeared.[30]

[23] *Ibid.*, p. 92.

[24] In McKay, *The Selected Poems of Claude McKay* (New York, 1953), p. 110.

[25] Joseph Freeman, *An American Testament, A Narrative of Rebels and Romantics* (New York, 1936), pp. 243, 245–46, 254.

[26] John Hope Franklin, *From Slavery to Freedom, A History of American Negroes* (New York, 1947), pp. 471–73.

[27] *Ibid.*

[28] *Ibid.*, pp. 473–74.

[29] *The Liberator* (July, 1919), 20–21.

[30] McKay, *A Long Way From Home*, pp. 59–91.

Upon his return to the United States in 1921, he became for a brief time co-editor of *The Liberator* with Michael Gold. Before leaving that job because of policy differences with Gold,[31] McKay's first American book of poems, *Harlem Shadows*,[32] appeared. During this period, he also made a brief first acquaintance with many leading Negro intellectuals, among them James W. Johnson and W. E. B. Du Bois.[33] But before the end of 1922, he was off again, this time to Russia.

McKay was among the first Negroes to go to Russia after the Civil War which had brought the Communists into undisputed power. He arrived during Lenin's period of ideological retrenchment, when the New Economic Policy allowed a limited amount of free enterprise and personal freedom. Because of his black complexion, McKay immediately attracted the attention of people in the street. Although not a party member, or even definitely committed to Marxist principles, McKay's popularity with the crowds in Moscow and Leningrad helped win him favor among higher party circles. Sen Katayama, then Japan's leading Communist, got McKay admitted to the Fourth Congress of the Communist International.[34] But above all, as McKay wrote James Weldon Johnson in 1935, "It was the popular interest that irresistibly pushed me forward."[35] His trip soon turned into one long triumph of personal popularity.

After meeting Trotsky in Moscow, he was sent on a long and elaborate tour of Soviet army and naval bases. Besides Trotsky, he met Zinoviev and other top Communists, as well as many leading Russian literary figures.

Despite McKay's sincere attraction to the Communist Revolution, he never fully committed himself to its ideology. In the 1930's, he was viciously attacked by American Communists for going back on his principles; but, as he wrote James Weldon Johnson in 1935, he went to Russia as "a writer and free spirit"[36] and left the same. He wrote Johnson then and later repeated in his autobiography that he had desired in 1922 the title, "creative writer," and had felt it would mean more to Negroes in the long run.[37]

Throughout the twenties, and to a large extent throughout his life, McKay remained what Frederick Hoffman called the "aesthetic radical."[38]

[31] *Ibid.*, pp. 138–41. See also, Aaron, *op. cit.*, p. 93.

[32] McKay, *Harlem Shadows* (New York, 1922).

[33] McKay, *A Long Way From Home, pp. 108–15*

[34] *Ibid.*, pp. 165–66.

[35] Letters from McKay to James Weldon Johnson, May 8, 1935, in the McKay folder of the Johnson Correspondence (James Weldon Johnson Collection, Yale University Library).

[36] *Ibid.*

[37] *Ibid.*

[38] Frederick J. Hoffman, *The Twenties, American Writings in the Postwar Decade* (New York, 1955), pp. 382–84.

This was the artist who, typical of the twenties, stoutly affirmed the value of his non-social personality. He considered himself "the natural man," willing in an age of conformity to be only himself. That McKay shared this attitude is evident in all his writings.

Like other Negro writers of the twenties (most notably, Langston Hughes), he shared, to some degree, the same feeling of alienation that characterized Gertrude Stein's "lost generation." Thus, in 1918, McKay could write: "And now this great catastrophe [World War I] has come upon the world, proving the real hollowness of nationhood, patriotism, racial pride, and most of the things one was taught to respect and reverence."[39] His affiliation with *The Liberator* and his trip to Russia were part of a personal search for new moral and social standards.

McKay's trip to Russia marked the beginning of his long twelve-year exile in Europe. From Russia, he went briefly to Germany, then to France, where he lived for a number of years. In the late twenties, he journeyed to Spain and then to Morocco in North Africa where he remained until his return to the United States in 1934.[40]

Why did McKay spend twelve years wandering through Europe and North Africa? He never felt himself to be a typical expatriate. In his autobiography, he gave perhaps the main reason for his long expatriation.

*Color consciousness was the fundamental of my restlessness . . . my white fellow-expatriates could sympathize but . . . they could not altogether understand . . . unable to see deep into the profundity of blackness, some even thought . . . I might have preferred to be white like them . . . they couldn't understand the instinctive . . . pride of a black person resolute in being himself and yet living a simple civilized life like themselves.*[41]

The place of Negroes in the modern world was the one great problem that obsessed McKay from his arrival in the United States until his death in 1948.[42] For a while after World War I, he undoubtedly thought that in Communism Negroes might find a great world brotherhood.

In the twenties, he turned from international communism but not from the common Negro, with whom he had always closely identified. He came to the conclusion that in Negro working people there existed an uninhibited creativity and joy in life which Europeans, including Americans, had lost. In their folk culture lay strength enough for their salvation. McKay

---

[39] *Pearson's Magazine* (September, 1918), 276.

[40] McKay, *A Long Way From Home*, pp. 153–341, contains an account of his travels through Europe and North Africa. A briefer account is in Wagner, *op. cit.*, pp. 215–17.

[41] McKay, *A Long Way From Home*, p. 245.

[42] For McKay's views on race toward the end of his life, his "Right Turn to Catholicism" (typewritten ms. in the Schomburg Collection, New York Public Library) is especially important.

felt Negroes should not lose sight of their own uniqueness and the value of their own creations while taking what was valuable from the larger European civilization. He laid much emphasis on the need of Negroes to develop a group spirit.[43]

Among Negro writers of the twenties, McKay was not alone in his discovery of the folk. In fact, of central importance to the Negro Renaissance was its emphasis on Negro folk culture. Jean Toomer, for example, celebrated the black peasants of Georgia. . . . In enthusiastic outbursts, youthful Langston Hughes was also loudly proclaiming the worth of the common folk.[44]

To a certain extent, the New Negro's emphasis on the folk was heightened by the new attitude toward Negroes exhibited by many white writers of the twenties. After World War I certain white writers such as Gertrude Stein and Waldo Frank thought they saw in Negroes beings whose naturally creative expressiveness had not been completely inhibited by the evil forces of modern civilization.[45] As the twenties progressed, Negroes and their arts enjoyed a considerable vogue. Primitive African art became popular in the twenties. Negro singers found a greater public receptivity, and the blues entered American music. In many respects, American Negroes had in the twenties a favorable opportunity for a reassessment of their past accomplishments and future potentials.

The great emphasis on the primitive and the folk led however to some naïve delusions. Just as whites had previously built a stereotype of the happy, simpleminded plantation Negro, many people in the twenties stereotyped Negroes as unfettered children of nature, bubbling over with uninhibited sexual joy and child-like originality. To the extent that Negro writers accepted such an image, they limited the depth and richness of their own evaluations of American Negro life.[46]

While he was in Europe, McKay produced three novels which reflected his own interest in the Negro folk. They were *Home to Harlem* (1928),[47] *Banjo* (1929), and *Banana Bottom* (1933). He also produced a volume of short stories entitled *Gingertown* in 1932.[48] To a considerable extent, McKay's view of the Negro common folk was influenced by the newer stereotype of Negroes. *Home to Harlem,* his first novel, is the story

---

[43] These ideas were presented by McKay in two novels, *Banjo* (New York, 1929), and *Banana Bottom* (New York, 1933). He discussed the idea of a "group soul" in *A Long Way From Home,* pp. 349–54.

[44] Langston Hughes, "The Negro Artist and the Racial Mountain," *The Nation* (June 23, 1926), 694.

[45] For a general discussion of this topic, see Wagner, *op. cit.,* pp. 174–77. Also, see Hoffman, *op. cit.,* pp. 269–71.

[46] Bone, *op. cit.,* pp. 58–61.

[47] *Home to Harlem* (New York, 1928).

[48] *Gingertown* (New York, 1932).

of Jake, a Negro doughboy, and his joyful return to Harlem after World War I. Jake seems to have been McKay's ideal type—an honest, carefree worker whose existence, if a rather aimless one, is not complicated by pettiness or unnecessary worry over things that do not immediately concern him. Contrasted to Jake is Ray (McKay himself), an educated Negro, who is torn between two ways of life—Jake's and the more serious though conventional one imposed upon him by education. While the virtues of the common folk are contrasted to the doubts and confusion of the educated, McKay takes the reader on a tour of Harlem cabarets and rent parties.

His unvarnished view of Harlem night life delighted many white readers of the twenties and dismayed not a few middle-class Negroes.[49] The latter felt that an undue emphasis on the Negro lower class would damage their fight for civil rights and further delay their just battle for liberty. McKay was not the only writer of the Negro Renaissance to upset respectable Negro society.[50] One of the chief results of the Negro Renaissance was to force the Negro middle class to reevaluate their relationship to the Negro masses.

McKay's second novel, Banjo, told the story of the Negro beachboys of Marseilles, and further contrasted the free life of common Negroes with the frustrations of those caught in the more sophisticated web of modern civilization. In his third novel, Banana Bottom, he idealized the folk culture of Jamaica.

In some ways, Claude McKay differed radically from the typical New Negro writer of the twenties. For one thing, he was a Jamaican and did not become an American citizen until 1940. For another, he was older by some ten years than most writers of the Negro Renaissance; and except for a brief period, he did not live in the United States at all in the twenties.

He was also unique in the extent to which he associated with the larger literary world. Most Negro writers of the twenties had depended on Negro publications for a start. McKay's first successes were in white magazines—Seven Arts, Pearson's, and The Liberator. As an editor of The Liberator for a brief while, he was probably the only Negro writer of the time to hold such a position on an important American publication. McKay was at least partly responsible for the greater degree of communication that

---

[49] Here are two extreme views of McKay's Home to Harlem. The first reflects Negro middle-class opinion.

Again, white people think we are buffoons, thugs and rotters anyway. Why should we waste so much energy to prove it? That's what Claude McKay has done. (Clipping from the Chicago Defender, March 17, 1928, in McKay Folder, Schomburg Collection, New York Public Library.)

Now, another view:

[Home to Harlem is] . . . beaten through with the rhythm of life that is the jazz rhythm . . . the real thing in rightness. . . . It is the real stuff, the low-down on Harlem, the dope from the inside. (John R. Chamberlain, Review of Home to Harlem, New York Times, March 11, 1928, p. 5.)

[50] Langston Hughes, The Big Sea, An Autobiography (New York, 1945), pp. 265–66.

existed between Negro and white writers in the twenties. On the eve of his departure for Russia in 1922, James Weldon Johnson gave him a farewell party, and invited prominent writers of both races. Years later Johnson wrote to McKay concerning that event:

*We often speak of that party back in '22. . . . Do you know that was the first getting together of the black and white literati on a purely social plane. Such parties are now common in New York, but I doubt if any has been more representative. You will remember there were present Heywood Broun, Ruth Hale, F. P. Adams, John Farrar, Carl Van Doren, Freda Kirchwey, Peggy Tucker, Roy Nash—on our side you, Du Bois, Walter White, Jessie Fauset, [Arthur] Schomburg, J. Rosamond Johnson—I think that party started something.*[51]

Although McKay's career differed somewhat from that of the typical Negro writer of the twenties, he represented much that was characteristic of the New Negro. His movement from rural Jamaica to the big city and the literary world of the twenties is itself symbolic of the larger movement by Negro people from the rural South to the broader horizons of the urban North. His early interest in Communism was only one indication that the New Negro would no longer be unaffected by world events. World War I had ended American isolation for both Negroes and whites.

In his prose, McKay stressed the value of the common Negro and joined other Negro Renaissance writers in a rediscovery of Negro folk culture. But it is for his poetry that McKay will be longest remembered. For in his poetry, he best expressed the New Negro's determination to protect his human dignity, his cultural worth, and his right to a decent life.

[51] Letter from Johnson to McKay, August 21, 1930, in the McKay Correspondence (Yale University Library).

# 26

## BLACK MOSES
### Edmund David Cronon

**A**LTHOUGH Marcus Garvey never set foot on African soil, the basis for his race philosophy was Africa, the Negro homeland. For out of the moist green depths of the African jungle had come the endless files of hapless Negro slaves, a seemingly inexhaustible

From Edmund David Cronon, *Black Moses: The Story of Marcus Garvey and the Universal Negro Improvement Association* (Madison: The University of Wisconsin Press; © 1955 by the Regents of the University of Wisconsin), pp. 170–174, 175–176, 177–180, 182–186, 187–191, 192–193, 195–197, 220–224.

labor force to be devoured by the hungry plantations of the Americas. And in spite of the substantial but largely unrecognized contribution of these black slaves to the building of a New World civilization, their life of servitude under white masters had tended to destroy their African culture and to tear down their national and personal self-respect. To Garvey it seemed axiomatic that a redemption of the Negroes of the world must come only through a rebuilding of their shattered racial pride and a restoration of a truly Negro culture. Race pride and African nationalism were inextricably woven together in the Garvey philosophy, therefore, and the program of the Universal Negro Improvement Association centered around these two complementary objectives.

To understand Marcus Garvey and his extraordinary movement, it is necessary to consider in detail this strong emphasis on racism and African nationalism. Such a study helps not only to illumine the ideas of the man but also to show the basis for his wide appeal. Garvey's unparalleled success in capturing the imagination of masses of Negroes throughout the world can be explained only by recognizing that he put into words—and what magnificent inspiring words they were—what large numbers of his people were thinking. Garveyism as a social movement, reflecting as it did the hopes and aspirations of a substantial section of the Negro world, may best be studied by considering the ideas of its founder and leader, since these contain the key to Garvey's remarkable success.

In trying to establish a philosophy of Garveyism, however, it is important to place the movement in the context of general Negro thought in the period immediately following World War I. This was the era of the New Negro reaction to the race riots and frustrated hopes of the war years, and it was an age distinguished by the great artistic and literary activity that has been justly called the Negro Renaissance. Garveyism was for the most part decisively repudiated by the Negro intellectuals and it is thus difficult to give Garvey any credit for the flowering of the Negro Renaissance. Certainly his unceasing efforts to restore a strong sense of pride in things Negro was a march down the same path as that trod by the New Negroes, however, and the same forces that stimulated the Negro Renaissance helped to create an audience for Garveyism. Garvey's bombastic efforts to whip up an intense black nationalism were a logical counterpart to the more subtle but equally militant contemporary verse of such Negro poets as Claude McKay, Langston Hughes, and Countee Cullen.

The significance of Garveyism lies in its appeal to the dreams of millions of Negroes throughout the world. The amazingly loyal support given Marcus Garvey by the Negro masses, particularly in the United States and the West Indies, was forthcoming because he told his followers what they most wanted to hear, or, as E. Franklin Frazier has said, he made them "feel like somebody among white people who have said they were nobody."[1] Two decades after Garvey's inglorious departure for Atlanta penitentiary a new Harlem generation still remembered him as the man

[1] Frazier, "The Garvey Movement," *Opportunity*, IV, 347.

who "brought to the Negro people for the first time a sense of pride in being black."[2] This is the core of Marcus Garvey's philosophy; around this ideal he centered his life.

Coming at a time when Negroes generally had so little of which to be proud, Garvey's appeal to race pride quite naturally stirred a powerful response in the hearts of his eager black listeners. "I am the equal of any white man," Garvey told his followers. "I want you to feel the same way."[3] "We have come now to the turning point of the Negro," he declared with calm assurance, "where we have changed from the old cringing weakling, and transformed into full-grown men, demanding our portion as MEN."[4] One of the delegates to the first U.N.I.A. convention in Harlem in 1920 served notice that "it takes 1,000 white men to lick one Negro" and gave an illuminating preview of the type of Negro leadership needed in the future. "The Uncle Tom nigger has got to go, and his place must be taken by the new leader of the Negro race," he asserted. "That man will not be a white man with a black heart, nor a black man with a white heart, but a black man with a black heart."[5]

Garvey felt strongly that only through concerted action could Negroes achieve any betterment of their lowly status. "The world ought to know that it could not keep 400,000,000 Negroes down forever,"[6] he once remarked, and he constantly spoke optimistically of the Negroes of the world "standing together as one man."[7] The black man could hope to better himself, Garvey believed, only by joining his own actions with those of others of his race. "It has been said that the Negro has never yet found cause to engage himself in anything in common with his brother," the U.N.I.A. founder admitted, "but the dawn of a new day is upon us and we see things differently. We see now, not as individuals, but as a collective whole, having one common interest."[8] One of his followers put it a little more strongly:

*Men and women of the Negro race, rouse ye in the name of your posterity, summon your every sense, collect your every faculty, thrust the scales from your eyes and be converted to the cause of Negro advancement and dig-*

[2] Adam Clayton Powell, Jr., *Marching Blacks* (New York: Dial, 1945), p. 50.

[3] Quoted in Rollin Hartt, "The Negro Moses and His Campaign to Lead the Black Millions into Their Promised Land," *Independent*, CV, 206.

[4] Amy Jacques-Garvey, *Philosophy and Opinions of Marcus Garvey* (New York: Universal Publishing House, 1923), I, 9.

[5] New York *World*, August 7, 1920.

[6] Garvey, *Philosophy and Opinions*, I, 9.

[7] *Ibid.*, II, 15.

[8] Quoted by Hartt in *Independent*, CV, 219.

*nity; Negro power and Sovereignty; Negro freedom and integrity; thereby becoming the giants of your own destiny! Your posterity is crying out to you.*[9]

This plea for racial solidarity was one in which Negroes of widely varying political persuasions could join.[10]

"It is obvious, according to the commonest principles of human action," Garvey told his followers, "that no man will do as much for you as you will do for yourself."[11] Accordingly, he counseled Negroes to work for a strong and united black nation able to demand justice instead of sympathy from the ruling powers of the world. "If we must have justice, we must be strong," he explained; "if we must be strong, we must come together; if we must come together, we can only do so through the system of organization." "Let us not waste time in breathless appeals to the strong while we are weak," he advised, "but lend our time, energy, and effort to the accumulation of strength among ourselves by which we will voluntarily attract the attention of others."[12] Create a strong Negro nation, Garvey said in essence, and never more will you fear oppression at the hands of other races.

This spirit of race confidence and solidarity pervaded all of the many activities of the Garvey movement. The Black Star Line and its successor, the Black Cross Navigation and Trading Company, the Negro Factories Corporation, and indeed the African Legion, the Black Cross Nurses, and the other components of the U.N.I.A. itself were all a part of the general plan to weld the Negro people into a racially conscious, united group for effective mass action. Outsiders might laugh or scoff at some of the antics of the various Garvey organizations, their serious members ludicrous with high-toned titles and elaborate uniforms, but the importance of this aspect of the movement in restoring the all but shattered Negro self-confidence should not be overlooked.

Garvey exalted everything black and exhorted Negroes to be proud of their distinctive features and color. Negroid characteristics were not shameful marks of inferiority to be camouflaged and altered; they were rather symbols of beauty and grace. . . .

One of the methods used by Garvey to build up a sense of pride in the Negro heritage was his constant reference to the exploits of Negro heroes and to the land from which the race had come. He angrily accused white scholars of distorting Negro history to make it unfavorable to colored people. "Every student of history, of impartial mind," Garvey taught,

---

[9] B. S. Clark, *Is It the Color of Our Skin?* (Pittsburgh: Clark, 1921), p. 20.

[10] See, for example, T. S. Boone, *Paramount Facts in Race Development* (Chicago: Hume, 1921), pp. 20–21.

[11] Quoted by Hartt in *Independent*, CV, 218.

[12] Garvey, *Philosophy and Opinions*, II, 12.

"knows that the Negro once ruled the world, when white men were savages and barbarians living in caves; that thousands of Negro professors . . . taught in the universities in Alexandria."[13] The intent Negro audiences in Liberty Hall delighted in Garvey's vivid recollections of a creative black civilization at a time when white men were nothing:

*When Europe was inhabited by a race of cannibals, a race of savages, naked men, heathens and pagans, Africa was peopled with a race of cultured black men, who were masters in art, science and literature; men who were cultured and refined; men, who, it was said, were like the gods. Even the great poets of old sang in beautiful sonnets of the delight it afforded the gods to be in companionship with the Ethiopians. Why, then, should we lose hope? Black men, you were once great; you shall be great again. Lose not courage, lose not faith, go forward. The thing to do is to get organized. . . .*[14]

Along with the reborn Negro pride in the glorious past and distinctive color of the race went a reorientation in religion as well. Garvey believed that Negroes should end their subserviency to the white man through the worship of his white God. This rejection of an alien deity embodying Caucasian features was not original with Garvey and was in fact a logical part of any intensely race-conscious movement of this nature. Religious workers in Africa had long noted the tendency of their converts to think of the deity in terms of Negro pigmentation and to reject the concept of a white God.[15] Indeed, many religious cults and sects among American Negroes had projected the idea of a black God long before Garvey arrived in the United States.[16] Even some whites had suggested that Negro ministers should think in black terms, one fastidious southerner going so far as to assert that the Negro's Bible "ought to teach him that he will become a black angel and go home at death to a black God."[17] Garvey's extreme racial nationalism demanded fulfillment in a truly Negro religion, for, as his widow explains, "It is really logical that although we all know God is a spirit, yet all religions more or less visualize Him in a likeness akin to their own race. . . .

[13] Garvey, *Philosophy and Opinions*, II, 19. See also p. 82.

[14] *Ibid.,* I, 77.

[15] Everett V. Stonequist, *The Marginal Man* (New York: Scribners, 1937), p. 21.

[16] Joel A. Rogers, *Sex and Race: Negro-Caucasian Mixing in All Ages and All Lands* (N.Y.: J. A. Rogers, 1940), I, 254–71; James M. Webb, *A Black Man Will Be the Coming Universal King: Proven by Biblical History* (Chicago: Author [1918]), p. 12; James H. A. Brazelton, *Self-Determination: The Salvation of the Race* (Oklahoma City: The Educator, 1918), pp. 248–49.

[17] Kelsey Blanton, *Color-Blind and Skin-Deep Democracy* ([Tampa, Fla.:] Kelsey Blanton, 1924), p. 60.

Hence it was most vital that pictures of God should be in the likeness of the [Negro] Race."[18]

To implement the black religion, Garvey called upon the Reverend George Alexander McGuire, a prominent Episcopal clergyman who left his Boston pulpit in 1920 to become Chaplain General of the Universal Negro Improvement Association. On September 28, 1921, in a service conducted by dignitaries of the Greek Orthodox Church, McGuire was ordained a bishop and consecrated as head of the new African Orthodox Church.[19] Probably because Garvey had been brought up a Roman Catholic and Bishop McGuire had formerly been associated with the Episcopalian Church, the ritual of the new black religion followed much the same pattern as the liturgy of those two churches.

From the first, however, Bishop McGuire urged the Garveyites to "forget the white gods." "Erase the white gods from your hearts," he told his congregation. "We must go back to the native church, to our own true God."[20] The new Negro religion would seek to be true to the principles of Christianity without the shameful hypocrisy of the white churches.[21] Garvey himself urged Negroes to adopt their own religion, "with God as a Being, not as a Creature," a religion that would show Him "made in our own image—black."[22] When queried by a white reporter as to his reputed belief in the Negro ancestry of Christ, Garvey hedged a bit and replied that he believed "simply that Christ's ancestry included all races, so that He was Divinity incarnate in the broadest sense of the word."[23] In spite of strong opposition from the regular Negro clergy, Garvey's African Orthodox Church was able to report in its monthly magazine, the *Negro Churchman*, that "in its first year" it had "extended its missions through several states, into Canada, Cuba, and Hayti." Bishop McGuire reported that he had already recruited "10 Priests, 4 Deacons, 2 Sub-deacons and several Deaconesses, Catechists and Seminarians in training."[24]

By the time the Fourth International Convention of the Negro Peoples of the World met in 1924, moreover, the leaders of the black religion were openly demanding that Negroes worship a Negro Christ. During the open-

[18] Amy Jacques-Garvey, Kingston, Jamaica, to the author, July 5, 1949.

[19] *Negro Churchman*, I (March, 1923), 1.

[20] Quoted in Claude McKay, *Harlem: Negro Metropolis* (New York: Dutton, 1940), p. 166; Roi Ottley, *"New World A-Coming": Inside Black America* (Boston: Houghton Mifflin, 1943), p. 73.

[21] See, for instance, Amy Jacques-Garvey, *Tragedy of White Injustice* (New York: Amy Jacques-Garvey, 1927), pp. 4–5; Garvey, *Philosophy and Opinions*, I, 27; Marcus Garvey, "The White, Sinful Church," *Black Man*, I (July, 1935), 8.

[22] Quoted in Truman H. Talley, "Marcus Garvey: the Negro Moses?" *World's Work*, XLI, 165; "A Black Moses and His Dream of a Promised Land," *Current Opinion*, LXX, 330.

[23] Quoted by Hartt in *Independent*, CV, 205.

[24] *Negro Churchman*, I (March, 1923), 1.

ing parade through the streets of Harlem, U.N.I.A. members marched under a large portrait of a black Madonna and Child.[25] The convention session of August 5, 1924, drew the attention of the white press when Bishop McGuire advised Negroes to name the day when all members of the race would tear down and burn any pictures of the white Madonna and the white Christ found in their homes. "Then let us start our Negro painters getting busy," the Bishop declared, "and supply a black Madonna and a black Christ for the training of our children." Bishop McGuire gave added weight to his words by speaking under a large oil painting that clearly portrayed the type of Madonna and Child he had in mind.[26]

Bishop McGuire told of an aged Negro woman who had gratefully offered her African Orthodox pastor five dollars for telling her of the black Christ, because she knew that "no white man would ever die on the cross for me." Speaking emphatically so that none of his listeners might fail to catch the import of his message, the Bishop declared that Christ had actually been a reddish brown in color, and he predicted that if the Saviour were to visit New York He would not be able to live on fashionable Riverside Drive but would have to go to Harlem, "because all the darker people live here in Harlem." Bishop McGuire complained that the western Negro was the only Negro in the world who accepted the white man's characterization of the devil as being black, and he announced that henceforth the Negro's devil would be white. Another speaker at the same meeting, the Reverend J. D. Barber of Ethiopia, prophesied that the Negro would soon have his own illustrated Bible, complete with inspiring pictures of Negro saints and angels. Reverend Barber recalled St. John's description of Christ as "a black man, with feet that shone as polished brass, hair of lamb's wool and eyes with flames of fire," a rather elastic reference to the account in the prologue of the Book of Revelation. . . .[27]

Except for an insignificant handful of converts to the African Orthodox Church, the regular Negro clergy firmly rejected the new black religion, and it has been estimated—"guess-timated" is doubtless a more precise term—that as many as four out of five American Negro preachers were opposed to the concept of a black God.[28] William Pickens suggests that this rejection of Garvey's spiritual leadership may have amounted more to a distrust of his political aims and business methods than to any indication of convictions on the subject of color.[29] More convincing is A. Philip Randolph's explanation that Negro preachers opposed the African Orthodox Church

[25] "Garvey," Opportunity, II (September, 1924), 284–85; Negro World, August 16, 1924.

[26] New York Times, August 6, 1924.

[27] Ibid.

[28] Talley in World's Work, XLI, 165; "Black Moses and His Dream," Current Opinion, LXX, 330; Harold E. Zickfoose, "The Garvey Movement," unpublished M.A. Thesis, Iowa State University, 1931, p. 62.

[29] William Pickens, Washington, to the author, May 27, 1949.

out of fear they would lose their following, since their congregations had been conditioned in a white civilization and had thus grown up believing in a white God and in a Christian religion that had been fashioned and proselytized by white men.[30] Garvey's widow believes that the antipathy resulted largely from economic considerations, since the consolidation of Negroes into one denomination would mean the end of individual power and prestige for the preachers leading the innumerable small sects and independent churches.[31] Another consideration might be the need to retain white support in areas such as the American South where the Negro preacher has traditionally looked to white leaders for his cue in matters of politics and social action.

Unwittingly Garvey demonstrated a keen awareness of social psychology when he used a black God of Israel to stimulate racial nationalism among the Negro masses. And in spite of the loud outcries from Negro intellectuals and the horrified regular clergy when he first launched the campaign for the new religion, Garvey had the satisfaction before he died of seeing a decided shift in favor of a Negro-oriented spiritualism among certain elements of the Negro intelligentsia.[32] An eminent Negro sociologist has summed up perhaps better than anyone else Garvey's shrewd awareness of the spiritual needs of his followers. "The intellectual can laugh, if he will," wrote E. Franklin Frazier of the black God, "but let him not forget the pragmatic value of such a symbol among the type of people Garvey was dealing with."[33]

Much more important in the stimulation of black nationalism was the U.N.I.A. program to lead Negroes back to their African homeland. With customary flamboyance Garvey assured his followers that a few years would see Africa as completely dominated by Negroes as Europe was by whites. "No one knows when the hour of Africa's Redemption cometh," he warned mysteriously. "It is in the wind. It is coming. One day, like a storm, it will be here."[34] To his Liberty Hall supporters Garvey exclaimed, "Let Africa be our guiding star—our star of destiny,"[35] while to the dark motherland he called, "Wake up Ethiopia! Wake up Africa! Let us work towards the one glorious end of a free, redeemed and mighty nation. Let Africa be a bright star among the constellation of nations."[36]

[30] A. Philip Randolph, New York, to the author, June 24, 1949.

[31] Amy Jacques-Garvey, Kingston, Jamaica, to the author, July 5, 1949.

[32] See, for example, Benjamin E. Mays, *The Negro's God as Reflected in His Literature* (Boston: Chapman and Grimes, 1938), pp. 184–85.

[33] Frazier in *Opportunity*, IV, 347.

[34] Garvey, *Philosophy and Opinions*, I, 10.

[35] *Ibid.*, p. 6.

[36] *Ibid.*, p. 5.

A great independent African nation was the essential ingredient in the Garvey recipe for race redemption and he was earnestly convinced that Negroes needed the dark continent to achieve their destiny as a great people. Like another ardent disciple of racial nationalism, Garvey demanded *Lebensraum* for his people. It fell to the U.N.I.A. to lead the struggle to regain Africa and in the fight Garvey foresaw divine intervention. "At this moment methinks I see Ethiopia stretching forth her hands unto God," he declared fervently, "and methinks I see the angel of God taking up the standard of the Red, the Black, and the Green, and saying, 'Men of the Negro race, Men of Ethiopia, follow me!' It falls to our lot to tear off the shackles that bind Mother Africa." "Climb ye the heights of liberty," Garvey exhorted the U.N.I.A. legions, "and cease not in well-doing until you have planted the banner of the Red, the Black, and the Green upon the hilltops of Africa."[37]

But what of the powerful European nations that had carved up the African continent and now controlled the homeland? Garvey frequently disclaimed any animus against the white race,[38] but at the same time he pointedly told his followers: "We shall not ask England or France or Italy or Belgium, 'Why are you here?' We shall only command them, 'Get out of here.'"[39] The barrier to a free Africa was the white man, and Garvey warned ominously: "We say to the white man who now dominates Africa that it is to his interest to clear out of Africa now, because we are coming . . . 400,000,000 strong."[40] Garvey loved to speculate on the tremendous power that would belong to the Negro people once they discovered what their numerical strength could do for them.[41] "We are going home after a long vacation," he told the U.N.I.A., "and are giving notice to the tenant to get out. If he doesn't there is such a thing as forcible ejection."[42] "You will find ten years from now, or 100 years from now," he warned a white audience, "Garvey was not an idle buffoon but was representing the new vision of the Negro who was looking forward to great accomplishments in the future."[43]

---

[37] Quoted in Mary White Ovington, *Portraits in Color* (New York: Viking, 1927) p. 18.

[38] See Garvey, *Philosophy and Opinions*, I, 13; Garvey, *Speech at Madison Square Garden* (New York, 1924); Garvey, *Speech at Royal Albert Hall* (London: U.N.I.A., 1928), pp. 26–27; "Black Moses and His Dream," *Current Opinion*, LXX, 331; Tuttle, "A New Nation in Harlem," *World Tomorrow*, IV, 279–81; Benjamin Brawley, *Short History of the American Negro* (New York: Macmillan, 1927), p. 266.

[39] New York *World*, August 3, 1920. See also Garvey, *Philosophy and Opinions*, 1, 40–41.

[40] Quoted in James Weldon Johnson, *Black Manhattan* (New York: Knopf, 1930), p. 254; *Revolutionary Radicalism*, II, 1513.

[41] Garvey, *Philosophy and Opinions*, I, 39.

[42] New York *World*, August 5, 1920.

[43] Garvey, *Minutes of a Speech at Century Theatre, London, 1928*, p. 29.

It was never Garvey's intention that all Negroes in the New World would return to Africa and in this sense it is misleading to call his scheme a Back to Africa movement. Rather he believed like many Zionists that once a strong African nation was established Negroes everywhere would automatically gain needed prestige and strength and could look to it for protection if necessary.[44] "At no time did he visualize all American Negroes returning to Africa," says his widow.[45] "We do not want all the Negroes in Africa, Garvey informed a U.N.I.A. audience in Madison Square Garden in 1924. "Some are no good here, and naturally will be no good there."[46] Those particularly needed for the work in Africa would be engineers, artisans, and willing workers of all sorts—in short, the pioneering elements upon which all civilizations are built.

Garvey's address at his inauguration as Provisional President of Africa in 1920 demonstrated his strong belief in a personal destiny as the liberator of Africa. "The signal honor of being Provisional President of Africa is mine," he exulted. "It is a political calling for me to redeem Africa. It is like asking Napoleon to take the world. . . . He failed and died at St. Helena. But may I not say that the lessons of Napoleon are but stepping stones by which we shall guide ourselves to African liberation?"[47] The possibility of going down in history as the father of his country fascinated Garvey, and after a visit to the grave of George Washington he described "a new thought, a new inspiration" that had come to him at Mount Vernon. "It was the vision of a day—near, probably—when hundreds of other men and women will be worshipping at a shrine. This time the vision leads me to the shrine of some black man, the father of African independence. . . ."[48]

Most American Negro editors scoffed at the Back to Africa talk and loudly proclaimed the desire of Negroes to remain in the United States. The Chicago *Defender,* which generally avoided use of the word Negro in its columns, announced proudly, "The Race considers itself African no more than white Americans consider themselves European." The *Defender* went on to suggest pointedly that "in the United States lunacy commissions still have legal standing."[49] An anti-Garvey cartoon showed a strong manly Negro holding a small nondescript "Back to Africa fanatic" and advising, "The best thing you can do is stay right *here* and fight out your salvation."[50] Even the white press, when it deigned to notice Garvey, was hostile to the

---

[44] Hartt in *Independent,* CV, 206.

[45] Amy Jacques Garvey, Kingston, Jamaica, to the author, February 19, 1949, and February 14, 1951.

[46] Garvey, *Speech at Madison Square Garden.*

[47] Quoted by W. E. B. Du Bois in "Marcus Garvey," *Crisis,* XXI, 114.

[48] Quoted by Hartt in *Independent,* CV, 218.

[49] Chicago *Defender,* September 13, 1924.

[50] *Ibid.,* September 2, 1922.

idea of a redemption of Africa.[51] Negro intellectuals generally opposed Garvey's methods if not his interest in Africa. Booker T. Washington had preached against any idea of a return to Africa and doubtless his philosophy still carried great weight with many American Negroes.[52] Sometimes, however, even Garvey's critics saw fascinating possibilities in the awakened interest in the ancestral homeland. Writing after Garvey's confinement in Atlanta, Professor Alain Locke declared, "Garveyism may be a transient, if spectacular, phenomenon, but the possible role of the American Negro in the future development of Africa is one of the most constructive and universally helpful missions that any modern people can lay claim to. . . ."[53]

Garvey's passionate interest in Africa was a logical development of his firm conviction that Negroes could expect no permanent progress in a land dominated by white men.[54] No doubt he would have agreed completely with Mr. Dooley's shrewd analysis of the American race problem: "Th' trouble is that th' naygurs iv th' North have lived too long among th' white people, an' th' white people iv th' South have lived too long among th' naygurs."[55] Garvey said essentially the same thing when he told Negroes to develop "a government, a nation of our own, strong enough to lend protection to the members of our race scattered all over the world, and to compel the respect of the nations and the races of the earth."[56] When Garvey spoke of discrimination, he touched a subject painfully familiar to every Negro: "If you cannot live alongside the white man in peace, if you cannot get the same chance and opportunity alongside the white man, even though you are his fellow citizen; if he claims that you are not entitled to this chance or opportunity because the country is his by force of numbers, then find a country of your own and rise to the highest position within that country."[57] The Garvey solution for Negro ills was to make the race "so strong as to strike fear" into the hearts of the oppressor white race.[58] Only when Negroes could compel respect and justice through their connection with a strong Negro government would the position of the race be secure.

Garvey had no illusions about the white man's Christian love and believed that it would be used only when conveniently suitable. The

[51] New York Times, August 4, 1920.

[52] See Victoria Earle Matthews, Black Belt Diamonds: Gems from the Speeches, Addresses, and Talks to Students of Booker T. Washington (N. Y.: Fortune and Scott, 1898), pp. 9, 19, 27, and 58–59.

[53] Alain Locke, "Enter the New Negro," Survey, LIII (March, 1925), 634; Locke (ed.), The New Negro (New York: Boni, 1925), p. 15.

[54] Garvey, Philosophy and Opinions, II, 3, 40, 46, 49, and 97.

[55] [Finley P. Dunne] Dissertations by Mr. Dooley (N. Y.: Harper & Row, 1906), p. 190.

[56] Quoted in Ovington, Portraits in Color, p. 30.

[57] Quoted by Hartt in Independent, CV, 206.

[58] Ibid., p. 218.

U.N.I.A. therefore conceded the right of whites to do as they pleased in their own lands provided that Negroes were allowed to develop a nation of their own in Africa.[59] "Political, social and industrial America," Garvey cautioned, "will never become so converted as to be willing to share up equitably between black and white."[60] Though Negroes might live as useful citizens in the United States for thousands of years, Garvey believed that as long as the white population was numerically superior to them the blacks could never hope for political justice or social equality.[61]

Garvey's plain abdication of Negro rights in America quickly brought him the open support of such white supremacy groups as the Ku Klux Klan and the Anglo-Saxon Clubs, both flourishing mightily in the postwar years. Garvey's major book, the second volume of his *Philosophy and Opinions,* carried an advertisement for Major Earnest Sevier Cox's *White America,* a polemical work strongly preaching the separation of the races. Major Cox sometimes spoke to U.N.I.A. audiences at Liberty Hall in New York, and he even dedicated a pamphlet on racial purity to Garvey, whom he called "a martyr for the independence and integrity of the Negro race."[62] Another white supporter was John Powell, the fanatical organizer of the Anglo-Saxon Clubs of America. Garvey expressed great admiration for men like Cox and Powell because of "their honesty and lack of hypocrisy" in openly working to maintain the power of the white race.[63] Speaking at Liberty Hall late in 1925, Powell congratulated the U.N.I.A. on its racial improvement program and reaffirmed the mutual desire of blacks and whites to preserve the purity of their respective races.[64] Garvey also received support from some southern whites who looked upon his movement with favor because it was likely to attract Negroes who might otherwise be resentful of their subordinate caste position in the United States.[65] After he was deported, some of Garvey's white friends were active in a campaign to permit the return of the exiled U.N.I.A. leader.[66]

"Lynchings and race riots," said Garvey with reference to the grim postwar period of racial strife and violence, "all work to our advantage by teaching the Negro that he must build a civilization of his own or forever

[59] Garvey, *Philosophy and Opinions,* II, 46.

[60] *Ibid.,* p. 49.

[61] *Ibid.,* pp. 97–98.

[62] E. S. Cox, *Let My People Go* (Richmond, Va.: White America Society, 1925), p. 4. See also Cox, *The South's Part in Mongrelizing the Nation* (Richmond Va.: White America Society, 1925) pp. 8–9, 93–94, 103, 108.

[63] Garvey, *Philosophy and Opinions,* II, 338.

[64] *Ibid.,* p. 347.

[65] Blanton, *Color-Blind and Skin-Deep Democracy,* pp. 61–62.

[66] E. S. Cox, *Lincoln's Negro Policy* (Richmond, Va.: Wm. Byrd Press, 1938), pp. 29–32; Cox, *South's Part in Mongrelizing,* pp. 93–94.

remain the white man's victim."[67] Bishop McGuire, the religious leader of the U.N.I.A. and spiritual head of the African Orthodox Church, declared frankly that the Ku Klux Klan's campaign of intimidation and violence would benefit the movement by driving harassed Negroes into the Garvey organization.[68] In 1922 Garvey indicated his tacit support of the dread Klan, an alliance his opponents had suspected for some time. "The Ku Klux Klan is going to make this a white man's country," Garvey asserted in stating his belief that the K.K.K. was the invisible government of America. "They are perfectly honest and frank about it. Fighting them is not going to get you anywhere."[69]

Early in 1922 Garvey went to Atlanta, Georgia, for a conference with Edward Young Clarke, Imperial Giant of the Klan.[70] The purpose of the meeting was apparently to see how strong the Klan was and whether or not Garvey could hope for its support for the Back to Africa program of the U.N.I.A. Garvey's widow explains that far from approving of the Klan's violent actions against Negroes, her husband merely believed "that the prejudice exhibited by the Klan in hysteria, hate, cruelty, and mob violence was the prejudice common to most white Americans, which deep in their hearts they felt, but culture and refinement prevented many from showing any trace of it."[71] The meeting was one of expediency, then, rather than of mutual admiration, but it was nonetheless a serious tactical blunder.

Although details of the Atlanta conference were withheld, the mere thought that a responsible Negro leader would collaborate with the leading avowed enemy of his race brought down a storm of criticism upon Garvey's head. Alderman George Harris, editor of the New York News, denounced Garvey as "misrepresenting the attitude of 100 per cent of our native-born Americans and 75 per cent of the foreign-born group" when he surrendered to Clarke. "When Garvey agrees with the Klan's theory that this is a white man's country," Harris complained angrily, "he sadly misrepresents our people."[72] William Pickens, who had at one time very nearly accepted a high U.N.I.A. post, now spurned with contempt a Garvey title of nobility because of this rumored alliance with the Ku Klux Klan.[73] W. E. B. Du Bois let go a powerful blast against the U.N.I.A. president in Crisis, the organ of the National Association for the Advancement of Colored People. "Marcus

---

[67] Quoted by Hartt in Independent, CV, 219.

[68] Chicago Defender, August 16, 1924.

[69] New York Times, July 10, 1922.

[70] Chicago Defender, July 8, 1922; New York Times, February 8, 1923; W. E. B. Du Bois, "Back to Africa," Century, CV, 547; Burgit Aron, "Garvey Movement," unpublished M.A. Thesis, Columbia University, 1947, p. 117.

[71] Amy Jacques-Garvey, Kingston, Jamaica, to the author, February 19, 1949.

[72] Quoted in Chicago Defender, July 22, 1922.

[73] Ibid., July 29, 1922.

Garvey is, without doubt, the most dangerous enemy of the Negro race in America and the world," sputtered the indignant editor of *Crisis*. "He is either a lunatic or a traitor."[74] Unperturbed by this barrage of Negro criticism, Garvey countered with a candid appraisal of white America. "I regard the Klan, the Anglo-Saxon Clubs and White American Societies," he maintained, "as better friends of the race than all other groups of hypocritical whites put together. I like honesty and fair play. You may call me a Klansman if you will, but, potentially every white man is a Klansman, as far as the Negro in competition with whites socially, economically and politically is concerned, and there is no use lying about it."[75]

The main reason that Garvey and his organization were acceptable to the Ku Klux Klan and other white supremacy groups was that the U.N.I.A. leader preached race purity to his followers. He thundered that racial amalgamation must cease forthwith and warned that any member of the Universal Negro Improvement Association who married a white would be summarily expelled.[76] Not only did Garvey advocate race purity, but as a Jamaican black he attempted to transfer the West Indian three-way color caste system to the United States by attacking mulatto leaders. He laughed at the light-skinned mulattoes, who, he said, were always seeking "excuses to get out of the Negro Race,"[77] and he scornfully accused his mulatto opponents of being "time-serving, boot-licking agencies of subserviency to the whites."[78] The average Negro leader, Garvey said, sought to establish himself as "the pet of some philanthropist of another race," thereby selling out the interests of his own people. . . .[79]

Garvey denounced other Negro leaders as being bent on cultural assimiliation, cravenly seeking white support, and miserably compromising between accommodation and protest.[80] The National Association for the Advancement of Colored People was the worst offender in Garvey's mind, because, he said, it "wants us all to become white by amalgamation, but they are not honest enough to come out with the truth." "To be a Negro is no disgrace, but an honor," Garvey indignantly affirmed, "and we of the U.N.I.A. do not want to become white."[81] He warned both whites and

---

[74] "A Lunatic or a Traitor," *Crisis*, XXVIII, 8–9.

[75] Garvey, *Philosophy and Opinions*, II, 71; Ottley, "*New World A-Coming*," p. 74.

[76] Hartt in *Independent*, CV, 219.

[77] Garvey, *Philosophy and Opinions*, I, 6.

[78] Quoted by Talley in *World's Work*, XLI, 163; "Black Moses and His Dream," *Current Opinion*, LXX, 330.

[79] Garvey, *Philosophy and Opinions*, I, 29–30.

[80] Garvey, *Philosophy and Opinions*, I, 29–30; Gunnar Myrdal, *American Dilemma*, (New York: Harper, 1944), p. 746.

[81] Garvey, *Philosophy and Opinions*, II, 325–26; John Hope Franklin, *From Slavery to Freedom* (New York: Knopf, 1947), p. 482.

blacks that the purity of the two races was endangered by the false prophets of amalgamation. "It is the duty of the virtuous and morally pure of both the white and black races," he announced, "to thoughtfully and actively protect the future of the two peoples, by vigorously opposing the destructive propaganda and vile efforts of the miscegenationists of the white race, and their associates, the hybrids of the Negro race."[82] "I believe in a pure black race," Garvey proclaimed loudly, "just as how all self-respecting whites believe in a pure white race, as far as that can be."[83] The U.N.I.A. chief felt constrained to warn the white world of the dangers inherent in social equality. "Some Negroes believe in social equality," he cautioned. "They want to intermarry with the white women of this country, and it is going to cause trouble later on. Some Negroes want the same jobs you have. They want to be Presidents of the nation. . . ."[84]

Garvey had a strong distaste for any alliance with white labor organizations, a skepticism that probably stemmed in part from his early failure as a strike leader in Jamaica. This distrust of the labor movement also reflected a feeling that the white worker was the Negro's greatest competitor and most dangerous rival.[85] Rather than seek an alliance with white workers, Garvey told Negroes that the white employer was their best friend until such time as the race had achieved economic independence.[86] The Negro Factories Corporation and the Black Star Line were direct moves to set up Negro-owned business enterprises so that Negroes would not have to beg for employment from whites. It seemed self-evident to Garvey that "the only convenient friend" of the American Negro worker was "the white capitalist," who "being selfish—seeking only the largest profit out of labor—is willing and glad to use Negro labor wherever possible on a scale 'reasonably' below the standard white union wage." The white employer would "tolerate the Negro" only if he accepted "a lower standard of wage than the white union man." Garvey's solution for the black worker, therefore, was to "keep his scale of wage a little lower than the whites" and thereby "keep the good-will of the white employer," all the time husbanding Negro resources so that the race could ultimately become economically free.[87] Needless to say, this cheerful rejection of trade unionism did little to endear Garvey to Negro labor leaders, and it early won

---

[82] Garvey, *Philosophy and Opinions*, II, 62; Ottley, "*New World A-Coming*," p. 73.

[83] Garvey, *Philosophy and Opinions*, I, 37.

[84] Quoted in Lens Nembhard, *Trials and Triumphs of Marcus Garvey* (Kingston, Jamaica: Gleaner, 1940), p. 84.

[85] Abram Harris and Sterling Spero, "Negro Problem," *Encyclopedia of the Social Sciences*, XI, 350.

[86] Ralph J. Bunche, "Programs, Ideologies, Tactics, and Achievements," unpublished monograph for the Carnegie-Myrdal study. Schomburg Collection, New York Public Library, p. 412; Harry Haywood, *Negro Liberation* (New York: International Publishers, 1948), p. 202.

[87] Garvey, *Philosophy and Opinions*, II, 69–70.

for him the bitter hostility of men like Chandler Owen and A. Philip Randolph, who were currently engaged in a successful campaign to establish a union of Negro sleeping car porters.

Similarly, Garvey refused to have anything to do with socialism and communism, despite the alarmist attempts of the Lusk Committee and the Department of Justice to portray him as a dangerous radical agitator. He felt that these movements of the left, although they made a pretense of helping the Negro, were inherently prejudiced against the black race, since they were dominated by whites. "Fundamentally what racial difference is there between a white Communist, Republican or Democrat?" Garvey demanded to know. "On the appeal of race interest the Communist is as ready as either to show his racial . . . superiority over the Negro."[88] The U.N.I.A. leader suspected that for all his fine talk the Communist would just as quickly join a lynch mob as would the less radical white citizen, and consequently he believed that communism must first prove itself as a really new reform movement before the Negro could safely accept it.[89] The Communists were not initially opposed to Garvey's Universal Negro Improvement Association, though they deplored his emphasis on African Zionism. Party members inside the U.N.I.A. were ordered to push the fight for Negro equality with the United States, but they were so few in number that they were never able either to "capture" the association or to challenge successfully Garvey's leadership.[90] The Communist Party was greatly impressed with the amazing lower-class appeal of the U.N.I.A., however, and after the organization had begun to disintegrate in 1926 Robert Minor wrote disconsolately: "A breaking up of this Negro association would be a calamity to the Negro people and to the working class as a whole. . . . It is composed very largely, if not almost entirely, of Negro workers and impoverished farmers, although there is a sprinkling of small business men. . . ."[91]

Amid the many conflicting interpretations of the meaning and importance of Garveyism, ranging from angry condemnation to uncritical praise, just what is Marcus Garvey's place in the pages of twentieth-century history? Certainly it may not be denied that here is one of the most interesting figures of our age. The sweeping range of his dreams, the startling audacity of his plans, the compelling authority of his inspired words, all acted to secure him a fanatically devoted following at a time when the despairing Negro people were awaiting a messiah. The extent of Garvey's following is itself significant, for it reflected the depth of the secret longings and bitter

[88] *Ibid.*; Garvey, "The Future," *Black Man,* II (July–August 1936), 8–9.

[89] Garvey, *Philosophy and Opinions,* II, 70.

[90] Wilson Record, *The Negro and the Communist Party* (Chapel Hill: University of North Carolina Press, 1951), pp. 40–41.

[91] Robert Minor, "Death or a Program," *Workers Monthly,* V, 270, quoted in *ibid.,* p. 41. Cf. I. Amter, *The World Liberative Movement of the Negroes* (Moscow: Soviet State Publishing House, 1925).

pessimism of the black masses. Marcus Garvey was an instrument through which the restless Negro world could express its discontent. His striking success in creating a powerful mass organization in a matter of months was possible only because he spoke the language of his people and told his followers what they wanted and needed to hear—that the black man was as good as any other.

And yet, despite Garvey's triumph as an unparalleled propagandist and organizer of the Negro masses, his success proved ephemeral, and his vaunted Universal Negro Improvement Association turned out to be only a transient, if extremely colorful, phenomenon. Personally honest, a sincere and dedicated visionary, Garvey might have hoped for more lasting success. Energy, imagination, daring, a commanding personality, superb oratorical skill—all these were his to use on behalf of the oppressed black people he yearned to serve. But his failings as a leader overbalanced the sounder aspects of his program. For all his impressive organizational activities, Marcus Garvey remains a tragic, even a pathetic figure, who is today remembered more for the size of his dreams than for the practical accomplishments of his once imposing race movement.

Garvey's reluctance to delegate responsibility, his difficulty in finding honest and capable subordinates, and his disinclination to listen to the advice and suggestions of men frequently better informed than he militated against any permanent gains from his work. By unconsciously seeking fawning courtiers rather than competent co-workers he opened wide the doors to blundering mismanagement and disloyal corruption. Garvey's egocentric, at times even arrogant, personality demanded that there be but one supreme U.N.I.A. leader and drove from his counsels those men who might have helped to avert the crippling misfortunes that ultimately overtook the movement. Those who remained were all too often dishonest and unscrupulous self-seekers who only accelerated the final collapse. The logical scapegoat for the Black Star fiasco, Garvey served a prison sentence for the financial chicanery of some of his two-faced associates and his own supremely confident but irresponsible and inexperienced leadership. A good lawyer could doubtless have won his acquittal, but Garvey's overweening conceit and irrational suspicions led him to reject his expert counsel and plead his own case—with disastrous results.

The inherent weaknesses of Garveyism itself also acted to limit its ultimate influence. Garvey sought to raise high the walls of racial nationalism at a time when most thoughtful men were seeking to tear down these barriers. His West Indian background led him rather ineptly to attempt to discredit much of the existing American Negro leadership by introducing a new and unfamiliar divisive symbolism based on the degree of color. The Back to Africa program provided an easy escape for Negroes hard pressed and weary of a life of oppression and frustration, but is was no real answer to the problems that beset the Negro world. Few American Negroes were seriously interested in a "return" to Africa, a mysterious land that none of them knew and few cared to see firsthand.

In effect Garvey asked his followers to abdicate their hard-won, admittedly incomplete rights in the United States and to turn the country over to white supremacists of the Ku Klux Klan variety. Whatever their feelings for the other parts of the Garvey program, most Negro Americans were inclined to agree with the sober appraisal of a respected Garvey critic, N.A.A.C.P. secretary James Weldon Johnson: "As the world is at present, the United States, with all its limitations, offers the millions of Negroes within its borders greater opportunities than any other land."[92]

Garvey's work was important largely because more than any other single leader he helped to give Negroes everywhere a reborn feeling of collective pride and a new awareness of individual worth. Young and unknown, this black Moses came out of the West Indies at a time when the shocking upturn in race riots and lynchings was graphically emphasizing to American Negroes the negation of their loyal contribution to the nation's victory in World War I. With the broken bodies of the victims of racial violence marking the broken hopes of the war years, the Negro world badly needed a message of hope and encouragement. This Marcus Garvey undertook to supply in terms bold and language uncompromising, with the result that in an astonishingly brief time he had captured the attention of his people to a degree no other Negro leader has ever attained. Because he made the Negro masses proud of their past and resolute to face the future, a surprising number of Garvey's devoted followers were willing to forget the erratic course steered by the Black Star Line and to forgive the vast sums that disappeared virtually without trace into the yawning emptiness of the U.N.I.A. treasury. Garvey appeared out of obscurity at a fortuitous moment in Negro history, at a time when American Negroes were ripe for a chauvinistic appeal to racial nationalism and ready for a black Zionism that could restore their shattered self-respect and promise a deliverance from present burdens.

Garvey demonstrated as no man before him had ever done the basic unrest within the Negro world. In capturing the imagination of millions of ordinary black men and women throughout the world, he showed the striking appeal that racial nationalism can, under certain circumstances, have for the Negro. Garvey helped to stir and set in motion much of the sweeping flood of race consciousness now inundating the colored world. His success in briefly harnessing the hopes and aspirations of large numbers of American Negroes to a wildly nationalistic program of African redemption, therefore, helps considerably to illumine an important chapter in the history of race relations in the United States. Garvey proved that the black masses could be organized through an emotional appeal based on racial chauvinism. But the steady decline in his following after 1925, in spite of Garvey's frantic efforts to revive and maintain the movement, suggests that the sort of appeal that worked so well in the years immediately after World War I was much less effective under later conditions. It is doubtful

[92] Johnson, *Black Manhattan*, p. 259.

whether Garvey could find today, in the United States at least, the ready response that greeted his early proselytizing efforts.

In assessing Marcus Garvey's work as a Negro leader, one is hard put to discover any tangible gain resulting from the impressive movement he created. Garvey may have brought a much needed spiritual uplift to masses of discouraged and despairing blacks in the early twenties, but there remains today little of practical significance as a fitting monument to his labors. By undercutting most of the existing Negro leadership, even those elements worthy of support, and by rejecting all but the most extreme white backing—the dubious championship of the Klan and other racist groups—Garvey nullified much of the potential value of his movement in creating better conditions for his people in the United States. Garveyism failed largely because it was unable to come up with a suitable alternative to the unsatisfactory conditions of American life as they affect the Negro. Escape, either emotional or physical, was neither a realistic nor a lasting answer.

## SUGGESTIONS FOR FURTHER READING

**A**S yet there is no comprehensive treatment of Afro-American history during the 1920s. The reader, therefore, must rely on works devoted to particular aspects of the decade. Especially valuable on the Negro Renaissance are *James Weldon Johnson's classic, Black Manhattan (New York, 1930); the personal memoir of Langston Hughes, The Big Sea (New York, 1940); the excellent collection of essays in *Alain Locke (ed.), The New Negro (New York, 1925); *Robert Bone's stimulating Negro Novel in America (rev. ed.; New Haven, Conn., 1966); and *Harold Cruse's controversial Crisis of the Negro Intellectual (New York, 1967).

An introduction to the black writers of the 1920s is provided in a number of anthologies. Among these are Sterling Brown, et al. (eds.), The Negro Caravan (New York, 1941) and James A. Emanuel and Theodore Gross (eds.), Dark Symphony: Negro Literature in America (New York, 1968). Two valuable studies by a participant in the Negro Renaissance are *Sterling Brown, The Negro in American Fiction (Washington, D.C., 1937) and Negro Poetry and Drama (Washington, D.C., 1937). One should also read the writings of the artists of the twenties such as Countee Cullen, Langston Hughes, Claude McKay, and Jean Toomer. A good introduction to the black authors before and since the twenties is *Herbert Hill (ed.), Anger And Beyond: The Negro Writer in the United States (New York, 1966). Also

* An asterisk indicates that the book is available in paperback.

consult the bibliographies in Emanuel and Gross, *Dark Symphony* and Bone, *Negro Novel* cited earlier.

The race riots of the period are analyzed in *Elliott M. Rudwick, *Race Riot at East St. Louis* (Carbondale, Ill., 1964) and *Arthur Waskow, *From Race Riot to Sit-In* (Garden City, N.Y., 1966). Still valuable is the Chicago Commission on Race Relations' investigation of that city's race riot of 1919, *The Negro in Chicago* (Chicago, 1922). Black reaction to white violence is discussed in Elliott M. Rudwick and August Meier, "Negro Retaliatory Violence in the Twentieth Century," *New Politics,* V (Winter 1966). Also valuable is Allen D. Grimshaw, "Lawlessness and Violence in America and Their Special Manifestations in Changing Negro-White Relations," *Journal of Negro History,* XLIV (January 1959). Studies of violence in a broader context are contained in *Hugh D. Graham and Ted R. Gurr (eds.), *History of Violence in America* (Washington, D. C., 1969).

There are a number of studies of the Klan. *David Chalmers, *Hooded Americanism: The History of the Ku Klux Klan* (New York, 1965) is a good introduction. More specialized are Emma Lou Thornbrough, "Segregation in Indiana During the Klan Era of the 1920s," *Mississippi Valley Historical Review,* XLVII (March 1961); Charles C. Alexander, *The Ku Klux Klan in the Southwest* (Lexington, Ky., 1965); and the revisionist interpretation of *Kenneth T. Jackson, *The Ku Klux Klan in the City, 1915–1930* (New York, 1967). Examinations of white attitudes in other areas include Robert Moats Miller, "The Attitudes of American Protestantism Toward the Negro, 1919–1939," *Journal of Negro History,* XLI (July 1956) and Richard B. Sherman, "Republicans and Negroes: The Lessons of Normalcy," *Phylon,* XXVII (Spring 1966).

A good way of getting directly into the philosophy of Marcus Garvey is *Amy Jacques-Garvey (ed.), *Philosophy and Opinions of Marcus Garvey* (New York, 1923). Important interpretive essays in addition to Cronon's *Black Moses* are E. Franklin Frazier, "The Garvey Movement," *Opportunity* (November 1926) and Elliott M. Rudwick, "Du Bois vs. Garvey: Racial Propagandists at War," *Journal of Negro Education,* XXVII (Fall 1959). Precedents for Garvey's black nationalism and back-to-Africa movement are discussed in August Meier, "The Emergence of Negro Nationalism (A Study in Ideologies)," *Midwest Journal,* IV (Winter 1951–1952) and (Summer 1952) and *Edwin S. Redkey, *Black Exodus: Black Nationalist and Back-to-Africa Movements, 1880–1910* (New Haven, Conn., 1969). E. U. Essien-Udom while devoting the major portion of his *Black Nationalism* (Chicago, 1962) to the Black Muslims, incorporates an excellent historical discussion of black nationalism. A comprehensive anthology on this subject is *John Bracey, Jr., August Meier, and Elliott M. Rudwick (eds.), *Black Nationalism in America* (Indianapolis, Ind., 1969).

* An asterisk indicates that the book is available in paperback.

# CHAPTER TEN

# The Great Depression and the New Deal

**F**OR most Americans, the Great Depression brought to a sudden end the apparent prosperity of the 1920s. Unemployment figures for Afro-Americans during the Depression confirmed the maxim: "last hired and first fired." Detroit in 1931 reported that 60 percent of the black working population as opposed to 32 percent of the white was jobless; for Houston the respective figures were 35 percent for blacks and 18 percent for whites. In the same year, 43.5 percent of Chicago's black males were unemployed as compared to 29.7 percent of the white males. Black and white women of that city were separated by an even wider gap—58.5 percent and 19.4 percent respectively. From the evidence available it appears that as the Depression became worse the higher unemployment rate for blacks persisted. By 1937 approximately 39 percent of employable blacks in the North were without work as against 18 percent of the whites in this category. The growing jobless rate for blacks led to an increase in the proportion of the black population on relief—from 18 percent in 1930 to 30 percent in 1935.

New Deal programs provided assistance for many blacks. They benefited from the relief, work, and youth projects. Moreover, many Afro-Americans found jobs with the federal government, possibly in greater numbers than at any previous time in American history. Most were on the nonprofessional level, but a significant number held appointive positions in cabinet departments and government agencies. Mary McLeod Bethune, for example, served as Director of Negro Affairs in the National Youth Administration, Robert Weaver worked in the Department of Interior, and Ira DeA. Reid was on the Social Security Board. Public statements condemning racial discrimination gave the Roosevelt Administration the appearance of standing for the equality of all men. Even though Roosevelt would not support the antilynching bill before Congress, he unequivocally condemned lynching as murder. "These things," remarked W. E. B. Du Bois, "give us hope." Two students of Afro-American studies have observed that the Roosevelt Administration's rhetoric mirrored "a clear-cut reversal in the attitudes of white Americans" toward black Americans during the 1930s.[1]

The actions of particular individuals within the administration strengthened this image. Harold Ickes, as Secretary of the Interior, appointed blacks to high-level positions in his department, attempted to limit discrimination on Interior Department projects, and served as Roosevelt's unofficial adviser on Negro relations. Mrs. Eleanor Roosevelt frequently communicated the opinions of black leaders, such as Walter White of the NAACP, to her husband. Her addresses before black audiences and her outspoken sympathy for the plight of blacks fostered the pro-equality posture of the New Deal.

The New Deal, though, is not without its negative side. Many New Deal agencies followed policies that denied blacks benefits equal to those secured by whites. Discrimination against blacks was usually more pronounced where there was a large degree of local control. As a result of the National Recovery Administration policy of adhering to the prevailing local wage rates, blacks received lower pay than whites for the same work. Black farmers and farm workers discovered that the same southern whites who supported that section's racial policy controlled the local boards that operated under the Agricultural Adjustment Administration. Even though many Afro-American youths and their families profited from the activities of the Civilian Conservation Corps, it was often on a segregated basis or on a level not proportionate to their needs. The Tennessee Valley Authority, "Democracy at Work," as one of the agency's directors, David Lillienthal, described it, excluded Afro-Americans from the model town at Norris, Tennessee, and generally limited black workers to unskilled jobs on segregated work gangs. The Federal Housing Administration discouraged its valuators from giving its backing to a home mortgage when such "adverse influences" as "inharmonious racial groups" existed. And for all its representations regarding racial equality, not a single piece of civil rights legislation was enacted during the Roosevelt years.

In their failure to receive much beyond relief, blacks shared a similar fate with white Americans at the bottom of the economic ladder. Tenant farmers were the biggest losers under the crop reduction programs of the AAA. Old age and unemployment insurance benefits of the Social Security Act as well as the minimum wage and maximum hours provisions of the Fair Labor Standards Act exempted domestic servants, the service trades, and agricultural workers—fields in which a substantial portion of the Afro-American population labored. Ralph J. Bunche's essay, selection 27, published in 1936 when he was a professor of political science at Howard University, discusses the limitations of the Roosevelt Administration. Taking a position that has certain similarities to that advanced by some scholars in recent years, Bunche asserts that the New Deal followed the "classical pattern of

[1] August Meier and Elliott M. Rudwick, *From Plantation to Ghetto* (New York, 1966), p. 211.

middle-class planning" that compromised with big business. Accordingly, it neglected the basic social problems faced by the working class. Bunche believes that most blacks share the same problems as the white proletariat, "but more of it" because of a caste system that compounds a class society. In support of his position, he examines the policies and activities of the NRA and AAA.

Despite the limitations of the New Deal mentioned above, the majority of Afro-American voters transferred their support from the Republican to the Democratic party during the Roosevelt years. Afro-Americans may have seen in the relief they received, the public utterances in behalf of equality, and the rhetoric of the "forgotten man," an improvement over past governmental policy. Democratic urban machines may provide an additional reason. As black settlement in northern cities increased, local Democrats courted the Negro vote more actively than their Republican counterparts who had come to take it for granted. Whatever the explanation, more and more black voters in the 1930s followed black publisher Robert Vann's advice to "go home and turn Lincoln's picture to the wall. The debt has been paid in full."

Despite the shift in allegiance of Negro voters during the 1930s, Negro organizations did not refrain from criticizing violations of the rights of black people. The NAACP pursued court actions against discrimination. It constantly brought to the Roosevelt Administration's attention discriminatory practices on the part of New Deal agencies. "Don't Buy Where You Can't Work" boycotts demanded that white merchants in the ghetto hire more black workers. Both the New Deal and the NAACP received criticism from the short-lived National Negro Congress. During World War II, the "forgotten years" Richard M. Dalfiume speaks of in selection 28, militancy became even more evident.

Dalfiume maintains that discrimination in war industries and the armed forces as well as all the talk of fighting racism and tyranny around the world made more apparent to Afro-Americans their second-class position in the United States. Against this background, Dalfiume examines Afro-American attitudes toward the war effort. Of interest is his comparison of the positions taken by blacks in World War I and World War II. The frame of mind of black Americans during World War II gravitated toward a combination of cynicism, hope, militancy, and increased race consciousness. All of these elements were evident in the March on Washington Movement. The MOWM, Dalfiume argues, marked a new direction in the civil rights movement. Its importance should be evaluated on the basis of the tactics it employed, its influence on other protest organizations, and as a reflection of the changing mood of Afro-Americans, not as to whether it achieved its immediate goals in the 1940s. For one can find in the MOWM the direct-action philosophy put into action by civil rights groups of the 1950s and 1960s. Accordingly, this essay should be read in conjunction with the articles in the next chapter.

While New Deal accomplishments were few in the area of civil rights, the Supreme Court handed down decisions chipping away at legal discrimination. The Court's rulings at this time also prepared the way for the 1950s and the 1960s. Thurgood Marshall traces civil rights decisions in selection 29, an article written three years before the Supreme Court announced its ruling in *Brown* v. *The Board of Education* overturning the "separate but equal" doctrine of *Plessy* v. *Ferguson*. Then special counsel for the NAACP and since appointed to the Supreme Court, Marshall concentrates on the equal protection clause of the Fourteenth Amendment as it relates to court decisions in such areas as jury service, public accommodations, and education. His article appears to anticipate the Supreme Court's decision in *Brown v. The Board of Education.* One should decide if the ruling in this case was a necessary prerequisite for the civil rights activities that will be discussed in the next chapter.

# 27

## A CRITIQUE OF NEW DEAL SOCIAL PLANNING AS IT AFFECTS NEGROES
*Ralph J. Bunche*

### NEW DEAL "EQUILIBRIUM"

THE New Deal, at its inception, confronting an economy of chaos, proclaimed its major purpose to be the application of planning to our entire social structure. In pursuance of this objective a whole series of complicated and contradictory mechanisms have been invented and set up with the purpose of effecting a regulated orderliness in the economic life of the nation. But after two years of frantic trial and error, the New Deal, and most of its elaborate machinery, remains suspended in mid-air, bewildered, and innocuous. Relief expenditures have continued to rise, and unemployment was greater at the end of the year 1934 than it was in December, 1933. Even the staunchest supporters of the New Deal, though still weakly professing optimism, are often compelled to admit that its ideology is illogical, inconsistent, vague, and confused; that its program is composed of a mass of self-contradictory experimentation, and that, in its unblushing rôle of political coquette, it turns now to the left, now to the right.

The explanations of the New Deal and of its apparent failure are not far to seek. The New Deal merely represents our domestic phase of the almost universal attempt in capitalistic countries to establish a new equilibrium in the social structure; an attempt made necessary by the fact that the collapse of the economic structures under the world-wide depression brought out, in bold relief, the sharp class antagonisms which the developing capitalistic economies had nurtured. The history of the operation of social forces in the Western world since the World War is sharply outlined in at least two particulars: (1) Capitalists, *i.e.*, Big Owners, have clearly indicated their inability and unwillingness to afford any leadership

Ralph J. Bunche, "A Critique of New Deal Social Planning at it Affects Negroes," *Journal of Negro Education,* V (January 1936), 59–65. Reprinted by permission of the publisher and the author.

in the society which would promise even a meager measure of social justice to the masses of population, though the productive and organizational
genius of capitalism is unchallenged; (2) on the other hand, the working
classes of the countries of Western Europe, Russia excepted, though winning their way to a position of real power in the state, completely failed to
take over the controls of the state, either through political channels or by
force. The result has been a significant upsurge of the middle classes of
the Western world, whose claim to national leadership is predicated on
their assumed ability to reconcile these conflicting interests in the society
through the establishment of a new equilibrium;—a new society, in fact,
in which conflicting group interests and inequalities will be merged in a
higher national purpose.

Unwittingly or not, President Roosevelt was responsive to these
social forces when he sounded the key note of the New Deal in his radio
address of May 7, 1933.

*It is wholly wrong to call the measures that we have taken government
control of transportation. It is rather a partnership in profits, for profits
would still go to the citizens, but rather a partnership in planning and a
partnership to see that the plans are carried out.*

The New Deal which was then visited upon us embraced no significant shift of ideas, traditions, or loyalties. In large degree it represented
merely an effort to refurbish the old individualistic-capitalistic system and
to entrust it again with the economic destinies and welfare of the American
people. It recognized, of course, that the American economy had slowed
down, and particularly that the forces within it were no longer in equilibrium—a rude awakening for our traditional class-consciousless society.
The intellectual pilots of the New Deal would remedy this condition, though
certainly not by revolution, nor even by fascist counter revolution, (not
immediately, at any rate); but in the words of one author: "abhorring the
thought of violence and having no conscious class interests of their own,
[they] have refused to agree that the mechanism has run down. They will
wind it up again and, having done that, will suspend in balance and for
all time the existing class relations in American society."[1]

### THE TENETS OF THE NEW DEAL

Certain postulates have been laid down as fundamental in the New
Deal program. The private ownership of the means of production is to
continue, but on the one hand, capitalism must be stopped from exploiting
the producers of its raw materials and, on the other, its labor supply. Agriculture, despite its over-capitalized plant and its reluctant but almost complete restriction to the domestic market, is to be permitted a large enough

[1] Hacker, *Short History on the New Deal.* p. 26.

return to allow for the meeting of fixed charges and the purchase of capital and consumer's goods. Wage-earners, although it is admitted that in a machine economy there are too many of them in the white-collar and laboring categories, are to be assured employment and at least the means of subsistence, with a large hope thrown in for incomes conducive to a decent standard of living.

Our own rather short experience with middle-class planning, not to mention the clearer and even more disastrous experiences of Italy, Germany, and Austria with similar schemes, permits us to raise a serious question concerning the ability of the middle classes to construct a new equilibrium which will afford a proper consideration of the interests of the masses of the population. The weakness of the middle classes is precisely that they are "in the middle," i.e., they hold an intermediate position between the working masses and the finance capitalists. Included in their ranks are many whose economic status is continually precarious, and who are weak, uncourageous, and unskillful. In the U.S. today they are largely petty bourgeois. There are many who would incline sympathetically toward the cause of the proletariat, but there are many others whose aspirations ally them ideologically with big business, thus adding greater confusion to the American scene.

Yet this rather ambiguous middle class,—opportunistic and ambitious, lacking class cohesion and ideology—whose members have been completely captivated by the lure of the American Dream, has but two alternatives in the present situation. The middle class itself must take over and operate industry or it must allow private industry to retain its tenacious grip on the economic structure of the nation. But the middle-class leadership is well aware of the violent nature of the struggle that would be necessary in any attempt to wrest industry out of the hands of big ownership. Consequently, the tendency is to take the easier path and to employ the power of the state to keep the masses in check while handling the industrialists with velvet gloves. That is merely another way of saying that the working masses become ever more dependent upon the intervention of the state in their struggle to obtain social justice from the owners and directors of industry. But coincidentally, the alliance between the middle-class political power and the economic power of big business, becomes more unholy. Italy and Nazi Germany afford classic illustrations of the sort of "balance" the working masses can expect from such a process.

The dilemma of the New Deal, then, merely reflects the basic dilemma of capitalism. Either capitalism must surrender itself to intelligent and scientific social planning, (and this it cannot do, for such planning involves a single ownership of the means of production for use rather than for profit), or else it must blunder on, repeating the errors and perpetuating the rigidities which inevitably lead a poorly planned industrial society into periodic depression.

The measures of intervention employed by the New Deal have really been measures of state capitalism which have already been employed by social democratic and fascist governments in Europe, and which obviously have not restored prosperity there, nor settled any of the fundamental conflicts within the modern capitalistic state.

Class lines are more sharply drawn, but state capitalism attempts to balance these class interests within the limits of middle-class democracy. The NRA, for example, began with sympathetic gestures toward labor, if section 7a can be so considered. But it soon became a means of preventing and settling strikes, usually to the disadvantage of labor, as witnessed by the defeat of labor in the settlements of the automobile, San Francisco, textile and other strikes.

American state capitalism has no choice but this, for it proposes to salvage the old order. It retains formal democracy and may make minor concessions to labor. The government intervenes to aid industry, to limit output. But this is not the planned economy of socialism, where all phases of economic activity are placed under planful regulation and control, because here class interests remain in bitter conflict and big ownership retains its economic power. It is not without great significance to the subject of middle-class planning under capitalism, that Secretary Wallace, in his book *New Frontiers*, readily acknowledges, with amazing frankness for one in his position, the enormous influence wielded over the New Deal administration and legislation by the paid lobbies of powerful industrial interests. He clearly suggests that several of the important features of the New Deal represent, not the mature wishes and policies of the Roosevelt administration, but the demands of self-seeking pressure groups, whose demands were too insistent and vigorous to be withstood. The NRA and its codes, he confesses, were not the brain-children of the brain-trusters, but were the products of a swarm of hard-headed business men intent on group price-fixing, who swooped down on Washington and its New Dealers. In America, then, the New Deal follows the classical pattern of middle-class planning by compromise with Big Business,—a policy fatal to the interests of labor.

### THE NEW DEAL AND THE NEGRO

For the Negro population, the New Deal means the same thing, but more of it. Striking at no fundamental social conditions, the New Deal at best can only fix the disadvantages, the differentials, the discriminations, under which the Negro population has labored all along. The traditional racial stereotypes,—which have been inherited from the master-slave tradition and which have been employed by the ruling class of large land-holders in the South and industrialists in the North to give effective expression to their determination to keep the Negro in a servile condition and as a profitable labor supply—remain, and are indeed, often heightened by the New Deal.

Intelligent analysis and the dictates of a purely selfish policy of promoting the profit motive should have made clear to the NRA that the competitive exploitation of any significant part of the population such as the Negro, would frustrate its efforts toward recovery. The poverty of the Negro is an ever-present obstacle to the prosperity of the dominant population. Therefore the first efforts of the NRA should have been directed toward assuring Negro workers that real wage which would make possible for them a decent standard of living.

### NEGRO WAGE EARNERS

To the contrary, however, from the beginning, relatively few Negro workers were even theoretically affected by the labor provisions of NRA. The evils of part-time work, irregular work and occupational and wage differentials, suffered especially by the great mass of Negro workers in the South, were perpetuated under NRA. Through the codes, occupational and geographical differentials were early used as a means of excluding Negro workers from the benefits of minimum wage and hour provisions. Subsequently, the continuation of the inferior economic status of the Negro was assured by NRA through code provisions basing wage rates on the habitual wage differential existing between Negro and white workers. Such measures failing to keep Negro wages at the desired low level, there was still the device of securing a specific exemption from the code of the Negro wage-earners in any given plant. In the power laundry code approved by the President, in an industry employing nearly 30,000 Negro women, a 14 cent per hour minimum wage was established, and even this miserable level was not enforced. Dr. Peck,[2] Executive Director of the Labor Advisory Board, who has maintained staunchly that the NRA has benefited Negro workers, in that the "rates in codes have greatly narrowed the differentials which existed before codes," admits however, that in the service industries in which so many Negroes are employed, "habit, standard of living, cost of living and the level of income of the local population may have a long-time result in a continuance of differential wages." To make still more illusory the theoretical benefits of the NRA to Negro wage-earners, the compliance machinery has been so constructed and operated as virtually to deny any just treatment to the Negro workman, especially in the South.

The FERA relief figures portray graphically enough the effect of NRA upon the Negro. In October, 1933, approximately 2,117,000 Negroes were in families registered on relief rolls, or about eighteen percent of the total Negro population in 1930. In January, 1935, about 3,500,000 Negroes in families on relief were reported, approximating twenty-nine percent of the 1930 population. Most significantly, too, the proportion of Negroes on relief in relation to total population was greater in rural than in urban centers. In addition, it is reliably estimated that there are now some 1,000,000 male Negroes unemployed, exclusive of agricultural pursuits.

[2] "The Negro Worker and the NRA," *Crisis*, S 1934.

AGRICULTURE

The dilemma of American Agriculture is the dilemma of the American economy. There are too many farmers and too much land in cultivation, just as there are too many industrial workers and too much industrial production. These surpluses exist because American agriculture and industry have developed too much efficiency for our profit-motivated economic system. The welfare of the Negro farmer is bound up in the government's solution to the basic dilemma of capitalism—the necessity of providing a decent standard of living, based on a much higher consumption level, for all of the surplus workers and farmers, while retaining an economic order which is founded on profit and not on use. The New Deal, in its agricultural program expressed through the AAA, grabbed vigorously at one horn of the dilemma, and the Negro farmer and farm worker have been left dangling precariously from the other. It goes without saying that the Negro tenant farmer has borne more than his share of this burden. The AAA bears the responsibility for other methods of fixing the Negro population as a poverty-stricken group. It has winked at wide-spread violations of the rights of tenant farmers under the crop-reduction contracts; though the acreage reductions under the government rental agreements dispensed with the need of a great number of the tenants, the government contract theoretically prescribed the reduction of tenants by the land owner. The AAA has blandly permitted the white owner to employ the traditional methods of intimidation of the Negro to deprive him of his benefits from the crop reduction program in payment of parity checks.

The apparent failure of the government's pay-as-you-*not*-grow agricultural program, the growing conviction that the European market for our agricultural products is gone for good, together with the ever-present worry of too many farmers and too much land—we could probably get along with about one-half the number of farmers we now have and could remove from cultivation one-third to one-half of the land now used through the application of efficiency and technical advances to the industry. It is these conditions which have compelled the administration in desperation to flirt with the essentially fantastic "planning" scheme of subsistence homesteads. This scheme proposes to move the inefficient farmers, who thereby are doomed, out of their present economic graveyards and transplant them to semi-rural villages, where they will establish "model" communities. Living on plots ranging from five to forty acres, they will continue to till the soil, but only for family consumption, and are supposed to undergo a sort of economic atavism by reviving the fine old peasant pastimes of pottery making, woodwork, spinning, weaving, etc. To keep life from becoming too monotonous, as it most certainly would under such positive economic security, the government will provide some "factory" seeds for them to plant in the early spring. After the transplanted farmers get through fiddling around in their garden plots, and have indulged in a bit of handicraft, they will thus have the chance to pick up a bit of pin money for automobiles, radios and electric refrigerators, by working in the factories. In this way the submarginal farmer is to be kept on the land and so prevented from swelling the steadily mounting ranks of the industrial unemployed, and likewise kept out of competitive production. In other words the subsistence homesteader will be lifted out of the mainstream of our economic life and laid up on an economic shelf to dry (rot).

The real catch to the scheme is of course in the fact that the bill for the construction, the equipment, repair, taxation, and provision of social services for these communities of "official" peasants, will be footed chiefly by the employed industrial wage earners and the producing commercial farmers; not to mention the serious consequences for a capitalism which thrives on markets and profits, resulting from the consequential contraction of its domestic market for both consumer's and capital goods. This policy Mr. Webster Powell and Mr. Harold M. Ware aptly call "planning for permanent poverty."

Insofar as the program has applied to Negroes it has followed the traditional patterns of racial discrimination and segregation, two Jim Crow projects for Negroes having been recently established.

Primarily, the New Deal is a great relief program which guarantees at level best only a precarious livelihood of the most meager essentials for the millions of distressed workers and farmers who are on the outside of our economic life looking in. Middle-class New Deal planning has adequately demonstrated an utter inability to attain its necessary objectives of lower prices, greater output, and elimination of unemployment in industry. The New Deal policy of planning by separate private industries inevitably tends to raise prices and restrict output—that is to say, it tends to perpetuate an economy of scarcity. Whether consciously or not, it has placed agricultural scarcity in competition with industrial scarcity, and the resultant increases in the prices of both agricultural and manufactured products have deepened the economic depression in which both agriculture and industry had sunk. It has shown only confusion when faced with the problem of administering prices and production in the interest of the whole population.

In the nature of the case it could at best do but little for the Negro within the existing social structure. The Negro does not even boast a significant middle class which, at least, might share some of the gains made for that class by the New Deal. For the Negro middle class exists, in the main, only psychologically, and can be briefly defined as "a hope, a wish and caricature." In fact, the New Deal planning only serves to crystallize those abuses and oppressions which the exploited Negro citizenry of America have long suffered under laissez-faire capitalism, and for the same reasons as in the past.

# 28

## THE "FORGOTTEN YEARS" OF THE NEGRO REVOLUTION
### Richard M. Dalfiume

A RECENT president of the American Sociological Society addressed himself to a puzzling question about what we know as the Civil Rights Revolution: "Why did social scientists—and sociologists in particular—not foresee the explosion of collective action of Negro Americans toward full integration into American society?" He pointed out that "it is the vigor and urgency of the Negro demand that is new, not its direction or supporting ideas."[1] Without arguing the point further, the lack of knowledge can be attributed to two groups—the ahistorical social scientists, and the historians who, until recently, have neglected modern Negro history.

The search for a "watershed" in recent Negro history ends at the years that comprised World War II, 1939–1945. James Baldwin has written of this period: "The treatment accorded the Negro during the Second World War marks, for me, a turning point in the Negro's relation to America. To put it briefly, and somewhat too simply, a certain hope died, a certain respect for white Americans faded."[2] Writing during World War II, Gunnar Myrdal predicted that the war would act as a "stimulant" to Negro protest, and he felt that "There is bound to be a redefinition of the Negro's status in America as a result of this War."[3] The Negro sociologist E. Franklin Frazier states that World War II marked the point where "The Negro was no longer willing to accept discrimination in employment and in housing without protest."[4] Charles E. Silberman writes that the war was a "turning point" in American race relations, in which "the seeds of the protest movements of the 1950s and 1960s were sown."[5] While a few writers have indicated the importance of these years in the recent Negro protest movement, the majority have failed to do so. Overlooking what went before, most recent books on the subject claim that a Negro "revolution" or "re-

Richard M. Dalfiume, "The 'Forgotten Years' of the Negro Revolution, " *Journal of American History*, LV (June 1968), 90–106. Reprinted by permission of the *Journal of American History* and the author.

[1] Everett C. Hughes, "Race Relations and the Sociological Imagination," *American Sociological Review*, XXVIII (Dec. 1963), 879.

[2] Quoted in J. Milton Yinger, *A Minority Group in American Society* (New York, 1965), 52. Many Negroes agreed with James Baldwin in recalling the bitterness they experienced. William Brink and Louis Harris, *The Negro Revolution in America* (New York, 1964), 50.

[3] Gunnar Myrdal, *An American Dilemma: The Negro Problem and Modern Democracy* (New York, 1944), 756, 997.

[4] E. Franklin Frazier, *The Negro in the United States* (rev. ed., New York, 1957), 682.

[5] Charles E. Silberman, *Crisis in Black and White* (New York, 1964), 60, 65.

volt" occurred in 1954, 1955, 1960, or 1963.[6] Because of the neglect of the war period, these years of transition in American race relations comprise the "forgotten years" of the Negro revolution.

To understand how the American Negro reacted to World War II, it is necessary to have some idea of the discrimination he faced. The defense build-up begun by the United States in 1940 was welcomed by Negroes who were disproportionately represented among the unemployed. Employment discrimination in the revived industries, however, was rampant. When Negroes sought jobs at aircraft factories where employers begged for workers, they were informed that "the Negro will be considered only as janitors and in other similar capacities. . . ."[7] Government financed training programs to overcome the shortages of skilled workers discriminated against Negro trainees. When government agencies issued orders against such discrimination, they were ignored.[8]

Increasing defense preparations also meant an expansion of the armed forces. Here, as in industry, however, Negroes faced restrictions. Black Americans were assigned a minimal role and rigidly segregated. In the navy, Negroes could enlist only in the all-Negro messman's branch. The marine and the air corps excluded Negroes entirely. In the army, black Americans were prevented from enlisting, except for a few vacancies in the four regular army Negro units that had been created shortly after the Civil War; and the strength of these had been reduced drastically in the 1920s and 1930s.[9]

Although the most important bread-and-butter issue for Negroes in this period was employment discrimination, their position in the armed forces was an important symbol. If one could not participate fully in the defense of his country, he could not lay claim to the rights of a full-fledged citizen. The NAACP organ, the *Crisis*, expressed this idea in its demand for unrestricted participation in the armed forces: "this is no fight merely to wear a uniform. This is a struggle for status, a struggle to take democracy off of parchment and give it life."[10] Herbert Garfinkel, a student of Negro

[6] See, for example, Lewis M. Killian and Charles Grigg, *Racial Crisis in America* (Englewood Cliffs, 1964); Louis E. Lomax, *The Negro Revolt* (New York, 1962); Leonard Broom and Norval D. Glenn, *Transformation of the Negro American* (New York, 1965); Brink and Harris, *Negro Revolution in America*.

[7] Quoted in Louis Coleridge Kesselman, *The Social Politics of FEPC: A Study in Reform Pressure Movements* (Chapel Hill, 1948), 7.

[8] Charles H. Thompson, "The American Negro and the National Defense," *Journal of Negro Education*, IX (Oct. 1940), 547–52; Frazier, *Negro in the United States*, 599–606; Robert C. Weaver, "Racial Employment Trends in National Defense," *Phylon*, II (4th Quarter, 1941), 337–58.

[9] See Richard M. Dalfiume, "Desegregation of the United States Armed Forces, 1939–1953" (doctoral dissertation, University of Missouri, 1966), 30–57; Ulysses Lee, *United States Army in World War II: Special Studies: The Employment of Negro Troops* (Washington, 1966), 32–87.

[10] "For Manhood in National Defense," *Crisis*, 47 (Dec. 1940), 375.

protest during this period, points out that "in many respects, the discriminatory practices against Negroes which characterized the military programs
. . . cut deeper into Negro feelings than did employment discrimination."[11]

Added to the rebuffs from industry and the armed services were a
hundred others. Negroes, anxious to contribute to the Red Cross blood
program, were turned away. Despite the fact that white and Negro blood
is the same biologically, it was deemed inadvisable "to collect and mix
caucasian and Negro blood indiscriminately."[12] When Negro citizens called
upon the governor of Tennessee to appoint some black members to the
state's draft boards, he told them: "This is a white man's country. . . . The
Negro had nothing to do with the settling of America."[13] At a time when
the United States claimed to be the last bulwark of democracy in a war-torn
world, the legislature of Mississippi passed a law requiring different text-
books for Negro schools: all references to voting, elections, and democracy
were to be excluded from the black student's books.[41]

The Negro's morale at the beginning of World War II is also partly
explained by his experience in World War I. Black America had gone into
that war with high morale, generated by the belief that the democratic
slogans literally meant what they said. Most Negroes succumbed to the
"close ranks" strategy announced by the crusading NAACP editor, W. E. B.
Du Bois, who advocated subduing racial grievances in order to give full
support to winning the war. But the image of a new democratic order was
smashed by the race riots, lynchings, and continued rigid discrimination.
The result was a mass trauma and a series of movements among Negroes in
the 1920s which were characterized by a desire to withdraw from a white
society which wanted little to do with them. When the war crisis of the
1940s came along, the bitter memories of World War I were recalled with
the result that there was a built-in cynicism among Negroes toward the
democratic slogans of the new war.[15]

Nevertheless, Negroes were part of the general population being
stimulated to come to the defense of democracy in the world. When they
responded and attempted to do their share, they were turned away. The
result was a widespread feeling of frustration and a general decline of the

[11] Herbert Garfinkel, *When Negroes March: The March on Washington Movement in the
Organizational Politics for FEPC* (Glencoe, Ill., 1959), 20.

[12] General James C. Magee, Surgeon General, to Assistant Secretary of War John J. McCloy,
Sept. 3, 1941, ASW, 291.2, Record Group 335 (National Archives); Pittsburgh *Courier,*
Jan. 3, 1942.

[13] Pittsburgh *Courier,* Nov. 2, 1940.

[14] "Text Books in Mississippi," *Opportunity,* XVIII (April 1940), 99.

[15] Kenneth B. Clark, "Morale of the Negro on the Home Front: World Wars I and II,"
*Journal of Negro Education,* XII (Summer 1943), 417–28; Walter White, " 'It's Our Country,
Too': The Negro Demands the Right to be Allowed to Fight for It," *Saturday Evening Post,*
213 (Dec. 14, 1940), 27, 61, 63, 66, 68; Metz T. P. Lochard, "Negroes and Defense," *Nation,*
152 (Jan. 4, 1941), 14–16.

Negro's morale toward the war effort, as compared with the rest of American society. But paradoxically, the Negro's general morale was both low and high.

While the morale of the Negro, as an American, was low in regard to the war effort, the Negro, as a member of a minority group, had high morale in his heightened race consciousness and determination to fight for a better position in American society. The same slogans which caused the Negro to react cynically also served to emphasize the disparity between the creed and the practice of democracy as far as the Negro in America was concerned. Because of his position in society, the Negro reacted to the war both as an American and as a Negro. Discrimination against him had given rise to "a sickly, negative attitude toward national goals, but at the same time a vibrantly positive attitude toward racial aims and aspirations."[16]

When war broke out in Europe in 1939, many black Americans tended to adopt an isolationist attitude. Those taking this position viewed the war as a "white man's war." George Schuyler, the iconoclastic columnist, was a typical spokesman for this view: "So far as the colored peoples of the earth are concerned," Schuyler wrote, "it is a toss-up between the 'democracies' and the dictatorships. . . . [W]hat is there to choose between the rule of the British in Africa and the rule of the Germans in Austria?"[17] Another Negro columnist claimed that it was a blessing to have war so that whites could "mow one another down" rather than "have them quietly murder hundreds of thousands of Africans, East Indians and Chinese. . . ."[18] This kind of isolationism took the form of anti-colonialism, particularly against the British. There was some sympathy for France, however, because of its more liberal treatment of black citizens.[19]

Another spur to isolationist sentiment was the obvious hypocrisy of calling for the defense of democracy abroad while it was not a reality at home. The NAACP bitterly expressed this point:

*The Crisis is sorry for brutality, blood, and death among the peoples of Europe, just as we were sorry for China and Ethiopia. But the hysterical cries of the preachers of democracy for Europe leave us cold. We want*

[16] Cornelius L. Golightly, "Negro Higher Education and Democratic Negro Morale," *Journal of Negro Education*, XI (July 1942), 324. See also Horace R. Cayton, "Negro Morale," *Opportunity*, XIX (Dec. 1941), 371–75; Louis Wirth, "Morale and Minority Groups," *American Journal of Sociology*, XLVII (Nov. 1941), 415–33; Kenneth B. Clark, "Morale Among Negroes," Goodwin Watson, ed., *Civilian Morale* (Boston, 1942), 228–48; Arnold M. Rose, *The Negro's Morale: Group Identification and Protest* (Minneapolis, 1949), 5–7, 54–55, 122–24, 141–44.

[17] Pittsburgh *Courier*, Sept. 9, 1939.

[18] P. L. Prattis in *ibid.*, Sept. 2, 1939. Similar sentiments were expressed by Chicago *Defender* editorials, May 25, June 15, 1940.

[19] Pittsburgh *Courier*, Sept. 9, 16, 1939.

[20] "Lynching and Liberty," *Crisis*, 47 (July 1940), 209.

*democracy in Alabama and Arkansas, in Mississippi and Michigan, in the District of Columbia*—in the Senate of the United States.[20]

The editor of the Pittsburgh *Courier* proclaimed that Negroes had their "own war" at home "against oppression and exploitation from without and against disorganization and lack of confidence within"; and the Chicago *Defender* thought that "peace at home" should be the main concern of black Americans.[21]

Many Negroes agreed with columnist Schuyler that "Our war is not against Hitler in Europe, but against the Hitlers in America."[22] The isolationist view of the war in Europe and the antagonism toward Great Britain led to an attitude that was rather neutral toward the Nazis and the Japanese, or, in some extreme cases, pro-Axis. Appealing to this latent feeling, isolationist periodicals tried to gain Negro support in their struggle against American entrance into the war.[23] By 1940 there were also Negro cults such as the Ethiopian Pacific Movement, the World Wide Friends of Africa, the Brotherhood of Liberty for the Black People of America, and many others, which preached unity among the world's darker people, including Japanese. Many of these groups exploited the latent anti-semitism common among Negroes in the urban ghettos by claiming that the racial policies of Germany were correct.[24]

Reports reached the public that some black Americans were expressing a vicarious pleasure over successes by the "yellow" Japanese and by Germany. In a quarrel with her employer in North Carolina, a Negro woman retorted: "I hope Hitler does come, because if he does he will get you first!" A Negro truck driver in Philadelphia was held on charges of treason after he was accused of telling a Negro soldier that he should not be in uniform and that "This is a white man's government and war and it's no damned good." After Pearl Harbor, a Negro share cropper told his landlord: "By the way, Captain, I hear the Japs done declared war on you white folks." Another Negro declared that he was going to get his eyes slanted so that the next time a white man shoved him around he could fight back.[25]

---

[21] Pittsburgh *Courier*, Sept. 9, 1939; Chicago *Defender*, May 25, 1940.

[22] Pittsburgh *Courier*, Dec. 21, 1940.

[23] Lee, *The Employment of Negro Troops*, 65–67; Horace Mann Bond, "Should the Negro Care Who Wins the War?" *Annals*, CCXXIII (Sept. 1942), 81–84; Adam Clayton Powell, Jr., "Is This a 'White Man's War'?" *Common Sense*, XI (April 1942), 111–13.

[24] Roi Ottley, "A White Folk's War?" *Common Ground*, II (Spring 1942), 28–31, and *'New World A-Coming'* (Boston, 1943), 322–42; Lunnabelle Wedlock, *The Reaction of Negro Publications and Organizations to German Anti-Semitism* (Washington, 1942), 116–93; Alfred M. Lee, "Subversive Individuals of Minority Status," *Annals*, CCXXIII (Sept. 1942), 167–68.

[25] St. Clair Drake and Horace R. Cayton, *Black Metropolis* (New York, 1945), 744–45; Ottley, *'New World A-Coming'*, 306–10; Horace R. Cayton, "Fighting for White Folks?" *Nation*, 155 (Sept. 26, 1942), 267–70.

It is impossible to determine the extent of this kind of pro-Axis senti-ment among Negroes, but it was widespread enough for the Negro press to make rather frequent mention of it.[26] In 1942 and 1943 the federal govern-ment did arrest the members of several pro-Japanese Negro cults in Chicago, New York, Newark, New Jersey, and East St. Louis, Illinois. Although the numbers involved were small, the evidence indicated that Japanese agents had been at work among these groups and had capitalized on Negro grievances.[27]

By the time of the Pearl Harbor attack, certain fundamental changes were taking place among American Negroes. Nowhere is this more evi-dent than in a comparison of Negroes' reactions to World Wars I and II. The dominant opinion among them toward World War I was expressed by Du Bois. In World War II, most Negroes looked upon the earlier stand as a great mistake. The dominant attitude during World War II was that the Negro must fight for democracy on two fronts—at home as well as abroad. This opinion had first appeared in reaction to the discriminatory treatment of Negro soldiers;[28] but with the attack on Pearl Harbor, this idea, stated in many different ways, became the slogan of black America.[29]

American Negroes took advantage of the war to tie their racial demands to the ideology for which the war was being fought. Before Pearl Harbor, the Negro press frequently pointed out the similarity of American treatment of Negroes and Nazi Germany's treatment of minorities. In 1940, the Chicago *Defender* featured a mock invasion of the United States by Germany in which the Nazis were victorious because a fifth column of southern senators and other racists aided them.[30] Later the *Crisis* printed an editorial which compared the white supremacy doctrine in America to the

---

[26] "The Negro and Nazism," *Opportunity*, XVIII (July 1940), 194–95; Horace R. Cayton in Pittsburgh *Courier*, Dec. 20, 1941; J. A. Rodgers in *ibid.*, Dec. 27, 1941; Chandler Owen in Norfolk *Journal and Guide*, Dec. 13, 1941; report in Baltimore *Afro-American*, Nov. 21, 1942.

[27] New York *Times*, Sept. 15, 22, 1942, Jan. 14, 28, 1943.

[28] "Conference Resolutions," *Crisis*, 47 (Sept. 1940), 296; "Where the Negro Stands," *Opportunity*, XIX (April 1941), 98; Lester M. Jones. "The Editorial Policy of Negro News-papers of 1917–18 as Compared with That of 1941–42," *Journal of Negro History*, XXIX (Jan. 1944), 24–31.

[29] Baltimore *Afro-American*, Dec. 20, 1941, Feb. 7, 1942; Norfolk *Journal and Guide*, March 21, 1942; "Now Is the Time Not to Be Silent," *Crisis*, 49 (Jan. 1942), 7; "The Fate of Democracy," *Opportunity*, XX (Jan. 1942), 2. Two Negro newspapers adopted this theme for their war slogans. The Pittsburgh *Courier*, Feb. 14, 1942, initiated a "Double V" campaign—"victory over our enemies at home and victory over our enemies on the battle-fields abroad." When a Negro was brutally lynched in Sikeston, Missouri, a few weeks after Pearl Harbor, the Chicago *Defender*, March 14, 1942, adopted as its war slogan: "Remember Pearl Harbor and Sikeston too." See also Ralph N. Davis, "The Negro News-papers and the War." *Sociology and Social Research*, XXVII (May–June 1943), 373–80.

[30] Chicago *Defender*, Sept. 25, 1940.

Nazi plan for Negroes, a comparison which indicated a marked similarity.[31] Even the periodical of the conservative Urban League made such comparisons.[32]

Many Negroes adopted a paradoxical stand on the meaning of the war. At the same time that it was labeled a "white man's war," Negroes often stated that they were bound to benefit from it. For example, Schuyler could argue that the war was not for democracy, but "Peace means . . . a continuation of the status quo . . . which must be ended if the Negro is to get free." And accordingly, the longer the war the better: "Perhaps in the shuffle we who have been on the bottom of the deck for so long will find ourselves at the top."[33]

Cynicism and hope existed side by side in the Negro mind. Cynicism was often the attitude expressed after some outrageous example of discrimination. After Pearl Harbor, however, a mixture of hope and certainty —great changes favorable to the Negro would result from the war and things would never be the same again—became the dominant attitude. Hope was evident in the growing realization that the war provided the Negro with an excellent opportunity to prick the conscience of white America. "What an opportunity the crisis has been . . . for one to persuade, embarrass, compel and shame our government and our nation . . . into a more enlightened attitude toward a tenth of its people!" the Pittsburgh Courier proclaimed.[34] Certainty that a better life would result from the war was based on the belief that revolutionary forces had been released throughout the world. It was no longer a "white man's world," and the "myth of white invincibility" had been shattered for good.[35]

There was a growing protest against the racial status quo by black Americans; this was evidenced by the reevaluation of segregation in all sections of the country. In the North there was self-criticism of past accep-

---

[31] "Nazi Plan for Negroes Copies Southern U. S. A.," Crisis, 48 (March 1941), 71.

[32] "American Nazism," Opportunity, XIX (Feb. 1941), 35. See also editorials in Pittsburgh Courier, March 15, April 19, 26, 1941, May 30, 1942; Chicago Defender, Sept. 7, 1940; Norfolk Journal and Guide, April 19, 1941; Baltimore Afro-American, Feb. 17, 1940, Sept. 6, 1941.

[33] Pittsburgh Courier, Oct. 5, 1940; George S. Schuyler, "A Long War Will Aid the Negro," Crisis, 50 (Nov. 1943), 328–29, 344. See also J. A. Rodgers in Pittsburgh Courier, June 28, 1941; Horace R. Cayton in ibid., March 22, 1941; Baltimore Afro-American, Sept. 12, 16, 1939; Guion Griffis Johnson, "The Impact of War Upon the Negro," Journal of Negro Education, X (July 1941), 596–611.

[34] Pittsburgh Courier, Jan. 10, Aug. 8, 1942. Charles S. Johnson, "The Negro and the Present Crisis," Journal of Negro Education, X (July 1941), 585–95. Opinion surveys indicated that most Negro soldiers expressed support for this kind of opportunism. Samuel A. Stouffer and others, The American Soldier (2 vols., Princeton, 1949), I, 516–17.

[35] Baltimore Afro-American, June 12, Oct. 31, 1942; Walter White in Pittsburgh Courier, May 23, 1942. The impact of world affairs on the American Negro is detailed in Harold R. Isaacs, The New World of Negro Americans (New York, 1963).

tance of certain forms of segregation.[36] Southern Negroes became bolder in openly questioning the sacredness of segregation. In October 1942, a group of southern Negro leaders met in Durham, North Carolina, and issued a statement on race relations. In addition to endorsing the idea that the Negro should fight for democracy at home as well as abroad, these leaders called for complete equality for the Negro in American life. While recognizing the "strength and age" of the South's racial customs, the Durham meeting was "fundamentally opposed to the principle and practice of compulsory segregation in our American society." In addition, there were reports of deep discontent among southern Negro college students and evidence that political activity among the blacks of the South, particularly on the local level, was increasing.[37]

The American Negro, stimulated by the democratic ideology of the war, was reexamining his position in American society. "It cannot be doubted that the spirit of American Negroes in all classes is different today from what it was a generation ago," Myrdal observed.[38] Part of this new spirit was an increased militancy, a readiness to protest loud and strong against grievances. The crisis gave Negroes more reason and opportunity to protest. Representative of all of the trends of black thought and action— the cynicism, the hope, the heightened race consciousness, the militancy —was the March on Washington Movement (MOWM).

The general idea of exerting mass pressure upon the government to end defense discrimination did not originate with A. Philip Randolph's call for a march on Washington, D.C., in early 1941.[39] Agitation for mass pressure had grown since the failure of a group of Negro leaders to gain any major concessions from President Franklin D. Roosevelt in September 1940.[40] Various organizations, such as the NAACP, the Committee for Participation of Negroes in the National Defense, and the Allied Commit-

---

[36] See editorials in Pittsburgh *Courier*, Dec. 28, 1940; Feb. 1, June 28, 1941; May 30, 1942; Baltimore *Afro-American*, May 23, 1942.

[37] Charles S. Johnson, *To Stem This Tide* (Boston, 1943), 131–39; Malcolm S. MacLean, president of Hampton Institute, to Marvin H. McIntyre, Nov. 20, 1942, OF 93, Roosevelt Papers (Franklin D. Roosevelt Library, Hyde Park); George B. Tindall, "The Significance of Howard W. Odum to Southern History: A Preliminary Estimate," *Journal of Southern History*, XXIV (Aug. 1958), 302. Anthropologist Hortense Powdermaker, *After Freedom: A Cultural Study of the Deep South* (New York, 1939), 331–33, 353, supports the observations of a tendency to rebel among the younger Negroes of the South. See also Ralph J. Bunche, "The Negro in the Political Life of the United States," *Journal of Negro Education*, X (July 1941), 567–84; Myrdal, *American Dilemma*, 499; Henry Lee Moon, *Balance of Power: The Negro Vote* (Garden City, 1948), 178–79.

[38] Myrdal, *American Dilemma*, 744.

[39] Garfinkel, *When Negroes March*, fails to emphasize this point.

[40] Walter White, *A Man Called White* (New York, 1948), 186–87; "White House Blesses Jim Crow," *Crisis*, 47 (Nov. 1940), 350–51, 357; Dalfiume, "Desegregation of the United States Armed Forces, 1939–1953," 46–51.

tees on National Defense, held mass protest meetings around the country in late 1940 and early 1941.[41] The weeks passed and these efforts did not seem to have any appreciable impact on the government; Walter White, Randolph, and other Negro leaders could not even secure an appointment to see the President. "Bitterness grew at an alarming pace throughout the country," White recalled.[42]

It remained, however, for Randolph to consolidate this protest. In January 1941, he wrote an article for the Negro press which pointed out the failure of committees and individuals to achieve action against defense discrimination. "Only power can effect the enforcement and adoption of a given policy," Randolph noted; and "Power is the active principle of only the organized masses, the masses united for a definite purpose." To focus the weight of the black masses, he suggested that 10,000 Negroes march on Washington, D.C., with the slogan: "We loyal Negro-American citizens demand the right to work and fight for our country."[43]

This march appeal led to the formation of one of the most significant —though today almost forgotten—Negro protest movements. The MOWM pioneered what has become the common denominator of today's Negro revolt—"the spontaneous involvement of large masses of Negroes in a political protest."[44] Furthermore, as August Meier and Elliott Rudwick have recently pointed out, the MOWM clearly foreshadowed "the goals, tactics, and strategy of the mid-twentieth-century civil rights movement." Whites were excluded purposely to make it an all-Negro movement; its main weapon was direct action on the part of the black masses. Furthermore, the MOWM took as its major concern the economic problems of urban slum-dwellers.[45]

Randolph's tactic of mass pressure through a demonstration of black power struck a response among the Negro masses. The number to march on Washington on July 1, 1941, was increased to 50,000, and only Roosevelt's agreement to issue an executive order establishing a President's Committee on Fair Employment Practices led to a cancellation of the march. Negroes then, and scholars later, generally interpreted this as a great victory. But the magnitude of the victory is diminished when one examines the original MOWM demands: an executive order forbidding government contracts to be awarded to a firm which practiced discrimination in hiring, an executive order abolishing discrimination in government defense training courses, an executive order requiring the United States Employment Service to supply workers without regard to race, an executive order abolishing segregation

[41] Pittsburgh *Courier*, Dec. 7, 14, 21, 1940; Jan. 4, 25, Feb. 8, 1941.

[42] White, *A Man Called White*, 189–90.

[43] Pittsburgh *Courier*, Jan. 25, 1941.

[44] Garfinkel, *When Negroes March*, 8.

[45] August Meier and Elliott M. Rudwick, *From Plantation to Ghetto: An Interpretative History of American Negroes* (New York, 1966), 222.

in the armed forces, an executive order abolishing discrimination and segregation on account of race in all departments of the federal government, and a request from the President to Congress to pass a law forbidding benefits of the National Labor Relations Act to unions denying Negroes membership. Regardless of the extent of the success of the MOWM, however, it represented something different in black protest. Unlike the older Negro movements, the MOWM had captured the imaginations of the masses.[46]

Although overlooked by most recent writers on civil rights, a mass militancy became characteristic of the American Negro in World War II. This was symbolized by the MOWM and was the reason for its wide appeal. Furthermore, older Negro organizations found themselves pushed into militant stands. For example, the NAACP underwent a tremendous growth in its membership and became representative of the Negro masses for the first time in its history. From 355 branches and a membership of 50,556 in 1940, the NAACP grew to 1,073 branches with a membership of slightly less than 450,000 in 1946.[47] The editors of the Pittsburgh *Courier* recognized that a new spirit was present in black America. In the past, Negroes

*made the mistake of relying entirely upon the gratitude and sense of fair play of the American people. Now we are disillusioned. We have neither*

[46] "Proposals of the Negro March-On-Washngiton Committee to President Roosevelt for Urgent Consideration," June 21, 1941, OF 391, Roosevelt Papers. The standard versions of a Negro "victory" are Garfinkel, *When Negroes March;* Kesselman, *The Social Politics of FEPC;* and Louis Ruchames, *Race, Jobs, & Politics: The Story of FEPC* (New York, 1953). For a different interpretation, see Dalfiume, "Desegregation of the United States Armed Forces, 1939–1953," 172–77. The Negro press generally recognized that the MOWM represented something new. The Pittsburgh *Courier,* July 5, 1941, claimed: "We begin to feel at last that the day when we shall gain full rights . . . of American citizenship is now not far distant." The Chicago *Defender,* June 28, July 12, 1941, felt that the white man will be convinced that "the American black man has decided henceforth and forever to abandon the timid role of Uncle-Tomism in his struggle. . . ." The tactics of the MOWM had "demonstrated to the doubting Thomases among us that only mass action can pry open the iron doors that have been erected against America's black minority."

[47] Frazier, *The Negro in the United States,* 537; Charles Radford Lawrence, "Negro Organizations in Crisis: Depression, New Deal, World War II" (doctoral dissertation, Columbia University, 1953), 103; Myrdal, *American Dilemma,* 851–52. Such close observers of American race relations as Will Alexander, Edwin Embree, and Charles S. Johnson recognized the changing character of Negro protest. They believed that "the characteristic movements among Negroes are now for the first time becoming proletarian, as contrasted to upper class or intellectual influence that was typical of previous movements. The present proletarian direction grows out of the increasing general feelings of protest against discrimination, especially in the armed forces and in our war activities generally. The present movements are led in part by such established leaders as A. Philip Randolph, Walter White, etc. There is likelihood (and danger) that the movement may be seized upon by some much more picturesque figure who may be less responsible and less interested in actual improvement of conditions. One of the most likely of the potential leaders is A. Clayton Powell, Jr." Memorandum of Conferences of Alexander, Johnson, and Embree on the Rosenwald Fund's Program in Race Relations, June 27, 1942, Race Relations folder, Rosenwald Fund Papers (Fisk University).

*faith in promises, nor a high opinion of the integrity of the American peo-
ple, where race is involved. Experience has taught us that we must rely
primarily upon our own efforts. . . . That is why we protest, agitate, and
demand that all forms of color prejudice be blotted out. . . .*[48]

By the time of the Japanese attack on Pearl Harbor, many in America,
both inside and outside of the government, were worried over the state of
Negro morale. There was fear that the Negro would be disloyal.[49] The
depth of white ignorance about the causes for the Negro's cynicism and
low morale is obvious from the fact that the black press was blamed for the
widespread discontent. The double victory attitude constantly displayed in
Negro newspapers throughout the war, and supported by most black Americans, was considered as verging on disloyalty by most whites. White
America, ignorant of the American Negroes' reaction to World War I,
thought that black citizens should subdue their grievances for the duration.

During World War II, there was pressure upon the White House and
the justice department from within the federal government to indict some
Negro editors for sedition and interference with the war effort. President
Roosevelt refused to sanction this, however. There was also an attempt to
deny newsprint to the more militant Negro newspapers, but the President
put an end to this when the matter was brought to his attenion.[50] The restriction of Negro newspapers from military installations became so widespread that the war department had to call a halt to this practice in 1943.[51]
These critics failed to realize that, although serving to unify black opinion,
the Negro press simply reflected the Negro mind.

One of the most widely publicized attacks on the Negro press was
made by the southern white liberal, Virginius Dabney, editor of the Richmond *Times Dispatch*. He charged that "extremist" Negro newspapers and
Negro leaders were "demanding an overnight revolution in race relations,"

[48] Pittsburgh *Courier*, Sept. 12, 1942. See also Roscoe E. Lewis, "The Role of Pressure Groups
in Maintaining Morale Among Negroes," *Journal of Negro Education*, XII (Summer 1943),
464–73; Earl Brown, "American Negroes and the War," *Harper's Magazine*, 184 (April 1942),
545–52; Roi Ottley, "Negro Morale," *New Republic*, 105 (Nov. 10, 1941), 613–15; Thomas
Sancton, "Something's Happened to the Negro," *New Republic*, 108 (Feb. 8, 1943), 175–79;
Stanley High, "How the Negro Fights for Freedom," *Reader's Digest*, 41 (July 1942), 113–18;
H. C. Brearley, "The Negro's New Belligerency," *Phylon*, V (4th Quarter 1944), 339–45.

[49] Memorandum to Assistant Secretary of War McCloy from G-2, June 27, 1942, ASW 291.2,
Record Group 335.

[50] White, *A Man Called White*, 207–08; R. Keith Kane to Ulric Bell, May 14, 1942, OFF
992.11, Record Group 208; Memorandum to Robert A. Lovett from McCloy, March 6,
1942, ASW 291.2, Record Group 335.

[51] Baltimore *Afro-American*, Sept. 30, 1941; Pittsburgh *Courier*, March 8, 1941, Nov. 13,
1943. Assistant Secretary of War McCloy, who was also head of the war department's
Advisory Committee on Negro Troop Policies, held a critical view of the Negro press that
was common in the army. McCloy to Herbert Elliston, editor of the Washington *Post*,
Aug. 5, 1943, ASW 292.2, Record Group 335.

and as a consequence they were "stirring up interracial hate." Dabney concluded his indictment by warning that "it is a foregone conclusion that if an attempt is made forcibly to abolish segregation throughout the South, violence and bloodshed will result."[52] The Negro press reacted vigorously to such charges. Admitting that there were "all-or-nothing" Negro leaders, the Norfolk *Journal and Guide* claimed they were created by the "nothing-at-all" attitude of whites.[53] The Chicago *Defender* and Baltimore *Afro-American* took the position that they were only pointing out the shortcomings of American democracy, and this was certainly not disloyal.[54] The NAACP and the Urban League claimed that it was patriotic for Negroes to protest against undemocratic practices, and those who sought to stifle this protest were the unpatriotic ones.[55]

The Negro masses simply did not support a strategy of moderating their grievances for the duration of the war. After attending an Office of Facts and Figures conference for Negro leaders in March 1942, Roy Wilkins of the NAACP wrote:

... it is a plain fact that no Negro leader with a constituency can face his members today and ask full support for the war in the light of the atmosphere the government has created. Some Negro educators who are responsible only to their boards or trustees might do so, but the heads of no organized groups would dare do so.[56]

[52] Virginius Dabney, "Nearer and Nearer the Precipice," *Atlantic Monthly*, 171 (Jan. 1943), 94–100; Virginius Dabney, "Press and Morale," *Saturday Review of Literature*, XXV (July 4, 1942), 5–6, 24–25.

[53] Norfolk *Journal and Guide*, Aug. 15, 1942. See also *Journal and Guide* editorials of Oct. 17, April 25, 1942; and March 6, 1943, for a defense of Negro militancy.

[54] Chicago *Defender*, Dec. 20, 1941; Baltimore *Afro-American*, Jan. 9, 1943.

[55] Pittsburgh *Courier*, May 8, June 19, 1943. A few conservative Negroes joined whites in criticizing the growing militancy. James E. Shepard, Negro president of North Carolina College for Negroes, asked the administration to do something to undercut the growing support of the militants among young Negroes: "Those who seek to stir them up about rights and not duties are their enemies." Shepard to Secretary of the Navy Frank Knox, Sept. 28, 1940, OF 93, Roosevelt Papers. Frederick D. Patterson, president of Tuskegee Institute, made it clear in his newspaper column and in talks with administration officials that he believed in all-out support for the war effort by Negroes regardless of segregation and discrimination. "Stimson Diary," Jan. 29, 1943 (Yale University Library), and columns by Patterson in the Pittsburgh *Courier*, Jan. 16, July 3, 1943. Such conservatives were bitterly attacked in the Negro press. The black leader who urged his people to relax their determination to win full participation in American life was a "misleader and a false prophet," the Norfolk *Journal and Guide*, May 2, 1942, proclaimed. Such people "endangered" the interests of Negroes by "compromising with the forces that promote and uphold segregation and discrimination," wrote the editor of the Chicago *Defender*, April 5, 1941. The *Crisis* charged that those Negroes who succumbed to segregation as "realism" provided a rationale for those whites who sought to perpetuate segregation. "Government Blesses Separatism," *Crisis*, 50 (April 1943), 105.

[56] Memorandum to White from Roy Wilkins, March 24, 1942, Stephen J. Spingarn Papers (Harry S. Truman Library, Independence).

By 1942, the federal government began investigating Negro morale in order to find out what could be done to improve it. This project was undertaken by the Office of Facts and Figures and its successor, the Office of War Information.[57] Surveys by these agencies indicated that the great amount of national publicity given the defense program only served to increase the Negro's awareness that he was not participating fully in that program. Black Americans found it increasingly difficult to reconcile their treatment with the announced war aims. Urban Negroes were the most resentful over defense discrimination, particularly against the treatment accorded black members of the armed forces. Never before had Negroes been so united behind a cause: the war had served to focus their attention on their unequal status in American society. Black Americans were almost unanimous in wanting a show of good intention from the federal government that changes would be made in the racial status quo.[58]

The government's inclination to take steps to improve Negro morale, and the Negro's desire for change, were frustrated by the general attitude of white Americans. In 1942, after two years of militant agitation by Negroes, six out of ten white Americans felt that black Americans were satisfied with things the way they were and that Negroes were receiving all of the opportunities they deserved. More than half of all whites interviewed in the Northeast and West believed that there should be separate schools, separate restaurants, and separate neighborhoods for the races. A majority of whites in all parts of the country believed that the Negro would not be treated any better after the war than in 1942 and that the Negro's lesser role in society was due to his own shortcomings rather than anything the whites had done.[59] The white opposition to racial change may have provided the rationale for governmental inactivity. Furthermore, the white obstinance must have added to the bitterness of black Americans.

Although few people recognized it, the war was working a revolution in American race relations. Sociologist Robert E. Park felt that the racial

---

[57] Memorandum to Archibald MacLeish from Kane, Feb. 14, 1942; Bell to Embree, Feb. 23, 1942, OFF 002.11, Record Group 208. Some government agencies displayed timidity when it came to a subject as controversial as the race question. Jonathan Daniels, Assistant Director in Charge of Civilian Mobilization, Office of Civilian Defense, urged the creation of a Division of American Unity within the OCD, but his superiors decided Negro morale was "too hot a potato." Memoranda to James Landis, April 1, 7, 1942; Daniels to Howard W. Odum, Aug. 24, 1942, Jonathan Daniels Papers (University of North Carolina).

[58] "Reports from the Special Services Division Submitted April 23, 1942: Negro Organizations and the War Effort"; Cornelius Golightly, "Negro Morale in Boston," Special Services Division Report No. 7, May 19, 1942; Special Services Division Report No. 5, May 15, 1942: "Negro Conference at Lincoln University"; Special Services Division Memorandum. "Report on Recent Factors Increasing Negro-White Tension," Nov. 2, 1942. All are in OFF and OWI files in Record Group 44.

[59] "Intelligence Report: White Attitudes Toward Negroes," OWI, Bureau of Intelligence, Aug. 5, 1942; same title dated July 28, 1942, Record Group 44. Hazel Gaudet Erskine, "The Polls: Race Relations," Public Opinion Quarterly, XXVI (Spring 1962), 137–48.

structure of society was "cracking," and the equilibrium reached after the Civil War seemed "to be under attack at a time and under conditions when it is particularly difficult to defend it."[60] Sociologist Howard W. Odum wrote from the South that there was "an unmeasurable and unbridgeable distance between the white South and the reasonable expectation of the Negro."[61] White southerners opposed to change in the racial mores sensed changes occurring among "their" Negroes. "Outsiders" from the North, Mrs. Franklin Roosevelt, and the Roosevelt Administration were all accused of attempting to undermine segregation under the pretense of wartime necessity.[62]

Racial tensions were common in all sections of the country during the war.[63] There were riots in 1943. Tensions were high because Negro Americans were challenging the status quo. When fourteen prominent Negroes, conservatives and liberals, southerners and northerners, were asked in 1944 what they thought the black American wanted, their responses were almost unanimous. Twelve of the fourteen said they thought that Negroes wanted full political equality, economic equality, equality of opportunity, and full social equality with the abolition of legal segregation.[64] The war had stimulated the race consciousness and the desire for change among Negroes.

Most American Negroes and their leaders wanted the government to institute a revolutionary change in its race policy. Whereas the policy had been acquiescence in segregation since the end of Reconstruction, the government was now asked to set the example for the rest of the nation by supporting integration. This was the demand voiced by the great majority of the Negro leaders called together in March 1942 by the Office of Facts and Figures.[65] *Crisis* magazine summarized the feelings of many black Americans: Negroes have "waited thus far in vain for some sharp and dramatic notice that this war is not to maintain the status quo here."[66]

The White House, and it was not alone, failed to respond to the revolutionary changes occurring among the nation's largest minority. When

[60] Robert E. Park, "Racial Ideologies," William Fielding Ogburn, ed., *American Society In Wartime* (Chicago, 1943), 174.

[61] Howard W. Odum, *Race and Rumors of Race: Challenge to American Crisis* (Chapel Hill, 1943), 7; for a similar view, see Johnson, *To Stem This Tide*, 67–68, 73, 89–107, 113, 117.

[62] John Temple Graves, "The Southern Negro and the War Crisis," *Virginia Quarterly Review*, 18 (Autumn 1942), 500–17; Clark Foreman, "Race Tension in the South," *New Republic*, 107 (Sept. 21, 1942), 340–42.

[63] Alfred McClung Lee and Norman Daymond Humphrey, *Race Riot* (New York, 1943); Carey McWilliams, "Race Tensions: Second Phase," *Common Ground*, IV (Autumn 1943), 7–12.

[64] Rayford W. Logan, ed., *What the Negro Wants* (Chapel Hill, 1944).

[65] Memorandum to White from Wilkins, March 23, 1942, Spingarn Papers; Pittsburgh *Courier*, March 28, 1942; Norfolk *Journal and Guide*, March 28, 1942.

[66] "U.S.A. Needs Sharp Break With the Past," *Crisis*, 49 (May 1942), 151.

the Fraternal Council of Negro Churches called upon President Roosevelt to end discrimination in the defense industries and armed forces, the position taken was that "it would be very bad to give encouragement beyond the point where actual results can be accomplished."[67] Roosevelt did bestir himself over particularly outrageous incidents. When Roland Hayes, a noted Negro singer, was beaten and jailed in a Georgia town, the President dashed off a note to his attorney general: "Will you have someone go down and check up . . . and see if any law was violated. I suggest you send a northerner."[68]

Roosevelt was not enthusiastic about major steps in the race relations field proposed by interested individuals within and without the government.[69] In February 1942 Edwin R. Embree of the Julius Rosenwald Fund, acutely aware of the growing crisis in American race relations, urged Roosevelt to create a commission of experts on race relations to advise him on what steps the government should take to improve matters. FDR's answer to this proposal indicates that he felt race relations was one of the reform areas that had to be sacrificed for the present in order to prosecute the war. He thought such a commission was "premature" and that "we must start winning the war . . . before we do much general planning for the future." The President believed that "there is a danger of such long-range planning becoming projects of wide influence in escape from the realities of war. I am not convinced that we can be realists about the war and planners for the future at this critical time."[70]

[67] "A Statement to the President of the United States Concerning the Present World Crisis by Negro Church Leaders Called by the Executive Committee of the Fraternal Council of Negro Churches of America," Feb. 17, 1942; McIntyre to MacLean, Chairman of the President's Committee on Fair Employment Practice, Feb. 19, 1942, OF 93, Roosevelt Papers.

[68] Memorandum to the Attorney General from the President, Aug. 26, 1942, OF 93, ibid.

[69] Franklin Roosevelt's conservative and "leave well enough alone" attitude toward Negro rights is discussed in Arthur M. Schlesinger, Jr., The Age of Roosevelt: The Politics of Upheaval (Boston, 1960), 431; Frank Freidel, F. D. R. and the South (Baton Rouge, 1965), 73, 81, 97; Mary McLeod Bethune, "My Secret Talks with F. D. R.," Ebony, IV (April 1949), 42–51. Perhaps Roosevelt's conservative attitude is responsible for his privately expressed dislike of the NAACP. In 1943 Arthur B. Spingarn, president of the NAACP, asked him to write a letter praising the twenty-five years of service by White to that organization. On one version of the proposed letter there is an attached note which reads: "Miss Tully brought this in. Says the President doesn't think too much of this organization—not to be to[o] fullsome—tone it down a bit." Roosevelt to Spingarn, Oct. 1, 1943, PPF 1226, Roosevelt papers.

[70] Roosevelt to Embree, March 16, 1942, in answer to Embree to Roosevelt, Feb. 3, 1942, OF 93, Roosevelt Papers. In his covering letter to the President's secretary, Embree emphasized that his proposed commission should address itself to the problem of race around the world as well as at home: "A serious weakness both in America and among the united nations is the low morale of the 'colored peoples' to whom this war is being pictured as simply another struggle of the white man for domination of the world. This condition is becoming acute among the Negro group at home and among important allies abroad, especially the Chinese and the residents of Malaya, the East Indies, and the Philippines."

After the race riots of 1943, numerous proposals for a national committee on race relations were put forward; but FDR refused to change his position. Instead, the President simply appointed Jonathan Daniels to gather information from all government departments on current race tensions and what they were doing to combat them.[71] This suggestion for what would eventually become a President's Committee on Civil Rights would have to wait until a President recognized that a revolution in race relations was occurring and that action by the government could no longer be put off. In the interim, many would share the shallow reasoning of Secretary of War Stimson that the cause of racial tension was "the deliberate effort . . . on the part of certain radical leaders of the colored race to use the war for obtaining . . . race equality and interracial marriages. . . ."[72]

The hypocrisy and paradox involved in fighting a world war for the four freedoms and against aggression by an enemy preaching a master race ideology, while at the same time upholding racial segregation and white supremacy, were too obvious. The war crisis provided American Negroes with a unique opportunity to point our, for all to see, the difference

---

Embree to McIntyre, Feb. 3, 1942, Commission on Race and Color folder, Rosenwald Fund Papers.

[71] In June 1943, Embree and John Collier, Commissioner of Indian Affairs, developed an idea for a committee established by the President "to assume special responsibility in implementing the Bill of Rights of the Constitution, particularly in defending racial minorities at a time of crisis." Memorandum to Johnson and Alexander from Embree, June 16, 1943, Race Relations folder, Rosenwald Fund Papers. See also John Collier and Saul K. Padover, "An Institute for Ethnic Democracy," Common Ground, IV (Autumn 1943), 3–7, for a more elaborate proposal.

Embree probably passed along his idea to Odum of the University of North Carolina so that he could discuss it with a fellow North Carolinian in the White House, Daniels, administrative assistant to the President. Odum and Daniels had a conference in August 1943 from which emerged a recommendation for a "President's Committee on Race and Minority Groups." Odum to Daniels, Aug. 23, 1943; Memorandum to Daniels from Odum, Aug. 30, 1943, Howard W. Odum Papers (University of North Carolina).

Although Daniels apparently gave Odum the impression that he was interested in a national committee, this was not the case. "It has been suggested that a committee of prominent men be named to study this situation," he wrote the President. "I am sure the naming of such a committee would not now halt the procession of angry outbreaks which are occurring. I doubt that any report could be made which would be so effective as a statement now from you would be. I am very much afraid, indeed, that any committee report would only serve as a new ground for controversy." Memorandum to the President from Daniels, Aug. 2, 1943, Daniels Papers. Roosevelt apparently agreed with Daniels, and Odum was informed that "My boss does not think well of the idea that we discussed." Daniels to Odum, Sept. 1, 1943, Odum Papers.

Daniels' appointment as White House coordinator of information on race relations was actually suggested by him to the President in June 1943. Memorandum to the President from Daniels, June 29, 1943, Daniels Papers. By July 1943, Roosevelt had approved of the new role for his administrative assistant, and Daniels was hard at work gathering information. Daniels to Secretary of War Stimson, July 28, 1943, ASW 291.2, Record Group 335.

[72] "Stimson Diary," June 24, 1943.

between the American creed and practice. The democratic ideology and rhetoric with which the war was fought stimulated a sense of hope and certainty in black Americans that the old race structure was destroyed forever. In part, this confidence was also the result of the mass militancy and race consciousness that developed in these years. When the expected white acquiescence in a new racial order did not occur, the ground was prepared for the civil rights revolution of the 1950s and 1960s; the seeds were indeed sown in the World War II years.

# 29

## THE SUPREME COURT AS PROTECTOR OF CIVIL RIGHTS
*Thurgood Marshall*

ALTHOUGH almost a century has elapsed since the Civil War and the abolition of slavery as an American institution, the transition of the Negro from a slave-chattel to a full-fledged free American citizen has been painfully retarded. The Fourteenth Amendment was adopted to assure that this change from slave status to citizenship would take place, and, in fact, to protect all persons against discrimination based on race, religion, color, blood, or national origin.

That many of the vestiges of slavery remain and that racial discrimination still is practiced in all sections of the United States is to a considerable extent the responsibility of the United States Supreme Court which spelled out the meaning of this new constitutional provision. The Court's narrow, cautious, and often rigid interpretation of the amendment's reach and thrust in the past gave constitutional sanction to practices of racial discrimination and prejudice. Thus such practices have been permitted to become a part of the pattern of contemporary American society, in effective nullification of the constitutional mandate.

Prime examples of this narrow and corrosive limitation of the amendment's effect are the *Civil Rights Cases*,[1] in which a federal civil rights act was declared unconstitutional on the ground that the Fourteenth Amendment could not affect the activities of private persons; *Plessy* v. *Ferguson*,[2] which condoned enforced racial segregation under the "sepa-

Thurgood Marshall, "The Supreme Court as Protector of Civil Rights: Equal Protection of the Laws," *Annals of the American Academy of Political and Social Science*, CLXXV (May 1951), 101–110. Reprinted by permission of the publisher and the author.

[1] 109 U. S. 3 (1883).

[2] 163 U. S. 537 (1896).

rate but equal" formula; and *Pace* v. *Alabama*,[3] which upheld the constitutionality of a legislative proscription of intermarriage between Negroes and white persons.

### CHANGE IN TREND

The harm which these decisions have done to the cause of civil rights, however, has been somewhat repaired in subsequent cases, for we are now reaching the point where it is possible to view it as likely that the constitutional interdiction against racial and color discrimination will be gven the high evaluation it deserves.

Many years after the passage of the Fourteenth Amendment, its mandate of equal protection of the laws was neglected, as the Court forged and sharpened the concept of due process into a formidable constitutional weapon to cut away governmental interference with private property and with the liberty of corporations. With the appointment of what has become popularly known as the "Roosevelt Court," this weapon was laid aside, and the due process clause, as a constitutional deterrent to governmental action, now seems to be of significance only in that area where the right being asserted is fundamental to and implicit in our concept of liberty.[4]

While now deferring to the legislative judgment in economic matters, however, the Court has begun to look upon the protection of personal liberty as one of its primary functions.[5] The requirement that equal protection of the laws be accorded, expressly required by the Fourteenth Amendment[6] and read into the Fifth Amendment by the Court itself,[7] is increasingly furnishing the means through which protection of a very vital phase of personal liberty may be realized—the right to be free from differences of treatment because of race, color, blood, or national origin.

In this special field the Supreme Court in the past decade has evidenced an increasing awareness of the brutal realities of racial discrimination and its contradiction of constitutional guarantees. A real effort is now being made to require that members of an unpopular color or racial minority be accorded the same treatment as anyone else.

[3] 106 U. S. 583 (1883).

[4] See Palko v. Connecticut, 302 U. S. 319, 325 (1937); Adamson v. California, 332 U.S. 46 (1947).

[5] See, e.g., Lowell v. Griffin, 303 U. S. 444 (1938); Hague v. C.I.O., 307 U. S. 496 (1939).

[6] The Fourteenth Amendment reads: "No state shall . . . deny to any person . . . the equal protection of the laws."

[7] See Hirabayashi v. United States, 320 U. S. 81 (1943); Korematsu v. United States, 323 U. S. 214 (1944); *Ex parte* Endo, 323 U. S. 283 (1944); United Public Works v. Mitchell, 330 U. S. 75, 100 (1947).

## NOT UNIFORMITY BUT IMPARTIALITY

The obligation to furnish equal protection of the law does not establish an abstract uniformity applicable alike to all persons without regard to circumstances or conditions. Equal protection requires that all persons be fairly treated in their relations with the state. But the concept makes allowance for dissimilarity of circumstances in order that legislation may fall with evenhandedness upon all persons. Special burdens and duties may be imposed upon a particular group or class for the benefit of the public as a whole. Arbitrary discrimination alone is prohibited.

If control or regulation of a particular group is undertaken, the classification or distinction upon which such legislation is founded must be based upon a real or substantial difference which has pertinence to the legislative objective.[8] This is an extremely flexible formula, and a classification's reasonableness is largely dependent upon the peculiar needs, the special difficulties, and the particular requirements of the local situation. Here again the Court must necessarily give great weight to legislative judgment in view of the necessity for familiarity with local conditions.

Where the legislature, however, attempts to single out persons because of their particular race, color, or national origin in order to subject them to discriminatory penalties, then a determination of the unreasonableness of these penalties within the purview of the Constitution is not precluded by lack of any special or specific familiarity with local conditions or needs. The Supreme Court of the United States, far removed from the stresses which keep racial animosity alive, is best able to determine whether the state in fact provides equal protection of the laws as required by the Constitution.

This was recognized in *United States* v. *Carolene Products Company,*[9] where Justice Stone stated:

*There may be narrower scope for operation of the presumption of constitutionality when legislation appears on its face to be within a specific prohibition of the Constitution, such as those of the first ten amendments, which are deemed equally specific when held to be embraced within the fourteenth. . . .*

*Nor need we inquire whether similar conditions enter into the review of statutes directed at particular religions . . ., or national . . ., or racial minorities . . .; whether prejudice against discrete and insular minorities may be a special condition, which tends seriously to curtail the operation of those political processes ordinarily to be relied upon to protect*

---

[8] Examples are legion: Puget Sound Power & Light Co. v. Seattle, 291 U. S. 619 (1934); Board of Tax Commissioners v. Jackson, 283 U. S. 527 (1931); Groessart v. Cleary, 335 U. S. 464 (1948); Smith v. Cahoon, 283 U. S. 553 (1931); Skinner v. Oklahoma, 316 U. S. 535 (1942).

[9] 304 U. S. 144, note 4 (1938).

*minorities, and which may call for a correspondingly more searching judicial inquiry.*

It is sometimes said that there is a presumption of unconstitutionality running against governmental action based upon race or color. This may be an overstatement of fact, but certainly this type of governmental action in terms of motivation, purpose, and effect is now subjected to a more searching scrutiny than is ordinarily the case with other kinds of state activity.[10] Here the Supreme Court now retains for itself the final word as to whether the state has violated constitutional standards of conduct, and therefore functions as the ultimate guardian of civil rights.

### THE EXCLUSION CASES

In giving effect to the equality requirement of the Fourteenth Amendment, the Supreme Court has had little difficulty in successfully dealing with total deprivation of rights or exclusion based on race and color. Since 1879 in *Strauder* v. *West Virginia,*[11] it has been enforcing the equal protection of the laws in this area with vigor and strength. There it said:

*[The equal protection clause of the Fourteenth Amendment] was designed to assure to the colored race the enjoyment of all civil rights that under the law are enjoyed by white persons, and to give to that race the protection of the General Government, in that enjoyment, whenever it should be denied by the States. . . .*
*. . . What is this but declaring . . . that all persons, whether colored or white, shall stand equal before the laws of the States, and, in regard to the colored race, for whose protection the amendment was primarily designed, that no discrimination shall be made against them by law because of their color?*[12]

Thus, exclusion of Negroes from jury service,[13] total deprivation of a right to educational opportunities furnished by the state,[14] or exclusion of Negroes from certain residential areas[15] have all been held to be a denial of equal protection.[16]

[10] See Korematsu v. United States, cited note 7 *supra.*

[11] 100 U. S. 303 (1880).

[12] *Ibid.,* pp. 306, 307.

[13] Norris v. Alabama, 294 U. S. 587 (1935); Hill v. Texas, 316 U. S. 400 (1942); Patton v. Mississippi, 332 U. S. 463 (1947).

[14] Missouri *ex rel.* Gaines v. Canada, 305 U. S. 337 (1938); Sipuel v. Board of Regents, 332 U. S. 631 (1948).

[15] Buchanan v. Warley, 245 U. S. 60 (1917).

[16] Although in Mitchell v. United States, 313 U. S. 80 (1941), no constitutional question was reached, the decision involved interpretation as to whether the Interstate Commerce Act

A glaring exception is the Japanese cases,[17] in which legal sanction was given to the governmental exclusion of American citizens of Japanese origin from the West Coast during World War II, although it seems evident that the Court recognized this action as going to the brink of constitutional power. This sweeping military interference with individual freedom was justified under the compulsion of a national emergency. Yet we unquestionably invite disaster if there are times when it is considered permissible to ignore or thrust aside constitutional guarantees and prohibitions.

Now, after the danger has passed, the United States Court of Appeals for the Ninth Circuit, in a sober and biting analysis of the military treatment of the Japanese, finds that their exclusion from the West Coast did not derive from any real apprehension of danger by sabotage, but was based upon General De Witt's belief in disloyalty by blood.[18] It is to be hoped that if the future poses a similar problem, the Court will have learned that in determining the permissible reach of constitutional safeguards with respect to civil rights, military judgment must be subjected to as searching an analysis as any other type of governmental interference.

Except for these cases, however, a total deprivation of rights or exclusion based upon race or color has been struck down with vigor and directness. Where, however, the infringement has been more subtly camouflaged, or where the Court has not considered the restriction a total deprivation or exclusion, its role as protector of civil rights has left, on the whole, much to be desired.[19] In four recent cases, however, which we will examine here, we see signs of the Court's growing maturity in its handling of civil rights problems.

## RIGHT TO GAINFUL OCCUPATION

In 1948 in *Takahashi* v. *Fish and Game Commission*,[20] the Court, in a 7–2 decision, held a California fish and game statute unconstitutional which prohibited the issuance of a license for commercial fishing to any person ineligible for citizenship. Controversy between Torao Takahashi and

---

prohibited an interstate carrier from denying Pullman space to Congressman Arthur Mitchell because of race, and falls in this category of exclusion cases. In the more recent opinion involving discrimination by interstate railroads under the Interstate Commerce Act, the Court seems to bar all regulations which subject persons to different treatment because of race—Henderson v. United States, 339 U. S. 816 (1950).

[17] Hirabayashi v. United States and Korematsu v. United States, cited note 7 *supra*.

[18] Acheson v. Murakami, 176 F 2d 953 (CCA 9th 1949). See particularly pp. 957–58.

[19] For an excellent detailed analysis of the United States Supreme Court's handling of constitutional questions affecting Negroes' rights, see Edward F. Waite, "The Negro and the Supreme Court," 30 *Minnesota Law Review* 219 (1946); and Morroe Berger, "The Supreme Court and Group Discrimination Since 1937," 49 *Columbia Law Review* 201 (1949).

[20] 334 U. S. 410 (1948).

the state centered upon the purpose of the statute. The former asserted that the statute was the outgrowth of racial animosity. The latter's claimed purpose was the conservation of fish. Of course, if racial antagonism was the statute's motivation, then it was illegal in its objective. If, on the other hand, the state was legitimately attempting to conserve its fish resources, classification of alien Japanese as ineligible for commercial fishing licenses bore no reasonable relation to the statute's objective. Hence the classification was invalid whatever its purpose.

The Court, however, refused to meet these issues, but chose to base decision upon an unconstitutional conflict between state and federal power with respect to the regulation of immigration; upon the state's obligation under the Fourteenth Amendment and federal laws passed thereunder to furnish equal protection of the laws to all persons in lawful residence within its jurisdiction; and upon an absence of a sufficient state interest to enact such legislation in any event.

Although the Court refused to repudiate the power of the state to deal with aliens exclusively as a class, it stated that this power must be held to narrow limits. This case can be distinguished from *Clarke v. Deckenbahc*,[21] in which prohibition of operation of billiard and pool halls by aliens was upheld on the ground that the special social problems incident to these establishments justified the state in excluding aliens as a class. It cannot be squared with *Heim v. McCall*,[22] however, in which the prohibition of employment to aliens in public works was permitted, or with *Patsone v. Pennsylvania*,[23] in which a statute prohibiting aliens from hunting wild game was held to meet the requirements of the equal protection of the laws. Nor is it correct to view the decision as merely the application of *Truax v. Raich*,[24] since the statute there was struck down because of its sweeping and indiscriminate effect upon all aliens and all businesses of more than a certain number of employees.

The decision can be explained only as a drastic restriction of state authority to discriminate against aliens as a class. If the rationale of *Takahashi v. Fish and Game Commission* is taken as a guide to future Court decisions, it is apparent that the state will have to prove the purity and the legitimacy of its motives, and show that there is a reasonable relationship between the classification on the basis of alienage and the statute's objectives, before the burdens imposed will be allowed to stand. If these formidable prerequisites are required in the future, the rights of aliens, lawfully in residence, to freedom from discrimination by the state because of their origin will be assured.

[21] 274 U. S. 392 (1927).
[22] 239 U. S. 175 (1915).

[23] 232 U. S. 138 (1914). See Milton R. Konvitz, "The Alien and the Asiatic in American Law" 190–207 (1946) for a summary of numerous occupations which various states now bar aliens from entering.

[24] 239 U. S. 33 (1915).

## RIGHT TO REAL PROPERTY

The decisions in *Oyama* v. *California*[25] and *Shelley* v. *Kraemer*[26] treat of different phases of the same problem—the right of a citizen to the ownership, use, and occupancy of real property.

In *Oyama* v. *California* the issue before the Court was the validity of California's statutory presumption that a conveyance of land to a citizen or to an alien eligible to take title by an ineligible alien, who had paid consideration for the land, was prima facie evidence of an evasion of the state's Alien Land Law, and the land would escheat to the state. The Court in a rather strange division[27] refused to decide the basic constitutional problem —the validity of the Alien Land Law which prohibited aliens ineligible for citizenship from taking title to real property in California—but rested decision on the narrow ground that an American citizen of Japanese origin is denied the equal protection of the laws when a gift of land to him from his father, ineligible to citizenship, is presumed to be an evasion of the law, no such presumption being operative when the parent is a citizen or is eligible for citizenship. Thus the citizen son was denied the equal protection of the laws in that the state took away his property because his father was an alien.

Although the narrow limitations of the majority opinion seem basically untenable, the effect of the decision was to protect the parties involved against the impact of the statute. Yet the reason for the Court's refusal to hold the Alien Land Law unconstitutional, as it would be required to do under the rationale of the *Takahashi* case, is extremely difficult to understand. The only plausible explanation seems to lie in Chief Justice Vinson and Justice Frankfurter's insistence that constitutional questions be decided only within the narrow limits of the facts before the Court. Adherence to that principle in this case, however, has caused the Court to reach a decision via a tortuous and circuitous route, whereas the more simple path of holding the Alien Land Law unconstitutional seems sounder and more inviting. If the state must now do all that we understand the subsequent decision in *Takahashi* v. *Fish and Game Commission* to mean that it must, before its subjection of aliens to special burdens will meet the test of constitutionality, the narrowness of the decision in the *Oyama* case seems particularly unnecessary.

[25] 332 U. S. 633 (1948).

[26] 334 U. S. 1 (1948).

[27] Chief Justice Vinson wrote the majority opinion, in which Justice Frankfurter joined. Two concurring opinions were written—one by Justice Black joined by Justice Douglas, and one by Justice Murphy joined in by Justice Rutledge—in which it was argued that the Alien Land Act should be declared unconstitutional. Justice Jackson dissented on the ground that the majority opinion made sense only if the Alien Land Act were declared unconstitutional, which he seemed to feel ought to have been done. Justice Reed dissented on the ground that the state had power to enact the statute in question in which Justice Burton joined.

In *Shelley* v. *Kraemer,* on the other hand, the Court met a much more difficult constitutional problem with unusual directness. Although enforced segregation in residential areas by legislative fiat had been held a denial of equal protection of the laws in *Buchanan* v. *Warley,*[28] private restrictive agreements which accomplished the same result through judicial enforcement had in effect been sustained in *Corrigan* v. *Buckley.*[29] Then for approximately twenty years the Supreme Court refused to meet this issue in subsequent cases.[30] In 1948, however, the Court felt that the question was ripe for decision, granted certiorari in *Shelley* v. *Kraemer* and its companion cases, and held that racial restrictive covenants, although valid as between private persons, when enforced by the state courts constituted a denial of the equal protection of the laws.[31]

## CONCEPT OF STATE ACTION

As we have seen, the guarantees of the Fourteenth Amendment can be infringed only through state machinery. Between the *Civil Rights Cases* and *Shelley* v. *Kraemer,* the concept of state action underwent considerable expansion. State action was found in acts of legislature,[32] judiciary,[33] executive,[34] administrative agencies,[35] and political subdivisions of the state;[36] in the action of government officials clothed with state power, even though their action may not have been sanctioned by the state;[37] in the refusal of a state to act where a duty required it to do so;[38] in attempts to effect discrimination by delegation of what is normally a state function to private agencies;[39] in the discriminatory acts of a labor union granted sole bargain-

[28] Cited note 15 *supra.*

[29] 271 U. S. 323 (1926).

[30] See Hansberry v. Lee, 311 U. S. 32 (1940); Mays v. Burgess, 147 F 2d 869 (App. D.C. 1944); cert. denied, 325 U. S. 868 (1945).

[31] Hurd v. Hodge, 334 U. S. 24 (1948), decided the same day, involved restrictive convenant enforcement in the District of Columbia. Such enforcement was held to be a violation of federal statutes.

[32] Nixon v. Herndon, 273 U. S. 536 (1927).

[33] Bridges v. California, 314 U. S. 252 (1941); Cantwell v. Connecticut, 310 U. S. 296 (1940).

[34] *Ex parte* Virginia, 100 U. S. 339 (1880).

[35] Home Telephone & Telegraph Co. v. Los Angeles, 227 U. S. 278 (1913); Yick Wo v. Hopkins, 118 U. S. 356 (1886).

[36] Hague v. C.I.O., 307 U. S. 496 (1939); Lowell v. Griffin, 303 U. S. 444 (1938).

[37] United States v. Classic, 313 U. S. 299 (1941); *cf.* Barney v. New York, 193 U. S. 430 (1904).

[38] Truax v. Corrigan, 257 U. S. 312 (1921).

[39] Smith v. Allwright, 321 U. S. 649 (1944).

ing rights under Congressional mandate;[40] and in the action of a private company maintaining a company-owned town.[41] To reach judicial enforcement of restrictive covenants, however, the Court had to expand the concept of state action to new limits.

In *Shelley* v. *Kraemer,* moreover, there apparently was no insistence upon narrowly limiting decision in order to avoid deciding a broader constitutional issue than the facts required. Had this been a consideration, it would seem that decision could have rested on public policy without reaching the state-action question, on the ground that private agreements which restrict use of property to persons because of race or color are at war with national policy evidenced in the Fourteenth Amendment, and no person can use the judicial machinery to enforce agreements so directly contrary to national policy. Yet the Court chose to find a specific denial of the equal protection of the laws in the enforcement of such agreements, and the *Shelley* v. *Kraemer* decision is a broad prohibition against any use of the state's judicial process to give effect to these agreements.[42]

The decision is unquestionably one of the most important in the whole field of civil rights. With judicial enforcement of restrictive covenants now held to be a denial of the equal protection of the laws, it becomes possible for colored minorities to break out of crowded ghettos into unsegregated residential areas, with consequent opportunity of acceptance as members of an integrated community. Thus increased opportunity is given for eventual solution of racial problems in this country.

### RIGHT TO AN EDUCATION

In *Sweatt* v. *Painter*[43] and *McLaurin* v. *Oklahoma State Regents for Higher Education et al.,*[44] effort was made to have the Court re-examine and overrule *Plessy* v. *Ferguson* and declare its "separate but equal" formula, under which racial segregation has flourished, to be violative of the constitutional requirement of equality of treatment.[45] In all the education cases decided

[40] Steele v. Louisville & N.R.R. Co., 323 U. S. 192 (1944).

[41] Marsh v. Alabama, 326 U. S. 501 (1946).

[42] In Weiss v. Leaon, 225 S.W. 127 (Mo. 1949), a Missouri Supreme Court upheld the right of a party to a restrictive covenant to bring an action for damage for breach of the agreement on the ground that all that Shelley v. Kraemer forbade was enforcement of specific performance of the covenant under an injunctive decree. Such a distinction is unrealistic. If the courts may be used to seek damages for breach of the covenant, then the ground will have been cut from under Shelley v. Kraemer and the decision will have been rendered relatively useless. It is our view that Shelley v. Kraemer bars any use whatsoever of the judicial process to give effect to restrictive agreements, and it is to be hoped that the Supreme Court will have an early occasion to settle this question.

[43] 339 U. S. 629 (1950).

[44] 339 U. S. 637 (1950).

[45] Under this formula segregation is considered permissible if the separate facilities set aside for Negroes are equal or substantially equal to those maintained for whites. Alabama,

by the Court for more than half a century after *Plessy* v. *Ferguson,* the "separate but equal" doctrine seemed at least tacitly accepted as a correct statement of the law. Yet in no case did the Court actually decide that the segregated facility was in fact equal.[46]

In *Sweatt* v. *Painter* the state urged that a segregated law school for Negroes was substantially equal to the law school of the University of Texas, and therefore met the requirements of equal protection of the laws under the "separate but equal" formula. The Court measured the law school for Negroes against the University of Texas and found

*in terms of number of the faculty, variety of courses and opportunity for specialization, size of the student body, scope of the library, availability of law review and similar activities, the University of Texas Law School was superior. . . . The law school, the proving ground for legal learning and practice, cannot be effective in isolation from the individuals and institutions with which the law interacts. Few students and no one who has practiced law would choose to study in an academic vacuum, removed from the interplay of ideas and the exchange of views with which the law is concerned.*

Sweatt's admission to the University of Texas Law School was therefore ordered.

In *McLaurin* v. *Oklahoma State Regents,* although McLaurin was admitted to the state university, he was subjected to special rules and regulations, because of his color, not applicable to other students. The Court held that the state had overreached the limits of its power in treating him differently from other students, and that the equal protection of the laws required that McLaurin be admitted subject only to the same terms and conditions as all other students.

### EDUCATIONAL SEGREGATION DEFEATED

The Court was content to solve only the specific problem presented, and explicitly refused to re-examine or reaffirm *Plessy* v. *Ferguson.* In its

---

Arkansas, Delaware, Florida, Georgia, Kentucky, Louisiana, Maryland, Mississippi, Missouri, North Carolina, Oklahoma, South Carolina, Tennessee, Texas, Virginia, West Virginia, and the District of Columbia, where enforced segregation in varying forms is required, supposedly operate under this formula. It is, of course, common knowledge that no separate facility maintained for Negroes is even remotely the physical equal of that maintained for whites.

[46] In the Gaines and Sipuel cases, there was no facility whatsoever for Negroes. An attempt was made to have the Court consider the question in Fisher v. Hurst, 333 U. S. 147 (1949), via an original writ of mandamus in the Supreme Court when the State of Oklahoma, in response to the Court's mandate in the Sipuel case, hastily established overnight a separate law school for Negroes allegedly the equal of that of the University of Oklahoma. The Court refused to decide the question, however, on technical grounds.

restricted context of constitutional protection as applied to state graduate and professional schools, however, it has set standards so high and so rigid that it seems highly improbable that racial segregation at these educational levels can successfully meet the test of constitutionality. Indeed, a careful reading of these two opinions forces the conclusion that *Plessy* v. *Ferguson's* "separate but equal" doctrine is now totally without significance at the professional and graduate school levels of state universities.

An indication of inequality was found in Sweatt's isolation from the ruling majority. Since it would seem that integration is of equal if not greater importance at the elementary, high school, and college levels, the whole structure of segregation in public education seems to have been dealt a shattering blow.

The Court, even in deciding the question presented in what seems to have been the "separate but equal" format, did break free from that philosophy in finding the enforced segregation of Negroes in a separate law school in the *Sweatt* case an inequality and in recognizing that McLaurin was denied equal treatment by virtue of the mental and psychological burdens he was forced to undergo in being required to conform to segregational practices within the classroom, the library, and the cafeteria at the University of Oklahoma. In that respect certainly these two decisions stand for the proposition that racial segregation in a state's educational system is a denial of the equal protection of the laws.

As a direct or indirect result of these decisions, Negroes are now attending graduate and professional state schools in Arkansas, Texas, Maryland, Delaware, Kentucky, Oklahoma, Virginia, West Virginia, and Louisiana. North Carolina, Tennessee, and Georgia have refused to accede to the inevitable, but it is doubtful that even the most rabid racist in those states does not now realize that the admission of Negroes into the state universities must soon take place. As far as we know, no effort has been made to test the issue in Alabama or Mississippi, and the situation in Florida is beclouded. On the whole, more than a thousand Negroes, heretofore denied opportunity for graduate and professional training, have already been accepted for that training along with other students. Thus a major modification in the pattern of American life is in the making.

### SOME REMAINING PROBLEMS

Constitutional protection against freedom from distinctions based upon race or color is still far from secure. The authority of the state to enforce segregation in theaters and other places of public amusement, restaurants, intrastate carriers, and recreational facilities,[47] and in colleges and elementary

---

[47] In Rice v. Arnold, 95 L. Ed. 37 decided Oct. 16, 1950, the Court granted certiorari to review a decision of the Florida Supreme Court which had ordered a public golf course in Miami to set aside one day per week for exclusive use of the course by Negroes. The cause was remanded in light of the opinion in McLaurin v. Oklahoma State Regents, 339 U. S. 637 (1950). The latter decision would seem to require opening of the golf course to all persons without distinction based upon race or color.

high schools, remains directly untouched. There also remains the question as to whether corporations which undertake to build huge housing developments and are thereby given certain governmental rights and concessions are still acting in a private capacity, so that exclusion of Negroes from these developments cannot be prohibited by the Constitution.[48] Yet, authority to practice discrimination in these areas should fall, if subjected to the same analysis which the Court applied to the *Sweatt* and *McLaurin* cases.

The fact that the Court did not decide segregation to be unconstitutional per se or in all areas is not fatal. The *Sweatt* and *McLaurin* cases indicate the Supreme Court's conviction that segregation is a denial of equality, and these decisions are potent weapons with which to continue the fight against segregation. The Court's present strategy may be to breach the pattern of segregation area by area by dealing with specific problems as they are presented. It may feel that in whittling away the legal foundation upon which segregation is based, in that fashion, the protection afforded to civil rights may be more palatable to the community and hence more lasting.

Surely segregation remains as the chief problem with which a civil rights attorney must deal, and our job would have been nearer conclusion had it been possible to convince the Court that it should overrule *Plessy* v. *Ferguson*. But having failed in that objective in the *Sweatt* and *McLaurin* cases, the Court must now be convinced as each new issue arises that the time is ripe for the "separate but equal" doctrine to be further delimited. The problem is carefully to marshal overwhelming evidence of the inequalities inherent in segregation in the particular areas involved, and thereby demonstrate that an extension of the principles of the *Sweatt* and *McLaurin* cases is timely. With each succeeding case, the Court must also be urged to overrule *Plessy* v. *Ferguson* and to break completely with the "separate but equal" philosophy.

### CONCLUSION

Any fair assessment of the Court's role in the past decade compels the conclusion that it has done considerably more than any other arm of the federal government to secure, preserve, and extend civil rights. Although its approach has been undeniably cautious, the Court seems to be making a real effort to deal effectively with our most disturbing problem with practical wisdom and insight. If it continues along the path blazed by its recent

---

[48] Dorsey v. Stuyvesant Town Corp., 229 N.Y. 512, 87 N.E. 2d 541 (1949). The New York Court of Appeals in a divided opinion held that no state action was involved in the refusal of the Metropolitan Life Insurance Co. to admit Negroes to Stuyvesant Town housing development in New York City. The land upon which the development is erected was secured through state condemnation proceedings, and the corporation had been granted tax exemption for a period of twenty-five years. There seems to be here a sufficient evidence of state action for the Fourteenth Amendment's mandate of equal protection to be properly invoked. However, the United States Supreme Court refused to grant petition for writ of certiorari. 339 U. S. 981 (1950).

decisions, the Constitution's mandate of equal protection of the laws will eventually accomplish the objective its framers intended—that of prohibiting all forms of community discriminatory action based upon race or color.

## SUGGESTIONS FOR
## FURTHER READING

&T HERE is need for a thorough examination of the effect of both the Depression and the New Deal on black Americans. Leslie Fishel, "The Negro in the New Deal Era," *Wisconsin Magazine of History*, XLVIII (Winter 1964–1965) is a brief survey. In the meantime, the reader can utilize studies of specific agencies and programs of the Roosevelt Administration. *Bernard Sternsher (ed.), *The Negro in Depression and War* (Chicago, 1969), brings together a wide variety of essays on the New Deal. The classic study of Gunnar Myrdal, *An American Dilemma* (New York, 1944) covers many elements of the thirties. Still of considerable interest are the articles in the January 1936 issue of the *Journal of Negro Education*. A recent study is Raymond Wolters, *Negroes and The Great Depression* (Westport, Conn., 1970).

Scholars have given substantial coverage to the Roosevelt Administration's agricultural policy and the status of black farm workers. See *Arthur F. Raper, *Preface to Peasantry* (Chapel Hill, N.C., 1933); Charles S. Johnson, *Shadow of the Plantation* (Chicago, 1934); Charles S. Johnson, et al., *The Collapse of Cotton Tenancy* (Chapel Hill, N.C., 1935); Arthur F. Raper and Ira DeA. Reid, *Share-croppers All* (Chapel Hill, N.C., 1941); and David E. Conrad, *The Forgotten Farmers: The Story of the Sharecroppers in the New Deal* (Urbana, Ill., 1965). Conrad's monograph along with M. S. Venkataramani, "Norman Thomas, Arkansas Sharecroppers, and the Roosevelt Agricultural Policies," *Mississippi Valley Historical Review*, XLVII (September 1960) and Louis Cantor, "A Prologue to the Protest Movement: The Missouri Sharecropper Roadside Demonstration of 1939," *Journal of American History*, LV (March 1969) cover black involvement in sharecropper protest groups. John A. Salmond, "The Civilian Conservation Corps and the Negro," *Journal of American History*, LII (June 1965) traces that agency's policy toward blacks.

For useful studies on labor unions and blacks, read Horace R. Cayton and George S. Mitchell, *Black Workers and the New Unions* (Chapel Hill, N.C., 1939); Herbert R. Northrup, *Organized Labor and the Negro* (New York, 1944); and Ray Marshall, *The Negro and Organized Labor* (New York, 1965). Essays on the New Deal era are included in *Julius Jacobson (ed.), *The Negro and the American Labor Movement* (New York, 1968) and the Summer 1969 issue of *Labor History*. An outstanding work that explores the relationship between blacks and unions before the 1930s is Sterling Spero and Abram Harris, *The Black Worker* (New York, 1931).

Critical evaluations by blacks of New Deal programs can be found in the

* An asterisk indicates that the book is available in paperback.

January 1936 issue of the *Journal of Negro Education*. A defense of the Roosevelt Administration by a member of the "black cabinet" is Robert C. Weaver, "The New Deal and the Negro: A Look at the Facts," *Opportunity*, XIII (July 1935). The differing views of Negro leaders toward the New Deal are presented in James A. Harrell, "Negro Leadership in the Election Year 1936," *Journal of Southern History*, XXXIV (November 1968).

Recent studies that offer critical appraisals of the Roosevelt Administration's policy toward blacks and the lower strata of American society are Barton J. Bernstein, "The New Deal: The Conservative Achievements of Liberal Reform," in *Bernstein (ed.), *Towards a New Past* (New York, 1968); *Paul Conkin, *The New Deal* (New York, 1967); and *Howard Zinn (ed.), *New Deal Thought* (Indianapolis, Ind., 1966), pp. xv–xxxvi. An attempt to rebut these critics is made by Jerold S. Auerbach, "New Deal, Old Deal, or Raw Deal: Some Thoughts on New Left Historiography," *Journal of Southern History*, XXV (February 1969).

There are a number of studies on the shift by the majority of black voters from the Republican to the Democratic party. See, for example, Ernest W. Collins, "Cincinnati Negroes and Presidential Politics," *Journal of Negro History*, XLI (April 1956); John M. Allswang, "The Chicago Negro Voter and the Democratic Consensus: A Case Study, 1918–1936," *Journal of the Illinois State Historical Society*, LX (Summer 1967); and Rita W. Gordon, "The Change in the Political Alignment of Chicago's Negroes During the New Deal," *Journal of American History*, LVI (December 1969).

*Wilson Record, *The Negro and the Communist Party* (Chapel Hill, N.C., 1951) discusses an important aspect of the 1930s. Harold Cruse presents critical observations of the left in his *Crisis of the Negro Intellectual* (New York, 1967). Communist participation in the Scottsboro trials is described in Dan T. Carter, *Scottsboro* (Baton Rouge, La., 1969). Carter's outstanding book also offers insights into the activities of black organizations in the thirties. Other studies of black protest organizations in the thirties and forties are *Herbert Garfinkel, *When Negroes March: The March on Washington Movement* (Glencoe, Ill., 1959); August Meier and Elliott M. Rudwick, "How CORE Began," *Social Science Quarterly*, XLIX (March 1969) and "The First Freedom Ride," *Phylon*, XXX (Fall 1969); Robert L. Zangrando, "The NAACP and a Federal Anti-Lynching Bill, 1934–1940," *Journal of Negro History*, L (April 1965); and Avrah Strickland, *History of the Chicago Urban League* (Urbana, Ill., 1966). Louis Ruchames, *Race, Jobs, and Politics: The Story of FEPC* (New York, 1953) is an examination of the agency established in response to the MOWM.

Two studies on Afro-Americans in the armed services are Ulysses Lee, *The United States Army in World War II: The Employment of Negro Troops* (Washington, D.C., 1966) and Richard M. Dalfiume, *Fighting on Two Fronts: Desegregation of the Armed Forces, 1939–1953* (Columbia, S.C., 1969).

For court decisions as well as local, state, and federal laws relative to the rights of blacks, see Clement E. Vose, *Caucasians Only: The Supreme Court, the NAACP, and the Restrictive Covenant Cases* (Berkeley, Calif., 1959); Jack Greenberg, *Race Relations and American Law* (New York, 1959); *Albert Blaustein and C. C. Ferguson, *Desegregation and the Law* (rev. ed.; New Brunswick, N.J., 1962); *Loren Miller, *The Petitioners* (New York, 1966); and *Monroe Berger, *Equality by Statute* (rev. ed.; New York, 1967).

* An asterisk indicates that the book is available in paperback.

# &CHAPTER ELEVEN&

# Since *Brown* vs. *The Board of Education*

W ITH its ruling in *Brown v. The Board of Education* the Supreme Court removed the cloak of legal respectability from segregation. Its decision, while limited to integration of schools, stimulated activity for desegregation in other areas of American life. Civil rights organizations in the late 1950s and the early 1960s put into operation the direct-action strategy advanced by the March on Washington Movement and the Congress of Racial Equality in the 1940s. The bus boycott in Montgomery led by Martin Luther King, the sit-ins by black college students, and the Freedom Rides were among the nonviolent direct-action techniques that captured national attention and resulted in wider participation among blacks and whites.

James A. Geschwender attempts to account for the growing militancy among Afro-Americans in selection 30. He uses the relative changes in education, occupations, and income of blacks and whites between 1940 and 1960 to test five hypotheses for the black-protest movement. In the two decades, blacks narrowed their disparity with whites in education and middle-status occupations but not in income or upper-status jobs. This led Afro-Americans to a greater awareness of their relative deprivation, which, in turn, resulted in a growing tendency for blacks to protest against their second-class status. Consider if Geschwender's framework can also be used to account for the ghetto riots and the black-power movement.

The shift toward black power from integration and nonviolent direct action is the subject of Allen J. Matusow's analysis of the Student Nonviolent Coordinating Committee in selection 31. Growing out of the early sit-ins in the Upper South, SNCC gradually extended its operations to the Deep South and the northern ghettos; its focus turned from white middle-class goals to concern for the black masses; its strategy of working with white liberals for integration changed to emphasis on black nationalism. What accounted for these changes among the blacks in SNCC? How did they affect the organization's relations with other civil rights groups and white liberals?

Matusow traces the story of SNCC's transformation into a black power organization. It is one of growing disillusionment with the political process, white liberals, and integration. An integrated society became less and less a goal for SNCC members. Estrangement from white supporters became particularly evident in the summer of 1964. Drawing upon the work of the black psychiatrist Alvin Pouissant, Matusow's essay presents evidence of friction between black and white civil rights workers. As the gap between white and black widened and as black nationalism gained a more favorable reception, SNCC turned into an all-black body concerned with the problem of the black masses.

Developments in the northern ghetto also contributed to the changed nature of SNCC. Affected only in a peripheral way by the civil rights legislation of the early 1960s, and yet more conscious of their inferior socioeconomic position, many northern blacks manifested their frustrations in ghetto uprisings. Responding to these grievances, in varying degree, old as well as new protest organizations devised strategies that were directed toward the black lower classes. One of the newer groups was the Black Panthers. Founded in 1966, the Panthers' future role in the black people's struggle is not clear at this time. As the decade of the seventies opens they share certain common attitudes with other black militants: they are disillusioned with the American political and economic system; they are suspicious of the motives of liberal and even radical whites; and they consider the struggle of black Americans part of the battle of Third World people against colonialism. But, as Ronald Steel in selection 32 points out, it would be a mistake to assume that the Panthers are just a carbon copy of SNCC and other black militant groups.

Unlike SNCC the Panthers have no middle-class heritage to reject; their backgrounds and experiences are those of the black lower classes. Scornful of cultural nationalists, they maintain that the cultural factor must be subsumed in revolutionary nationalism. Although advocates of black unity, the Panthers welcome, unlike SNCC, alliances with white radicals. Yet such alliances have problems. Steel devotes a substantial portion of his article to the differences between the white radicals and the Panthers. In contrast to the white radicals, the Panthers have definite goals; they are not visionaries. Separated from their revolutionary rhetoric, the Panthers want protection of constitutional rights and economic justice for black Americans—"what most middle-class Americans take for granted." Steel believes that this and other aspects of the Black Panther movement are overlooked by a large segment of the mass media and political leaders set upon destroying the Panthers.

Finally, to what extent do the Panthers draw upon earlier traditions in the black experience in America? As will be apparent from the selections in this volume, there are precedents for much of the Panther program. They did not originate black pride, self-help, and economic cooperation. Thus, the reader should ponder in what ways the Panthers follow and depart from earlier movements in the history of the black American.

# 30

## SOCIAL STRUCTURE AND THE NEGRO REVOLUTION
*James A. Geschwender*

T HE summer of 1963 has been referred to as "The Summer of the Negro Revolt." Negroes have rebelled against their status in the United States from the earliest days of slavery to the present time,[1] but this rebellion reached its peak to date the summer of 1963, when it became a nationwide movement with protests and demonstrations in three-fourths of our states in all mainland regions of the country.[2]

It is true that this revolt did not simply emerge spontaneously and full-blown in one summer. Yet, we cannot validly view this present protest as a simple continuation of the protest begun during slavery. Intense and widespread support makes today's protest basically different. Lomax chooses to date today's revolt from December 1, 1955, when Mrs. Rosa Parks refused to give up her seat on a Montgomery, Alabama, bus.[3] Others might prefer other dates, but this seems as good as any. The major question is not the precise date of its inception but rather the reasons for its existence.

James A. Geschwender, "Social Structure and the Negro Revolution: An Examination of Some Hypotheses," *Social Forces*, XLIII (December 1964), 248–256. Reprinted by permission of the publisher.

I am indebted to Elwood Guernsey for compiling much of the data upon which Tables 1 and 3 are based and to the Institute for Social Research, Florida State University, for the use of graduate assistants and machines. I have benefited from the critical comments on earlier drafts generously given by William A. Rushing and Henry J. Watts.

[1] For information on the slave revolts see Herbert Aptheker, *American Negro Slave Revolts* (New York: Columbia University Press, 1945), and for a brief history of other Negro protest activity see Gunnar Myrdal, *An American Dilemma* (New York: Harper & Row, 1944), pp. 736–937.

[2] See files of *The New York Times* throughout the period from May to August, 1963.

[3] Louis E. Lomax, *The Negro Revolt* (New York: New American Library, 1963), p. 92.

Journalists have speculated as to these reasons.[4] It is time for a sociologist to attempt a structural explanation. The present writer will attempt to do this by searching the literature for sociological hypotheses which purport to be able to explain such revolts, examining empirical evidence pertaining to the living conditions of the Negro in order to test and evaluate these hypotheses, and drawing some general conclusions.

## PROPOSED EXPLANATORY HYPOTHESES

Five general types of hypotheses which attempt to explain this type of revolt have appeared in the sociological literature.

The first of these might be called "The Vulgar Marxist Hypothesis." It could be so named because of the general belief that this is the manner in which Marx believed revolutions originate.[5] This hypothesis may be stated: *As a group experiences a worsening of its conditions of life, it will become increasingly dissatisfied until it eventually rebels.* It is questionable if this is the correct interpretation of Marx's analysis of the cause of the revolutions.[6] Nevertheless, this hypothesis has received support from Sorokin in his analysis of revolution and qualifies as a candidate hypothesis.[7]

The second type of hypothesis might be called "The Rising Expectation Hypothesis." This hypothesis may be stated: *As a group experiences an improvement in its conditions of life it will also experience a rise in its level of desires. The latter will rise more rapidly than the former, leading to dissatisfaction and rebellion.* The classic statement of this hypothesis was presented by L. P. Edwards though others have presented similar formulations.[8]

The third kind of explanation might be called "The Sophisticated Marxist Hypothesis," after its author, or "The Relative Deprivation Hypothesis," after its nature. This hypothesis may be stated: *As a group experiences an improvement in its conditions of life and simultaneously observes a second group experiencing a more rapid rate of improvement, it will become dissatisfied with its rate of improvement and rebel.* Marx saw the chain of events—including the alienation of labor, the development of class consciousness, and the proletarian revolution—as having its inception with

---

[4] Lomax, op. cit., and Dan Wakefield, *Revolt in the South* (New York: Grove, 1960), are just two examples among many.

[5] Cf. James C. Davies, "Toward a Theory of Revolution," *American Sociological Review*, 27 (February 1962), pp. 5–18, esp. p. 5.

[6] Cf. Reinhard Bendix and Seymour Martin Lipset, " 'Karl Marx' Theory of Social Classes," Reinhard Bendix and Seymour Martin Lipset (eds.), *Class, Status and Power* (New York: Free Press, 1953), pp. 26–75, esp. pp. 32–33.

[7] Pitirim A. Sorokin, *The Sociology of Revolution* (Philadelphia: Lippincott, 1925), p. 367.

[8] Lyford P. Edwards, *The Natural History of Revolution* (Chicago: University of Chicago Press, 1927). See also the passage quoted from A. de Tocqueville in Davies, *op. cit.*, p. 6, and Crane Brinton, *The Anatomy of Revolution* (New York: Norton, 1938), esp. pp. 74–78 and pp. 44–46.

feelings of relative deprivation resulting from a set of changes in objective conditions.[9]

The fourth type of hypothesis might be called "The Rise and Drop Hypothesis." It may be worded: *As a group experiences an improvement in its conditions of life followed by a sharp reversal of this improvement, it will become dissatisfied and rebel.* James C. Davies formulated this hypothesis.[10]

The fifth type of hypothesis might be called "The Status Inconsistency Hypothesis," and may be worded: *A group which possesses a number of status attributes which are differently ranked on the various status hierarchies will be dissatisfied and prone toward rebellion.* This hypothesis is probably best known through Lenski's work in status crystallization but is similar to propositions of Broom, Hughes, and Sorokin.[11]

## THE POSITION OF THE NEGRO IN THE UNITED STATES

Having listed the various hypotheses purporting to explain phenomena such as "The Negro Revolt," it is time to examine the data which permit an evaluation of these hypotheses. Let us examine the position of the Negro in the United States in terms of the categories: education, occupation, and income. These particular categories are chosen for analysis because of the belief that they are most crucial in determining one's life chances and one's style of life[12]

Unfortunately, direct data on Negroes are not available in most areas one would wish to examine. One is forced to rely upon data for non-whites and infer to Negroes. This will introduce some distortion into the data. This distortion, however, should not be overestimated. The number of non-Negro nonwhites has been less than ten percent of the nonwhites throughout the time period with which we will be concerned. Furthermore, data are available showing both nonwhite and Negro occupational distributions for 1940 and 1950, and in no occupational category for either year do the two frequencies differ by over seven-tenths of one percent.[13] This lends support to the belief that the position of the nonwhite may be taken as a reasonable approximation of that of the Negro.

[9] See citations in Davies, *op. cit.*, p. 5; Bendix and Lipset, *op. cit.*, pp. 32–33.

[10] Davies, *op. cit.*, p. 6.

[11] Gerhard Lenski, "Status Crystallization: A Non-Vertical Dimension of Social Status," *American Sociological Review*, 19 (August 1954), p. 412; Leonard Broom, "Social Differentiation and Stratification," Robert K. Merton, Leonard Broom and Leonard S. Cottrell (eds.), *Sociology Today* (New York: Basic Books, 1959), pp. 429–41; Everett C. Hughes, "Social Change and Status Protest: An Essay on the Marginal Man," *Phylon*, 10 (First Quarter 1949), pp. 58–65; Pitirim A. Sorokin, *Society, Culture and Personality* (New York: Harper & Row, 1947).

[12] The crucial role played by the status dimensions of ethnicity, education, occupation, and income is supported by Lenski, *op. cit.*, and Broom, *op. cit.*, p. 431.

[13] These data were compiled from census data and are available from the present writer upon request.

Table 1. Level of education by color, males, 1940 and 1960

| Level of Education | White | | | Nonwhite | | | Nonwhites as Percent of Total | | Ratio[a] |
|---|---|---|---|---|---|---|---|---|---|
| | 1940 | 1960 | % Change | 1940 | 1960 | % Change | 1940 | 1960 | |
| No schooling | 3.2 | 2.0 | − 1.2 | 11.7 | 6.6 | − 5.1 | 26.1 | 26.3 | 0.94 |
| ELEM 1–4 yrs | 8.8 | 5.5 | − 3.3 | 34.5 | 21.1 | −13.4 | 27.7 | 28.9 | 0.97 |
| 5–6 yrs | 11.1 | 7.1 | − 4.0 | 20.6 | 14.8 | − 5.8 | 15.3 | 17.9 | 1.09 |
| 7 yrs | 7.0 | 6.6 | − 0.4 | 7.5 | 8.5 | + 1.0 | 9.5 | 11.8 | 1.16 |
| 8 yrs | 30.5 | 18.4 | −12.1 | 11.4 | 12.3 | + 0.9 | 3.5 | 6.6 | 1.77 |
| HIGH 1–3 yrs | 15.1 | 18.9 | + 3.8 | 7.4 | 17.1 | + 9.7 | 4.6 | 8.7 | 1.77 |
| 4 yrs. | 13.0 | 22.1 | + 9.1 | 3.8 | 11.7 | + 7.9 | 2.8 | 5.3 | 1.77 |
| COLL 1–3 yrs | 5.3 | 9.0 | + 3.7 | 1.7 | 4.4 | + 2.7 | 3.0 | 4.9 | 1.52 |
| 4 yrs | 5.9 | 10.3 | + 4.4 | 1.4 | 3.4 | + 2.0 | 2.3 | 3.4 | 1.38 |
| Total Reporting | 99.9 | 99.9 | | 99.9 | 99.9 | | 8.9 | 9.5 | 1.00 |
| | 33,59 | 5,150 | −43,157,862 | 3,27 | 9,786 | −4,547,539 | | | |

[a] Standardized by number reporting education.
Source: United States Bureau of the Census. Characteristics of the Population, United States Summary, 1940, 1960, Alaska and Hawaii excluded.

Table 1 portrays the changes that have taken place in male level of education by race between 1940 and 1960. There are two approaches one could take to the analysis of comparative rates of educational improvements of whites and nonwhites. One could compare the proportional distributions of whites and nonwhites by educational categories or one could examine rates based upon nonwhite proportional representation within educational categories. Each technique has its merits and they can be used to supplement one another. The first six columns of Table 1 represent the former and the last three columns represent the latter.

In analyzing the ethnic distributions by educational categories, levels of education may profitably be broken into three broad categories: low—from none to six years of elementary school; middle—seventh grade through eleventh grade; and high—high school graduates through four or more years of college. A much larger percentage of nonwhites than whites (24.3 to 8.5 percent) are moving out of the lower educational category. The middle educational category shows an increase in the proportion of nonwhites (11.6 percent) and a decrease in the proportion of whites (8.7 percent). This suggests that nonwhites are moving in larger numbers than whites out of the lower educational categories; that they are moving into the middle educational categories which the whites are moving out of; and that the nonwhites are moving into the upper educational categories in smaller numbers than whites.

Changes in the proportional representation of nonwhites in each educational category are measured by ratios comparing 1960 proportions to 1940 proportions standardized by numbers reporting education. The standardized ratios give a precise way of measuring the rate of educational improvement of nonwhites relative to that of the society as a whole. A ratio of one represents proportional improvement; less than one, improvement at a slower rate; and more than one, improvement at a more rapid rate. There was a net gain in proportion of nonwhites in all educational levels above the fourth grade. The size of the gain at the two highest levels was less than that for the three middle levels. Thus, it would appear that nonwhites are improving their level of education at a more rapid rate than whites.

The use of census data for comparing changing educational levels over time has one major weakness. Age distributions are not controlled, so it is not possible to know how much of the result is a reflection of different age distributions. Table 2 presents median years of schooling completed by age, sex, and color for 1959 and sheds some light on this difficulty. A comparison of the ratios of the nonwhite median to the white median for each of the age categories reveals that, with the singular exception of the 55 to 64 age category, there is a steady progression toward greater equality in level of education between white and nonwhite as age decreases. This can only reflect a situation in which nonwhites are improving their educational accomplishments relative to whites.

Thus, it may be concluded that the nonwhite is improving his educa-

Table 2. Median years of schooling completed age 25 years and over by age, sex, and color, March 1959

| Age | Male | | | Female | | |
|---|---|---|---|---|---|---|
| | Total | Nonwhite | Nonwhite as percent of total | Total | Nonwhite | Nonwhite as percent of total |
| 25–29 | 12.4 | 10.9 | 88 | 12.3 | 11.0 | 89 |
| 30–34 | 12.2 | 9.5 | 78 | 12.2 | 10.0 | 82 |
| 35–44 | 12.1 | 8.1 | 67 | 12.1 | 8.8 | 73 |
| 45–54 | 10.2 | 6.7 | 66 | 10.8 | 7.7 | 71 |
| 55–64 | 8.7 | 6.7 | 77 | 8.9 | 6.6 | 74 |
| 65 and over | 8.2 | 3.8 | 46 | 8.4 | 5.4 | 64 |

Source: Data taken from Murray Gendell and Hand L. Zetterberg, A Sociological Alamanac for the United States (New York: Bedminster Press, 1961), Table 68, p. 70.

tional level relative to previous generations of nonwhites and also is improving his educational level relative to whites. The data are ambiguous as to proportional gains in the upper educational categories.

## OCCUPATION

Table 3 presents the changes which have taken place in male occupations by race from 1940 to 1960. It presents the data in the same two ways that were used earlier in the analysis of data on education. The first three columns portray the changes in the distribution of persons into occupational categories by race. It may be noted that nonwhites have increased their representation in all non-farm occupational categories and that whites have increased their representation in all non-farm occupational categories except labor. This makes it difficult to determine whether the increase in numbers of nonwhite professionals and managers represents occupational upgrading. Nonwhites increased their representation in the highest status non-farm occupations (professional-technical) and (manager-official-proprietor) by 13.8 percent but decreased their representation in the highest status category of farm occupations (farmer and farm manager) by 16.3 percent.

The second three columns present the distribution of persons into occupational categories by race when non-farm occupations only are considered. We now note that there is a decrease in the proportion of nonwhites in the two lowest status occupational categories (service and labor); an increase in representation in the upper blue collar and lower white collar categories (operatives, craftsmen-foremen, clerical-sales); an increase in the professional-technical occupational category and a negligible decrease in the manager-official-proprietor category.

These figures appear to demonstrate an occupational upgrading of nonwhites. The data are unclear as to relative rates of upgrading. Nonwhites are shifting from farm to non-farm occupations in larger numbers than whites; shifting into the highest status occupations less rapidly than whites; shifting into the middle status occupations more rapidly than whites; and shifting out of the lowest status occupations more rapidly than whites, if we consider non-farm occupational data and, less rapidly than whites if we consider data on all occupations.

The seventh and eighth columns in Table 3 present the proportion of nonwhites in each occupational category for 1940 and 1960. The final two columns present ratios of the 1960 proportions to the 1940 proportions standardized by numbers reporting occupations for all occupations and non-farm occupations only. As in the case of education, a ratio of one represents changes at the same rate as the larger society; more than one, increase in proportional representation; less than one, decrease in proportional representation. The ratios computed on the basis of all occupations show a decrease in nonwhite representation in the farmer-farm manager occupational category and an increase in all other occupational categories

Table 3. Occupation by color, United States males, 1940 and 1960

| Occupation | Color | All occupations 1940 | 1960 | Change | Non-farm only 1940 | 1960 | Change | Nonwhites as percent of total 1940 | 1960 | All occupations Ratio[a] | Non-farm only Ratio[b] |
|---|---|---|---|---|---|---|---|---|---|---|---|
| Professional Technical | White | 6.0 | 11.4 | + 5.4 | 7.6 | 12.5 | + 4.9 | 3.0 | 3.3 | 1.16 | 0.82 |
|  | Nonwhite | 1.9 | 4.1 | + 2.2 | 3.2 | 4.7 | + 1.5 |  |  |  |  |
| Farm-Farm Managers | White | 14.2 | 5.9 | − 8.3 |  |  |  | 13.1 | 7.3 | 0.59 |  |
|  | Nonwhite | 21.2 | 4.9 | −16.3 |  |  |  |  |  |  |  |
| Managers-Prop Officials | White | 10.7 | 12.0 | + 1.3 | 13.6 | 13.1 | − 0.5 | 1.5 | 1.8 | 1.26 | 1.01 |
|  | Nonwhite | 1.7 | 0.6 | + 0.6 | 2.9 | 2.6 | − 0.3 |  |  |  |  |
| Clerical-Sales | White | 14.1 | 15.2 | + 1.1 | 17.9 | 16.5 | − 1.4 | 1.5 | 4.1 | 2.87 | 2.29 |
|  | Nonwhite | 2.2 | 6.9 | + 4.7 | 3.7 | 7.9 | + 4.2 |  |  |  |  |
| Craftsmen-Foremen | White | 15.8 | 21.4 | + 5.6 | 20.1 | 23.3 | + 3.2 | 2.7 | 4.5 | 1.76 | 1.40 |
|  | Nonwhite | 4.4 | 10.7 | + 6.3 | 7.5 | 12.2 | + 4.7 |  |  |  |  |
| Operatives | White | 19.1 | 20.4 | + 1.3 | 24.3 | 22.2 | − 2.1 | 6.2 | 10.7 | 1.82 | 1.45 |
|  | Nonwhite | 12.5 | 25.9 | +13.4 | 21.3 | 29.6 | + 8.3 |  |  |  |  |
| Service | White | 5.4 | 5.5 | + 0.1 | 6.9 | 6.0 | − 0.9 | 22.2 | 21.5 | 1.02 | 0.82 |
|  | Nonwhite | 15.3 | 16.0 | + 0.7 | 26.1 | 18.3 | − 7.8 |  |  |  |  |
| Farm Labor | White | 7.1 | 2.4 | − 4.7 |  |  |  | 22.3 | 23.3 | 1.09 |  |
|  | Nonwhite | 20.1 | 7.8 | −12.3 |  |  |  |  |  |  |  |
| Labor | White | 7.6 | 5.9 | − 1.7 | 9.7 | 6.4 | − 3.3 | 21.5 | 25.6 | 1.25 | 1.00 |
|  | Nonwhite | 20.7 | 21.4 | +10.7 | 35.3 | 24.5 | −10.8 |  |  |  |  |
| Total | White | 30,480,640 | 37,846,254 |  | 24,000,434 | 34,620,227 |  | 9.1 | 8.6 | 1.00 | 1.00 |
|  | Nonwhite | 3,072,606 | 3,558,946 |  | 1,801,092 | 3,107,859 |  |  |  |  |  |

[a] Standardized by number reporting occupations.

[b] Standardized by number reporting non-farm occupations.

Source: United States Bureau of the Census, Characteristics of the Population, United States Summary, 1940, 1960, Alaska and Hawaii excluded.

(but a negligible increase in the service category). The ratios computed on the basis of non-farm occupations show a decrease in nonwhite representation in the occupational categories of professional-technical and service; relative stability in the occupational categories of labor and manager-official-proprietor; and an increase in proportional representation in all other occupational categories.

When considered as a totality, the data on occupational changes indicate that nonwhites are leaving the farms more rapidly than whites, are being occupationally upgraded relative to previous generations of non-whites; and are experiencing some occupational upgrading relative to whites but possibly not at the highest occupational status levels.

INCOME

It is difficult to examine income changes over extended periods of time because of the large number of different techniques of reporting income that are used, the difficulty in getting data from the same technique for many consecutive years, and the shifting value of the dollar in terms of purchasing power. We will consider the technique of measuring income which was reported over the longest time span, analyzed in both current and constant dollars. Constant dollars are computed by translating the purchasing power of current dollars into the average purchasing power of the dollar from 1947 to 1949.

Table 4 presents median income of males 14 and over having wage

*Table 4. Median income males 14 and over having wage or salary income in current and constant dollars in the United States for 1939 to 1961*

| | White | | Nonwhite | | |
|---|---|---|---|---|---|
| Year | Current dollars | Constant dollars | Current dollars | Constant dollars | White minus nonwhite in constant dollars |
| 1939 | 1112 | 2176 | 460 | 900 | 1276 |
| *** | *** | *** | *** | *** | *** |
| 1947 | 2357 | 2468 | 1279 | 1339 | 1189 |
| 1948 | 2711 | 2637 | 1615 | 1571 | 1066 |
| 1949 | 2735 | 2686 | 1367 | 1342 | 1344 |
| 1950 | 2982 | 2901 | 1828 | 1779 | 1122 |
| 1951 | 3345 | 3014 | 2060 | 1856 | 1158 |
| 1952 | 3507 | 3090 | 2038 | 1795 | 1295 |
| 1953 | 3760 | 3286 | 2833 | 1826 | 1460 |
| 1954 | 3754 | 3270 | 2131 | 1856 | 1414 |
| 1955 | 3986 | 3480 | 2342 | 2045 | 1435 |
| *** | *** | *** | *** | *** | *** |
| 1961 | 5287 | 4134 | 3015 | 2358 | 1776 |

Source: *Statistical Abstract of the United States,* Washington, D.C.: United States Department of Commerce, Bureau of the Census, 1962, and earlier editions. 1961 income data from P.60 Series, *Current Population Reports,* 1962.

or salary income by color for those years in which such data were available from 1939 to 1961. Nonwhite income has shown a relatively steady increase in both current and constant dollars from 1939 to 1961. White income has shown a similar increase on both current and constant dollars. The difference between white and nonwhite median incomes in constant dollars increased from $1,276 in 1939 to $1,776 in 1961. Thus, nonwhite males have improved their income in both current and constant dollars, but have fallen further behind white males in so doing.[14] In other words, nonwhites are raising their standard of living, but less rapidly than whites.

### EVALUATION OF HYPOTHESES

Now that the changing position of the Negro (nonwhite) in the United States has been examined, we are in a position to evaluate the hypotheses presented earlier.

"The Vulgar Marxist Hypothesis," which predicted rebellion as a result of a worsening of conditions of life, is clearly inconsistent with these data. The position of the Negro is improving educationally, occupationally, and income-wise.

"The Rising Expectations Hypothesis," which predicted rebellion as a result of improvements in conditions of life, is consistent with the data examined. Negroes have improved their level of education; they have better jobs, and they are earning more money with which they may purchase more things. One might assume a more rapid rise in level of aspirations but data are lacking to either substantiate or refute the assumption.

"The Sophisticated Marxist Hypothesis," which gave a relative deprivation basis for its prediction of rebellion, is also consistent with these data. Negroes have improved their level of education and have done so more rapidly than have whites. But education is not a direct measure of living conditions either socially or economically. It is one source of status and, as such, it carries with it certain satisfactions. Occupation may be viewed as a second source of status. The Negro has improved his occupational level, thus improving his status rewards as well as receiving other rewards in terms of better working conditions. The evidence is not clear as to the relative occupational gains or losses experienced by the Negro. He appears to be moving more rapidly than whites into the middle status occupations, but if urban occupations only are considered, he is moving more slowly into the higher status occupations. Whether this situation would produce feelings of relative loss or relative gain is a moot question which could only be settled through further empirical studies.

The area of income most directly affects conditions of life and presents the clearest picture. Negroes are improving their incomes in terms

---

[14] This same general pattern emerges regardless of the choice of income data. It holds for median family income, female income, urban income, as well as the combined individual and family income.

of both current and constant dollars. The gap between white and Negro incomes is also increasing in terms of both current and constant dollars. Thus, Negroes are improving their material conditions of life but are not doing so at the same rate as whites. This is the perfect situation to create feelings of relative deprivation leading to rebellion.

"The Rise and Drop Hypothesis," which predicted rebellion as a result of the reversal of past progress in conditions of life, is not consistent with the data examined. There appears to be a relatively steady improvement in level of education, level of occupation, and income in both current and constant dollars. No reversal may be observed.

"The Status Inconsistency Hypothesis," which predicted rebellion as a result of an increase in the proportion of status inconsistents, is consistent with the data examined. There has been an increase in the proportion of status inconsistents among Negroes. This is true in both a trivial and a significant sense. Current research in status inconsistency emphasizes the dimensions of occupation, income, education, and ethnicity as the crucial ones for American society. Negroes have retained their low ethnic status, but they have improved their position on each of the other status dimensions. Thus, they have increased their status inconsistency in the trivial sense. They have increased the combination of low ethnic status with higher rankings on other dimensions.

Negroes have also increased their status inconsistency in a more significant sense. These data show that they are not only improving their level of education, but they are doing so at a more rapid rate than whites; while in the area of occupational gains there has not been as significant a gain relative to that of whites. Table 1 shows that nonwhites are increasing their proportional representation in the educational category of one-to-three-years-of-college 1.53 times as rapidly as is the total society, and they are increasing their representation in the four-or-more-years-of-college 1.38 times as rapidly. When the category of all those with any college is considered, nonwhites are increasing their representation 1.48 times as rapidly as is the general society. Yet Table 3, which covers the same time span, shows that nonwhites are increasing their representation in the occupational category of professional-technical workers only 1.16 times as rapidly as the general society, when all occupations are considered, or 0.82 times as rapidly when only non-farm occupations are considered. They are increasing their representation in the combined managerial and professional categories 1.19 times as rapidly as whites, when all occupations are considered, and 1.00 times as rapidly for non-farm occupations. This shows that nonwhites (and presumably Negroes) are improving their educational qualifications for professional and technical jobs more rapidly than they are receiving these jobs, thus causing an increased disparity between educational qualifications for jobs and level of occupational achievement.[15]

---

[15] I say an increased discrepancy because Turner has already demonstrated the existence of the discrepancy in 1940. He showed that only thirty-nine percent of the nonwhites' lower

We may observe the same pattern if we consider proportional distributions of whites and nonwhites into educational and occupational categories. Nonwhites increased their representation in the category of some college or college graduate by 4.7 percent. These would presumably be the categories best qualifying them for upper white collar jobs. They increased their representation in the professional-technical occupational category by 2.2 percent (a gain which is 44.7 percent of the educational gain), and they increased their representation in the combined manager and professional-technical categories by 2.8 percent (59.6 percent of the educational gain). The corresponding figures for whites show an increase of 8.1 percent in the some college or college graduate category and an increase of 5.4 percent (66.7 percent of the educational gain) in the professional-technical categories and an increase in the combined professional-technical and manager categories of 6.7 percent (82.7 percent of the educational gain). These data show that whites are making gains in the occupational realm which are much more in proportion to their educational gains than are nonwhites. Data on non-farm occupations reveal the same pattern.[16] Nonwhites are increasing their discrepancy between education and occupation and becoming more status inconsistent.

It was shown in Table 4 that Negroes are not increasing their income level as rapidly as whites. Further evidence that improved educational achievements are not rewarded by increased incomes as rapidly for nonwhites as for whites may be derived from Table 5. Not only do nonwhites

Table 5. Median income by level of education and color—males 14 and over, 1961

| Level of Education | White | Nonwhite | Difference |
|---|---|---|---|
| Elementary: | | | |
| Less than 8 years | 2303 | 1554 | 749 |
| 8 years | 3617 | 2505 | 1112 |
| High School: | | | |
| 1–3 years | 4090 | 2427 | 1663 |
| 4 years | 5155 | 3381 | 1774 |
| Some College | 6379 | 4246 | 2133 |
| Total | 4432 | 2292 | 2140 |

Source: Current Population Reports, P60 Series, United States Bureau of the Census, #39, p. 4.

receive a lower median income than whites at each level of education, but the dollar gap between medians increases as level of education increases.

---

job status could be attributed to their lesser amount of education. See Ralph H. Turner, "Foci of Discrimination in the Employment of Non-Whites," American Journal of Sociology, 58 (November 1952), pp. 247–56.

[16] Nonwhites: Professional-technical—1.5 percent (31.5 percent of educational gains). Combined Manager and Professional-technical—1.2 percent (25.6 percent of educational gains). Whites: Professional-technical—4.9 percent (60.5 percent of educational gains). Combined Manager and Professional-technical—4.4 percent (54.3 percent of educational gains).

Even if we ignore their ethnicity, Negroes are becoming increasingly status inconsistent as a result of the fact that they are raising their level of education but are being denied the occupational mobility or income level which would "normally" be associated with such progress.

## DISCUSSION

Only two out of the five proposed hypotheses have been rejected. This leaves the task of either choosing among the remaining hypotheses or somehow reconciling them. It is a relatively simple task to reconcile the "Sophisticated Marxist Hypothesis" with "The Status Inconsistency Hypothesis," as the essence of each is the concept of the relative deprivation. The former is explicitly stated in these terms, while the latter's thesis is implied. It is the association between statuses which generally prevails in a society that determines what is status consistency. Deviations from this prevailing association are what constitute status inconsistency. It is the experiencing of these deviations to one's own detriment which causes the propensity to revolt among status inconsistents.[17]

It is also possible to reconcile "The Rising Expectations Hypothesis" with the "Status Inconsistency Hypothesis." Both Edwards and Brinton see blockages of social mobility as an essential basis for "The Rising Expectations Hypothesis."[18] People feel that they have legitimate aspirations which are blocked, thus interfering with the circulation of the elite, and creating a status inconsistent group. This is very similar to the interpretation that Broom gives to "The Status Inconsistency Hypothesis."[19]

It seems that "relative deprivation" is the essence of all three hypotheses that are consistent with the observed data. It is only by observing the process of social mobility in society that one will develop aspirations for such mobility. Observation of the criteria used to select successful aspirants allows development of feelings that one's aspirations are legitimate. Possession of these characteristics without subsequent mobility creates status inconsistency. Without comparing one's own experiences with those of others in society and subsequently developing feelings of relative deprivation, no rebellion would take place.

## CONCLUSIONS

Five hypotheses which purport to account for the current "Negro Revolt" were taken from the literature. Data were examined which resulted in

[17] Cf., George C. Homans, *Social Behavior: Its Elementary Forms* (New York: Harcourt, 1961), pp. 232–264. Homans points out that anger leading to rebellion will result from the experiencing of this deviance to one's detriment, while guilt (which is a weaker emotion not calculated to lead to rebellion) will result from the experiencing of this deviance to one's benefit.

[18] Brinton, *op. cit.,* pp. 78–79; Edwards, *op. cit.,* p. 30.

[19] Broom, *op. cit.,* p. 439.

the rejection of two of these. The three which remained were reconciled with each other in terms of their common basis in the concept of relative deprivation. This should not be misinterpreted as a claim that the psychological state of possessing feelings of relative deprivation will, regardless of objective conditions, produce rebellion. In contrast, the suggestion proposed herein is that certain types of objective conditions will produce feelings of relative deprivation, which will, in turn, produce rebellion.

The Negro in the United States has been exposed to just such a set of objective conditions. He is handicapped by blockages in the circulation of the elite, especially in the area of the professions. He is acquiring the education which is normally the key to occupational mobility and economic gain. He is not experiencing as rapid a rate of occupational mobility to which he feels he is entitled. He is not receiving the economic rewards which he feels he has earned. As a result, he is becoming increasingly status inconsistent and he sees himself falling further and further behind the white. He feels relatively deprived and unjustly so. Therefore, he revolts in order to correct the situation.

# 31

## FROM CIVIL RIGHTS TO BLACK POWER
### Allen J. Matusow

**T**HE transformation of black protest in the 1960's from civil rights to black power has seemed in retrospect an inevitable development. When the inherent limitations of the civil rights movement finally became apparent and when the expectations that the movement created met frustration, some kind of militant reaction in the black community seemed certain. However predictable this development may have been, it tells little about the concrete events that led to the abandonment of the civil rights program and to the adoption of a doctrine that is in many ways its opposite. For black power was not plucked whole from impersonal historical forces; nor was its content the only possible expression of rising black militancy. Rather, black power both as a slogan and a doctrine was in large measure the creation of a small group of civil rights workers who in the early 1960's manned the barricades

Allen J. Matusow, "From Civil Rights to Black Power; The Case of SNCC, 1960–1966," in Barton J. Bernstein and Allen J. Matusow, eds., *Twentieth-Century America: Recent Interpretations* (New York: Harcourt, Brace & Jovanovich, Inc., 1969), pp. 533–556. Reprinted by permission of the author.

of black protest in the Deep South. The group was called the Student Nonviolent Coordinating Committee (SNCC). Through its spokesman, Stokely Carmichael, SNCC first proclaimed black power and then became its foremost theoretician. Others would offer glosses on black power that differed from SNCC's concept, but because SNCC had contributed so much to the civil rights movement, no other group could speak with so much authority or command a comparable audience. Although SNCC borrowed freely from many sources to fashion black power into a doctrine, the elements of that doctrine were in the main the results of SNCC's own history. An examination of that history reveals not only the roots of black power but also the sad fate of the whole civil rights movement.

Founded in 1960, SNCC was an outgrowth of the historic sit-in movement, which began in Greensboro, North Carolina, on February 4 of that year. Four freshmen from a local Negro college attempted to desegregate the lunch counter at a Woolworth's five and ten store. The example of these four sent shock waves through the black colleges of the South and created overnight a base for a campaign of massive civil disobedience. The new generation of black students seemed suddenly unwilling to wait any longer for emancipation at the hands of the federal courts and in the next months supplied most of the recruits for the nonviolent army of 50,000 that rose spontaneously and integrated public facilities in 140 Southern cities. For the students on the picket lines, the prophet of the sit-in movement was Dr. Martin Luther King, the leader of the successful Montgomery bus boycott of 1955–56. The students found in King's nonviolent philosophy a ready-made ethic, a tactic, and a conviction of righteousness strong enough to sustain them on a sometimes hazardous mission.[1] It was King's organization, the Southern Christian Leadership Conference (SCLC), that first suggested the need for some central direction of the sit-in movement. At the invitation of SCLC's executive secretary, some 300 activist students from throughout the South met in Raleigh, North Carolina, in April 1960, to discuss their problems. The students agreed to form a coordinating body, which became SNCC, and in May 1960, hired a secretary and opened an office in Atlanta. In October the organization decided to become a permanent one, and 235 delegates approved a founding statement inspired by King's philosophy:

*We affirm the philosophical or religious ideal of nonviolence as the foundation of our purpose, the presupposition of our belief, and the manner of our action. . . . Through nonviolence, courage displaces fear. Love transcends hate. Acceptance dissipates prejudice; hope ends despair. Faith*

---

[1] For accounts of the sit-ins see Howard Zinn, *SNCC: The Abolitionists* (Beacon, 1965), Chapter 2; Jack Newfield, *A Prophetic Minority* (Signet, 1966), Chapter 3; August Meier, "The Successful Sit-Ins in a Border City: A Study in Social Causation," *The Journal of Intergroup Relations,* II (Summer, 1961), 230–37; Charles U. Smith, "The Sit-Ins and the New Negro Student," *ibid.,* 223–29; James Peck, *Freedom Ride* (Simon and Schuster, 1962), Chapter 6.

*reconciles doubt. Peace dominates war. Mutual regards cancel enmity. Justice for all overwhelms injustice. The redemptive community supersedes immoral social systems.*[2]

In truth, the Christian rhetoric of SNCC's founding statement was not appropriate. The author of the statement was James Lawson, a young minister who never actually belonged to SNCC.[3] Most of the students who rallied to the sit-ins in 1960 accepted King's teachings more out of convenience than conviction and respected his courage more than his philosophy. For while King believed that Christian love was an end in itself and that Negro nonviolence would redeem American society, the students preferred to participate in America rather than to transform it. Sociologists who examined the attitudes of protesters in the black colleges found not alienation from American middle-class values but a desire to share fully in middle-class life.[4] In a perceptive piece written for *Dissent,* Michael Walzer supported these findings from his own first-hand impressions of the sit-ins. Walzer concluded that the students were materialistic as well as moral, were "willing to take risks in the name of both prosperity and virtue," and had as their goal "assimilation into American society." As for nonviolence, Walzer wrote, "I was told often that 'when one side has all the guns, then the other side is nonviolent.' "[5]

In the beginning, the philosophical inconsistencies of the sit-ins did not trouble SNCC, for it stood at the forefront of a movement whose ultimate triumph seemed not far distant. But within months, as mysteriously as it began, the sit-in movement vanished. By the spring of 1961 the black campuses had lapsed into their customary quiescence, their contribution to the civil rights movement at an end. As for SNCC, since October 1960, the student representatives from each Southern state had been meeting monthly to squander their energies trying to coordinate a movement that was first too amorphous and then suddenly moribund. SNCC's attempt in early 1961 to raise up new hosts of students proved ineffectual, and lacking followers, the organization seemed without a future.[6] Then in May 1961, the Freedom Rides restored a sense of urgency to the civil rights movement and gave SNCC a second life.

[2] Quoted in Newfield, *A Prophetic Minority,* p. 47.

[3] Emily Schottenfeld Stoper, "The Student Nonviolent Coordinating Committee: The Growth of Radicalism in a Civil Rights Organization," unpublished dissertation, Harvard University, 1968, pp. 35–36.

[4] Ruth Searles and J. Allen Williams, Jr., "Negro College Students' Participation in Sit-Ins," *Social Forces,* (Dec., 1966), 215–20.

[5] Michael Walzer, "The Politics of the New Negro," *Dissent,* VII (Summer, 1960), 235–43.

[6] Anne Braden, "The Southern Freedom Movement in Perspective," *Monthly Review,* XVII (July–Aug., 1965), 31–32; also James Howard Laue, "Direct Action and Desegregation: Toward a Theory of the Rationalization of Protest," unpublished dissertation, Harvard University, 1965, p. 128.

On May 14, 1961, members of the Congress of Racial Equality (CORE) began the Freedom Rides to test a Supreme Court decision outlawing segregation in transportation terminals. On May 20, after one of CORE's integrated buses was bombed near Anniston, Alabama, and another was mobbed in Birmingham, CORE decided to call off its rides. But amid sensational publicity, students from Nashville and Atlanta, many associated with SNCC, rushed to Birmingham to continue the journey to New Orleans. After mobs assaulted this second wave of riders, the Federal Government stepped in to protect them, and they were permitted to go as far as Jackson, where local authorities put them in jail for defying segregation ordinances. Throughout the summer of 1961 some 300 citizens from all over America took Freedom Rides that brought them to the jails of Jackson.[7] For SNCC the Freedom Rides provided a temporary outlet for activism and, more important, inspired radical changes in the structure and purpose of the organization.

Perhaps the most important result of the Freedom Rides for SNCC was to focus its attention on the Deep South. Most of the sit-ins had occurred in the cities and larger towns of the Upper South, and the victories there had come with relative ease. Now the magnitude of the task confronting the civil rights movement became clearer. As some in SNCC had already perceived, sit-ins to desegregate public places offered no meaningful benefits to poverty-stricken tenant farmers in, say, Mississippi. In order to mobilize the black communities in the Deep South to fight for their rights, sporadic student demonstrations would be less useful than sustained efforts by full time field workers.[8] In the summer of 1961, as SNCC was beginning to grope toward the concept of community action, the Federal Government stepped in with an attractive suggestion.

Embarrassed by the Freedom Rides, Attorney General Robert F. Kennedy moved to direct the civil rights movement into paths that, in his view, were more constructive. Kennedy suggested that the civil rights organizations jointly sponsor a campaign to register Southern black voters. Such a drive, its proponents argued, would be difficult for even extreme segregationists to oppose and eventually might liberalize the Southern delegation in Congress. When the Justice Department seemed to offer federal protection for registration workers and when white liberals outside the Administration procured foundation money to finance anticipated costs, the civil rights groups agreed to undertake the project.[9] Within SNCC, advocates of direct action fought acceptance of the project, but the issue was compromised and a threatened split was averted. SNCC's decision to

---

[7] For accounts of the Freedom Rides, see Zinn, *SNCC,* Chapter 3; and Peck, *Freedom Ride,* Chapters 8 and 9.

[8] Laue, "Direct Action and Desegregation," pp. 154, 160, 167–68.

[9] On origins of the voter registration drive, see Pat Watters and Reece Cleghorn, *Climbing Jacob's Ladder* (Harcourt, 1967), pp. 44–59; and Louis Lomax, *The Negro Revolt* (Signet, 1963), pp. 246–50.

mobilize black communities behind efforts to secure political rights decisively changed the character of the organization. It thereafter ceased to be
an extracurricular activity of student leaders and became instead the voca-
tion of dedicated young men and women who temporarily abandoned
their careers to become full time paid workers (or "field secretaries") in
the movement. Moreover, as SNCC workers drifted away from the black
campuses and began living among Deep South blacks, they cast aside the
middle-class goals that had motivated the sit-ins of 1960 and put on the
overalls of the poor. Begun as middle-class protest, SNCC was developing
revolutionary potential.[10]

In Mississippi the major civil rights groups (NAACP, SCLC, CORE
and SNCC) ostensibly joined together to form the Council of Federated
Organizations (COFO) to register black voters. But in reality, except for
one Mississippi congressional district where CORE had a project of its own,
COFO was manned almost entirely by SNCC people. The director of
COFO was SNCC's now legendary Robert Moses, a product of Harlem
with a Masters degree in philosophy from Harvard, whose courage and
humanity made him the most respected figure in the organization. Moses
had entered Pike County, Mississippi, alone in 1961, stayed on in spite of
a beating and a jail term, and in the spring of 1962 became COFO's
director in charge of voting projects in Vicksburg, Cleveland, Greenwood,
and a few other Mississippi towns.[11] Although SNCC also had registration
projects in Arkansas, Alabama, and Georgia, it concentrated on Mississippi,
where the obstacles were greatest.

Throughout 1962 and into 1963 SNCC workers endured assaults,
offered brave challenges to local power structures, and exhorted local
blacks to shake off fear and stand up for freedom. But SNCC scored no
breakthroughs to sustain morale, and while its goals remained outwardly
unchanged, its mood was turning bitter. To SNCC the hostility of local
racists was not nearly so infuriating as the apparent betrayal that it suffered at the hands of the Justice Department. SNCC believed that in 1961
the Kennedy Administration had guaranteed protection to registration
workers, but in Mississippi in 1962 and 1963, SNCC's only contact with
federal authority consisted of the FBI agents who stood by taking notes
while local policemen beat up SNCC members. SNCC and its supporters
insisted that existing law empowered the Federal Government to intervene,
but the Justice Department contended that it was in fact powerless. SNCC
doubted the sincerity of the Government's arguments and became convinced that the Kennedys had broken a solemn promise for political
reasons.[12] Thus by 1963 SNCC was already becoming estranged from
established authority and suspicious of liberal politicians.

[10] Braden, "Southern Freedom Movement," p. 36; Laue, "Direct Action and Desegregation,"
p. 171; Stoper, "The Student Nonviolent Coordinating Committee," pp. 6 and 8.

[11] For an account of Moses in Mississippi, see Zinn, *SNCC*, Chapter 4.

[12] See *ibid.*, Chapter 10; and Watters and Cleghorn, *Climbing Jacob's Ladder*, p. 58.

SNCC's growing sense of alienation cut it off even from other civil rights organizations and most importantly from Dr. King, who by 1963 had become a fallen idol for SNCC workers. They believed that King was too willing to compromise, wielded too much power, and too successfully monopolized the funds of the movement. Doubts about King had arisen as early as the Freedom Rides, when students turned to him for advice and leadership and received what they considered only vague sympathy. In fact, after CORE called off the first ride, King privately supported Robert Kennedy's plea for a "cooling-off" period. But much to SNCC's annoyance, when militant voices prevailed and the rides continued, the press gave King all the credit.[13] In Albany, Georgia, in December 1961, after SNCC aroused the black population to pack the local jails for freedom, King came to town, got arrested, monopolized the headlines, and almost stole the leadership of the Albany campaign from SNCC.[14] In SNCC's view, dependence on King's charisma actually weakened the civil rights movement, for it discouraged development of leadership at the grass-roots level. Why, SNCC asked, did King use his huge share of civil rights money to maintain a large staff in Atlanta, and why did he never account for the funds that he so skillfully collected?[15] As King lost influence on SNCC, dissenting attitudes about nonviolence, implicit since 1960, came to be frankly articulated. When Robert Penn Warren asked Robert Moses what he thought of King's philosophy, Moses replied,

*We don't agree with it, in a sense. The majority of the students are not sympathetic to the idea that they have to love the white people that they are struggling against. . . . For most of the members, it is tactical, it's a question of being able to have a method of attack rather than to be always on the defensive.*[16]

During the March on Washington in August 1963, the nation almost caught a glimpse of SNCC's growing anger. John Lewis, the chairman of SNCC and one of the scheduled speakers, threatened to disrupt the harmony of that happy occasion by saying what he really thought. Only with difficulty did moderates persuade Lewis to delete the harshest passages of his address. So the nation did not know that SNCC scorned Kennedy's civil rights bill as "too little and too late." Lewis had intended to ask the 250,000 people gathered at the Lincoln Memorial,

[13] Laue, "Direct Action and Desegregation," pp. 179, 338.

[14] Stoper, "The Student Nonviolent Coordinating Committee," p. 104; *New York Times* (Dec. 24, 1961), section IV, 5.

[15] "Integration: Hotter Fires," *Newsweek,* LXII (July 1, 1963), 19–21.

[16] Robert Penn Warren, *Who Speaks for the Negro* (Random House, Inc., 1965), p. 91.

*What is there in this bill to insure the equality of a maid who earns $5 a week in the home of a family whose income is $100,000 a year? . . . This nation is still a place of cheap political leaders who build their careers on immoral compromises and ally themselves with open forms of political, economic, and social exploitation. . . . The party of Kennedy is also the party of Eastland. The party of Javits is also the party of Goldwater. Where is our party? . . . We cannot depend on any political party, for the Democrats and the Republicans have betrayed the basic principles of the Declaration of Independence.*

In those remarks that he never delivered, Lewis used both the language of Christian protest and images alive with the rage of SNCC field workers. "In the struggle we must seek more than mere civil rights; we must work for the community of love, peace, and true brotherhood." And,

*the time will come when we will not confine our marching to Washington. We will march through the South, through the heart of Dixie, the way Sherman did. We shall pursue our "scorched earth" policy and burn Jim Crow to the ground—nonviolently. We shall fragment the South into a thousand pieces and put them back together in the image of democracy.*[17]

The crucial milestone of SNCC's road to radicalism was the Freedom Summer of 1964. Freedom Summer grew out of a remarkable mock election sponsored by SNCC in the autumn of 1963. Because the mass of Mississippi's black population could not legally participate in choosing the state's governor that year, Robert Moses conceived a freedom election to protest mass disfranchisement and to educate Mississippi's blacks to the mechanics of the political process. COFO organized a new party called the Mississippi Freedom Democrats, printed its own ballots, and in October conducted its own poll. Overwhelming the regular party candidates, Aaron Henry, head of the state NAACP and Freedom Democratic nominee for governor, received 70,000 votes, a tremendous protest against the denial of equal political rights. One reason for the success of the project was the presence in the state of 100 Yale and Stanford students, who worked for two weeks with SNCC on the election. SNCC was sufficiently impressed by the student contribution to consider inviting hundreds more to spend an entire summer in Mississippi. Sponsors of this plan hoped not only for workers but for publicity that might at last focus national attention on Mississippi.[18] By the winter of 1963–64, however, rising militancy in SNCC had begun to take on overtones of black nationalism, and some of the membership resisted the summer project on the grounds that most of the volunteers would be white. Present from the beginning, by mid-1964 whites made up one-fifth

[17] Quoted in Watters and Cleghorn, *Climbing Jacob's Ladder,* pp. xiv–xv.

[18] On freedom ballot, see Len Holt, *The Summer That Didn't End* (William Morrow, 1965), pp. 35–36, 152–53.

of SNCC's approximately 150 full time field secretaries. Though whites had suffered their fair share of beatings, some blacks in SNCC were expressing doubts about the role of white men in a movement for black freedom. At a staff meeting at Greenville, Mississippi, in November 1963, a debate on the proposed Freedom Summer brought the issue of white-black relations into the open. In his book *SNCC: The New Abolitionists,* Howard Zinn, who attended this meeting, summarizes the views of the militants:

*Four or five of the Negro staff members now urged that the role of whites be limited. For whites to talk to Mississippi Negroes about voter registration, they said, only reinforced the Southern Negro's tendency to believe that whites were superior. Whites tended to take over leadership roles in the movement, thus preventing Southern Negroes from being trained to lead. Why didn't whites just work in the white Southern community? One man noted that in Africa the new nations were training black Africans to take over all important government positions. Another told of meeting a Black Muslim in Atlanta who warned him that whites were taking over the movement. "I had the feeling inside. I felt what he said was true."*

But Fannie Lou Hamer disagreed. Mrs. Hamer had been a time-keeper on a cotton plantation and was one of the local Mississippi blacks whom SNCC discovered and elevated to leadership. Speaking for the majority of the meeting, she said, "If we're trying to break down this barrier of segregation, we can't segregate ourselves." Thus in February 1964, SNCC sent an invitation to Northern college students to spend their summer vacation in Mississippi.[19]

In retrospect, the summer of 1964 was a turning point in the civil rights movement. When the summer began, SNCC was still operating within the framework of liberal America, still committed to integration and equal political rights for all citizens. But by the end of the summer of 1964, the fraying cords that bound SNCC to liberal goals and values finally snapped. In a sense, much of later black power thought was merely a postcript to SNCC's ill-fated summer project.

In June 1964, more than 700 selected students, judged by a staff psychiatrist at MIT to be "an extraordinarily healthy bunch of kids,"[20] came to Oxford, Ohio, for two week-long orientation sessions conducted by veteran SNCC workers. The atmosphere in Oxford, tense from the outset, became on June 22 pervaded with gloom. Robert Moses quietly told the volunteers that three workers had gone into Neshoba county in Mississippi the day before and had not been heard from since. One was Michael

[19] Zinn, *SNCC,* pp. 8–9, 186–88; see also Calvin Trillin, "Letter from Jackson," *New Yorker,* XL (Aug. 29, 1964), 80–105.

[20] Quoted in James Atwater, "If We Can Crack Mississippi . . . ," *Saturday Evening Post,* CCXXXVII (July 25, 1964), 16.

Schwerner, a CORE staff member; the second was James Chaney, a black SNCC worker from Mississippi; and the third was Andrew Goodman, a student volunteer who had finished his orientation in Ohio a few days before.[21] (In August the bodies of these three were discovered in their shallow graves near Philadelphia, Mississippi.)

The volunteers in Ohio had to face not only their own fear but also unanticipated hostility from the SNCC workers whom they had come to assist. Tensions between black workers and white volunteers seethed under the surface for some days and then finally erupted. One night SNCC showed a film of a grotesque voting registrar turning away black applicants. When the student audience laughed at the scene, six SNCC people walked out, enraged at what they considered an insensitive response. There followed an exchange between the workers and the volunteers, in which the students complained that the staff was distant, uncommunicative, and "looked down on us for not having been through what they had." A SNCC worker replied,

*If you get mad at us for walking out, just wait until they break your head in, and see if you don't have something to get mad about. Ask Jimmy Travis over there what he thinks about the project. What does he think about Mississippi? He has six slugs in him, man, and the last one went right through the back of his neck when he was driving a car outside Greenwood. Ask Jesse here—he has been beaten so that we wouldn't recognize him time and time and time and time again. If you don't get scared, pack up and get the hell out of here because we don't need any favors of people who don't know what they are doing here in the first place.*

The bitter words seemed to have a cathartic effect, and the meeting culminated in emotional singing. Said one volunteer a bit too optimistically, "The crisis is past, I think."[22]

From one perspective the story of the two months that followed is one of the human spirit triumphant. Though three more people were killed, eighty others were beaten, thirty-five churches were burned, and thirty other buildings bombed, few turned back; black and white together, the civil rights workers in Mississippi worked for racial justice.[23] The student volunteers taught in Freedom Schools, where 3,000 children were given their first glimpse of a world beyond Mississippi. They organized the disfranchised to march on county courthouses to face unyielding registrars. Most importantly, they walked the roads of Mississippi for the Freedom Democratic Party (FDP). Denying the legitimacy of the segregated Democratic party, COFO opened the FDP to members of all races and declared the party's loyalty to Lyndon Johnson. The goal of the FDP in the summer

[21] Sally Belfrage, *Freedom Summer* (Viking, 1965), p. 11.

[22] Elizabeth Sutherland, ed., *Letters from Mississippi* (McGraw-Hill, 1965), pp. 5–6.

[23] Watters and Cleghorn, *Climbing Jacob's Ladder*, p. 139.

of 1964 was to send a delegation to the Democratic convention in Atlantic City to challenge the credentials of the regular Democrats and cast the state's vote for the party's nominees. To mount this challenge against the racist Democrats of Mississippi, COFO enrolled 60,000 members in the FDP and then organized precinct, county, and state conventions to choose 68 integrated delegates to go north. The FDP, in which tens of thousands of black Mississippi citizens invested tremendous hopes, was a true grass-roots political movement and the greatest achievement of Freedom Summer.[24]

Although the FDP brought to Atlantic City little more than a sense of moral outrage, it nevertheless managed to transform its challenge of the Mississippi regulars into a major threat to the peace of the national party. Mrs. Hamer helped make this feat possible by her electrifying (and televised) testimony before the credentials committee on how Mississippi policemen had beaten her up for trying to register to vote. As Northern liberals began rallying to the FDP, the managers of the conventions sought a compromise that would satisfy the liberals and at the same time keep the bulk of the Southern delegations in the convention. President Johnson favored a pro-posal to seat all the Mississippi regulars who pledged their loyalty to the party, to deny any voting rights to the FDP delegates, but to permit them to sit on the floor of the convention. In addition, he proposed that at future conventions no state delegations chosen by racially discriminatory pro-cedures would be accredited. But because this compromise denied the FDP's claims of legitimacy, the FDP and many liberals declared it unaccep-table and threatened to take their case to the floor of the convention, a prospect that greatly displeased the President. Johnson then sent Senator Hubert Humphrey to Atlantic City to act as his agent in settling the contro-versy. Unsubstantiated rumors had it that if Humphrey's mission failed, the President would deny the Senator the party's vice-presidential nomination. In close touch with both the White House and the credentials committee, Humphrey proposed altering the original compromise by permitting two FDP delegates to sit in the convention as delegates at large with full voting rights. This was as far as Johnson would go, and at the time it seemed far enough. Though the Mississippi white regulars walked out, no Southern delegations followed them, and, at the same time, most liberals felt that the Administration had made a genuine concession. Black leaders, including Dr. King, pleaded with the FDP to accept Humphrey's compromise. But the FDP denied that the compromise was in any sense a victory.[25] Angered at Humphrey's insistence that he alone choose the two at-large delegates, the FDP announced that it had not come to Atlantic City "begging for crumbs."[26] Mrs. Hamer, by now a minor national celebrity, said of Humphrey's efforts,

---

[24] Holt, *The Summer That Didn't End,* Chapter 8; Zinn, *SNCC,* p. 251.

[25] Holt, *The Summer That Didn't End,* pp. 16–17; Watters and Cleghorn, *Climbing Jacob's Ladder,* pp. 290–92; *New York Times* (Aug. 25, 1964), 23.

[26] William McCord, *Mississippi: The Long Hot Summer* (Norton, 1965), p. 117.

"It's a token of rights on the back row that we get in Mississippi. We didn't come all this way for that mess again."[27]

To the general public the FDP appeared to be a band of moral zealots hostile to reasonable compromise and ungrateful for the real concession that the party had offered. The true story was more complicated. Aware that total victory was impossible, the FDP had in fact been quite willing to accept any proposal that recognized its legitimacy. At the beginning of the controversy Oregon's Congresswoman Edith Green offered a compromise that the FDP found entirely acceptable. Mrs. Green proposed that the convention seat every member of both delegations who signed a pledge of loyalty and that Mississippi's vote be divided between the two groups according to the number of seated delegates in each. Since only eleven members of the credentials committee (10 percent of the total) had to sign a minority report to dislodge the Green compromise from committee, the FDP seemed assured that its case would reach the convention floor, where many believed that the Green compromise would prevail over Johnson's original proposal. FDP's hopes for a minority report rested chiefly on Joseph Rauh, a member of the credentials committee, leader of the Democratic party in the District of Columbia, veteran of innumerable liberal crusades, and, happily, adviser and legal counsel of the FDP. But Rauh was also a friend of Hubert Humphrey and an attorney for Humphrey's strong supporter, Walter Reuther. After Humphrey came on the scene with his compromise, Rauh backed away from the minority report.

In his semi-official history of the Mississippi Summer Project, *The Summer That Didn't End,* Len Holt presents the FDP and SNCC interpretation of what happened. Presumably pressured by his powerful friends, Rauh broke a promise to the FDP and would not support the Green compromise. One by one the FDP's other allies on the committee backed away —some to protect jobs, others to keep alive hopes for federal judgeships, and one because he feared the loss of a local antipoverty program. In the end the FDP failed to collect the needed signatures, and there was no minority report. The angry rhetoric that the FDP delegates let loose in Atlantic City was in reality inspired less by Humphrey's compromise than by what the FDP regarded as its betrayal at the hands of the white liberals on the credentials committee. By the end of the Democratic convention SNCC was convinced that membership in the Democratic coalition held little hope for Southern blacks and that, lacking power, they would always be sold out by the liberals. In Atlantic City the phrase "white power structure" took on concrete meaning. Freedom Summer, which began with SNCC fighting for entrance into the American political system, ended with the radical conviction that that system was beyond redemption.[28]

[27] Mrs. Hamer is quoted in Holt, *The Summer That Didn't End,* p. 174.

[28] *New York Times* (Aug. 25, 1964), 23; Holt, *The Summer That Didn't End,* pp. 171–78; see also Zinn, *SNCC,* pp. 251–56; and Stoper, "The Student Nonviolent Coordinating Committee," pp. 74, 77–79, 81.

In the end the Freedom Summer Project of 1964 not only destroyed SNCC's faith in the American political system; it also undermined its commitment to integration. Within the project racial tensions between white and black workers were never successfully resolved. Though many white volunteers established warm relationships with the local black families that housed them,[29] healthy communication between students and veteran SNCC workers proved difficult at best. Staff members resented the officious manner of better-educated volunteers and feared that the white students were taking over the movement. "Several times," one volunteer wrote, "I've had to completely re-do press statements or letters written by one of them."[30] Said a SNCC worker, "Look at those fly-by-night freedom fighters bossing everybody around."[31] SNCC people found it hard to respect the efforts of volunteers who they knew would retreat at the end of the summer to their safe middle-class world. One sensitive white female volunteer wrote that SNCC workers "were automatically suspicious of us, the white volunteers; throughout the summer they put us to the test, and few, if any, could pass. . . . It humbled, if not humiliated, one to realize that *finally they will never accept me.*"[32] By the end of the summer a spirit akin to black nationalism was rising inside the SNCC organization.

The overall failure of Freedom Summer administered a blow to SNCC's morale from which the organization almost did not recover. In November 1964, Robert Coles, a psychiatrist who had worked closely with SNCC, wrote about the tendency of veteran workers to develop battle fatigue. Even heroic temperaments, he said, could not escape the depression that inevitably results from long periods of unremitting dangers and disappointments. But by the fall of 1964 battle fatigue was no longer just the problem of individual SNCC members; it was pervading the entire organization. One patient told Coles,

*I'm tired, but so is the whole movement. We're busy worrying about our position or our finances, so we don't do anything. . . . We're becoming lifeless, just like all revolutions when they lose their first momentum and become more interested in preserving what they've won than going on to new challenges. . . . Only with us we haven't won that much, and we're either holding to the little we have as an organization, or we get bitter, and want to create a new revolution. . . . You know, one like the Muslims want which is the opposite of what we say we're for. It's as if we completely reverse ourselves because we can't get what we want.*[33]

[29] See, for instance, Sutherland, *Letters from Mississippi,* p. 48.

[30] Quoted in *ibid.,* p. 202.

[31] Quoted in Pat Watters, *Encounter with the Future* (Southern Regional Council, May, 1965), p. 32.

[32] Belfrage, *Freedom Summer,* p. 80.

[33] Robert Coles, "Social Struggle and Awareness," *Psychiatry,* XXVII (Nov., 1964), 305–15.

Uncertain of their purpose, SNCC workers in the winter of 1964–65 grew introspective. Months were consumed in discussing the future of whites in the movement and the proper structure of the organization. Fresh from a trip to Africa where he met the black nationalist Malcolm X, John Lewis, Chairman of SNCC, spoke for the majority in early 1965 when he demanded that blacks lead their own movement.[34] At the same time, quarrels over organization almost tore SNCC apart. Some workers became "high on freedom" and advocated a romantic anarchism that rejected bureaucratic structure and leadership. Robert Moses, for instance, believed that SNCC workers should "go where the spirit say go, and do what the spirit say do." Moses was so disturbed by his own prestige in the movement that he changed his name, drifted into Alabama, and thereafter was only vaguely connected with SNCC. Meanwhile SNCC's field work tended to fall into neglect.[35]

In the summer of 1965 SNCC brought 300 white volunteers into Mississippi for its second and last summer project. The result was a shambles. Racial tensions caused some projects to break up and prevented serious work in others. Problems only dimly perceived a year before assumed stark clarity, and SNCC's resentment of the volunteers became overt and unambiguous. At staff meetings blacks would silence students with such remarks as "How long have you been here?" and "How do you know what it's like being black?" and "if you don't like the way we do it, get the hell out of the state."[36] Not all the blame for the final breakdown of race relations in SNCC, however, belonged to the black staff. The questionable motivation of some of the white students led Alvin Poussaint, a black psychiatrist close to SNCC, to add a new neurosis to medical terminology—the white African Queen or Tarzan complex. The victim of this neurosis harbored repressed delusions of himself as an "intelligent, brave, and handsome white man or woman, leading the poor down-trodden and oppressed black men to freedom and salvation.[37]

But the most serious obstacle to healthy race relations inside SNCC was sex, and in this dimension, as really in all others, the villain was neither black worker nor white student, but rather the sad and twisted history of race relations in America. The white girl who came South to help SNCC found herself, according to Dr. Poussaint, "at the center of an emotionally

[34] Watters, *Encounter with the Future*, pp. 29–31; see also Lerone Bennett, Jr., "SNCC, Rebels with a Cause," *Ebony*, XX (July, 1965), 146–53.

[35] For the Moses quote, see Gene Roberts, "From Freedom High to 'Black Power,'" *New York Times Magazine* (Sept. 25, 1966), 21; see also Bruce Payne, "The Student Nonviolent Coordinating Committee: An Overview Two Years Later," *The Activist* (Nov., 1965), 6–7; and Stoper, "Student Nonviolent Coordinating Committee," pp. 126–27.

[36] These quotations are from transcripts of informal taped interviews conducted in the South in 1965 by students of Stanford University. The tapes are stored at Stanford.

[37] Alvin F. Poussaint, "Problems of White Civil Rights Workers in the South," *Psychiatric Opinion*, III (Dec., 1966), 21.

shattering crossfire of racial tensions that have been nurtured for centuries."[38] In the summer of 1965 a veteran black civil rights worker in SCLC tried to warn white girls of the perils that awaited them in their dealings with black men in the movement:

*What you have here is a man who had no possible way of being a man in the society in which he lives, save one. And that's the problem. The only way or place a Negro man has been able to express his manhood is sexually and so you find a tremendous sexual aggressiveness. And I say quite frankly, don't get carried away by it and don't get afraid of it either. I mean, don't think it's because you're so beautiful and so ravishing that this man is so enamoured of you. It's not that at all. He's just trying to find his manhood and he goes especially to the places that have robbed him of it. . . . And so, in a sense, what passes itself as desire is probably a combination of hostility and resentment—because he resents what the society has done to him and he wants to take it out on somebody who symbolizes the establishment of society.*[39]

At the end of the summer a white girl spoke of her experiences:

*Well, I think that the white female should be very well prepared before she comes down here to be bombarded. And she also has to be well prepared to tell them to go to hell and be prepared to have them not give up. . . . I've never met such forward men as I have in Mississippi.*[40]

The problem was complicated by the jealousy of black girls toward their white rivals, and by neurotic whites who sought to ease their guilt by permitting blacks to exploit them sexually and financially.[41] On leaving their projects to go home, a few white girls told Poussaint, "I hate Negroes."[42] By the end of the summer of 1965 no one could any longer doubt that the blacks reciprocated the feeling.

The year 1965 was a lost one for SNCC. For the first time since its founding, it was no longer on the frontier of protest, no longer the keeper of the nation's conscience, no longer the driving force of a moral revolution. The civil rights acts of 1964 and 1965 brought the civil rights movement, for which SNCC had suffered so much, to a triumphant conclusion, but SNCC had lost interest in integrated public accommodations and equal political rights. SNCC seemed to be losing its sense of mission and after years of providing heroes for the black protest movement, it now needed

[38] Alvin F. Poussaint, "The Stresses of the White Female Worker in the Civil Rights Movement in the South," *American Journal of Psychiatry*, CXXIII (Oct., 1966), 401.

[39] Taped by Stanford students in 1965.

[40] *Ibid.*

[41] Poussaint, "Problems of White Civil Rights Workers in the South," 20–21.

[42] Poussaint, "Stresses of the White Female Worker," 404.

a hero of its own. Significantly it chose Malcolm X, the black nationalist who had been assassinated by Muslim rivals in February 1965.[43] Only a few years before, SNCC and Malcolm X had seemed to occupy opposite poles of black protest. Thus while SNCC's John Lewis was toning down his speech at the March on Washington, Malcolm X was saying,

*Who ever heard of angry revolutionists all harmonizing "We Shall Overcome . . . Suum Day . . ." while tripping and swaying along arm-in-arm with the very people they were supposed to be angrily revolting against? Who ever heard of angry revolutionists swinging their bare feet together with their oppressors in lily-pad park pools, with gospels and guitars and "I Have a Dream" speeches?[44]*

While policemen were clubbing SNCC workers in Mississippi, Malcolm X was saying, "If someone puts a hand on you, send him to the cemetery."[45] While SNCC was pondering the meaning of Atlantic City, Malcolm X was saying, "We *need* a Mau Mau. If they don't want to deal with the Mississippi Freedom Democratic Party, then we'll give them something else to deal with." While black nationalists were still a minority in SNCC, Malcolm X was calling for black control of black politicians in black communities, black ownership of ghetto businesses, and black unity "to lift the level of our community, to make our society beautiful so that we will be satisfied in our own social circles and won't be running around here trying to knock our way into a social circle where we're not wanted."[46] This was the language that had made Malcolm X the hero of the urban ghetto, and it was the language appropriate in 1965 to SNCC's militant mood. In a certain sense Malcolm X was the link that connected SNCC with the black radicalism that was arising in the North.

Unlike SNCC, the ghetto masses never had to disabuse themselves of the colorblind assumptions of the civil rights movement. Trapped permanently in their neighborhoods, the poor blacks of the North have always been painfully conscious of their racial separateness. As Essien-Udom, a historian of black nationalism, has written, blackness "is the stuff of their lives and an omnipresent, harsh reality. For this reason the Negro masses are instinctively 'race men.' "[47] But the civil rights movement nevertheless had its consequences in the ghetto. The spectacle of Southern blacks defying their white tormentors apparently inspired among Northern blacks race pride and resurgent outrage at the gap between American ideals and black

[43] On influence of Malcolm X on SNCC, see Stoper, "The Student Nonviolent Coordinating Committee," p. 181.

[44] *The Autobiography of Malcolm X* (Grove, 1966), pp. 280–81.

[45] *Malcolm X Speaks: Selected Speeches and Statements* (Merit, 1965), p. 12.

[46] *Ibid.,* 38–39.

[47] E. U. Essien-Udom, *Black Nationalism* (University of Chicago Press, 1962), p. 3.

realities. Thus the civil rights movement had the ironic effect of feeding the nationalist tendency in the ghetto to turn inward, to separate, and to identify the white men outside as the enemy. SNCC's frustrations exploded intellectually in the formulation of black power doctrines, but ghetto rage took the form of riot.

The riot of August 1965, in Watts (the sprawling ghetto of Los Angeles) dwarfed the violent outbursts of the previous year and awakened America to the race crisis in her big cities. A social trauma of the first order, the Watts riot resulted in 35 deaths, 600 burned and looted buildings, and 4,000 persons arrested.[48] Above all it revealed the dangerous racial hatred that had been accumulating unnoticed in the nation's black ghettos. The official autopsy of Watts denied by implication that it was a revolt against white oppression. The McCone Commission (after its chairman, John McCone), appointed by California's Governor Pat Brown to investigate the riot, estimated that only 10,000 Watts residents, or two percent of the population in the riot area, had actually been on the streets during the uprising. This minor fraction, the Commission contended, was not protesting specific grievances, which admittedly existed in abundance, but was engaged in an "insensate rage of destruction" that was "formless, quite senseless."[49] Critics of the McCone report have ably challenged these findings. (For example, Robert Fogelson points out that "to claim that only 10,000 Negroes rioted when about 4,000 were arrested is to presume that the police apprehended fully forty percent of the rioters.")[50] In reality, a rather large minority of the riot-age population in Watts was on the streets during the riot, and as one of the Commission's own staff reports revealed, the riot had significant support inside the ghetto, especially in the worst slum areas.[51]

On the crucial question of the riot's causes, observers on the scene agreed that the rioters were animated by a common anger against whites.[52] Robert Blauner, a staff member of the McCone Commission and its severest critic, has written,

*Most of the actions of the rioters appear to have been informed by the desire to clear out an alien presence, white men, rather than to kill them. . . . It was primarily an attack on property, particularly white-owned businesses.*

[48] A Report by the Governor's Commission on the Los Angeles Riot, *Violence in the City—An End or a Beginning?* (Dec. 2, 1965), pp. 1–2. (Referred to hereafter as the McCone Report.)

[49] McCone Report, pp. 1, 4–5.

[50] Robert M. Fogelson, "White on Black: A Critique of the McCone Commission Report on the Los Angeles Riots," *Political Science Quarterly*, LXXXII (September, 1967), 345.

[51] E. Edward Ransford, *Attitudes and Other Characteristics of Negroes in Watts, South Central, and Crenshaw Areas of Los Angeles* (a staff study prepared for the McCone Commission), p. 2.

[52] See, for instance, Robert Conot, *Rivers of Blood, Years of Darkness* (Bantam Books, 1967), p. 204.

*. . . The spirit of the Watts rioters appears similar to that of anti-colonial crowds demonstrating against foreign masters.*[53]

Said Bayard Rustin, a moderate black intellectual who was in Watts during the riot, "The whole point of the outbursts in Watts was that it marked the first major rebellion of Negroes against their masochism and was carried on with the express purpose of asserting that they would no longer quietly submit to the deprivation of slum life."[54] Thus in 1965, for different reasons, both the ghetto masses and the members of SNCC were seized by militant anti-white feelings, and it was this congruence of mood that would shortly permit SNCC to appeal to a nation-wide black audience.

After a year on the periphery of the black protest movement, SNCC in 1966 moved again to the forefront. In May 1966, at a time when the organization was apparently disintegrating, 135 staff members (twenty-five of them white) met in Nashville to thrash out their future. Early in the emotional conference, by a vote of sixty to twenty-two, John Lewis, the gentle advocate of nonviolence, retained the chairmanship of SNCC by defeating the challenge of the militant Stokely Carmichael. But as the conference went on, the arguments of the militants began to prevail. When the staff voted to boycott the coming White House conference on civil rights, Lewis announced that he would attend anyway, and the question of the chairmanship was then reopened. This time SNCC workers chose Carmichael as their new leader by a vote of sixty to twelve. The conference next issued a statement calling, among other things, for "black Americans to begin building independent political, economic, and cultural institutions that they will control and use as instruments of social change in this country."[55]

A few weeks later the full meaning of Carmichael's election became clear to the whole nation. The occasion was the famous Meredith march through Mississippi in June of 1966. James Meredith, the man who integrated the University of Mississippi in 1962 with the help of the United States Army, embarked on a 200-mile walk from Memphis to Jackson to show the black people of Mississippi that they could walk to the voting booths without fear. On June 6, twenty-eight miles out of Memphis, a white man felled Meredith with buckshot. Erroneously believing that Meredith had been killed, civil rights leaders immediately flew to Mississippi to continue his walk against fear. So it was that arm in arm, Martin Luther King of SCLC, Floyd McKissick of CORE, and Stokely Carmichael of SNCC marched down U.S. Highway 51.

Early efforts of the three leaders to maintain surface unity rapidly

[53] Quoted in Robert Blauner, "Whitewash over Watts: The Failure of the McCone Commission Report," *Transaction*, III (March–April, 1966), 9.

[54] Bayard Rustin, "The Watts 'Manifesto' and the McCone Report," *Commentary*, XLI (March, 1966), 30.

[55] This account of Carmichael's election and the quotations from SNCC's statement are from Newfield, *A Prophetic Minority*, pp. 75–77.

broke down. Significantly, the first issue that divided them was the role of white people in the Meredith march. King's workers publicly thanked Northern whites for joining the procession. McKissick also thanked the Northerners but announced that black men must now lead the civil rights movement. And Carmichael mused aloud that maybe the whites should go home. As the column moved onto the back roads and Southern white hostility increased, the leadership of the march failed to agree on how to respond to violence. In Philadelphia, Mississippi, Dr. King conducted a memorial service for Goodman, Chaney, and Schwerner and told a crowd of 300 jeering whites that the murderers of the three men were no doubt "somewhere around me at this moment." Declaring that "I am not afraid of any man," King then delivered a Christian sermon. But after the service was over and local whites got rough, the marchers returned punch for punch.

The real spokesman for the march, it soon developed, was not King but Stokely Carmichael. In one town, after spending a few hours in jail, Carmichael told a crowd, 'I ain't going to jail no more. I ain't going to jail no more," and he announced, "Every courthouse in Mississippi ought to be burned down to get rid of the dirt." Carmichael then issued the cry that would make him famous. Five times he shouted "Black Power!" and the *New York Times* reported, "each time the younger members of the audience shouted back, 'Black Power.'" Informed of this new slogan, Dr. King expressed disapproval, and SCLC workers exhorted crowds to call not for black power but for "freedom now." Nevertheless, by the end of the Meredith march, black power had become a force to reckon with.[56]

At its inception in June, 1966, black power was not a systematic doctrine but a cry of rage. In an article in the *New York Times Magazine*, Dr. Poussaint tried to explain the psychological origin of the anger expressed in the new slogan:

I remember treating Negro workers after they had been beaten viciously by white toughs or policemen while conducting civil rights demonstrations. I would frequently comment, "You must feel pretty angry getting beaten up like that by those bigots." Often I received a reply such as: "No, I don't hate those white men, I love them because they must really be suffering with all that hatred in their souls. Dr. King says the only way we can win our freedom is through love. Anger and hatred has never solved anything."

I used to sit there and wonder, "Now, what do they really do with their rage?"

Poussaint reported that after a while these workers vented their mounting rage against each other.

While they were talking about being nonviolent and "loving" the sheriff that just hit them over the head, they rampaged around the project houses

[56] For the Meredith march, see *New York Times*, June 7, 1966, p. 1; June 8, pp. 1 and 26; June 9, p. 1; June 12, pp. 1 and 82; June 17, p. 1; June 21, p. 30; June 22, p. 25.

*beating up each other. I frequently had to calm Negro civil rights workers
with large doses of tranquilizers for what I can describe clinically only as
acute attacks of rage.*

In time the civil rights workers began to direct their anger against white
racists, the Federal Government, and finally white people in the movement.
Said Poussaint:

*This rage was at a fever pitch for many months, before it became crystallized
in the "Black Power" slogan. The workers who shouted it the loudest were
those with the oldest battle scars from the terror, demoralization, and castration which they experienced through continual direct confrontation with
Southern white racists. Furthermore, some of the most bellicose chanters of
the slogan had been, just a few years before, examples of nonviolent, loving
passive resistance in their struggle against white supremacy. These workers
appeared to be seeking a sense of inner psychological emancipation from
racists through self-assertion and release of aggressive angry feelings.*[57]

In the months following the Meredith march, SNCC found itself at
the center of a bitter national controversy and spokesman for an enlarged
constituency. The anger implicit in the slogan "black power" assured SNCC
a following in the ghettos of the North and ended its regional confinement.
Through its leader, Stokely Carmichael, SNCC labored through 1966 and
into 1967 to give intellectual substance to the black power slogan, seeking
especially to frame an analysis that would be relevant to black Americans
of all sections. Although his speeches were often inflammatory, Carmichael
in his writings attempted serious, even restrained, argument suitable for
an educated audience. But the elements of black power were not, in truth,
derived from rational reflection but from wretched experience—from the
beatings, jailhouses, and abortive crusades that SNCC veterans had endured
for six years. SNCC had tried nonviolence and found it psychologically
destructive. (The "days of the free head-whipping are over," Carmichael
and his collaborator Charles Hamilton wrote. "Black people should and
must fight back."[58]) SNCC, for example, had believed in integration and tried
it within its own organization, but black and white together had not
worked. (Integration, said Carmichael, "is a subterfuge for the maintenance
of white supremacy" and "reinforces, among both black and white, the
idea that 'white' is automatically better and 'black' is by definition inferior."[59]) SNCC had allied with white liberals in the Democratic party and
had come away convinced that it had been betrayed. (In dealing with
blacks, Carmichael said, white liberals "perpetuate a paternalistic, colonial

---

[57] Alvin F. Poussaint, "A Negro Psychiatrist Explains the Negro Psyche," *New York Times
Magazine* (Aug. 20, 1967), 55 ff.

[58] Stokely Carmichael and Charles V. Hamilton, *Black Power: The Politics of Liberation*
(Vintage, 1967), p. 52.

[59] Stokely Carmichael, "What We Want," *New York Review of Books* (Sept. 22, 1966), 6.

relationship."[60]) SNCC had struggled for equal political rights but concluded finally that political inequality was less oppressive than economic exploitation. In 1966 SNCC felt it was necessary to go beyond the assertion of these hard conclusions and to attempt to impose on them systematic form. So it was that after years of activism divorced from ideology, SNCC began to reduce its field work and concentrate on fashioning an intellectual rationale for its new militancy. At a time when the black protest movement was floundering and its future direction was uncertain, SNCC stepped forward to contribute the doctrines of black power, which were really the culmination of its career. No history of SNCC would be complete, therefore, without some consideration of those doctrines.

According to Stokely Carmichael, the black masses suffer from two different but reinforcing forms of oppression: class exploitation and white racism. To illustrate this point, he relies on an analogy apparently inspired by Franz Fanon's *Wretched of the Earth,* a book with considerable influence in black power circles. The black communities of contemporary America, Carmichael says, share many of the characteristics of African colonies under European rule. Thus as Africa once enriched its imperialist masters by exporting valuable raw materials to Europe, so now do the American ghettos "export" their labor for the profit of American capitalists. In both Africa and America, white men own local businesses and use them to drain away any wealth somehow possessed by the subject population. As in Africa, there exists in the ghetto a white power structure that is no abstraction, but is a visible and concrete presence—the white landlords, for instance, who collect rent and ignore needed repairs, the city agencies and school systems that systematically neglect black people, the policemen who abuse black citizens and collect payoffs from white racketeers. By far the most insidious method devised by the white imperialists for perpetuating class exploitation has been the use of race as a badge of inferiority. Colonial masters, says Carmichael, "purposely, maliciously, and with reckless abandon relegated the black man to a subordinated, inferior status in society. . . . White America's School for Slavery and Segregation, like the School of Colonialism, has taught the subject to hate himself and deny his humanity." As the colonies of Africa have done, black Americans must undergo "political modernization," liberate their communities, and achieve self-determination. And like Africa, the ghetto must win the struggle by its own effort.[61]

For Carmichael, liberation begins with eradication of the effects of white racism. To overcome the shame of race bred in them by white men, blacks must develop a cultural identity, rediscover the rich African civilization from which they originally came, and learn from their history that they are a "vibrant, valiant people."[62] Freed of their damaging self-image, they

[60] Carmichael and Hamilton, *Black Power,* p. 65.

[61] For the colonial analogy, see *ibid.,* Chapter 1.

[62] *Ibid.,* pp. 37–39.

can begin to challenge the capitalist values that have enslaved them as a class. The white middle class, says Carmichael, has fostered esteem for "material aggrandizement," is "without a viable conscience as regards humanity," and constitutes "the backbone of institutional reason in this country." Black men, however, will develop values emphasizing "the dignity of man, not . . . the sanctity of property," "free people," not "free enterprise."[63] "The society we seek to build among black people, then, is not a capitalist one. It is a society in which the spirit of community and humanistic love prevail."[64] To complete the process of liberation, black men will have to purge the ghetto of exploiting institutions and develop structures that conform to their new values.

The reconstruction of the black community, Carmichael contends, should be in the hands of black people in order to "convey the revolutionary idea . . . that black people are able to do things themselves." Among other acts of liberation that they can perform, ghetto blacks should conduct rent strikes against slum landlords and boycotts against the ghetto merchant who refuses to " 'invest' say forty to fifty percent of his net profit in the indigenous community." Governmental structures that have violated the humanity of blacks will have to be either eliminated from the ghetto or made responsive to their black constituency. The school system must be taken from professionals, most of whom have demonstrated "insensitivity to the needs and problems of the black child" and given to black parents, who will control personnel and curriculum. The indifference of the existing political parties to black people necessitates formation of separate (parallel) black organizations, both in the 110 Southern counties with black majorities and in the ghettos of the North.[65] According to Carmichael, it is simply naive to think that poor and powerless blacks have anything in common with the other components of the Democratic coalition. White liberals inevitably fall under the "overpowering influence" of their racist environment, and their demands for civil rights are "doing for blacks." Labor unions accept the existing order and, in the case of the AFL, even discriminate against black workers. Black political parties, Carmichael believes, will alone be devoted to real change and will in fact make possible emancipation from dominant American values and power centers.[66]

Carmichael professes to believe that black power is not really a departure from American practice. "Traditionally," he writes, "for each new ethnic group, the route to social and political integration into America's pluralistic society has been through the organization of their own institutions with which to represent their communal needs within the larger

---

[63] Ibid., pp. 40–4.

[64] Carmichael, "What We Want," 7.

[65] Carmichael and Hamilton, Black Power, Chapter 8 and p. 166.

[66] Ibid., pp. 60–66.

society."[67] Once in possession of power, blacks then could reenter the old coalitions for specific goals. But "let any ghetto group contemplating coalition be so tightly organized, so strong, that . . . it is an 'undigestible body' which cannot be absorbed or swallowed up." Given Carmichael's scheme for a radical reconstruction of American society, it is not surprising that the only group that he someday hopes to make his allay is the poor whites.[68]

As several critics have pointed out,[69] Carmichael's version of black power is hardly more than a collection of fragments, often lacking in clarity, consistency, and conviction. Thus, for example, Carmichael talks about the need for parallel institutions but offers only one example—black political organizations. He claims that these organizations can regenerate the entire political system but typically neglects to explain concretely how this regeneration is to be achieved. He calls for radical rejection of American values and institutions but at the same time portrays the black community as merely another ethnic group turning temporarily inward to prepare for later integration into American society. According to Carmichael, ghetto blacks are an exploited proletariat kept in bondage to enrich America's capitalist class; yet black workers seem more like a *lumpenproletariat* threatened with loss of economic function and forced to the margin of the American economy. Carmichael fails to reveal the mechanisms by which big business keeps the black man exploited, and indeed it seems doubtful that big business especially profits from the depressed condition of such a large group of potential consumers. But the real criticism of black power is not that as a body of thought it lacks coherence and sustained argument. Its greatest weakness is its failure to propose adequate solutions.

Carmichael began his argument by maintaining that black men suffer from two separate but related forms of discrimination—racial and economic. When Carmichael proposes ways for black men to undo the effects of racism, he makes good sense. Certainly black men should uncover their cultural roots and take pride in what has been of worth in their heritage. Certainly liberal paternalism is now anachronistic and black men should lead their own organizations. Nonviolence probably *was* psychologically damaging to many who practiced it, and integration into a hostile white society is not only an unrealistic goal but demeaning to a self-respecting people. Furthermore, some middle-class values, as Carmichael maintains, are less than ennobling, and elements of the black man's life style do have intrinsic merit. But it is doubtful whether black self-respect can ever be achieved without a solution of the second problem confronting ghetto

[67] Stokely Carmichael, "Toward Black Liberation," *The Massachusetts Review*, VII (Autumn, 1966), 642.

[68] Carmichael and Hamilton, *Black Power*, pp. 80, 82.

[69] For critiques of black power, see, for instance, Paul Feldman, "The Pathos of 'Black Power,'" *Dissent* (Jan.–Feb., 1967), 69–79; Bayard Rustin, "'Black Power' and Coalition Politics," *Commentary*, XLII (Sept., 1966), 35–40; Christopher Lasch, "The Trouble with Black Power," *New York Review of Books*, X (Feb. 29, 1968), 4 ff.

blacks, and it is here that Carmichael's version of black power is most deficient.

Concerned primarily with humanizing social and governmental structures inside the ghetto, Carmichael has little to say about ending poverty in black America. Although more responsive policemen and schoolteachers and less dishonest slum lords and merchants will no doubt be a great step forward, these aspects of ghetto life are of less consequence than unemployment or poverty wages. Within the ghetto the resources for economic reconstruction are simply not available, and since Carmichael rejects coalitions outside the ghetto, he is barred from offering a realistic economic strategy. It is this weakness that led the black intellectual and long-time civil rights leader Bayard Rustin to oppose black power. Pointing to the futility of separatist politics in a society in which the black man is a minority, Rustin calls for "a liberal-labor-civil rights coalition which would work to make the Democratic party truly responsive to the aspirations of the poor, and which would develop support for programs (specifically those outlined in A. Philip Randolph's $100 billion Freedom Budget) aimed at the reconstruction of American society in the interest of greater social justice."[70] Rustin's goals are considerably less apocalyptic than Carmichael's, but they are far more realistic. Carmichael's radical ruminations about a socialist alliance of poor whites and poor blacks seem fantasies irrelevant to American social realities. Although Carmichael's vision holds out hope for some distant time, it offers no meaningful proposals for the present.

The true significance of black power lies not in the doctrines into which it evolved but in the historical circumstances that gave it birth. The real message of black power is that after years of struggle to make America an open and just society, an important group of civil rights workers, instructed by the brute facts of its own history, gave up the fight. Black power was a cry of rage directed against white bigots who overcame righteous men by force, a cry of bitterness against white liberals who had only a stunted comprehension of the plight of the black poor, and a cry of frustration against gains that seemed meager when compared to needs. It is possible, however, that even rage can perform a useful function, and if the black power slogan brings about a constructive catharsis and helps rouse the black masses from apathy, then the intellectual shortcomings of black power doctrines may seem of little consequence, and what began as a cry of despair may yet play a creative role in the black protest movement. Therefore, whether the history of SNCC in this decade will be considered triumph or tragedy depends on events yet to occur.

---

[70] Bayard Rustin, " 'Black Power' and Coalition Politics," 36.

# 32

LETTER FROM OAKLAND: THE PANTHERS
*Ronald Steel*

I WENT to Oakland, dead end of the westward course of empire, and home of the Black Panthers, to take a look at a conference of the revolutionary Left. Oakland, where the American dream ends at the Pacific, and the nightmare begins, is a familiar kind of industrial city: high-rise office buildings and apartments downtown, plasticene shopping centers on the fringe, and slowly decaying wooden houses in between. West Oakland, facing the Bay and the gleaming hills of San Francisco beyond, is the ghetto where the Black Panthers were born. It is a California-style ghetto, with one-family houses and neglected yards, where poverty wears a more casual face and despair is masked by sunshine.

The Panthers in July [1969] summoned their friends—a mixed bag of revolutionaries, radicals, pacifists, and liberals—to assemble in Oakland to form what they called a "united front against fascism." The phrase itself had a defensive ring, reminiscent of the ill-fated Popular Fronts of the 1930s, and it seemed to indicate that the Panthers were in trouble. White radicals, few of whom were consulted about the agenda, privately expressed doubts about the usefulness of such a conference, and many SDS chapters did not send representatives. As it turned out, they would not have had much of a role to play anyway, since the Panthers were very much running their own show and not accepting criticism from those who came to hear them.

Like so many other gatherings of the radical Left, the conference produced little unity but a great deal of dissatisfaction. Most of the sessions were disorganized and, with a few exceptions, the speeches were little more than an interminable series of spot announcements denouncing the evils of rampant fascism. No one seemed interested in discussing whether fascism had indeed arrived in America. This, like so much of the other rhetoric of the revolutionary Left, was simply taken for granted.

When the three-day conference finally rambled to an end, the dwindling band of white radicals dirfted away in dismay, wondering what kind of bag the Panthers had got themselves into. The more militant radicals from Berkeley feared that the Panthers had turned reformist, while socialists and Trotskyites complained about their dictatorial methods. The "united front," whose creation was the ostensible purpose of the conference, had not been formed and most participants expressed doubts that it ever would be. The general consensus was that the Panthers didn't have a very clear idea of what they were up to. They wanted to enlist allies, and they hoped that some kind of united front would develop. But they had no real plan worked out, and certainly no intention of letting anyone else supply one.

From Ronald Steel, "Letter from Oakland: The Panthers," *The New York Review of Books*, XIII (September 1969), 14–23. Reprinted with permission from *The New York Review of Books*. Copyright © 1969 The New York Review.

Why did the Panthers call such a conference in the first place? At least in part because they have been under increasing harassment and intimidation by the police and the FBI. During the past few months more than forty leaders and 100 members have been arrested, and some of them are now facing life imprisonment or the death penalty. The party's founder and chief theorist, twenty-seven-year-old Huey P. Newton, is serving a fourteen-year sentence for allegedly shooting an Oakland policeman. Its most articulate spokesman, Eldridge Cleaver, has chosen to go into exile rather than return to prison on dubious charges of parole violation. Its treasurer, seventeen-year-old Bobby Hutton, was killed by police during last year's Oakland shootout. And its acting chairman, Bobby Seale, is under federal indictment for conspiring to incite a riot at last year's Democratic convention, although he was not a member of any of the organizations sponsoring the protests and spent less than a day in Chicago. . . .

The Panthers are absolutely serious when they talk of the need for "socialism"; and this is what distinguishes them from the other black militant and black power groups. They see themselves as "revolutionary nationalists," who seek black pride in separatist movements, religious cults, and emulation of ancient African culture. "The revolutionary nationalist," according to Huey Newton, "sees that there is no hope for cultural or individual expression, or even hope that his people can exist as a unique entity in a complex whole as long as the bureaucratic capitalist is in control." On the other hand: "cultural nationalism," explained David Hilliard, "is basically related to the physiological need for a return back to Africa in the culture, and we don't see that that is really relevant to any revolution, because culture never frees anyone. As Fanon says, the only culture is that of the revolution."

The reference to Fanon is instructive, for the Panthers, as can readily be seen from the writings of Huey Newton and Eldridge Cleaver, have been deeply influenced by the black psychiatrist from Martinique who died in the service of the Algerian revolution. *The Wretched of the Earth* is a kind of revolutionary Bible for them, and one with far more emotional impact than the Little Red Books which are so often quoted. Both Newton and Cleaver, freely acknowledging their debt to Fanon, have described black people as forming an oppressed colony within the white mother country, the United States. The colony is kept in line by an occupying army—white policemen who live outside the ghetto—and is exploited by businessmen and politicians.

The exploiters can be black as well as white, for the enemy, they insist, is not so much racism as capitalism, which creates and nourishes it. As would be expected of socialist revolutionaries, the Panthers are opposed to black capitalism, which Huey Newton has described as a "giant stride *away* from liberation . . ." since ". . . the rules of black capitalism, and the limits of black capitalism are set by the white power structure." Explaining his opposition, Newton has written:

*There can be no real black capitalism because no blacks control the means of production. All blacks can do is have illusions. They can dream of the day when they might share ownership of the means of production. But there is no free enterprise in America. We have monopoly capitalism which is a closed society of white industrialists and their protectors, white politicians in Washington.*

According to the Panthers, black power has been absorbed into the establishment, shorn of its horns, and transformed into innocent black capitalism, which even Richard Nixon can praise because it poses no threat to the white power structure.

As an alternative they offer "revolution," to liberate oppressed minorities in the United States and break the stranglehold of capitalism on the economically underdeveloped countries of the Third World. Until there is some form of socialist "revolution" in America, they believe, small countries will remain prey to neo-colonialism and imperialism. The revolutionary in America, therefore, carries the world upon his shoulders. The black man in America will not be free until the white man is free, and until the white man is free, until America is transformed by a socialist revolution, the underdeveloped countries of the world will remain in economic chains.

Such a comprehensive theory clearly has its inadequacies. Although blacks can be described as forming an internal colony within the United States, they do not supply raw materials, labor, or markets to capitalism in the same way as the colonies did. There is, moreover, no evidence at present that the US is entering a revolutionary crisis that will involve the mass of workers. Nor can the Panthers have much success in breaking away into a separate state. What happens, as has been asked, when there's a border dispute? (It is not fair, however, to charge the Panthers with advocating political separatism. They claim neither to favor it nor to discourage it; they simply demand that a UN-supervised plebescite be held on the issue in the black colony. In any case, this is not an immediate problem, and certainly not a major objective for them.)

The Panthers' Marxist-Leninist language, combined with their Fanonist theories of psychological alienation and Third World solidarity, makes them particularly appealing to middle-class white militants, who share their ideology but lack their discipline. White radicals also lack the black man's non-reducible commitment to black liberation: the fact that he is black. A white radical can cop out any time he wants by cutting his hair and behaving like a square. A black man cannot escape. In fighting against the system he becomes, by his very act of resistance, a hero to white radicals. As Huey Newton has explained:[1]

---

[1] The quotations from Huey Newton are from an interview in *The Movement*, August 1968, republished as a pamphlet, and available from SDS.

*Black people in America, in the black colony, are oppressed because we're black and we're exploited. The whites are rebels, many of them from the middle class, and as far as any overt oppression this is not the case. So therefore I call their rejection of the system somewhat of an abstract thing. They're looking for new heroes. . . . In pressing for new heroes the young white revolution found the heroes in the black colony at home and in the colonies throughout the world. . . .*

While Newton favors alliances with white radicals, he points out that "there can be no black-white unity until there first is black unity." Only blacks can decide the proper strategy for the black community.

White radicals, divided on tactics and ideology, and split into a plethora of competing, often hostile, groups, have only recently begun to deal with some of the problems of "black liberation." There has always been sympathy for the black struggle, and even participation when it was permitted during the civil rights movement. But things have changed greatly since Stokely Carmichael kicked the whites out of SNCC and the Panthers moved into the streets with guns. Unable to lead the black movement, white radicals are no longer even sure how they can aid it. Uncertain of their tactics, and confused about their goals, they revert to ready-made formulas, like "revolution," to deal with a multitude of complexities that are too difficult to analyze right now. Some assert that groups like the Panthers are the "vanguard" of the revolution—as though this justified white radicals' inability to work out a coherent theory or strategy.

The Vietnam war no longer serves as the great rallying point for the Left that it used to. Radicals have a good deal to protest about, but they seem to focus their energies on largely symbolic issues, such as the People's Park, or on the predictable seizure of university administration buildings. The radical Left is hung up on revolution, but doesn't seem to have the vaguest idea of how it should be organized, or how the country would be run if such an event ever took place. . . .

The major program they are now emphasizing is community control of police, with cities divided into districts, each with its own police force controlled by an elected neighborhood council, and with policemen living in the district they control. "If a policeman's brutalizing somebody in the community and has to come back home and sleep that night," Bobby Seale explained, "we can deal with him in our community." Participants at the conference were urged to get out and work on such petitions for decentralization—whites in white communities, browns in Latin communities, and blacks in the ghettos. For blacks and other minority groups such decentralization makes sense. It would not bring about the millennium, but it could sharply reduce the slaying and beating of ghetto people by trigger-happy, frightened, or racist white cops.

The white revolutionaries, however, were put off by such reformist proposals—particularly the Berkeley contingent, which seemed hung up on violence, with some members talking about guerrilla warfare in the streets.

Even the pro-Panther SDS leadership felt that decentralization, however good it might be for the ghettos, was a bad policy for white neighborhoods, where it might lead to the creation of vigilante teams under the guise of police forces. The SDS interim committee voted against endorsement of the petition campaign unless it were limited to black and brown communities.

This didn't go down well with the Panthers. On his return from Algiers, where he attended the Pan-African Arts Festival, chief of staff David Hilliard told newsmen that "The Black Panther Party will not be dictated to by people who are obviously bourgeois procrastinators, seeking made-to-order revolution which is abstract, metaphysical and doesn't exist in the black or white community." He derided the SDS argument that community control would make police forces in white areas worse than they already are, and defined the issue as one of revolutionary solidarity. "We're not going to let SDS worm their way out of their revolutionary duties," he warned. "If they are revolutionary, then this is what we, as the vanguard of the revolution in Babylon, dictate—that they circulate that petition, not in our communities, but in their own."

Never very comfortable with SDS, the Panthers feel much more at home with the "brothers off the block," the street people, the lumpenprole-tariat, to use another phrase they are fond of, than with the guilt-ridden children of the white bourgeoisie. With a few exceptions, such as Huey Newton and Bobby Seale, they have had little formal education beyond high school, and some of the most intelligent do not even have that. "We got our education on the street, in the service, or in jail," the Panthers' soft-spoken minister of education, Ray "Masai" Hewitt, told me. The Panther leaders are self-made intellectuals or, in political scientist Martin Kilson's term, "paraintellectuals."[2]

"We relate to the Young Patriots" (a white, recently radicalized Chicago group that is organizing nationally), David Hilliard stated, "because they're operating on the same class level as the Black Panther Party." They also share a similar rhetoric. Speaking at the conference on the eve of the moon landing, a leader of the Young Patriots named Preacherman, in black

---

[2] Describing such leaders as Malcolm X and Eldridge Cleaver, Kilson has written: "Unlike the established elements in the Negro intelligentsia, the paraintellectuals share a cultural experience similar to that of the black lower classes. They share too the lower classes' brutalizing experience with the coercive arm of white-controlled cities, especially the police power. These common experiences enabled the paraintellectuals to be spokesmen for the Negro masses as they emerged into a militant politicalization through riots. The paraintellectuals came onto the scene as legitimate and *natural* leaders. Moreover, they advance the politicalization of the black urban masses, after a fashion, by formulating descriptions of black-white relations, past and present, and policies for altering these relations that the Negro lower class finds meaningful. Few of the established elements among the black intelligentsia have, until very recently, had such success." (Martin Kilson, "The New Black Intellectuals," *Dissent*, July–August 1969, p. 307.)

beret and shades, gave a moving speech which was, in effect, a tribute to the Panthers' ability to reach traditionally apolitical, racist white groups:

*Our struggle is beyond comprehension to me sometimes, and I felt that poor whites was (and maybe we felt wrongly, but we felt it) was forgotten, and that certain places we walked there were certain organizations that nobody saw us until we met the Illinois chapter of the Black Panther Party and they met us. And we said, "Let's put that theory into practice about riddin' ourselves of that racism." You see, otherwise, otherwise to us, freeing political prisoners would be hypocrisy. That's what it'd be. We want to stand by our brothers, dig? And, I don't know. I'd even like to say something to church people. I think one of the brothers last night said, "Jesus Christ was a bad motherfucker." Man, we all don't want to go that route, understand. He laid back and he said, "Put that fuckin' nail right there, man. That's the people's nail. I'm takin' it." But we've gone beyond it. . . .*

The Young Patriots started out as a street gang and gradually developed a political consciousness that led them in the direction of the Panthers. A similar attempt at radicalizing organized labor is being made with the creation of the League of Revolutionary Black Workers, a federation of several Detroit-based workers' groups such as the Dodge Revolutionary Union Movement (DRUM) and its equivalents at Ford (FRUM), Chrysler (CRUM), and elsewhere. The all-black League was started, according to John Watson, one of its founders, "because the working class is already divided between the races, and because it is necessary for black workers to be able to act independently of white workers."

White workers have been encouraged to form radical organizations of their own to work out a common strategy with black union revolutionaries, but progress has been slow. Speaking of such a group at the Detroit *News,* Watson observed, ". . . although a number of the white guys who were down there had risen above the levels of racism and understood the exploitative nature of the company and of the system, they had very little experience in organizing to fight oppression and exploitation." As with the Panthers, these black workers consider themselves to be in the "vanguard of the revolutionary movement," and see most whites still on the fringes of the real struggle.

These "revolutionary" union groups were started to protect black workers who felt they were being treated unfairly and even victimized by racist white union leaders. Also, they believed, together with like-minded white workers, that union chiefs were in collusion with the bosses to speed up work schedules and ignore grievances over intolerable working conditions. The radical union groups are, first of all, self-protective associations for people unprotected or abused by the regular, bureaucratized unions. Secondly, they hope to stimulate a political awareness that will lead to a revolutionary situation in America.

For the time being, however, it is clear that the ghettos are potentially the most explosive places in the country. This is where the Panthers are organized (although they are trying to establish close contacts with the revolutionary union movements, as well as with student groups) and where they draw their main support. Much of their appeal for ghetto youths (shared by many whites) is their image of a powerful black man with a rifle. In his recent book of essays[3] Eldridge Cleaver describes his own first encounter with the Panthers at a meeting in the Fillmore district ghetto of San Francisco: "I spun round in my seat and saw the most beautiful sight I had ever seen: four black men wearing black berets, powder blue shirts, black leather jackets, black trousers, shiny black shoes—and each with a gun!"

Since then Cleaver has learned that there is more to being a Panther than carrying a gun. But the image of power and violence is still the basic one created by the Panthers. When ghetto youths learn that party membership is not like joining a street gang but more like taking religious vows, many of them become disillusioned and turn away from the Panthers. They are put off by the strict discipline,[4] the political indoctrination, the discouragement of racism, and such community service projects as the Panther program to provide free breakfast to ghetto children. The Panthers have had to purge people who turned out to be basically criminals or racists unable to relate to the party's political and intellectual program.

Unlike many of the ghetto youth, who want action, retribution, and loot, young black idealists are drawn to the Panthers' philosophy of social justice and equality through power. Where there have been spontaneous black riots, such as those following the assassination of Martin Luther King, the Panthers have tried to cool it, to discourage violence that could lead only to further repression without any political gains. Unfortunately the political leadership in most cities is too dense to realize that the Panthers are actually a force for stability in the ghettos. An intelligent white ruling class would encourage the Panthers rather than try to destroy them; that it has failed to understand this does indeed argue for its own inherent instability.

Lately the Panthers have been emphasizing programs directly related

---

[3] *Eldridge Cleaver,* Random, 211 pp., $5.95.

[4] There are twenty-six rules of discipline that all members must follow, of which the first is "no party member can have narcotics or weed in his possession while doing party work." In addition, there are eight "points of attention":

1. Speak politely.
2. Pay fairly for what you buy.
3. Return everything you borrow.
4. Pay for anything you damage.
5. Do not hit or swear at people.
6. Do not damage property or crops of the poor, oppressed masses.
7. Do not take liberties with women.
8. If we ever have to take captives, do not ill-treat them.

to the needs of the ghetto community, such as free breakfasts and health clinics. This summer they have also been setting up black "liberation schools," where children between two and sixteen are taught some things about American history, economics, and politics that they never learn in the public schools. Clearly much of this is indoctrination, although the Panthers claim that they are correcting the distorted image that black children receive of themselves and their society.

White middle-class revolutionaries tend to patronize such activities as reformist. But the breakfasts, the schools, and the clinics have won the Panthers support within the ghetto that they never could have gained by guns alone or by Marxist-Leninist analyses of the internal contradictions of capitalism. In Oakland, where the party has existed for nearly three years, it is an important element of the black community, respected even though it is not often fully understood. Just as the police have been forced to respect the power of the Panthers, so the white power elite has had to deal with an organized, politically conscious force within the black community. Throughout much of the Bay area, where the Panthers are particularly well organized, they are an articulate, alert defender of black people's interests. The Panthers are there when the community needs them, and they are there when no one else seems to be listening.

An example that comes to mind, simply because it occurred while I was in San Francisco, concerned a sixteen-year-old boy who was shot in the back by a member of San Francisco's Tactical Squad while he was fleeing the scene of an alleged auto theft. The shooting occurred near his home and was heard by his mother, a practical nurse, who was thrown to the ground by the police when she ran to his side screaming, "Don't shoot my boy again." The wounded boy was thrown into a police truck and nearly an hour elapsed before he actually reached the hospital. It is the sort of thing that happens every day in Hunter's Point and a hundred other black ghettos around America. The only difference is that, miraculously, the bullet was deflected by a rib bone and the boy was not killed, and that the Panthers brought it to the attention of the public by calling a press conference which Bobby Seale, David Hilliard, and Masai, the party's three top leaders, attended.

At the conference were a few representatives of the local press (the television stations were invited but refrained from sending anyone), myself, a few Panthers, their lawyer, Charles Garry, the boy, Jimmie Conner, and his parents. The boy, soft-spoken and composed, spoke of the incident as though it were a normal part of life, and when asked why he ran away, replied, with the tedium of one explaining the obvious, "Why did I run? Because I'm scared of police." With him sat his parents, an attractive, quiet woman in her mid-thirties and a handsome, somewhat stocky, graying man who works in aircraft maintenance. Both very light-skinned, eminently respectable, and both bitter and confused about what had happened to them.

Had they been white, their son would have been reprimanded, or at most taken to court. But they are black and their son was almost killed, as other boys have been killed in Hunter's Point and elsewhere for even lesser crimes—if indeed Jimmie Conner was guilty of a crime. When asked about the incident, Mrs. Conner replied, "Just another Negro gone, that's the way we believe that they think about the kids up here. Too many of our kids are dying for nothing. They see police three blocks away and they start running because they're scared. I'm gonna fight them. If I have to go to jail OK. If I have to work for the rest of my life, I will. If they shoot me that's fine. I'm gonna fight, this has got to stop." This is a story with many morals, but it could be called the radicalization of Mrs. Orzella Conner, housewife, mother, nurse, and now friend of the Black Panthers.

How did the Panthers get involved in this incident, although none of the Conners is a member of the party? Because a doctor at the hospital where Jimmie was taken was so shocked at his treatment by the police that he called Charles Garry, who in turn called Bobby Seale. What followed was a press conference, followed by a lawsuit under the 1964 Civil Rights Act, followed by press coverage—which of course could never have occurred had the Panthers not been called in.

The cynical would say that the Panthers have something to gain from this publicity, which indeed they have. But that is to miss the point, which is that by such actions they are establishing themselves, in the eyes of the black community, as the defenders of the black man too humble to interest anyone else. They can sink their roots in the black community and win its allegiance partly because no one else is fulfilling that role. This is one of the things that the Panthers mean by "educating" the people, informing them of their rights and making them activist defenders rather than passive victims. This education is carried on through meetings, discussions, leaflets, and the party newspaper. While their tactics have shifted several times since the formation of the party in October 1966, their objectives remain the ones set out in their ten-point program of black liberation.[5]

---

[5] 1. We want freedom. We want power to determine the destiny of our Black Community.
2. We want full employment for our people.
3. We want an end to the robbery by the CAPITALIST of our Black Community. [N.B. Recently changed to "capitalist" from "white man."]
4. We want decent housing, fit for shelter of human beings.
5. We want education for our people that exposes the true nature of this decadent American society. We want education that teaches us our true history and our role in the present day society.
6. We want all black men to be exempt from military service.
7. We want an immediate end to POLICE BRUTALITY and MURDER of black people.
8. We want freedom for all black men held in federal, state, county and city prisons and jails.
9. We want all black people when brought to trial to be tried in court by a jury of their peer group or people from their black communities, as defined by the Constitution of the United States.
10. We want land, bread, housing, education, clothing, justice and peace. And as our major political objective, a United Nations-supervised plebiscite to be held throughout the black

Looking at this program and talking to the Panthers, as well as reading their newspaper, *The Black Panther* (which everyone interested enough to read this essay ought to do in order to gain, if nothing else, an idea of the atrocities that are going on under the name of law and order), make one realize that the "revolution" they talk about is not necessarily the cataclysmic upheaval that sends the white middle class into spasms. Rather, it is the achievement of constitutional guarantees and economic justice for black people. These gun-carrying, Mao-quoting revolutionaries want what most middle-class Americans take for granted. As Huey Newton has said, if reformist politicians like the Kennedys and Lindsay could solve the problems of housing, employment, and justice for blacks and other Americans at the bottom of the social heap, there would be no need for a revolution. And, it goes without saying, little support for such groups as the Black Panther Party.

The Panthers have a voice in the black community (although not necessarily so large as many whites imagine) because they offer hope for change to ghetto people whom the civil rights movement and the poverty program bureaucrats have been unable to touch. They walk proudly through the streets of Oakland in their black leather jackets, and they hold mass rallies for the liberation of Huey Newton in the shadow of the Alameda County Court House where he was sentenced. They speak to the black man's image of himself. They tell him that he is no longer powerless against the forces that oppress him, and that his struggle for freedom is part of a world-wide liberation movement. In this sense they fulfill a real psychological need.

While they have not yet shed white blood, except in self-defense, does this mean that they never will, that their talk of guerrilla warfare is simply rhetoric? It would be rash to say so, for the Panthers have declared that they are ready to kill anyone who stands in the way of "black liberation." And they are convinced that racism in this society is so pervasive and deeply rooted that there can be no freedom for black people until it is extirpated by some form of revolution. Even Gene Marine, who, in his highly informative book, *The Black Panthers*,[6] freely admits his admiration for the Panthers, confesses, "I am frightened by them." Like some of the white revolutionaries who emulate them, the Panthers seem to have over-learned *The Battle of Algiers,* and have tried to apply its lesson to a society where the situation is totally different. The United States today is not Algeria of 1954, nor Cuba of 1958, nor even France of 1968. It is a deeply troubled, but nonetheless largely stable society which is capable of putting down an insurrection ruthlessly and quickly.

---

colony in which only black colonial subjects will be allowed to participate, for the purpose of determining the will of black people as to their national destiny. [Followed by an explanatory paragraph taken from the US Constitution: "When in the course of human events. . . ."]

[6] Signet, 1969, 224 pp., $.95 (paper).

Don't the Panthers realize this? They seem to, at the present moment anyway. This is why they are serving free breakfasts to ghetto children; attempting to form alliances with white radicals, liberals, workers, and pacifists; and urging people to sign petitions for the decentralization of the police. They may be going through a temporary stage, but the direction in which they are heading is clearly marked reformism. Right now they seem interested in maximum publicity, which is why they hold meetings and press conferences, and complain about the way the mass media ignores or distorts their actions. Some of their sympathizers fear that the Panthers are pushing themselves too much in the public eye, and that this only aids the enemies who are trying to destroy them. But since the police and politicians are out to get the Panthers in any case, perhaps such an effort to convince the public that they are not really monsters is their only chance for survival.

It is curious, to say the least, that the federal government has decided to come down hard on the Panthers at the very time that they are emphasizing ballots and petitions, community self-help, and political alliances, rather than shoot-outs. The severe harassment and repression they are now suffering may, if anything, improve the Panthers' appeal among the black bourgeoisie and white liberals. It would be one of the ironies of our irrational political life if John Mitchell and J. Edgar Hoover, together with the so-called "liberal" mayors of cities like San Francisco and Chicago, succeeded in giving the Panthers a new vitality just at the time when the party seemed in difficulty.

Mention of the word "revolution" is enough to send most politicians and police officers into a rage. Like radicals in general, the Panthers naturally talk a good deal about revolution, and use such other catch-words as facism, imperialism, and the dictatorship of the proletariat. They connect racism with the evils of capitalism, and quote freely from the sacred texts of Marx, Lenin, and Mao. Walk into any Panther office and you are likely to find not only Little Red Books lying about, but the officer of the day with his nose buried in the works of Mao, or one of Lenin's many pamphlets. Slogans, often vague and even meaningless in the context in which they are used, become part of the revolutionary vocabulary. This is true not only of the Panthers, who use such slogans to reach an audience with little formal education, but of young radicals generally. The deliberate inflation and distortion of language is a disease of the Left.

The Panthers, however, realize that racism is deeply embedded in the cultural history of Europe and America and is not, as certain Marxists still argue, simply a by-product of class society. As Huey Newton has said, "Until you get rid of racism . . . no matter what kind of economic system you have, black people will still be oppressed." What revolution seems to mean for the Panthers is the transformation of the ghetto and the "liberation" of black people, and of all oppressed people, from lives of poverty, degradation, and despair. The steps by which this will take place are not specified precisely, but they need not be violent ones unless every other road to radical change is closed. Having defined the problem, the Panthers now ask white America what kind of solution it proposes. So far as the Panthers are concerned, the answer has been harassment, repression, and even murder.

The Panthers are not racist, but they refuse to take any instructions from their white sympathizers. Indeed, this may be what makes it possible for them to be anti-racist. Commenting on the anti-white sentiment in SNCC before it became an all-black organization, Huey Newton recently said, "We have never been controlled by whites, and therefore we don't fear the white mother-country radicals." Their willingness to work with allied white radicals is not shared by most black militant groups. When Stokely Carmichael recently left the Panthers, his stormy letter of departure[7] centered on just this issue.

As the Carmichael-Cleaver exchange indicated, the black militants are just as fragmented into feuding factions as are the whites. Their rivalry, however, is a good deal more violent, and the struggle between the Panthers and the "cultural nationalist" US group of Ron Karenga led to the murder of two Panthers in Los Angeles last year. The Panthers are serious about wanting to carry on programs of education, and in spite of the terrible repression they are now facing have an enduring faith in the democratic system of petitions and ballots—far more than do the young white radicals. But like most revolutionaries, they are highly authoritarian and want loyal and unquestioning followers (as Stokely Carmichael rightly pointed out in his letter) rather than critical colleagues.

Unlike the white revolutionaries, however, the Panthers do have some fairly clear ideas of what they want—even though they are uncertain about the best way to get it. Whatever their shortcomings, they did not seem to me self-indulgent, romantic, or part-time players at revolution. They are in this struggle for keeps. Anyone who is a Panther today, or who

---

[7] In spite of his official title of Prime Minister, Stokely Carmichael was not much more than a figurehead in the party. From his self-chosen exile in Guinea, he sent an open letter to the party, distributed by his wife at Kennedy airport to the press, in which he declared:

The alliances being formed by the party are alliances which I cannot politically agree with, because the history of Africans living in the US has shown that any premature alliance with white radicals has led to complete subversion of blacks by the whites through their direct or indirect control of the black organization.

He also criticized the "present tactics and methods which the party is using to coerce and force everyone to submit to its authority," and declared that unless the Panthers change their political direction they "will at best become a reformist party and at worst a tool of racist imperialists used against the black masses."

To this denunciation Eldridge Cleaver, Minister of Information in enforced exile, replied in the pages of *Ramparts:*

That you know nothing about the revolutionary process is clear, that you know less about the United States and its people is clearer, and that you know even less about humanity than you do about the rest is clearest of all. . . . You should know that suffering is color blind and that the victims of imperialism, racism, colonialism, and neo-colonialism come in all colors and that they need unity based on revolutionary principles rather than skin color.

contemplates joining the party, knows that there is a good chance that he will be jailed or die a violent death. Panthers have already been murdered by the police, many have been beaten and wounded, and others are almost certain to be killed in the months and years ahead. It takes courage to join the party, to submit to its discipline, and to face the likely prospect of imprisonment or death. But for some there is no other way. As Eldridge Cleaver has written, "A slave who dies of natural causes will not balance two dead flies on the scale of eternity."

The Panthers have come a long way since Huey Newton and Bobby Seale first formed the party three years ago in Oakland. It has spread across the nation and has eclipsed such groups as SNCC and CORE to become the most powerful black militant organization in America. This rapid expansion has created problems—not only increasing police harassment and repression as the Panthers become more influential within the black community, but also the difficulty of maintaining the high standard of membership that its leaders would like. Not all Panthers have the organizing ability of Bobby Seale or the analytical minds of David Hilliard, Eldridge Cleaver, and Huey Newton. Which is to say that the Panthers are not super-human, as some white radicals would like to believe, any more than they are devils.

Beneath an inflammatory vocabulary of ghetto hyperbole and a good deal of facile Marxist sloganizing, the Panthers seemed to me serious, hard-working, disciplined, and essentially humanistic in their work within the black community and in their vision of a more just society. For the Panthers, weapons are an instrument of self-protection, and ultimately the means to achieve the revolution that, in the absence of a peaceful alternative, will make liberation possible. For some of the white militants I spoke to around Berkeley, however, it seemed that revolution is the means, and denouncing or shooting up the "fascists" (who seem to include just about everyone who disagrees on tactics or strategy . . .) is conceived as the end. Since Chicago, and particularly since the brutal suppression by the police during the battle of People's Park, some West Coast militants seem to have become traumatized by violence, convinced there is no other way to carry on radical politics.

But Che's prescription is no more relevant in the tree-lined streets of Berkeley or Cambridge than it was in the mountains of Bolivia. The Panthers are prepared for guerrilla warfare, as a last-ditch stand, because they think they may have no other alternative. There are white revolutionaries, on the West Coast and elsewhere, who, in the impatience of their rage and their inability seriously to change a society whose policies they find oppressive, accept this prescription uncritically, and, in view of the forces marshalled against them on the Right, with a half-conscious quest for martyrdom. As its frustration increases, the New Left becomes more shrill in its rhetoric and dogmatic in its politics. Instead of focusing on the most blatant inequalities and injustices of American life, it is assaulting the periphery. Instead of trying to educate the people to inequities of the social-economic system and the cost of maintaining an empire, it has success-fully alienated the working class without whose support no radical change, let alone "revolution," is possible.

In its resistance to the draft, the war, and racism, the radical Left has aroused parts of the nation. More people now realize there is something seriously wrong with American society but are not certain how to deal with it. Many are frightened and attribute all unrest to a conspiracy of "troublemakers." Others know that change must come, but would like it to be as unobtrusive as possible. It remains to be seen how many can be reached, whether it be on the plane of morality or self-interest, and con-vinced that change need not be personally threatening to them. To do this radicals must have plausible ideas on how a transformed society would produce a better existence for the mass of people. It does little good for the radical Left to dismiss everyone who disagrees as "fascist," for these are a majority, and if they are treated as fascists long enough, they may begin behaving in such a way as to make the current repression seem like libertarianism in comparison.

America is not now a "fascist" country, nor is it likely soon to become one, although this is not impossible. Probably it will continue to be an advanced capitalist society in which cruel inequalities and repression, unliv-able cities, and inhuman conditions of work continue to exist along with considerable liberty to take political action, while our rulers control an empire of poor nations abroad. It is the duty of the Left to find ways to change this system: to educate people rather than simply abuse them; to understand what is happening in the factories and farms and lower-middle-class neighborhoods and be in touch with the people in them; to use the universities as places where the complex problems of replacing repressive capitalism and imperialism with a better system can be studied seriously; to stop playing Minutemen and begin acting like radicals. If there is ever going to be a revolution in this country, it will have to happen first in people's heads. What takes place in the streets of a society like this one has another name. It is called repression.

## SUGGESTIONS FOR FURTHER READING

&T HE literature on the decade and a half since *Brown* v. *The Board of Education* is extensive; therefore, the following list of suggested read-ings is quite selective. Good introductions to the period are Benjamin Muse, *Ten Years of Prelude* (New York, 1964); Muse, *The American Negro Revolu-*

* An asterisk indicates that the book is available in paperback.

*tion: From Non-violence to Black Power, 1963–1967* (Bloomington, Ind., 1968);
and *Anthony Lewis, *Portraits of a Decade* (New York, 1964). Especially valuable
are *Thomas F. Pettigrew, *A Profile of the Negro American* (Princeton, N.J., 1964)
and *Charles E. Silberman, *Crisis in Black and White* (New York, 1964).

Examinations of the reasons for black participation in the nonviolent protest
movement are presented by Ruth Searles and J. Allen Williams, "Negro College
Students Participation in Sit-Ins," *Social Forces,* XL (March 1962); James W. Vander
Zanden, "The Non-Violent Movement Against Segregation," *American Journal of
Sociology,* LXVIII (March 1963); and Donald R. Matthews and James W. Prothro,
*Negroes and the New Southern Politics* (New York, 1966). There are a number of
investigations on whether or not the civil rights revolution brought about changes
in black leadership. Among these are Lewis Killian and Charles U. Smith, "Negro
Protest Leaders in a Southern Community," *Social Forces,* XXXVIII (March 1960);
*Lewis Killian and Charles Grigg, *Racial Crisis in America* (Englewood Cliffs, N.J.,
1964); Jack L. Walker, *Sit-Ins in Alabama: A Study in the Negro Revolt* (New
Brunswick, N.J., 1964); *Daniel C. Thompson, *The Negro Leadership Class* (Englewood Cliffs, N.J., 1963); and *Louis Lomax, *The Negro Revolt* (New York, 1962).
Lomax's volume should be read in conjunction with August Meier, "Negro Pro-
test Movements and Organizations," *Journal of Negro Education,* XXXII (Fall 1963).

The reader interested in the participants, organizations, and campaigns of
the civil rights movement will find a wealth of writings. *James Peck, *Freedom
Ride* (New York, 1962) and *Howard Zinn's pre-Carmichael study of *SNCC: The
New Abolitionists* cover two important groups. One should consult the writings of
Martin Luther King, *Stride Toward Freedom* (New York, 1958); *Why We Can't
Wait* (New York, 1964); and *Where Do We Go From Here* (New York, 1967). The
two best studies of King are David L. Lewis's biography *King* (New York, 1970) and
August Meier's essay, "On the Role of Martin Luther King," *New Politics,* IV (Winter
1965). Also useful are James Farmer, *Freedom—When?* (New York, 1966) and
*Whitney M. Young, Jr., *To Be Equal* (New York, 1964). Two studies of the best-
known black-nationalist organization of the early 1960s are *C. Eric Lincoln, *The
Black Muslims in America* (Boston, 1961) and *E. U. Essien-Udom, *Black Nationalism* (Chicago, 1962). Any investigation of the Muslims must make use of the writ-
ings of Malcolm X. Read *The Autobiography of Malcolm X* (New York, 1964);
George Breitman, *Malcolm X Speaks* (New York, 1966) and *The Last Year of
Malcolm X* (New York, 1968).

The ghetto riots of the 1960s have received wide coverage. Two studies are
*Report of the National Advisory Commission on Civil Disorders* (Washington, D.C.,
1968) and Robert M. Fogelson and Robert B. Hill, "Who Riots? A Study of Participation in the 1967 Riots," *Supplemental Studies for the National Advisory Commission on Civil Disorders* (Washington, D.C., 1968). *Hugh D. Graham and Ted R.
Gurr (eds.), *History of Violence in America* (Washington, D.C., 1969) and *Jerome
H. Skolnick, *The Politics of Protest* (New York, 1969) contain discussions of the
ghetto uprisings in a broader framework. Economic developments are important
for an understanding of the ghetto riots as well as the civil rights movement. A
collection of excellent essays is offered in *Arthur Ross and Herbert Hill (eds.),
*Race, Jobs and Poverty* (New York, 1967).

The literature on the black-power movement is increasing almost daily. The
essays incorporated in *Floyd Barbour (ed.), *The Black Power Revolt* (New York,

* An asterisk indicates that the book is available in paperback.

1968) are a good introduction. *Stokely Carmichael and Charles V. Hamilton, *Black Power* (New York, 1967) is one of the most widely read statements on the subject. One should not overlook the writings of Malcolm X. Among the many criticisms and defenses of black power are Bayard Rustin, "Black Power and Coalition Politics," *Commentary*, XLII (September 1966); Martin Duberman, "Black Power in America," *Partisan Review*, XXXV (Winter 1968); Christopher Lasch, "The Trouble with Black Power," *New York Review of Books*, X (February 1968); Howard Dratch, "The Emergence of Black Power," *International Socialist Journal*, XXVI (July 1968); and David Danzig, "In Defense of Black Power," *Commentary*, XLII (September 1966). For information on the Black Panthers, see *Eldridge Cleaver, *Soul on Ice* (New York, 1968) and Gene Marine, *The Black Panthers* (New York, 1969).

* An asterisk indicates that the book is available in paperback.

## DATE DUE

| MR 26'84 | | | |
|---|---|---|---|
| | | | |
| | | | |
| | | | |
| | | | |
| | | | |
| | | | |
| | | | |
| | | | |
| | | | |
| | | | |
| | | | |
| | | | |
| | | | |
| | | | |
| | | | |
| GAYLORD | | | PRINTED IN U.S.A. |